BARRON'S

HOW TO PREPARE FOR THE

TOEFL®

iBT

TEST OF ENGLISH
AS A FOREIGN LANGUAGE
Internet-Based Test

12TH EDITION

Pamela J. Sharpe, Ph.D.

BARRON'S

To my students at home and abroad with best wishes for success on the TOEFL and after the TOEFL

Pamela Sharpe

About the Author

Dr. Pamela Sharpe is an internationally recognized educator in the field of English as a Second Language (ESL). She has taught at many prestigious colleges and universities in the United States including the University of Florida, the University of Toledo, Miami Dade Community College, Arizona Western College, the Ohio State University, and the University of Texas, as well as several universities abroad. She has also taught on the statewide educational television network at Northern Arizona University. Dr. Sharpe is the author of twelve textbooks that have been used successfully by millions of students worldwide. She is a preeminent authority in test preparation for the TOEFL. For more information about Dr. Sharpe or to contact her, visit her web site at *www.teflprep.com*.

© Copyright 2006 by Barron's Educational Series, Inc.

Previous edition under the title *How to Prepare for the TOEFL Test: Test of English as a Foreign Language*
© copyright 2004, 2001, 1999, 1996, 1994, 1989, 1986, 1983, 1979, 1977 by Barron's Educational Series, Inc.

All inquiries should be addressed to:
Barron's Educational Series, Inc.
250 Wireless Boulevard
Hauppauge, New York 11788
http://www.barronseduc.com

Library of Congress Catalog Card No. 2005054551

ISBN-13: 978-0-7641-3374-9 (book only)
ISBN-10: 0-7641-3374-8 (book only)
ISBN-13: 978-0-7641-7917-4 (book with compact disks)
ISBN-10: 0-7641-7917-9 (book with compact disks)
ISBN-13: 978-0-7641-7905-1 (book with CD-ROM)
ISBN-10: 0-7641-7905-5 (book with CD-ROM)
ISBN-13: 978-0-7641-7918-1 (compact disks only package)
ISBN-10: 0-7641-7918-7 (compact disks only package)

Library of Congress Cataloging-in-Publication Data
Sharpe, Pamela J.
    How to prepare for the TOEFL iBT / Pamela J. Sharpe. — 12th ed.
       p.   cm.
    Rev. ed. of: How to prepare for the TOEFL test. 11th ed. 2004.
    ISBN-13: 978-0-7641-3374-9 (book)
    ISBN-10: 0-7641-3374-8 (book)
    ISBN-13: 978-0-7641-7905-1 (book with CD-ROM)
    ISBN-10: 0-7641-7905-5 (book with CD-ROM)
    1. English language—Textbooks for foreign speakers. 2. Test of English as a Foreign Language—
Study guides. 3. English language—Examinations—Study guides. I. Sharpe, Pamela J.
How to prepare for the TOEFL test. II. Title.

PE1128.S5   2006
428.0076—dc22   2005054551

PRINTED IN THE UNITED STATES OF AMERICA
9 8 7 6 5 4 3 2 1

BRIEF TABLE OF CONTENTS

EXTENDED TABLE OF CONTENTS

4 MODEL TEST 2: PROGRESS TEST   153

5 REVIEW OF TOEFL® iBT SECTIONS   201

6 MORE MODEL TESTS   273

7 ANSWERS AND AUDIO SCRIPTS FOR ACTIVITIES, QUIZZES, AND MODEL TESTS   503

8   SCORE ESTIMATES   775

9   RESOURCES   783

ACKNOWLEDGMENTS

With affection and appreciation, I acknowledge my indebtedness to the friends, family, and colleagues who have been part of the TOEFL team for so many years.

The late Dr. Jayne Harder, former Director of the English Language Institute at the University of Florida for initiating me into the science of linguistics and the art of teaching English as a second language;

Robert and Lillie Sharpe, my parents for their assistance in typing and proofreading previous editions and for their enthusiastic encouragement throughout my career;

The late Dr. Tom Clapp, former Dean of Continuing Education at the University of Toledo for the maturity and confidence that I gained during our marriage because he believed in me;

Carole Berglie, former Editor at Barron's Educational Series for her guidance in seeing the first edition of the manuscript through to publication;

Marcy Rosenbaum, Project Editor at Barron's Educational Series for her invaluable insights and wise counsel during every stage of development and production;

Debby Becak, Production Manager at Barron's Educational Series for the creative suggestions and designs, large and small, that have improved every chapter;

Bob O'Sullivan, Managing Editor at Barron's Educational Series for making important decisions at critical times during the project;

Mark Miele, Editorial Director at Barron's Educational Series for consulting on the project and for providing indispensable advice on legal questions;

Carlos Moreno, Carlos Moreno Photography for the photographs that provided the TOEFL-like context for the audio questions;

Joan Franklin, President, and John Rockwell, Editor, at Cinema Sound for casting and directing the talented voices and bringing the script to life;

Sara Black, Copy Editor for her constructive criticism and helpful corrections throughout the manuscript;

Kathy Telford, Proofreader at Proofreaders Plus for her attention to the important details, her positive approach to errors, and her friendship;

Dennis Oliver, Professor at Estrella Mountain Community College for coauthoring the *Glossary of Campus Vocabulary*;

Erin Osterman Fitzgerald, Legal Assistant for securing the reprint permissions and organizing the legal files;

David John Osterman, Technology Consultant for helping me to transform my office for the 21st century;

John T. Osterman, my husband—a special thank you for the unconditional love and the daily interest in and support for my writing career, as well as for checking my math in the evaluation tables. Each revision of this book is better than the last, and every new and revised year with John is the best year of my life.

PERMISSIONS

TIMETABLE FOR THE TOEFL® iBT

Test Section	Questions	Time
Reading	3–5 passages with 12–14 questions	60–100 minutes
Listening	2–3 conversations with 5 questions each 4–6 lectures with 6 questions each	60–90 minutes
BREAK		5–10 minutes
Speaking	2 independent tasks 4 integrated tasks	20 minutes
Writing	1 integrated task 1 independent task	20 minutes 30 minutes

Note: The tests in this book contain three reading passages, three conversations, and six lectures *or* five reading passages, two conversations, and four lectures because that is the standard length for an official TOEFL. Every official test includes either reading or listening material that is being field-tested for future use. There is no tutorial on the new iBT.

1
ORIENTATION

TO THE STUDENT: HOW TO USE THIS BOOK TO SUCCEED

A STUDY PLAN

Many students do not prepare for the TOEFL before they take the exam. They do not even read the *TOEFL® iBT Information and Registration Bulletin* when they register. You have an advantage. Using this book, you have a study plan for success.

STEPS TO SUCCESS

This book is easy to use. More than one million Barron's students have succeeded on the TOEFL. You can be successful too, by following twelve steps.

➤ 1. Inform yourself about the test.

Read the answers to "FAQs—Frequently Asked Questions About the TOEFL® iBT" in this chapter. Then, if you cannot find a copy locally, visit the TOEFL web site at **www.ets.org/toefl** to download a copy of the *TOEFL Information and Registration Bulletin*. Research demonstrates that students who know what to expect will perform better on an examination.

➤ 2. Invest time in your study plan.

Be realistic about how much time you need to prepare for the TOEFL. Choose a syllabus from the choices in this chapter. Use distributed practice—two hours every day for four months will give you better results than twelve hours every day for forty days, even though you will be studying 120 hours for both schedules.

➤ 3. Develop study habits.

The study habits explained at the end of this chapter will help you succeed on the TOEFL and after the TOEFL when you are admitted to a college or university, or when you continue your professional training to keep your licenses current. Successful students understand the value of these habits.

1

➤ 4. Evaluate your strengths and weaknesses.

Take the Pretest, Model Test 1 in Chapter 2 and check your answers using the Explanatory or Example Answers and Audio Scripts for Model Tests in Chapter 7. Which sections of the TOEFL were easier for you? Which were more difficult? Plan to spend more time on the sections on which you received lower scores.

➤ 5. Master academic skills.

Chapter 3 contains a summary of the academic skills that you will need to complete the tasks on the Next Generation TOEFL. Read the strategies, complete the practice activities, and check your answers. By going systematically through this chapter, you will acquire valuable academic skills. Take your time and learn them well.

➤ 6. Check your progress.

After you finish the work in Chapter 3, you will be ready to check your progress. Take the first Progress Test, Model Test 2 in Chapter 4 and check your answers using the Explanatory or Example Answers in Chapter 7. You should begin to see how the academic skills are used on the new TOEFL® iBT.

➤ 7. Improve English proficiency.

Chapter 5 will show you how your English proficiency is tested on the TOEFL. Review important language problems and identify strategies for the language skill that corresponds to each section—Reading, Listening, Speaking, and Writing. Take the quizzes and check your answers. Although you need to know more English than it is possible to include in one chapter, this review will help you apply the English you know to the test situation. You will improve your English proficiency as measured by the TOEFL.

➤ 8. Understand the directions.

Take the time to read and understand the directions for each problem in Chapter 5 and each section on the model tests. If you already understand what to do in order to complete a certain type of question, you will not have to spend as much valuable time reading and analyzing the directions when you take the official TOEFL.

➤ 9. Practice taking model tests.

Students who have an opportunity to take at least one model test will almost always increase their scores significantly on the official TOEFL test. Experience is a great teacher. This book provides you with seven model tests for practice. In order to take advantage of the experience, you should always follow the test directions carefully and time each section. Take each model test without stopping for a break until you finish the Reading and Listening sections. Then take a five-minute break and work without stopping until you complete the Speaking and Writing sections. By simulating the test conditions, you will become familiar with the way that it feels to take the TOEFL and you will be able to concentrate on the questions instead of trying to figure out what is going to happen next. You will also learn to pace yourself so that you can finish each section within the time limits. Remember, you should not try to memorize the questions on the model tests. You will find similar questions on the official TOEFL, but you will not find exactly the same questions. Try to improve your skills, not your memory.

➤ 10. Estimate your TOEFL score.

Chapter 8 gives you a method for estimating your TOEFL score from scores on the model tests in this book. If you do not have a teacher or a reliable grader to evaluate your speaking and writing sections, you may want to consider using one of the services listed at the end of the chapter. You need to know how your speaking and writing will factor into the total score.

➤ 11. Maintain a positive attitude.

Throughout the book, you will find advice for staying positive and motivated. Most of it can be found under the heading "Advisor's Office." Take the time to read the suggestions and think about them. Other successful students have benefited from the same advice.

➤ 12. Take the test when you are ready.

Some students try to succeed on the TOEFL before they are ready. Be realistic about your study schedule. If you are not scoring very well on the model tests and the estimates of your TOEFL scores are below the minimum for you to achieve your goal, you should reconsider your registration date. Knowing when to take the test is part of a successful study plan. If you give yourself the time you need and if you follow the study plan using this book, you will reach your goal. In the future, you will not be asked whether you took the TOEFL a month earlier or later but you *will* be asked to produce the required score. You can do it! Take the test when you are ready.

TO THE TEACHER: RECOMMENDATIONS AND RESOURCES

PERSPECTIVES

In the Middle Ages, a man approached two stonemasons and asked them what they were doing. The first stonemason replied, "I am laying stones." The other answered, "I am building a cathedral."

I have been teaching TOEFL preparation classes since 1970 and writing TOEFL materials since 1975. As I go into my classes, I ask myself: Am I teaching TOEFL prep or am I helping students achieve their career goals? As I prepare each new edition of my books, I ask myself: Am I writing TOEFL preparation books or am I making tools that will help students succeed on the TOEFL and *after* the TOEFL? It is a very different perspective and inspires in a different way.

Certainly, we have seen many changes in the TOEFL across the decades. Often Educational Testing Service has revised the TOEFL in an effort to keep pace with changes in our ESL/EFL teaching paradigms, and occasionally the revisions in the TOEFL have produced changes in our teaching paradigms in something referred to as a *washback effect*.

This is probably the most challenging time in TOEFL preparation that I have experienced because the Next Generation Internet-Based TOEFL (iBT) is more than a revision. It is a completely different kind of test, which requires a new approach to learning. Our students will have demonstrate their ability to integrate the language skills by completing tasks similar to those that they will be expected to accomplish in academic settings. They will have to speak and write at high levels of proficiency.

Eventually, I believe that the changes on the TOEFL will be beneficial for our students and for us, their teachers. During the initial transition period, however, it could be difficult to plan appropriate lessons and adjust our teaching styles.

TEACHING TIPS

These ideas work for me. I invite you to try some of them in your classes.

➤ 1. Begin with a positive message.

It can be very simple. For instance, "The highest tower is built one brick at a time."
If you put a new message in the same place every time—on an overhead or on the board—students will learn to look for it when they come into the room. Music serves the same purpose. It sets a positive mood for the session.

➤ 2. Write three important goals for the class so that students can see them.

Three goals are manageable for one class session. When they are visible, they keep us all on track. At the end of the class, referring to the goals gives everyone a sense of progress and closure for the day.

➤ 3. Arrange for model tests to be taken in a lab or at home on the honor system.

Your time with students is too valuable for you to spend four hours proctoring each model test. That would add up to twenty-eight hours of class time for all of the model tests in this book.

➤ 4. Allow students to grade the Reading and Listening sections of their model tests.

If students take responsibility for grading the objective sections of their model tests, and for referring to the explanatory answers, you will save hours that you would have had to use doing routine clerical tasks. If the students take the model tests on the computer, the scoring for these sections will be done automatically; if they are using the book, the answer key is printed in Chapter 7. This will afford you the time you need to concentrate on answering questions.

➤ 5. Ask students to write their questions on note cards and bring them to class.

When students refer to the explanatory answers, many questions are resolved for them without asking the teacher. If students write down their questions, sometimes the answer becomes apparent to them at this stage. The questions that they bring to class are really worth discussion. If you have them on cards, you can prepare your answers for the question-and-answer session at the beginning of the next class. You always have the answer!

➤ 6. When several students have the same question, prepare a short presentation.

When the question is repeated, it gives us an indication of what our students need to know. By using their questions for class preparation, we show that we are teaching people, not subjects.

➤ 7. Make overheads of test questions and show the students how you choose an answer.

Let the students "listen in" on your thought processes as you decide why answers are incorrect and which answer choice is correct. Use the explanatory answers in the book to help you. For example, you might say, "I know that A is not correct because the professor did not include this research in his lecture. Choice B looks possible, but it is not complete. The choice leaves out the second part of the answer. That means it must be either Choice C or D. I know that D is not correct because the professor said that there were three types, not two. It must be Choice C." Modeling *how* to think helps students *learn* to think when they see similar test items.

➤ 8. Use class time to teach and practice academic skills.

Make overheads of material from Chapter 3 and go over it in class. Take the quizzes in class, using "Think, Answer, Compare, Discuss." Students have time to think and respond to each answer independently, and then they compare their answers to the correct answer and discuss why that choice is a good one.

➤ 9. Focus on speaking and writing in class.

Provide many good models of responses to speaking and writing questions in class. Show students how to use the checklists to evaluate speaking and writing.

➤ 10. Assign speaking tasks and writing tasks as homework.

Have students turn in tapes and essays. If you have voice mail and choose to use it for homework assignments, students can phone you and leave a one-minute response to a speaking task. Spend grading time on these important sections. Bring samples of good work to class—good organization, good openings, good support statements, good closings. Catch your students doing something good and use it as an example.

➤ 11. Don't worry about covering all the material in the book.

This book has more material than most teachers need for a course, but all of it was written for self-study as well as for classroom instruction. That means that students can work on their own for "extra credit," and all of the pages don't have to be referred to in class. In my experience, when we teachers try to cover too much, we are the only ones who can keep up. The material gets covered, but the students don't understand it. I trust that teachers know which pages to select for the students in their classes.

12. Provide counseling and encouragement as part of the class routine.

Ideally, one minute at the end of class can be used for a pep talk, a cheer, or a success story about a former student. This is one of my favorite cheers: T-O-E-F-L. We're making progress. We're doing well. T-O-E-F-L. I also like to stand by a poster at the door when students are leaving my class. The last thing they see is the affirmation on the poster: "I know more today than I did yesterday. I am preparing. I will succeed." Some students want a handshake, a high five, or a hug. Others just smile and say good-bye. Some hang by the door, and I know that they need to talk. Every excellent TOEFL prep teacher I know is also a very good counselor. You probably are, too.

RESOURCES

Several resources for teachers are listed in Chapter 8. Four syllabus options are listed in the next section. It is also worthwhile to read the "Steps to Success" for students printed on the previous pages. The most frequently asked questions (FAQs) are answered at the end of this chapter. If I can be of help to you or your students, please contact me by visiting my web site at *www.teflprep.com*.

SYLLABUS OPTIONS

A *syllabus* is a "study plan." There are four options from which to choose. The estimated number of hours for each option is the minimum time that is required to complete the plan.

The Standard Syllabus requires 16 weeks and 80 hours of your time. It is the best option because it allows you to study about 5 hours each week, and you can build in some review if you need it.

The Accelerated Syllabus also requires 80 hours, but it is possible to complete it in half the number of weeks by making a commitment to studying about ten hours each week. *Accelerated* means "fast." This calendar does not include time for review.

The Abbreviated Syllabus should be chosen only when you cannot find the time in your schedule to follow one of the other calendars. *Abbreviated* means "shorter." This calendar does not allow you to complete all the study materials in the book. A concise version of this book, *Barron's Pass Key to the TOEFL, 6th Edition*, contains only the material in the abbreviated syllabus.

The Individualized Syllabus is often chosen when you have already taken the TOEFL and you are very sure which sections will be most difficult for you when you take it again. This calendar allows you to concentrate on one or two sections without repeating information that you have already mastered on other sections.

Standard Syllabus — 16 Weeks/80 Hours

Week	Topic	Reference Pages	Class Hours
1	Orientation		5 hours
	How to Use This Book to Succeed		
	Study Habits		
	Frequently Asked Questions		
	Model Test 1: Pretest—With Explanatory Answers		
	Academic Skills—With Activities		
2	Taking Notes		5 hours
3	Paraphrasing		5 hours
4	Summarizing		5 hours
5	Synthesizing		5 hours
6	Model Test 2: Progress Test—With Explanatory Answers		5 hours
	Review of TOEFL Sections— With Quizzes and Glossaries		
7	Reading		5 hours
8	Listening		5 hours
9	Speaking		5 hours
10	Writing		5 hours
	Model Tests—With Explanatory Answers		
11	Model Test 3: Progress Test		5 hours
12	Model Test 4: Progress Test		5 hours
13	Model Test 5: Progress Test		5 hours
14	Model Test 6: Progress Test		5 hours
15	Model Test 7: Progress Test		5 hours
16	Individualized Review		5 hours

Accelerated Syllabus — 8 Weeks/80 Hours

Week	Topic	Reference Pages	Class Hours
1	Orientation		5 hours
	How to Use This Book to Succeed		
	Study Habits		
	Frequently Asked Questions		
	Model Test 1: Pretest—With Explanatory Answers		
	Academic Skills—With Activities		
2	Taking Notes		10 hours
	Paraphrasing		
3	Summarizing		10 hours
	Synthesizing		
4	Model Test 2: Progress Test—With Explanatory Answers		10 hours
	Review of TOEFL Sections—With Quizzes and Glossaries		
	Reading		
	Listening		
5	Speaking		10 hours
	Writing		
6	Model Tests—With Explanatory Answers		
	Model Test 3—Progress Test		10 hours
	Model Test 4—Progress Test		
7	Model Test 5—Progress Test		10 hours
	Model Test 6—Progress Test		
8	Model Test 7—Progress Test		15 hours
	Individualized Review		

Abbreviated Syllabus — 4 Weeks/50 Hours

Week	Topic	Reference Pages	Class Hours
1	Orientation		4 hours
	Frequently Asked Questions		
	Model Test 1: Pretest—With Explanatory Answers		
	Academic Skills—Read Only		
	Taking Notes		2 hours
	Paraphrasing		2 hours
	Summarizing		2 hours
	Synthesizing		2 hours
2	Model Test 2: Progress Test—With Explanatory Answers		5 hours
	Review of TOEFL Sections—Read Only Quizzes and Glossaries		
	Reading		2 hours
	Listening		2 hours
	Speaking		2 hours
	Writing		2 hours
3	Model Tests—With Explanatory Answers		
	Model Test 3—Go on to Model Test 4		0 hours
	Model Test 4—Progress Test		5 hours
	Model Test 5—Progress Test		5 hours
4	Model Test 6—Progress Test		5 hours
	Model Test 7—Progress Test		5 hours
	Individualized Review		5 hours

Individualized Syllabus — Variable Weeks/Hours

Week	Topic	Reference Pages	Class Hours
1	Orientation		4 hours
	Frequently Asked Questions		
	Model Test 1: Pretest		
2	Group and Individual Assignments		As needed

Barron's How to Prepare for the TOEFL, 12th Edition, is designed to support self-study. After analyzing the Pretest, the teacher can assign individualized review by selecting the chapters and pages that focus on the most challenging sections of the test for each student. It is often helpful to divide the class into groups of students who have similar patterns of error on the Pretest. Model tests provide a process for monitoring individual progress and redirecting student effort. *Barron's Practice Exercises for the TOEFL, 5th Edition,* is an additional resource for individual practice.

FAQs—FREQUENTLY ASKED QUESTIONS ABOUT THE TOEFL® iBT

The TOEFL is the Test of English as a Foreign Language. Almost one million students from 180 countries register to take the TOEFL every year at test centers throughout the world. Some of them do not score well because they do not understand enough English. Others do not score well because they do not understand the examination. The following questions are frequently asked by students as they prepare for the TOEFL.

TOEFL PROGRAMS

➤ What is the purpose of the TOEFL?

Since 1963, the TOEFL has been used by scholarship selection committees of governments, universities, and agencies such as Fulbright, the Agency for International Development, AMIDEAST, and Latin American Scholarship Programs as a standard measure of the English proficiency of their candidates. Some professional licensing and certification agencies also use TOEFL scores to evaluate English proficiency. The admissions committees of more than 4500 colleges and universities in the United States, Canada, Australia, Great Britain, and many other countries worldwide require foreign applicants to submit TOEFL scores along with transcripts and recommendations in order to be considered for admission.

➤ When was the Internet-Based TOEFL (iBT) launched?

The Internet-Based TOEFL (iBT), also called the Next Generation TOEFL, was launched on September 24, 2005, in the United States. The following month, it was administered in Canada, Germany, Italy, and France. The iBT is being introduced throughout the world in phases during 2006.

➤ When will the iBT be introduced in my country?

Five months before the test is introduced in a new area, notices will be published. To see a schedule of times and test centers, visit the TOEFL web site or check the *TOEFL® iBT Registration and Information Bulletin* on the TOEFL web site at *www.ets.org/toefl*. A revised timeline is continuously updated on the TOEFL web site.

➤ When and where will the iBT be offered?

Eventually, more than fifty test dates will be scheduled. Times during mornings, afternoons, and evenings will be available on both weekdays and weekends.

➤ When will the CBT and the PBT be discontinued?

The Computer-Based TOEFL (CBT) and the Paper-Based TOEFL (PBT) will be discontinued in each country when the Internet-Based TOEFL is introduced.

➤ Which language skills are tested on the TOEFL?

Computer-Based TOEFL	Paper-Based TOEFL	Internet-Based TOEFL
Listening	Listening	Listening
Structure	Structure	Speaking
Reading	Reading	Reading
Writing	Test of Written English	Writing

➤ Does the TOEFL have a Speaking section?

The Internet-Based TOEFL includes a Speaking section with six questions. If the Paper-Based TOEFL must be used in a remote area, it will also contain a Speaking section.

➤ Why was the Structure section removed from the new TOEFL?

Grammar is now tested as part of the other sections. It is important to use good grammar in the Speaking and the Writing sections.

➤ Will the TOEFL® iBT writing topics be published?

Not at this time. However, many of the topics that were previously published for the Computer-Based TOEFL are similar to the types of topics found on the independent writing task for the iBT.

➤ Is it possible to take the iBT without the Speaking or the Writing sections?

The Speaking section and the Writing section are required on the Internet-Based TOEFL. You must take all sections of the TOEFL in order to receive a score.

➤ Is the Internet-Based TOEFL more difficult than previous TOEFL formats?

Although the Reading and Listening sections contain longer passages, the questions are not very different from those on previous TOEFL formats. However, most students find the Speaking and Writing sections more challenging. That is why it is a good idea to practice, using this book.

REGISTRATION

➤ How do I register for the TOEFL?

You can register for the Internet-Based TOEFL online, by mail, or by telephone.

Online	*www.ets.org/toefl* for testing worldwide
Phone	1-800-GO-TOEFL (1-800-468-6335) for testing in the United States and Canada
	1-443-751-4862 for testing outside the United States and Canada
Mail	ETS-TOEFL iBT Registration Office, P.O. Box 6152, Princeton, NJ 08541-6152 USA
	Regional Registration Centers worldwide (addresses listed in the *TOEFL® iBT Registration and Information Bulletin*)

➤ Where can I find a free TOEFL® iBT Registration and Information Bulletin?

This important bulletin includes the information that you will need to register for the TOEFL. It can be downloaded free from the TOEFL web site *www.ets.org/toefl*. In addition, all Regional Registration Centers have paper copies of the bulletin, or it can be found at many libraries, universities, and educational counseling centers around the world. It is also possible to order a bulletin from Educational Testing Service, but the shipping can take as long as eight weeks.

➤ Where are the Regional Registration Centers?

Eight Regional Registration Centers (RRCs) are planned to support the test sites and counseling centers in their region. They will be listed on the web site soon.

➤ Will my registration be confirmed?

Your registration number can be printed when you register online, or you can receive your number by e-mail, if you prefer.

➤ When should I register for the TOEFL?

You must register at least seven days before the test date. Because test centers fill rapidly during desirable times, it is a good idea to register several months in advance. You may choose as many as four test centers for the same date so that you have a greater probability of completing your registration. If you are taking the TOEFL as part of the application process for college or university admission, you should plan to take the test early enough for your score to be received by the admission office before the application deadline.

➤ May I change the date or cancel my registration?

To receive a refund, you must reschedule or cancel three full days before your test date. For example, if your test is on Friday, you must call to cancel your registration on Monday. You will be charged a $40 fee for this service.

➤ What are the fees for the TOEFL® iBT?

The fee for the test administration, including four score reports is $140 U.S.

➤ How may I pay the fees?

You may pay by credit card, e-check from bank accounts in the United States, money order, or the current exchange rate for the U.S. dollar in one of the following currencies: Australian dollar, British pound, Canadian dollar, Danish krone, Euro, Hong Kong dollar, Japanese yen, New Zealand dollar, Norwegian kroner, Singapore dollar, Swedish krona, Swiss franc.

TEST ADMINISTRATION

➤ How will the TOEFL® iBT be administered?

The TOEFL will be offered on a schedule of dates in a network of test centers throughout the world. Most areas will have between thirty and forty administrations every year. The room in which the TOEFL is administered is usually a computer lab. You will be assigned a seat. If you are late, you will probably not be admitted.

➤ Where can I take the TOEFL?

The TOEFL web site at *www.ets.org/toefl* lists test centers and schedules.

➤ In what room will the test be offered?

The room may be a computer lab or a language laboratory. It may be a classroom with about fifteen computers at least four feet apart.

➤ What should I take with me to the test room?

You are not permitted to take anything with you when you enter the test room. No cell phones, paper, dictionaries, pens, or pencils are allowed. The test supervisor will give you a headset, paper, and pencils.

➤ What kind of identification is required?

In the United States, only your valid passport will be accepted for admission to the TOEFL. In other countries, your valid passport is still the best identification, but if you do not have a passport, you may refer to the TOEFL web site for special directions. Your photograph will be taken at the test center and reproduced on all official score reports, along with your signature. Be sure to use the same spelling and order of your name on your registration materials, the test center log that you will sign when you enter and leave the test area, the forms on the computer screens, and any correspondence that you may have with the TOEFL office. You should also use the same spelling on applications for schools and documents for agencies that will receive your score reports. Even a small difference can cause serious delays or even denial of the applications.

➤ How long is the testing session?

The TOEFL® iBT takes about four hours to administer, including the time required for giving directions and the break between the Listening and the Speaking sections.

EXAMINATION

➤ What kinds of questions are found on the iBT?

The majority of the questions on the iBT are multiple choice. Some other types of questions are also on the iBT. These questions have special directions on the screen. You will have many examples of them in the model tests in this book.

➤ Are all of the TOEFL® iBT tests the same?

Unlike the Computer-Based TOEFL (CBT), which presented questions based on your responses to previous questions, the iBT is a linear test. That means that on the same form, all of the test questions are the same.

➤ Why are some of the Reading and Listening sections longer?

The test developers include experimental questions for either the Reading or the Listening section on most TOEFL forms. You must do your best on all the questions because you will not know which questions are experimental and which are test questions that will be scored. For example, you may be taking the iBT with someone who has experimental questions in Reading, but you may have experimental questions in Listening. For this reason, your friend's test may have a longer Reading section, and your test may have a longer Listening section. The experimental questions may be at the beginning, middle, or end of the section.

➤ May I choose the order of the sections on my TOEFL?

You may not choose the order. Reading, Listening, Speaking, and Writing are tested in that order on the TOEFL, with a ten-minute break between the Listening and Speaking.

➤ What kinds of questions are found on the iBT?

Most of the questions are multiple choice, but some questions have special directions on the screen. You will have examples of the most frequently tested items in Chapter 5 in this book.

➤ May I take notes?

You are permitted to take notes and use them to answer the questions on the iBT. You will be given paper for that purpose when you enter the test room. Your notes will be collected and shredded after the test.

➤ May I change an answer?

On the Listening section, you can change your answer by clicking on a new answer. You can change your answer as many times as you wish until you click on the **Confirm Answer** button. On the Reading section, you can change your answer by clicking on the new answer. You can change your answer as many times as you wish, and you can go back to previous answers on the same reading passage. When you begin a new reading passage, you may not return to the previous passage to change answers. On the Speaking section, you will be cued with a beep to begin and end speaking. Everything that you say during the recording time will be submitted. You cannot change an answer. On the Writing section, you can revise your essays as much as you wish until the clock indicates that no time is remaining. If you submit your essays before time is up, you cannot return to them. The CD-ROM that supplements this book will provide you with practice in choosing and changing answers on the computer screen.

➤ If I am not sure of an answer, should I guess?

If you are not sure of an answer, you should guess. The number of incorrect answers is not subtracted from your score. First, eliminate all the possibilities that you know are NOT correct. Then, if you are almost sure of an answer, guess that one. If you have no idea of the correct answer for a question, choose one letter and use it for your "guess answer" throughout the entire examination. The "guess answer" is especially useful for finishing a section quickly.

➤ Why do some of the TOEFL tests have additional questions?

Some of the tests include questions that are being field-tested for use in future TOEFL administrations. These tests have more questions, but your answers to the additional field-test questions are not calculated as part of your score.

➤ What if I cannot hear the audio for the Listening section?

You will receive your own headphones with a microphone attached. Before the Listening section begins, you will have an opportunity to adjust the volume yourself. Be careful to adjust the volume when you are prompted to do so. If you wait until the test begins, you may not be able to adjust it. If there is a problem with your headset, raise your hand, and ask the test supervisor to provide you with another headset.

➤ What can I do if there is a problem during the test?

If there is a problem with the Internet connection or the power that supplies the computers, and if the test must be discontinued, everyone who is taking the test at that site is entitled to a refund or a free test on another date. This does not happen very often.

➤ What if I have a personal problem during the test?

If you become ill or you are being disturbed by the behavior of another person in the room, tell your test supervisor immediately. If you think that your score may be affected by the problem, ask the supervisor to file an Irregularities Report.

➤ Are breaks scheduled during the TOEFL?

A 10-minute break is scheduled between the Listening and the Speaking sections.

➤ How often may I take the iBT?

You may take the TOEFL as many times as you wish to score to your satisfaction. Although there were restrictions on when you could take the Computer-Based TOEFL (CBT), you can take the iBT more than once each month if you choose to do so.

➤ If I have already taken the TOEFL, how will the previous scores affect my new score?

TOEFL scores are valid for two years. If you have taken the TOEFL more than once but your first score report is more than two years ago, the first score will not be reported. If you have taken the TOEFL more than once in the past two years, a report will be sent for the test date that you request.

➤ May I keep my test?

You cannot save your test to a disk or send it to an e-mail address. If you try to do so, the TOEFL office may take legal action. There are examples of the official TOEFL test questions on the web site at *www.ets.org/toefl*.

➤ What happens to someone who cheats on the iBT?

Entering the room with false identification, tampering with the computer, using a camera, giving or receiving help, or trying to remove test materials or notes is considered cheating. Do not cheat. In spite of opportunity, knowledge that others are doing it, the desire to help a friend, or fear that you will not make a good score, *do not cheat*. On the TOEFL, cheating is a very serious matter. If you are discovered, you will be dismissed from the room, your score will be canceled, and you may not be able to take the test again on a future date.

SCORE REPORTS

➤ How is the Speaking section scored?

Trained raters listen to each of the speaking responses and assign them a number 0–4. The scores for all six responses are averaged and converted to a total section score 0–30. The raters grade the Speaking section using checklists similar to those printed in this book.

➤ How is the Writing section scored?

Trained raters read your essays and assign them a number 0–5. If there is disagreement about your score, a team leader will also read your essays. The scores for each essay are combined and converted to a section score 0–30. Raters grade the Writing section using checklists similar to those printed in this book.

➤ How is the total TOEFL score calculated?

The iBT has converted section scores for each of the four sections. The range for each section score is 0–30. When the scores for the four sections are added together, the total score range will be 0–120.

➤ How do I interpret my score?

You cannot pass or fail the TOEFL. Each school or agency will evaluate the scores according to its own requirements. Even at the same university, the requirements may vary for different programs of study, levels of study (graduate or undergraduate), and degrees of responsibility (student or teaching assistant). Many universities are setting minimum requirements for each section. The following range of requirements is typical of admissions policies for North American universities. This assumes, of course, that the applicant's documents other than English proficiency are acceptable.

Reading	19–21
Listening	17–21
Speaking	20–23
Writing	20–25
TOTAL	76–90

To be certain of the requirements for your school or agency, contact them directly.

➤ How do the scores compare on the iBT, CBT, and PBT formats?

The following chart compares TOEFL scores on the three most recent formats—the Internet-Based TOEFL (iBT), the Computer-Based TOEFL (CBT), and the Paper-Based TOEFL (PBT). More detailed charts are posted on the web site maintained by Educational Testing Service at *www.ets.org*.

iBT	CBT	PBT
111–120	273–300	640–677
96–110	243–272	590–639
79–95	213–242	550–589
65–78	183–212	513–549
53–64	153–182	477–512
41–52 *48*	123–152 *140*	437–476 *460*
30–40	93–122	397–436
19–29	63–92	347–396
6–18	23–62	311–346
0–5	0–22	310

➤ When can I see my scores?

You will be able to see your score report online fifteen business days after the test date. Score reports will be mailed to you and to the schools and agencies that you designate on the day they are posted online. You are entitled to five copies of your test results, including one copy for you and four official score reports.

➤ May I cancel my scores?

After you view your estimated score on the screen, you will be given the option to report or cancel your scores. If you choose to report your scores, you will then choose four institutions or agencies to receive score reports. All of this is arranged by responding to questions on the computer screen. If you do not want your scores to be reported, click on cancel when this option appears on the screen.

➤ How can I send additional score reports?

If you need more than four score reports, which are provided as part of your test fee, you may order more at $17 each. Order online or mail in the order form that you will find in your *TOEFL® iBT Registration and Information Bulletin*. Reports are sent in four days when you order them online. Allow at least two weeks for mail orders.

➤ Is there a direct correspondence between proficiency in English and a TOEFL score?

There is not always a direct correspondence between proficiency in English and a score on the TOEFL. Many students who are proficient in English are not proficient in how to approach the examination. That is why it is important to prepare by using this book.

➤ Can I estimate my TOEFL score before I take the official test?

To estimate your TOEFL score, after you complete each of the seven model tests, use the score estimates in Chapter 8 of this book. If you complete Model Tests 1–7 on the CD-ROM that supplements this book, you will see an estimate of your TOEFL score on the screen.

➤ Will I succeed on the TOEFL?

You will receive from your study what you give to your study. The information is here. Now, it is up to you to devote the time and the effort. More than one million students have succeeded by using *Barron's How to Prepare for the TOEFL*. You can be successful, too.

STUDY HABITS

A habit is a pattern of behavior that is acquired through repetition. Research indicates that it takes about twenty-one days to form a habit. The following study habits are characteristic of successful students. Be successful! Form these habits now. They will help you on the TOEFL and after the TOEFL.

➤ Accept responsibility.

Successful students understand that the score on the TOEFL is their responsibility. It doesn't happen because of luck. It is the result of their own efforts. Take responsibility for your TOEFL score. Don't leave it to chance.

- Don't rely on luck.
- Work diligently.

➤ Get organized.

You will need a place to study where you can concentrate. Try to find a quiet place where you can arrange your study materials and leave them until the next study session. If that is not practical, then find a bag that you can use to store all your materials so that you can have everything you need when you go to the library or another place to study. Don't use the bag for anything else. This will save time because you will not be looking for everything in different areas of your house or room, and you will not be trying to find TOEFL preparation material among other things in the bag. You are less likely to lose important notes.

- Find a study area.
- Keep your materials in one place.

➤ Set realistic goals.

Be honest about your preparation. Students who are just beginning to learn English are not prepared to take the TOEFL. Give yourself the time you need to prepare. By setting an unrealistic goal, for example, to finish preparing with this book in one week, you will probably be very disappointed. Even advanced students need time to learn academic skills and review language skills as well as to take model tests.

- Evaluate your English.
- Set a goal that you can achieve.

➤ Make a plan.

It is not enough to have a goal, even a realistic goal. Successful students also have a plan to accomplish a goal. What are you going to do to achieve the goal you have set? You will need to have time and resources. What are they? To help you make your plan, look at the options for a syllabus on page 6.

- Dedicate time and resources.
- Select a syllabus.

➤ Establish priorities.

The pretest on pages 21–65 in this book will be helpful to you when you set priorities. By analyzing your strengths and weaknesses on the test, you will know which sections of the test will be the most difficult and which will be easy for you. You will also know which problems within each section require the most study. By focusing on those sections and problems, you can set priorities and use your time wisely.

- Take the pretest.
- Analyze your strengths and weaknesses.

➤ Manage time.

How do you spend time? Clearly, a certain amount of your time should be spent sleeping or relaxing. That is important to good health. However, you should think about how much time you spend worrying or procrastinating. That is not a healthy way to spend time. Successful students have a schedule that helps them manage their time. Preparing for the TOEFL is written down on the schedule. TOEFL preparation is planned for on a regular basis just like a standing appointment. If it is written down, it is more probable that you will give it the time necessary to achieve your goal. When you start to worry, use that energy to do something positive. Learn to use time while you are waiting for an appointment or commuting on public transportation to study. Even a five-minute review will help you.

- Schedule study time.
- Use unscheduled time well.

➤ Learn from mistakes.

If you knew everything, you wouldn't need this book. Expect to make mistakes on the quizzes and on the model tests. Read the explanatory answers, and learn from your mistakes. If you do this, you will be less likely to make those mistakes again on the official TOEFL.

- Study the explanatory answers.
- Review your errors.

➤ Stay motivated.

It is easy to begin with enthusiasm, but it is more difficult to maintain your initial commitment. How do you stay motivated? To keep their energy up, some students give themselves some incentives. Without small rewards along the way, it may be more difficult to stay motivated. Just be sure that the reward doesn't take more time than the study. Remember, an incentive is supposed to keep you moving, not slow you down.

- Give yourself small incentives.
- Keep moving.

➤ Choose to be positive.

Your attitude will influence your success on the TOEFL examination. To be successful, you must develop patterns of positive thinking. To help develop a positive attitude, memorize the following sentences and bring them to mind after each study session. Bring them to mind when you begin to have negative thoughts:

I know more today that I did yesterday.
I am preparing.
I will succeed.

Remember, some tension is normal and good. Accept it. Use it constructively. It will motivate you to study. But don't panic or worry. Panic will cause loss of concentration and poor performance. Avoid people who panic and worry. Don't listen to them. They will encourage negative thoughts.

You know more today than you did yesterday.
You are preparing.
You will succeed.

There is more advice for success in the "Advisor's Office" throughout the book. Please read and consider the advice as you continue your TOEFL preparation.

2
MODEL TEST 1: PRETEST

READING SECTION

The Reading section tests your ability to understand reading passages like those in college textbooks. The passages are about 700 words in length.

This is the short format for the Reading section. On the short format, you will respond to three passages. After each passage, you will answer 12–14 questions about it.

Most questions are worth 1 point, but the last question in each passage is worth more than 1 point.

You will have 60 minutes to read all of the passages and answer the questions. You may take notes while you read, but notes are not graded. You may use your notes to answer the questions. Some passages may include a word or phrase that is underlined in blue. Click on the word or phrase to see a glossary definition or explanation.

Choose the best answer for multiple-choice questions. Follow the directions on the page or on the screen for computer-assisted questions. Click on **Next** to go to the next question. Click on **Back** to return to the previous question. You may return to previous questions for all of the passages in the same reading part, but after you go to the next part, you will not be able to return to passages in a previous part. Be sure that you have answered all of the questions for the passages in each part before you click on **Next** at the end of the passage to move to the next part.

You can click on **Review** to see a chart of the questions you have answered and the questions you have not answered in each part. From this screen, you can return to the question you want to answer in the part that is open.

A clock on the screen will show you how much time you have to complete the Reading section.

PART I

Reading 1 "Beowulf"

Historical Background

→ The epic poem *Beowulf*, written in Old English, is the earliest existing Germanic epic and one of four surviving Anglo-Saxon manuscripts. Although *Beowulf* was written by an anonymous Englishman in Old English, the tale takes place in that part of Scandinavia from which Germanic tribes emigrated to England. Beowulf comes from Geatland, the southeastern part of what is now Sweden. Hrothgar, king of the Danes, lives near what is now Leire, on Zealand, Denmark's largest island. The *Beowulf* epic contains three major tales about Beowulf and several minor tales that reflect a rich Germanic oral tradition of myths, legends, and folklore.

→ The *Beowulf* warriors have a foot in both the Bronze and Iron Ages. Their mead-halls reflect the wealthy living of the Bronze Age Northmen, and their wooden shields, wood-shafted spears, and bronze-hilted swords are those of the Bronze Age warrior. However, they carry iron-tipped spears, and their best swords have iron or iron-edged blades. Beowulf also orders an iron shield for his fight with a dragon. Iron replaced bronze because it produced a blade with a cutting edge that was stronger and sharper. The Northmen learned how to forge iron in about 500 B.C. Although they had been superior to the European Celts in bronze work, it was the Celts who taught them how to make and design iron work. Iron was accessible everywhere in Scandinavia, usually in the form of "bog-iron" found in the layers of peat in peat bogs.

The *Beowulf* epic also reveals interesting aspects of the lives of the Anglo-Saxons who lived in England at the time of the anonymous *Beowulf* poet. The Germanic tribes, including the Angles, the Saxons, and the Jutes, invaded England from about A.D. 450 to 600. By the time of the *Beowulf* poet, Anglo-Saxon society in England was neither primitive nor uncultured. [A]

→ Although the *Beowulf* manuscript was written in about A.D. 1000, it was not discovered until the seventeenth century. [B] Scholars do not know whether *Beowulf* is the sole surviving epic from a flourishing Anglo-Saxon literary period that produced other great epics or whether it was unique even in its own time. [C] Many scholars think that the epic was probably written sometime between the late seventh century and the early ninth century. If they are correct, the original manuscript was probably lost during the ninth-century Viking invasions of Anglia, in which the Danes destroyed the Anglo-Saxon monasteries and their great libraries. However, other scholars think that the poet's favorable attitude toward the Danes must place the epic's composition after the Viking invasions and at the start of the eleventh century, when this *Beowulf* manuscript was written.

→ The identity of the *Beowulf* poet is also uncertain. ☐D He apparently was a Christian who loved the pagan heroic tradition of his ancestors and blended the values of the pagan hero with the Christian values of his own country and time. Because he wrote in the Anglian dialect, he probably was either a monk in a monastery or a poet in an Anglo-Saxon court located north of the Thames River.

Appeal and Value

Beowulf interests contemporary readers for many reasons. First, it is an outstanding adventure story. Grendel, Grendel's mother, and the dragon are marvelous characters, and each fight is unique, action-packed, and exciting. Second, Beowulf is a very appealing hero. He is the perfect warrior, combining extraordinary strength, skill, courage, and loyalty. Like Hercules, he devotes his life to making the world a safer place. He chooses to risk death in order to help other people, and he faces his inevitable death with heroism and dignity. Third, the *Beowulf* poet is interested in the psychological aspects of human behavior. For example, the Danish hero's welcoming speech illustrates his jealousy of Beowulf. The behavior of Beowulf's warriors in the dragon fight reveals their cowardice. Beowulf's attitudes toward heroism reflect his maturity and experience, while King Hrothgar's attitudes toward life show the experiences of an aged nobleman.

Finally, the *Beowulf* poet exhibits a mature appreciation of the transitory nature of human life and achievement. In Beowulf, as in the major epics of other cultures, the hero must create a meaningful life in a world that is often dangerous and uncaring. He must accept the inevitability of death. He chooses to reject despair; instead, he takes pride in himself and in his accomplishments, and he values human relationships.

1. According to paragraph 1, which of the following is true about *Beowulf*?

   Ⓐ It is the only manuscript from the Anglo-Saxon period.
   Ⓑ The original story was written in a German dialect.
 ✓ Ⓒ The author did not sign his name to the poem.
 • Ⓓ It is one of several epics from the first century.

   Paragraph 1 is marked with an arrow [→].

2. The word <u>which</u> in the passage refers to

 • Ⓐ tale
 ✓ Ⓑ Scandinavia
   Ⓒ manuscripts
   Ⓓ Old English

3. Why does the author mention "bog-iron" in paragraph 2?

  Ⓐ To demonstrate the availability of iron in Scandinavia
  Ⓑ To prove that iron was better than bronze for weapons
  Ⓒ To argue that the Celts provided the materials to make iron
  Ⓓ To suggest that 500 B.C. was the date that the Iron Age began

  Paragraph 2 is marked with an arrow [➔].

4. Which of the sentences below best expresses the information in the highlighted statement in the passage? The other choices change the meaning or leave out important information.

  Ⓐ Society in Anglo-Saxon England was both advanced and cultured.
  Ⓑ The society of the Anglo-Saxons was not primitive or cultured.
  Ⓒ The Anglo-Saxons had a society that was primitive, not cultured.
  Ⓓ England during the Anglo-Saxon society was advanced, not cultured.

5. The word <u>unique</u> in the passage is closest in meaning to

  Ⓐ old
  Ⓑ rare
  Ⓒ perfect
  Ⓓ weak

6. According to paragraph 4, why do many scholars believe that the original manuscript for *Beowulf* was lost?

  Ⓐ Because it is not like other manuscripts
  Ⓑ Because many libraries were burned
  Ⓒ Because the Danes were allies of the Anglo-Saxons
  Ⓓ Because no copies were found in monasteries

  Paragraph 4 is marked with an arrow [➔].

7. In paragraph 4, the author suggests that *Beowulf* was discovered in the

  Ⓐ first century
  Ⓑ ninth century
  Ⓒ eleventh century
  Ⓓ seventeenth century

  Paragraph 4 is marked with an arrow [➔].

8. Why does the author of this passage use the word "apparently" in paragraph 5?

   ⒜ He is not certain that the author of *Beowulf* was a Christian.
   ⒝ He is mentioning facts that are obvious to the readers.
   ⒞ He is giving an example from a historical reference.
   ⒟ He is introducing evidence about the author of *Beowulf.*

   Paragraph 5 is marked with an arrow [➔].

9. The author compared the Beowulf character to Hercules because

   ⒜ they are both examples of the ideal hero
   ⒝ their adventures with a dragon are very similar
   ⒞ the speeches that they make are inspiring
   ⒟ they lived at about the same time

10. The word <u>exhibits</u> in the passage is closest in meaning to

    ⒜ creates
    ⒝ demonstrates
    ⒞ assumes
    ⒟ terminates

11. The word <u>reject</u> in the passage is closest in meaning to

    ⒜ manage
    ⒝ evaluate
    ⒞ refuse
    ⒟ confront

12. Look at the four squares [■] that show where the following sentence could be inserted in the passage.

    Moreover, they disagree as to whether this *Beowulf* is a copy of an earlier manuscript.

    Where could the sentence best be added?

    Click on a square [■] to insert the sentence in the passage.

13. **Directions:** An introduction for a short summary of the passage appears below. Complete the summary by selecting the THREE answer choices that mention the most important points in the passage. Some sentences do not belong in the summary because they express ideas that are not included in the passage or are minor points from the passage. *This question is worth 2 points.*

Beowulf is the oldest Anglo-Saxon epic poem that has survived to the present day.

• *E*

•

•

Answer Choices

A The Northmen were adept in crafting tools and weapons made of bronze, but the Celts were superior in designing and working in iron.

B In the Viking invasions of England, the Danish armies destroyed monasteries, some of which contained extensive libraries.

C King Hrothgar and Beowulf become friends at the end of their lives, after having spent decades opposing each other on the battlefield.

D The poem chronicles life in Anglo-Saxon society during the Bronze and Iron Ages when Germanic tribes were invading England.

E Although *Beowulf* was written by an anonymous poet, probably a Christian, about 1000 A.D., it was not found until the seventeenth century.

F *Beowulf* is still interesting because it has engaging characters, an adventurous plot, and an appreciation for human behavior and relationships.

PART II

Reading 2 "Thermoregulation"

→ Mammals and birds generally maintain body temperature within a narrow range (36–38°C for most mammals and 39–42°C for most birds) that is usually considerably warmer than the environment. Because heat always flows from a warm object to cooler surroundings, birds and mammals must counteract the constant heat loss. This maintenance of warm body temperature depends on several key adaptations. The most basic mechanism is the high metabolic rate of endothermy itself. Endotherms can produce large amounts of metabolic heat that replace the flow of heat to the environment, and they can vary heat production to match changing rates of heat loss. Heat production is increased by such muscle activity as moving or shivering. In some mammals, certain hormones can cause mitochondria to increase their metabolic activity and produce heat instead of ATP. This **nonshivering thermogenesis (NST)** takes place throughout the body, but some mammals also have a tissue called **brown fat** in the neck and between the shoulders that is specialized for rapid heat production. Through shivering and NST, mammals and birds in cold environments can increase their metabolic heat production by as much as 5 to 10 times above the minimal levels that occur in warm conditions.

→ Another major thermoregulatory adaptation that evolved in mammals and birds is insulation (hair, feathers, and fat layers), which reduces the flow of heat and lowers the energy cost of keeping warm. Most land mammals and birds react to cold by raising their fur or feathers, thereby trapping a thicker layer of air. A Humans rely more on a layer of fat just beneath the skin as insulation; goose bumps are a vestige of hair-raising left over from our furry ancestors. B Vasodilation and vasoconstriction also regulate heat exchange and may contribute to regional temperature differences within the animal. C For example, heat loss from a human is reduced when arms and legs cool to several degrees below the temperature of the body core, where most vital organs are located. D

→ Hair loses most of its insulating power when wet. Marine mammals such as whales and seals have a very thick layer of insulation fat called blubber, just under the skin. Marine mammals swim in water colder than their body core temperature, and many species spend at least part of the year in nearly freezing polar seas. The loss of heat to water occurs 50 to 100 times more rapidly than heat loss to air, and the skin temperature of a marine mammal is close to water temperature. Even so, the blubber insulation is so effective that marine mammals maintain body core temperatures of about 36–38°C with metabolic rates about the same as those of land mammals of similar size. The flippers or tail of a whale or seal lack insulating blubber, but countercurrent heat exchangers greatly reduce heat loss in these extremities, as they do in the legs of many birds.

➔ Through metabolic heat production, insulation, and vascular adjustments, birds and mammals are capable of astonishing feats of thermoregulation. For example, small birds called chickadees, which weigh only 20 grams, can remain active and hold body temperature nearly constant at 40°C in environmental temperatures as low as –40°C—as long as they have enough food to supply the large amount of energy necessary for heat production.

Many mammals and birds live in places where thermoregulation requires cooling off as well as warming. For example, when a marine mammal moves into warm seas, as many whales do when they reproduce, excess metabolic heat is removed by vasodilation of numerous blood vessels in the outer layer of the skin. In hot climates or when vigorous exercise adds large amounts of metabolic heat to the body, many terrestrial mammals and birds may allow body temperature to rise by several degrees, which enhances heat loss by increasing the temperature gradient between the body and a warm environment.

➔ Evaporative cooling often plays a key role in dissipating the body heat. If environmental temperature is above body temperature, animals gain heat from the environment as well as from metabolism, and evaporation is the only way to keep body temperature from rising rapidly. Panting is important in birds and many mammals. Some birds have a pouch richly supplied with blood vessels in the floor of the mouth; fluttering the pouch increases evaporation. Pigeons can use evaporative cooling to keep body temperature close to 40°C in air temperatures as high as 60°C, as long as they have sufficient water. Many terrestrial mammals have sweat glands controlled by the nervous system. Other mechanisms that promote evaporative cooling include spreading saliva on body surfaces, an adaptation of some kangaroos and rodents for combating severe heat stress. Some bats use both saliva and urine to enhance evaporative cooling.

Glossary
ATP: energy that drives certain reactions in cells
mitochondria: a membrane of ATP

14. According to paragraph 1, the most fundamental adaptation to maintain body temperature is

  Ⓐ the heat generated by the metabolism
  Ⓑ a shivering reflex in the muscles
  Ⓒ migration to a warmer environment
  Ⓓ higher caloric intake to match heat loss

Paragraph 1 is marked with an arrow [➔].

15. Based on information in paragraph 1, which of the following best explains the term "thermogenesis"?

    Ⓐ Heat loss that must be reversed
    Ⓑ The adaptation of brown fat tissue in the neck
    Ⓒ The maintenance of healthy environmental conditions
    Ⓓ Conditions that affect the metabolism

Paragraph 1 is marked with an arrow [➜].

16. Which of the sentences below best expresses the information in the highlighted statement in the passage? The other choices change the meaning or leave out important information.

    Ⓐ An increase in heat production causes muscle activity such as moving or shivering.
    Ⓑ Muscle activity like moving and shivering will increase heat production.
    Ⓒ Moving and shivering are muscle activities that increase with heat.
    Ⓓ When heat increases, the production of muscle activity also increases.

17. The word <u>minimal</u> in the passage is closest in meaning to

    Ⓐ most recent
    Ⓑ most active
    Ⓒ newest
    Ⓓ smallest

18. In paragraph 2, the author explains the concept of vasodilation and vasoconstriction by

    Ⓐ describing the evolution in our ancestors
    Ⓑ giving an example of heat loss in the extremities
    Ⓒ comparing the process in humans and animals
    Ⓓ identifying various types of insulation

Paragraph 2 is marked with an arrow [➜].

19. The word <u>regulate</u> in the passage is closest in meaning to

    Ⓐ protect
    Ⓑ create
    Ⓒ reduce
    Ⓓ control

20. According to paragraph 3, why do many marine animals require a layer of blubber?

    Ⓐ Because marine animals have lost their hair during evolution
    Ⓑ Because heat is lost in water twice as fast as it is in air
    Ⓒ Because dry hair does not insulate marine animals
    Ⓓ Because they are so large that they require more insulation

    Paragraph 3 is marked with an arrow [➔].

21. The word <u>those</u> in the passage refers to

    Ⓐ marine animals
    Ⓑ core temperatures
    Ⓒ land mammals
    Ⓓ metabolic rates

22. Why does the author mention chickadees in paragraph 4?

    Ⓐ To discuss an animal that regulates heat very well
    Ⓑ To demonstrate why chickadees have to eat so much
    Ⓒ To mention an exception to the rules of thermoregulation
    Ⓓ To give a reason for heat production in small animals

    Paragraph 4 is marked with an arrow [➔].

23. In paragraph 6, the author states that evaporative cooling is often accomplished by all of the following methods EXCEPT

    Ⓐ by spreading saliva over the area
    Ⓑ by urinating on the body
    Ⓒ by panting or fluttering a pouch
    Ⓓ by immersing themselves in water

    Paragraph 6 is marked with an arrow [➔].

24. The word <u>enhance</u> in the passage is closest in meaning to

    Ⓐ simplify
    Ⓑ improve
    Ⓒ replace
    Ⓓ interrupt

25. Look at the four squares [■] that show where the following sentence could be inserted in the passage.

    The insulating power of a layer of fur or feathers mainly depends on how much still air the layer traps.

    Where could the sentence best be added?

    Click on a square [■] to insert the sentence in the passage.

26. **Directions:** An introduction for a short summary of the passage appears below. Complete the summary by selecting the THREE answer choices that mention the most important points in the passage. Some sentences do not belong in the summary because they express ideas that are not included in the passage or are minor points from the passage. *This question is worth 2 points.*

    Thermoregulation is the process by which animals control body temperatures within healthy limits.

    -
    -
    -

Answer Choices

Ⓐ Although hair can be a very efficient insulation when it is dry and it can be raised, hair becomes ineffective when it is submerged in cold water.

Ⓑ Some animals with few adaptations for thermoregulation migrate to moderate climates to avoid the extreme weather in the polar regions and the tropics.

Ⓒ Mammals and birds use insulation to mitigate heat loss, including hair and feathers that can be raised to trap air as well as fat or blubber under the skin.

Ⓓ Some birds have a special pouch in the mouth, which can be fluttered to increase evaporation and decrease their body temperatures by as much as 20°C.

Ⓔ Endotherms generate heat by increasing muscle activity, by releasing hormones into their blood streams, or by producing heat in brown fat tissues.

Ⓕ Panting, sweating, and spreading saliva or urine on their bodies are all options for the evaporative cooling of animals in hot environmental conditions.

Reading 3 "Social Readjustment Scales"

→ Holmes and Rahe (1967) developed the Social Readjustment Rating Scale (SRRS) to measure life change as a form of stress. Ⓐ The scale assigns numerical values to 43 major life events that are supposed to reflect the magnitude of the readjustment required by each change. In responding to the scale, respondents are asked to indicate how often they experienced any of these 43 events during a certain time period (typically, the past year). The person then adds up the numbers associated with each event checked. Ⓑ

→ The SRRS and similar scales have been used in thousands of studies by researchers all over the world. Ⓒ Overall, these studies have shown that people with higher scores on the SRRS tend to be more vulnerable to many kinds of physical illness—and many types of psychological problems as well (Derogatis & Coons, 1993; Gruen, 1993; Scully, Tosi & Banning, 2000). Ⓓ More recently, however, experts have criticized this research, citing problems with the methods used and raising questions about the meaning of the findings (Critelli & Ee, 1996; Monroe & McQuaid, 1994; Wethington, 2000).

First, the assumption that the SRRS measures change exclusively has been shown to be inaccurate. We now have ample evidence that the desirability of events affects adaptational outcomes more than the amount of change that they require (Turner & Wheaton, 1995). Thus, it seems prudent to view the SRRS as a measure of diverse forms of stress, rather than as a measure of change-related stress (McLean & Link, 1994).

→ Second, the SRRS fails to take into account differences among people in their subjective perception of how stressful an event is. For instance, while divorce may deserve a stress value of 73 for *most* people, a particular person's divorce might generate much less stress and merit a value of only 25.

→ Third, many of the events listed on the SRRS and similar scales are highly ambiguous, leading people to be inconsistent as to which events they report experiencing (Monroe & McQuaid, 1994). For instance, what qualifies as "trouble with the boss"? Should you check that because you're sick and tired of your supervisor? What constitutes a "change in living conditions"? Does your purchase of a great new sound system qualify? As you can see, the SRRS includes many "events" that are described inadequately, producing considerable ambiguity about the meaning of one's response. Problems in recalling events over a period of a year also lead to inconsistent responding on stress scales, thus lowering their reliability (Klein & Rubovits, 1987).

Fourth, the SRRS does not sample from the domain of stressful events very thoroughly. Do the 43 events listed on the SRRS exhaust all the major stresses that people typically experience? Studies designed to explore that question have found many significant omissions (Dohrenwend et al., 1993; Wheaton, 1994).

→ Fifth, the correlation between SRRS scores and health outcomes may be inflated because subjects' neuroticism affects both their responses to stress scales and their self-reports of health problems. Neurotic individuals have a tendency to recall more stress than others and to recall more symptoms of illness than others (Watson, David, & Suls, 1999). These tendencies mean that some of the correlation between high stress and high illness may simply reflect the effects of subjects' neuroticism (Critelli & Ee, 1996). The possible contaminating effects of neuroticism obscure the meaning of scores on the SRRS and similar measures of stress.

The Life Experiences Survey

In the light of these problems, a number of researchers have attempted to develop improved versions of the SRRS. For example, the Life Experiences Survey (LES), assembled by Irwin Sarason and colleagues (1978), has become a widely used measure of stress in contemporary research (for examples see Ames et al., 2001; Denisoff & Endler, 2000; Malefo, 2000). The LES revises and builds on the SRRS survey in a variety of ways that correct, at least in part, most of the problems just discussed.

→ Specifically, the LES recognizes that stress involves more than mere change and asks respondents to indicate whether events had a positive or negative impact on them. This strategy permits the computation of positive change, negative change, and total change scores, which helps researchers gain much more insight into which facets of stress are most crucial. The LES also takes into consideration differences among people in their appraisal of stress, by dropping the normative weights and replacing them with personally assigned weightings of the impact of relevant events. Ambiguity in items is decreased by providing more elaborate descriptions of many items to clarify their meaning.

The LES deals with the failure of the SRRS to sample the full domain of stressful events in several ways. First, some significant omissions from the SRRS have been added to the LES. Second, the LES allows the respondent to write in personally important events that are not included on the scale. Third, the LES has an extra section just for students. Sarason et al. (1978) suggest that special, tailored sections of this sort be added for specific populations whenever it is useful.

27. Based on the information in paragraph 1 and paragraph 2, what can be inferred about a person with a score of 30 on the SRRS?

    Ⓐ A person with a higher score will experience less stress than this person will.
    Ⓑ It is likely that this person has not suffered any major problems in the past year.
    Ⓒ The amount of positive change is greater than that of a person with a score of 40.
    Ⓓ This person has a greater probability to be ill than a person with a 20 score.

Paragraph 1 and Paragraph 2 are marked with arrows [→].

28. The word <u>they</u> in the passage refers to

    Ⓐ changes
    Ⓑ measures
    ✓ Ⓒ events
    Ⓓ outcomes

29. The word <u>diverse</u> in the passage is closest in meaning to

    Ⓐ necessary
    Ⓑ steady
    Ⓒ limited
    ✓ Ⓓ different

30. In paragraph 4, the author uses divorce as an example to show

    Ⓐ how most people respond to high stress situations in their lives
    Ⓑ the serious nature of a situation that is listed as a stressful event
    ✓ Ⓒ the subjective importance of a situation listed on the scale
    Ⓓ the numerical value for a stressful event on the SRRS

    Paragraph 4 is marked with an arrow [➔].

31. In paragraph 5, how does the author demonstrate that the response events on the SRRS are not consistent?

    ✓ Ⓐ By asking questions that could be answered in more than one way
    Ⓑ By giving examples of responses that are confusing
    Ⓒ By comparing several ways to score the stress scales
    Ⓓ By suggesting that people do not respond carefully

    Paragraph 5 is marked with an arrow [➔].

32. According to paragraph 7, why is the SRRS inappropriate for people with neuroses?

    Ⓐ They are ill more often, which affects their scores on the scale.
    ✓ Ⓑ Their self-reporting on the scale is affected by their neuroses.
    Ⓒ They tend to suffer more stress than people without neuroses.
    Ⓓ Their response to stress will probably not be recorded on the scale.

    Paragraph 7 is marked with an arrow [➔].

33. The word <u>assembled</u> in the passage is closest in meaning to

    Ⓐ announced
    Ⓑ influenced
    ✓ Ⓒ arranged
    Ⓓ distributed

34. The word <u>relevant</u> in the passage is closest in meaning to

    Ⓐ occasional
    Ⓑ modern
    Ⓒ related
    Ⓓ unusual

35. According to paragraph 9, why does the LES ask respondents to classify change as positive or negative?

    Ⓐ To analyze the long-term consequences of change
    Ⓑ To determine which aspects of change are personally significant
    Ⓒ To explain why some people handle stress better than others
    Ⓓ To introduce normative weighting of stress events

Paragraph 9 is marked with an arrow [➔].

36. According to the passage, which of the following is true about the SRRS as compared with the LES?

    Ⓐ The SRRS includes a space to write in personal events that have not been listed.
    Ⓑ The SRRS features a section for specific populations such as students.
    Ⓒ The SRRS assigns numbers to calculate the stress associated with events.
    Ⓓ The SRRS has hints to help people recall events that happened over a year ago.

37. Which of the following statements most accurately reflects the author's opinion of the SRRS?

    Ⓐ There are many problems associated with it.
    Ⓑ It is superior to the LES.
    Ⓒ It should be studied more carefully.
    Ⓓ The scale is most useful for students.

38. Look at the four squares [■] that show where the following sentence could be inserted in the passage.

This sum is an index of the amount of change-related stress the person has recently experienced.

Where could the sentence best be added?

Click on a square [■] to insert the sentence in the passage.

39. **Directions**: Complete the table by matching the phrases on the left with the headings on the right. Select the appropriate answer choices and drag them to the surveys to which they relate. TWO of the answer choices will NOT be used. *This question is worth 4 points.*

To delete an answer choice, click on it. To see the passage, click on **View Text**.

Answer Choices	**SRRS**
A Limits the events to forty-three major life changes	•
B Calculates subscores for negative and positive changes	•
C Must be taken twice in one year for a reliable score	•
D Incorporates a space to write in additional events	**LES**
E Provides for subjective interpretation of the changes	•
F Is no longer being used by psychologists	•
G Includes sections for specialized populations	•
H Consists of a scale developed in the 1960s	•
I Assigns a standard numerical value to events	

LISTENING SECTION

 Model Test 1, Listening Section, CD 1, Track 1

The Listening section tests your ability to understand spoken English that is typical of interactions and academic speech on college campuses. During the test, you will respond to conversations and lectures.

This is the long format for the Listening section. On the long format, you will respond to three conversations and six lectures. After each listening passage, you will answer 5–6 questions about it. Only two conversations and four lectures will be graded. The other conversation and lectures are part of an experimental section for future tests. Because you will not know which conversations and lectures will be graded, you must try to do your best on all of them.

You will hear each conversation or lecture one time. You may take notes while you listen, but notes are not graded. You may use your notes to answer the questions.

Choose the best answer for multiple-choice questions. Follow the directions on the page or on the screen for computer-assisted questions. Click on **Next** and **OK** to go to the next question. You cannot return to previous questions. You have 20–30 minutes to answer all of the questions. A clock on the screen will show you how much time you have to complete your answers for the section. The clock does not count the time you are listening to the conversations and lectures.

PART I

Listening 1 "Learning Center"

1. What does the woman need?

    Ⓐ A meeting with Professor Simpson
    Ⓑ An English composition class
    Ⓒ An appointment for tutoring
    Ⓓ Information about the Learning Center

2. Why does the woman say this:

    Ⓐ She is worried that she cannot afford the service.
    Ⓑ She is trying to negotiate the cost of the sessions.
    Ⓒ She is showing particular interest in the man.
    Ⓓ She is expressing surprise about the arrangement.

3. Why is the man concerned about the woman's attendance?

    Ⓐ If she is absent, her grade will be lowered.
    Ⓑ He will not get a paycheck if she is absent.
    Ⓒ She has been sick a lot during the semester.
    Ⓓ Her grades need to be improved.

4. What does the man agree to do?

    Ⓐ He will show the woman how to use the library.
    Ⓑ He will write some compositions for the woman.
    Ⓒ He will talk with the woman's English professor.
    Ⓓ He will show the woman how to improve her writing.

5. What does the man imply about the woman's teacher?

    Ⓐ The professor is very difficult to understand.
    Ⓑ He does not know where she came from.
    Ⓒ Her students seem to like her teaching style.
    Ⓓ He is familiar with her requirements.

Listening 2 "Geology Class"

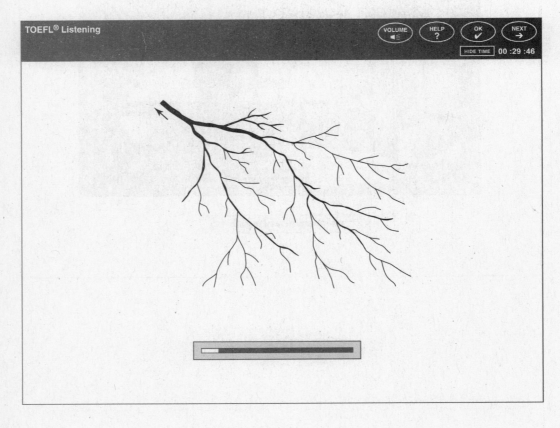

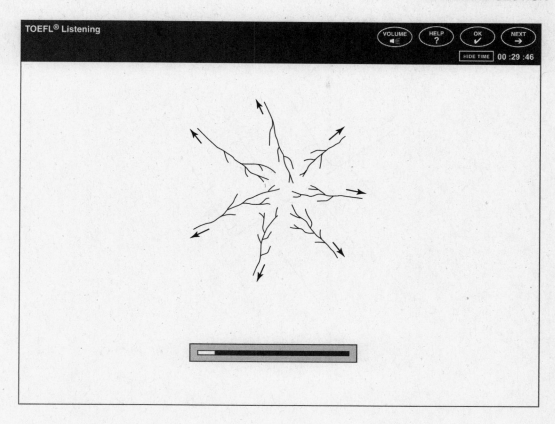

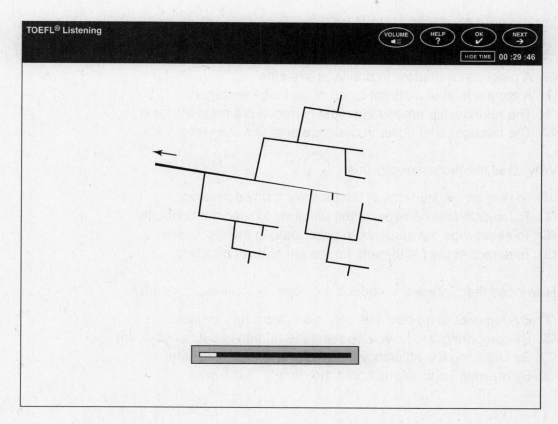

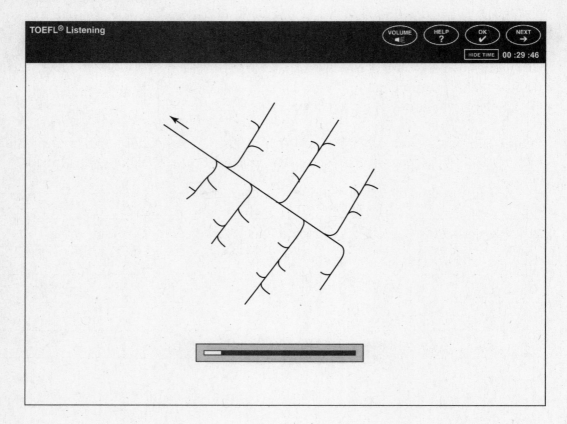

6. What is this lecture mainly about?

    Ⓐ A process for improving drainage systems
    Ⓑ A comparison of different types of drainage systems
    Ⓒ The relationship among the most common drainage systems
    Ⓓ The changes that occur in drainage systems over time

7. Why does the professor say this:

    Ⓐ To remind the students of the topic for today's session
    Ⓑ To indicate that he expects the students to read the textbook
    Ⓒ To encourage the students to participate in the discussion
    Ⓓ To demonstrate his respect for the students in his class

8. How does the professor introduce the dendritic drainage system?

    Ⓐ By demonstrating how this very old system has evolved
    Ⓑ By comparing it to both a tree and the human circulatory system
    Ⓒ By criticizing the efficiency of the branches in the system
    Ⓓ By drawing conclusions about the climate in the area

9. Why does the professor mention the spokes of a wheel?

   Ⓐ To make a point about the stream beds in a trellis pattern
   Ⓑ To contrast the formation with that of a rectangular one
   Ⓒ To explain the structure of a radial drainage system
   Ⓓ To give an example of a dendritic drainage system

10. In the lecture, the professor discusses the trellis drainage pattern. Indicate whether each of the following is typical of this pattern. Click in the correct box for each phrase.

		Yes	No
A	Parallel stream beds flowing beside each other		
B	Stream beds with sharp 90 degree turns		
C	Drainage from the top of a central peak		
D	Hard rock formations on top of soft rock formations		
E	Geological evidence of folding with outcroppings		

11. What does the professor imply when he says this:

   Ⓐ The test questions will be very difficult.
   Ⓑ The students should read their textbooks before the test.
   Ⓒ The basic patterns from the notes will be on the test.
   Ⓓ The test will influence the final grade.

Listening 3 "Art Class"

12. What is the lecture mainly about?

    Ⓐ The way that drawing has influenced art
    Ⓑ The relationship between drawing and other art
    Ⓒ The distinct purposes of drawing
    Ⓓ The reason that artists prefer drawing

13. According to the professor, why do architects use sketches?

    Ⓐ Architects are not clear about the final design at the beginning.
    Ⓑ To design large buildings, architects must work in a smaller scale.
    Ⓒ Engineers use the architect's sketches to implement the details.
    Ⓓ Sketches are used as a record of the stages in development.

14. What does the professor mean when she says this:

    Ⓐ She is checking to be sure that the students understand.
    Ⓑ She is expressing uncertainty about the information.
    Ⓒ She is inviting the students to disagree with her.
    Ⓓ She is indicating that she is in a hurry to continue.

15. Why does the professor mention the drawing of Marie Antoinette?

    Ⓐ It is an example of a work copied in another medium.
    Ⓑ Drawing was typical of the way that artists were educated.
    Ⓒ The sketch was a historical account of an important event.
    Ⓓ The size of the drawing made it an exceptional work of art.

16. What is the professor's opinion of Picasso?

    Ⓐ Picasso was probably playing a joke by offering drawings for sale.
    Ⓑ At the end of his career, Picasso may have chosen drawing because it was easy.
    Ⓒ Picasso's drawings required the confidence and skill of a master artist.
    Ⓓ Cave drawings were the inspiration for many of Picasso's works.

17. According to the lecture, what are the major functions of drawing?

Click on 3 answer choices.

A̲ A technique to remember parts of a large work

B̲ A method to preserve a historical record

C̲ An example of earlier forms of art

D̲ An educational approach to train artists

E̲ A process for experimenting with media

PART II

Listening 4 "Professor's Office"

18. Why does the woman go to see her professor?

    Ⓐ To get notes from a class that she has missed
    Ⓑ To clarify some of the information from a lecture
    Ⓒ To talk about her career in international business
    Ⓓ To ask some questions about a paper she is writing

19. According to the professor, which factor causes staffing patterns to vary?

    Ⓐ The yearly earnings for all of the branch offices
    Ⓑ The number of employees in a multinational company
    Ⓒ The place where a company has its home office
    Ⓓ The number of years that a company has been in business

20. Why does the professor say this:

    Ⓐ To indicate that he is getting impatient
    Ⓑ To encourage the woman to continue
    Ⓒ To show that he does not understand
    Ⓓ To correct the woman's previous comment

21. Which of the following would be an example of a third-country pattern?

    Click on 2 answer choices.

    Ⓐ A Scottish manager in an American company in Africa

    Ⓑ A German manager in a Swiss company in Germany

    Ⓒ A British manager in an American company in India

    Ⓓ A French manager in a French company in Canada

22. According to the professor, how do senior-level Japanese managers view their assignments abroad?

    Ⓐ They consider them to be permanent career opportunities.
    Ⓑ They use them to learn skills that they will use in Japan.
    Ⓒ They understand that the assignment is only temporary.
    Ⓓ They see them as a strategy for their retirement.

Listening 5 "Astronomy Class"

23. What is the discussion mainly about?

   Ⓐ The discovery of the Alpha Centauri system
   Ⓑ The reason solar systems are confused with galaxies
   Ⓒ The vast expanse of the universe around us
   Ⓓ The model at the National Air and Space Museum

24. Why does the professor say this:

   Ⓐ The students can read the details in the textbook.
   Ⓑ The professor wants the students to concentrate on listening.
   Ⓒ The facts are probably already familiar to most of the class.
   Ⓓ This lecture is a review of material from a previous session.

25. Why wouldn't a photograph capture a true picture of the solar system walk?

   Ⓐ It would not show the distances between the bodies in space.
   Ⓑ The information on the markers would not be visible in a picture.
   Ⓒ The scale for the model was not large enough to be accurate.
   Ⓓ A photograph would make the exhibit appear much smaller.

26. How does the professor explain the term *solar system*?

   Ⓐ He identifies the key features of a solar system.
   Ⓑ He refers to the glossary in the textbook.
   Ⓒ He gives several examples of solar systems.
   Ⓓ He contrasts a solar system with a galaxy.

27. Why does the professor say this:

   Ⓐ He is trying to get the students to pay attention.
   Ⓑ He is correcting something that he said earlier in the lecture.
   Ⓒ He is beginning a summary of the important points.
   Ⓓ He is joking with the students about the lecture.

28. What can be inferred about the professor?

   Ⓐ The professor used to teach in Washington, D.C.
   Ⓑ The professor likes his students to participate in the discussion.
   Ⓒ The professor wants the students to take notes on every detail.
   Ⓓ The professor is not very interested in the subject of the lecture.

Listening 6 "Psychology Class"

29. What is the discussion mainly about?

    Ⓐ The difference between suppression and repression
    Ⓑ Why Freud's theories of defense mechanisms are correct
    Ⓒ Some of the more common types of defense mechanisms
    Ⓓ How to solve a student's problem with an unfair professor

30. How does the student explain the term *repression*?

    Ⓐ He contrasts it with suppression.
    Ⓑ He identifies it as a conscious response.
    Ⓒ He gives several examples of it.
    Ⓓ He refers to a study by Freud.

31. Why does the professor say this:

    Ⓐ She is getting the class to pay attention.
    Ⓑ She is making a joke about herself.
    Ⓒ She is asking for a compliment.
    Ⓓ She is criticizing a colleague.

32. Which of the following is an example of *displacement* that was used in the lecture?

    Ⓐ Insisting that the professor dislikes you, when you really dislike him
    Ⓑ Defending the professor even when you are angry about his behavior
    Ⓒ Blaming someone in your study group instead of blaming the professor
    Ⓓ Refusing to acknowledge that a problem exists because of the low grade

33. According to the professor, what happened in the 1990s?

    Ⓐ The concept of defense mechanisms was abandoned.
    Ⓑ New terms were introduced for the same mechanisms.
    Ⓒ Modern researchers improved upon Freud's theory.
    Ⓓ Additional categories were introduced by researchers.

34. How does the professor organize the lecture?

    Ⓐ She has visual aids to explain each point.
    Ⓑ She uses a scenario that students can relate to.
    Ⓒ She provides a handout with an outline.
    Ⓓ She helps students read the textbook.

PART III

Listening 7 "Bookstore"

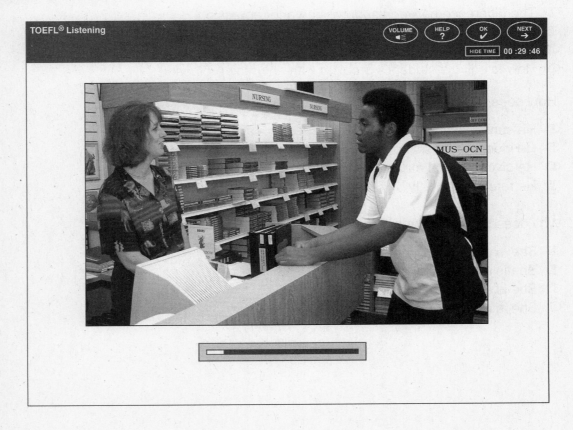

35. What does the man need from the bookstore?

    Ⓐ A schedule of classes for next term
    Ⓑ A form to order books
    Ⓒ Specific books for his classes
    Ⓓ Information about employment

36. What does the man need if he wants a full refund?

    Click on 2 answer choices.

    Ⓐ Identification

    Ⓑ His registration form

    Ⓒ A receipt for the purchase

    Ⓓ Proof of his deposit

37. What does the woman mean when she says this:

    Ⓐ She is not sure that the student employee will give her the form.
    Ⓑ She thinks that he will have to wait for the student employees.
    Ⓒ She does not want the man to bother her because she is busy.
    Ⓓ She is is not sure that the man understands what to do.

38. What does the woman imply about the used books she sells?

    Ⓐ They are purchased before new books.
    Ⓑ They do not have marks in them.
    Ⓒ She does not recommend buying them.
    Ⓓ She would rather sell new books.

39. What does the man need to do now?

    Ⓐ Go to the bank to get money for the deposit
    Ⓑ Sit down and fill out the form to order books
    Ⓒ Take his books back to the dormitory
    Ⓓ Locate the schedule numbers for his classes

Listening 8 "Environmental Science Class"

40. What is this lecture mainly about?

    ⓐ An overview of fuel cell technology
    ⓑ A process for producing fuel cells
    ⓒ A comparison of fuel cell models
    ⓓ Some problems in fuel cell distribution

41. What does the professor mean when he says this:

    ⓐ He wants the students to take notes.
    ⓑ He would like the students to participate.
    ⓒ He is impressed with these options.
    ⓓ He does not plan to talk about the alternatives.

42. Why does the professor mention the STEP program in Australia?

    ⓐ He has personal experience in this project.
    ⓑ He is referring to information from a previous discussion.
    ⓒ He is comparing it to a successful program in Japan.
    ⓓ He thinks it is a very good example of a project.

43. Why does the professor say this:

    ⓐ To indicate that the date is not important
    ⓑ To provide a specific date for the contract
    ⓒ To correct a previous statement about the date
    ⓓ To show that he is uncertain about the date

44. What are some of the problems associated with fuel cell technology?

    Click on 2 answer choices.

    Ⓐ Noise pollution

    Ⓑ Public acceptance

    Ⓒ Supplies of hydrogen

    Ⓓ Investment in infrastructures

45. What is the professor's attitude toward fuel cells?

    ⓐ He thinks that the technology is not very efficient.
    ⓑ He is hopeful about their development in the future.
    ⓒ He is doubtful that fuel cells will replace fossil fuels.
    ⓓ He is discouraged because of the delays in production.

Listening 9 "Philosophy Class"

TOEFL® Listening   VOLUME   HELP   OK   NEXT
                            ◄≡   ?   ✔   →
                                          HIDE TIME 00 :29 :46

Renaissance

46. What is the main focus of this discussion?

    Ⓐ The Renaissance
    Ⓑ Important scholars
    Ⓒ Humanism
    Ⓓ Political reform

47. Why does the professor say this:

    Ⓐ She thinks that the spelling of the term is not important.
    Ⓑ She assumes that the students know how to spell the term.
    Ⓒ She knows that the term can be found in the textbook.
    Ⓓ She does not want to spend time explaining the term.

48. Why does the professor mention the drawing by Leonardo da Vinci?

    Ⓐ She wants the students to refer to their textbook more often.
    Ⓑ She uses it as an example of the union of art and science.
    Ⓒ She says that it is one of her personal favorites.
    Ⓓ She contrasts his work with that of other artists.

49. According to the professor, what was the effect of using Latin as a universal language of scholarship?

    Ⓐ It facilitated communication among intellectuals in many countries.
    Ⓑ It made Rome the capital of the world during the Renaissance.
    Ⓒ It caused class distinctions to be apparent throughout Europe.
    Ⓓ It created an environment in which new ideas were suppressed.

50. According to the professor, what can be inferred about a Renaissance man?

    Ⓐ He would probably be a master craftsman.
    Ⓑ He would have an aptitude for both art and science.
    Ⓒ He would be interested in classical philosophers.
    Ⓓ He would value logic at the expense of creativity.

51. All of the following characteristics are true of humanism EXCEPT

    Ⓐ Mankind is innately good.
    Ⓑ Scholars must serve society.
    Ⓒ The individual is important.
    Ⓓ Human beings are rational.

 Please turn off the audio. There is a 10-minute break between the Listening section and the Speaking section.

SPEAKING SECTION

 Model Test 1, Speaking Section, CD 1, Track 2, continued on CD 2, Track 1

The Speaking section tests your ability to communicate in English in an academic setting. During the test, you will be presented with six speaking questions. The questions ask for a response to a single question, a conversation, a talk, or a lecture.

You may take notes as you listen, but notes are not graded. You may use your notes to answer the questions. Some of the questions ask for a response to a reading passage and a talk or a lecture. The reading passages and the questions are written, but most of the directions will be spoken.

Your speaking will be evaluated on both the fluency of the language and the accuracy of the content. You will have 15–20 seconds to prepare and 45–60 seconds to respond to each question. Typically, a good response will require all of the response time but the answer will be complete by the end of the response time.

The time for the Speaking section is about 20 minutes. A clock on the screen will show you how much time you have to prepare your answer and how much time you have to record it.

Independent Speaking Question 1 "A Marriage Partner"

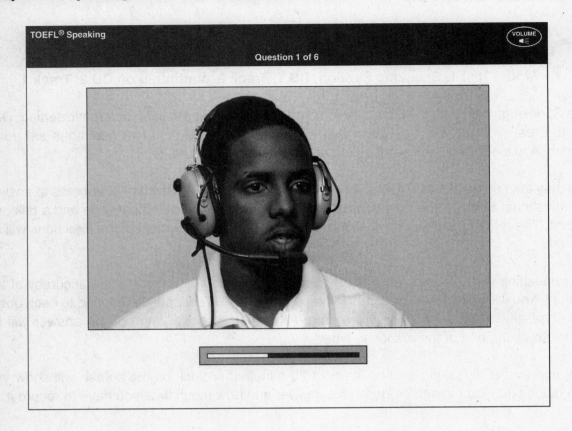

   Listen for a question about a familiar topic.

Question
Describe an ideal marriage partner. What qualities do you think are most important for a husband or wife? Use specific reasons and details to explain your choices.

Preparation Time: 15 seconds
Recording Time: 45 seconds

Independent Speaking Question 2 "News"

 Listen for a question that asks your opinion about a familiar topic.

Question

Some people like to watch the news on television. Other people prefer to read the news in a newspaper. Still others use their computers to get the news. How do you prefer to be informed about the news and why? Use specific reasons and examples to support your choice.

Preparation Time: 15 seconds
Recording Time: 45 seconds

Integrated Speaking Question 3 "Meal Plan"

Read a short passage and listen to a talk on the same topic.

Reading Time: 45 seconds

<u>Change in Meal Plans</u>
Residence hall students are no longer required to purchase seven-day meal plans. Now two meal plan options will be offered. The traditional seven-day plan will still be available, including three meals every day at a cost of $168 per month. In addition, a five-day plan will be offered, including three meals Monday–Friday at a cost of $120 per month. Students who elect to use the five-day plan may purchase meals on the weekend at three dollars per meal. The food court in the College Union provides several fast-food alternatives. In addition to burgers and pizza, Chinese food, Mexican food, and a salad bar are also available.

TOEFL® Speaking

Question 3 of 6

VOLUME

 Now listen to two students who are talking about the plan.

Question
The man expresses his opinion of the new meal plan. Report his opinion, and explain the reasons that he gives for having that opinion.

Preparation Time: 30 seconds
Recording Time: 60 seconds

Integrated Speaking Question 4 "Aboriginal People"

Read a short passage and listen to part of a lecture on the same topic.

Reading Time: 45 seconds

Aboriginal People

Although the first inhabitants of Australia have been identified by physical characteristics, culture, language, and locale, none of these attributes truly establishes a person as a member of the Aboriginal People. Because the Aboriginal groups settled in various geographical areas and developed customs and lifestyles that reflected the resources available to them, there is great diversity among those groups, including more than 200 linguistic varieties. Probably the most striking comparison is that of the Aboriginal People who inhabit the desert terrain of the Australian Outback with those who live along the coast. Clearly, their societies have developed very different cultures. According to the Department of Education, the best way to establish identity as a member of the Aboriginal People is to be identified and accepted as such by the Aboriginal community.

 Now listen to part of a lecture in an anthropology class. The professor is talking about Aboriginal People.

Question

Explain how the Aboriginal People are identified. Draw upon information in both the reading and the lecture.

Preparation Time: 30 seconds
Recording Time: 60 seconds

Integrated Speaking Question 5 "Scheduling Conflict"

 Now listen to a short conversation between a student and his friend.

Question

Describe the man's problem and the two suggestions that his friend makes about how to handle it. What do you think the man should do, and why?

Preparation Time: 20 seconds
Recording Time: 60 seconds

Integrated Speaking Question 6 "Laboratory Microscope"

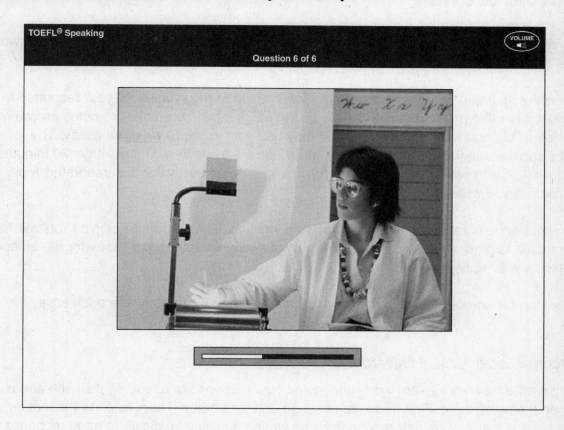

 Now listen to part of a talk in a biology laboratory. The teaching assistant is explaining how to use the microscope.

Question
Using the main points and examples from the talk, describe the two major systems of the laboratory microscope, and then explain how to use it.

Preparation Time: 20 seconds
Recording Time: 60 seconds

WRITING SECTION

The Writing section tests your ability to write essays in English similar to those that you would write in college courses.

During the test, you will write two essays. The integrated essay asks for your response to an academic reading passage and a lecture on the same topic. You may take notes as you read and listen, but notes are not graded. You may use your notes to write the essay. The lecture will be spoken, but the directions and the questions will be written. You will have 20 minutes to plan, write, and revise your response. Typically, a good essay for the integrated topic will require that you write 150–225 words.

The independent essay usually asks for your opinion about a familiar topic. You will have 30 minutes to plan, write, and revise your response. Typically, a good essay for the independent topic will require that you write 300–350 words.

A clock on the screen will show you how much time you have to complete each essay.

Integrated Essay "School Organization"

You have 20 minutes to plan, write, and revise your response to a reading passage and a lecture on the same topic. First, read the passage and take notes. Then, listen to the lecture and take notes. Finally, write your response to the writing question. Typically, a good response will require that you write 150–225 words.

Reading Passage
Time: 3 minutes

Historically, schools in the United States have borrowed the European system of school organization, a system that separates students into grades by chronological age. In general, children begin formal schooling at the age of six in what is referred to as the first grade. For the most part, students progress through twelve grades; however, some students who do not meet minimum requirements for a particular grade may be asked to repeat the year.

Graded schools are divided into primary grades, intermediate grades, and secondary grades. Primary education includes grades 1 through 5 or 6, and may also provide kindergarten as a preparation for first grade. Referred to as elementary school, these grades are usually taught by one teacher in a self-contained classroom. Intermediate grades begin with grade 6 or 7 and offer three years of instruction. At this level, teams of teachers may collaborate to provide subject-based classes similar to those offered in high school. Viewed as a preparation for high school, intermediate education is known as junior high school. At grade 9 or 10, secondary school begins. Classes taught by subject specialists usually last about fifty minutes to allow a student ten minutes to move to the next class before it begins at the top of the hour. At the end of twelve successful grades of instruction, students are eligible for a secondary school diploma, more commonly called a high school diploma.

Model Test 1, Writing Section, CD 2, Track 2

 Now listen to a lecture on the same topic as the passage that you have just read.

Question
Summarize the main points in the lecture, explaining how they cast doubt on the ideas in the reading passage.

Independent Essay "An Important Leader"

Question
Leaders like John F. Kennedy and Martin Luther King have made important contributions to the people of the United States. Name another world leader you think is important. Give specific reasons for your choice.

 This is the end of Model Test 1.
To check your answers, refer to "Explanatory or Example Answers and Audio Scripts for Model Tests: Model Test 1," Chapter 7, pages 552–585.

3

ACADEMIC SKILLS

TAKING NOTES

Taking notes is writing down information while you are listening or reading. There are three problems that you will confront when you are taking notes.

1. **The professor determines the pace of a lecture**. This means that you have to take notes as quickly as the professor speaks.
2. **The notes must include all the main ideas and major facts**. This means that you have to know how to identify important information when you hear it or read it.
3. **The notes may be used for different reasons**. This means that you have to organize the notes to help you remember, to add to the information from another assignment, or to plan a speech or an essay.

This chapter will help you improve your note taking skills. You will learn how to

- **Organize your notes**
- **Identify important information**
- **Take notes quickly**

How will these strategies help you on the TOEFL? By learning to take better notes when you hear lectures, you will have the information you need to respond to the listening comprehension questions and to prepare your speaking and writing questions. You will even improve your reading comprehension. Taking excellent notes is one of the most important academic skills for success on the TOEFL and after the TOEFL when you are enrolled in a college or university program.

ORGANIZE YOUR NOTES

Strategies to Use
- ➤ Anticipate the purpose
- ➤ Divide the paper into columns
- ➤ Separate the major and minor points

➤ Anticipate the purpose

If you can anticipate the purpose of a reading or a lecture, you will be able to prepare your mind to receive the information, and you will already know how to organize your notes.

PRACTICAL STRATEGY

The most common purposes for academic English are to provide the answers to basic questions. These questions are answered in textbooks and lectures to help you learn the academic subjects.

Purpose	Question
Definition	What is it?
Description and Example	What are the characteristics?
Classification	Which group does it belong to?
Sequence	What is the order—first, second, and so on?
Comparison and Contrast	How is it the same or different from something else?
Cause and Effect	How does it cause something? What happens?
Problem and Solution	Why is it a problem? What is the solution?
Persuasion or Evaluation	Why should it be supported or rejected?

The headings and subheadings in textbooks help you anticipate the purpose of the chapter or the sections within a chapter. For example, a heading in an earth science textbook that includes only one noun, **The Atmosphere**, will probably be a definition or a description of the atmosphere. A heading such as **Forces Within the Atmosphere** implies that several forces will be discussed and further implies that this will be a classification or perhaps a comparison and contrast of the forces. **Atmospheric Patterns of Motion** introduces a process and could anticipate a sequence or even a cause and effect. **Problems in Predicting Weather** is a heading that contains the purpose in the word *problems.* You know that this is a problem and solution section. Persuasion can usually be identified because of words like *should* and *must* as well as subjective or judgmental phrases like *better* or *worse*, whereas evaluation contains both sides of an issue.

PRACTICE ACTIVITY 1

Did you understand? Try to anticipate the purpose of each section in a textbook by reading the headings and subheadings. Here are some headings and subheadings for practice. The first one is completed to give you an example. The answers are printed in Chapter 7 on page 503.

Sometimes you will make a mistake anticipating the purpose. Your prediction will be different from the way that the reading or lecture proceeds. Don't worry. Trying to predict is still a good idea, and you will become more skilled as you practice using other activities and tests in this book.

EXAMPLE

Subheading: The Enlightenment   **Purpose:** definition *or* description

1. Settlement Patterns

2. The Functions of Art

3. Language Development

4. How Important Is Relativity?

5. Causes of Schizophrenia

6. Evaluating Kohlberg's Theory

7. Types of Financial Services

8. A History of Plate Tectonics

9. Estimating Population

10. Black Holes

PRACTICAL STRATEGY

The lectures on the TOEFL begin with an introductory screen followed by a narrator's introduction. They will give you a general direction for your listening. Most of the time, the narrator will tell you in which class the lecture is given. Sometimes the narrator will also provide the main topic.

PRACTICE ACTIVITY 2

Did you understand? Try to anticipate part of the narrator's introduction by viewing the introductory screen. Here are some introductions to lectures for practice. The first one is completed to give you an example. The answers are printed in Chapter 7 on pages 503–504.

EXAMPLE

Astronomy

"Listen to part of a lecture in an astronomy class."

Activity 2, CD 2, Track 4

1. | **Business** |

   Listen to part of a lecture in _____.

2. | **Music Appreciation** |

   Listen to part of a lecture in _____.

3. | **Biology** |

   Listen to part of a lecture in _____.

4. | **Anthropology** |

   Listen to part of a lecture in _____.

5. | **Engineering** |

   Listen to part of a lecture in _____.

6. | **Linguistics** |

   Listen to part of a lecture in _____.

7. | **Art History** |

   Listen to part of a lecture in _____.

8. | **Psychology** |

   Listen to part of a lecture in _____.

9. | **Geology** |

   Listen to part of a lecture in _____.

10. | **History** |

   Listen to part of a lecture in _____.

PRACTICAL STRATEGY

A good lecturer will also give you ways to anticipate the purpose of a lecture or part of a lecture with verbal cues. Sometimes the lecturer will announce the topic in such a way that the purpose is directly stated. Other times you will have to draw a conclusion. Although the topic is stated at the beginning of the lecture, there may be some references to previous lectures or some classroom business to conclude before the topic is announced. When the topic for a lecture is stated, the lecturer may either pause just before saying the topic or stress the topic by raising the volume or using very clear pronunciation.

To be a good listener, you should prepare your mind to accept the information. If you know which class the lecturer is teaching, you already know how to focus your attention. By hearing the cue that identifies the topic, you have a context for the rest of the lecture.

PRACTICE ACTIVITY 3

Did you understand? Try to anticipate the purpose of a lecture by listening to the beginning of it. Here are some short introductions to lectures for practice. The first one is completed to give you an example. The answers are printed in Chapter 7 on page 504.

EXAMPLE

"Okay then, let's get started. Uh, today we're going to talk about the *biosphere*."

 Activity 3, CD 2, Track 5

1.

2.

3.

4.

5.

6.

7.

8.

9.

10.

➤ Divide the paper into columns

There are many variations of column note taking. This style is very simple and effective. Draw a line down your note paper from the top to the bottom about two inches from the left margin, as shown on the next page. This is called two-column notes. When you are taking notes, put the topics or main ideas in the left column and add details and examples in the right column. This system helps you take notes more quickly because you don't have to identify the main ideas and the details or examples by writing out words or by using a more complicated outline format that requires letters and numbers. Placement to the left or to the right of the line sorts the ideas in order of importance and shows their relationship.

PRACTICAL STRATEGY

Draw a line across the paper from the left to the right about two inches from the top. This is a space for the main idea. Draw another line about two inches from the bottom, as shown. This is a space that you can use for your thoughts and ideas as you are taking notes. Later, when you look at your notes, you will know which ideas are from the textbook or lecture and which are yours.

Main Idea

Major point 1	Examples and details
Major point 2	Examples and details
Major point 3	Examples and details

My Ideas

PRACTICE ACTIVITY 4

Did you understand? Try to put the information in the following sentence outline into two-column notes. Refer to the two-column format above as an example. The answers are printed in Chapter 7 on page 504.

There are three arguments in support of protecting endangered species.

I. Aesthetic justification states that the various forms of nature influence the life experience of human beings in a positive way.
   A. Many endangered species are uniquely beautiful.
   B. They are appreciated universally in art and literature.
   C. Some are important to the religious community.

II. Ecological self-interest assumes that a balance of nature benefits all species.
   A. All species perform essential functions.
      1. For example, an endangered species may be the unique carrier of a cure for a human disease.
   B. In order to protect ourselves, we must protect other species.

III. Moral justification asserts that the creatures themselves have rights.
   A. The United Nations World Charter for Nature declares that all species have the right to exist.
   B. Human beings have the responsibility to preserve all species.

IV. The professor does not directly promote any argument, but advocacy for the protection of endangered species is implied in the lecture.

➤ Separate the major and minor points

In order to use two columns for notes, you must be able to classify the ideas into major and minor points. There are usually three or four major points in a short lecture or reading passage. Each of the major points is supported by examples and details. The examples and details are minor points.

PRACTICAL STRATEGY

When you hear a major point, write it on the left. When you hear a minor point, write it on the right.

PRACTICE ACTIVITY 5

Did you understand? Look at the notes under each topic. The sentences in the notes refer to either the major points or the minor points. Try to organize the notes under the topic by putting the major points in the left column and the minor points in the right column. Your answer is correct if the points are placed correctly on either the left or right. The points do not have to be in exactly the same order. The first one is completed to give you an example. The answers are printed in Chapter 7 on pages 505–506.

EXAMPLE

There are three types of managers in addition to the general manager.

The line manager is responsible for production.
For example, a production manager is a line manager.
A staff manager is in charge of support activities such as human resources.
Information systems is also overseen by a staff manager.
A functional manager is the head of a department.
A department chair at a college is a functional manager.
The manager of a sales department at a company is also a functional manager.

3 managers

line manager production	production manager
staff manager support activities	human resources information systems
functional manager head dept	dept chair college sales dept company

1.   According to Mead, the self has two sides: the "I" and the "me."

     It is predictable because social conformity is expected.
     This part of the self is less predictable because it is unique.
     This part of the self is formed through socialization by others.
     The "I" represents the individuality of a person.
     For instance, a spontaneous reaction might reveal the "I."
     The "me" represents the expectations and attitudes of others.

2.   The mystery of pulsars was resolved in the 1960s.

     We see pulses of light each time the beam sweeps past the Earth.
     The pulsar in the Crab Nebula, for example, currently spins about thirty times per second.
     We also know that pulsars are not perfectly timed because each revolution of a pulsar takes a little longer.
     We know that pulsars are neutron stars, like lighthouses left by supernova explosions.
     It will probably spin about half as fast two thousand years from now.
     Like a lighthouse, the neutron star revolves.

3.   Britain transported convicts to Australia in an effort to solve the problems of overcrowding in prisons.

     There were 11 ships with 750 prisoners aboard.
     Four companies of marines sailed with them as guards.
     They took enough supplies for two years.
     In 1787, the first fleet left for Botany Bay in New South Wales.
     Shortly after arriving in 1788, the colony was moved to Sydney Cove.
     In Sydney, the water supply and soil were better.
     Although Sydney was the new site, for many years it was called Botany Bay.

4.   Frederick Carl Frieseke was an American impressionist.

     In Normandy, he began to paint indoor settings.
     In 1905, Frieseke moved to Giverney where he lived until 1920.
     He studied with Whistler in the late 1800s.
     Born in Michigan, he went to Paris in 1897.
     In his later work, he began to use a darker palette.
     From Whistler, he learned the academic style of the salons.
     At Giverney, Frieseke was influenced by Monet.
     Monet was experimenting with the effects of sunlight.
     The style of Monet and his school is known as impressionism.
     By 1920, Frieseke had left Giverney for Normandy.

5.   Two types of weathering will break down rock masses into smaller particles.

     Interaction between surface or ground water and chemicals causes chemical weathering.
     With increased precipitation or temperature, chemicals tend to break down faster.
     Mechanical weathering occurs when force and pressure grind rocks down.
     A common example is the wearing away of granite facades on buildings.
     The weathering of feldspar in granite can be caused by a reaction to acids in rain.
     Pressure from freezing and thawing causes rocks to expand and contract.
     When a rock is broken in two by physical forces, it is more vulnerable to weathering.

IDENTIFY IMPORTANT INFORMATION

> **Strategies to Use**
> ➤ Pay attention to key words
> ➤ Notice cues in speech and writing

➤ Pay attention to key words

Key words help you identify the important information in a textbook or a lecture. Certain key words appear more often in a reading passage or a lecture with a particular purpose.

PRACTICAL STRATEGY

The key words below are listed under the purpose for which they are frequently used. These key words are not 100 percent accurate, but they do give you a starting point. Key words are especially important in lectures since the sentences that the professor uses in speech are not edited like the sentences in textbooks, and are, therefore, more difficult to follow.

Definition
Is known as
Is called
Is
Refers to
Means

Description and Example
Consists of
Adjective
For example
For instance
Namely
Specifically
That is

Classification
Kinds of
Types of
Classes of
Groups of
Parts of
Properties of
Characteristics of
Varieties of

Sequence—Chronology or Process
First, second, third
Next, then, last
Finally
Before
After
At the same time
Meanwhile
Now
As soon as
Later
Subsequently
Eventually
Step
Stage
Phase

Comparison and Contrast
Like
Similar to
Differ from
Compared with
In comparison
Similarly
In the same way
In contrast
Whereas
Adjective + -er
Although
But
Conversely
In spite of
Even though
However
Instead
On the contrary
On the other hand
Despite

Cause and Effect
As a consequence
As a result
Thus
Therefore
Because
Because of
For this reason
Consequently
Since
So

Problem and Solution
Problem

Persuasion or Evaluation
First, second, third
Should, must, ought to
Therefore
In conclusion, in summary

PRACTICE ACTIVITY 6

Did you understand? Try to identify the key words in the sentences. Underline them. Then decide in which kind of reading passage they might be found. Here are some sentences for practice. The first one is completed to give you an example. The answers are printed in Chapter 7 on page 506.

EXAMPLE

Mesopotamia <u>refers to</u> the land between two rivers. *Definition*

1. There are two types of mixtures—heterogeneous and homogeneous.

2. As a result, the litmus paper turns blue when the solution is a base.

3. In contrast, a counterculture exhibits behavior that is contrary to the dominant culture.

4. The first stage of sleep produces alpha waves.

5. The main properties of soil include color, texture, and structure.

6. Community service should be a requirement for graduation from the College of Education.

7. For example, the Navajo create sacred images in colored sand in order to restore the spiritual and physical health of the sick.

8. The maximum amount of water that air can hold at a given temperature and pressure is known as saturation.

9. Whereas an objective is specific and measurable, a goal is broader and is usually not time specific.

10. Dutch explorers in the early seventeenth century called the west coast of Australia "New Holland," a name that was used to describe the continent until the beginning of the nineteenth century.

➤ Notice cues in speech and writing

Sometimes professors will tell you that a point is important while they are presenting their lectures. Some phrases to listen for include the following:

Pay particular attention to
Be sure to
Especially important is
And this is important
And this is the key point

Written cues will also appear in textbooks. Look for headings, bold letters, and italics.

PRACTICAL STRATEGY

Underline the information or put a star beside it to indicate that the professor has identified it as an important point.

PRACTICE ACTIVITY 7

Did you understand? Listen to the beginning of a lecture on language and try to identify the important information in the notes. Underline it or put a star beside it. A sentence from the lecture is shown here along with a star beside the corresponding point in the notes to give you an example. The answers are printed in Chapter 7 on pages 506–507.

EXAMPLE

"And this is important—standard language is appropriate in both speech and writing."
Notes: *appropriate speech + writing

Listen to the beginning of a lecture in a linguistics class.

Activity 7, CD 2, Track 6

Definition + comparison = three types of language

Standard usage	definitions words + phrases found in dictionary
Permanent core	used formal + informal situations
	*appropriate speech + writing
Colloquial language	included in dictionary marked as colloquial idioms
Often evolves into standard	understood + used in informal situations, not formal
	more common in speech
Slang expressions	sometimes in dictionary marked as slang
Temporary phenomenon	used by some speakers in informal situations
	more common in speech
Continuum	Most Formal—Least Formal
	Standard—Colloquial—Slang

TAKE NOTES QUICKLY

Strategies to Use
➤ Know what to ignore
➤ Use abbreviations and symbols
➤ Draw relationships

➤ Know what to ignore

Sometimes professors will pause to think before they continue their lectures. Some professors will use verbal pauses, for example, *uh* and *um*, as well as words like *now, so, okay, well*. Other professors will use repetition or restatement as a way to gather their thoughts or to clarify a previous point. In repetition, the professor will use the same words or phrases several times. In restatement, the professor will say the same thing in a slightly different way. Since repetition and restatement do not add to the meaning, you can ignore them.

PRACTICAL STRATEGY

The time that the professor uses to think is advantageous to you because you can ignore these pauses, repetitions, and restatements and you can use the additional time to take notes.

PRACTICE ACTIVITY 8

Did you understand? Try to identify the important information in the lecture. Cross out everything in the transcript that you could ignore. The first sentence from the lecture is shown to give you an example. The answers are printed in Chapter 7 on pages 507–508.

EXAMPLE

Status ▮▮▮▮▮▮ position ▮ society ▮▮▮▮ group.

Sociology

Listen to the beginning of a lecture in a sociology class as you read the transcript. The professor is discussing status and roles.

 Activity 8, CD 2, Track 7

Status refers to, uh, a position in society or . . . or in a group. But there are really two types of status—ascribed status and achieved status. Okay, in ascribed status, the status is automatic, so you don't have a choice. In other words, it's an involuntary status. And some examples that come to mind are status because of race or sex. Not much you can do about that. On the other hand, achieved status requires some effort, and there's a choice involved. For instance, a marriage partner, or the type of education, or, for that matter, uh, the length of time in school. Well, these are choices, uh, achievements, and so they fall under the category of achieved status. So, that brings us to the status set. A status set is the combination of all statuses that an individual has. Me, for example. I'm a professor, but I'm also a husband and a father, and, and a, uh, son, since my mother is still living.

So, in each of these statuses, I, I have certain behaviors that are expected, uh, because of the status. Okay, all of the behaviors are roles, I mean, a role is the behavior expected because of status. Okay, back to status set. All of the statuses—husband, father, son, professor—combine to form the status set, and each of the statuses have certain expectations. Let me use that professor status again. So, as a professor, I have a teaching role, and I have to prepare classes. That's expected. I also advise students, grade assignments, and evaluate my students. But this role has very different expectations. Uh, as a researcher, I, I have to design studies, raise funds for grants, and uh, then perform the research, and, and, finally, I write articles and reports. So, I think you see what I mean.

But, one more thing, and this is important, sometimes role conflict can occur. Let me say that again, role conflict. And that means that meeting the expectations for one role will cause problems for an individual who is trying to meet other expectations in a different role. Okay, let's say that one of my students is dating my daughter. I don't recommend this. But anyway, I may have role strain that could even develop into role conflict because it will be difficult for me to meet the expectations for my role as teacher and uh, when the student comes to my house, I'll have to remember my status as father and my role that requires me to welcome a guest into my home, and, well, form an opinion about someone who wants to take my daughter out on a date. The textbook actually . . .

➤ Use abbreviations and symbols

Use abbreviations for important words and phrases that are repeated. There are two ways to do this. You can use capital letters that will remind you of the word or phrase. For example, in a lecture about Colonial America, you might use C M as an abbreviation for the phrase; in a lecture about the philosophy of John Dewey, you could use D as an abbreviation for the name. Or you can write the beginning of the word or phrase. For Colonial America, you could write

Col Am; for John Dewey, J Dew. The abbreviation can be anything that will remind you of the word or phrase when you are reading your notes.

You should also use symbols and abbreviations for small words that are common in the language. The following list includes some of the most commonly used words in English. The abbreviations here are shortened forms for these frequently heard words.

+	and
w	with
w/o	without
=	is, are, means, refers to, like, is called
≠	different, not
#	number
X	times
→	results in, causes, produces, therefore
←	comes from, derives from
ex	example
@	at
1,2,3	first, second, third
<	less, smaller
>	more, larger
btw	between

PRACTICAL STRATEGY

The abbreviations in the list printed above are part of my system for taking notes and some of my students use it, but I encourage you to create your own system because you will probably come up with symbols and abbreviations that will have meaning to you, and you will understand them later when you are reading your notes. There is space for additional words. Be sure to choose something that makes sense to you.

Symbol	Word
	and
	with
	without
	is, are, means, refers to, like, is called
	different, not
	number
	times
	results in, causes, produces, therefore
	comes from, derives from
	example
	at
	first, second, third
	less, smaller
	more, larger
	between

PRACTICE ACTIVITY 9

Did you understand? Now practice taking notes with your system. First, listen to each of the sentences and write your notes here. When you are finished taking notes for all ten sentences, try to write the original sentences using only your notes. Then compare your sentences with the sentences printed in the answer key. An example is shown using my system. Your answer is correct if *you* can read it and if the meaning is the same as the original sentence. The words do not have to be exactly the same. Example answers are printed in Chapter 7 on page 509.

Listen to some sentences from college lectures. Take notes as quickly as you can.

 Activity 9, CD 2, Track 8

EXAMPLE

Friction between moving air and the ocean surface generates undulations of water called *waves*.

Short: Friction btw air + ocean surface → waves
Very short: Fric btw air + Ø surf → waves

Friction between air and the ocean surface causes *waves*.

1.

2.

3.

4.

5.

6.

7.

8.

9.

10.

➤ Draw relationships

To take notes, you can use symbols and diagrams. By using this system, you can reduce the number of words that you have to write. Here are some examples of notes for each of the common relationships.

DEFINITION

Definitions are part of every academic subject because the vocabulary must be introduced in order to understand and learn new concepts. Definitions often appear in italic or bold print in textbooks. Many textbooks have a glossary of specialized vocabulary in the back of the book.

Professors often give new words special emphasis in their lectures by pausing after the word and before the definition or by stressing the word the first time it is introduced. Look at these examples of definitions and notice the diagrams that show the relationship between the word and the definition.

A *menu* is a list of computer functions that appears on the screen.
Menu = list /functions on screen

The *id* consists of instincts.
Id = instincts

CLASSIFICATION

Classifications are also found in every subject. To classify means to organize into groups with similar characteristics. Look at these examples of classifications and notice how the diagrams show the relationship between the main category and the classification of types or kinds.

This chapter explores four highly specialized forms of fungus, which include molds, yeasts, lichens, and mycorrhizae.

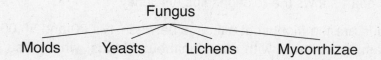

Two types of motivation have been identified by cognitive psychologists. *Intrinsic motivation* is based on internal factors, as for example curiosity or the challenge to succeed, whereas *extrinsic motivation* involves external incentives such as rewards or even punishments.

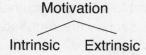

Sometimes this diagram is enough for you to remember other details, but a word or a brief phrase can help you recall a definition for each type.

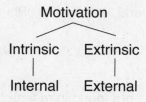

SEQUENCE

Sequence is often found in narrations of historical events, in descriptions of research studies, and in directions for scientific experiments or processes.

The Roman Empire was built in three stages, which consisted of the conquest of Italy, the conflict with Carthage and expansion into the Western Mediterranean, and, finally, the domination of the Greek kingdoms and the Eastern Mediterranean.

Roman Empire

- Conquest Italy
- Conflict Carthage + expansion W Med
- Domination Greek + E Med

The history of Cubism falls into three phases—the Cezanne phase, which lasted only two years from 1907 to 1909, followed by the Analytical phase from 1910 to 1912, which, by the way, was the phase in which the most abstract purification of the form was realized, and finally, the Synthetic phase, beginning in 1913.

Cubism

- Cezanne phase 1907–9
- Analytical phase 1910–12
    abstract purification
- Synthetic phase 1913

COMPARISON AND CONTRAST

Comparison and contrast identifies how two or more objects or ideas are the same or different. A side-by-side chart shows the relationships efficiently.

Cirrus clouds are the highest at altitudes between 17,000 and 50,000 feet, but they don't produce rain, in contrast with cumulonimbus clouds, which also penetrate the upper atmosphere, but cause lightning storms, rain, and tornados.

Cirrus   _Cumulonimbus_
17–50,000 ft   upper atmos
Ø rain   rain–lightning–tornados

Although each person is responsible for one instrument in most sections of the orchestra, the members of the percussion section are required to play several instruments in one concert or even for one composition.

Orchestra

Percussion   Other Sections
Play several   Play one

CAUSE AND EFFECT

Cause and effect or cause and result are found in research studies for all subjects, but the natural sciences contain many examples.

Mercantilism is an economic concept that assumes that the total volume of trade is unchangeable and, therefore, that trade causes conflict.

Mercantilism = total volume trade unchangeable
Trade → Conflict

When the temperatures on Earth dropped below the melting point of the rocks on the surface, the outer crust gradually solidified.

Temp Earth < melt pt rocks → crust solid

PROBLEM AND SOLUTION

A problem and solution relationship is similar to a cause and effect relationship and can be represented by a similar drawing.

Because employees can begin to expect incentives simply for doing their jobs, and this can become a problem, it is better to reserve incentives for occasions that require exceptional effort.

Expect incentives/job → Reserve incentives/exceptional

The problem is that most populations of ginseng in Canada are too small to survive unless they are completely protected from harvesting by humans.

Ginseng survive → Ø human harvesting

Practical Strategy

Sometimes it is faster to represent an idea with a symbol or a diagram than it is to write notes in words. This is especially true of relationships.

Practice Activity 10

Did you understand? Now practice drawing diagrams to represent relationships. First listen to each of the sentences from lectures on different topics. Then stop the audio and draw your diagram. Compare your drawings with the drawings in the answer key. The first one is completed to give you an example. Your answer is correct if it shows the same relationship as the drawings in the answer key, even if the diagram is not exactly the same. The answers are printed in Chapter 7 on pages 509–511.

Example

The nervous system is divided into two major parts: the central nervous system and the peripheral nervous system.

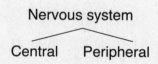

Nervous system

Central   Peripheral

Listen to some sentences from college lectures. Take notes by drawing diagrams.

Activity 10, CD 2, Track 9

1.

2.

3.

4.

5.

6.

7.

8.

9.

10.

ADVISOR'S OFFICE

This advice from Dr. Charles Swindell is framed on the wall of my office near my computer so that I can see it every day. I am happy to share it with you.

The longer I live, the more I realize the impact of attitude on life. Attitude to me is more important than facts. It is more important then the past, than education, than money, than circumstances, than failures, than successes, than what other people think or say or do. It is more important then appearance, giftedness, or skill. The remarkable thing is, we have a choice every day regarding the attitude we embrace for that day. We cannot change our past. We cannot change the fact that people may act in a certain way. We cannot change the inevitable. The only thing we can do is play on the one string we have, and that is our attitude. I am convinced that life is 10 percent what happens to me and 90 percent how I react to it. And so it is with you. We are in charge of our attitudes.

Henry Ford said it another way: "If you think you can or you think you can't, you are probably right."

PARAPHRASING

Paraphrasing means using different words to express the same meaning. When you paraphrase, you express an idea that you have heard or read, but you say or write it in your own words. Because you are including all of the information when you paraphrase, the paraphrase is usually about the same length as the original. There are three problems that you will confront when you are paraphrasing.

1. **There is a natural tendency to repeat the same words instead of paraphrasing them.** This means that you need to listen and read for meaning instead of focusing on individual words and grammatical structures.
2. **Reference materials such as a thesaurus may not be used on the TOEFL.** This means that you have to know synonyms for words and phrases.
3. **Sometimes it is not possible to think of a paraphrase.** This means that you must learn how to give credit to sources when you use them in speaking or writing.

This chapter will help you improve your paraphrasing skills. You will learn how to

- **Choose synonyms for words and phrases**
- **Use alternative grammatical structures**
- **Cite expressions and ideas**

How will these strategies help you on the TOEFL? By learning to paraphrase well, you will achieve a higher score on all four sections of the TOEFL. There are questions that require you to recognize or produce paraphrases on the Reading, Listening, Writing, and Speaking sections. Paraphrasing is a very important academic skill for success in college or university classes as well. Using someone else's words is called *plagiarizing.* Plagiarizing is a very serious offense and can result in your being expelled from school.

CHOOSE SYNONYMS FOR WORDS AND PHRASES

Strategies to Use
➤ Substitute multiple synonyms
➤ Use phrases
➤ Make an explanation

➤ Substitute multiple synonyms

When you use the strategy of substituting synonyms, you must substitute more than one word or phrase. An excellent paraphrase will also be expressed by a different grammatical structure. You will learn about using alternative structures later in this chapter.

PRACTICAL STRATEGY

Paraphrases with synonyms must be restatements. Substituting only one vocabulary word in a sentence is not a restatement. It is so close to the original that it is not an acceptable paraphrase. Here is an example statement and an unacceptable paraphrase:

Original Statement:	The hardest woodwind instrument to learn is the oboe.

Unacceptable Paraphrase:	The *most difficult* woodwind instrument to learn is the oboe.

Why is the first paraphrase unacceptable? Did you notice that only one word was different from the original statement? Remember that substituting one synonym is not a restatement and not an acceptable paraphrase.

Now look at an acceptable paraphrase:

Original Statement:	The hardest woodwind instrument to learn is the oboe

Acceptable Paraphrase:	The *most difficult* woodwind instrument to *master* is the oboe.

Why is the second paraphrase acceptable? Did you notice that more than one synonym was different? The phrase *most difficult* was substituted for the word *hardest* and the word *master* was substituted for the word *learn*. But this paraphrase is still very close to the original sentence.

This is an improvement in paraphrasing:

Original Statement:	The hardest woodwind instrument to learn is the oboe.

Excellent Paraphrase:	The oboe is the most difficult woodwind instrument to master.

Why is this paraphrase considered excellent? Like the acceptable paraphrase, more than one synonym was different. The phrase *most difficult* was substituted for the word *hardest* and the word *master* was substituted for the word *learn.* Did you also see how the structure of the sentence changed? The subject of the original statement was *the hardest woodwind instrument* and the complement was *the oboe.* In the excellent paraphrase, *the oboe* was the subject and *the hardest woodwind instrument* was the complement.

PRACTICE ACTIVITY 11

Did you understand? Try to rewrite each sentence that you may see in a textbook by substituting synonyms for the underlined words and phrases. As you have learned, an excellent paraphrase will also change the structure of the sentence, but in this practice activity, let's begin by writing acceptable paraphrases. Substitute multiple synonyms. The first one is completed to give you an example. Your answer is correct if the words or phrases you use are synonyms for the underlined words or phrases and the meaning of the sentence is the same. The synonyms do not have to be the ones that are used in the answer key. Example answers are printed in Chapter 7 on page 511.

EXAMPLE

Original: Thomas Edison was a very <u>curious</u> child, <u>performing</u> his first experiment <u>when he was only three years old.</u>

Paraphrase: Thomas Edison was a very <u>inquisitive</u> child, <u>conducting</u> his first experiment <u>at the age of three</u>.

1. The copperhead, a snake that <u>strikes</u> without warning, is <u>considered</u> much more <u>dangerous</u> than the rattlesnake.

2. Because J. P. Morgan was known as a <u>reputable</u> and <u>prudent</u> businessman, he was able to <u>persuade</u> others to <u>remain</u> in the market even after the crash had <u>begun</u>.

3. Phosphorus is <u>used</u> in paint on highway signs and markers because it is <u>bright</u> <u>at night</u>.

4. Rain forests are <u>often</u> <u>located</u> <u>near</u> the equator.

5. By the mid-<u>nineteenth century</u>, land was so <u>expensive</u> in <u>large</u> cities that architects <u>began to conserve</u> space by <u>building</u> skyscrapers.

6. <u>Research studies</u> of vertebrates <u>show</u> <u>development</u> from a very <u>simple</u> heart in fish to a <u>complex</u> four-chamber heart in humans.

7. When two products are <u>fundamentally</u> <u>the same</u>, advertising can <u>influence</u> the <u>choice</u> that the public makes.

8. <u>As a whole</u>, in birds, the male of the species is <u>more brilliantly</u> colored.

9. The <u>price</u> of gold on the world market <u>is subject to</u> several <u>variables</u>, including but not <u>limited to</u> supply and demand.

10. The <u>idea</u> of a submarine is not <u>recent</u>, dating from the <u>1400s</u> when Drebbel and da Vinci <u>drew</u> <u>initial</u> <u>sketches</u>.

➤ Use phrases

There is a tendency to try to find one word to paraphrase, but phrases can be a useful alternative.

PRACTICAL STRATEGY

The English language contains many phrasal verbs that express the same meaning as a one-word verb. In general, the phrasal verb is used for informal writing and speaking, and the one-word verb is used for more formal language. Some of the phrasal verbs that are common to academic language are listed here.

Bring about	cause
Carry on	transact; continue
Carry out	complete; accomplish
Clear up	clarify
Come about	happen
Come across	find
Come by	find accidentally
Come out with	publish; produce
Come up with	create
Cut down on	reduce
Fall through	fail
Figure out	understand
Find out	discover
Give off	emit
Go after	follow
Go back	return
Go before	precede
Go down	decrease
Go on	continue; happen
Go over	review
Go through	experience; penetrate
Go up	increase
Keep on	continue
Keep up	remain current
Leave out	exclude; omit
Look for	seek
Look into	investigate
Look like	resemble
Look over	examine
Look up	locate information
Look up to	respect
Make out	understand with difficulty
Make up	invent; compose
Pick out	select
Point out	show; indicate
Put off	postpone

Put up with	tolerate
Rule out	eliminate
Run across	find accidentally
Run into	meet by accident
Set up	arrange
Show up	appear unexpectedly
Spell out	state in detail
Stand for	represent
Stick out	protrude
Take into account	consider
Take over	assume control
Take place	occur
Think through	reason
Throw away	discard
Touch on	mention briefly
Try out	test
Turn into	transform
Turn out	conclude
Turn up	discover
Wind up	finish
Work out	active
Write up	report

PRACTICE ACTIVITY 12

Did you understand? First read each sentence. Then try to say each sentence using a phrase instead of a one-word verb. The first one is completed to give you an example. Your answer is correct if the phrases that you use are synonyms for the underlined words and the meaning of the sentence is the same. The phrases do not have to be the ones that are used in the answer key. Example answers are recorded on Track 10 of the audio and also printed in Chapter 7 on pages 511–512.

PHRASAL VERBS

EXAMPLE

Written: A balance of international payment refers to the net result of the business that a nation <u>transacts</u> with other nations in a given period.

Spoken: A balance of international payment refers to the net result of the business that a nation <u>carries on</u> with other nations in a given period.

Activity 12, CD 2, Track 10

1. Because light travels faster than sound, lightning appears to <u>precede</u> thunder.

2. Congress <u>respected</u> Jefferson because of his intelligence and creativity.

3. The lower teeth in crocodiles <u>protrude</u> when their mouths are closed.

4. Some sponges <u>resemble</u> plants.

5. The first census was <u>accomplished</u> in Great Britain in 1801.

6. People who have <u>experienced</u> a traumatic event may have recurring images of it.

7. In algebra, letters and other symbols <u>represent</u> numbers.

8. During periods of stress or excitement, the heart rate <u>increases</u> and airways to the lungs become dilated.

9. Theories of prehistory and early humans are constantly changing as we <u>consider</u> the new evidence from archeological finds.

10. Dreams may have been the inspiration for the Surrealists to <u>create</u> their works of art.

➤ Make an explanation

Sometimes even native speakers cannot retrieve a word from memory when they are paraphrasing, especially when they are speaking. When this happens to you, there are several ways to compensate for the word that has slipped your mind. Make an explanation.

PRACTICAL STRATEGY

If it is an adjective, you can use an opposite adjective with the word *not*. For example, if a synonym for the adjective *large* slips your mind, you can say, *not small. The sum was not small.* If it is a verb, you can use a general verb instead of a specific synonym. For example, if you forget the synonym for the verb *rely on*, you can say, *use*, which is a very general verb that includes many meanings. Early traders *used* barter instead of money to exchange goods. If it is a noun, you can describe the noun with a descriptive phrase or clause. For example, if you forget the synonym for the noun *farmer* or if the word *farmer* slips your mind, you can describe it by saying, *the person who engages in agriculture.*

These compensatory strategies are used to get out of a problem when you are speaking. They should be used as a last resort instead of stopping when you are speaking.

Practice Activity 13

Did you understand? Try to restate each sentence that you may see in a textbook by explaining the meaning instead of substituting a synonym for the underlined word. The first one is completed to give you an example. Example answers are recorded on Track 11 of the audio and also printed in Chapter 7 on page 512.

Example

The Constitution guarantees that private homes will not be searched without a <u>warrant</u>.
The Constitution guarantees that private homes will not be searched without <u>written authorization</u>.

 Activity 13, CD 2, Track 11

ADJECTIVES

Use an opposite.

Example

The second movement of a symphony is usually <u>slow</u>.
The second movement of a symphony is usually <u>not fast</u>.

1. The temperature in many desert regions is <u>cold</u> at night.

2. Facial expressions may be <u>common</u> across cultures.

3. Obsidian is <u>shiny</u> because it cools too quickly for crystals to form.

4. <u>Few</u> musical instruments play louder than 100 decibels or softer than 20 decibels.

5. The people who have adapted to life at very high altitudes are usually <u>short</u>.

NOUNS

Use a phrase.

Example

<u>Skyscrapers</u> are representative of the International Style of architecture.
<u>Tall buildings</u> are representative of the International Style of architecture.

1. In many cities, <u>vendors</u> must have a license to set up their booths in public places.

2. Studies show that small <u>pets</u> are a positive influence in elderly people's lives.

3. Staircases were an important feature of the <u>palaces</u> constructed during the Baroque period.

4. Global wind patterns are affected by the <u>Earth's rotation</u>.

5. <u>Bilingual education</u> is more common in regions where language minorities live.

VERBS

Use a general verb.

EXAMPLE

Many managers <u>employ</u> teams to accomplish complex goals.
Many managers <u>use</u> teams to accomplish complex goals.

1. Unlike cast iron, pure wrought iron <u>contains</u> no carbon.

2. Hypnosis <u>achieves</u> a heightened state of suggestibility in a willing participant.

3. Productivity increases when fewer employees are required to <u>accomplish</u> the work.

4. Normally, the plasma in human blood <u>constitutes</u> 50–60 percent of the total blood volume.

5. Three fourths of the goods <u>manufactured</u> in Canada for export are sold to the United States.

USE ALTERNATIVE GRAMMATICAL STRUCTURES

> **Strategies to Use**
> ➤ Produce restatements
> ➤ Read and listen for meaning
> ➤ Edit problem paraphrases

➤ Produce restatements

Learning to identify possibilities for alternative structures will improve your paraphrasing skills. A restatement with an alternative structure is not a paraphrase because it uses too many of the same words and phrases. Later in this chapter, you will use restatements with synonyms to produce paraphrases.

PRACTICAL STRATEGY

Study the examples of restatements in each of the categories below. Learn to make restatements using alternative structures. When you can use both synonyms and alternative structures, you will be able to paraphrase appropriately. For now, focus on alternative structures.

Chronology	before/after/during
Coordination	not only-but also/neither-nor/not-but/both-and/as well as
Cause	because/because of/since/as a result
Comparison	similar/like/the same/differ/different/more/less
Concession	although/even though/despite/in spite of/but/whereas
Negatives	not + un-/not once/not one/very rarely/very seldom
Passives	BE + past participle

CHRONOLOGY

Original:

After the Missouri Compromise was abandoned by Congress, the Republican party was formed in 1854, partly in opposition to the spread of slavery in the United States.

Restatement:

Before the Republican party was formed in 1854, in part to oppose the spread of slavery in the United States, the Missouri Compromise had already been abandoned by Congress.

COORDINATION

Original:

Byzantine art consisted not only of oriental style but also of Greek ideas that maintained its popularity for more than eleven centuries.

Restatement:

Popular for more than eleven hundred years, Byzantine art consisted of both oriental style and Greek ideas.

CAUSE

Original:

In the classic experiment in operant conditioning, Pavlov's dog salivated when he heard a bell because he associated the sound with food.

Restatement:

Since Pavlov's dog associated the sound of a bell with being fed, he salivated when he heard it in the classic experiment in operant conditioning.

COMPARISON

Original:

As a conductor of heat and electricity, aluminum exceeds all metals except silver, copper, and gold.

Restatement:

Silver, copper, and gold are better conductors of heat and electricity than aluminum is.

CONCESSION

Original:	Despite the great differences in size, shape, and function, all human cells have the same forty-six chromosomes.
Restatement:	Although the forty-six chromosomes are the same in all human cells, there are differences in the size, shape, and function.

NEGATIVE

Original:	It is not illegal in some cultures to be married to more than one woman at the same time, but the monogamous relationship is the most common.
Restatement:	In some cultures, it is legal to be married to several women at once, but it is more common to be married to just one woman.

PASSIVE

Original:	The explosive properties of nitroglycerin, later one of the components of dynamite, were discovered by Ascanio Sobrero, an Italian chemistry professor.
Restatement:	Italian chemistry professor Ascanio Sobrero discovered that nitroglycerin, later used in the production of dynamite, had explosive properties.

PRACTICE EXERCISE 14

Did you understand? Try to restate each sentence that you may see in a textbook by writing an alternative grammatical structure. Make changes to the grammar but do not make changes in the meaning of the sentence. The first one for each structure is completed to give you an example. Example answers are printed in Chapter 7 on pages 512–513.

CHRONOLOGY

EXAMPLE

Chronology:	After the death of Queen Mary in 1558, her half-sister Elizabeth ascended the throne of England.
Chronology Restatement:	Before Elizabeth ascended the throne of England in 1558, her half-sister Mary ruled.

1. Not until the Triassic Period did the first primitive mammals appear.

2. Glass became a major construction material during the late Middle Ages.

3. Helium replaced hydrogen as a power source for dirigibles because it was safer.

4. The Moriori people settled the Chatham Islands off the coast of New Zealand long before the Europeans arrived in 1791.

5. Always rinse your test tubes and pipettes with a small amount of distilled water before you store them in the lab cabinets.

COORDINATION

EXAMPLE

Coordination: Before the introduction of the musical staff, composers preserved their work not only by writing it down but also by teaching it to a younger musician.

Coordination
Restatement: Before the introduction of the musical staff, composers preserved their work by teaching it to a younger musician, not by writing a book.

1. Both genes and viruses are made of essential chemicals called nucleoproteins.

2. Successful managers neither proceed without a plan nor ignore opportunities that arise.

3. Technically, not only glass but also water are considered minerals.

4. Neither corn nor winter wheat are native to the Americas.

5. Ethnicity is usually based on race and religion as well as national origin.

CAUSE

EXAMPLE

Cause: The diesel engine that runs on oil is more efficient than most other engines because it converts more of the useful energy stored in the fuel.

Cause
Restatement: The diesel engine runs more efficiently than most other engines because of the oil that converts more useful energy.

1. Psychologists suggest that incentives cause workers to increase productivity.

2. Because many flakes have been found in excavations of Stone Age settlements, anthropologists conclude that they were used as tools for cutting and scraping.

3. Too much water can cause plants to turn brown on the edges.

4. Blood pressure can become elevated as a result of increased salt consumption.

5. Since the interstate highway system linking roads across the country was built in the 1930s, most of the roads in the system need to be repaired.

COMPARISON

EXAMPLE

Comparison: Although they are smaller in size, for the most part, chipmunks are like most other ground squirrels.

Comparison
Restatement: Chipmunks are mostly like other ground squirrels except for their smaller size.

1. Viruses and the first life forms that appeared on Earth millions of years ago have a similar structure.

2. The lungs have a higher oxygen concentration than the blood does.

3. The Indian Ocean is smaller but deeper than the Atlantic Ocean.

4. Picasso's work was not the same during various artistic periods.

5. The difference in the gravitational attraction of various places on the Earth's surface is the reason that the weight of objects is not the same.

CONCESSION

EXAMPLE

Concession: Although oil paint tends to yellow with age, tempera colors retain their vibrancy for centuries.

Concession
Restatement: Oil paint tends to yellow with age, but tempera colors retain their vibrancy for centuries.

1. Whereas insulin levels are close to or above normal in type 2 diabetes, target cells cannot respond adequately.

2. Although the idea of an English language academy is regularly proposed, the response has never been very positive.

3. Even though the Jovian planets are grouped together, each one has had a very different evolutionary history.

4. Despite the advantage that young people enjoy for recall in vocabulary studies, older people appear to be better at word recognition.

5. In spite of the fact that interviews are the most common strategy for assessing job applicants, they tend to have low validity.

NEGATIVE

EXAMPLE

Negative: The addiction to gambling is not unlike the addiction to substances.

Affirmative
Restatement: The addiction to gambling is like the addiction to substances.

1. Not once has the geyser known as Old Faithful failed to erupt on time.

2. Nonstandard dialects are not used as educational models in schools.

3. Never has there been such wide access to news from so many media.

4. The construction of a city on the ruins of a previous settlement is not uncommon.

5. Not until the Triassic Period did the first primitive mammals develop.

PASSIVE

EXAMPLE

Active statement: Sea gulls need either fresh or salt water for them to survive.

Passive
Restatement: Either fresh or salt water is needed by sea gulls for them to survive.

1. It is interesting that people over the age of 65 experience fewer mental health disorders.

2. In the stringed instruments, a bow produces the tones when it is played across a set of strings made of wire or gut.

3. High-frequency radiation from the Sun and other sources partly ionize gases in the ionosphere.

4. Architects can use a domed roof to conserve floor space.

5. The Egyptians used papyrus to make paper, sails, baskets, and clothing.

➤ Read and listen for meaning

When you read or listen for meaning, you learn to think about the ideas that the writer or speaker is communicating, not the individual words or grammar used.

PRACTICE STRATEGY

Practice reading and listening for meaning. By focusing on sentences or even paragraphs, you will train your mind to make connections and comprehend the ideas instead of trying to understand word by word. The important question is this: What does the author or the lecturer mean? What ideas are being expressed?

PRACTICAL ACTIVITY 15

Did you understand? Try to identify the sentences that express the same idea. The first one is completed to give you an example. Example answers are printed in Chapter 7 on page 514.

EXAMPLE

What does the professor mean by the following statement:

> Poet and humorist Ogden Nash tried but failed to adapt himself to the academic and later the business world.

    Ⓐ He was a better businessman than he was a teacher.
    ● He did not succeed in either teaching or business.
    Ⓒ He tried teaching before he finally succeeded in business.
    Ⓓ He made no effort to succeed in teaching and business.

1.   What does the professor mean by the following statement:

> After hitting a bar several times with similar results, an animal learns that it can get food by pressing the bar.

    Ⓐ An animal is able to press the bar more after it is fed three or four times.
    Ⓑ Three or four animals are used in the experiment with similar results.
    Ⓒ There are several trials by an animal before the food is released.
    Ⓓ An animal learns how to get food by hitting a bar.

2.   What does the professor mean by the following statement:

> Although he wrote many short stories, it was a poem, "The Raven," that brought Poe his greatest recognition as a writer.

    Ⓐ Poe is remembered more for a poem than for his short stories.
    Ⓑ "The Raven" is less well-known than Poe's short stories.
    Ⓒ Poe is famous for writing both short stories and poetry.
    Ⓓ Poe wrote more short stories than poems during his career.

3. What does the professor mean by the following statement:

    It was an atom that contained in the form of pure energy the fundamental components of the entire universe.

    Ⓐ The universe was made up of many atoms of pure energy.
    Ⓑ The effect of a pure atom in the universe was to produce energy.
    Ⓒ Everything in the universe was reduced to pure energy in one atom.
    Ⓓ The energy in the universe was stored in pure atoms.

4. What does the professor mean by the following statement:

    Although a bear does not eat during the winter, sustaining itself from body fat, its temperature remains almost normal, and it breathes regularly.

    Ⓐ When a bear survives on body fat instead of eating, its temperature and respiration are reduced.
    Ⓑ Not eating during the winter does not affect the bear's breathing, but it does affect its temperature.
    Ⓒ During the winter, the bear's temperature is normal and its respiration is regular, but it does not require food.
    Ⓓ The bear's diet of fat during the winter does not affect its temperature and respiration.

5. What does the professor mean by the following statement:

    It is generally true that as long as the CEO maintains the confidence of the board of directors, they will not intervene to dictate specific policies.

    Ⓐ Policies are dictated by the board with the approval of the CEO.
    Ⓑ The board will assume control only if they lose confidence in the CEO.
    Ⓒ The confidence of the CEO is important to decisions that the board makes.
    Ⓓ The intervention by the CEO in board policies does not occur often.

6. What does the professor mean by the following statement:

    Temperature variations cause pressure differences in the air.

    Ⓐ Fluctuations in the air pressure are a result of changes in temperature.
    Ⓑ Changes in the air pressure and temperature vary at different times.
    Ⓒ The temperature is usually different from the air pressure.
    Ⓓ Changeable temperatures are caused by reversals in the wind.

7. What does the professor mean by the following statement:

    To maintain a healthy body weight, an animal must balance energy intake with energy output, largely by metabolic activity and regular physical exertion.

    Ⓐ Metabolism regulates activity and exercise reduces body weight for a healthy life style.
    Ⓑ A healthy life style includes exercise in order to control weight gain that is caused by the metabolism.
    Ⓒ Metabolism and exercise are ways to stabilize consumption and production of energy for a healthy weight.
    Ⓓ Animals generally balance their metabolisms by healthy eating and exercise, which also controls their weight.

8. What does the professor mean by the following statement:

An example of children's literature that supports the natural inclination to play with language is the *nursery rhyme*.

Ⓐ The nursery rhyme is a good example of children's literature because it is fun.
Ⓑ Children like nursery rhymes because they enjoy them during playtime.
Ⓒ Children's literature is written in language that the child can understand.
Ⓓ The child's interest in playing with language is encouraged by the nursery rhyme.

9. What does the professor mean by the following statement:

For employees whose jobs involve sitting at a computer terminal entering data or typing reports, the location of the computer relative to the company is of no consequence.

Ⓐ Employees who work at their computers like to choose their locations.
Ⓑ It does not matter where employees work at their computers.
Ⓒ The location of their computers should be comfortable to employees.
Ⓓ Computer terminals must be located near each other in a company.

10. What does the professor mean by the following statement:

Ireland was first settled around 7500 B.C. by hunting tribes from Scotland, followed by people from the Mediterranean know as the Firbolgs.

Ⓐ The Firbolgs arrived in Ireland from the Mediterranean after the Scottish people had already settled there.
Ⓑ Irish tribes went to Scotland and then followed a hunting route all the way to the Mediterranean area called Firbolgs.
Ⓒ The Irish and Scottish people explored Europe, reaching as far as the Mediterranean where they settled.
Ⓓ Looking for a place to live, the Firbolgs went to Scotland and then to Ireland where they finally settled.

➤ Edit problem paraphrases

Here are some problems that you can learn to avoid:

- Don't change the meaning
- Don't leave out information
- Don't use too much of the original wording
- Don't copy the original

Original Sentence:

Sometimes students plagiarize material from lectures and reading passages because they don't understand how to make the appropriate changes for an excellent paraphrase.

DON'T CHANGE THE MEANING

This is not an excellent paraphrase because the meaning has been changed from the original:

> On occasion, students use paraphrases of excellent lectures and reading passages without understanding the purpose of the changes that they have made in them.

DON'T LEAVE OUT IMPORTANT INFORMATION

This is not an excellent paraphrase because it does not include all of the important information in the original:

> On occasion, students use lecture and reading material verbatim.

DON'T USE TOO MUCH OF THE ORIGINAL WORDING

This is not an excellent paraphrase because it looks and sounds too much like the original:

> On occasion, students plagiarize material from lectures and reading passages because they don't comprehend how to make the necessary changes for an excellent paraphrase.

DON'T COPY THE ORIGINAL

This is not an excellent paraphrase because it is an exact copy of the original.

> Sometimes students plagiarize material from lectures and reading passages because they don't understand how to make the appropriate changes for an excellent paraphrase.

PRACTICE ACTIVITY 16

Did you understand? Try to find the problem in each paraphrase and edit it. The first one is completed to give you an example. Example answers are printed in Chapter 7 on pages 514–515.

EXAMPLE

Original:	Tides are caused by the gravitational pull of both the Sun and the Moon.
Paraphrase:	Tides are produced by the gravitational pull of both the Sun and the Moon.
Problem:	The paraphrase is too much like the original. Only one word was changed.
Edited Paraphrase:	The combined gravitational effects of the Sun and Moon produce tides on Earth.

Why is this better? Because synonyms have been substituted, and an alternative grammatical structure has been used, but the meaning has not changed.

1. Original: Proteins are molecules that regulate the movement of materials across cell walls.

     Paraphrase: Molecules that regulate the movement of materials across cell walls are proteins.

2. Original: The invention of the steam engine played a major role in the Industrial Revolution because it caused the factory system to extend itself to many areas of production apart from the cotton industry.

   Paraphrase: The invention of the steam engine was a primary influence in the Industrial Revolution.

3. Original: Although big companies are trying to maintain a balance between traditional advertising and some of the newer alternatives like blogging, it is often the smaller entrepreneurs who are using bloggers as an efficient way to stack their competition.

   Paraphrase: Big companies are using bloggers to defeat their smaller rivals.

4. Original: Fossils of bones have the appearance of stone, but the holes and pores are actually infused with mineral deposits from the surrounding sediments.

   Paraphrase: Fossils of bones look like stone, but there are mineral deposits from the surrounding sediments in the holes and pores.

5. Original: Pictograms found in many parts of the world about 1500 B.C. constitute the earliest system of writing, although written symbols have been discovered that date from as early as 3500 B.C.

   Paraphrase: Pictograms found in various parts of the world are the earliest evidence of a written system despite the discovery of written symbols.

6. Original: The modern atmosphere is probably the fourth atmosphere in the history of the Earth.

   Paraphrase: The modern atmosphere is probably the fourth atmosphere in the history of the Earth.

7. Original: Whereas alcohol is a depressant, coffee is a stimulant.
   Paraphrase: Alcohol is not like coffee.

8. Original: The Pacific Basin, which includes the continent of Australia and the thousands of islands grouped together as Oceania, covers one third of the surface of the Earth.

   Paraphrase: The Pacific Basin is also called Oceania because it encompasses one third of the Pacific Ocean.

9. Original: In fresco painting, the pigments may be mixed with water and applied to the plaster before it dries so that the lime in the plaster fuses with the pigments on the surface.

   Paraphrase: The lime in wet plaster bonds with the pigments on the surface when the colors are mixed.

10. Original: As Linnaeus originally conceived the biological classification chart, he segregated all living creatures solely according to their degree of physical similarity.

    Paraphrase: Linnaeus originally created the biological classification chart by categorizing all living creatures according to their degree of physical similarity.

CITE EXPRESSIONS AND IDEAS

Strategies to Use
➤ Introduce the source before quoting
➤ Mark quotations in writing and in speaking
➤ Use strong verbs to report ideas
➤ Mention the source appropriately

➤ Introduce the source before quoting

It is important to cite the expressions and ideas of others. To cite means to give credit to the source. This is especially true when the idea is a definition, an opinion, a unique expression, or research data that is not common knowledge.

PRACTICAL STRATEGY

There are several phrases and clauses that can be used to introduce the source of your ideas. Let's say that Professor Thompson makes the following statement in a lecture: "The shift from manufacturing to service has resulted in lower paying jobs and a decline in the strength of labor unions." You may want to quote this opinion. If you do, the words in the quotation must be exactly the same as those in the original. Here are five ways to introduce the source before the quotation.

According to Professor Thompson, "The shift from manufacturing to service has resulted in lower paying jobs and a decline in the strength of labor unions."

In the words of Professor Thompson, "The shift from manufacturing to service has resulted in lower paying jobs and a decline in the strength of labor unions."

To quote Professor Thompson, "The shift from manufacturing to service has resulted in lower paying jobs and a decline in the strength of labor unions."

As Professor Thompson puts it, "The shift from manufacturing to service has resulted in lower paying jobs and a decline in the strength of labor unions."

Professor Thompson said, "The shift from manufacturing to service has resulted in lower paying jobs and a decline in the strength of labor unions."

On the TOEFL examination, sometimes the professor is not named. In that case, you can still introduce your source by changing the introductions slightly:

According to the professor,
In the words of the professor,
To quote the professor,
As the professor puts it,
The professor said,

PRACTICE ACTIVITY 17

Did you understand? Try to quote each sentence that you hear in a lecture by an unnamed professor. Be sure to use one of the introductory phrases or clauses before you begin your quotation. The first one is completed to give you an example. Your answer is correct if you write any of the introductions and if the words in your quotations are exactly the same as those of the professor. Example answers are printed in Chapter 7 on pages 515–516.

EXAMPLE

"Communicating is the act of transmitting information."

According to the professor, "Communicating is the act of transmitting information."

Also correct:

In the words of the professor, "Communicating is the act of transmitting information."

To quote the professor, "Communicating is the act of transmitting information."

As the professor puts it, "Communicating is the act of transmitting information."

The professor said, "Communicating is the act of transmitting information."

1. A stock is equity in a company, and, therefore, it represents ownership.

2. The desalination of the ocean is going to be a crucial aspect of water management.

3. The theme of a worldwide flood is found in the mythology of many cultures.

4. Psychology focuses on the individual, whereas sociology focuses on social groups.

5. The ethics of science will become more important in this decade.

6. I call my idea the simplification principle.

7. The three-domain system is superior to the five-domain system of classification in biology.

8. The term *relief* describes any printing method with a raised image.

9. Training programs must address the issue of technology in the workplace.

10. Quasars are difficult to study because they are so far away.

➤ Mark quotations in writing and in speaking

Quotation marks are used before and after the words that you are quoting. This is easy to see when you are quoting in the written language. But when you are quoting in the spoken language, you need to *hear* the quotation marks. Words and phrases must be used to mark quotations in speaking.

PRACTICAL STRATEGY

There are several phrases and clauses that can be used to mark quotations. Let's say that Professor Smith makes the following statement in a lecture: "Additives are chemicals that manufacturers add to food and other products." You may want to quote this definition. If you use the quotation in writing, you must use quotation marks before and after the words that you are quoting. If you use the quotation in speaking, you must use words and phrases in place of the quotation marks. The words in the quotation must be exactly the same as those in the original. Here are several ways to mark the beginning and ending of a quotation in speaking:

According to Professor Smith, *and I am quoting here,* "Additives are chemicals that manufacturers add to food and other products." *End quote.*

According to Professor Smith, *and I quote,* "Additives are chemicals that manufacturers add to food and other products." *End quote.*

To quote Professor Smith, "Additives are chemicals that manufacturers add to food and other products." *End quote.*

PRACTICE ACTIVITY 18

Did you understand? Try to quote each sentence. First, put the quotation marks around the written quote. Be sure to put them above the line, not on the line. Then use verbal quotation marks for a spoken quote. The first one is completed to give you an example. Your answer is correct if you use any of the verbal quotation marks and if the words in your quotation are exactly the same as those of the source. Spoken answers are recorded on Track 12 of the audio. Example answers are printed in Chapter 7 on pages 516–517.

EXAMPLE

A mirage is an optical illusion in the atmosphere.

Written quote: According to Professor Brown, "A mirage is an optical illusion in the atmosphere."

Spoken quotes: According to Professor Brown, *and I quote,* "A mirage is an optical illusion in the atmosphere." *End quote.*

According to Professor Brown, *and I am quoting here,* "A mirage is an optical illusion in the atmosphere." *End quote.*

To quote Professor Brown, "A mirage is an optical illusion in the atmosphere." *End quote.*

Activity 18, CD 2, Track 12

1. According to a study by Professor Carter, patients can lower their blood pressure by losing weight and decreasing their intake of salt.

2. According to Professor Jones, over fourteen billion Euros were introduced into the world economy in January, 2002.

3. To quote a study in the *Journal of Psychology,* many people who have achieved their career ambitions by midlife are afflicted by depression.

4. According to the textbook, an organ is a group of tissues capable of performing some special function.

5. According to Professor Stephens, John Philip Sousa was the greatest composer of marches for bands.

6. In Professor Davison's opinion, Ben Johnson may be the author of several plays attributed to William Shakespeare.

7. Professor Davis said that statistical data can be very difficult to interpret because correlations are not causes.

8. As Professor Gray puts it, the prime minister serves at the pleasure of the parliament.

9. According to the reading passage, moving water is the single most important factor in determining the surface features of the Earth.

10. In Professor Russell's opinion, the most important quality for a scientist is the ability to make careful observations.

➤ Use strong verbs to report ideas

PRACTICAL STRATEGY

Sometimes you will want to refer to the ideas and research of others without using a direct quotation. When the ideas are specific to an author or researcher, it is still necessary to cite the source. Choose verbs that report the idea and convey the meaning that you wish to attach to the idea. You may choose verbs that express doubt, neutrality, or certainty.

Doubtful	**Neutral**	**Certain**
Allege	Indicate	Advance
Assume	Illustrate	Argue
Believe	Mention	Assert
Claim	Note	Conclude
Imply	Observe	Confirm
Predict	Point out	Demonstrate
Propose	Report	Discover
Suggest	Say	Find
Suppose	Show	Maintain
Suspect	State	Verify

PRACTICE ACTIVITY 19

Did you understand? Try to report each quotation. Choose a verb to express doubt, neutrality, or certainty. The first one is completed to give you an example. Your answer is correct if you use any of the verbs listed under the correct heading—doubtful, neutral, certain. Notice that both verbs in reported language are in the past tense. Example answers are printed in Chapter 7 on page 517.

EXAMPLE

Quotation: Psychologist Carl Rogers said, "Negative feedback causes people to develop a poor self-concept."

Certain Report: Carl Rogers <u>argued</u> that negative feedback <u>caused</u> people to develop a poor self-concept.

Also Correct: Carl Rogers <u>maintained</u> that negative feedback <u>caused</u> people to develop a poor self-concept.

1. Sociologist Lee Clark said, "When danger arises, the rule is for people to help those next to them before they help themselves." "Panic: Myth or Reality," *Contexts I* (Fall 2002), p. 21.
   Neutral report:

2. Biological anthropologist Barry Bogin said, "We can use the average height of any group of people as a barometer of the health of their society." "The Tall and Short of It," *Applying Anthropology: An Introductory Reader,* Mountain View, California: Mayfield Publishing Company, 2001, p. 54.
   Doubtful report:

3. Physician Stanley Joel Reiser said, "Machines direct the attention of both doctor and patient to the measurable aspect of illness, but away from the human factors that are at least equally important." *Medicine and the Reign of Technology,* New York: Cambridge University Press, 1978, p. 229.
   Certain report:

4. Educator Harry Wong said, "There is but one correlation with success, and that is attitude." *The First Days of School: How to Be an Effective Teacher,* Sunnyvale, California: Harry K. Wong Publications, 1991, p. 35.
   Certain report:

5. Choreographer Martha Graham said, "Technique and training have never been a substitute for that condition of awareness which is talent." *Dance as a Theatre Art,* Hightstown, New Jersey: Princeton Book Company, 1974, p. 136.
   Doubtful report:

6. Psychologist Carl Jung said, "The collective unconscious seems to be something like an unceasing stream or perhaps an ocean of images and figures which drift into consciousness in our dreams." "The Basic Postulates of Analytical Psychology," *Modern Man in Search of a Soul,* Routledge and Kegan Paul, 1933.
   Doubtful report:

7. Computer entrepreneur Bill Gates said, "The key for Microsoft™ has always been hiring very smart people." Transcript of video history interview, National Museum of American History, January 11, 2005.
   Neutral report:

8. Geneticists James Watson and Francis Crick said, "DNA structure has two helical chains each coiled around the same axis." "A Structure for Deoxyribose Nucleic Acid," *Nature,* Volume 171 (April 2), 1953, p. 737.
   Doubtful report:

9. Environmentalist John Sinclair said, "Many politicians are hostile to the environmental movement because they see it in conflict with the economic model they support." "The Legacy of Voluntary Conservationists." 1998 Romeo Lahey Lecture for the National Parks Association of Queensland, Australia.
Neutral report:

10. Astrophysicist Carl Sagan said, "Even a relatively small nuclear war may be capable of producing a global climatic catastrophe." Speech before the Commonwealth Club, February 8, 1985.
Certain report:

➤ Mention the source appropriately

You already know how to introduce a source, but sometimes you need to mention the source more than one time. In that case, there is a pattern that is customarily used to mention the source appropriately.

PRACTICAL STRATEGY

When you cite the source the first time, use the first and last name. The title is optional. When you site the second time, use the last name only. If you cite a third time, use a pronoun, for example, *he* or *she.* After the third citation, you may use the pronoun again if the meaning is clear, or you may repeat the last name for clarity.

In the case of speakers or writers who are not named, the source should still be cited. You may be able to identify and cite the source as a professor, a speaker, an author, a writer, or a student, based on the context in which the information is presented. Use this general description the first time that you cite the source. If it is clear that the person is a man or woman, you can use the correct pronoun when you cite the source a second or third time. After the third citation, you may use the pronoun again if the meaning is clear, or you may repeat the general description for clarity.

PRACTICE ACTIVITY 20

Did you understand? Try to report the information in the notes. Cite the source appropriately. The first report is completed to give you an example. Listen to the example answers on Track 13, and read the script printed in Chapter 7 on pages 517–518.

EXAMPLE

Source: Edwin Hubble (man) astronomer

- demonstrated Andromeda nebula located outside our galaxy
- established the islands universe theory = galaxies exist outside our own
- study resulted in Hubble's constant = standard relationship/galaxy's distance from Earth and speed recession

Astronomer <u>Edwin Hubble</u> demonstrated that the Andromeda nebula was located outside our galaxy. <u>Hubble</u> established the islands universe theory, which states that galaxies exist outside our own. <u>He</u> published a study that resulted in what is now called Hubble's constant, a standard relationship between a galaxy's distance from Earth and its speed of recession.

 Activity 20, CD 2, Track 13

1. Source: Theodore White (man)
   Book—*The Making of the President*

   • 1960 presidential debate—press conference
   • Nixon proceeded—personal debate
   • Kennedy spoke directly to TV viewers
   • estimated Kennedy gained 2 mil votes

2. Source: Paul Cezanne (man)

   • all forms in nature—based on geometric shapes
   • cone, sphere, cylinder primary
   • used outlining to emphasize shapes

3. Source: Marie Curie (woman)

   • won Nobel p physics 1903 w/husband—discovery of radium
   • won Nobel p chemistry 1911—isolation pure radium
   • 1st person 2 Nobel p

4. Source: Erik Erikson (man) psychologist

   • proposed eight stages/personal development
   • psychological crises/each stage shaped sense/self
   • lifelong process

5. Source: Margaret Mead (woman)

   • first fieldwork in Samoa 1925
   • book *Coming of Age in Samoa* best seller—translated many languages
   • still one/most well-known anthropologists
   • people/simple societies provide valuable lessons/industrialized

6. Source: Leonardo da Vinci (man)

   • quintessential Renaissance man
   • brilliant painter
   • interested in mechanics
   • work in math clear in perspective

7. Source: Peter Drucker (man) author
    * *Management Challenges for the 21st Century*
    * five transforming forces
    * trends have major implications for long-term strategies of companies

8. Source: Freidrich Mohs (man)

    * devised hardness scale/10 minerals
    * assigned 10 to diamond—hardest known
    * lesser values other min
    * scale still useful/relative hardness

9. Source: Maria Montessori (woman)

    * proposed educational model
    * not transmission knowledge
    * free to develop
    * success child working independently

10. Source: Jane Goodall (woman)

    * collaboration Louis Leaky
    * years living w/chimpanzees—Gombe Reserve
    * imitated behaviors
    * discovered chimp complex social organization
    * first document chimp making/using tools
    * also identified 20 different sounds/communication

ADVISOR'S OFFICE

Do you talk to yourself? Of course you do. Maybe not aloud, but all of us have mental conversations with ourselves. So the question is *how* do you talk to yourself?

Negative Talk	*Positive Talk*
I can't study all of this.	I am studying every day.
My English is poor.	My English is improving.
I won't get a good score.	I will do my best.
If I fail, I will be so ashamed.	If I need a higher score, I can try again.

How would you talk to good friends to encourage and support them? Be a good friend to yourself. When negative talk comes to mind, substitute positive talk. Encourage yourself to learn from mistakes.

SUMMARIZING

Summarizing is related to paraphrasing because you are using your own words to express an idea that you have heard or read. Remember that when you paraphrase, you are including all of the information, but when you summarize, you are including only the main ideas. A paraphrase is about the same length as the original, but a summary is shorter than the original. There are three problems that you will confront when you are summarizing.

1. **A summary does not include everything in the original.** This means that you should not try to write too much.
2. **Details and examples that support the main points are usually not included in a summary.** This means that you have to be able to discriminate between the main points and the details or examples.
3. **The author's point of view must be maintained.** This means that you cannot express your opinion when you report the information.

This chapter will help you improve your summarizing skills. You will learn how to

- **Condense the ideas**
- **Identify the main points**
- **Report the information**

How will these strategies help you on the TOEFL? By learning to summarize, you will be able to answer the questions that are worth the most points on the Reading section. There are also questions that require you to produce summaries on the Writing and Speaking sections. Moreover, research demonstrates that students who understand how to summarize and use this skill when they prepare for tests will be able to remember information better.

CONDENSE THE IDEAS

Strategies to Use
➤ Be brief
➤ Combine sentences

➤ Be brief

A summary is a shorter version of the original. For example, if the original is 1000 words, a summary would be 200–500 words. A paraphrase is about the same number of words as the original, but a summary should be brief and concise.

PRACTICAL STRATEGY

Details and examples are used to explain and extend the main points in a reading or a lecture. To be brief, delete the details and examples in a summary.

Practice Activity 21

Did you understand? Try to mark out all the example sentences in the following passage and lecture. Then recopy the remaining sentences below the originals. You will have a good start for writing your summaries. But remember that you cannot use someone else's words. You still need to paraphrase when you summarize. The answers are printed in Chapter 7 on page 518. Your answers are correct if you have paraphrased the same ideas.

1. Reading

Although speech is the most advanced form of communication, there are many ways of communicating without using speech. Signals, signs, and symbols may be found in every known culture. The basic function of a signal is to impinge upon the environment in such a way that it attracts attention. For example, the flashing lights at an intersection are designed to direct the driver's attention to the road. Smoke from a distant fire can also send a message, as does the more detailed version in the dots and dashes of a telegraph. Unlike signals, which, in general, are coded to refer to speech, signs contain meaning in and of themselves. A barber pole or a picture of a loaf of bread can convey meaning quickly and conveniently when placed in front of a shop. A stop sign means *stop* even though the words may not be written out on the red octagon. Finally, gestures are actions, which are more difficult to describe because of their relationship with cultural perceptions. For instance, in some cultures, applauding in a theater provides performers with an auditory symbol of approval. In other cultures, applauding can mean that the performance was not well received.

2. Lecture

Listen to part of a lecture in a botany class. Write down the major points but do not take notes on the examples. Then write a summary.

   Activity 21, CD 2, Track 14

➤ Combine sentences

Another good way to condense the ideas is to combine sentences. Connecting words put sentences together and show the relationships between them. There are several types of sentences with connecting words for each type. Connecting words for clauses introduce a subject and a verb. Connecting words for phrases introduce a noun.

Clauses of Addition
and	addition
moreover	addition

1. Penguins are the most highly specialized of all aquatic birds.
2. Penguins may live for twenty years.

Penguins are the most highly specialized of all aquatic birds, and they may live for twenty years.
or
Penguins are the most highly specialized of all aquatic birds; moreover, they may live for twenty years.

Clauses of Reversal

but	reversal
however	reversal

1.   Penguins may live for twenty years.
2.   Penguins have several obstacles to their survival.

Penguins may live for twenty years, but they have several obstacles to their survival.
or
Penguins may live for twenty years; however, they have several obstacles to their survival.

Clauses of Result

although	unexpected result	
even though	unexpected result	
because	expected result	
since	expected result	
when	absolute scientific result	

Phrase of Result

because of + noun	expected result

1.   Both parents have brown eyes.
2.   Their children may be born with blue eyes.

Although both parents have brown eyes, their children may be born with blue eyes.
or
Their children may be born with blue eyes although both parents have brown eyes.

Even though both parents have brown eyes, their children may be born with blue eyes.
or
Their children may be born with blue eyes even though both parents have brown eyes.

1.   Their children are born with blue eyes.
2.   Both brown-eyed parents have recessive genes for blue eyes.

Because both brown-eyed parents have recessive genes for blue eyes, their children are born with blue eyes.
or
Their children are born with blue eyes because both brown-eyed parents have recessive genes for blue eyes.

Since both brown-eyed parents have recessive genes for blue eyes, their children are born with blue eyes.

or

Their children are born with blue eyes since both brown-eyed parents have recessive genes for blue eyes.

Because of recessive genes, their children are born with blue eyes.

or

Their children are born with blue eyes because of recessive genes.

When both brown-eyed parents have recessive genes for blue eyes, their children are born with blue eyes.

or

Their children are born with blue eyes when both brown-eyed parents have recessive genes.

Clauses of Contrast

whereas   on the contrary

Phrases of Contrast

in spite of + noun   contradiction
despite

1. Many Native American tribes waged isolated battles against white settlers.
2. Under Chief Tecumseh, the Shawnees tried to establish a confederacy to unify resistance against white settlers.

Whereas many Native American tribes waged isolated battles against white settlers, under Chief Tecumseh the Shawnees tried to establish a confederacy to unify resistance against them.

1. Tecumseh's fearless opposition.
2. Tecumseh's coalition was defeated at the Battle of Fallen Timbers.

In spite of Tecumseh's fearless opposition, his coalition was defeated at the Battle of Fallen Timbers.

or

Despite Tecumseh's fearless opposition, his coalition was defeated at the Battle of Fallen Timbers.

Descriptive Clauses

which   not human
who   human

1. Magnesium is the lightest of the structural metals.
2. Magnesium is important in engineering industries.

Magnesium, which is the lightest of the structural metals, is important in engineering industries.

1. Engineers often need lightweight metals.
2. Engineers use magnesium for their designs.

Engineers, who often need lightweight metals, use magnesium for their designs.

More Descriptive Clauses
that   human or not human

1. The bill was not passed until 1920.
2. The bill allowed women the right to vote in the United States.

The bill that granted women the right to vote in the United States was not passed until 1920.

Chronology Clauses
while   same time
before   earlier time
after   later time

Chronology Phrases
during   same time

1. The Romans invaded England.
2. The Celts were living in England.

The Romans invaded England while the Celts were living there.
or
The Romans invaded England during the Celtic occupation.

1. First the Iberians had been living in England.
2. Then the Angles and Saxons came to England.

The Iberians had been living in England before the Angles and Saxons came there.
or
The Angles and Saxons came to England after the Iberians had been living there.

Conclusion Clauses
therefore   logical conclusion
thus   logical conclusion

1. The amount of land cannot be increased.
2. The amount of water cannot be increased.
3. Efficient agricultural methods must be employed.

The amount of land and water cannot be increased; therefore, efficient agricultural methods must be employed.
or
The amount of land and water cannot be increased; thus, efficient agricultural methods must be employed.

Parallel Structures
Similar structures connected by commas
Nouns
Verbs
Adjectives

1. Best known for creating the Sherlock Holmes mysteries, British author Sir Arthur Conan Doyle was a physician.
2. Sir Arthur Conan Doyle was also a world traveler.
3. Sir Arthur Conan Doyle wrote numerous adventure stories.

Best known for creating the Sherlock Holmes mysteries, British author Sir Arthur Conan Doyle was <u>a physician</u>, <u>a world traveler</u>, and <u>a writer</u> of numerous adventure stories.
or
Best known for creating the Sherlock Holmes mysteries, British author Sir Arthur Conan Doyle <u>practiced</u> medicine, <u>traveled</u> the world, and <u>wrote</u> numerous adventure stories.
or
Best known for creating the Sherlock Holmes mysteries, British author Sir Arthur Conan Doyle was well <u>educated</u>, <u>adventuresome</u>, and <u>prolific</u>.

Introductory Verbal Modifiers (-ing and -ed)

-ing forms and *-ed* forms may be used as verbals. Verbals function as modifiers. An introductory verbal modifier with *-ing* or *-ed* should immediately precede the noun it modifies. Otherwise, the relationship between the noun and the modifier is unclear, and the sentence is illogical.

1. Lindbergh designed his own plane, the *Spirit of St. Louis.*
2. Lindbergh flew from Roosevelt Field in New York to Le Bourget Field outside Paris.

Having designed his own plane, the *Spirit of St. Louis*, Lindbergh flew from Roosevelt Field in New York to Le Bourget Field outside Paris.

The plane was designed by Lindbergh.
The plane flew across the ocean with few problems.

Designed by Lindbergh, the plane flew across the ocean with few problems.

Practice Activity 22

Did you understand? Try to combine the sentences. Copy the combined sentences below the originals. The first sentence is completed to give you an example. The answers are printed in Chapter 7 on pages 519–520.

Example

An attitude is a positive or negative evaluation.
A positive or negative attitude may affect behavior.
An attitude may play an important role in perception.
which

An attitude, which is a positive or negative evaluation, may affect behavior and play an important role in perception.

1. Charlie Chaplin was a comedian.
   Charlie Chaplin was best known for his work in silent movies.
   who

2. Water is heated to 212 degrees F.
   Water becomes steam.
   when

3. Quasars are relatively small objects.
   Quasars emit an enormous amount of energy.
   which

4. The Earth moves into the shadow of the Moon.
   A total eclipse occurs.
   during

5. The Jamestown colony was founded by John Smith.
   Jamestown became the first successful English colony in America.
   -ed introductory verbal modifier

6. Many of the names of cities in California are adapted from the Spanish language.
   Early missionaries and settlers from Spain had extended their influence in the area.
   since/because/because of

7. The oceans cover two thirds of the Earth's surface.
   The oceans are the object of study for oceanographers.
   which

8. A chameleon is a tree lizard.
   The chameleon can change colors to conceal itself in vegetation.
   that

9. First cultural nationalism arose among people with similar languages and traditions.
   Then political nationalism threatened the existing order.
   before/after

10. Empowerment increases the autonomy of employees in organizations.
    Empowerment improves communication between workers and management.
    and/moreover

11. Monogamy means being married to one spouse.
    Serial monogamy involves marriage, divorce, and remarriage.
    whereas

12. Humor is associated with fun.
    Humor is also used as a coping strategy to relieve stress.
    but/however

13. Solar panels can convert sunlight into electricity.
    Solar panels are still not being exploited fully.
    although/even though

14. The root system of the alfalfa plant allows it to survive.
    Drought conditions do not kill alfalfa.
    despite/in spite of

15. Pain warns the victim before further damage is done.
    Pain has a positive function.
    therefore/thus

IDENTIFY THE MAIN POINTS

Strategies to Use
➤ Find a topic sentence
➤ Identify the major points
➤ Identify the minor points

➤ Find a topic sentence

The topic answers the question: What is this reading or lecture about? A topic sentence is a very general statement that includes the subject of the reading or lecture and also the way that the author or speaker plans to develop the topic. For example, a topic might be *management strategies in business*. This topic could be developed in a number of different ways. For example, *management strategies* could be developed by listing several types of strategies or by comparing different strategies. When you are looking for the topic, you should look for a sentence that includes a subject and a verb. *Management strategies in business* is a subject, but without a verb in the sentence, we still don't know how the topic will be developed. Some books call this kind of topic sentence *a controlling idea*.

PRACTICAL STRATEGY

The first sentence in a summary should be a direct statement. It should give the reader or listener a general idea of the topic for the reading or lecture and the way that the topic will be developed. Sometimes you can paraphrase a topic sentence from the original reading or lecture, but sometimes you must create it yourself from several sentences in the original.

PRACTICE ACTIVITY 23

Did you understand? Try to write one sentence that summarizes the entire reading or lecture. Example answers are printed in Chapter 7 on pages 520–521. Your answers are correct if your ideas are the same as the example answers.

1. Reading

The nuclear family, consisting of a mother, father, and their children, may be more an ideal than a reality. Although the so-called traditional family was always more varied than we had been led to believe, reflecting the very different racial, ethnic, class, and religious customs among different American groups, today the diversity is even more obvious.

The most recent government census statistics reveal that only about one third of all current American families fits the traditional mold of two parents and their children, and another third consists of married couples who either have no children or have none still living at home. An analysis of the remaining one third of the population reveals that about 20 percent of the total number of American households are single people, the most common descriptor being women over sixty-five years of age. A small percentage, about 3 percent of the total, consists of unmarried people who choose to live together, and the rest, about 7 percent, are single parents, with at least one child.

There are several easily identifiable reasons for the growing number of single-parent households. First, the sociological phenomenon of single-parent households reflects changes in cultural attitudes toward divorce and also toward unmarried mothers. A substantial number of adults become single parents as a result of divorce. In addition, the number of children born to unmarried women who choose to keep their babies and rear them by themselves has increased dramatically. Finally, there is a small percentage of single-parent families that have resulted from untimely death. Today, these varied family types are typical and, therefore, normal.

Moreover, because many families live far from relatives, close friends have become a more important part of family life than ever before. The vast majority of Americans claim that they have people in their lives whom they regard as family although they are not related. A view of family that only accepts the traditional nuclear arrangement not only ignores the reality of modern American family life but also undervalues the familial bonds created in alternative family arrangements. Apparently, many Americans are achieving supportive relationships in family forms other than the traditional one.

2. Lecture

Listen to part of a lecture in a chemistry class. Then summarize the lecture in one sentence.

 Activity 23, CD 2, Track 15

➤ Identify the major points

PRACTICAL STRATEGY

A major point is almost always directly stated. A major point has examples and details that refer to it. A major point is often found at the beginning of a new paragraph. Inferences and conclusions or examples and details are usually NOT major points.

PRACTICE ACTIVITY 24

Did you understand? Try to identify the major points. Answers are printed in Chapter 7 on pages 521–523.

1. Reading

The body of an adult insect is subdivided into three sections, including a head, a three-segment thorax, and a segmented abdomen. Ordinarily, the thorax bears three pairs of legs and a single or double pair of wings. The vision of most adult insects is specialized through two large compound eyes and multiple simple eyes.

Features of an insect's mouth parts are used in classifying insects into types. Biting mouth parts called mandibles, such as the mouth parts found in grasshoppers and beetles, are common among insects. Behind the mandibles are located the maxillae or lower jaw parts, which serve to direct food into the mouth between the jaws. A labrum above and one below are similar to another animal's upper and lower lips. In an insect with a sucking mouth function, the mandibles, maxillae, labrum, and labium are modified in such a way that they constitute a tube through which liquid such as water, blood, or flower nectar can be drawn. In a butterfly or moth, this coiled drinking tube is called the proboscis because of its resemblance, in miniature, to the trunk of an elephant or a very large nose. Composed chiefly of modified maxillae fitted together, the insect's proboscis can be flexed and extended to reach nectar deep in a flower. In mosquitoes or aphids, mandibles and maxillae are modified to sharp stylets with which the insect can drill through surfaces like human or vegetable membranes to reach juice. In a housefly, the expanding labium forms a spongelike mouth pad that it can use to stamp over the surface of food, sopping up food particles and juices.

- Ⓐ An adult insect has a three-section body that includes a head, a thorax, and an abdomen.
- Ⓑ Mandibles are mouth parts that facilitate biting and usually include upper and lower labrum.
- Ⓒ A mouth pad similar to a sponge allows flies to attract crumbs and juice on the surface of food.
- Ⓓ Insects are classified according to their mouth parts, which are specialized for feeding.
- Ⓔ Insects are the most numerous creatures on the planet and also the most adaptable.
- Ⓕ A proboscis is a tube that stretches to penetrate flowers where nectar is stored.
- Ⓖ The three-part thorax usually has six legs and two or four wings attached to it.
- Ⓗ The pointed stylets of mosquitoes and aphids facilitate drilling through skin on plants and humans.

2. Lecture

Listen to part of a lecture in an English class. Then identify the major points from the options below.

Activity 24, CD 2, Track 16

Ⓐ Noah Webster had a degree in law and practiced for a short time before he became a school teacher.

Ⓑ *The American Spelling Book*, Webster's first successful textbook, afforded him an income while he was writing his dictionary.

Ⓒ *An American Dictionary of the English Language* was written to demonstrate the unique usage of English in the United States.

Ⓓ *An American Dictionary of the English Language* has had many revised editions.

Ⓔ *The Compendious Dictionary of the English Language*, published in 1807, provided Webster with practice in compiling a dictionary.

Ⓕ Although he had a copyright for *The American Spelling Book*, ironically Webster did not have a copyright for the original dictionary and subsequent editions that bear his name.

Ⓖ Webster graduated from Yale only two years after the end of the Revolution that won independence for the United States from England.

➤ Identify the minor points

A minor point can be an example or a detail that supports a major point, or it can be a point that is not very well developed. A minor point may be mentioned without supporting examples or details in the original reading or lecture.

PRACTICAL STRATEGY

Minor points are usually not included in a summary. If you can identify the minor points, you can eliminate them. You can shorten your summary.

PRACTICE ACTIVITY 25

Did you understand? Try to identify the minor points. Then write a summary that includes only the major points. The answers are printed in Chapter 7 on pages 523–524. Your summary is correct if it includes the same ideas.

1. Reading

In the 15th century, two important advances in painting were introduced. Prior to that time, most paintings were created on wood panels; however, in the second half of the century, many artists began to prefer linen canvas. The canvas offered several important advantages. Whereas wood panels were heavy and difficult to transport and hang, the lighter linen canvas could be rolled up for shipment and was relatively easy to transport, frame, and mount. Moreover, if patrons were at a distance from the artist, the finished work might have to be hauled in a cart. It was difficult to protect it from damage as it bumped along the primitive roads. In addition, the patrons were demanding larger and larger works and the large wood pieces had a tendency to crack. In contrast, the linen canvases could be stretched to almost any size and remained perfectly smooth.

The oil paints themselves were also superior to previous paints. One of the most obvious improvements was the fact that the paint dried slowly, and thus, layers of paint could be brushed on top of previously applied layers, allowing the artist to erase a section that was not perfect. Another refinement was the range of consistencies possible with oils. Thin oil paints take on the characteristics of a glaze, but thick oils look like paste and can be layered to create a three-dimensional aspect.

2. Lecture

Listen to part of a lecture in an engineering class. Then write a summary. Do not include the minor points.

    Activity 25, CD 2, Track 17

REPORT THE INFORMATION

> **Strategies to Use**
> ➤ Use the same organization as the original
> ➤ Report the content accurately
> ➤ Retain the original emphasis
> ➤ Maintain an objective point of view
> ➤ Check the summary

➤ Use the same organization as the original

A summary should retain the same organization as the original reading or lecture. For example, if the passage identifies three different types of evergreen trees, then the organization is classification. Your summary should also be organized to classify the three different types of trees. If the passage explains the cause of deforestation in Canada, then the organization of the passage is cause and effect. Your summary should also be organized to demonstrate cause and effect. If the passage explains the life cycle of a pine tree, then the organization is chronological. Your summary should also be organized in chronological order. It is also important NOT to rearrange the order. A good summary begins with the first major point and follows with each major point in the order that it appears in the original.

PRACTICAL STRATEGY

First, determine the organization of the reading or lecture. Then list the major points in the order in which you read or heard them. This list gives you an outline for your summary.

PRACTICE ACTIVITY 26

Did you understand? Put the major points in the order that they should appear in a summary. The answers are printed in Chapter 7 on page 524. Your answers are correct if they are in the same order as the original.

1. Reading

Although stage plays have been set to music since the era of the ancient Greeks when the dramas of Sophocles and Aeschylus were accompanied by lyres and flutes, the usually accepted date for the beginning of opera as we know it is 1600. As part of the celebration of the marriage of King Henry IV of France to the Italian aristocrat Maria de Medici, the Florentine composer Jacopo Peri produced his famous *Euridice*, generally considered to be the first opera. Following his example, a group of Italian musicians, poets, and noblemen called the Camerata revived the style of musical story that had been used in Greek tragedy. Taking most of the plots for their operas from Greek and Roman history and mythology, they began the process of creating an opera by writing a libretto or drama that could be used to establish the framework for the music. They called their compositions *opera in musica* or musical works. It is from this phrase that the word *opera* was borrowed and abbreviated.

For several years, the center of opera was Florence in northern Italy, but gradually, during the baroque period, it spread throughout Italy. By the late 1600s, operas were being written and performed in many places throughout Europe, especially in England, France, and Germany. However, for many years, the Italian opera was considered the ideal, and many non-Italian composers continued to use Italian librettos. The European form de-emphasized the dramatic aspect of the Italian model, however, introducing new orchestral effects and even some ballet.

Furthermore, composers acquiesced to the demands of singers, writing many operas that were little more than a succession of brilliant tricks for the voice, designed to showcase the splendid vocal talent of the singers who had requested them. It was thus that complicated arias, recitatives, and duets evolved. The aria, which is a long solo, may be compared to a song in which the characters express their thoughts and feelings. The recitative, which is also a solo of sorts, is a recitation set to music, the purpose of which is to continue the story line. The duet is a musical piece written for two voices, a musical device that may serve the function of either an aria or a recitative within the opera.

Major Points

- Ⓐ Three types of musical pieces in opera
- Ⓑ The first opera in Italy
- Ⓒ The growth of opera throughout Europe

2. Lecture

Listen to part of a lecture in a biology class. Then put the major points in the same order as the lecture.

 Activity 26, CD 2, Track 18

Major Points

- Ⓐ A method of classification for protozoans—the three types motility
- Ⓑ Current research—questions, redefinitions
- Ⓒ Similarity to plants—make food from water/CO_2
- Ⓓ A definition of protozoans—single cell
- Ⓔ Considered animals—eating, breathing, reproducing

➤ Report the content accurately

You will be evaluated not only on how well you use language to write a summary but also on how accurately you understand and report the content of the original.

PRACTICAL STRATEGY

Read and listen for meaning. When you have finished reading or listening, review the content. Ask yourself some basic questions. Include the questions that reporters use in their writing— *who, what, when, where, why, how?* The content may not include answers to all of the questions, but, with practice, you will be able to identify the questions that are important to the content you have read or heard.

PRACTICE ACTIVITY 27

Did you understand? Answer the content questions. Then, copy the answers to the questions in paragraph form to make a summary. The answers and the example summaries are printed in Chapter 7 on pages 525–526.

1. Reading

According to the controversial sunspot theory, great storms on the surface of the Sun hurl streams of solar particles into space and eventually into the atmosphere of our planet, causing shifts in the weather on the Earth and interference with radio and television communications.

A typical sunspot consists of a dark central umbra, a word derived from the Latin word for shadow, which is surrounded by a lighter penumbra of light and dark threads extending out from the center like the spokes of a wheel. Actually, the sunspots are cooler than the rest of the photosphere, which may account for their apparently darker color. Typically, the temperature in a sunspot umbra is about 4000 K, whereas the temperature in a penumbra registers 5500 K, and the granules outside the spot are 6000 K.

Sunspots range in size from tiny grains to complex structures with areas stretching for billions of square miles. About 5 percent of all sunspots are large enough so that they can be seen from Earth without instruments; consequently, observations of sunspots have been recorded for thousands of years. They have been observed in arrangements of one to more than one hundred spots, but they tend to occur in pairs. There is also a marked tendency for the two spots of a pair to have opposite magnetic polarities. Furthermore, the strength of the magnetic field associated with any given sunspot is closely related to the spot's size.

Sunspots have also been observed to occur in cycles, over a period of eleven years. At the beginning of a cycle, the storms occur between 20 and 40 degrees north and south of the equator on the Sun. As the cycle continues, some of the storms move closer to the equator. As the cycle diminishes, the number of sunspots decreases to a minimum, and they cluster between 5 and 15 degrees north and south latitude.

Although there is no theory that completely explains the nature and function of sunspots, several models show scientists' attempts to relate the phenomenon to magnetic field lines along the lines of longitude from the north and south poles of the Sun.

1. What is the author's main purpose in the passage?

    Ⓐ To describe the nature of sunspots
    Ⓑ To propose a model for cycles in the solar year
    Ⓒ To compare the umbra and the penumbra in sunspots
    Ⓓ To argue for the existence of magnetic fields in sunspots

2. Why are solar particles hurled into space?

    Ⓐ Undetermined causes on Earth
    Ⓑ Disturbances of wind on the Sun
    Ⓒ Small rivers on the surface of the Sun
    Ⓓ Changes in the Earth's atmosphere

3. How can we describe the effect of matter from the Sun that enters the Earth's atmosphere?

    Ⓐ It causes volcanic eruptions on the surface of the Earth.
    Ⓑ It affects changes in the weather patterns on Earth.
    Ⓒ It results in shadows across the Earth's surface.
    Ⓓ It produces higher temperatures on the Earth.

4. How would you describe most sunspots?

    Ⓐ A shadow encircled by bright and dark lines extending out like spokes in a wheel
    Ⓑ A bright wheel with a dark shadow that covers part of the spokes that extend out
    Ⓒ A wheel with alternating spokes of dark shadows and bright spaces in between
    Ⓓ A spoke of a wheel with a bright trail partially covered by a dark shadow

5. What does the author mean by the statement "Actually, the sunspots are cooler than the rest of the photosphere, which may account for their apparently darker color"?

    Ⓐ Neither sunspots nor the photosphere is hot.
    Ⓑ Sunspots in the photosphere do not have any color.
    Ⓒ The color of sunspots could be affected by their temperature.
    Ⓓ The size of a sunspot affects its temperature.

6. In which configuration do sunspots usually occur?

    Ⓐ In one spot of varying size
    Ⓑ In a configuration of two spots
    Ⓒ In arrangements of one hundred or more spots
    Ⓓ In groups of several thousand spots

7. How are sunspots explained?

    Ⓐ Sunspots appear to be related to the pull of highly magnetic fields on the Earth.
    Ⓑ Sunspots may be related to magnetic fields that follow longitudinal lines on the Sun.
    Ⓒ Sunspots are explained by large storms that occur on the surface of the Earth.
    Ⓓ Sunspots have no theory or model to explain their occurrence or reappearance.

8. The sunspot theory is

  Ⓐ not very important
  Ⓑ widely accepted
  Ⓒ subject to debate
  Ⓓ relatively new

2. Lecture

Listen to part of a lecture in an anthropology class. Then answer the questions and use the answers to write a summary.

 Activity 27, CD 2, Track 19

1. According to the lecturer, fossils are considered valuable for all of the following reasons EXCEPT

  Ⓐ They suggest how the climate may have been.
  Ⓑ They provide information about migration.
  Ⓒ They document the evolution of the horse.
  Ⓓ They maintain a record of life prior to the Miocene.

2. What does the lecturer mean by the statement, "Geologists believe that the first horses appeared on Earth about sixty million years ago as compared with only two million years ago for the appearance of human beings."

  Ⓐ Geologists claim that horses appeared on Earth millions of years before human beings.
  Ⓑ Both horses and human beings appeared several million years ago, if we believe geologists.
  Ⓒ The geological records for the appearance of horses and human beings are not very accurate.
  Ⓓ Horses and human beings cannot be compared by geologists because they appeared too long ago.

3. According to the lecture, the anchitheres

  Ⓐ never lived in the North American continent
  Ⓑ had migrated to Europe in the Miocene Period from North America
  Ⓒ developed larger bodies than the hipparion from North America
  Ⓓ were only about the size of a small dog when they invaded North America

4. Which of the following conclusions may be made on the basis of information in the lecture?

  Ⓐ Following the same route, the hipparion migrated to Europe in the Pliocene.
  Ⓑ There are no fossil remains of either the anchitheres or the hipparion in Europe.
  Ⓒ Both horses were in North America when the first European colonists arrived.
  Ⓓ Very little is conclusively known about the evolution of the horse in Europe.

5. What happened to the anchitheres when the hipparion invaded Europe?

   Ⓐ They interbred with the hipparion.
   Ⓑ They migrated into Asia.
   Ⓒ They did not survive.
   Ⓓ They evolved into large horses.

6. What do we know about horses in North America during the Pleistocene?

   Ⓐ They were very large and strong.
   Ⓑ They were already extinct.
   Ⓒ They lived in the Bering Straits.
   Ⓓ They migrated south from Alaska.

7. What happened to the hipparion in Europe?

   Ⓐ They developed into a sturdy animal, like modern breeds of horses.
   Ⓑ They were replaced by other larger, stronger animals.
   Ⓒ They evolved into modern ponies instead of modern horses.
   Ⓓ They disappeared because they were hunted into extinction.

8. How was the domesticated horse introduced in North America?

   Ⓐ Early hunting tribes from Europe herded them across the Bering Straits.
   Ⓑ They were used as transportation by immigrants who used a land route.
   Ⓒ Europeans returned the horse to the American colonies on ships.
   Ⓓ They migrated to find better grasslands than they had in Europe and Asia.

➤ Retain the original emphasis

The emphasis should be the same in both the original and the summary. For example, a passage about the three different types of leaves may include all three types, but it may dedicate half of the passage to one type—palmate leaves. In this case, your summary should retain the same emphasis by dedicating half of the summary to palmate leaves.

PRACTICAL STRATEGY

When you read, think in terms of space. How much space does the author devote to each point? When you listen, think in terms of time. How much time does the speaker devote to each point? When you do this, you are determining the emphasis for each point in the original, and you will know how much emphasis to give to these points in your summary.

PRACTICE ACTIVITY 28

Did you understand? Try to identify the emphasis for each part of the original and assign percentages. Then write a summary that retains the original emphasis. The answers and example summaries are printed in Chapter 7 on pages 526–527.

1. Reading

The Federal Reserve System, commonly called the Fed, is an independent agency of the United States government charged with overseeing the national banking system. Since 1913, the Federal Reserve System has served as the central bank for the United States. The Fed's primary function is to control monetary policy by influencing the cost and availability of money and credit through the purchase and sale of government securities. If the Federal Reserve provides too little money, interest rates tend to be high, borrowing is expensive, business activity slows down, unemployment goes up, and the danger of a recession is augmented. On the other hand, if there is too much money, interest rates decline, and borrowing can lead to excess demand, pushing up prices and fueling inflation. In addition to controlling the money supply, the Fed has several other responsibilities. In collaboration with the U.S. Department of the Treasury, the Fed puts new coins and paper currency into circulation by issuing them to banks. It also supervises the activities of member banks abroad and regulates certain aspects of international finance.

The Federal Reserve System consists of twelve district reserve banks and their branch offices along with several committees and councils. All national commercial banks are required by law to be members of the Fed, and all deposit-taking institutions like credit unions are subject to regulation by the Fed regarding the amount of deposited funds that must be held in reserve and that, by definition, therefore, are not available for loans. The most powerful body is the seven-member board of governors in Washington, appointed by the President and confirmed by the Senate. Although it is true that the Federal Reserve does not depend on Congress for budget allocations, and therefore is free from the partisan politics that influence most of the other governmental bodies, it is still responsible for frequent reports to the Congress on the conduct of monetary policies.

In many ways, the Federal Reserve is like a fourth branch of the United States government because it is composed of national policy makers. However, in practice, the Fed does not stray from the financial policies established by the executive branch of the government.

Major Points

- The function and responsibilities of the Fed
- The composition of the Fed
- A comparison of the Fed to a fourth branch of government

2. Lecture

Listen to part of a lecture in a psychology class. Then assign a percentage to each of the following points from the lecture and write a summary using the percentages to determine how much to write on each point.

 Activity 28, CD 2, Track 20

Major Points

- The level of sophistication for human memory
- The memory trace
- Working memory

➤ Maintain an objective point of view

An objective point of view is a neutral position. A summary is not an analysis or a commentary. A summary does not invite an opinion.

PRACTICAL STRATEGY

In your summary, you should not agree or disagree with the author's or the speaker's ideas. Don't make judgments. Don't add information. When you report, you should not include *your* opinions or comments. The conclusion should be the author's or the speaker's conclusion, not yours.

PRACTICE ACTIVITY 29

Did you understand? Try to find the opinions in the summary and delete them. Use the original reading to compare the content. The answers are printed in Chapter 7 on pages 528–529.

1. Reading

Charles Ives, who is now acclaimed as the first great American composer of the twentieth century, had to wait many years for the public recognition he deserved. Born to music as the son of a bandmaster, Ives played drums in his father's community band and organ at the local church. He entered Yale University at twenty to study musical composition with Horatio Parker, but after graduation he chose not to pursue a career in music. He suspected correctly that the public would not accept the music he wrote because Ives did not follow the musical fashion of his times. While his contemporaries wrote lyrical songs, Ives transfigured music and musical form. He quoted, combined, insinuated, and distorted familiar hymns, marches, and battle songs, while experimenting with the effects of polytonality, or the simultaneous use of keys with conflicting rhythms and time. Even when he could convince some musicians to show some interest in his compositions, after assessing them conductors and performers said that they were essentially unplayable.

Ives turned his attention to business. He became a successful insurance executive, building his company into the largest agency in the country in only two decades. Although he occasionally hired musicians to play one of his works privately for him, he usually heard his music only in his imagination. After he recovered from a serious heart attack, he became reconciled to the fact that his ideas, especially the use of dissonance and special effects, were just too different for the musical mainstream to accept. Determined to share his music with the few people who might appreciate it, he published his work privately and distributed it free.

In 1939, when Ives was sixty-five, American pianist John Kirkpatrick played *Concord Sonata* in Town Hall. The reviews were laudatory. One reviewer proclaimed it "the greatest music composed by an American." By 1947, Ives was famous. His *Second Symphony* was presented to the public in a performance by the New York Philharmonic, fifty years after it had been written. The same year, Ives received the Pulitzer Prize. He was seventy-three.

Summary

Charles Ives started his musical career as a member of his father's band and received a degree from Yale University in music, but he became a businessman instead because he was afraid that his music would not be well accepted. His music was very different from the popular songs of his era because he used small phrases from well-known music with unusual rhythms and tones. Fifty years after he wrote his *Second Symphony*, it was performed by the New York Philharmonic, and he was awarded the Pulitzer Prize.

I think that Charles Ives was wrong not to pursue his musical career from the beginning. If he had continued writing music instead of selling insurance, we would have more pieces now.

2. Lecture

Listen to part of a lecture in a geology class. Then delete the opinions from the summary.

 Activity 29, CD 3, Track 1

In my opinion, geysers are interesting. They happen when underground water gets hot and pressure from above causes the water to get hotter and lighter so it goes up to the surface and explodes out. Then, the water runs back into the ground and starts all over again. Geysers have to have heat, a place to store water, an opening where the water can shoot up, and cracks in the ground for the water to go back down into a pool. Geysers are in New Zealand, Iceland, and the United States. Old Faithful in Yellowstone is the most famous geyser, but the best place to see geysers is in New Zealand. I saw the Pohutu Geyser there on my vacation two years ago, and it was awesome.

➤ Check the summary

If you know how your summary will be evaluated, you can use the same criteria to check it before you submit it.

PRACTICAL STRATEGY

Save some time at the end of your written summary to re-read it and check it. Keep a short checklist in mind as you review your content and organization.

PRACTICE ACTIVITY 30

Did you understand? Try to find the problems in the following summaries. Use the original reading to compare the content and the short checklist to identify which problems to correct. The answers are printed in Chapter 7 on page 529.

Short Checklist for Summaries

✔ Be brief
✔ Use the same organization as the original
✔ Include the major points
✔ Report the content accurately
✔ Retain the original emphasis
✔ Paraphrase using your own words
✔ Maintain an objective point of view

Reading

Very few people in the modern world obtain their food supply by hunting and gathering in the natural environment surrounding their homes. This method of harvesting from nature's provision, however, is not only the oldest known subsistence strategy but also the one that has been practiced continuously in some parts of the world for at least the last two million years. It was, indeed, the only way to obtain food until rudimentary farming and very crude methods for the domestication of animals were introduced about 10,000 years ago.

Because hunter-gatherers have fared poorly in comparison with their agricultural cousins, their numbers have dwindled, and they have been forced to live in the marginal wastelands. In higher latitudes, the shorter growing season has restricted the availability of plant life. Such conditions have caused a greater dependence on hunting and, along the coasts and waterways, on fishing. The abundance of vegetation in the lower latitudes of the tropics, on the other hand, has provided a greater opportunity for gathering a variety of plants. In short, the environmental differences have restricted the diet and have limited possibilities for the development of subsistence societies.

Contemporary hunter-gatherers may help us understand our prehistoric ancestors. We know from observation of modern hunter-gatherers in both Africa and Alaska that a society based on hunting and gathering must be very mobile. Following the food supply can be a way of life. If a particular kind of wild herding animal is the basis of the food for a group of people, those people must move to stay within reach of those animals. For many of the native people of the great central plains of North America, following the buffalo, who were in turn following the growth of grazing foods, determined their way of life.

For gathering societies, seasonal changes mean a great deal. While the entire community camps in a central location, a smaller party harvests the food within a reasonable distance from the camp. When the food in the area is exhausted, the community moves on to exploit another site. We also notice a seasonal migration pattern evolving for most hunter-gatherers, along with a strict division of labor between the sexes. These patterns of behavior may be similar to those practiced by humankind during the Paleolithic Period.

Summary 1

By studying hunter-gatherers in today's world, we can better understand the people from prehistoric times. In a hunter-gatherer society, the surrounding vegetation limits the dietary options. In addition, the length of the growing season restricts the amount of gathering that can be done and requires more hunting and fishing for groups to survive. We note that groups must follow the herds and travel to new sites where edible plants are in season. Although few people are now dependent upon hunting and gathering, it is the most ancient lifestyle, and perhaps the only way to subsist before agricultural communities arose during the past 10,000 years. Furthermore, men and women have specialized tasks. Competition with agricultural societies has crowded hunter-gatherers into harsh terrains.

Summary 2

Although few people are now dependent upon hunting and gathering, it is the most ancient lifestyle, and perhaps the only way to subsist before agricultural communities arose during the past 10,000 years. Competition with agricultural societies has crowded hunter-gatherers into harsh terrains. In a hunter-gatherer society, the surrounding vegetation limits the dietary options. In addition, the length of the growing season restricts the amount of gathering that can be done and requires more hunting and fishing for groups to survive. By studying hunter-gatherers in today's world, we can better understand the people from prehistoric times. We note that groups must follow the herds and travel to new sites where edible plants are in season. Furthermore, men and women have specialized tasks.

Summary 3

Few people are now dependent upon hunting and gathering; however, it is the most ancient lifestyle, and perhaps the only way to subsist before agricultural communities arose during the past 10,000 years. Competition with agricultural societies has crowded hunter-gatherers into harsh terrains. In my opinion, we should help these groups to learn how to grow their own crops so that they will not have to have limited diets and will not have to move to new sites where edible plants are in season. By studying hunter-gatherers in today's world, we can better understand the people from prehistoric times, and that is good, but we should help them, too.

Summary 4

Although very few people in the modern world obtain their food supply by hunting and gathering, this method is the oldest known subsistence strategy. Because hunter-gatherers have fared poorly, they have been forced to live in harsh environments with limited possibilities for their diet. By observation of modern hunter-gatherers, we know that people must move to stay within reach of the herds they hunt. When the food in the area is exhausted, the community moves on to exploit another site.

Summary 5

Few people are now dependent upon hunting and gathering, but it is the most ancient lifestyle, and perhaps the only way to subsist before agricultural communities arose during the past 10,000 years. It has been part of human cultures beginning two million years ago and continues to the present in some parts of the world. Modern hunter-gatherers provide us with information about prehistoric people. They probably moved to stay close to the herds they hunted and moved to take advantage of seasonal plants.

ADVISOR'S OFFICE

Why are you preparing for the TOEFL? What goal is motivating you to study and improve your score? Do you want to attend a university in an English-speaking country? Do you want to try for a scholarship from a sponsor in your country or region? Is the TOEFL required for graduation from your high school? Do you plan to apply for an assistantship at a graduate school? Do you need the score for a professional license?

Goals can be experienced as mental images. You can close your eyes and imagine everything, just like a movie. See yourself achieving your goal. Watch yourself as you attend school or practice your profession in your ideal environment. See other people congratulating you. Enjoy the success.

Understand that you cannot control reality with visualization. However, it does change your attitude, it helps you to focus, provides motivation, and reduces stress. Positive visualization is an excellent way to take a short break from studying.

SYNTHESIZING

Synthesizing means to combine two or more sources in order to create something new. It is probably the most complex academic skill because it includes all of the other academic skills that you have studied—taking notes, paraphrasing, and summarizing. In addition, the result of a synthesis should be more than the sum of the parts. There are three problems that you will confront when you are synthesizing.

1. **The relationship between the sources may not be obvious**. This means that you may have to figure out the connection.
2. **One source appears to contain all of the necessary information**. This means that you need to be sure to balance the information so that all of the sources are used.
3. **Synthesis requires a high level of thinking**. This means that you should have a plan in order to create a synthesis.

This chapter will help you improve your synthesizing. You will learn how to

- **Identify themes and connections**
- **Select information from both sources**
- **Follow a plan**

How will these strategies help you on the TOEFL? By learning to synthesize information from readings and lectures, you will develop ways of thinking that will help you prepare important integrated speaking and writing questions. The ability to synthesize is also required for success in making presentations and writing research papers for college or university classes.

IDENTIFY THEMES AND CONNECTIONS

Strategies to Use
➤ Identify the primary source
➤ Analyze the task
➤ Clarify the relationships
➤ Get organized

➤ Identify the primary source

At least two sources are required for a synthesis. The primary source presents the major points, and the secondary source provides additional information. The directions for a task or a question on a test will help you identify the primary source.

PRACTICAL STRATEGY

Read the directions very carefully to determine which source you are being asked to use as your primary source. The primary source is usually but not always mentioned first.

<u>EXAMPLE</u>

Primary source: Summarize the points that the *lecturer* makes,
Secondary source: explaining how they cast doubt on the information in the *reading.*

In this case, the primary source is the lecture and the secondary source is the reading.

PRACTICE ACTIVITY 31

Did you understand? Read the directions and underline the primary source. The first one is completed to give you an example. The answers are printed in Chapter 7 on pages 529–530.

<u>EXAMPLE</u>

Summarize the theory explained in the <u>reading</u>, showing how the lecturer casts doubt on the theory.

1. Summarize the points in the lecture, explaining how they support the data in the reading.

2. Explain the model described in the reading, and then show how the lecture contradicts it.

3. Explaining how they provide evidence for the information in the reading, summarize the points made in the lecture you have just heard.

4. Summarize the hypothesis outlined in the reading, explaining how the lecture supports it.

5. Summarize the major points in the reading, explaining how the lecture contradicts them.

6. Explain how the lecturer's view substantiates the opinions expressed in the reading.

7. Summarize the points made in the lecture you have just heard, explaining how they differ from the points made in the reading.

8. Summarize the points from the lecture, explaining how they cast doubt on the reading.

9. Referring to the main points in the lecture, summarize the professor's opinion, contrasting it with the views expressed in the reading.

10. Summarize the concept in the reading, referring to the examples provided in the lecture you have just heard.

➤ Analyze the task

The wording of the question or the assignment will direct your thinking. Some words and phrases that refer to the secondary source demonstrate agreement and extension, but other words and phrases show disagreement and contrast. Occasionally neutral words are used. It is important to understand the meaning of these words and phrases in order to analyze the task. The way that you relate the secondary source to the primary source depends on these words.

PRACTICAL STRATEGY

Start your thinking by categorizing words in the question or assignment as *extension* words or *contrast* words. The following lists will help you.

Agreement/Extension

Add to	include more evidence
Affirm	maintain to be true
Agree with	have the same opinion
Concur with	have the same opinion
Confirm	establish that something is true
Corroborate	show the same evidence
Prove	show that something is true
Provide an example of	give an illustration
Provide evidence for	give proof
Reinforce	make stronger
Substantiate	give proof
Support	maintain a position
Validate	show the facts
Verify	show the truth

Disagreement/Contrast

Cast doubt on	show uncertainty
Contradict	maintain the opposite
Contrast with	show difference
Counter	show the opposite
Differ from	show difference
Disagree with	give a different opinion
Discredit	show that something is not true
Disprove	establish that something is not true
Dispute	argue that something is wrong
Oppose	argue the opposite
Provide an alternative to	give a different option

Neutrality

Describe
Explain
List
Outline
Relate
Summarize

PRACTICE ACTIVITY 32

Did you understand? Without looking at the lists above, try to put these sentences into categories—*agreement and extension* or *disagreement and contrast*. First underline the word or phrase that refers to the secondary source. This word or phrase will show you how to relate the secondary source to the primary source. It will help you analyze the task. The first one is completed to give you an example. The answers are printed in Chapter 7 on page 530.

EXAMPLE

Summarize the major points in the reading and explain how the lecturer <u>casts doubt on</u> those points.
Disagreement/contrast

1. Summarize the points that the lecturer makes, explaining how they support the information in the reading.

2. Explain the theory proposed in the reading, and then contrast the ideas in the theory with the views expressed in the lecture.

3. Summarize the points made in the lecture you have just heard, explaining how they support the information in the reading.

4. Referring to the main points in the lecture, summarize the professor's views, contrasting them with the opinion expressed in the reading.

5. Summarize the hypothesis outlined in the lecture, explaining how the reading casts doubt on its validity.

6. Summarize the points in the lecture you have just heard, referring to the examples provided in the reading.

7. Summarize the major points in the reading, explaining how the lecture contradicts them.

8. Explain how the lecturer's ideas differ from those in the reading.

9. Summarize the points made in the lecture you have just heard, explaining how they reinforce the points made in the reading.

10. Summarize the points from the lecture, explaining how they cast doubt on the reading.

➤ Clarify the relationships

The relationship between the primary source and the secondary source is usually more specific than an extension or a contrast. Some of the most common relationships are listed in the chart below.

PRACTICAL STRATEGY

Using the chart below to help you, determine the specific relationship between the primary source and the secondary source.

Extension/Agreement

Primary Source	Secondary Source
Concept	Example/Case Study
Theory	Research Study/Proof
Definition	Example/Characteristics
Cause	Effect/Result
Problem	Solution
Issue/Situation	Explanation/Example

Contrast/Disagreement

Definition/Explanation	Comparison
Issue/Situation	Comparison/Contrast
Opinion	Contrasting opinion
Advantages	Disadvantages

PRACTICE ACTIVITY 33

Did you understand? Try to clarify the relationship between the sources in your synthesis. Refer to the chart above if you need to. The first one is completed to give you an example. The answers are printed in Chapter 7 on pages 530–531.

EXAMPLE

Primary source: Definition	Definition of a folk song
Secondary source: Example/Characteristics	Characteristics of "Barbara Allen"

1. Primary source: The advantages of cooperative learning in schools
   Secondary source: The disadvantages of cooperative learning in schools

2. Primary source: An explanation of theoretical linguistics
   Secondary source: An explanation of applied linguistics

3. Primary source: The eradication of diseases on a worldwide basis
   Secondary source: The World Health Organization's campaign against smallpox

4. Primary source: The problem of noise pollution in a technological society
   Secondary source: European noise ordinances that limit noise pollution

5. Primary source: Advertising products abroad
    Secondary source: The marketing plan for Toyota in the United States

6. Primary source: The theory of flow
    Secondary source: A Harvard University study on flow

7. Primary source: The impact of a large meteor on Earth
    Secondary source: The disappearance of dinosaurs after the meteor

8. Primary source: Nuclear power plants are dangerous.
    Secondary source: Nuclear power is a good source of energy.

9. Primary source: Qualitative research designs in the social sciences
    Secondary source: The Hawthorne effect as a limiting factor in qualitative research

10. Primary source: The size, price, and power of early computers
    Secondary source: The size, price, and power of modern computers

➤ Get organized

Use the skills that you have already learned to get organized before you begin your synthesis.

PRACTICAL STRATEGY

First, read the directions for your assignment or the question for your test. Ask yourself these questions:

1. What is the primary source?
2. What is the secondary source?
3. What is the task? Extension or contrast?
4. What is the specific relationship between the primary and secondary sources?

PRACTICE ACTIVITY 34

Read the directions for a synthesis of the reading and lecture below. Then prepare to respond by asking the four questions you have learned to use:

1. What is the primary source?
2. What is the secondary source?
3. What is the task? Extension or contrast?
4. What is the specific relationship between the primary and secondary sources?

The answers are printed in Chapter 7 on pages 531–532.

Directions: Summarize the points in the reading, explaining how the lecture supports them.

Reading

Marsupials are a group of mammals that are born alive after a very short gestation period. Since a marsupial appears quite early in its life cycle, it must complete its embryonic development while nursing. In order to survive, the young underdeveloped marsupial must crawl from the exit of the reproductive tract over its mother's body to attach itself to a nipple inside a fold of skin called the *marsupium* but better known as a pouch. During embryonic development, which can be weeks or months, depending on the species, a marsupial nurses and grows inside the pouch. Most marsupials do not form family groups. It is the female marsupial that cares for the offspring. The young marsupial may stay with the mother for more than a year, climbing in and out of the pouch to nurse or sleep.

Although marsupials once ranged throughout North and South America, as well as in Antarctica, only a few species now live outside of New Zealand and Australia where more than 250 species are still found. There is quite a diversity of marsupials within these species, and they have adapted to a number of different habitats; however, some characteristics are universal among them. Auditory and olfactory senses are very important to marsupials because they are nocturnal creatures that depend on their ears and eyes to locate their food at night. Some marsupials prefer plants, although others eat insects or meat. Like other mammals, marsupials are covered with hair. Unlike their placental cousins, however, marsupials have additional bones that project from the pelvis, a support that may strengthen the wall of the abdomen to reinforce the pouch that is their unique adaptation.

Lecture

Listen to part of a lecture in a biology class.

    Activity 34, CD 3, Track 2

SELECT INFORMATION FROM BOTH SOURCES

> **Strategies to Use**
> ➤ Summarize the primary source
> ➤ Use transition sentences
> ➤ Include the secondary source

➤ Summarize the primary source

You will often be asked to summarize the main points in the primary source and then relate the secondary source to it. Even if you are not asked to summarize the primary source, you should still begin by using your notes from the primary source.

PRACTICAL STRATEGY

After you have taken notes on both sources, direct your attention to the notes for the primary source. If the directions for your assignment or the question for your test instruct you to summarize the primary source, begin with a summary, using your notes.

PRACTICE ACTIVITY 35

Using the notes from the primary source, write a summary. In this case, the primary source is the reading in Activity 34. Do not use the notes from the secondary source in the summary. Compare your summary with the example summary printed in Chapter 7 on page 532.

Notes for Reading—Primary Source

- marsupials = mammals
- short gestation
    completes embryonic development nursing
    reproductive tract → marsupium/pouch w/nipple
- no family groups
    mother 1 yr +
- once NA, SA, Antarc
    now few outside NZ + Aust 250 species+
- diversity habitats
- universal characteristics
    nocturnal
    smell, hearing important
    hair
    additional bones project pelvis, reinforce pouch

Notes for Lecture—Secondary Source

- koala = marsupial ∅ bear
- gestation 35 d
- pink/no fur
- 19 mm
- birth canal → pouch/1 of 2 nipples
- 6–7 mo develop/explore
- 8 mo too big for pouch
- 4+ mo rides back/stomach
- 1 yr independent
- Teddy Bear = size, fur, round ears/large nose
- keen hearing, smell
- sleeps trees day
- combs eucalyptus leaves night

➤ Use transition sentences

Transition sentences are very useful in a synthesis. They can be used to connect information from the primary source with information from the secondary source. Transition sentences show the specific relationship between the two sources.

PRACTICAL STRATEGY

Learning some patterns for forming transitional sentences can be helpful. The charts below are examples for you to study.

Extension/Agreement
Primary Source   *Secondary Source*

Theory   **Research Study**

A research study on_____   was carried out _____.   According to _____,

A research study on flow was carried out at Harvard University. According to the study, . . .

Definition   **Example**

An example of _____   is_____.   According to _____,

An example of a familiar opera is "Carmen." According to the lecturer, "Carmen . . . "

Case study   **Concept**

_____ is a case study of   _____.   According to _____,

The Toyota company's campaign in the United States is a case study of advertising products abroad. According to the lecturer, Toyota . . .

Cause   **Effect**

_____ may have caused   _____.   According to _____.

The impact of a large meteor on Earth may have caused the disappearance of dinosaurs. According to the lecturer, the meteor . . .

Solution   **Problem**

_____ may offer a solution for   _____.   According to _____.

European noise ordinances may offer a solution for the problem of noise pollution in a techno-logical society. According to the lecturer, . . .

Opinion   **Opposing Opinion**

_____. However, a case may be made for the opposing view.   According to_____.

. . . the view that nuclear power plants are dangerous. However, a case may be made for the opposing view. According to the lecturer, . . .

Advantages   **Disadvantages**

_____. On the other hand, several disadvantages were mentioned_____.

. . . is also an advantage of cooperative learning. On the other hand, several disadvantages were mentioned in the lecture. First, . . .

Idea   **Comparison**

_____. In comparison,   _____.   According to_____.

. . . theoretical linguistics. In comparison, applied linguistics answers practical questions. According to the reading, an applied linguist . . .

➤ Include the secondary source

A synthesis is not complete unless information from the secondary source is included.

PRACTICAL STRATEGY

Proofread your synthesis. Look for information from both the primary source and the secondary source.

PRACTICE ACTIVITY 36

Use the information about the primary source and the secondary source to write transition sentences that will connect them. Compare your answers with the example answers printed in Chapter 7 on page 532. Your answers may be slightly different, but you should see the same patterns that you find in the examples.

EXAMPLE

Primary source: Reading
The advantage of observation is the natural setting.
Secondary source: Lecture
The disadvantage of observation is the potential for the researcher to be biased.
Transition sentence to connect advantages with disadvantages.

The advantage of observation is the natural setting. On the other hand, several disadvantages were mentioned in the lecture. First, there is the potential for the researcher to be biased.

1. Primary source:　　Reading
   A biogeographic realm is a land mass.
   Secondary source:　Lecture
   A biome is a major regional ecosystem.
   Transition sentence to connect one concept with another concept in a comparison.

2. Primary source:　　Reading
   Innovations in industrial production in the 19th century
   Secondary source:　Lecture
   Henry Ford's assembly line
   Transition sentence to connect a concept with an example.

3. Primary source:　　Lecture
   Advantages of stone for sculpture
   Secondary source:　Reading
   Disadvantages of stone for sculpture
   Transition sentence to connect the advantages with the disadvantages.

4. Primary source:　　Reading
   Horticultural societies grow crops using hand tools.
   Secondary source:　Lecture
   Agrarian societies cultivate crops with draft animals and plows.
   Transition sentence to connect one concept with another in a contrast.

5. Primary source:　　Reading
   Changes in the climate of the North American coastline.
   Secondary source:　Lecture
   El Nino
   Transition sentence to connect a cause (El Nino) with an effect (changes in climate).

6. Primary source:　　Reading
   Franchises
   Secondary source:　Lecture
   Kentucky Fried Chicken chain
   Transition sentence to connect a business concept with a case study of a restaurant franchise.

7. Primary source:　　Reading
   Risks for heart problems
   Secondary source:　Lecture
   Research on Type A and Type B personalities
   Transition sentence to connect a concept with a research study.

8. Primary source: Lecture
    The United States should convert to metrics.
    Secondary source: Reading
    The United States should retain the English system.
    Transition sentence to connect one opinion with an opposing opinion.

9. Primary source: Reading
    South Africa's natural resources
    Secondary source: Lecture
    Gold mining
    Transition sentence to connect a concept with an example.

10. Primary source: Reading
    Commuting to work
    Secondary source: Lecture
    Home offices
    Transition sentence to connect a problem (commuting) with a solution (home offices).

FOLLOW A PLAN

Strategies to Use
➤ Memorize a procedure
➤ Work within time limits
➤ Practice using the procedure

➤ Memorize a procedure

In order to accomplish a complex task, it helps to have a procedure. The first step in using a new procedure is putting the steps in order and learning them.

PRACTICAL STRATEGY

Tell yourself what you are going to do to create a synthesis of two sources. Read the following steps until you can recite them without looking at this page.

Read the assignment or test question.

  1. Identify the primary source.
  2. Identify the secondary source.
  3. Decide whether the task is extension or contrast.
  4. Determine the specific relationship between the primary and secondary sources.

Read the passage and take notes.
Listen to the lecture and take notes.
Plan and write a synthesis.

  5. Summarize the primary source.
  6. Create a transition sentence to connect the primary source with the secondary source.
  7. Summarize the secondary source while making references to the primary source.

PRACTICE ACTIVITY 37

Use the procedure to write a synthesis of a reading and a lecture. Take as much time as you need to complete the synthesis. Write 150–225 words. Compare your synthesis with the example answer in Chapter 7 on page 533.

Reading

The *Out of Africa hypothesis*, also called the *replacement hypothesis*, contends that modern humans originated in Africa, probably from a common ancestor. From there, they migrated to other regions, eventually replacing the populations of Neanderthals and other groups of earlier humans that may have survived.

Geneticists who support the *replacement hypothesis* argue that the similarities shared by all of the modern human populations confirm the existence of a common gene pool, and perhaps even one common female ancestor. They point to the fact that many modern human traits have evolved within the past 200,000 years as evidence of the replacement hypothesis. Furthermore, they cite studies of DNA in cell structures called mitochondria, which codes most of the inherited traits from ancestors. Most of these studies demonstrate that the diversity among human populations is very small as compared with other species. They conclude that there was only one small population from which all other populations descended. From their point of view, the evidence supports the theory that modern humans migrated from a relatively small area in Africa almost 150,000 years ago, moving along a route through the Middle East 100,000 years ago, and slowly populating regions throughout the world by displacing the communities of less developed humanlike species that they encountered.

Paleoanthropologists concede that, to date, the oldest fossil remains of modern *Homo sapiens* have been found in Africa, with the next oldest discovered in the Middle East. European fossils are dated at about 50,000 years after the African fossils. Thus, it would appear that the *replacement hypothesis* is substantiated by archaeological evidence.

Lecture

Now that you have read the explanation of human migration patterns in the reading, listen to part of a lecture on a similar topic.

 Activity 37, CD 3, Track 3

Synthesis

Summarize the major points in the reading and explain how the lecturer casts doubt on those points.

➤ Work within time limits

If you are synthesizing for an assignment that is due in several weeks, you will have plenty of time to think, write, and revise, but if you are synthesizing information for a test question, you will have to work within time limits, and you need to understand what those limits are.

PRACTICAL STRATEGY

The procedure is listed again but this time the time limits are shown. Pay attention to the timing when you practice using the procedure.

Read the assignment or test question—10 seconds

1. Identify the primary source.
2. Identify the secondary source.
3. Decide whether the task is extension or contrast.
4. Determine the specific relationship between the primary and secondary sources.

Read the passage and take notes—3 minutes
Listen to the lecture and take notes—3–5 minutes
Plan and write a synthesis—20 minutes

5. Summarize the primary source.
6. Create a transition sentence to connect the primary source with the secondary source.
7. Summarize the secondary source while making references to the primary source.

PRACTICE ACTIVITY 38

Use the procedure again to write another synthesis of a reading and a lecture. Write 150–225 words. Try to stay within the time limits to complete the activity this time. Compare your synthesis with the example answer in Chapter 7 on page 534.

Reading

In 1798, Thomas Malthus published an *Essay on the Principle of Population*, arguably one of the most important works ever written on the consequences of population growth. According to Malthus, without intervention, population will tend to exceed the supply of food because, whereas population increases exponentially, food supplies do not. He also observed that disasters, disease, famine, and war could have a beneficial effect on population by increasing mortality rates, and thus slowing population growth. In addition, he pointed out that the sector of the population at the highest standard of living tended to exercise preventive measures to control fertility, but the sector at the lowest standard of living had the largest number of children, thereby relinquishing any possibility of improvement in living conditions, and perhaps even serving as a stimulus for the disease and other factors that check population growth.

Citing the fact that the wealthy and better-educated sectors of society already controlled population, Malthus pointed out the benefits of universal education to solve the population problem. He recommended raising the minimum wage and providing an incentive for the poor to choose between having more children, which they could support at a low standard of living, or having smaller families, which they could provide with a higher standard of living. Malthus believed that the ambition to improve their standard of living would direct those at the lowest income levels to limit the number of children they brought into the world once they understood the relationship between their life style and the size of their family.

Lecture

Now that you have read the explanation of population in the reading, listen to part of a lecture on a similar topic.

 Activity 38, CD 3, Track 4

Synthesis

Summarize the major points in the lecture that you have just heard, explaining how they cast doubt on the ideas in the reading passage.

➤ Practice using the procedure

For a plan to be useful, you need to practice using it. With a little practice, the procedure will feel very natural to you. With a lot of practice, it will become automatic.

PRACTICAL STRATEGY

Continue using the procedure to gain competence and confidence. Remember, if you still have to think about the steps while you are going through them, and if it takes you longer than the time limit to complete the synthesis, you have two more practice activities in this chapter. In addition, all of the model tests have opportunities for you to practice synthesis. It will get easier.

PRACTICE ACTIVITY 39

Practice using the procedure again. Write another synthesis of a reading and a lecture. Try to stay within the time limits to complete the activity. Compare your synthesis with the example answer in Chapter 7 on page 535.

Reading

Crop circles are not a modern phenomenon. As early as the late 17th century, circular designs were found in grain crops and recorded in academic texts. However, the large number of eyewitness reports from England to Australia since 1970 has encouraged a more thorough examination of this phenomenon. To date, reports of more than 10,000 crop circles from almost thirty countries have been collected. Within the past thirty years, the designs have increased in complexity, including rings, lines and geometrical figures.

One of the problems associated with a serious scientific study of crop circles is the large number of hoaxers who have been discovered or who have admitted to having been a part of elaborate deceptions. Besides the famous team of Doug and Dave, who were attributed with creating a large number of circles in Britain, groups in New Zealand and in North America have been identified. Apparently, they flattened the crops by tromping through the field with heavy boots or by fastening planks of wood onto their boots to create intricate patterns without making footprints. In several experiments, most notably the 1998 demonstration supported by the Discovery Channel, a group of trained circle makers was paid to create patterns. The Discovery Channel test in New Zealand was mounted to prove that it was possible for teams to create patterns in a relatively short period of time. In less than four hours, they were able to make 100 circles intersecting in a pattern thirty feet in diameter. Critics pointed out that the location lent itself to secrecy, unlike other more populated sites where circles had been discovered. They also criticized the demonstration because, although the team worked at night, the area was very well-lighted.

Lecture

Now that you have read the passage on crop circles, listen to part of a lecture on a similar topic.

 Activity 39, CD 3, Track 5

Synthesis

Summarize the major points in the lecture that you have just heard, explaining how they cast doubt on the ideas in the reading passage.

PRACTICE ACTIVITY 40

Practice using the procedure again. Write another synthesis of a reading and a lecture. Try to stay within the time limits to complete the activity. Compare your synthesis with the example answer in Chapter 7 on page 536.

Reading

In an age of globalization, collaboration and strategic alliances may be essential to success. Of course, there have traditionally been a number of ways to cooperate, including mergers in which two companies form a legal union, or a joint venture where several companies pool resources to create a separate entity. However, a strategic alliance is much less involved than either a merger or a joint venture. Quite simply, a strategic alliance is a mutual agreement between two or more companies in order to work more effectively toward their goals. This usually involves a plan to share resources for mutual benefit. For example, one company may have financial resources and another company may have technical expertise. By combining these resources, both companies would increase profit. In some cases, one company may possess a brand name that would provide a marketing advantage to another company whose product is relatively unknown but has huge sales potential. In other cases, international strategic alliances open new markets abroad to companies that have a product but lack expertise in advertising for that market segment.

As compared with other options for cooperation, the major advantage of strategic alliances is that they may be easily formed and easily dissolved, which makes them a perfect vehicle in a rapidly changing business environment. When a mutual goal has been attained, the alliance may no longer be beneficial, and, unlike mergers or joint ventures, which have more long-term implications, partners in an alliance can come together for short-term collaboration and then realign themselves with other strategic partners when the markets shift or new technologies require different strategies.

Lecture

Now that you have read the passage on business collaboration, listen to part of a lecture on a similar topic.

 Activity 40, CD 3, Track 6

Synthesis

Summarize the major points in the reading, explaining how the lecture supports these ideas.

ADVISOR'S OFFICE

Perspective means "the way you view experiences." Have you heard the story about the teacup? Two people sit down at a table. There is only enough tea for one cup so they each have half a cup of tea to drink. One person looks at the cup and says, "Oh my, the cup is half empty." The other person looks at the cup and says, "Oh, look, the cup is half full." Which kind of person are you?

At this point in your review, it is easy to become discouraged. However, if you choose the "half full" perspective, you will have more energy to continue your studies. Yes, there is certainly a lot to review. If you understand half of the strategies, you have a choice. You can say, "Oh my, I know only half of this." Instead, you can say, "Oh look, I already know half of this!" You choose.

My advice is *believe in yourself*. Don't look at the long distance you have yet to travel. Celebrate the long distance that you have already traveled. Then you will have the energy and the courage to keep going.

4

MODEL TEST 2: PROGRESS TEST

READING SECTION

The Reading section tests your ability to understand reading passages like those in college textbooks. The passages are about 700 words in length.

This is the long format for the Reading section. On the long format, you will respond to five passages. After each passage, you will answer 12–14 questions about it. Only three passages will be graded. The other passages are part of an experimental section for future tests. Because you will now know which passages will be graded, you must try to do your best on all of them.

Most questions are worth 1 point, but the last question in each passage is worth more than 1 point.

You will have 100 minutes to read all of the passages and answer the questions. You may take notes while you read, but notes are not graded. You may use your notes to answer the questions. Some passages may include a word or phrase that is underlined in blue. Click on the word or phrase to see a glossary definition or explanation.

Choose the best answer for multiple-choice questions. Follow the directions on the page or on the screen for computer-assisted questions. Click on **Next** to go to the next question. Click on **Back** to return to the previous question. You may return to previous questions for all of the passages in the same reading part, but after you go to the next part, you will not be able to return to passages in a previous part. Be sure that you have answered all of the questions for the passages in each part before you click on **Next** at the end of the passage to move to the next part.

You can click on **Review** to see a chart of the questions you have answered and the questions you have not answered in each part. From this screen, you can return to the question you want to answer in the part that is open.

A clock on the screen will show you how much time you have to complete the Reading section.

PART I

Reading 1 "Resources and Industrialism in Canada"

→ While the much-anticipated expansion of the western frontier was unfolding in accordance with the design of the National Policy, a new northern frontier was opening up to enhance the prospects of Canadian industrial development. Ⓐ Long the preserve of the fur trade, the Canadian Shield and the western Cordilleras became a treasury of minerals, timber and hydroelectric power in the late 19th and early 20th centuries. As early as 1883, CPR [Canadian Pacific Railway] construction crews blasting through the rugged terrain of northern Ontario discovered copper and nickel deposits in the vicinity of Sudbury. Ⓑ As refining processes, uses, and markets for the metal developed, Sudbury became the world's largest nickel producer. The building of the Temiskaming and Northern Ontario Railway led to the discovery of rich silver deposits around Cobalt north of Lake Nipissing in 1903 and touched off a mining boom that spread northward to Kirkland Lake and the Porcupine district. Ⓒ Although the economic importance of these mining operations was enduring, they did not capture the public imagination to the same extent as the Klondike gold rush of the late 1890s. Ⓓ

→ Fortune-seekers from all parts of the world flocked to the Klondike and Yukon River valleys to pan for gold starting in 1896. At the height of the gold rush in 1898, the previously unsettled subarctic frontier had a population of about 30,000, more than half of which was concentrated in the newly established town of Dawson. In the same year, the federal government created the Yukon Territory, administered by an appointed commissioner, in an effort to ward off the prospect of annexation to Alaska. Even if the economic significance of the Klondike strike was somewhat exaggerated and short-lived, the tales of sudden riches, heroic and tragic exploits, and the rowdiness and lawlessness of the mining frontier were immortalized through popular fiction and folklore, notably the poetic verses of Robert W. Service.

→ Perhaps less romantic than the mining booms, the exploitation of forest and water resources was just as vital to national development. The Douglas fir, spruce, and cedar stands of British Columbia along with the white pine forests of Ontario satisfied construction demands on the treeless prairies as well as in the growing cities and towns of central Canada and the United States. British Columbia's forests also supplied lumber to Asia. In addition, the softwood forest wealth of the Cordilleras and the Shield was a valuable source of pulpwood for the development of the pulp and paper industry, which made Canada one of the world's leading exporters of newsprint. Furthermore, the fast flowing rivers of the Shield and Cordilleras could readily be harnessed as sources of hydroelectric power, replacing coal in the booming factories of central Canada as well as in the evolving mining and pulp and paper industries. The age of electricity under public ownership and control was ushered in by the creation of the Ontario Hydro-Electric Power Commission (now Ontario Hydro) in 1906 to distribute and eventually to produce this vital source of energy.

→   Western settlement and the opening of the northern resource frontier stimulated industrial expansion, particularly in central Canada. As the National Policy had intended, a growing agricultural population in the West increased the demand for eastern manufactured goods, thereby giving rise to agricultural implements works, iron and steel foundries, machine shops, railway yards, textile mills, boot and shoe factories, and numerous smaller manufacturing enterprises that supplied consumer goods. By keeping out lower-priced foreign manufactured goods, the high tariff policies of the federal government received much credit for protecting existing industries and encouraging the creation of new enterprises. To climb the tariff wall, large American industrial firms opened branches in Canada, and the governments of Ontario and Quebec aggressively urged them on by offering bonuses, subsidies, and guarantees to locate new plants within their borders. Canadian industrial enterprises became increasingly attractive to foreign investors, especially from the United States and Great Britain. Much of the over $600 million of American capital that flowed into Canada from 1900 to 1913 was earmarked for mining and the pulp and paper industry, while British investors contributed near $1.8 billion, mostly in railway building, business development, and the construction of urban infrastructure. As a result, the gross value of Canadian manufactured products quadrupled from 1891 to 1916.

1. Why does the author mention the railroads in paragraph 1?

Ⓐ Because miners were traveling to camps in the West
Ⓑ Because mineral deposits were discovered when the railroads were built
Ⓒ Because the western frontier was being settled by families
Ⓓ Because traders used the railroads to transport their goods

Paragraph 1 is marked with an arrow [→].

2. In paragraph 1, the author identifies Sudbury as

Ⓐ an important stop on the new railroad line
Ⓑ a large market for the metals produced in Ontario
Ⓒ a major industrial center for the production of nickel
Ⓓ a mining town in the Klondike region

Paragraph 1 is marked with an arrow [→].

3. The word enhance in the passage is closest in meaning to

Ⓐ disrupt
Ⓑ restore
Ⓒ identify
Ⓓ improve

4. According to paragraph 2, why was the Yukon Territory created?

   Ⓐ To encourage people to settle the region
   Ⓑ To prevent Alaska from acquiring it
   Ⓒ To establish law and order in the area
   Ⓓ To legalize the mining claims

   Paragraph 2 is marked with an arrow [➜].

5. The word <u>previously</u> in the passage is closest in meaning to

   Ⓐ frequently
   Ⓑ suddenly
   Ⓒ routinely
   Ⓓ formerly

6. How did the poetry by Robert Service contribute to the development of Canada?

   Ⓐ It made the Klondike gold rush famous.
   Ⓑ It encouraged families to settle in the Klondike.
   Ⓒ It captured the beauty of the western Klondike.
   Ⓓ It prevented the Klondike's annexation to Alaska.

7. According to paragraph 3, the forest industry supported the development of Canada in all of the following ways EXCEPT

   Ⓐ by supplying wood for the construction of homes and buildings
   Ⓑ by clearing the land for expanded agricultural uses
   Ⓒ by producing the power for the hydroelectric plants
   Ⓓ by exporting wood and newsprint to foreign markets

   Paragraph 3 is marked with an arrow [➜].

8. The word <u>Furthermore</u> in the passage is closest in meaning to

   Ⓐ Although
   Ⓑ Because
   Ⓒ Therefore
   Ⓓ Moreover

9. Which of the sentences below best expresses the information in the highlighted statement in the passage? The other choices change the meaning or leave out important information.

    (A) New businesses and industries were created by the federal government to keep the prices of manufactured goods low.
    (B) The lower price of manufacturing attracted many foreign businesses and new industries to the area.
    (C) Federal taxes on cheaper imported goods were responsible for protecting domestic industries and supporting new businesses.
    (D) The federal tax laws made it difficult for manufacturers to sell their goods to foreign markets.

10. The word them in the passage refers to

    (A) governments
    (B) plants
    (C) firms
    (D) policies

11. According to paragraph 4, British and American businesses opened affiliates in Canada because

    (A) the Canadian government offered incentives
    (B) the raw materials were available in Canada
    (C) the consumers in Canada were eager to buy their goods
    (D) the infrastructure was attractive to investors

    Paragraph 4 is marked with an arrow [→].

12. Look at the four squares [■] that show where the following sentence could be inserted in the passage.

    Railway construction through the Kootenay region of southeastern British Columbia also led to significant discoveries of gold, silver, copper, lead, and zinc.

    Where could the sentence best be added?

    Click on a square [■] to insert the sentence in the passage.

13. **Directions:** An introduction for a short summary of the passage appears below. Complete the summary by selecting the THREE answer choices that mention the most important points in the passage. Some sentences do not belong in the summary because they express ideas that are not included in the passage or are minor points from the passage. *This question is worth 2 points.*

The northern frontier provided many natural resources that contributed to industrial expansion of Canada.

-
-
-

Answer Choices

A The Yukon Territory was created in 1898 during the gold rush in the Klondike and Yukon River valleys.

B The frontier was documented in the popular press, which published tales of heroes and gold strikes.

C Significant discoveries of mineral deposits encouraged prospectors and settlers to move into the territories.

D Wheat and other agricultural crops were planted after the forests were cleared, creating the central plains.

E Powered by hydroelectricity, lumber and paper mills exploited the forests for both domestic and foreign markets.

F Incentives encouraged American and British investors to help expand manufacturing plants in Canada.

PART II

Reading 2 "Looking at Theatre History"

→ One of the primary ways of approaching the Greek theatre is through archeology, the systematic study of material remains such as architecture, inscriptions, sculpture, vase painting, and other forms of decorative art. A Serious on-site excavations began in Greece around 1870, but W. Dörpfeld did not begin the first extensive study of the Theatre of Dionysus until 1886. B Since that time, more than 167 other Greek theatres have been identified and many of them have been excavated. C Nevertheless, they still do not permit us to describe the precise appearance of the *skene* (illustrations printed in books are conjectural reconstructions), since many pieces are irrevocably lost because the buildings in later periods became sources of stone for other projects and what remains is usually broken and scattered. D That most of the buildings were remodeled many times has created great problems for those seeking to date both the parts and the successive versions. Despite these drawbacks, archeology provides the most concrete evidence we have about the theatre structures of ancient Greece. But, if they have told us much, archeologists have not completed their work, and many sites have scarcely been touched.

→ Perhaps the most controversial use of archeological evidence in theatre history is vase paintings, thousands of which have survived from ancient Greece. (Most of those used by theatre scholars are reproduced in Margarete Bieber's *The History of the Greek and Roman Theatre.*) Depicting scenes from mythology and daily life, the vases are the most graphic pictorial evidence we have. But they are also easy to misinterpret. Some scholars have considered any vase that depicts a subject treated in a surviving drama or any scene showing masks, flute players, or ceremonials to be valid evidence of theatrical practice. This is a highly questionable assumption, since the Greeks made widespread use of masks, dances, and music outside the theatre and since the myths on which dramatists drew were known to everyone, including vase painters, who might well depict the same subjects as dramatists without being indebted to them. Those vases showing scenes unquestionably theatrical are few in number.

→ Written evidence about ancient Greek theatre is often treated as less reliable than archeological evidence because most written accounts are separated so far in time from the events they describe and because they provide no information about their own sources. Of the written evidence, the surviving plays are usually treated as the most reliable. But the oldest surviving manuscripts of Greek plays date from around the tenth century, C.E., some 1500 years after they were first performed. Since printing did not exist during this time span, copies of plays had to be made by hand, and therefore the possibility of textual errors creeping in was magnified. Nevertheless, the scripts offer us our readiest access to the cultural and theatrical conditions out of which they came. But these scripts, like other kinds of evidence, are subject to varying interpretations. Certainly performances embodied a male perspective, for example, since the plays were written, selected, staged, and acted by men. Yet the existing plays feature numerous choruses of women and many feature strong female characters. Because these characters often seem victims of their own powerlessness and appear to be governed, especially in the comedies, by sexual desire, some critics have seen these plays as rationalizations by the male-dominated culture for keeping women segregated and cloistered. Other critics, however, have seen in these same plays an attempt by male authors to force their male audiences to examine and call into question this segregation and cloistering of Athenian women.

→ By far the majority of written references to Greek theatre date from several hundred years after the events they report. The writers seldom mention their sources of evidence, and thus we do not know what credence to give them. In the absence of material nearer in time to the events, however, historians have used the accounts and have been grateful to have them. Overall, historical treatment of the Greek theatre is something like assembling a jigsaw puzzle from which many pieces are missing: historians arrange what they have and imagine (with the aid of the remaining evidence and logic) what has been lost. As a result, though the broad outlines of Greek theatre history are reasonably clear, many of the details remain open to doubt.

Glossary

skene: a stage building where actors store their masks and change their costumes

14. According to paragraph 1, why is it impossible to identify the time period for theatres in Greece?

Ⓐ There are too few sites that have been excavated and very little data collected about them.

Ⓑ The archeologists from earlier periods were not careful, and many artifacts were broken.

Ⓒ It is confusing because stones from early sites were used to build later structures.

Ⓓ Because it is very difficult to date the concrete that was used in construction during early periods.

Paragraph 1 is marked with an arrow [→].

15. What can be inferred from paragraph 1 about the *skene* in theatre history?

Ⓐ Drawings in books are the only accurate visual records.

Ⓑ Not enough evidence is available to make a precise model.

Ⓒ Archaeologists have excavated a large number of them.

Ⓓ It was not identified or studied until the early 1800s.

Paragraph 1 is marked with an arrow [→].

16. The word primary in the passage is closest in meaning to

Ⓐ reliable

Ⓑ important

Ⓒ unusual

Ⓓ accepted

17. The word precise in the passage is closest in meaning to

Ⓐ attractive

Ⓑ simple

Ⓒ difficult

Ⓓ exact

18. In paragraph 2, the author explains that all vases with paintings of masks or musicians may not be evidence of theatrical subjects by

  Ⓐ arguing that the subjects could have been used by artists without reference to a drama
  Ⓑ identifying some of the vases as reproductions that were painted years after the originals
  Ⓒ casting doubt on the qualifications of the scholars who produced the vases as evidence
  Ⓓ pointing out that there are very few vases that have survived from the time of early dramas

Paragraph 2 is marked with an arrow [➜].

19. The word <u>controversial</u> in the passage is closest in meaning to

  Ⓐ accepted
  Ⓑ debated
  Ⓒ limited
  Ⓓ complicated

20. In paragraph 3, the author states that female characters in Greek theatre

  Ⓐ had no featured parts in plays
  Ⓑ were mostly ignored by critics
  Ⓒ did not participate in the chorus
  Ⓓ frequently played the part of victims

Paragraph 3 is marked with an arrow [➜].

21. According to paragraph 3, scripts of plays may not be accurate because

  Ⓐ the sources cited are not well known
  Ⓑ copies by hand may contain many errors
  Ⓒ they are written in very old language
  Ⓓ the printing is difficult to read

Paragraph 3 is marked with an arrow [➜].

22. The word <u>them</u> in the passage refers to

  Ⓐ events
  Ⓑ sources
  Ⓒ writers
  Ⓓ references

23. Why does the author mention a jigsaw puzzle in paragraph 4?

  Ⓐ To demonstrate the difficulty in drawing conclusions from partial evidence
  Ⓑ To compare the written references for plays to the paintings on vases
  Ⓒ To justify using accounts and records that historians have located
  Ⓓ To introduce the topic for the next reading passage in the textbook

Paragraph 4 is marked with an arrow [➜].

24. Which of the following statements most accurately reflects the author's opinion about vase paintings?

   Ⓐ Evidence from written documents is older than evidence from vase paintings.
   Ⓑ The sources for vase paintings are clear because of the images on them.
   Ⓒ The details in vase paintings are not obvious because of their age.
   Ⓓ There is disagreement among scholars regarding vase paintings.

25. Look at the four squares [■] that show where the following sentence could be inserted in the passage.

   These excavations have revealed much that was previously unknown, especially about the dimensions and layout of theatres.

   Where could the sentence best be added?

   Click on a square [■] to insert the sentence in the passage.

26. **Directions:** An introduction for a short summary of the passage appears below. Complete the summary by selecting the THREE answer choices that mention the most important points in the passage. Some sentences do not belong in the summary because they express ideas that are not included in the passage or are minor points from the passage. *This question is worth 2 points.*

   Greek theatre has been studied by a variety of methods.

   •

   •

   •

Answer Choices

Ⓐ Because the Greeks enjoyed dancing and music for entertainment outside of the theatre, many scenes on vases are ambiguous.

Ⓑ Historical accounts assembled many years after the actual theatrical works were presented give us a broad perspective of the earlier theatre.

Ⓒ Although considered less reliable, written records, including scripts, provide insights into the cultural aspects of theatre.

Ⓓ Archaeological excavations have uncovered buildings and artifacts, many of which were vases with theatrical scenes painted on them.

Ⓔ For the most part, men wrote the plays for Greek theatre, but choruses and even strong roles were played by women.

Ⓕ Computer simulations can recreate the image of a building that is crumbling as long as the dimensions and layout are known.

Reading 3 "Geothermal Energy"

→ Geothermal energy is natural heat from the interior of the Earth that is converted to heat buildings and generate electricity. The idea of harnessing Earth's internal heat is not new. As early as 1904, geothermal power was used in Italy. Today, Earth's natural internal heat is being used to generate electricity in 21 countries, including Russia, Japan, New Zealand, Iceland, Mexico, Ethiopia, Guatemala, El Salvador, the Philippines, and the United States. Total worldwide production is approaching 9,000 MW (equivalent to nine large modern coal-burning or nuclear power plants)—double the amount in 1980. Some 40 million people today receive their electricity from geothermal energy at a cost competitive with that of other energy sources. In El Salvador, geothermal energy is supplying 30% of the total electric energy used. However, at the global level, geothermal energy supplies less than 0.15% of the total energy supply.

→ Geothermal energy may be considered a nonrenewable energy source when rates of extraction are greater than rates of natural replenishment. However, geothermal energy has its origin in the natural heat production within Earth, and only a small fraction of the vast total resource base is being utilized today. Although most geothermal energy production involves the tapping of high heat sources, people are also using the low-temperature geothermal energy of groundwater in some applications.

Geothermal Systems

→ Ⓐ The average heat flow from the interior of the Earth is very low, about 0.06 W/m^2. Ⓑ This amount is trivial compared with the 177 W/m^2 from solar heat at the surface in the United States. However, in some areas, heat flow is sufficiently high to be useful for producing energy. For the most part, areas of high heat flow are associated with plate tectonic boundaries. Oceanic ridge systems (divergent plate boundaries) and areas where mountains are being uplifted and volcanic island arcs are forming (convergent plate boundaries) are areas where this natural heat flow is anomalously high. Ⓒ

On the basis of geological criteria, several types of hot geothermal systems (with temperatures greater than about 80°C, or 176°F) have been defined, and the resource base is larger than that of fossil fuels and nuclear energy combined. A common system for energy development is hydrothermal convection, characterized by the circulation of steam and/or hot water that transfers heat from depths to the surface. Ⓓ

Geothermal Energy and the Environment

→ The environmental impact of geothermal energy may not be as extensive as that of other sources of energy, but it can be considerable. When geothermal energy is developed at a particular site, environmental problems include on-site noise, emissions of gas, and disturbance of the land at drilling sites, disposal sites, roads and pipelines, and power plants. Development of geothermal energy does not require large-scale transportation of raw materials or refining of chemicals, as development of fossil fuels does. Furthermore, geothermal energy does not produce the atmospheric pollutants associated with burning fossil fuels or the radioactive waste associated with nuclear energy. However, geothermal development often does produce considerable thermal pollution from hot waste-waters, which may be saline or highly corrosive, producing disposal and treatment problems.

→ Geothermal power is not very popular in some locations among some people. For instance, geothermal energy has been produced for years on the island of Hawaii, where active volcanic processes provide abundant near-surface heat. There is controversy, however, over further exploration and development. Native Hawaiians and others have argued that the exploration and development of geothermal energy degrade the tropical forest as developers construct roads, build facilities, and drill wells. In addition, religious and cultural issues in Hawaii relate to the use of geothermal energy. For example, some people are offended by using the "breath and water of Pele" (the volcano goddess) to make electricity. This issue points out the importance of being sensitive to the values and cultures of people where development is planned.

Future of Geothermal Energy

At present, geothermal energy supplies only a small fraction of the electrical energy produced in the United States. However, if developed, known geothermal resources in the United States could produce about 20,000 MW which is about 10% of the electricity needed for the western states. Geohydrothermal resources not yet discovered could conservatively provide four times that amount (approximately 10% of total U.S. electric capacity), about equivalent to the electricity produced from water power today.

27. In paragraph 1, the author introduces the concept of geothermal energy by

Ⓐ explaining the history of this energy source worldwide
Ⓑ arguing that this energy source has been tried unsuccessfully
Ⓒ comparing the production with that of other energy sources
Ⓓ describing the alternatives for generating electric power

Paragraph 1 is marked with an arrow [→].

28. What is true about geothermal energy production worldwide?

Ⓐ Because it is a new idea, very few countries are developing geothermal energy sources.
Ⓑ Only countries in the Southern Hemisphere are using geothermal energy on a large scale.
Ⓒ Until the cost of geothermal energy becomes competitive, it will not be used globally.
Ⓓ Geothermal energy is already being used in a number of nations, but it is not yet a major source of power.

23

• 29. The word <u>approaching</u> in the passage is closest in meaning to

    Ⓐ hardly
    Ⓑ mostly
✓• Ⓒ nearly
    Ⓓ briefly

24

• 30. The word <u>that</u> in the passage refers to

    Ⓐ electricity
✓• Ⓑ cost
    Ⓒ energy
    Ⓓ people

25

15 • 31. In paragraph 2, the author states that geothermal energy is considered a nonrenewable resource because

    Ⓐ the production of geothermal energy is a natural process
    Ⓑ geothermal energy comes from the Earth
    Ⓒ we are not using very much geothermal energy now
    Ⓓ we could use more geothermal energy than is naturally replaced

Paragraph 2 is marked with an arrow [➜].

26

16 • 32. Which of the sentences below best expresses the information in the highlighted statement in the passage? The other choices change the meaning or leave out important information.

    Ⓐ High heat is the source of most of the geothermal energy but low heat groundwater is also used sometimes.
    Ⓑ Even though low temperatures are possible, high heat is the best resource for energy production for groundwater.
    Ⓒ Both high heat and low heat sources are used for the production of geothermal energy from groundwater.
    Ⓓ Most high heat sources for geothermal energy are tapped from applications that involve low heat in groundwater.

27

17 • 33. According to paragraph 3, the heat flow necessary for the production of geothermal energy

    Ⓐ is like solar heat on the Earth's surface
    Ⓑ happens near tectonic plate boundaries
    Ⓒ must always be artificially increased
    Ⓓ may be impractical because of its location

Paragraph 3 is marked with an arrow [➜].

34. The word <u>considerable</u> in the passage is closest in meaning to

    Ⓐ large
    Ⓑ dangerous
    Ⓒ steady
    Ⓓ unexpected

35. In paragraph 5, the author mentions the atmospheric pollution and waste products for fossil fuel and nuclear power

    Ⓐ to introduce the discussion of pollution caused by geothermal energy development and production
    Ⓑ to contrast pollution caused by fossil fuels and nuclear power with pollution caused by geothermal energy
    Ⓒ to argue that geothermal production does not cause pollution like other sources of energy do
    Ⓓ to discourage the use of raw materials and chemicals in the production of energy because of pollution

    Paragraph 5 is marked with an arrow [➜].

36. According to paragraph 6, the production of geothermal energy in Hawaii is controversial for all of the following reasons EXCEPT

    Ⓐ The volcanoes in Hawaii could be disrupted by the rapid release of geothermal energy.
    Ⓑ The rainforest might be damaged during the construction of the geothermal energy plant.
    Ⓒ The native people are concerned that geothermal energy is disrespectful to their cultural traditions.
    Ⓓ Some Hawaiians oppose using geothermal energy because of their religious beliefs.

    Paragraph 6 is marked with an arrow [➜].

37. What is the author's opinion of geothermal energy?

    Ⓐ Geothermal energy has some disadvantages, but it is probably going to be used in the future.
    Ⓑ Geothermal energy is a source that should be explored further before large-scale production begins.
    Ⓒ Geothermal energy offers an opportunity to supply a significant amount of power in the future.
    Ⓓ Geothermal energy should replace water power in the production of electricity for the United States.

38. Look at the four squares [■] that show where the following sentence could be inserted in the passage.

    One such region is located in the western United States, where recent tectonic and volcanic activity has occurred.

    Where could the sentence best be added?

    Click on a square [■] to insert the sentence in the passage.

39. **Directions**: Complete the table by matching the phrases on the left with the headings on the right. Select the appropriate answer choices and drag them to Fossil Fuels or Geothermal Energy. TWO of the answer choices will NOT be used. ***This question is worth 4 points.***

    To delete an answer choice, click on it. To see the passage, click on **View Text**.

Answer Choices

Ⓐ Radioactive waste materials must be buried.

Ⓑ Only a small amount of electricity is currently generated.

Ⓒ Transportation of raw materials is usually very costly.

Ⓓ Cultural beliefs question the use of this natural resource.

Ⓔ Gas emissions and disposal sites are problematic.

Ⓕ Water treatment problems occur as a result.

Ⓖ It is a renewable resource for power.

Ⓗ Refinement of chemicals is necessary.

Ⓘ Air pollution is a by-product of the process.

Fossil Fuels
-
-
-

Geothermal Energy
-
-
-
-

PART III

Reading 4 *"Migration from Asia"*

The Asian migration hypothesis is today supported by most of the scientific evidence. The first "hard" data linking American Indians with Asians appeared in the 1980s with the finding that Indians and northeast Asians share a common and distinctive pattern in the arrangement of the teeth. But perhaps the most compelling support for the hypothesis comes from genetic research. Studies comparing the DNA variation of populations around the world consistently demonstrate the close genetic relationship of the two populations, and recently geneticists studying a virus sequestered in the kidneys of all humans found that the strain of virus carried by Navajos and Japanese is nearly identical, while that carried by Europeans and Africans is quite different.

➔ The migration could have begun over a land bridge connecting the continents. During the last Ice Age 70,000 to 10,000 years ago, huge glaciers locked up massive volumes of water and sea levels were as much as 300 feet lower than today. Asia and North America were joined by a huge subcontinent of ice-free, treeless grassland, 750 miles wide. Geologists have named this area Beringia, from the Bering Straits. Summers there were warm, winters were cold, dry and almost snow-free. This was a perfect environment for large mammals—mammoth and mastodon, bison, horse, reindeer, camel, and saiga (a goatlike antelope). Small bands of Stone Age hunter-gatherers were attracted by these animal populations, which provided them not only with food but with hides for clothing and shelter, dung for fuel, and bones for tools and weapons. Accompanied by a husky-like species of dog, hunting bands gradually moved as far east as the Yukon River basin of northern Canada, where field excavations have uncovered the fossilized jawbones of several dogs and bone tools estimated to be about 27,000 years old.

➔ Other evidence suggests that the migration from Asia began about 30,000 years ago—around the same time that Japan and Scandinavia were being settled. This evidence is based on blood type. The vast majority of modern Native Americans have type O blood and a few have type A, but almost none have type B. Because modern Asian populations include all three blood types, however, the migrations must have begun before the evolution of type B, which geneticists believe occurred about 30,000 years ago.

By 25,000 years ago human communities were established in western Beringia, which is present-day Alaska. Ⓐ But access to the south was blocked by a huge glacial sheet covering much of what is today Canada. How did the hunters get over those 2,000 miles of deep ice? The argument is that the climate began to warm with the passing of the Ice Age, and about 13,000 B.C.E. glacial melting created an ice-free corridor along the eastern front range of the Rocky Mountains. Ⓑ Soon hunters of big game had reached the Great Plains.

→   In the past several years, however, new archaeological finds along the Pacific coast of North and South America have thrown this theory into question. Ⓒ The most spectacular find, at Monte Verde in southern Chile, produced striking evidence of tool making, house building, rock painting, and human footprints conservatively dated at 12,500 years ago, long before the highway had been cleared of ice. Ⓓ Many archaeologists now believe that migrants moved south in boats along a coastal route rather than overland. These people were probably gatherers and fishers rather than hunters of big game.

→   There were two later migrations into North America. About 5000 B.C.E. the Athapascan or Na-Dene people began to settle the forests in the northwestern area of the continent. Eventually Athapascan speakers, the ancestors of the Navajos and Apaches, migrated across the Great Plains to the Southwest. The final migration began about 3000 B.C.E. after Beringia had been submerged, when a maritime hunting people crossed the Bering Straits in small boats. The Inuits (also known as the Eskimos) colonized the polar coasts of the Arctic, the Yupiks the coast of southwestern Alaska, and the Aleuts the Aleutian Islands.

While scientists debate the timing and mapping of these migrations, many Indian people hold to oral traditions that include a long journey from a distant place of origin to a new homeland.

40. The word <u>distinctive</u> in the passage is closest in meaning to

    Ⓐ new
    Ⓑ simple
    Ⓒ different
    Ⓓ particular

41. According to paragraph 2, why did Stone Age tribes begin to migrate into Beringia?

    Ⓐ To intermarry with tribes living there
    Ⓑ To trade with tribes that made tools
    Ⓒ To hunt for animals in the area
    Ⓓ To capture domesticated dogs

Paragraph 2 is marked with an arrow [→].

42. The phrase <u>Accompanied by</u> in the passage is closest in meaning to

    Ⓐ Found with
    Ⓑ Joined by
    Ⓒ Threatened by
    Ⓓ Detoured with

43. The word <u>which</u> in the passage refers to

   Ⓐ migrations
   Ⓑ evolution
   Ⓒ geneticists
   Ⓓ populations

44. Why does the author mention blood types in paragraph 3?

   Ⓐ Blood types offered proof that the migration had come from Scandinavia.
   Ⓑ The presence of type B in Native Americans was evidence of the migration.
   Ⓒ The blood typing was similar to data from both Japan and Scandinavia.
   Ⓓ Comparisons of blood types in Asia and North America established the date of migration.

   Paragraph 3 is marked with an arrow [➔].

45. How did groups migrate into the Great Plains?

   Ⓐ By walking on a corridor covered with ice
   Ⓑ By using the path that big game had made
   Ⓒ By detouring around a huge ice sheet
   Ⓓ By following a mountain trail

46. Why does the author mention the settlement at Monte Verde, Chile, in paragraph 5?

   Ⓐ The remains of boats suggest that people may have lived there.
   Ⓑ Artifacts suggest that humans reached this area before the ice melted on land.
   Ⓒ Bones and footprints from large animals confirm that the people were hunters.
   Ⓓ The houses and tools excavated prove that the early humans were intelligent.

   Paragraph 5 is marked with an arrow [➔].

47. The word <u>Eventually</u> in the passage is closest in meaning to

   Ⓐ In the end
   Ⓑ Nevertheless
   Ⓒ Without doubt
   Ⓓ In this way

48. Which of the sentences below best expresses the information in the highlighted statement in the passage? The other choices change the meaning or leave out important information.

    Ⓐ Beringia was under water when the last people crossed the straits in boats about 3000 B.C.E.

    Ⓑ Beringia sank after the last people had crossed the straits in their boats about 3000 B.C.E.

    Ⓒ About 3000 B.C.E., the final migration of people in small boats across Beringia had ended.

    Ⓓ About 3000 B.C.E., Beringia was flooded, preventing the last people from migrating in small boats.

49. According to paragraph 6, all of the following are true about the later migrations EXCEPT

    Ⓐ The Athapascans traveled into the Southwest United States.

    Ⓑ The Eskimos established homes in the Arctic polar region.

    Ⓒ The Aleuts migrated in small boats to settle coastal islands.

    Ⓓ The Yupiks established settlements on the Great Plains.

Paragraph 6 is marked with an arrow [→].

50. Which of the following statements most accurately reflects the author's opinion about the settlement of the North American continent?

    Ⓐ The oral traditions do not support the migration theory.

    Ⓑ The anthropological evidence for migration should be reexamined.

    Ⓒ Migration theories are probably not valid explanations for the physical evidence.

    Ⓓ Genetic markers are the best evidence of a migration from Asia.

51. Look at the four squares [■] that show where the following sentence could be inserted in the passage.

Newly excavated early human sites in Washington State, California, and Peru have been radiocarbon dated to be 11,000 to 12,000 years old.

Where could the sentence best be added?

Click on a square [■] to insert the sentence in the passage.

52. **Directions:** An introduction for a short summary of the passage appears below. Complete the summary by selecting the THREE answer choices that mention the most important points in the passage. Some sentences do not belong in the summary because they express ideas that are not included in the passage or are minor points from the passage. *This question is worth 2 points.*

There is considerable evidence supporting a theory of multiple migrations from Asia to the Americas.

-
-
-

Answer Choices

Ⓐ Ancient stories of migrations from a far-away place are common in the cultures of many Native American nations.

Ⓑ The people who inhabited Monte Verde in southern Chile were a highly evolved culture as evidenced by their tools and homes.

Ⓒ Genetic similarities between Native American peoples and Asians include the arrangement of teeth, viruses, and blood types.

Ⓓ Hunters followed the herds of big game from Beringia south along the Rocky Mountains into what is now called the Great Plains.

Ⓔ Excavations at archaeological sites provide artifacts that can be used to date the various migrations that occurred by land and sea.

Ⓕ The climate began to get warmer and warmer, melting the glacial ice about 13,000 B.C.E.

Reading 5 "Physical and Chemical Properties and Changes"

→ Sugar, water, and aluminum are different substances. Each substance has specific properties that do not depend on the *quantity* of the substance. Properties that can be used to identify or characterize a substance—and distinguish that substance from other substances—are called **characteristic properties**. They are subdivided into two categories: physical properties and chemical properties.

The characteristic physical properties of a substance are those that identify the substance without causing a change in the composition of the substance. They do not depend on the quantity of substance. Ⓐ Color, odor, density, melting point, boiling point, hardness, metallic luster or shininess, ductility, malleability, and viscosity are all characteristic physical properties. For example, aluminum is a metal that is both ductile and malleable. B Another example of a physical property is water. Whether a small pan of water is raised to its boiling point or a very large kettle of water is raised to its boiling point, the temperature at which the water boils is the same value, 100 degrees C or 212 degrees F. C Similarly, the freezing point of water is 0 degrees C or 32 degrees F. These values are independent of quantity. D

Characteristic properties that relate to changes in the composition of a substance or to how it reacts with other substances are called chemical properties. The following questions pertain to the chemical properties of a substance.

1. Does it burn in air?
2. Does it decompose (break up into smaller substances) when heated?
3. What happens when it is placed in an acid?
4. What other chemicals will it react with, and what substances are obtained from the reaction?

Characteristic physical and chemical properties—also called **intensive properties**—are used to identify a substance. In addition to the characteristic physical properties already mentioned, some intensive physical properties include the tendency to dissolve in water, electrical conductivity, and density, which is the ratio of mass to volume.

Additional intensive chemical properties include the tendency of a substance to react with another substance, to tarnish, to corrode, to explode, or to act as a poison or carcinogen (cancer-causing agent).

Extensive properties of substances are those that depend on the quantity of the sample, including measurements of mass, volume, and length. Whereas intensive properties help identify or characterize a particular kind of matter, extensive properties relate to the amount present.

If a lump of candle wax is cut or broken into smaller pieces, or if it is melted (a change of state), the sample remaining is still candle wax. When cooled, the molten wax returns to a solid. In these examples, only a physical change has taken place; that is, the composition of the substance was not affected.

→ When a candle is burned, there are both physical and chemical changes. After the candle is lighted, the solid wax near the burning wick melts. This is a physical change; the composition of the wax does not change as it goes from solid to liquid. Some of the wax is drawn into the burning wick where a chemical change occurs. Here, wax in the candle flame reacts chemically with oxygen in the air to form carbon dioxide gas and water vapor. In any chemical change, one or more substances are used up while one or more new substances are formed. The new substances produced have their own unique physical and chemical properties.

The apparent disappearance of something, like the candle wax, however, is not necessarily a sign that we are observing a chemical change. For example, when water evaporates from a glass and disappears, it has changed from a liquid to a gas (called water vapor), but in both forms it is water. This is a phase change (liquid to gas), which is a physical change. When attempting to determine whether a change is physical or chemical, one should ask the critical question: Has the fundamental composition of the substance changed? In a chemical change (a reaction), it has, but in a physical change, it has not.

Glossary
ductility: can be drawn into wire
malleability: can be shaped
viscosity: thick, resistant to flow

53. According to paragraph 1, what do physical properties and chemical properties have in common?

   Ⓐ They are both used to create most of the substances.
   Ⓑ They include basic substances like sugar and water.
   Ⓒ They are classified as characteristic properties of substances.
   Ⓓ They change in proportion to the amount of the substance.

Paragraph 1 is marked with an arrow [➜].

54. The word <u>pertain</u> in the passage is closest in meaning to

   Ⓐ compare
   Ⓑ relate
   Ⓒ explain
   Ⓓ change

55. The word <u>which</u> in the passage refers to

   Ⓐ properties
   Ⓑ tendency
   Ⓒ density
   Ⓓ ratio

56. According to the passage, a *carcinogen*

   Ⓐ explodes under pressure
   Ⓑ conducts electricity
   Ⓒ causes cancer
   Ⓓ tarnishes in air

57. Which of the sentences below best expresses the information in the highlighted statement in the passage? The other choices change the meaning or leave out important information.

   Ⓐ Properties that are classified as intensive identify the type of substance and the extent of it present in the surrounding matter.
   Ⓑ The quantity of a substance influences its extensive properties, but the characteristics of the substance define the intensive properties.
   Ⓒ Where the intensive and extensive properties are found in substances is important in identifying their characteristics.
   Ⓓ Both intensive and extensive properties tend to have quantitative rather than qualitative characteristics present.

58. In paragraph 8, the author contrasts the concepts of physical and chemical changes by

   Ⓐ listing several types for each concept
   Ⓑ providing clear definitions for them
   Ⓒ identifying the common characteristics
   Ⓓ using a wax candle as an example

   Paragraph 8 is marked with an arrow [➔].

59. The word unique in the passage is closest in meaning to

   Ⓐ distinctive
   Ⓑ idealized
   Ⓒ primary
   Ⓓ significant

60. What can be inferred about phase changes?

   Ⓐ They are always chemical changes.
   Ⓑ They are sometimes physical changes.
   Ⓒ They are dependent on extensive properties.
   Ⓓ They usually produce new substances.

61. The word critical in the passage is closest in meaning to

   Ⓐ last
   Ⓑ important
   Ⓒ difficult
   Ⓓ simple

62. According to the passage, the classification of characteristic properties as "physical" or "chemical" is determined by

    Ⓐ whether there has been a change in the structure of the substance
    Ⓑ what happens when the quantity of the substance is increased
    Ⓒ their classification as either extensive or intensive samples
    Ⓓ the disappearance of a substance from one form to another

63. All of the following are mentioned as characteristic physical properties EXCEPT

    Ⓐ dissolving in water
    Ⓑ carrying an electrical charge
    Ⓒ resisting continuous flow
    Ⓓ decomposing when heated

64. Look at the four squares [■] that show where the following sentence could be inserted in the passage.

    It can be made into wire or thin, flexible sheets.

    Where could the sentence best be added?

    Click on a square [■] to insert the sentence in the passage.

65. **Directions:** Complete the table by matching the phrases on the left with the headings on the right. Select the appropriate answer choices and drag them to the characteristic properties to which they refer. TWO of the answer choices will NOT be used. *This question is worth 4 points.*

    To delete an answer choice, click on it. To see the passage, click on **View Text**.

Properties   **Physical Properties**

Ⓐ Color of the substance   •

Ⓑ Reaction in an acid   •

Ⓒ Decomposition in heat   •

Ⓓ Temperature at which it boils   **Chemical Properties**

Ⓔ The tendency to shine   •

Ⓕ The inclination to tarnish   •

Ⓖ The shape of the substance   •

Ⓗ Toxic if swallowed or inhaled   •

Ⓘ The relative amount in nature

LISTENING SECTION

 Model Test 2, Listening Section, CD 3, Track 7

The Listening section tests your ability to understand spoken English that is typical of interactions and academic speech on college campuses. During the test, you will respond to conversations and lectures.

This is the short format for the Listening section. On the short format, you will respond to two conversations and four lectures. After each listening passage, you will answer 5–6 questions about it.

You will hear each conversation or lecture one time. You may take notes while you listen, but notes are not graded. You may use your notes to answer the questions.

Choose the best answer for multiple-choice questions. Follow the directions on the page or on the screen for computer-assisted questions. Click on **Next** and **OK** to go to the next question. You cannot return to previous questions. You have 20–30 minutes to answer all of the questions. A clock on the screen will show you how much time you have to complete your answers for the section. The clock does not count the time you are listening to the conversations and lectures.

Rd.Q
30√ ← 50Q

PART I

Listening 1 "Professor's Office"

1. Why does the man go to see his professor?

   Ⓐ To prepare for the next midterm
   Ⓑ To clarify a question from the midterm
   Ⓒ To find out his grade on the midterm
   Ⓓ To complain about his grade on the midterm

2. Why does the man say this:

   Ⓐ He is giving something to the professor.
   Ⓑ He is trying to justify his position.
   Ⓒ He is apologizing because he does not understand.
   Ⓓ He is signaling that he will explain his problem.

3. What did the man do wrong?

   Ⓐ He did not finish the test within the time limit.
   Ⓑ He did not study enough before the test.
   Ⓒ He did not answer one question completely.
   Ⓓ He did not understand a major concept.

4. According to the student, what is *divergent evolution*?

    Ⓐ A population that evolves differently does not have a common ancestor.
    Ⓑ A similar environment can affect the evolution of different species.
    Ⓒ A similar group that is separated may develop different characteristics.
    Ⓓ The climate of an area will allow scientists to predict the life forms.

5. What will Jerry probably do on the next test?

    Ⓐ He will look for questions with several parts.
    Ⓑ He will read the entire test before he begins.
    Ⓒ He will ask for more time to finish.
    Ⓓ He will write an outline for each essay.

Listening 2 "Art History Class"

6. What is the discussion mainly about?

   Ⓐ Catherine de Medici's entertainments
   Ⓑ The figures for court dancing
   Ⓒ The development of the ballet
   Ⓓ The relationship between dance and meals

7. Why does the professor say this:

   Ⓐ To end his explanation and begin the lecture
   Ⓑ To apologize to the students about their tests
   Ⓒ To comment about the students' grades
   Ⓓ To regain the attention of the class

8. According to the professor, what does the term *balletti* mean?

   Ⓐ A dramatic story
   Ⓑ A parade of horses
   Ⓒ A dance done in figures
   Ⓓ An outdoor entertainment

9. How did the early choreographers accommodate the abilities of amateur performers?

   Ⓐ The steps were quite simple.
   Ⓑ The same performance was repeated.
   Ⓒ Practice sessions were lengthy.
   Ⓓ The dance was seen from a distance.

10. Why does the professor mention that he checked several references about the length of *Queen Louise's Ballet*?

    Ⓐ He was very interested in the ballet.
    Ⓑ He did not know much about it.
    Ⓒ He wasn't sure that it was accurate.
    Ⓓ He wanted to impress the class.

11. What can be inferred about the professor?

    Ⓐ He is not very polite to his class.
    Ⓑ He encourages the students to participate.
    Ⓒ He is not very interested in the topic.
    Ⓓ He is probably a good dancer.

Listening 3 "Linguistics Class"

12. What is the discussion mainly about?

  Ⓐ The history of the English language
  Ⓑ Different types of grammar
  Ⓒ A linguistic perspective for Latin
  Ⓓ Standard language in schools

13. How does the professor make his point about *native intuition*?

  Ⓐ He explains how to perform an easy experiment.
  Ⓑ He tells the class about his personal experience.
  Ⓒ He provides several examples of sentences.
  Ⓓ He contrasts it with non-native intuition.

14. What are two key problems for descriptive grammar?

  Click on 2 answer choices.

  Ⓐ The information is very complicated and subject to change.

  Ⓑ The formal language must be enforced in all situations.

  Ⓒ The language can be organized correctly in more than one way.

  Ⓓ The description takes time because linguists must agree.

15. Why does the student say this: 🎧

   Ⓐ She is disagreeing with the professor.
   Ⓑ She is confirming that she has understood.
   Ⓒ She is trying to impress the other students.
   Ⓓ She is adding information to the lecture.

16. According to the professor, why were Latin rules used for English grammar?

   Ⓐ Latin was a written language with rules that did not change.
   Ⓑ The Romans had conquered England and enforced using Latin.
   Ⓒ English and Latin had many vocabulary words in common.
   Ⓓ English was taking the place of Latin among educated Europeans.

17. Why does the professor discuss the rule to avoid ending a sentence with a preposition?

   Ⓐ It is a good example of the way that descriptive grammar is used.
   Ⓑ It shows the students how to use formal grammar in their speech.
   Ⓒ It is a way to introduce a humorous story into the lecture.
   Ⓓ It demonstrates the problem in using Latin rules for English.

PART II

Listening 4 "College Campus"

18. What is the purpose of this conversation?

   Ⓐ The woman is encouraging the man to be more serious about his studies.
   Ⓑ The woman is looking for alternatives to living in dormitory housing.
   Ⓒ The man is convincing the woman to join the International Student Association.
   Ⓓ The man is trying to find out why the woman didn't go to the talent show.

19. What does the man imply about the house where he is living?

   Ⓐ He prefers the house to the dorm.
   Ⓑ He is living at the house to save money.
   Ⓒ He does not like doing chores at the house.
   Ⓓ He thinks that the house is very crowded.

20. How does the man feel about the International Student Association?

   Ⓐ He is sorry that only women can join the club.
   Ⓑ He enjoys meeting people with different backgrounds.
   Ⓒ He wishes that they would have more activities.
   Ⓓ He will probably join the organization.

21. What does the woman mean when she says this:

   Ⓐ She is trying to persuade the man.
   Ⓑ She is not sure that she understood.
   Ⓒ She is expressing doubt about the time.
   Ⓓ She is changing her mind about going.

22. What does the woman agree to do?

   Ⓐ Join the club
   Ⓑ Eat at a restaurant
   Ⓒ Go to a meeting
   Ⓓ Study with the man

Listening 5 "Zoology Class"

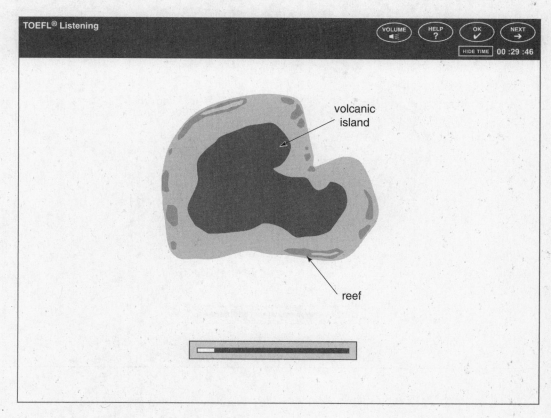

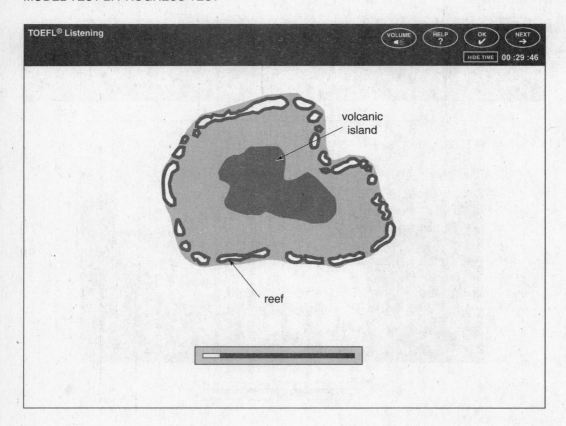

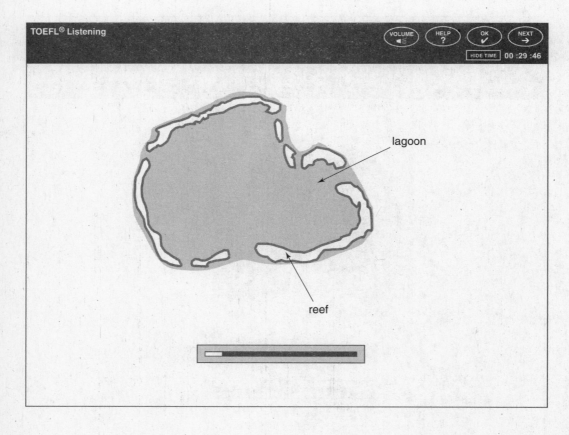

23. According to the professor, how do coral reefs grow?

   Ⓐ They become very large by eating other species.
   Ⓑ They connect coralite shells to build structures.
   Ⓒ They fill with ocean water to expand their size.
   Ⓓ They collect debris from ocean life in their habitat.

24. Why are so many egg bundles released during mass spawning?

   Ⓐ Some of the egg bundles will not be fertilized.
   Ⓑ Half of the egg bundles will not float.
   Ⓒ A number of the egg bundles will be eaten.
   Ⓓ Most of the egg bundles will break open.

25. According to the professor, what is *budding*?

   Ⓐ The division of a polyp in half to reproduce itself.
   Ⓑ The growth of limestone between the shells of polyps.
   Ⓒ The diversity that occurs within a coral reef.
   Ⓓ The increase in size of a polyp as it matures.

26. What is the relationship between zooxanthella and coral polyps?

   Click on 2 answer choices.

   Ⓐ The coral and the zooxanthella compete for the same food.

   Ⓑ The zooxanthella uses the coral for a shelter from enemies.

   Ⓒ The coral eats food produced by the zooxanthella.

   Ⓓ The same predators attack both coral and zooxanthella.

27. Which of the following reefs is probably an atoll?

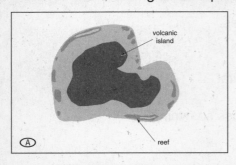

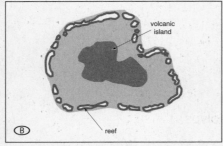

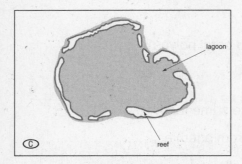

28. In the lecture, the professor explains coral reefs. Indicate whether each of the following is a true statement about coral reefs. Click in the correct box for each phrase.

		Yes	No
A	In general, the organism is quite simple.		
B	The structure of a reef can be very large.		
C	The living coral grows on top of dead shells.		
D	Mass spawning is not very effective.		

Listening 6 "Business Class"

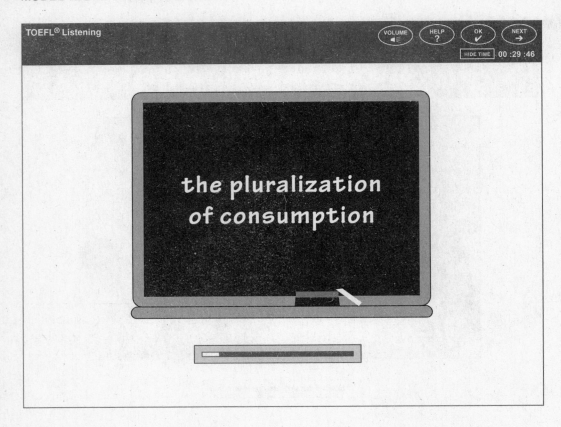

29. What is the discussion mainly about?

    Ⓐ Global marketing of food products
    Ⓑ International business in Europe
    Ⓒ Surprises in food preferences abroad
    Ⓓ Packaging food for exportation

30. How does the professor organize the lecture?

    Ⓐ He compares domestic and foreign products.
    Ⓑ He relates the textbook to his professional experience.
    Ⓒ He refers to case studies from the textbook.
    Ⓓ He presents information from most to least important.

31. Why does the student say this:

    Ⓐ She is asking the professor a question about his previous point.
    Ⓑ She is offering a possible answer to the professor's question.
    Ⓒ She is changing the subject of the class discussion.
    Ⓓ She is checking her comprehension of the professor's opinion.

32. What technique does the professor use to encourage student discussion?

    Ⓐ He gives students positive reinforcement by praising their efforts.
    Ⓑ He asks the students to talk among themselves in small groups.
    Ⓒ He assigns a different part of the textbook to each student.
    Ⓓ He calls on each student by name to contribute to the discussion.

33. What did Ted Levitt mean by "the pluralization of consumption"?

     Ⓐ More people would begin to travel.
     Ⓑ More multinational corporations would produce brands.
     Ⓒ More consumers will have the means to afford goods.
     Ⓓ More people will want the same products.

34. What does the professor say about television and movie companies?

     Ⓐ He indicates that some companies hire foreign marketing experts.
     Ⓑ He criticizes the way that they advertise their programs and films.
     Ⓒ He notes that they are one of the most widely distributed exports.
     Ⓓ He points out that they are paid to display brand-name products.

 Please turn off the audio. There is a 10-minute break between the Listening section and the Speaking section.

SPEAKING SECTION

 Model Test 2, Speaking Section, CD 3, Track 8, continued on CD 4, Track 1

The Speaking section tests your ability to communicate in English in an academic setting. During the test, you will be presented with six speaking questions. The questions ask for a response to a single question, a conversation, a talk, or a lecture.

You may take notes as you listen, but notes are not graded. You may use your notes to answer the questions. Some of the questions ask for a response to a reading passage and a talk or a lecture. The reading passages and the questions are written, but most of the directions will be spoken.

Your speaking will be evaluated on both the fluency of the language and the accuracy of the content. You will have 15–20 seconds to prepare and 45–60 seconds to respond to each question. Typically, a good response will require all of the response time, but the answer will be complete by the end of the response time.

The time for the Speaking section is about 20 minutes. A clock on the screen will show you how much time you have to prepare your answer and how much time you have to record it.

Independent Speaking Question 1 "A Birthday"

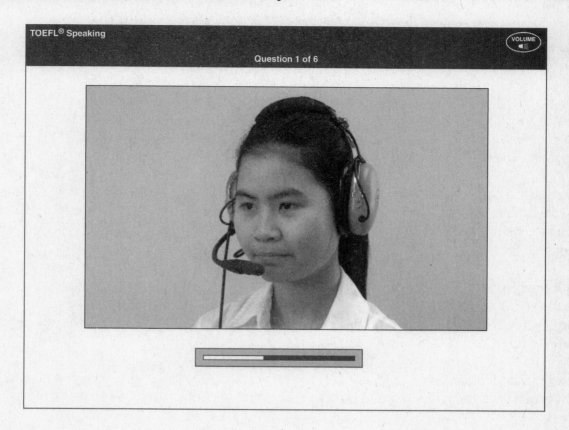

  Listen for a question about a familiar topic.

Question
Explain how birthdays are celebrated in your country. Use specific examples and details in your explanation.

Preparation Time: 15 seconds
Recording Time: 45 seconds

Independent Speaking Question 2 "Course Requirements"

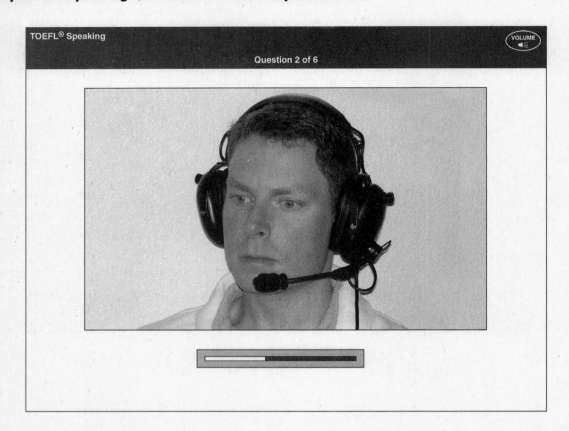

 Listen for a question that asks your opinion about a familiar topic.

Question

Some students would rather write a paper than take a test. Other students would rather take a test instead of writing a paper. Which option do you prefer and why? Use specific reasons and examples to support your opinion.

Preparation Time: 15 seconds
Recording Time: 45 seconds

Integrated Speaking Question 3 "Health Insurance"

Read a short passage and listen to a talk on the same topic.

Reading Time: 45 seconds

Health Insurance

All students may purchase health insurance at the time of registration by marking the insurance box on the course request form. Those students who choose not to use the health insurance option may still use the services of the Student Health Center, but their accounts must be settled at the time of each visit, and the alternative health insurance carrier must be billed directly by the students for reimbursement. International students are required to purchase student health insurance from the university and will be charged automatically at registration. Alternative health insurance carriers may not be substituted. No exceptions will be made.

TOEFL® Speaking

VOLUME

Question 3 of 6

 Now listen to the foreign student advisor. He is explaining the policy and expressing his opinion about it.

Question

The foreign student advisor expresses his opinion of the policy for health insurance. Report his opinion and explain the reasons that he gives for having that opinion.

Preparation Time: 30 seconds
Recording Time: 60 seconds

Integrated Speaking Question 4 "Antarctica"

Read a short passage and then listen to part of a lecture on the same topic.

Reading Time: 45 seconds

> Antarctica
>
> Antarctica and the ocean that surrounds it constitute 40 percent of the planet, but in spite of its vast area, it has remained a frontier with no permanent towns or transportation networks. Between 1895 and 1914, explorers planted their flags, claiming various sectors and the raw materials in them for their countries. Nevertheless, the remote location and the harsh environment have encouraged a spirit of cooperation among nations who maintain claims. Furthermore, because Antarctica plays a crucial role in the global environmental system, the exploitation of resources could have unpredictable consequences for the entire world. The Antarctic Treaty, signed in 1961 and expanded in 1991, ensures scientific collaboration, protects the environment, and prohibits military activities.

 Now listen to part of a lecture in a geography class. The professor is talking about Antarctica.

Question

Explain why many countries have staked claims in Antarctica, and why national interests have not been pursued.

Preparation Time: 30 seconds
Recording Time: 60 seconds

Integrated Speaking Question 5 "Extra Money"

 Now listen to a short conversation between a student and her friend.

Question
Describe the woman's problem and the two suggestions that her friend makes about how to handle it. What do you think the woman should do, and why?

Preparation Time: 20 seconds
Recording Time: 60 seconds

Integrated Speaking Question 6 "Research References"

Now listen to part of a lecture in a sociology class. The professor is discussing the criteria for using older research references.

Question
Using the main points and examples from the lecture, describe the two criteria for using an older research reference presented by the professor.

Preparation Time: 20 seconds
Recording Time: 60 seconds

WRITING SECTION

The Writing section tests your ability to write essays in English similar to those that you would write in college courses.

During the test, you will write two essays. The integrated essay asks for your response to an academic reading passage and a lecture on the same topic. You may take notes as you read and listen, but notes are not graded. You may use your notes to write the essay. The lecture will be spoken, but the directions and the questions will be written. You will have 20 minutes to plan, write, and revise your response. Typically, a good essay for the integrated topic will require that you write 150–225 words.

The independent essay usually asks for your opinion about a familiar topic. You will have 30 minutes to plan, write, and revise your response. Typically, a good essay for the independent topic will require that you write 300–350 words.

A clock on the screen will show you how much time you have to complete each essay.

Integrated Essay "The Turing Test"

You have 20 minutes to plan, write, and revise your response to a reading passage and a lecture on the same topic. First, read the passage and take notes. Then, listen to the lecture and take notes. Finally, write your response to the writing question. Typically, a good response will require that you write 150–225 words.

Reading Passage
Time: 3 minutes

Do computers think? It isn't a new question. In fact, Alan Turing, a British mathematician, proposed an experiment to answer the question in 1950, and the test, known as the Turing Test, is still used today. In the experiment, a group of people are asked to interact with something in another room through a computer terminal. They don't know whether it is another person or a computer that they are interacting with. They can ask any questions that they want. They can type their questions onto a computer screen, or they can ask their questions by speaking into a microphone. In response, they see the answers on a computer screen or they hear them played back by a voice synthesizer. At the end of the test, the people have to decide whether they have been talking to a person or to a computer. If they judge the computer to be a person, or if they can't determine the difference, then the machine has passed the Turing Test.

Since 1950, a number of contests have been organized in which machines are challenged to the Turing Test. In 1990, Hugh Loebner sponsored a prize to be awarded by the Cambridge Center for Behavioral Studies—a gold medal and a cash award of $100,000 to the designer of the computer that could pass the Turing Test; however, so far, no computer has passed the test.

Model Test 2, Writing Section, CD 4, Track 2

   Now listen to a lecture on the same topic as the passage that you have just read.

Question

Summarize the main points in the reading passage, and then explain how the lecture casts doubt on the ideas in the reading.

Independent Essay   "Family Pets"

Question

Read and think about the following statement:

Pets should be treated like family members.

Do you agree or disagree with this statement? Give reasons to support your opinion.

   This is the end of Model Test 2.
To check your answers, refer to "Explanatory or Example Answers and
Audio Scripts for Model Tests: Model Test 2," Chapter 7, pages 586–616.

5
REVIEW OF TOEFL® iBT SECTIONS

READING

OVERVIEW OF THE READING SECTION

The Reading section tests your ability to understand reading passages like those in college textbooks. The passages are about 700 words in length.

There are two formats for the Reading section. On the short format, you will respond to three passages. On the long format, you will respond to five passages. After each passage, you will answer 12–14 questions about it. Only three passages will be graded. The other passages are part of an experimental section for future tests. Because you will not know which passages will be graded, you must try to do your best on all of them.

Most questions are worth one point, but the last question in each passage is worth more than one point.

You will have 60 minutes to read all of the passages and answer the questions on the short format and 100 minutes to read all of the passages and answer the questions on the long format. You may take notes while you read, but notes are not graded. You may use your notes to answer the questions. Some passages may include a word or phrase that is underlined in blue. Click on the word or phrase to see a glossary definition or explanation.

Choose the best answer for multiple-choice questions. Follow the directions on the page or on the screen for computer-assisted questions. Click on **Next** to go to the next question. Click on **Back** to return to the previous question. You may return to previous questions for all of the passages in the same reading part, but after you go to the next part, you may not return to passages in a previous part. Be sure that you have answered all of the questions for the passages in each part before you click on **Next** at the end of the passage to move to the next part.

You can click on **Review** to see a chart of the questions you have answered and the questions you have not answered in each part. From this screen, you can return to the question you want to answer in the part that is open.

A clock on the screen will show you how much time you have to complete the Reading section.

REVIEW OF PROBLEMS FOR THE READING SECTION

➤ Prompts

A prompt for the Reading section is usually a passage from an undergraduate college textbook in one of the natural sciences, social sciences, humanities, or arts. The length of the passage is from 650 to 800 words. If there are technical words, they are explained in a glossary after the passage. There are either three or five prompts in the Reading section with twelve to fourteen questions after each prompt. When you are presented with three prompts, all three will be graded. When you are presented with five prompts, only three will be graded, and two will be used for experimental purposes. You should do your best on all five prompts because you will not know which of them will be graded. Problems 1–14 in this review refer to the following prompt:

"Producers, Consumers, and Decomposers"

➔ Organisms that are capable of using carbon dioxide as their sole source of carbon are called *autotrophs* (self-feeders), or **producers**. These are the plants. They chemically fix carbon through photosynthesis. Organisms that depend on producers as their carbon source are called *heterotrophs* (feed on others), or **consumers**. Generally, these are animals. From the producers, which manufacture their own food, energy flows through the system along a circuit called the **food chain**, reaching consumers and eventually *decomposers*. Ecosystems generally are structured in a **food web**, a complex network of interconnected food chains, comprising both strong interactions and weak interactions between species in the food web.

Primary consumers feed on producers. Ⓐ Because producers are always plants, the primary consumer is called an **herbivore**, or plant eater. A **carnivore** is a secondary consumer and primarily eats meat. Ⓑ A consumer that feeds on both producers (plants) and consumers (meat) is called an **omnivore**. Ⓒ

Decomposers are the final link in the chain. They renew the entire system by releasing inorganic materials from organic debris. Ⓓ **Decomposers** are bacteria and fungi that digest and recycle the organic debris and waste in the environment. In addition, the *detritus feeders*—worms, mites, termites, centipedes, and others—participate like a small army of workers. Waste products, dead plants and animals, and other organic remains are the principal food source for all these *detritivores*. Inorganic compounds are released in the process and the cycle continues.

➔ An example of a complex community is the oceanic food web that includes krill, a primary consumer. *Krill* is a shrimplike crustacean that is a major food for an interrelated group of organisms, including whales, fish, seabirds, seals, and squid in the Antarctic region. All of these organisms participate in numerous other food chains as well, some consuming and some being consumed. *Phytoplankton* begin this chain by harvesting solar energy in photosynthesis. Phytoplankton are eaten by *herbivorous zooplankton* such as krill and other organisms. Krill are eaten by consumers at the next <u>trophic level</u>. Because krill are a protein-rich, plentiful food, increasingly factory ships seek them out, such as those from Japan and Russia. The annual krill harvest currently surpasses a million tons, principally as feed for chickens and livestock and as protein for human consumption.

Efficiency in a Food Web

Any assessment of world food resources depends on the level of consumer being targeted. Let us use humans as an example. Many people can be fed if wheat is eaten directly. However, if the grain is first fed to cattle (herbivores) and then we eat the beef, the yield of available food energy is cut by 90% (810 kg of grain is reduced to 82 kg of meat); far fewer people can be fed from the same land area.

In terms of energy, only about 10% of the kilocalories (food calories, not heat calories) in plant matter survive from the primary to the secondary trophic level. When humans consume meat instead of grain, there is a further loss of biomass and added inefficiency. More energy is lost to the environment at each progressive step in the food chain. You can see that an omnivorous diet such as ours is quite expensive in terms of biomass and energy.

→ Food web concepts are becoming politicized as world food issues grow more critical. Today, approximately half of the cultivated acreage in the United States and Canada is planted for animal consumption—beef and dairy cattle, hogs, chickens, and turkeys. Livestock feed includes approximately 80% of the annual corn and nonexported soybean harvest. In addition, some lands cleared of rain forest in Central and South America were converted to pasture to produce beef for export to restaurants, stores, and fast-food outlets in developed countries. Thus, lifestyle decisions and dietary patterns in North America and Europe are perpetuating inefficient food webs, not to mention the destruction of valuable resources, both here and overseas.

Clearly, some food webs are exceptionally simple, such as eating grains directly, whereas others are more complex. The home gardener's tomatoes may be eaten by a tomato hornworm, which is then plucked off by a passing Robin, which is later eaten by a hawk—and so it goes, in endless cycles.

Glossary
phytoplankton: a plant that lives in the sea and produces its own energy source
trophic level: category measured in steps away from the energy input in an ecosystem

➤ Problems

The problems in this review represent the types of questions that are most frequently tested on the TOEFL. They will appear randomly after a reading passage. Directions will appear with the questions, but if you already recognize the type of problem in the question presented, and you are familiar with the directions, you will save time. The less time you have to spend reading directions, the more time you will have to read the passages and answer the questions. The number of points assigned to each problem is based on the evaluation system for the TOEFL. The frequency level for each problem is based on the average number of thirty-nine questions that are usually included in a Reading section of three prompts.

Average	1–2
High	3–4
Very high	5+

PROBLEM 1: TRUE-FALSE

A *True-False* problem asks you to identify the true statement.
Choose from four sentences.
Points—1
Frequency Level—Average

1. According to paragraph 1, which of the following is true about autotrophs?

    ● They use a chemical process to produce their own food.
    Ⓑ They require plant matter in order to survive.
    Ⓒ They need producers to provide them with carbon.
    Ⓓ They do not interact with other organisms in the food chain.

    Paragraph 1 is marked with an arrow [→].

PROBLEM 2: VOCABULARY

A *Vocabulary* problem asks you to choose a general synonym.
Choose from four words or phrases.
Points—1
Frequency Level—Very high

2. The word <u>sole</u> in the passage is closest in meaning to

    Ⓐ major
    Ⓑ steady
    ● only
    Ⓓ ideal

PROBLEM 3: TERMS

A *Terms* problem asks you to explain a word that is specific to the reading passage.
Choose from four definitions.
Points—1
Frequency Level—Average

3. Based on the information in paragraph 1, which of the following best explains the term "food web"?

  Ⓐ Energy manufactured by producer organisms in the food chain
  Ⓑ Another term that defines the food chain
  ● An interactive system of food chains
  Ⓓ Primary and secondary consumers in the food chain

  Paragraph 1 is marked with an arrow [➜].

PROBLEM 4: INFERENCE

An *Inference* problem asks you to draw a conclusion based on information in the passage.
Choose from four possibilities.
Points—1
Frequency Level— Very High

4. It may be concluded that human beings are omnivores because

  Ⓐ people feed on producers for the most part
  Ⓑ people are usually tertiary consumers
  ● people generally eat both producers and consumers
  Ⓓ most people are the top carnivores in the food chain

PROBLEM 5: PURPOSE

A *Purpose* problem asks you to understand why the author organizes a passage or explains a concept in a specific way.
Choose from four reasons.
Points—1
Frequency Level—Average

5. Why does the author mention krill in paragraph 4?

  Ⓐ To suggest a solution for a problem in the food chain
  Ⓑ To provide evidence that contradicts previously stated opinions
  Ⓒ To present an explanation for the killing of krill
  ● To give an example of a complex food web

  Paragraph 4 is marked with an arrow [➜].

PROBLEM 6: PARAPHRASE

A *Paraphrase* problem asks you to choose the best restatement.
Choose from four statements.
Points—1
Frequency Level—High

6. Which of the sentences below best expresses the information in the highlighted statement in the passage? The other choices change the meaning or leave out important information.

    Ⓐ Part of the one million tons of krill harvested annually is used for protein in animal feed.
    Ⓑ Both livestock and chickens as well as humans eat krill as a main part of their diets.
    Ⓒ The principal use of krill is for animal feed, although some of the one million tons is eaten by people.
    ● More than one million tons of krill is eaten by both animals and humans every year.

PROBLEM 7: DETAIL

A *Detail* problem asks you to answer a question about a specific point in the passage.
Choose from four possible answers.
Points—1
Frequency Level—Very high

7. According to paragraph 7, how much land is used to grow crops for animal feed?

    Ⓐ 80 percent of the acreage in Europe
    Ⓑ Most of the rain forest in Central America
    ● 50 percent of the farm land in Canada and the United States
    Ⓓ Half of the land in North and South America

    Paragraph 7 is marked with an arrow [➜].

PROBLEM 8: CAUSE

A *Cause* problem asks you to explain why something in the passage occurred.
Choose from four reasons.
Points—1
Frequency Level—Average

8. According to paragraph 7, food webs are inefficient because

    ● consumers in developed nations prefer animal protein
    Ⓑ politicians are not paying attention to the issues
    Ⓒ there are not enough acres to grow crops efficiently
    Ⓓ too much of the corn and soybean harvests are exported

    Paragraph 7 is marked with an arrow [➜].

PROBLEM 9: REFERENCE

A *Reference* problem asks you to identify a word or phrase in the passage that refers to a pronoun.
Choose from four words or phrases in the passage.
Points—1
Frequency Level—High

9. The word <u>others</u> in the passage refers to

   Ⓐ resources
   ● food webs
   Ⓒ grains
   Ⓓ cycles

PROBLEM 10: OPINION

An *Opinion* problem asks you to recognize the author's point of view.
Choose from four statements.
Points—1
Frequency Level—Average

10. Which of the following statements most accurately reflects the author's opinion about food issues?

   Ⓐ Too much grain is being exported to provide food for developed nations.
   Ⓑ More forested land needs to be cleared for food production in developing nations.
   ● Food choices in developed nations are very costly in terms of the environment.
   Ⓓ More animal protein is needed in the diets of people in developing nations.

PROBLEM 11: INSERT

An *Insert* problem asks you to locate a place in the passage to insert a sentence.
Choose from four options marked with a square.
Points—1
Frequency Level—High

11. Look at the four squares [■] that show where the following sentence could be inserted in the passage.

   A tertiary consumer eats primary and secondary consumers and is referred to as the "top carnivore" in the food chain.

   Where could the sentence best be added?   Ⓑ

   Click on a square [■] to insert the sentence in the passage.

PROBLEM 12: EXCEPTION

An *Exception* problem asks you to select a statement that includes information NOT in the passage.
Choose from four sentences.
Points—1
Frequency Level—Average

12. According to the passage, all of the following characteristics describe producers EXCEPT

    Ⓐ Producers serve as food for consumers.
    Ⓑ Producers make their own food.
    Ⓒ Producers form the first trophic level.
    ● Producers include bacteria and fungi.

PROBLEM 13: CLASSIFICATION

A *Classification* problem asks you to match phrases with the category to which they refer.
Choose phrases for two or three categories. Two phrases will not be used.

Points—1–4 points for seven choices   Points—1–3 points for five choices
1 point for 4 correct answers   1 point for 3 correct answers
2 points for 5 correct answers   2 points for 4 correct answers
3 points for 6 correct answers   3 points for 5 correct answers
4 points for 7 correct answers
Frequency Level—Average

13. **Directions:** Complete the table by matching the phrases on the left with the headings on the right. Select the appropriate answer choices and drag them to the type of organism to which they relate. TWO of the answer choices will NOT be used. *This question is worth 4 points.*

    To delete an answer choice, click on it. To see the passage, click on **View Text.**

Answer Choices

Ⓐ   Depend upon photosynthesis to survive

Ⓑ   Has a weak interaction among species

Ⓒ   Generally consist of animal life forms

Ⓓ   Include both herbivores and carnivores

Ⓔ   Form the last link in the food chain

Ⓕ   Eat meat as one of its primary food sources

Ⓖ   Feed on dead plants and animals

Ⓗ   Are always some variety of plant life

Ⓘ   Made exclusively of inorganic materials

Producers

• Ⓐ

• Ⓗ

Consumers

• Ⓒ

• Ⓓ

• Ⓕ

Decomposers

• Ⓔ

• Ⓖ

PROBLEM 14: SUMMARY

A *Summary* problem asks you to complete a summary of the passage.
Choose three sentences from six choices. Three sentences will not be used.
Points—1–2
1 point for 2 correct answers
2 points for 3 correct answers
Frequency Level—Average

14. **Directions:** An introduction for a short summary of the passage appears below. Complete the summary by selecting the THREE answer choices that mention the most important points in the passage. Some sentences do not belong in the summary because they express ideas that are not included in the passage or are minor points from the passage. *This question is worth 2 points.*

    The food web is comprised of producers, consumers, and decomposers, which interact in endless cycles.

    - A
    - B
    - C

Answer Choices

A Consumers, primarily animals, feed on producers, plants which manufacture their own food source through photosynthesis.

B Decomposers digest and recycle dead plants and animals, releasing inorganic compounds into the food chain.

C Since more energy is depleted into the environment at each level in the food chain, dietary choices affect the efficiency of food webs.

D Among consumers, human beings are considered omnivores because they eat not only plants but also animals.

E An example of an undersea food web includes phytoplankton, krill, and fish as well as birds, seals, and whales.

F Rain forests are being cut down in order to clear pastureland for cattle that can be exported to countries with fast-food restaurants.

READING STRATEGIES

In addition to the academic skills that you learned in Chapter 3, there are several reading strategies that will help you succeed on the TOEFL and after the TOEFL.

➤ Preview

Research shows that it is easier to understand what you are reading if you begin with a general idea of what the passage is about. Previewing helps you form a general idea of the topic. To preview, first read the title, the headings and subheadings, and any words in bold print or italics. You should do this as quickly as possible. Remember, you are reading not for specific information but for an impression of the topic. Next, read the first sentence of each paragraph and the last sentence of the passage. Again, this should take seconds, not minutes, to complete. This time you are looking for the main idea.

- Look at the title and headings
- Read the first sentence of every paragraph
- Read the last sentence of the passage

➤ Read faster

To read faster, read for meaning. Try to understand sentences or even paragraphs, not individual words. To do this, you should read phrases instead of reading word by word. Practice using the vision that allows you to see on either side of the word you are focusing on with your eyes. This is called *peripheral vision*. When you drive a car, you are looking ahead of you but you are really taking in the traffic situation on both sides. You are using peripheral vision to move forward. This is also important in learning to read faster. Your mind can take in more than one word at the same time. Just think if you stopped your car every time you wanted to know what was going on in the next lane! You would never get to your destination. To read faster, you have to read for ideas. If you don't know the meaning of a word but you understand the sentence, move on. Don't stop to look up the word in your dictionary. Don't stop your car.

- Use peripheral vision
- Read for meaning

➤ Use contexts

Before you can use a context, you must understand what a context is. In English, a *context* is the combination of vocabulary and grammar that surrounds a word. Context can be a sentence or a paragraph or a passage. Context helps you make a general prediction about meaning. If you know the general meaning of a sentence, you also know the general meaning of the words in the sentence. Making predictions from contexts is very important when you are reading a foreign language. In this way, you can read and understand the meaning of a passage without stopping to look up every new word in a dictionary. On an examination like the TOEFL, dictionaries are not permitted in the room. Of course, you have to know some of the words in order to have a context for the words that you don't know. That means that you need to work on learning a basic vocabulary, and then you can make an educated guess about the meaning of new words by using the context.

- Learn basic vocabulary
- Learn new words in context

➤ Make inferences

Sometimes you will find a direct statement of fact in a reading passage. Other times, you will not find a direct statement. Then you will need to use the facts as evidence to make an inference. An *inference* is a logical conclusion based on evidence. It can be about the passage itself or about the author's viewpoint. For example, you may begin reading a passage about the Native Americans who lived on the plains. You continue reading and note that they used buffalo for food. Later, you read that they used buffalo for clothing and shelter. From these facts, you can draw the conclusion that the buffalo was very important in the culture of the plains people. The author did not state this fact directly, but the evidence allows you to make an inference.

- Locate the evidence
- Draw conclusions

➤ Skim and scan

To *scan* is to let your eyes travel quickly over a passage in order to find something specific that you are looking for. By scanning, you can find the place in a reading passage where the answer to a question is found. First, read the question and look for a reference. A reference in the TOEFL will identify a paragraph where the answer to the question is found. For example, you may read, *Paragraph 2 is marked with an arrow [→].* You know that you need to scan for the arrow at the beginning of paragraph 2 in the passage. The paraphrased sentences and the vocabulary words on the TOEFL are shaded to help you find them.

If a question does not have a reference like an arrow or shading, then you should find the important content words in the question. *Content words* are usually nouns, verbs, or adjectives. They are called content words because they contain the meaning of a sentence. Now scan the passage for the same content words or synonyms of the words in the questions. Finally, read those specific sentences carefully, and choose the answer that corresponds to the meaning of the sentences you have read.

- Refer to arrows and shading
- Locate the details
- Check for exceptions

➤ Make connections

Reading is like having a conversation with the author. Your mind makes connections with the passage. Sometimes this will happen when you are reading and a word or phrase refers back to a previous point in the passage. On the TOEFL, one question requires you to insert a sentence at the most logical place in a passage. In this case, you are connecting a new sentence with the ideas in the passage. Active readers are always thinking about how the next sentence fits in with what they have already read.

- Find references
- Insert sentences

➤ Summarize

A summary includes only the main idea and the major points in a passage. Although a passage may contain many points, only the most important are included in a summary. In English, many writers tend to use a formula with one main idea and three major points. It is customary to find between two and four major points in a short passage.

When you are reading content material in textbooks or on examinations, pause at the end of a section to summarize. First, re-read the title or the section heading. State the main idea. Then, summarize the major points from that section. You can summarize by speaking or writing. The last question on the TOEFL is often a summary of the entire passage.

- State the main idea
- List the major points

APPLYING THE ACADEMIC SKILLS TO THE TOEFL

➤ Taking Notes

For some people, taking notes while they read the passage is a good strategy. For other people, it is not a good use of their time. They prefer to read once to get a general idea of the passage and then to go back and scan for each question. The way that you use your time is a very personal choice. When you take the model tests in the next chapter, practice by taking notes on some passages and by scanning on other passages. Use the model tests to determine whether you should spend time taking notes on the reading passages.

➤ Paraphrasing

This is the most important academic skill for the Reading section. Many of the questions and answer choices are paraphrases of information from the passage. Your ability to recognize paraphrases will be essential for you to score well on this section.

➤ Summarizing

The last question for every reading passage will require you to summarize the passage either by classifying information or by distinguishing between major points and minor points. Your skill in summarizing will be important because the last question is worth more points than the other questions.

➤ Synthesizing

This important skill is tested in other sections of the TOEFL® iBT.

QUIZ FOR THE READING SECTION

This is a quiz for the Reading section of the Next Generation TOEFL (iBT). This section tests your ability to understand reading passages like those in college textbooks. During the quiz, you will read one reading passage and respond to 14 questions about it. You will have 25 minutes to read the passage and answer the questions. You may take notes while you read. You may use your notes to answer the questions.

"The Heredity Versus Environment Debate"

During the past century, there has been heated controversy about whether intelligence is determined primarily by heredity or by environment. A When IQ tests were undergoing rapid development early in the twentieth century, many psychologists believed that intelligence was determined primarily by heredity. B

→ **Environmentalist view.** By the middle of the twentieth century, numerous studies had counteracted the hereditarian view, and most social scientists took the position that environment is as important as or even more important than heredity in determining intelligence. C Social scientists who stress the **environmentalist view of intelligence** generally emphasize the need for compensatory programs on a continual basis beginning in infancy. Many also criticize the use of IQ tests on the grounds that these tests are culturally biased. D

James Flynn found that "massive" gains have occurred during the twentieth century in the IQ scores of the population in fourteen nations. The major cause of these improvements, according to Flynn's analysis, is not genetic improvement in the population but environmental changes that led to gains in the kinds of skills assessed by IQ tests. Torsten Husen and his colleagues also have concluded, after reviewing large amounts of data, that improvements in economic and social conditions, and particularly in the availability of schooling, can produce substantial gains in average IQ from one generation to the next. In general, educators committed to improving the performance of low-achieving students are encouraged by these studies.

→ **Hereditarian view.** The **hereditarian view of intelligence** underwent a major revival in the 1970s and 1980s, based particularly on the writings of Arthur Jensen, Richard Herrnstein, and a group of researchers who have been conducting the Minnesota Study of Twins. Summarizing previous research as well as their own studies, these researchers concluded that heredity is the major factor in determining intelligence—accounting for up to 80 percent of the variation in IQ scores.

One very controversial study was published by Jensen in the *Harvard Educational Review* in 1969. Pointing out that African-Americans averaged about 15 points below whites on IQ tests, Jensen attributed this gap to a genetic difference between the two races in learning abilities and patterns. Critics countered Jensen's arguments by contending that IQ is affected by a host of environmental factors, such as malnutrition and prenatal care, that are difficult to measure and impossible to separate from hereditary factors. IQ tests are biased, they said, and do not necessarily even measure intelligence. Since his 1969 article, Jensen has continued to cite data that he believes link intelligence primarily to heredity. His critics continue to respond with evidence that environmental factors, and schooling in particular, have a major influence on IQ.

→ **Synthesizers' view.** A number of social scientists have taken a middle, or "synthesizing," position in this controversy. The **synthesizers' view of intelligence** holds that both heredity and environment contribute to differences in measured intelligence. For example, Christopher Jencks, after reviewing a large amount of data, divided the IQ variance into 0.45 due to heredity, 0.35 due to environment, and 0.20 due to interaction between the two ("interaction" meaning that particular abilities thrive or wither in specific environments). Robert Nichols reviewed all these and other data and concluded that the true value for heredity may be anywhere between 0.40 and 0.80 but that the exact value has little importance for policy. In general, Nichols and other synthesizers maintain that heredity determines the fixed limits of a range; within those limits, the interaction between environment and heredity yields the individual's intelligence. In this view, even if we cannot specify exactly how much of a child's intelligence is the result of environmental factors, teachers (and parents) should provide each child with a productive environment in which to realize her or his maximum potential.

Glossary
IQ: intelligence quotient; a numerical value for intelligence

1. According to paragraph 2, which of the following is true about environmentalists?

   Ⓐ They had only a few studies to prove their viewpoint.
   Ⓑ They did not agree with the use of IQ tests to measure intelligence.
   Ⓒ They did not believe that educational programs could raise IQ scores.
   Ⓓ They were already less popular by the mid twentieth century.

Paragraph 2 is marked with an arrow [→].

2. Which of the sentences below best expresses the information in the highlighted statement in the passage? The other choices change the meaning or leave out important information.

   Ⓐ Changes in the environment rather than genetic progress caused an increase in IQ scores, according to studies by Flynn.
   Ⓑ Flynn's studies were not conclusive in identifying the skills that resulted in improvements on IQ tests.
   Ⓒ IQ test results in research by Flynn did not improve because of genetics and environment.
   Ⓓ The reason that gains in IQ tests occurred was because of the changes in skills that were tested.

2

3. The word <u>data</u> in the passage is closest in meaning to

   Ⓐ experts
   Ⓑ advice
   Ⓒ arguments
   Ⓓ information

3

4. Why does the author mention the Minnesota Study of Twins in paragraph 4?

   Ⓐ To argue that environment is more important than heredity
   Ⓑ To prove the importance of heredity in measuring IQ
   Ⓒ To establish the synthesizer's view of intelligence
   Ⓓ To summarize previous research before designing a new study

Paragraph 4 is marked with an arrow [➜].

4

5. According to paragraph 4, what can be inferred about the results of the Minnesota Study of Twins?

   Ⓐ Twins brought up in different environments probably had similar IQ scores.
   Ⓑ The environments were more important to IQ than the genetic similarity of twins.
   Ⓒ The study did not support the previous work by Jensen and Herrnstein.
   Ⓓ The IQ scores of twins can vary by as much as 80 percent.

Paragraph 4 is marked with an arrow [➜].

5

6. According to Jensen's opponents, IQ tests are not reliable because

   Ⓐ heredity is not measured on the current forms of IQ tests
   Ⓑ it is difficult to determine whether a factor is due to heredity or environment
   Ⓒ learning abilities and patterns are different for people of diverse racial heredity
   Ⓓ they only measure intelligence and not many other important factors

6

7. The word <u>that</u> in the passage refers to

   Ⓐ Jensen's arguments
   Ⓑ IQ tests
   Ⓒ environmental factors
   Ⓓ Jensen's colleagues

7

8. Based on the information in paragraph 6, which of the following best explains the term <u>synthesizing</u>?

   Ⓐ A moderate position between the two extremes
   Ⓑ A position for which the evidence is overwhelming
   Ⓒ A controversial position that is hotly debated
   Ⓓ A modern revision of an outdated position

Paragraph 6 is marked with an arrow [➜].

9. According to a synthesizer's view, how does heredity influence intelligence?

    Ⓐ Heredity is very important but not as influential as environment.
    Ⓑ Heredity sets limits on intelligence, but environment can overcome them.
    Ⓒ A productive environment influences intelligence more than any other factor.
    Ⓓ Heredity and environment interact within the limits set at birth. ✓

10. According to the passage, all of the following are true of the hereditarian view EXCEPT

    Ⓐ Studies by Jensen and Herrnstein support this point of view. ✓
    Ⓑ Many psychologists in the early twentieth century were hereditarians. ✓
    Ⓒ Intelligence as measured by IQ tests is a result of genetic predisposition. ✓
    Ⓓ Environmental factors are not able to be separated from heredity. ✓

11. Which of the following statements most accurately reflects the author's opinion about IQ tests?

    Ⓐ The author believes that IQ tests should be used continuously from infancy.
    Ⓑ According to the author, there are too many disadvantages to IQ testing. –
    Ⓒ The author maintains a neutral point of view about IQ tests in the discussion. —
    Ⓓ IQ tests should be used in research studies but they should not be used in schools.

12. Look at the four squares [■] that show where the following sentence could be inserted in the passage.

These *hereditarians* thought that IQ tests and similar instruments measured innate differences in people's capacity.

Where could the sentence best be added?

Click on a square [■] to insert the sentence in the passage.

13. Complete the table by matching the phrases on the left with the headings on the right. Select the appropriate answer choices and drag them to the views of intelligence to which they relate. TWO of the answer choices will NOT be used. **This question is worth 4 points.**

To delete an answer choice, click on it. To see the passage, click on **View Text**.

Answer Choices	Hereditarian
Ⓐ Proposed interaction between heredity and environment.	•
Ⓑ Attributed lower IQ to malnutrition and lack of health care.	•
Ⓒ Suggested an innate range of IQ was influenced by environment.	•

D̲ Was supported by the Minnesota
Twins study in the 1970s.

E̲ Claimed racial composition was
a factor in measured IQ.

F̲ Maintained that IQ tests were often
biased in favor of the majority culture.

G̲ Cited schooling as a positive
consideration in the gains in IQ.

H̲ Stated that social improvements improve
performance on IQ tests.

I̲ Advanced this viewpoint when IQ
tests were being developed.

Environmentalist

-
-
-
-

14. **Directions:** An introduction for a short summary of the passage appears below. Complete the summary by selecting the THREE answer choices that mention the most important points in the passage. Some sentences do not belong in the summary because they express ideas that are not included in the passage or are minor points from the passage. *This question is worth 2 points.*

Historically, psychologists have proposed three viewpoints to explain the influence of heredity and environment on IQ scores.

-
-
-

Answer Choices

A̲ Studies by James Flynn verified significant increases in IQ scores among populations in fourteen nations in the last century.

B̲ By the 1970s, psychologists reversed their position, citing heredity as the primary determiner of intelligence as measured by IQ tests.

C̲ Because IQ tests are unfair to minority cultures, the current view is to disregard previous studies that use them as a basis for measurement.

D̲ In the mid 1900s, the popular view was that environment was the more important factor in the development of intelligence.

E̲ Before the development of IQ tests, both heredity and environment were thought to influence the relative intelligence of children.

F̲ Some modern psychologists have proposed a theory that relies on the interaction between heredity and environment to determine IQ.

This is the end of the Reading Quiz. To check your answers, refer to the Progress Chart for the Reading Quiz, Chapter 7, page 537.

STUDY PLAN

What did you learn from taking the quiz? What will you do differently when you take the model tests in the next chapter? Take a few minutes to think, and then write a sentence or two to help you revise your study plan.

EXTRA CREDIT

After you have completed this chapter, you may want to continue a review of reading. Here are some suggestions.

Practice reading on a computer screen. Reading on a computer screen is different from reading on a page. First, there is generally less text visible. Second, you must scroll instead of turning pages. Finally, there may be quite a few icons or other distracting visuals surrounding the passage. To become comfortable with reading on a computer screen, you should take advantage of every opportunity you have to practice. If you have a computer, spend time reading on the screen. Everything you read will help you improve this new skill.

Practice reading the kinds of topics that you will find in the Reading section. The reading passages are similar to the information that you will find in textbooks from general courses taught in colleges and universities during the first two years. If you can borrow English language textbooks, read passages from natural sciences, social sciences, the humanities, and the arts. The kinds of passages in encyclopedias are usually at a reading level slightly below that of textbooks, but they offer an inexpensive way to obtain a lot of reading material for different content areas. If you have access to the Internet, free encyclopedias are available online. An encyclopedia on CD-ROM is another option, which you may be able to use at a local library. If you purchase an encyclopedia on CD-ROM, an edition from a previous year will be cheaper and just as useful for your purposes.

ADVISOR'S OFFICE

If your body is relaxed, your mind can relax more easily. During the TOEFL examination, if you find yourself pursing your lips, frowning, and tightening your shoulders, then use a few seconds to stretch. Clasp your hands and put your arms over your head. Then turn your palms up to the ceiling and look up at your fingers. Pull your arms up as high as you can to stretch your muscles. Be sure not to look at anything but your own hands and the ceiling. That way, you won't be suspected of signaling to a friend. Even a two-second stretch can make a difference. Now, yawn or take a deep breath in and out, and you'll be more relaxed and ready to go on.

LISTENING

OVERVIEW OF THE LISTENING SECTION

The Listening section tests your ability to understand spoken English that is typical of interactions and academic speech on college campuses. During the test, you will respond to conversations and lectures.

There are two formats for the Listening section. On the short format, you will respond to two conversations and four lectures. On the long format, you will respond to three conversations and six lectures. After each listening passage, you will answer 5–6 questions about it. Only two conversations and four lectures will be graded. The other conversation and lectures are part of an experimental section for future tests. Because you will not know which conversations and lectures will be graded, you must try to do your best on all of them.

You will hear each conversation or lecture one time. You may take notes while you listen, but notes are not graded. You may use your notes to answer the questions.

Choose the best answer for multiple-choice questions. Follow the directions on the page or on the screen for computer-assisted questions. Click on **Next** and **OK** to go to the next question. You cannot return to previous questions. You have 20 minutes to answer all of the questions on the short format and 30 minutes to answer all of the questions on the long format. A clock on the screen will show you how much time you have to complete your answers for the section. The clock does not count the time you are listening to the conversations and lectures.

REVIEW OF PROBLEMS FOR THE LISTENING SECTION

➤ Prompts

A prompt for the Listening section is either a conversation on a college campus or part of a lecture in a college classroom on one of the natural sciences, social sciences, humanities, or arts. Each conversation or lecture is between three and six minutes long. There are either 6 or 9 prompts in the Listening section with 5–6 questions after each prompt. When you are presented with 6 prompts, all 6 will be graded. When you are presented with 9 prompts, only 6 will be graded, and 3 will be used for experimental purposes. You should do your best on all 9 prompts because you will not know which of them will be graded. Problems 15–18 in this review refer to the first prompt. Problems 19–24 refer to the second prompt. The scripts for the prompts in this review chapter have been printed for you to study while you listen to them. On the official TOEFL® iBT, you will not see the prompts, but you will see the questions while you hear them. The quiz at the end of this review and the model tests are like the official TOEFL® iBT. You will not see the scripts while you listen to the prompts for the quiz and the model tests.

CONVERSATION

 Problems 15–18, Conversation, CD 4, Track 4. Listen to a conversation on campus between two students.

Man:	Wait up. I need to ask you about something.
Woman:	Oh, hi Jack.
Man:	Hi. Listen, I was just wondering whether you understood what Professor Carson was saying about the review session next Monday?
Woman:	Sure. Why?
Man:	Well, the way I get it, it's optional.
Woman:	Right. He said if we didn't have any questions, we should just use the time to study on our own.
Man:	Okay. That's what I thought. Maybe I'll just skip it then.
Woman:	Well, it's up to you, but the thing is . . . sometimes at a review session, someone else will ask a question, and, you know, the way the professor explains it, it's really helpful, I mean, to figure out what he wants on the test.
Man:	Oh I didn't think about it that way, but it makes sense. So, you're going to go then.
Woman:	Absolutely. Um, I've had a couple of other classes with Carson and the review sessions always helped me get organized for the test.
Man:	Oh.
Woman:	And, if you've missed any of the lectures, he usually has extra handouts from all the classes. So . . .
Man:	Well, I haven't missed any of the sessions.
Woman:	Me neither. But I'm still going to be there. Look, uh, if it's like the other review sessions, the first hour he's going to go over the main points for each class, kind of like an outline of the course. Then from five-thirty to six-thirty, he'll take questions. That's the best part. And the last half hour, he'll stay for individual conferences with people who need extra help. I usually don't stay for that.
Man:	Okay. So we just show up at the regular time and place for class?
Woman:	Or not, if you decide to study on your own.
Man:	Right. But, don't you think he'll notice who's there?
Woman:	He said he wasn't going to take attendance.
Man:	Yeah, but still . . .
Woman:	It's a fairly large class.
Man:	But if he's grading your final and he remembers you were at the review, it might make a difference.
Woman:	Maybe. I think the important thing is just to study really hard and do your best. But, the review sessions help me study. I think they're really good.
Man:	Okay. Thanks. I guess I'll go, too.
Woman:	So I'll see you there.
Man:	Yeah, I think I . . . I'd better go.

➤ Problems

The problems in this review represent the types of questions that are most frequently tested on the TOEFL. The number of points assigned to each problem is based on the evaluation system for the TOEFL. The frequency level for each problem is based on the average number of thirty-four questions that are usually included in a Listening section of six prompts.

Average   1–2
High   3–4
Very high   5+

PROBLEM 15: PURPOSE

A *Purpose* problem asks you to explain why the speakers are having a conversation or why the professor is presenting the material in a lecture. Choose from four reasons.
Points—1
Frequency Level—Average

1. Why does the man want to talk with the woman?

   Ⓐ To ask her to help him study for the exam
   Ⓑ To get some handouts for a class he has missed
   ● To clarify his understanding of the review session
   Ⓓ To find out her opinion of Professor Carson

PROBLEM 16: DETAIL

A *Detail* problem asks you to answer a question about a specific point in the conversation or lecture.
Choose from four possible answers.
Points—1
Frequency Level—Very high

2. Why does the woman think that the review session will be helpful?

   Ⓐ Because she has some questions that she wants to ask the professor
   Ⓑ Because Professor Carson will tell them some of the test questions
   ● Because it helps to hear the answers to questions that other people ask
   Ⓓ Because she needs an individual conference with the professor

PROBLEM 17: INFERENCE

An *Inference* problem asks you to draw a conclusion based on information in the conversation or lecture. Choose from four possible answers.
Points—1
Frequency Level—Very high

3. Why does the man decide to go to the review session?

Ⓐ Because the review session will make up for absences
● Because the woman convinces him that it is a good idea
Ⓒ Because the professor has recommended the session
Ⓓ Because he needs help to organize his class notes

PROBLEM 18: PRAGMATICS

A *Pragmatics* problem asks you to comprehend the function of language on a level deeper than the surface meaning. You may need to understand the purpose or motivation of the speaker, or you may need to interpret the speaker's attitude or doubt about something in the conversation or lecture. Listen to a replay of the sentence or sentences that you must interpret.
Choose from four possible answers.
Points—1
Frequency Level—Very high

4. Listen again to part of the conversation. Then answer the following question.

Woman: He said he wasn't going to take attendance.
Man: Yeah, but still . . .
Woman: It's a fairly large class.

Why does the man say this: "Yeah, but still . . ."?

● He thinks that the professor will notice if a student is absent.
Ⓑ He agrees with the woman about the attendance policy.
Ⓒ He wants to change the subject that they are discussing.
Ⓓ He tries to encourage the woman to explain her opinion.

LECTURE

 Problems 19–24, Lecture, CD 4, Track 5. Listen to part of a lecture in a zoology class.

Professor:

As you know from the textbook, mimicry isn't limited to insects, but it's most common among them, and by mimicry I'm referring to the likeness between two insects that aren't closely related but look very much alike. The insects that engage in mimicry are usually very brightly colored. One of the insects, the one that's characterized by an unpleasant taste, a bad smell, a sting or bite, that insect is called the *model*. The mimic looks like the model but doesn't share the characteristic that protects the model from predators. But, of course, the predators associate the color pattern or some other trait with the unpleasant characteristic and leave both insects alone.

Henry Bates was one of the first naturalists who noticed that some butterflies that closely resembled each other were actually unrelated, so mimicry in which one species copies another is called Batesian mimicry. I have some lab specimens of a few common mimics in the cases here in the front of the room, and I want you to have a chance to look at them before the end of the class. There's a day flying moth with brown and white and yellow markings. And this moth is the model because it has a very unpleasant taste and tends to be avoided by moth eaters. But you'll notice that the swallowtail butterfly mounted beside it has very similar coloration, and actually the swallowtail doesn't have the unpleasant taste at all. Another example is the monarch butterfly, which is probably more familiar to you since they pass through this area when they're migrating. But you may not know that they have a very nasty taste because I seriously doubt that any of you have eaten one. But for the predators who *do* eat butterflies, this orange and black pattern on the monarch is a warning signal not to sample it. So, the viceroy butterfly here is a mimic. Same type of coloring but no nasty taste. Nevertheless, the viceroy isn't bothered by predators either, because it's mistaken for the monarch. So how does a predator know that the day flying moth and the monarch aren't good to eat? Well, a bird only has to eat one to start avoiding them all—models and mimics.

A stinging bumblebee is another model insect. The sting is painful and occasionally even fatal for predators. So there are a large number of mimics. For example, there's a beetle that mimics bumblebees by beating its wings to make noise, and the astonishing thing is that it's able to do this at the same rate as the bumblebee so exactly the same buzzing sound is created. I don't have a specimen of that beetle, but I do have a specimen of the hoverfly, which is a mimic of the honeybee, and it makes a similar buzzing sound, too. When you compare the bee with the fly, you'll notice that the honeybee has two sets of wings, and the hoverfly has only one set of wings, but as you can imagine, the noise and the more or less similar body and color will keep most predators from approaching closely enough to count the wings.

Some insects without stingers have body parts that mimic the sharp stinger of wasps or bees. Although the hawk moth is harmless, it has a bundle of hairs that protrudes from the rear of its body. The actual purpose of these hairs is to spread scent, but to predators, the bundle mimics a stinger closely enough to keep them away, especially if the hawk moth is moving in a threatening way as if it were about to sting. There's a hawk moth here in the case, and to me at least, it doesn't look that much like the wasp mounted beside it, but remember when you're looking at a specimen, it's stationary, and in nature the *movement* is also part of the mimicry.

Oh, here's a specimen of an ant, and this is interesting. Another naturalist, Fritz Muller, hypothesized that similarity among a large number of species could help protect *all* of them. Here's what he meant. After a few battles with a stinging or biting ant, especially when the entire colony comes to the aid of the ant being attacked, a predator will learn to avoid ants, even those that don't sting or bite, because they all look alike and the predator associates the bad experience with the group. And by extension, the predator will also avoid insects that mimic ants, like harmless beetles and spiders.

Look at this.

Ant   Spider

I have a drawing of a specimen of a stinging ant beside a specimen of a brownish spider and the front legs of the spider are mounted so they look more like antennae because that's just what the spider does to mimic an ant. That way it appears to have six legs like an ant instead of eight like a spider.

Okay, we have about ten minutes left, and I want you to take this opportunity to look at the specimen cases here in the front of the room. I'll be available for questions if you have them. How about forming two lines on either side of the cases so more of you can see at the same time?

PROBLEM 19: MAIN IDEA

A *Main Idea* problem asks you to identify the topic of the lecture, that is, what the lecture is mainly about.
Choose from four possible answers.
Points—1
Frequency Level—High

5. What is the lecture mainly about?

  ● An explanation of mimicry among species in the insect world
  Ⓑ A comparison of the features of the viceroy and the monarch butterfly
  Ⓒ A hypothesis to explain why similarity among species protects them all
  Ⓓ A response to questions about the specimens displayed in the cases

PROBLEM 20: ORGANIZATION

An *Organization* problem asks you recognize the rhetorical structure of a lecture or part of a lecture. For example, chronological order, steps in a sequence, cause and effect, comparison.
Choose from four possible answers.
Points—1
Frequency Level—Average

6. How does the professor organize the lecture?

  ● He shows specimens to demonstrate his points.
  Ⓑ He compares the theories of two naturalists.
  Ⓒ He classifies different types of mimics.
  Ⓓ He puts the ideas in chronological order.

PROBLEM 21: DETAILS

A *Details* problem asks you to answer a question about a specific point in the conversation or lecture.
Choose two or three answers from four to six possibilities.
Points—1
Frequency Level—Average

7. According to the lecture, what are some characteristics of a *model*?

  Click on 3 answer choices.

  Ⓐ A pair of wings
  ■ A foul odor
  ■ A bad taste
  Ⓓ A drab color
  ■ A painful sting

PROBLEM 22: TECHNIQUE

A *Technique* problem asks you to identify the way that a professor makes a point, for example, by comparing, by providing a definition, by giving an example.
Choose from four possible answers.
Points—1
Frequency Level—Average

8. How does the professor explain Batesian mimicry?

   Ⓐ By giving a precise definition
   ● By providing several examples
   © By referring to the textbook
   Ⓓ By contrasting it with another hypothesis

PROBLEM 23: YES-NO

A *Yes-No* problem asks you to decide whether statements agree or disagree with information in the lecture.
Mark a list of statements in a chart as either *Yes* or *No*.
Points—1–2
Frequency Level—Average

9. In the lecture, the professor explains Fritz Muller's hypothesis. Indicate whether each of the following supports the hypothesis.
   Click in the correct box for each choice.

		Yes	No
A	Predators avoid species of insects that have harmed them in the past by stinging or biting them.	✔	
B	Predators may be killed when an entire colony of insects joins forces against them.		✔
C	Predators leave harmless insects alone if they are part of a group that includes stinging insects.	✔	
D	Predators will refrain from attacking harmless insects if they look like insects that have stung them before.	✔	
E	Predators protect themselves from harmful insects by stinging or biting them before they are attacked.		✔

PROBLEM 24: CONNECTIONS

A *Connections* problem asks you to relate ideas or information in the lecture.
Match answers with categories, list the order of events or steps in a process, and show relationships on a chart.
Points—1–4
Frequency Level—Average

10. Indicate whether each insect below refers to a model or a mimic.
    Click in the correct box for each phrase.

Insects	Mimic	Model
A A viceroy butterfly	→	
B A brown spider	→	
C A hawk moth	→	
D A bumblebee		→
E A biting ant		→

LISTENING STRATEGIES

In addition to the academic skills that you learned in the previous chapter, there are several listening strategies that will help you succeed on the TOEFL and after the TOEFL.

➤ Get organized

Before you begin the Listening section on the official TOEFL, you will have an opportunity to adjust the volume on your headset. Be sure to do it before you dismiss the directions and begin the test. After the test has begun, you may not be able to adjust the volume. When you practice using the model tests in this book, adjust the volume at the beginning. Learn to get it right without touching the volume button again during practice. Then, prepare to listen. The directions tend to be long and boring, especially if you have experience taking model tests and know what to do. Don't get distracted. Be ready to hear the first word in the introduction to the first listening passage.

- Adjust the volume first
- Prepare to listen

➤ Preview

The introductions for the conversations and lecture contain important information that will help you prepare your mind to listen. For example, the narrator may say, "Now get ready to listen to part of a lecture in a history class." When you hear the introduction, you learn two useful facts. First, you know that you will be listening to a lecture. Second, you know that the lecture will be about history. This is helpful because it is a preview for the listening passage.

- Pay attention to the introductions
- Glance at the photo

➤ Use visuals

The photographs and other visuals are there to provide a context for the conversations and lectures. In general, the pictures of people are for orientation to the conversations and lectures, whereas the visuals of objects, art, specimens, maps, charts, and drawings support the meaning of the conversations and lectures. Do *not* focus on the pictures of people. *Do* focus on the other visuals that appear during the conversations and lectures. They could reappear in a question. When you take the model tests, practice selective attention. Look briefly at the pictures of the professor and the students, but be alert to the other visuals. If you become too involved in looking at the people, you may pay less attention to the audio, and you could miss part of the passage.

- Glance at the photos of people
- Focus on content visuals

➤ Read screen text

During the questions for conversations and lectures, watch the screen carefully. You will hear the questions, and you will also see them as text on the screen. If you find that it is to your advantage to close your eyes or look away from the photo during the short conversations, be sure to give your full attention to the screen again while the questions are being asked and the answer choices are presented. By using the model tests, you will be able to develop a rhythm for interacting with the screen that is best for you.

- Read the questions
- Develop a rhythm

➤ Understand campus context

The conversations and lectures take place in a campus context. A glossary at the end of this book contains a listing of campus vocabulary. These words and phrases will help you understand the conversations between campus personnel, professors, and students. Pragmatic understanding will help you understand the function of a sentence. A few examples of function are an apology, an explanation, or a way to get the listener's attention or to change the topic. Pragmatic understanding will also help you interpret the speaker's attitude and the nature of the information—a fact or an opinion. Studying the glossary is an important strategy for the Listening section. Start now.

- Learn campus vocabulary
- Study pragmatic cues for lectures

➤ Concentrate

Sometimes the environment for the TOEFL is not ideal. If the room is small, you may hear a very low hum from another headset or the scratch of pencils on paper when others are taking notes. These sounds can be distracting, especially during the Listening section. The earphones on your headset should suppress most of the noise, but it will be helpful if you have some strategies to help you concentrate. Some students press their earphones more tightly to their ears by holding them with their hands during long listening passages, but this may be clumsy for you when you reach for the mouse to answer questions. Other students train themselves to concentrate in a somewhat distracting environment by taking at least one model test in a small room where other people are studying, such as a library or a study lounge in a dormitory. Remember, you may not be able to control the test environment, but you can control your response to it. By keeping your eyes on the screen and the scratch paper and by remaining calm, you will be able to concentrate better. If the test situation is noisy, don't get angry and start negative talk in your mind. Don't let your emotions interfere with your concentration.

- Focus on the test materials
- Stay calm

APPLYING THE ACADEMIC SKILLS TO THE TOEFL

➤ Taking Notes

Taking notes is probably the most important academic skill for the Listening section. When you take notes, you will organize the information into major points and minor points. You will also record information that you can refer to when you answer questions. Your ability to take notes will be critical for you to score well on this section.

➤ Paraphrasing

Many of the answer choices are paraphrases of information from the passage. Your ability to recognize paraphrases will be helpful as you choose your answers.

➤ Summarizing

The first question in each conversation usually requires you to understand the purpose of the conversation, and the first question in each lecture usually requires you to recognize a summary of the main idea. By mastering the academic skill of summarizing, you will be able to respond correctly to the first question in each prompt. You will also be better prepared to relate ideas and make connections.

➤ Synthesizing

This important skill is tested in other sections of the TOEFL® iBT.

QUIZ FOR THE LISTENING SECTION

This is a quiz for the Listening section of the Next Generation TOEFL (iBT). This section tests your ability to understand campus conversations and academic lectures. During the quiz, you listen to one conversation and one lecture. You will hear each conversation or lecture one time and respond to questions about them. You may take notes while you listen. You may use your notes to answer the questions.

CONVERSATION

 Questions 1–4, Conversation, CD 4, Track 6. Listen to a conversation on campus between a professor and a student.

1. Why does the man go to see his professor?

    Ⓐ To borrow a reference book that he needs
    Ⓑ To ask a question about the material
    Ⓒ To get advice about studying for a test
    Ⓓ To pick up some handouts from the class

2. Why does the student say this:

    Ⓐ To challenge the professor's idea
    Ⓑ To encourage the professor to explain
    Ⓒ To try to change the subject
    Ⓓ To interrupt the professor respectfully

3. How should Jack prepare for the test?

    Ⓐ He should memorize the material in the book.
    Ⓑ He should study the questions before the test.
    Ⓒ He should organize his notes by topic.
    Ⓓ He should not change his usual study plan.

4. Why does the professor give open-book tests?

    Ⓐ Because she believes it helps students with memorization
    Ⓑ Because her tests contain a large number of small facts
    Ⓒ Because her students are more successful with the course
    Ⓓ Because she thinks it provides a better learning experience

Lecture

Questions 5–14, Lecture, CD 4, Track 6 continued. Listen to part of a lecture in an economics class.

5. What is the lecture mainly about?

    Ⓐ Changes in economic systems
    Ⓑ Tax incentives for business
    Ⓒ Supply-side economics
    Ⓓ A favorable balance of trade

6. How does the professor organize the lecture?

    Ⓐ By contrasting several economic systems
    Ⓑ By taking a historical perspective
    Ⓒ By arguing against Friedman and Asmus
    Ⓓ By pointing out the benefits of Reaganomics

7. According to the lecturer, what did Kennedy and Reagan have in common?

    Ⓐ They were both honored as Nobel laureates in economics.
    Ⓑ They cut taxes to spur the economy during their administrations.
    Ⓒ They identified themselves with supply-side economics.
    Ⓓ They both taught at the Chicago School of Economics.

8. What would Milton Freidman most likely say about moving a manufacturing plant from the United States to a site abroad?

    Ⓐ He would oppose it because it would cause people to lose their jobs.
    Ⓑ He would consider it an opportunity for business to cut costs.
    Ⓒ He would view it as a natural process in the shift to technology.
    Ⓓ He would be concerned about the decrease in productivity.

9. According to Barry Asmus, what are two key ways that consumers contribute to the creation of new jobs?

    Click on 2 answer choices.

    Ⓐ By investing their tax savings

    Ⓑ By purchasing cheaper goods

    Ⓒ By moving on to better paying jobs

    Ⓓ By spending more money

10. How does the professor explain the shift from manufacturing to technology?

    Ⓐ He points to the global economy as the explanation for it.
    Ⓑ He disagrees with most economists about the long-term effects.
    Ⓒ He compares it with the change from agriculture to manufacturing.
    Ⓓ He believes that it is too soon to draw any conclusions about it.

11. Why does the professor mention the General Electric plant?

    Ⓐ Because the plant is a good example of increased productivity
    Ⓑ Because unemployment resulted from company decisions
    Ⓒ Because the company was able to retrain their employees
    Ⓓ Because the plant was down-sized and many jobs were lost

12. Why does the professor say this:

    Ⓐ He would like the students to answer the question.
    Ⓑ He is joking with the students about the supply-siders.
    Ⓒ He wants the students to follow his logical answer.
    Ⓓ He is impatient because the students aren't paying attention.

13. In the lecture, the professor explains supply-side economics. Indicate whether each of the following strategies supports the theory.
Click in the correct box for each choice.

		Yes	No
A	Reduce tax rates		
B	Cut government spending		
C	Increase productivity		
D	Tolerate temporary unemployment		
E	Discourage consumer spending		

14. Put the following events in the correct order.

    Ⓐ Businesses hire more employees with the tax savings.
    Ⓑ The government works to affect a reduction in taxes.
    Ⓒ The businesses and their employees pay more taxes.
    Ⓓ Profits increase because of the growth in businesses.

STOP **This is the end of the Listening Quiz. To check your answers, refer to the Progress Chart for the Listening Quiz, Chapter 7, page 542.**

STUDY PLAN

What did you learn from taking the quiz? What will you do differently when you take the model tests in the next chapter? Take a few minutes to think, and then write a sentence or two to help you revise your study plan.

EXTRA CREDIT

After you have completed this chapter, you may want to continue a review of listening. Here are some suggestions.

Listen to an international news broadcast in English. Be sure to select a television or radio program that includes reporters from various English-speaking countries, especially Canada, the United States, Australia, and Great Britain. The Listening section of the TOEFL now includes voices that represent a variety of English accents. The purpose of this activity is to understand diverse speech. Don't take notes. Just listen and try to understand as much as you can.

Watch educational television programs. The Learning Channel, Discovery, PBS, BBC, and others provide narrated programming with visuals on subjects that simulate lecture topics on the TOEFL. Take notes while you watch the program. During commercial breaks, mute the program and try to summarize the major points that you have heard, using your notes.

Attend lectures in English. Local colleges and clubs often have free lectures in English. Choose to attend lectures that simulate college classrooms. In addition, several web sites offer lectures and talks. Select topics from natural science, social science, humanities, and the arts.

www.npr.org; click on *archives*

www.c-span.org; click on *booknotes*

ADVISOR'S OFFICE

There is usually a ten-minute break after the Listening section. What you do during the break is important. If you start to talk in your language with friends who are nervous or negative, you will go back into the Speaking section nervous and negative. Choose a friend who is willing to speak English with you during the break. Use the time to encourage each other with positive talk. If you speak English, you will continue thinking in English, and you will make a smooth transition into the next section of the TOEFL. If you are also thinking positively, you will be ready to do your best.

SPEAKING

OVERVIEW OF THE SPEAKING SECTION

The Speaking section tests your ability to communicate in English in an academic setting. During the test, you will be presented with six speaking questions. The questions ask for a response to a single question, a conversation, a talk, or a lecture.

You may take notes as you listen, but notes are not graded. You may use your notes to answer the questions. Some of the questions ask for a response to a reading passage and a talk or a lecture. The reading passages and the questions are written, but most of the directions will be spoken.

Your speaking will be evaluated on both the fluency of the language and the accuracy of the content. You will have 15–20 seconds to prepare and 45–60 seconds to respond to each question. Typically, a good response will require all of the response time, but the answer will be complete by the end of the response time. You will have about 20 minutes to complete the Speaking section.

A clock on the screen will show you how much time you have to prepare your answer and how much time you have to record it.

REVIEW OF PROBLEMS FOR THE SPEAKING SECTION

➤ Prompts

A prompt for the Speaking section is either spoken or written. For example, a prompt might be a question, a conversation, part of a lecture, a written announcement, or part of a textbook passage. Each question has a slightly different prompt. There are six sets of prompts in the Speaking section with 1 question after each set. Problems 1–6 in this review refer to the kinds of prompts that are typical on the TOEFL® iBT. The scripts for the spoken prompts have been printed for you to study while you listen to them. On the official TOEFL, you will not see the spoken prompts. You will see the written announcements and textbook passages, and you will also see the questions while you hear them. The quiz at the end of this review and the model tests are like the official TOEFL® iBT. You will not see the scripts while you listen to the prompts for the quiz and the model tests.

➤ Problems

The problems in this review represent the types of questions that are most frequently tested on the TOEFL. The task for each problem is explained. Each problem appears as one of the 6 questions included in the Speaking section.

PROBLEM 25: EXPERIENCES

In this question, you will be asked to speak about a personal experience. This may be a place, a person, a possession, a situation, or an occasion. After you hear the question, you will make a choice from your experience and then explain why you made that choice.

You will have 15 seconds to prepare and 45 seconds to speak.

Task

- Describe your experience
- Explain the reasons for your choice

 Problem 25, Example Question, CD 4, Track 7

Where would you like to study in the United States?

Example Notes—Answer and Reasons

Washington, D.C.

- Family in the area—advice, help
- International city—food, stores
- Tours—sites, trains to other cities
- Universities—excellent, accepted at 1

 Problem 25, Example Answer, CD 4, Track 7 continued.

I'd like to study at a university in Washington, D.C., because I have family in the area, and . . . and it would be nice to have them close by so I could visit them on holidays and in case I need advice or help. I've been to Washington several times, and I like it there. It's an international city with restaurants and stores where I can buy food and other things from my country while, uh, while I'm living abroad. And Washington is an exciting place. I've gone on several tours, but I still have many places on my list of sites to see. Also, um, there are trains to New York and Florida so I could take advantage of my free time to see other cities. Um, as for the universities, there are several, uh, several excellent schools in Washington and . . . and I'd probably be accepted at one of them.

Checklist 1

✔ The talk answers the topic question.
✔ The point of view or position is clear.
✔ The talk is direct and well-organized.
✔ The sentences are logically connected.
✔ Details and examples support the main idea.
✔ The speaker expresses complete thoughts.

✔ The meaning is easy to comprehend.
✔ A wide range of vocabulary is used.
✔ There are only minor errors in grammar.
✔ The talk is within a range of 125–150 words.

PROBLEM 26: PREFERENCES

In this question, you will be asked to speak about a personal preference. This may be a situation, an activity, or an event. After you hear the question, you will make a choice between two options presented and then explain why you made that choice.

You will have 15 seconds to prepare and 45 seconds to speak.

Task

- Choose between two options
- Explain the reasons for your preference

 Problem 26, Example Question, CD 4, Track 8

Some students live in dormitories on campus. Other students live in apartments off campus. Which living situation do you think is better and why?

Example Notes—Choice and Reasons

Dormitories

- More interaction—practice English, study
- Less responsibility—meals, laundry, cleaning
- Better location—library, recreation, classroom buildings

 Problem 26, Example Answer, CD 4, Track 8 continued

A lot of my friends live off campus, but I think that living in a dormitory is a better situation, uh, especially for the first year at a new college. Dormitories are structured to provide opportunities for interaction and for making friends. As a foreign student, it would be an advantage to be in a dormitory to practice English with other residents and to find study groups in the dormitory. And dorm students have, uh, less responsibility for meals, laundry, and . . . and, uh, cleaning because there are meal plans and services available, uh, as part of the fees. Besides, there's only one check to write so, uh, the book, uh, the bookkeeping . . . it's minimal. And the dormitory offers an ideal location near the library and, um, all the recreational facilities, and . . . and the classroom buildings.

Checklist 2

✔ The talk answers the topic question.
✔ The point of view or position is clear.
✔ The talk is direct and well-organized.
✔ The sentences are logically connected.
✔ Details and examples support the main idea.
✔ The speaker expresses complete thoughts.
✔ The meaning is easy to comprehend.
✔ A wide range of vocabulary is used.
✔ There are only minor errors in grammar.
✔ The talk is within a range of 125–150 words.

PROBLEM 27: REPORTS

In this question, you will be asked to read a short passage and listen to a speaker on the same topic. The topic usually involves a campus situation and the speaker's opinion about it. After you hear the question, you will be asked to report the speaker's opinion and relate it to the reading passage.

You will have 45 seconds to read the passage. After you have listened to the talk, you will have 30 seconds to prepare and 60 seconds to speak.

Task

- Summarize a situation and an opinion about it
- Explain the reason or the background
- Connect listening and reading passages

Reading
45 seconds

Announcement concerning a proposal for a branch campus
The university is soliciting state and local funding to build a branch campus on the west side of the city where the I-19 expressway crosses the 201 loop. This location should provide convenient educational opportunities for students who live closer to the new campus as well as for those students who may choose to live on the west side once the campus is established. The city plan for the next ten years indicates that there will be major growth near the proposed site, including housing and a shopping area. By building a branch campus, some of the crowding on the main campus may be resolved.

Problem 27, Talk, CD 4, Track 9

I understand that a branch campus on the city's west side would be convenient for students who live near the proposed site, and it might attract more local students, but I oppose the plan because it will redirect funds from the main campus where several classroom buildings need repair. Hanover Hall for one. And, uh, a lot of the equipment in the chemistry and physics labs should be replaced. In my lab classes, we don't do some of the experiments because, uh, because we don't have enough equipment. And we need more teachers on the main campus. I'd like to see the branch campus funding allocated for teachers' salaries in order to decrease the student-teacher ratios. Most of the freshman classes are huge, and there's very little inter-action with professors. Um, a branch campus would be a good addition, but not until some of the problems on the main campus have been taken care of.

Example Notes—Situation and Opinion

Plans to open a branch campus

- convenient for students near
- might attract more students
- relieve crowding on main campus

But will redirect funds from main campus

- buildings need repair
- equipment should be replaced
- more teachers—smaller classes

 Problem 27, Example Question, CD 4, Track 9 continued

The man expresses his opinion of the proposal in the announcement. Report his opinion and explain the reasons he gives for having that opinion.

 Problem 27, Example Answer, CD 4, Track 9 continued

The man concedes that the branch campus might be advantageous for students living close to the new location, but he's concerned that the funding for a branch campus will affect funding on main campus for . . . for important capital improvements such as classroom buildings that are, uh, in need of repair. Um, and equipment in the science labs is getting old, so it needs to be replaced. And he also points out that more teachers are needed for the main campus in order to reduce student-teacher ratios, which . . . which would improve the quality of the teaching and the, uh, amount of interaction in classes. So the man feels that more attention should be given to the main campus and funding should be directed to improve the main campus before a branch campus is considered.

Checklist 3

✔ The talk summarizes the situation and opinion.
✔ The point of view or position is clear.
✔ The talk is direct and well-organized.
✔ The sentences are logically connected.
✔ Details and examples support the opinion.
✔ The speaker expresses complete thoughts.
✔ The meaning is easy to comprehend.
✔ A wide range of vocabulary is used.
✔ Errors in grammar are minor.
✔ The talk is within a range of 125–150 words.

PROBLEM 28: EXAMPLES

In this question, you will be asked to listen to a speaker and read a short passage on the same topic. The topic usually involves a general concept and a specific example of it. Sometimes the speaker provides a contradictory point of view. After you hear the question, you will be asked to explain the example and relate it to the concept or contrast the opposing views.

You will have 45 seconds to read the passage. After you have listened to the talk, you will have 30 seconds to prepare and 60 seconds to speak.

Task

- Explain how an example supports a concept OR
  Contrast one view with another view
- Connect listening and reading passages

Reading
45 seconds

> The telegraphic nature of early sentences in child language is a result of the omission of grammatical words such as the article *the* and auxiliary verbs *is* and *are* as well as word endings such as *-ing, -ed,* or *-s.* By the end of the third year, these grammatical forms begin to appear in the speech of most children. It is evident that a great deal of grammatical knowledge is required before these structures can be used correctly, and errors are commonly observed. The correction of grammatical errors is a feature of the speech of preschoolers four and five years old. The study of the errors in child language is interesting because it demonstrates when and how grammar is acquired.

Problem 28, Lecture, CD 4, Track 10

English uses a system of about a dozen word endings to express grammatical meaning—the *–ing* for present time, *-s* for possession and plurality, and, uh, the *–ed* for the past, to mention only a few. But, um, how and when do children learn them? Well, in a classic study by Berko in the 1950s, investigators . . . they elicited a series of forms that required the target endings. For example, a picture was shown of a bird, and . . . and the investigator identified it by saying, "This is a Wug." Then the children were shown two similar birds, to, uh, . . . to elicit the sentence, "There are two____." And if the children completed the sentence by saying "Wugs," well, then it was inferred that they had learned the *–s* ending. Okay. Essential to that study was the use of nonsense words like "Wug," since the manipulation of the endings could have been supported by words that the children had . . . had already heard. In any case, charts were developed to demonstrate the, uh, the gradual natural of grammatical acquisition. And the performance by children from eighteen months to four years confirmed the basic theory of child language that the, uh, . . . the gradual reduction of grammatical errors . . . that these are evidence of language acquisition.

Example Notes—Concept and Example

Word endings—grammatical relationships

- *-ed* past
- *-s* plural

Wug experiment—Berko

- Nonsense words—not influenced by familiar
- Manipulated endings
- Data about development

Problem 28, Example Question, CD 4, Track 10 continued

Describe the Wug experiment and explain why the results supported the basic theory of child language acquisition.

Problem 28, Example Answer, CD 4, Track 10 continued

In English, there are several important word endings that express grammatical relationships, for example, the *-ed* ending signals that the speaker's talking about the past and the *-s* ending means "more than one," uh, when it's used at the end of a noun. So, when children learn English, they, um, they make errors in these endings, but they gradually refine their use until they master them. In the Wug experiment, Berko created nonsense words to get children to use endings . . . so . . . so the researchers could, uh, follow their development. It was important not to use *real* words because the children might have been influenced by a word they'd heard before. So this experiment provided data about the time it takes and the age when endings are learned. It supported the basic theory of child language that, um, sorting out grammatical errors is a feature of the speech of . . . of four-year-olds . . . and a stage in language acquisition.

Checklist 4

✔ The talk relates an example to a concept.
✔ Inaccuracies in the content are minor.
✔ The talk is direct and well-organized.
✔ The sentences are logically connected.
✔ Details and examples support the opinion.
✔ The speaker expresses complete thoughts.
✔ The meaning is easy to comprehend.
✔ A wide range of vocabulary is used.
✔ The speaker paraphrases in his/her own words.
✔ The speaker credits the lecturer with wording.
✔ Errors in grammar are minor.
✔ The talk is within a range of 125–150 words.

PROBLEM 29: PROBLEMS

In this question, you will be asked to listen to a conversation and explain a problem as well as the solutions that are proposed.

After you have listened to the conversation, you will have 20 seconds to prepare and 60 seconds to speak.

Task

- Describe a problem and several recommendations
- Express an opinion about the better solution OR
  Propose an alternative solution

 Problem 29, Conversation, CD 4, Track 11

Student 1:   Did your scholarship check come yet?
Student 2:   Yeah, it came last week. Didn't yours?
Student 1:   No. That's the problem. And everything's due at the same time—tuition, my dorm fee, and let's not forget about books. I need about four hundred dollars just for books.
Student 2:   Well, do you have any money left from last semester, in your checking account, I mean?
Student 1:   Some, but not nearly enough. The check probably won't be here until the end of the month and I won't get paid at work for two more weeks . . . I don't know what I'm going to do.

Student 2:   How about your credit card? Could you use that?

Student 1:   Maybe, but I'm afraid I'll get the credit card bill before I get the scholarship check; then I'll be in worse trouble because of, you know, the interest rate for the credit card on top of everything else.

Student 2:   I see your point. Still, the check might come before the credit card bill. You might have to gamble, unless . . .

Student 1:   I'm listening.

Student 2:   Well, unless you take out a student loan. A short-term loan. They have them set up at the Student Credit Union. Isn't that where you have your checking account?

Student 1:   Umhum.

Student 2:   So you could take out a short-term loan and pay it off on the day that you get your check. It wouldn't cost that much for interest because it would probably be only a few weeks. That's what I'd do.

Example Notes—Problem and Possible Solutions, Opinion, and Reasons

Problem—not enough money

- Scholarship check late
- Books, tuition, dorm due

Solutions

- Use credit card
- Take out student loan

Opinion—support student loan

- Paid same day
- $ not much

Problem 29, Example Question, CD 4, Track 11 continued

Describe the woman's budgeting problem and the two suggestions that the man makes. What do you think the woman should do and why?

Problem 29, Example Answer, CD 4, Track 11 continued

The woman doesn't have enough money for her expenses. Um, she has to pay tuition and her dorm fee is due at the same time. Besides that, she needs to buy books. So the problem is everything has to be paid now, and she won't get her scholarship check until the end of the month, and she won't get her paycheck for two weeks. Um, the man suggests that she use her credit card because she won't have to pay it off until the end of the month, but the problem is . . . the . . . the interest would be substantial if the scholarship check is delayed. The other idea—to take out a student loan—that seems better because the loan could be paid off on the day the check arrives instead of a fixed date, and it wouldn't cost much to get a short-term loan at the Student Credit Union. So . . . I support applying for a student loan.

Checklist 5

✔ The talk summarizes the problem and recommendations.
✔ The speaker's point of view or position is clear.
✔ The talk is direct and well-organized.
✔ The sentences are logically connected.
✔ Details and examples support the opinion.
✔ The speaker expresses complete thoughts.
✔ The meaning is easy to comprehend.
✔ A wide range of vocabulary is used.
✔ Errors in grammar are minor.
✔ The talk is within a range of 125–150 words.

PROBLEM 30: SUMMARIES

In this question, you will be asked to listen to part of an academic lecture and to give a summary of it.

After you have listened to the lecture, you will have 20 seconds to prepare and 60 seconds to speak.

Task

- Comprehend part of an academic lecture
- Summarize the main points

 Problem 30, Lecture, CD 4, Track 12

Two types of irrigation methods that are used worldwide are mentioned in your textbook. Flood irrigation—that's been a method in use since ancient times—and we still use it today where water's cheap. Basically, canals connect a water supply like a river or a reservoir to the fields where ditches are constructed with valves, uh, valves that allow farmers to siphon water from the canal, sending it down through the ditches. So that way the field can be totally flooded, or smaller, narrow ditches along the rows can be filled with water to irrigate the crop. But, this method does have quite a few disadvantages. Like I said, it's contingent upon cheap water because it isn't very efficient and the flooding isn't easy to control, I mean, the rows closer to the canal usually receive much more water, and of course, if the field isn't flat, then the water won't be evenly distributed. Not to mention the cost of building canals and ditches and maintaining the system. So let's consider the alternative—the sprinkler system. In this method of irrigation, it's easier to control the water and more efficient since the water's directed only on the plants. But, in hot climates, some of the water can evaporate in the air. Still, the main problem with sprinklers is the expense for installation and maintenance because there's a very complicated pipe system and that usually involves a lot more repair and even replacement of parts, and of course, we have to factor in the labor costs in feasibility studies for sprinklers.

Example Notes—Main Points

Flood

- Not efficient
- Difficult to control—flat fields
- Initial expense to build canals, ditches
- Requires maintenance

Sprinkler

- Complicated pipe system
- Expensive to install, maintain, repair, replace
- Labor cost

 Problem 30, Example Question, CD 4, Track 12 continued

Using examples from the lecture, describe two general types of irrigation systems. Then explain the disadvantages of each type.

 Problem 30, Example Answer, CD 4, Track 12 continued

Two methods of irrigation were discussed in the lecture. First, flood irrigation. It involves the release of water into canals and drainage ditches that flow into the fields. The disadvantages of the flood method, um, well, it isn't very efficient since more water is used in flooding than the crops actually, uh, need, and also it isn't easy to control. Another problem is the initial expense for the construction of the canals and the connecting ditches as well as . . . as maintenance. And besides that, if the fields aren't flat, the water doesn't—I mean, it isn't distributed evenly. The second method is sprinkler irrigation, which uses less water and provides better control, but there is some evaporation, and the pipe system's complicated and can be expensive to install and maintain. So . . . there's usually a lot more labor cost because the equipment must be repaired and replaced more often that a canal system.

Checklist 6

✔ The talk summarizes a short lecture.
✔ Inaccuracies in the content are minor.
✔ The talk is direct and well-organized.
✔ The sentences are logically connected.
✔ Details and examples support the opinion.
✔ The speaker expresses complete thoughts.
✔ The meaning is easy to comprehend.
✔ A wide range of vocabulary is used.
✔ The speaker paraphrases in his/her own words.
✔ The speaker credits the lecturer with wording.

✔ Errors in grammar are minor.
✔ The talk is within a range of 125–150 words.

SPEAKING STRATEGIES

In addition to the academic skills that you learned in the previous chapter, there are several speaking strategies that will help you succeed on the TOEFL and after the TOEFL.

➤ Anticipate the first question

You will probably be asked to talk about familiar topics at the beginning of the Speaking section. If you think about some of these topics, you will know how to answer when you hear the questions. A few seconds to prepare does not give you enough time to organize your thoughts unless you have the advantage of prior preparation.

You may be asked to choose a favorite person, place, activity, or item to talk about. To prepare for this question, spend a few minutes thinking about your personal favorites.

- Prepare some answers
- Read them aloud

EXAMPLE

My favorite pastime is _____*traveling*_____.

1. My favorite teacher is _____.

2. My favorite city is _____.

3. My favorite class is _____.

4. My favorite book is _____.

5. My favorite movie is _____.

6. My favorite sport is _____.

7. My favorite vacation place is _____.

8. My favorite holiday is _____.

9. My favorite music is _____.

10. My favorite person is _____.

➤ Support your answers

The directions in speaking questions usually ask you to give examples or reasons to support your answers. Develop the habit of adding the word *because* after your opinions, and provide at least two reasons to support your position. You will become a better thinker and a better speaker. For example, "My favorite pastime is traveling *because* I like to meet people and I enjoy learning about different places." "My favorite city is San Diego *because* the climate is beautiful year round and there are many interesting sights in or near the city."

* Use the word *because*
* Give two or three examples or reasons

➤ Understand the task

You must listen to the question to understand how to organize your answer. If you are being asked to state an opinion, you should state your opinion and argue only one side of the issue. If you are being asked to argue both sides of the issue and take a stand, then the task is very different. In that case, you will have to make a case for both sides before you state your opinion.

* Read the question carefully
* Respond to the topic

➤ Pronounce to communicate

Everyone has an accent in English. People from Australia have an Australian accent. People from the United States have an American accent. People from Britain have a British accent. See what I mean? The important point is that your accent is okay as long as the listener can understand you. It is good to try to improve your pronunciation, but communication is more important for the TOEFL and for your academic and professional life.

* Accept your accent
* Improve communication

➤ Sound confident

If you speak in a very low voice, hesitating and apologizing, the listener makes some negative assumptions. This person is not confident. This person probably doesn't know the answer. Try to speak up and sound assertive without being aggressive. It helps to start with a smile on your face.

* Speak up
* Be assertive

➤ Read 135 words per minute

Yes, this is a speaking strategy. To succeed on the Speaking section, you will be asked to read short passages of about 100 words each, and you will have about 45 seconds in which to complete the reading. This reading speed is not impossibly fast, but you will have to avoid re-reading phrases in order to finish within the time limit. When you take the quiz at the end of this section, you will hear a cue to start reading, and a question at the end of 45 seconds. This will help you time yourself. You probably already read 135 words per minute. If not, work on reading faster, using the reading strategies at the beginning of this chapter.

- Time yourself
- Increase speed to 135

➤ Adapt notes

The system for taking notes that you learned in Chapter 3 can be made more effective by adapting it for each question. Use the task and the question to anticipate an outline for your notes. Refer to the example notes for Problems 25–30 on pages 235–244 for models of adapted notes.

- Use a system for taking notes
- Adapt the format for each question

➤ Pace yourself

There is no time for a long introduction. You have one minute or less to make your point. Start immediately with a direct statement. For example, "The lecturer compares bacteria and viruses." Include the most important points. When you practice speaking, using the model tests in this book, you will hear a prompt to start and a beep to end your speech. On the TOEFL, you must stop when the beep sounds. Always time yourself when you are practicing for the Speaking section. If you are not using the audio timing, then set a kitchen timer for the number of seconds that corresponds to the type of test problem that you are practicing—45 or 60—and then begin speaking. When the bell rings, stop speaking. Did you complete your thought or did you have more to say? Learn to pace yourself. Soon you will develop a sense of timing for the questions and you will know how much you can say in a short answer.

- Start with a direct statement
- Make a few major points
- Set a timer

➤ Prepare key phrases

Some key phrases are useful for each of the problems in the Speaking section. Refer to pages 75–76 for additional words and phrases.

Question 1: Experiences

My favorite _____ is _____ because _____ .

Question 2: Preferences

Although some people _____ , I prefer _____ because _____ .

Although there are many good reasons why _____ , I favor _____ because _____ .

Although a good argument can be made for _____ , my preference is _____ because _____ .

Question 3: Reports

The speaker supports _____ because _____ .

The speaker opposes _____ because _____ .

Question 4: Examples

According to the (reading, lecture) _____ .

_____ is an example of _____ .

Question 5: Problems

The problem is that _____ .

According to _____ , one solution is to _____ .

Another possibility is to _____ .

I think that the best solution is to _____ because _____ .

It seems to me that _____ is the best solution because _____ .

Question 6: Summaries

Definition: According to the lecturer, a _____ is _____ .

Description: According to the lecturer, a _____ has (three) characteristics.

Classification: (Two) types of _____ were discussed in the lecture.

Chronology: The lecturer explained the sequence of events for _____ .

Comparison: The lecturer compared _____ with _____ .

Contrast: The lecturer contrasted _____ with _____ .

Cause and Effect: The lecturer explains why _____ .

Problem and Solution: The lecturer presents several solutions for the problem
                             of _____ .

- Study the key phrases
- Practice using them

➤ Use verbal pauses

If you get to a point where you don't know what to say, it is better to use some verbal pauses to think instead of stopping and thinking in silence. Silence on the tape is going to lose points for you. You can say, *Okay, Now, Um, And,* or *Uh.* All of these verbal pauses are very common in the speech of native speakers. Of course, if you use these too often, you will also lose points because they will distract the listener and you won't have enough time to answer the question completely.

- Learn verbal pauses
- Use them when necessary

➤ Correct yourself

How can you correct yourself while you are speaking? First, recognize the difference between mistakes and slips. Most of the time, you *don't know* that you have made a mistake, but you *do know* when you make a slip. Even native speakers make mistakes and slips in grammar. In a very long sentence, we can forget whether the subject was singular or plural, and we can make a mistake. But sometimes we hear our mistake, and we correct slips by backing up and starting over. Some commonly used phrases to correct a previous grammatical slip are *I mean* or *that is.* For example, "The worker bees that take care of the young is called, I mean are called, nurses." These phrases can be used to correct content, too. For example, "Drones are female bees, I mean, male bees." A good rule is to always correct slips in content and correct slips in grammar and word choice if you can do it quickly and move along without interrupting the flow of your speech.

- Correct slips
- Use common phrases

➤ Speak to the criteria for evaluation

There are checklists for each question on the Speaking section. Use these checklists to evaluate your speaking. If you do not know how to use the checklist, get some extra help. For other options to evaluate your speaking, see page 781.

- Keep the checklists in mind
- Take advantage of other options

➤ Stay positive

It is natural to be a little anxious about speaking in a second language, but it is important not to become negative and frightened. Negative thoughts can interfere with your concentration, and you may not hear the questions correctly. Take some deep breaths before each question and say this in your mind: "I am a good speaker. I am ready to speak." If you begin to have negative thoughts during the test, take another deep breath and think "confidence" as you breathe in. Focus on listening to the questions. Focus on taking notes.

- Take deep breaths
- Use positive self-talk

APPLYING THE ACADEMIC SKILLS TO THE TOEFL

➤ Taking notes

Taking notes is an important academic skill for the Speaking section because you will use them to organize your talk and you will refer to them while you are speaking. When you take notes, it will help you to adapt to the type of question presented. Use the example notes in this chapter to help you. Your ability to take notes will support your success on every question in the Speaking section.

➤ Paraphrasing

Many of the answer choices are paraphrases of information from the passage. Your ability to recognize paraphrases will be helpful as you choose your answers.

➤ Summarizing

You will be speaking a minute or less in response to each question. You must be brief, but you must also include all of your major points. In other words, you must summarize. The first two questions in the Speaking section require you to talk about familiar topics. In these questions, you can summarize your experiences. The last two questions require you to summarize the information in a conversation and a lecture. Your ability to summarize will be crucial for you to score well on this section.

➤ Synthesizing

This important skill is tested in two questions on the Speaking section. Question 3 requires you to synthesize the information in a talk and in a short reading. Question 4 requires you to synthesize the information in a reading passage and in a lecture. You will receive points not only for speaking well but also for including accurate content. The ability to integrate reading and listening by synthesizing information will be necessary for you to achieve a high score on the Speaking section.

QUIZ FOR THE SPEAKING SECTION

This is a quiz for the Speaking section of the Next Generation TOEFL (iBT). This section tests your ability to communicate in English in an academic context. During the quiz, you will respond to six speaking questions. You may take notes as you listen. You may use your notes to answer the questions. The reading passages and the questions are printed in the book, but most of the directions will be spoken. Once you begin, do not pause the audio.

 Quiz for the Speaking Section, CD 4, Track 13

QUESTION 1

If you were asked to choose one movie that has influenced your thinking, which one would you choose? Why? What was especially impressive about the movie? Use specific reasons and details to explain your choice.

Preparation Time: 15 seconds
Recording Time: 45 seconds

QUESTION 2

Some people think that teachers should be evaluated by the performance of their students on standardized tests at the end of the term. Other people maintain that teachers should be judged by their own performance in the classroom, and not by the scores that their students achieve on tests. Which approach do you think is better and why? Use specific reasons and examples to support your opinion.

Preparation Time: 15 seconds
Recording Time: 45 seconds

QUESTION 3

Reading Time: 45 seconds

Policy for Tuition
In order to qualify for instate tuition, a student must have lived within this state for a period of not less than one year. Furthermore, the instate address must be the permanent residence of the student. College campus addresses may not be used as permanent residences. The student's driver's license and any vehicles must be registered in the state, and the previous year's state tax form must have been submitted to this state. Voter registration and a high school diploma may also be used as evidence of instate status. Spouses and children of military personnel qualify for instate tuition without residence requirements.

The student expresses his opinion of the policy for instate tuition. Report his opinion and explain the reasons that he gives for having that opinion.

Preparation Time: 30 seconds
Recording Time: 60 seconds

QUESTION 4

Reading Time: 45 seconds

Communication with Primates
Early experiments to teach primates to communicate with their voices failed because of the differences in their vocal organs, not their intellectual capacity. Dramatic progress was observed when researchers began to communicate by using American Sign Language. Some chimpanzees were able to learn several hundred signs that they put together to express a number of relationships similar to the initial language acqusition of children. In addition, success was achieved by using plastic symbols on a magnetic board, each of which represented a word. For example, a small blue triangle represented an apple. Chimpanzees were able to respond correctly to basic sequences and even to form some higher-level concepts by using the representative system.

Explain the importance of the Kanzi experiment in the context of research on primate communication.

Preparation Time: 30 seconds
Recording Time: 60 seconds

QUESTION 5

Describe the woman's problem and the two suggestions that her friend makes about how to handle it. What do you think the woman should do, and why?

Preparation Time: 20 seconds
Recording Time: 60 seconds

QUESTION 6

Using the main points and examples from the lecture, describe the habitable zone, and then explain how the definition has been expanded by modern scientists.

Preparation Time: 20 seconds
Recording Time: 60 seconds

This is the end of the Speaking Quiz. To check your answers, refer to the Progress Chart for the Speaking Quiz, Chapter 7, page 547.

STUDY PLAN

What did you learn from taking the quiz? What will you do differently when you take the model tests in the next chapter? Take a few minutes to think and then write a sentence or two to help you revise your study plan.

EXTRA CREDIT

After you have completed this chapter, you may want to continue a review of speaking. Here are some suggestions.

Listen to good models of speaking in similar situations. Research is clearly on the side of those who advocate listening as a method to improve speaking. This means that one of the best ways to learn to speak well is to listen to good speakers. It is also important to simulate the kind of speaking situation that you will be required to complete. On the TOEFL, you have six questions and six situations. If you ask similar questions to excellent speakers and listen carefully to their responses, you will learn a great deal. That is why this book contains recorded examples of the answers that excellent speakers might provide for the questions in this review chapter and in the Speaking section of each model test. For extra credit and improvement, ask teachers or English-speaking friends to record their answers to the Speaking questions in this book. Don't give them the questions in advance. Use the same presentation and timing that you are using for the model tests. Then listen to their answers.

Practice using the telephone to speak. Call a friend to practice some of the speaking questions by phone. Speak directly into the phone. Ask your friend to confirm that you are speaking at a good volume to be heard clearly and that you sound confident, but not arrogant. If your friend is a native speaker, you can ask some of the Speaking questions and listen to the responses. Some telephones have a recording option. With your friend's permission, you can record the call.

OPTIONS FOR EVALUATION

It is difficult to evaluate your own speaking. If you are taking an English class, ask your teacher to use the checklists in this chapter to evaluate your speaking. You need to know how you are progressing in relationship to the criteria on the checklists because that is how you will be evaluated on the TOEFL iBT.

If you do not have good options to have your speaking evaluated without a fee, there is a fee-based option that will provide professional evaluations. See page 781 for details.

ADVISOR'S OFFICE

When you face a challenge, "fake it until you can make it." This means that you should act as though everything were working out well, even when you have doubts. Put a smile on your face, even if it isn't real, and eventually it will be a real smile. Stand up straight with your head high and walk with purpose. You will start to actually feel more confident. If you are acting like a successful person, it may feel strange at first. But the more you practice your role as a successful person, the more comfortable you will be. Soon, when you reach your goals and you are truly successful, you will have practiced the role, and you will be the person you have been playing.

WRITING

OVERVIEW OF THE WRITING SECTION

The Writing section tests your ability to write essays in English similar to those that you would write in college courses.

During the test, you will write two essays. The integrated essay asks for your response to an academic reading passage and a lecture on the same topic. You may take notes as you read and listen, but notes are not graded. You may use your notes to write the essay. The lecture will be spoken, but the directions and the questions will be written. You will have 20 minutes to plan, write, and revise your response. Typically, a good essay for the integrated topic will require that you write 150–225 words.

The independent essay usually asks for your opinion about a familiar topic. You will have 30 minutes to plan, write, and revise your response. Typically, a good essay for the independent topic will require that you write 300–350 words.

A clock on the screen will show you how much time you have to complete each essay.

REVIEW OF PROBLEMS FOR THE WRITING SECTION

➤ Prompts

A prompt for the Writing section is either a question that refers to both a spoken and written text for the integrated essay or a written question for the independent essay. Problems 31–34 in this review refer to the kind of prompts that are typical on the TOEFL. On the official TOEFL® iBT, you will be asked to respond to one integrated question and one independent question. The scripts for the spoken prompts have been printed for you to study while you listen to them. On the official TOEFL® iBT, you will not see the spoken prompt. You will see the written question and textbook passage.

➤ Problems

The problems in this review represent the types of questions that are most frequently tested on the TOEFL. The task for each problem is explained. Each problem appears as one of the two questions included in the Writing section.

PROBLEM 31: SYNTHESIS OF OPPOSING IDEAS

In this integrated essay question, you will be asked to read a short passage from a textbook and then listen to part of a short lecture about the same topic. The ideas in the textbook and the lecture will not agree. After you read the question, you write an essay that includes information from both the reading and the lecture.

You will have 20 minutes to plan, write, and revise your essay. Typically, a good response will require that you write 150–225 words.

Task

- Read a short passage and take notes
- Listen to a short lecture and take notes
- Answer a question using information from *both* the reading and the lecture

Reading Passage
Time: 3 minutes

> In his classic book *The Interpretation of Dreams*, published in 1900, Sigmund Freud identified wish fulfillment as the origin of many dreams. For example, a student who is concerned about taking an important exam may dream about the exam, or, more likely, some type of symbol for the exam will appear in a dream. Since thoughts must be translated into concrete images, dreams are expressed in pictures rather than in words. Freud advanced the notion of dream symbols, that is, images with deep symbolic meaning. In the case of the exam, it might be expressed as an obstacle or a hurdle in a race. In Freud's view, dreams have much in common with daydreams. There is a wish that is forbidden or repressed in some way, and forces that oppose it. In the case of dreams while sleeping, they offer a compromise, that is, a way for the wish to be expressed safely.
>
> According to Freud, dreams can be viewed as a way to reveal the unconscious. To that end, there are two levels to every dream, including the manifest content, which is obvious and direct, and the latent content, which is symbolic. To return to the example of the student's dream, the manifest content would be the hurdle in the race, but the latent content would be the exam that is in the dreamer's subconscious. Because some wishes and desires are too disturbing or too socially inappropriate to surface from the unconscious to the conscious mind, the symbols that are employed may make the wish difficult to expose. The student may actually want to cheat in order to succeed on the exam, but in a dream, borrowing a friend's book may be a more acceptable way to express that desire. In a sense, the dream serves to protect the mind from a conflict in the unconscious.

Reading Passage Notes
Freud 1900 <u>Interp. Dreams</u>

- wish fulfillment ← d

Ex

- student d exam or symbol
- d = pictures Ø words
- symbols images
- exam = obstacle in race

D = daydreams

- wish repressed
- d safe express
- d reveal unconscious

2 levels = manifest content = obvious, direct/obstacle race
        latent content = symbolic/exam

- wishes disturbing or inapprop
- symbols protect from conflict

Problem 31, Lecture, CD 5, Track 2. Now listen to a lecture on the same topic as the passage you have just read.

As you will recall from the reading in your textbook, Freud's psychodynamic theory is premised on the assumption that dreams arise from a troubled subconscious mind, and so they have deep meaning. But there are other points of view that you should be familiar with. Allan Hobson and Robert McCarley propose a very different theory of dreams. They turn to biochemical research and physiology for answers. Using data from their study of sleep activity in cats, and by the way, they used cats because cats have brain waves and muscle movements during sleep that are very similar to those of humans. In any case, Hobson and McCarley determined that the kind of sleep associated with dreams is controlled from the brain stem and, furthermore, that there are chemicals in the stem that regulate the firing of certain neurons. So they posit that during dream sleep, brain cells that control movement and balance are activated, but the messages do not transfer to the body and, consequently, no movement is initiated. Still, the brain is trying to interpret the messages, so dreams occur.

But how does this explain what we dream about? I mean the content. Well, let's take the example of a common dream. Let's say, you are trying to escape from something. The brain receives a message to run, but the legs don't respond. According to the activation-synthesis theory, the dream that results will probably include something about being chased and running away. In other words, you will play out the physical movement in a dream. But, according to the proponents of the activation-synthesis theory, there isn't any hidden meaning in your dream. Your unfulfilled desires have nothing to do with it. For the neurophysiologists, a dream is just a chemical response to brain cells.

Lecture Notes
Hobsin + MacKarly

- biochemical research + physiology
- sleep activity cats/brain waves, muscle movements = humans
- dreams ←
- chemicals → firing neurons   brain cells → movement
- ∅ transfer body = no movement/interpret message dream

Ex

- escape dream
- brain message – run $\emptyset$ legs → chase + run
- activation synthesis theory
- no hidden meaning or unfulfilled desires
- chem. response to brain cells

Essay Question

Summarize the main points in the lecture, contrasting them with the ideas in the reading passage.

Integrated Essay

In research with cats, Hobsin and MacKarly concluded that dreams are the result of chemicals in the brain that cause neurons to fire. Although the brain is signaling the body to move, the message does not reach the muscles. Instead, it is interpreted in a dream. The example the lecturer cited was a dream in which a person wants to escape. The brain signals the legs to run, but instead, the dreamer sees images of himself being chased. According to the theory, dreams are simply a chemical response to neurological activity.

This new model, called activation synthesis theory, contrasts sharply with the earlier theory that Freud put forward in his classic book *The Interpretation of Dreams*, in which he explained dreaming as symbolic images that reveal repressed desires and unfulfilled wishes. Furthermore, Freud interpreted dreams on two levels. The first, manifest content, was the literal or direct interpretation, whereas the second, latent content, exposed the symbolic nature of the image. For example, a student who is worried about an exam may dream about an obstacle in a race, creating the manifest content of the obstacle on a race track because of the underlying latent content associated with the exam.

For Hobsin and MacKarly, no unfulfilled wishes are relevant in the student's dream. The chemistry of the brain and not the psyche causes the vision of the race track and all other images in dreams.

Checklist for Integrated Essay

✔ The essay answers the topic question.
✔ Inaccuracies in the content are minor.
✔ The essay is direct and well-organized.
✔ The sentences are logically connected.
✔ Details and examples support the main idea.
✔ The writer expresses complete thoughts.
✔ The meaning is easy to comprehend.
✔ A wide range of vocabulary is used.
✔ The writer paraphrases in his/her own words.
✔ The writer credits the author with wording.
✔ Errors in grammar and idioms are minor.
✔ The academic topic essay is within a range of 150–225 words.

Evaluator's Comments

The essay answers the topic question and the content is accurate. The writer credits the researchers and paraphrases ideas. It is a well-organized essay with logically connected sentences. The meaning is clear.

PROBLEM 32: SYNTHESIS OF SUPPORTING IDEAS

In this integrated essay question, you will be asked to read a short passage from a textbook and then listen to part of a short lecture about the same topic. The ideas in the textbook and the lecture will agree. After you read the question, you write an essay that includes information from both the reading and the lecture.

You will have 20 minutes to plan, write, and revise your essay. Typically, a good response will require that you write 150–225 words.

Task

- Read a short passage and take notes
- Listen to a short lecture and take notes
- Answer a question using information from *both* the reading and the lecture

Reading Passage
Time: 3 minutes

According to the nebular hypothesis, between 4 and 5 million years ago, a large cloud of dust and gas collected around the region in which the current solar system is positioned. Although similar clouds of dust and gas referred to as nebulae are relatively common and may be found throughout the galaxy, in this cloud as much as 99 percent of the material consisted of hydrogen and helium, and all other naturally occurring elements were also included in small proportions.

Gravity initiated a collapse in the cloud, which in turn caused it to spin rapidly. This spinning resulted in a disk shape with a rounded middle and flat edges. Random regions exerted a stronger gravitational pull and solid elements began to connect and, ultimately, to break apart into small objects called planetesimals ranging in size from a few feet to a few miles. As these planetesimals collided and captured each other, distinct masses concentrated in areas approximately where the planets are now found.

At the same time that the planets were forming, the Sun began to transform itself into a star. The star, which had retained almost 99 percent of the nebula's original mass, radiated light and heat. The planets nearest the center, which we call the terrestrial planets, were formed from materials that did not disintegrate at higher temperatures, whereas the planets farther away, called the Jovian planets, contained virtually the same mix of helium, hydrogen, and trace elements as the original nebula and were able to condense at much lower temperatures. Asteroids and comets were also swirling around the system, including matter that was not collected by collision with a planet or the gravitational pull of a planet. The fact that the orbits of all the planets lie near the same plane is further evidence of the solar system's rapid rotation when the nebular cloud began to flatten out.

Reading Passage Notes
Nebular Hypothesis

- 4–5 m yrs ago
- cloud dust + gas → solar system
- 99% hydrogen + helium w/all elements
- gravity collapse → spin/disk rounded mid + flat edges
- random regions = strong gravity → connect + break apart planetisimals
- planetisimals collided + captured → planets
- Sun 99% nebula's mass → light + heat
- planets near = terrestrial/not disintegrate higher temp
          far = Jovian/same mix hydrogen + helium etc as cloud/condense lower temp
- asteroids + comets swirl
- orbits near same plane = evidence rapid rotation

Problem 32, Lecture, CD 5, Track 3. Now listen to a lecture on the same topic as the passage you have just read.

Newer high-speed computers have allowed us to perform experiments by modeling events that would be very difficult to duplicate under natural conditions. And we have been able to do some interesting research with models of the collapse of an interstellar cloud under the influence of its own gravitational pull. The modeling has led to a general consensus that stars form in that way—a process of collapse, I mean. So, although the experiments are not definitive, they lead us to the logical conclusion that when a star is born, it will probably have a circumstellar nebula with conditions that are very favorable to the formation of planets. In effect, we have been able to watch the conditions that existed at the beginning of the formation of the solar system, and observe how the planets were formed. And that's pretty amazing. Furthermore, the modeling suggests that the planetary formation seems to be a natural consequence of the process that initiates the formation of a star. So, this suggests that planetary systems are the rule, rather than the exception. And that means that an organized search for other planetary systems should yield some rather interesting results. We may find that the nebular hypothesis is valid not only for our solar system but also for other systems in the universe. Besides that, when we do the math, we have to assume that at least some of the stars would produce solar systems with planets that could support life.

Lecture Notes
Computer model

- research collapse interstellar cloud influence gravity
- stars form = process collapse
- star born probably nebula = conditions form planets
- natural result process initiates formation star
- planetary systems rule, not exception
- N H other systems universe
- math → some stars → solar systems → support life

Essay Question

Summarize the nebular hypothesis that is described in the reading and then explain how the lecture supports the hypothesis.

Integrated Essay

The nebular hypothesis posits that between four and five million years ago a cloud of dust and gas containing all of the elements in the solar system collapsed under the force of gravity, an event which caused the cloud to spin and flatten into a disk. Then, a stronger gravitational pull caused bodies to merge and pull apart, forming planetesimals that eventually shaped the planets that exist today. The planets near the Sun, which we call the terrestrial planets, tolerated higher temperatures, but the planets farther away had a composition more similar to the original cloud and condensed when exposed to the lower temperature. The fact that the planets orbit close to the same plane is evidence for the hypothesis. Furthermore, new technologies have allowed us to test the hypothesis with a computer model, which replicates the original conditions. According to scientists, the formation of planets is a natural result of the process that occurs in the formation of a star. Moreover, the nebular hypothesis suggests that there are other solar systems in the universe, some of which could support life.

Checklist for Integrated Essay

✔ The essay answers the topic question.
✔ Inaccuracies in the content are minor.
✔ The essay is direct and well-organized.
✔ The sentences are logically connected.
✔ Details and examples support the main idea.
✔ The writer expresses complete thoughts.
✔ The meaning is easy to comprehend.
✔ A wide range of vocabulary is used.
✔ The writer paraphrases in his/her own words.
✔ The writer credits the author with wording.
✔ Errors in grammar and idioms are minor.
✔ The essay is within a range of 150–225 words.

Evaluator's Comments

The writer has responded to both parts of the question, using transition words to connect the sentences logically. The content is accurate and easy to understand. Excellent vocabulary selection and variety of grammatical structures support the well-paraphrased essay.

PROBLEM 33: OPINION

In this independent essay question, you will be asked to write an essay about a familiar topic. This may be a place, a person, a possession, a situation, or an occasion. After you read the question, you will state your opinion and then explain why you have that opinion.

You will have 30 minutes to plan, write, and revise your essay. Typically, a good response will require that you write a minimum of 300 words.

Task

- State your opinion
- Explain the reasons for your opinion

Question

Some students apply for admission only to their first-choice school, while others apply to several schools. Which plan do you agree with, and why? Be sure to include details and examples to support your opinion.

Example Notes

Several schools

- application Ø guarantee admission
  competitive standards
  no space
  w/o school 1 semester
  $ but saves time
- learn about options
  communications
  discover advantages
  assistantships
  negative experience
- I plan 3 schools
  1 choice happy
  options open

Independent Essay

Although I understand students who desire to concentrate all of their energy on applications to their first-choice schools, I support making application to several different schools. There are two reasons why I feel this is important. First, application does not guarantee admission, even for a very highly qualified applicant. The school that a student prefers may have very competitive standards for acceptance. In spite excellent academic credentials, high scores on admissions tests such as the SAT and the TOEFL, and exceptional supporting documents, some qualified applicants may be turned away because not enough space to accommodate them. If students apply to their first-choice schools, and they are not accepted for reasons that could not be anticipated, they may find themselves in the position of being without a school for at least a semester while they scramble to apply to the schools they had considered as second or third choices. It is expensive to apply to a large number of schools because of the application fees, but making application to three schools can save time, which is also a valuable commodity.

Another reason to apply to several schools is the opportunity to learn more about each the educational options during the application process. While materials are being submitted and communication is occurring between the student and the school officials, advantages at the second- or third-choice school may be discovered as a result of the information exchanged. Scholarships, grants, and other opportunities may be extended when the committee is reviewing the application at one of the schools. For example, an unpublicized research assistantship may be available because of the prior work experience that an applicant has included on the application form. Conversely, the experience that the student has in applying to the first-choice school may be so negative that another school will be more attractive than the first-choice institution.

When I am ready to study at a university, I plan to apply to three schools—two with very competitive standards, and one with moderate standards. If I am admitted at my first-choice school, I will be happy, but I will leave my options open during the application process just in case I discover some advantages at one of the other schools.

Checklist for Independent Essay

✔ The essay answers the topic question.
✔ The point of view or position is clear.
✔ The essay is direct and well-organized.
✔ The sentences are logically connected.
✔ Details and examples support the main idea.
✔ The writer expresses complete thoughts.
✔ The meaning is easy to comprehend.
✔ A wide range of vocabulary is used.
✔ Various types of sentences are included.
✔ Errors in grammar and idioms are minor.
✔ The essay is within a range of 300–350 words.

Evaluator's Comments

The writing sample is well-organized. It addresses the question and does not digress from the topic. There is a logical progression of ideas, and the writer uses good transitions. Opinions are supported by examples. The writer demonstrates excellent language proficiency, as evidenced by a variety of grammatical structures and acceptable vocabulary. The reader can understand this opinion without re-reading. There are only a few grammatical errors that appear to have occurred because of time constraints. They have been corrected below:

Line 5	in spite of
Line 7	because there is not enough space
Line 14	each of the educational options

PROBLEM 34: ARGUMENT

In this independent essay question, you will be asked to argue both sides of an issue and then take a stand for one side.

You will have 30 minutes to plan, write, and revise your essay. Typically, a good response will require that you write a minimum of 300 words.

Task

- Argue one side—advantages and disadvantages
- Argue the other side—advantages and disadvantages
- Take a stand for one of the arguments
- Explain the reasons for your preference

Question
Some students like to take distance-learning courses by computer. Other students prefer to study in traditional classroom settings with a teacher. Consider the advantages of both options, and make an argument for the way that students should organize their schedules.

Example Notes
Advantages distance

- attend class at your convenience
- complete assignments at own pace
- repeat lectures

Advantages traditional

- structured environment
- more personal relationship
- immediate response to questions
- study groups + friendships

Independent Essay
Both distance-learning courses and traditional classes provide important but different experiences for college students. On the one hand, there are many advantages to distance-learning courses. One of the most important benefits is the opportunity to attend class on your convenience. This is very important for students who hold full-time jobs since they can choose to take their classes on a schedule that allows them to continue working. Another advantage is the chance to complete assignments at your own pace. For students who can work more quick than their classmates, it is possible to earn more credits during the semester. A huge advantage to international students is the option of listen to lectures more than once.

On the other hand, there are advantages to attending a traditional class. The structured environment is beneficial, especially for students who are not as highly motivating. In addition, it is more likely that you will develop a personal relationship with the teacher, an advantage not only for the course but also after the course when you need a recommendation. By seeing you and talking with you face-to-face, the teacher will remember you better. It is also easier to get an immediate response to questions because you only have to raise your hand instead sending e-mail and waiting for an answer. Last, the opportunity for study groups and friendships is different and more personal when you sit in the same room.

Given all the advantages of both types of courses, I think that students would be wise to register for distance-learning courses and traditional classroom courses during their college experiences. By participating in distance-learning courses, they can work independently in classes that may be more difficult for them, repeating the lectures on computer at convenient times. By attending traditional classes, they can get to know the teachers personally and will have good references when they need them. They will also make friends in the class. By sharing information with other students, they can organize their schedules for the following semester, chosing the best classes and including both distance-learning and traditional courses.

Checklist for Independent Essay

✔ The essay answers the topic question.
✔ The point of view or position is clear.
✔ The essay is direct and well-organized.
✔ The sentences are logically connected.
✔ Details and examples support the main idea.
✔ The writer expresses complete thoughts.
✔ The meaning is easy to comprehend.
✔ A wide range of vocabulary is used.
✔ Various types of sentences are included.
✔ Errors in grammar and idioms are minor.
✔ The general topic essay is within a range of 300–350 words.

Evaluator's Comments

The writing sample is well-organized with a good topic sentence and good support statements. It addresses both sides of the question and does not digress from the topic. There is a logical progression of ideas and excellent language proficiency, as evidenced by a variety of grammatical structures and appropriate vocabulary. Transition words and phrases support the reader's comprehension of the arguments without re-reading. There are only a few grammatical errors that have been corrected below:

Line 3	at your convenience
Line 6	more quickly
Line 8	the option of listening
Line 10	motivated
Line 14	instead of
Line 24	choosing

WRITING STRATEGIES

In addition to the academic skills that you learned in the previous chapter, there are several writing strategies that will help you succeed on the TOEFL and after the TOEFL. Some of the strategies are more appropriate for the integrated essay and others are more useful for the independent essay.

Integrated Essay

The integrated question asks for a synthesis of the content in a lecture and a reading passage. It is usually the first essay question.

➤ Report

When you are writing about content, it is important not to offer your opinions. To do this, you must distinguish between content and opinion. Content may include both facts and the ideas of the author or lecturer. Opinion is what *you* think. Your job in an integrated essay is to report the facts and ideas without making judgments and without expressing your opinions.

- State the facts and ideas
- Avoid expressing your opinions

➤ Identify sources

In the question for the integrated essay, you will be directed to the primary source. For example, the question may ask you to summarize content *from the reading* or to summarize the main points *in the lecture*. This is a cue to begin with a summary from the primary source identified in the question—either the reading or the lecture. Then, you will be asked to support or contrast the information in the primary source with the information in the secondary source. Go to the other source after you have completed your summary. Be sure to include information from both sources, but begin with the primary source.

- Begin with the primary source
- Include both sources

➤ Make connections

Supporting Transitions	Opposing Transitions
When the secondary source agrees with the primary source, use supporting transitions.	When the secondary source does not agree with the primary source, use opposing transitions.
Moreover,	In contrast,
Furthermore,	On the other hand,
In addition,	

- Establish the relationship between sources
- Choose appropriate transitions

➤ Include a variety of structures

Essays with a variety of sentence structures are more interesting, and they receive higher scores. Complex sentence structures, achieved by combining simple sentences, also improve scores. Refer to pages 115–119 to review sentence combining.

- Vary sentence structures
- Combine sentences

➤ Edit your writing

If you use all of your time to write, you won't have enough time to edit your writing. Students who take the time to read what they have written will find some of their own mistakes and can correct them before submitting the final essays. Be sure to edit both the independent essay and the integrated essay. To edit most effectively, use the grading checklist that raters will use to evaluate your writing.

- Re-read your essay
- Edit with the checklist

Independent Essay

The independent question on the TOEFL asks for your opinion. It is usually the second essay question.

➤ Respond to the topic

It is very important to read the question carefully and analyze the topic. If you write on a topic other than the one that you have been assigned, your essay will not be scored.

- Analyze the topic
- Write on the assigned topic

➤ Be direct

When you are asked for your *opinion*, it is appropriate to begin with a direct statement. The following phrases and clauses introduce an opinion:

Introduction	Opinion
Introductory phrase, In my opinion, In my view, From my point of view, From my perspective,	**Direct statement = Subject + Verb** school uniforms are a good idea.
Introductory Clause I agree that I disagree that I think that I believe that I support the idea that I am convinced that It is clear to me that	**Direct statement = Subject + Verb** school uniforms are a good idea.

- Begin with an introductory phrase or clause
- Make a direct statement of opinion

➤ Concede the opposing view

Sometimes you will be offered two choices. When stating a *preference*, it is polite to concede that the opposing view has merit. The following words and phrases express concession: *although, even though, despite,* and *in spite of.* For example:

Concession	Opinion
Concession clause	**Direct statement = Subject + Verb**
Although there are many advantages to living in the city,	I prefer life in a small town.
Even though technology can damage the environment,	I think it causes more good than harm.
Despite the differences among cultures,	I believe that peace is possible.
In spite of the benefits of studying in a group,	I prefer to study alone.

- Begin with a concession clause
- Make a direct statement of opinion

➤ Use an outline sentence

Some books call the second sentence in an essay the *topic sentence,* the *controlling sentence,* the *thesis statement,* or the *organizing sentence.* The purpose of this sentence is to outline the essay for the reader. Here are some examples of outline sentences.

First sentence:
Although there are many advantages to living in the city, I prefer life in a small town.
Outline sentence:
Three personal experiences convince me that small towns provide a better life style.

First sentence:
Despite the differences among cultures, I believe that peace is possible.
Outline sentence:
History provides several encouraging examples.

First sentence:
In spite of the benefits of studying in a group, I prefer to study alone.
Outline sentence:
There are three reasons why I have this preference.

- Outline the essay for the reader
- Write an outline sentence

➤ Think in English

How do English-speaking writers think? According to research by Robert Kaplan, they organize their thoughts in a linear pattern. This means that they think in a straight line. Details and examples must relate to the main points. Digressions are not included.

For essays that require an opinion, the organization would look like this:

Opinion	In my view, school uniforms are a good idea.
↓	
Outline Sentence	Three reasons convince me that wearing uniforms will improve the educational experience of students.
↓	
Reason 1	In the first place, uniforms are not as expensive as brand name clothing.
↓	
Example/Detail	For example, a new school uniform costs about $30, but designer jeans and a name-brand shirt cost five times that amount. An expensive book would be a better investment.
Reason 2	Second, it is easier to get ready for school.
↓	
Example/Detail	When there are five choices, it requires time and thought to decide what to wear. Uniforms simplify the problem of choosing a shirt to complement a certain pair of pants and, furthermore, selecting socks and shoes to go with them. All of these decisions take time and divert attention from preparing for classes.
Reason 3	Finally, students who wear uniforms identify themselves with their school.
↓	
Example/Detail	Wearing the school colors establishes that each student is part of the group.
Conclusion	In conclusion, I think schools that require uniforms send a positive message to their students. They communicate that it is more important to be the best student than it is to have the best clothing.

- Think in a straight line
- Connect each idea with the next

➤ Write a strong conclusion

In TOEFL essays, it is not appropriate to apologize for not having written enough, for not having enough time, or for not using good English skills. An apology will cause you to lose points. In addition, a good conclusion does not add new information. It does not introduce a new idea. A strong conclusion is more like a summary of the ideas in one last sentence.

- Summarize the main idea
- Avoid apologies and new topics

APPLYING THE ACADEMIC SKILLS TO THE TOEFL

➤ Taking Notes

Taking notes is an important academic skill for the Writing section because you will use them to organize your essay. Because you will not be graded on the notes, you should not worry about making them perfect. It is more important for them to be useful to you.

➤ Paraphrasing

In the integrated essay, you must be careful not to use the exact words from the reading or the lecture. Plagiarizing will result in a failing score on the essay. You must use the skills that you learned to paraphrase in your essay.

➤ Summarizing

As you will remember, summarizing is one of the steps in synthesizing. You will often be asked to summarize the primary source before you relate it to the secondary source.

➤ Synthesizing

Part 1 of the Writing section is the integrated essay. It is a synthesis of information from a reading passage and a lecture. Synthesizing is the most important academic skill for the integrated essay.

QUIZ FOR THE WRITING SECTION

This is a quiz for the Writing section of the Next Generation TOEFL (iBT). This section tests your ability to write essays in English. During the quiz, you will respond to two writing questions. You may take notes as you read and listen to academic information. You may use your notes to write the essays. Once you begin, you have 20 minutes to write the first essay and 30 minutes to write the second essay.

QUESTION 1

Reading Passage
Time: 3 minutes

A win-win negotiation is concluded when both parties gain something of value in exchange for making concessions. Although the balance of power may change during the negotiation process, negotiators on both sides must remain open to options that will ultimately allow for a fair exchange. To achieve a resolution that benefits both parties, everyone involved must be willing to listen carefully to each other's concerns. To arrive at a conclusion that is good for everyone, negotiators must reveal what they value and what they don't value. Good negotiators look for something that their side does not value but to which the other side assigns a high value. By offering it, they lose nothing, but the other side gains something, thereby feeling more disposed to concede something that the other side perceives as valuable. In addition to listening for ways to help the other side, everyone has to be aware of the limitations that both sides may bring to the table. There are some options that cannot be explored because they are not possible for one of the parties. For example, a price that does not allow a profit margin for the company that manufactures it is not a point of negotiation, unless the other side can offer a way to increase profits or productivity. If that isn't possible, then perhaps a service that saves the buyer money might be a way to balance the firm pricing structure of the goods.

A win-win negotiation allows both parties to feel that they made a good deal, but another positive outcome is the way that the people involved feel about each other. In traditional bargaining, people on opposite sides of a negotiation tend to view each other as adversaries, a relationship that is often difficult to change after the negotiation has ended and the collaboration is supposed to begin. In a win-win setting, the parties approach the negotiation as colleagues who want to support each other's success. When the deal has been made and the collaboration begins, the people involved are already committed to working together for their mutual benefit.

 Question 1, Lecture, CD 5, Track 4. Now listen to a lecture on the same topic as the passage you have just read.

Question
Summarize the points made in the reading passage, and then explain how the case study from the lecture supports the reading.

Writing Time: 20 minutes
Typical Response: 150–225 words

Question 2
Some people like to communicate by e-mail and voice mail. Other people like to communicate by telephone or face-to-face. Which type of communication do you prefer, and why? Be sure to include details and examples to support your opinion.

Writing Time: 30 minutes
Typical Response: 300–350 words

 This is the end of the Writing Quiz. To check your answers, refer to the Progress Chart for the Writing Quiz, Chapter 7, page 550.

STUDY PLAN

What did you learn from taking the quiz? What will you do differently when you take the model tests in the next chapter? Take a few minutes to think and then write a sentence or two to help you revise your study plan.

EXTRA CREDIT

After you have completed this chapter, you may want to continue a review of writing. Here are some suggestions.

Become familiar with the independent writing topics. Topics previously used for independent questions on the CBT TOEFL Writing section are listed in the TOEFL *Information Bulletin* available free from Educational Testing Service. They are also listed on the web site at *www.ets.org.* Read through the questions, and think about how you would respond to each of the topics. Since most of them require you to state an opinion, it is helpful to form a general opinion on each topic.

Read good examples of expository writing. Research confirms that reading is important to the development of writing. This means that one of the best ways to learn to write well is to read good models of writing. By being exposed to good writing, you will acquire good techniques. That is why this book contains examples of the answers that excellent writers might create in response to the questions in this review chapter and in the Writing section of each model test. It is important to read these example answers carefully. Remember that you will be asked to produce expository, not literary essays. For this reason, you should read opinion essays instead of short stories. It is also a good idea to read summaries of content material. Many popular college textbooks in English provide summaries at the end of the chapters. In general, these summaries are good models for you to read.

OPTIONS FOR EVALUATION

It is difficult to evaluate your own writing. If you are taking an English class, ask your teacher to use the checklists in this chapter to evaluate your writing. You need to know how you are progressing in relationship to the criteria on the checklists because that is how you will be evaluated on the TOEFL.

If you do not have good options to have your writing evaluated without a fee, there are fee-based options that will provide professional evaluations. See page 781 for details.

ADVISOR'S OFFICE

Keep your eyes on the destination, not on the road. There are short roads and long roads to the same destination, but the important point is to arrive where you want to be. Of course, there are several reasons why you prefer to achieve a successful score on the TOEFL the first time that you attempt it. It is costly to take the test again, and you are eager to begin your academic studies or professional life. Nevertheless, a goal is seldom destroyed by a delay, so don't destroy your positive attitude, either. If you take the time to prepare, you will probably be able to take the short road, but if you have not studied English very long, you may need more practice. Please don't compare yourself to anyone else. They are on their road, and you are on yours. Just keep going. You will get there.

6

MORE MODEL TESTS

MODEL TEST 3: PROGRESS TEST

READING SECTION

The Reading section tests your ability to understand reading passages like those in college textbooks. The passages are about 700 words in length.

This is the short format for the Reading section. On the short format, you will respond to three passages. After each passage, you will answer 12–14 questions about it.

Most questions are worth 1 point, but the last question in each passage is worth more than 1 point.

You will have 60 minutes to read all of the passages and answer the questions. You may take notes while you read, but notes are not graded. You may use your notes to answer the questions. Some passages may include a word or phrase that is underlined in blue. Click on the word or phrase to see a glossary definition or explanation.

Choose the best answer for multiple-choice questions. Follow the directions on the page or on the screen for computer-assisted questions. Click on **Next** to go to the next question. Click on **Back** to return to the previous question. You may return to previous questions for all of the passages in the same reading part, but after you go to the next part, you will not be able to return to passages in a previous part. Be sure that you have answered all of the questions for the passages in each part before you click on **Next** at the end of the passage to move to the next part.

You can click on **Review** to see a chart of the questions you have answered and the questions you have not answered in each part. From this screen, you can return to the question you want to answer in the part that is open.

A clock on the screen will show you how much time to have to complete the Reading section.

PART I

Reading 1 "Symbiotic Relationships"

Symbiosis is a close, long-lasting physical relationship between two different species. In other words, the two species are usually in physical contact and at least one of them derives some sort of benefit from this contact. There are three different categories of symbiotic relationships: parasitism, commensalism, and mutualism.

Parasitism is a relationship in which one organism, known as the parasite, lives in or on another organism, known as the host, from which it derives nourishment. Generally, the parasite is much smaller than the host. Although the host is harmed by the interaction, it is generally not killed immediately by the parasite, and some host individuals may live a long time and be relatively little affected by their parasites. Some parasites are much more destructive than others, however. Newly established parasite/host relationships are likely to be more destructive than those that have a long evolutionary history. With a long-standing interaction between the parasite and the host, the two species generally evolve in such a way that they can accommodate one another. It is not in the parasite's best interest to kill its host. If it does, it must find another. Likewise, the host evolves defenses against the parasite, often reducing the harm done by the parasite to a level the host can tolerate.

→ Parasites that live on the surface of their hosts are known as **ectoparasites**. Fleas, lice, and some molds and mildews are examples of ectoparasites. Ⓐ Many other parasites, like tapeworms, malaria parasites, many kinds of bacteria, and some fungi, are called **endoparasites** because they live inside the bodies of their hosts. Ⓑ A tapeworm lives in the intestines of its host where it is able to resist being digested and makes use of the nutrients in the intestine. Ⓒ

Even plants can be parasites. Mistletoe is a flowering plant that is parasitic on trees. It establishes itself on the surface of a tree when a bird transfers the seed to the tree. It then grows down into the water-conducting tissues of the tree and uses the water and minerals it obtains from these tissues to support its own growth. Ⓓ

If the relationship between organisms is one in which one organism benefits while the other is not affected, it is called **commensalism**. It is possible to visualize a parasitic relationship evolving into a commensal one. Since parasites generally evolve to do as little harm to their host as possible and the host is combating the negative effects of the parasite, they might eventually evolve to the point where the host is not harmed at all. There are many examples of commensal relationships. Orchids often use trees as a surface upon which to grow. The tree is not harmed or helped, but the orchid needs a surface upon which to establish itself and also benefits by being close to the top of the tree, where it can get more sunlight and rain. Some mosses, ferns, and many vines also make use of the surfaces of trees in this way.

In the ocean, many sharks have a smaller fish known as a remora attached to them. Remoras have a <u>sucker</u> on the top of their heads that they can use to attach to the shark. In this way, they can hitchhike a ride as the shark swims along. When the shark feeds, the remora frees itself and obtains small bits of food that the shark misses. Then, the remora reattaches. The shark does not appear to be positively or negatively affected by remoras.

→ **Mutualism** is another kind of symbiotic relationship and is actually benefi-cial to both species involved. In many mutualistic relationships, the relationship is obligatory; the species cannot live without each other. In others, the species can exist separately but are more successful when they are involved in a mutu-alistic relationship. Some species of Acacia, a thorny tree, provide food in the form of sugar solutions in little structures on their stems. Certain species of ants feed on the solutions and live in the tree, which they will protect from other ani-mals by attacking any animal that begins to feed on the tree. Both organisms benefit; the ants receive food and a place to live, and the tree is protected from animals that would use it as food.

→ One soil nutrient that is usually a limiting factor for plant growth is nitrogen. Many kinds of plants, such as beans, clover, and alder trees, have bacteria that live in their roots in little <u>nodules</u>. The roots form these nodules when they are infected with certain kinds of bacteria. The bacteria do not cause disease but provide the plants with nitrogen-containing molecules that the plants can use for growth. The nitrogen-fixing bacteria from the living site and nutrients that the plants provide, and the plants benefit from the nitrogen they receive.

Glossary
sucker: an adaptation for sucking nourishment or sticking to a surface
nodules: growths in the form of knots

1. The word <u>derives</u> in the passage is closest in meaning to

   Ⓐ requests
   Ⓑ pursues
   Ⓒ obtains
   Ⓓ rejects

2. The word <u>it</u> in the passage refers to

   Ⓐ host
   Ⓑ organism
   Ⓒ parasite
   Ⓓ relationship

3. The word <u>relatively</u> in the passage is closest in meaning to

    Ⓐ comparatively
    Ⓑ routinely
    Ⓒ adversely
    Ⓓ frequently

4. Which of the sentences below best expresses the information in the highlighted statement in the passage? The other choices change the meaning or leave out important information.

    Ⓐ A parasite is less likely to destroy the host when it attaches itself at first.
    Ⓑ Parasites that have lived on a host for a long time have probably done a lot of damage.
    Ⓒ The most destructive phase for a host is when the parasite first invades it.
    Ⓓ The relationship between a parasite and a host will evolve over time.

5. The word <u>tolerate</u> in the passage is closest in meaning to

    Ⓐ permit
    Ⓑ oppose
    Ⓒ profit
    Ⓓ avoid

6. According to paragraph 3, how do ectoparasites survive?

    Ⓐ They live in mold and mildew on their hosts.
    Ⓑ They digest food in the intestines of their hosts.
    Ⓒ They live on the nutrients in their bacterial hosts.
    Ⓓ They inhabit the outside parts of their hosts.

    Paragraph 3 is marked with an arrow [➔].

7. Which of the following is mentioned as an example of a commensal relationship?

    Ⓐ Orchids
    Ⓑ Mistletoe
    Ⓒ Ants
    Ⓓ Fungus

8. The word <u>actually</u> in the passage is closest in meaning to

    Ⓐ frequently
    Ⓑ initially
    Ⓒ really
    Ⓓ usually

9. In paragraph 7, why does the author use the example of the *Acacia* tree?

   Ⓐ To demonstrate how ants survive by living in trees
   Ⓑ To explain how two species can benefit from contact
   Ⓒ To show the relationship between plants and animals
   Ⓓ To present a problem that occurs often in nature

   Paragraph 7 is marked with an arrow [→].

10. According to paragraph 8, how does bacteria affect beans and clover?

   Ⓐ It causes many of the plants to die.
   Ⓑ It limits the growth of young plants.
   Ⓒ It supplies nitrogen to the crops.
   Ⓓ It infects the roots with harmful nodules.

   Paragraph 8 is marked with an arrow [→].

11. Look at the four squares [■] that show where the following sentence could be inserted in the passage.

   They live on the feathers of birds or the fur of animals.

   Where could the sentence best be added?

   Click on a square [■] to insert the sentence in the passage.

12. In which of the following chapters would this passage most probably appear?

   Ⓐ Environment and Organisms
   Ⓑ Pollution and Policies
   Ⓒ Human Influences on Ecosystems
   Ⓓ Energy Resources

13. **Directions:** Complete the table by matching the phrases on the left with the headings on the right. Select the appropriate answer choices and drag them to the type of relationship to which they refer. TWO of the answer choices will NOT be used. **This question is worth 4 points.**

To delete an answer choice, click on it. To see the passage, click on **View Text**.

Answer Choices

A One species benefits and the other is not harmed.

B Both species benefit from their contact.

C Both species harm each other in the relationship.

D One species is harmed while the other species benefits.

E Often one of the species is destroyed by the relationship.

F During evolution, this relationship may become symbiotic.

G Both species may require their relationship for survival.

H In this relationship, the host may evolve defenses to avoid harm.

I Both species are more successful when they form this relationship.

Parasitic

•

•

•

Commensal

•

•

•

Mutualistic

•

PART II

Reading 2 "Civilization"

Between 4000 and 3000 B.C., significant technological developments began to transform the Neolithic towns. The invention of writing enabled records to be kept, and the use of metals marked a new level of human control over the environment and its resources. Already before 4000 B.C., craftspeople had discovered that metal-bearing rocks could be heated to liquefy metals, which could then be cast in molds to produce tools and weapons that were more useful than stone instruments. Although copper was the first metal to be utilized in producing tools, after 4000 B.C. craftspeople in western Asia discovered that a combination of copper and tin produced bronze, a much harder and more durable metal than copper. Its widespread use has led historians to speak of a Bronze Age from around 3000 to 1200 B.C., when bronze was increasingly replaced by iron.

→ At first, Neolithic settlements were hardly more than villages. But as their inhabitants mastered the art of farming, they gradually began to give birth to more complex human societies. As wealth increased, such societies began to develop armies and to build walled cities. By the beginning of the Bronze Age, the concentration of larger numbers of people in the river valleys of Mesopotamia and Egypt was leading to a whole new pattern for human life.

→ As we have seen, early human beings formed small groups that developed a simple culture that enabled them to survive. As human societies grew and developed greater complexity, a new form of human existence—called civilization—came into being. A civilization is a complex culture in which large numbers of human beings share a number of common elements. Historians have identified a number of basic characteristics of civilization, most of which are evident in the Mesopotamian and Egyptian civilizations. These include (1) an urban revolution; cities became the focal points for political, economic, social, cultural, and religious development; (2) a distinct religious structure; the gods were deemed crucial to the community's success, and professional priestly classes, as stewards of the gods' property, regulated relations with the gods; (3) new political and military structures; an organized government bureaucracy arose to meet the administrative demands of the growing population while armies were organized to gain land and power; (4) a new social structure based on economic power; while kings and an upper class of priests, political leaders, and warriors dominated, there also existed large groups of free people (farmers, artisans, craftspeople) and at the very bottom, socially, a class of slaves; (5) the development of writing; kings, priests, merchants, and artisans used writing to keep records; and (6) new forms of significant artistic and intellectual activity, such as monumental architectural structures, usually religious, occupied a prominent place in urban environments.

→ Why early civilizations developed remains difficult to explain. Ⓐ Since civilizations developed independently in India, China, Mesopotamia, and Egypt, can general causes be identified that would explain why all of these civilizations emerged? Ⓑ A number of possible explanations of the beginning of civilization have been suggested. A theory of challenge and response maintains that challenges forced human beings to make efforts that resulted in the rise of civilization. Some scholars have adhered to a material explanation. Ⓒ Material forces, such as the growth of food surpluses, made possible the specialization of labor and development of large communities with bureaucratic organization. Ⓓ But the area of the Fertile Crescent, in which Mesopotamian civilization emerged, was not naturally conducive to agriculture. Abundant food could only be produced with a massive human effort to carefully manage the water, an effort that created the need for organization and bureaucratic control and led to civilized cities. Some historians have argued that nonmaterial forces, primarily religious, provided the sense of unity and purpose that made such organized activities possible. Finally, some scholars doubt that we are capable of ever discovering the actual causes of early civilization.

14. Which of the following is the best definition of a civilization?

    Ⓐ Neolithic towns and cities
    Ⓑ Types of complex cultures
    Ⓒ An agricultural community
    Ⓓ Large population centers

15. The word <u>its</u> in the passage refers to

    Ⓐ copper
    Ⓑ bronze
    Ⓒ metal
    Ⓓ iron

16. According to paragraph 2, what happens as societies become more prosperous?

    Ⓐ More goods are produced.
    Ⓑ Walled cities are built.
    Ⓒ Laws are instituted.
    Ⓓ The size of families increased.

Paragraph 2 is marked with an arrow [➜].

17. The word <u>hardly</u> in the passage is closest in meaning to

    Ⓐ frequently
    Ⓑ likely
    Ⓒ barely
    Ⓓ obviously

18. Why does the author mention Neolithic towns in paragraph 2?

    Ⓐ To give an example of a civilization
    Ⓑ To explain the invention of writing systems
    Ⓒ To argue that they should be classified as villages
    Ⓓ To contrast them with the civilizations that evolved

Paragraph 2 is marked with an arrow [➜].

19. According to paragraph 3, how was the class system structured?

    Ⓐ An upper class and a lower class
    Ⓑ Slaves, free people, and a ruling class
    Ⓒ A king, an army, and slaves
    Ⓓ Intellectuals and uneducated farmers and workers

Paragraph 3 is marked with an arrow [➜].

20. Which of the sentences below best expresses the information in the highlighted statement in the passage? The other choices change the meaning or leave out important information.

    Ⓐ Mesopotamian and Egyptian civilizations exhibit the majority of the characteristics identified by historians.

    Ⓑ The characteristics that historians have identified are not found in the Egyptian and Mesopotamian cultures.

    Ⓒ Civilizations in Mesopotamia and Egypt were identified by historians who were studying the characteristics of early cultures.

    Ⓓ The identification of most historical civilizations includes either Egypt or Mesopotamia on the list.

21. The word <u>crucial</u> in the passage is closest in meaning to

    Ⓐ fundamental
    Ⓑ arbitrary
    Ⓒ disruptive
    Ⓓ suitable

22. The word <u>prominent</u> in the passage is closest in meaning to

    Ⓐ weak
    Ⓑ important
    Ⓒ small
    Ⓓ new

23. According to paragraph 4, how can the independent development of civilization in different geographic regions be explained?

    Ⓐ Scholars agree that food surpluses encouraged populations to be concentrated in certain areas.

    Ⓑ There are several theories that explain the rise of civilization in the ancient world.

    Ⓒ The model of civilization was probably carried from one region to another along trade routes.

    Ⓓ Historians attribute the emergence of early cities at about the same time as a coincidence.

Paragraph 4 is marked with an arrow [→].

24. All of the following are cited as reasons why civilizations developed EXCEPT

    Ⓐ Religious practices unified the population.
    Ⓑ The management of water required organization.
    Ⓒ A major climate change made living in groups necessary.
    Ⓓ Extra food resulted in the expansion of population centers.

25. Look at the four squares [■] that show where the following sentence could be inserted in the passage.

   Some historians believe they can be established.

   Where could the sentence best be added?

   Click on a square [■] to insert the sentence in the passage.

26. **Directions:** An introduction for a short summary of the passage appears below. Complete the summary by selecting the THREE answer choices that mention the most important points in the passage. Some sentences do not belong in the summary because they express ideas that are not included in the passage or they are minor points from the passage. *This question is worth 2 points.*

   Certain qualities appear to define a civilization.

   -
   -
   -

Answer Choices

Ⓐ Free citizens who work in professions for pay

Ⓑ Bureaucracies for the government and armies

Ⓒ Libraries to house art and written records

Ⓓ A strategic location near rivers or the sea

Ⓔ Organized religion, writing, and art

Ⓕ A densely populated group with a class structure

Reading 3 "Life in Our Solar System"

Although we can imagine life based on something other than carbon chemistry, we know of no examples to tell us how such life might arise and survive. We must limit our discussion to life as we know it and the conditions it requires. The most important requirement is the presence of liquid water, not only as part of the chemical reactions of life, but also as a medium to transport nutrients and wastes within the organism.

The water requirement automatically eliminates many worlds in our solar system. The moon is airless, and although some data suggest ice frozen in the soil at its poles, it has never had liquid water on its surface. In the vacuum of the lunar surface, liquid water would boil away rapidly. Mercury too is airless and cannot have had liquid water on its surface for long periods of time. Venus has some traces of water vapor in its atmosphere, but it is much too hot for liquid water to survive. If there were any lakes or oceans of water on its surface when it was young, they must have evaporated quickly. Even if life began there, no traces would be left now.

The inner solar system seems too hot, and the outer solar system seems too cold. The Jovian planets have deep atmospheres, and at a certain level, they have moderate temperatures where water might condense into liquid droplets. But it seems unlikely that life could begin there. The Jovian planets have no surfaces where oceans could nurture the beginning of life, and currents in the atmosphere seem destined to circulate gas and water droplets from regions of moderate temperature to other levels that are much too hot or too cold for life to survive.

A few of the satellites of the Jovian planets might have suitable conditions for life. Jupiter's moon Europa seems to have a liquid-water ocean below its icy crust, and minerals dissolved in that water would provide a rich broth of possibilities for chemical evolution. [A] Nevertheless, Europa is not a promising site to search for life because conditions may not have remained stable for the billions of years needed for life to evolve beyond the microscopic stage. [B] If Jupiter's moons interact gravitationally and modify their orbits, Europa may have been frozen solid at some points in history. [C]

→ Saturn's moon Titan has an atmosphere of nitrogen, argon, and methane and may have oceans of liquid methane and ethane on its surface. [D] The chemistry of life that might crawl or swim on such a world is unknown, but life there may be unlikely because of the temperature. The surface of Titan is a deadly −179°C (−290°F). Chemical reactions occur slowly or not at all at such low temperatures, so the chemical evolution needed to begin life may never have occurred on Titan.

→ Mars is the most likely place for life in our solar system. The evidence, however, is not encouraging. Meteorite ALH84001 was found on the Antarctic ice in 1984. It was probably part of debris ejected into space by a large impact on Mars. ALH84001 is important because a team of scientists studied it and announced in 1996 that it contained chemical and physical traces of ancient life on Mars.

Scientists were excited too, but being professionally skeptical, they began testing the results immediately. In many cases, the results did not confirm the conclusion that life once existed on Mars. Some chemical contamination from water on Earth has occurred, and some chemicals in the meteorite may have originated without the presence of life. The physical features that look like fossil bacteria may be mineral formations in the rock.

Spacecraft now visiting Mars may help us understand the past history of water there and paint a more detailed picture of present conditions. Nevertheless, conclusive evidence may have to wait until a geologist in a space suit can wander the dry streambeds of Mars cracking open rocks and searching for fossils.

We are left to conclude that, so far as we know, our solar system is bare of life except for Earth. Consequently, our search for life in the universe takes us to other planetary systems.

27. The word <u>automatically</u> in the passage is closest in meaning to

    Ⓐ partially
    Ⓑ actually
    Ⓒ occasionally
    Ⓓ naturally

28. The word <u>it</u> in the passage refers to

    Ⓐ ice
    Ⓑ soil
    Ⓒ moon
    Ⓓ solar system

29. Which of the following statements about the water on Venus is true?

    Ⓐ The water evaporated because of the high temperatures.
    Ⓑ The water became frozen in the polar regions.
    Ⓒ Only a little water is left in small lakes on the surface.
    Ⓓ Rain does not fall because there is no atmosphere.

30. The word <u>stable</u> in the passage is closest in meaning to

    Ⓐ visible
    Ⓑ active
    Ⓒ constant
    Ⓓ strong

31. What can be inferred from the passage about the Jovian planets?

    Ⓐ Some of the Jovian planets may have conditions that could support life.
    Ⓑ Jupiter is classified as one of the Jovian planets.
    Ⓒ Europa is the largest of the moons that revolve around Jupiter.
    Ⓓ The orbits of the Jovian planets have changed over time.

32. According to paragraph 5, why would life on Titan be improbable?

    Ⓐ It does not have an ocean.
    Ⓑ It is not a planet.
    Ⓒ It is too cold.
    Ⓓ It has a low atmosphere.

    Paragraph 5 is marked with an arrow [→].

33. Which of the sentences below best expresses the information in the highlighted statement in the passage? The other choices change the meaning or leave out important information.

    Ⓐ Life on Mars was found as a result of research in many cases.
    Ⓑ The evidence did not demonstrate that there was life on Mars in the past.
    Ⓒ Many cases of life were concluded in the history of Mars.
    Ⓓ The conclusion was that only one instance of life on Mars was verified.

34. The word <u>originated</u> in the passage is closest in meaning to

    Ⓐ turned
    Ⓑ changed
    Ⓒ begun
    Ⓓ disappeared

35. Why does the author mention the meteorite ALH84001 in paragraph 6?

    Ⓐ Because it was found in Antarctica about fifty years ago
    Ⓑ Because it was evidence of a recent impact on Mars
    Ⓒ Because scientists thought that it contained evidence of life on Mars
    Ⓓ Because the meteorite probably came from Mars a long time ago

    Paragraph 6 is marked with an arrow [→].

36. How will scientists confirm the existence of life on Mars?

    Ⓐ By sending unmanned spacecraft to Mars
    Ⓑ By looking at fossils on Mars
    Ⓒ By viewing pictures taken of Mars
    Ⓓ By studying the present conditions on Mars

37. Which of the following statements most accurately reflects the author's opinion about life in our solar system?

    Ⓐ Life is probably limited to planets in the inner solar system.
    Ⓑ There is a large body of evidence supporting life on Mars.
    Ⓒ There is little probability of life on other planets.
    Ⓓ We should explore our solar system for conditions that support life.

38. Look at the four squares [■] that show where the following sentence could be inserted in the passage.

Such periods of freezing would probably prevent life from developing.

Where could the sentence best be added?

Click on a square [■] to insert the sentence in the passage.

39. **Directions:** An introduction for a short summary of the passage appears below. Complete the summary by selecting the THREE answer choices that mention the most important points in the passage. Some sentences do not belong in the summary because they express ideas that are not included in the passage or are minor points from the passage. *This question is worth 2 points.*

Current evidence does not support the theory of life in our solar system.

-
-
-

Answer Choices

A The meteorite that was discovered in the Antarctic in the 1980s was thought to contain evidence of early life on Mars, but it was later disputed.

B The planet that has the greatest probability for life in the past or now is Mars, but more investigation is required to draw conclusions.

C Europa has an ocean under the ice on the surface of the moon, which may contain the chemical combinations required for life to evolve.

D Although some of the moons that revolve around Saturn and Jupiter have conditions that might support life, the evidence contradicts this possibility.

E Other planetary systems must have life that is similar to that which has evolved on Earth because of the principles of carbon chemistry.

F It is too hot for life on the planets near the Sun in the inner solar system and too cold on the planets most removed from the Sun in the outer solar system.

LISTENING SECTION

 Model Test 3, Listening Section, CD 5, Track 5

The Listening section tests your ability to understand spoken English that is typical of interactions and academic speech on college campuses. During the test, you will respond to conversations and lectures.

This is the long format for the Listening section. On the long format, you will respond to three conversations and six lectures. After each listening passage, you will answer 5–6 questions about it. Only two conversations and four lectures will be graded. The other conversation and lectures are part of an experimental section for future tests. Because you will not know which conversations and lectures will be graded, you must try to do your best on all of them.

You will hear each conversation or lecture one time. You may take notes while you listen, but notes are not graded. You may use your notes to answer the questions.

Choose the best answer for multiple-choice questions. Follow the directions on the page or on the screen for computer-assisted questions. Click on **Next** and **OK** to go to the next question. You cannot return to previous questions. You have 20–30 minutes to answer all of the questions. A clock on the screen will show you how much time you have to complete your answers for the section. The clock does not count the time you are listening to the conversations and lectures.

PART I

Listening 1 "Students on Campus"

1. What are the students mainly discussing?

   Ⓐ Group sessions in the Office of Career Development
   Ⓑ The advantages of career counseling for the man
   Ⓒ The woman's internship in the Office of Career Development
   Ⓓ How to find employment in the field of career counseling

2. What is the man's problem?

   Ⓐ He does not have time to see an advisor.
   Ⓑ He does not have an internship yet.
   Ⓒ He does not know which career to choose.
   Ⓓ He does not have a job offer after graduation.

3. Why does the woman tell the man about her experience?

   Ⓐ To demonstrate the benefits of going to the Office of Career Development
   Ⓑ To encourage the man to talk with an advisor about an internship
   Ⓒ To suggest that he change his major from math to library science
   Ⓓ To give the man her opinion about his career decision

4. What is the woman's attitude toward her internship?

    Ⓐ She would rather go to graduate school.
    Ⓑ She is looking forward to interning.
    Ⓒ She thinks that it is a very positive experience.
    Ⓓ She will be happy when she completes it.

5. What will the man probably do?

    Ⓐ He will make an appointment with his academic advisor.
    Ⓑ He will go to the Office of Career Development.
    Ⓒ He will apply for a job at the library.
    Ⓓ He will ask the woman to help him with his tests.

Listening 2 "Sociology Class"

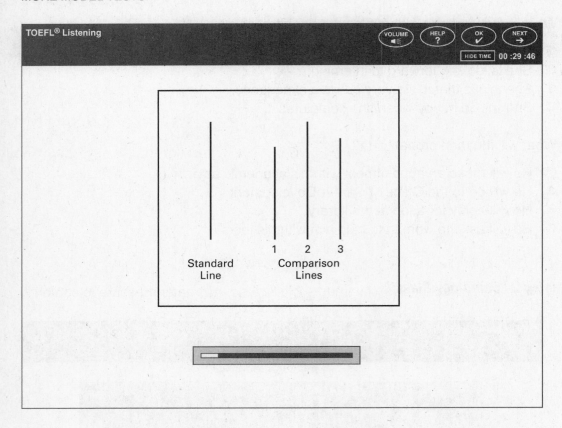

6. What is the main topic of the lecture?

Ⓐ The problems inherent in group decisions
Ⓑ Ways that individuals become popular in groups
Ⓒ The influence of groups on individual behavior
Ⓓ The differences in social influence across cultures

7. According to the professor, what two results were reported in the Asch and Abrams studies?

Click on 2 answer choices.

Ⓐ A larger group exerts significantly more pressure than a smaller group.

Ⓑ Subjects conformed to group opinion in more than one-third of the trials.

Ⓒ When the subject knows the group socially, there is greater pressure to conform.

Ⓓ A majority opinion has as much influence as a unanimous opinion.

8. Why does the professor say this:

Ⓐ She regretted the result of the experiment.
Ⓑ She knew that the students would not like the information.
Ⓒ She needed to correct what she had said in a previous statement.
Ⓓ She neglected to mention important facts.

9. What generally happens after a group makes a decision?

Ⓐ Some group members regret their decision.
Ⓑ At least one group member presents a new idea.
Ⓒ As a whole, the group is even more united in its judgment.
Ⓓ The popular group members compete for leadership.

10. Based on information in the lecture, indicate whether the statements describe the Asch study.

For each sentence, click in the Yes or No column.

		Yes	No
A	Only one subject is being tested.		
B	The cards can be interpreted several ways.		
C	Some of the group collaborate with the experimenter.		

11. What is the professor's attitude about the studies on social influence?

Ⓐ She seems surprised by the results.
Ⓑ She appears to be very interested in them.
Ⓒ She needs more information about them.
Ⓓ She doubts that there is practical application.

Listening 3 "Art History Class"

12. What is the main topic of this lecture?

    Ⓐ The process of fixing a photograph
    Ⓑ The problem of exposure time
    Ⓒ The experiments by Louis Daguerre
    Ⓓ The history of early photography

13. According to the professor, what two limitations were noted in Daguerre's process for developing and fixing latent images?

    Click on 2 answer choices.

    Ⓐ The photograph disappeared after a few minutes.

    Ⓑ The images were very delicate and easily fell apart.

    Ⓒ Multiple images could not be made from the plate.

    Ⓓ The exposure time was still several hours long.

14. Why does the professor say this:

    Ⓐ He is trying to generate interest in the topic.
    Ⓑ He makes reference to a story in the textbook.
    Ⓒ He is not sure whether the information is accurate.
    Ⓓ He wants the students to use their imaginations.

15. What substance was first used to fix the images?

    Ⓐ Copper powder
    Ⓑ Table salt
    Ⓒ Mercury vapor
    Ⓓ Hot water

16. What can we assume about photographers in the 1800s?

    Ⓐ Most of them had originally been painters before they became interested in photography.
    Ⓑ Portrait photographers were in the highest demand since people wanted images of their families.
    Ⓒ There were only a few photographers who were willing to work in such a new profession.
    Ⓓ Some of them must have experienced health problems as a result of their laboratory work.

17. In what order does the professor explain photographic principles?

    Ⓐ From the least to the most important facts
    Ⓑ In a chronological sequence of events
    Ⓒ The order of the steps in the photographic process
    Ⓓ The advantages before the disadvantages

PART II

Listening 4 "Admissions Office"

18. Why does the student go to the admissions office?

   Ⓐ He is applying for financial aid.
   Ⓑ He is requesting an official transcript.
   Ⓒ He is transferring to another college.
   Ⓓ He is trying to enroll in classes.

19. What is missing from the student's file?

   Ⓐ A financial aid application
   Ⓑ A transcript from County Community College
   Ⓒ Grades from Regional College
   Ⓓ An official copy of the application

20. Why does the woman say this:

   Ⓐ She is asking the man to finish explaining the situation.
   Ⓑ She is confirming that she understands the problem.
   Ⓒ She is expressing impatience with the man's explanation.
   Ⓓ She is trying to comprehend a difficult question.

21. What does the woman suggest that the man do?

  (A) Make a copy of his transcripts for his personal file
  (B) Complete all of the admissions forms as soon as possible
  (C) Change his provisional status to regular status before registering
  (D) Continue to request an official transcript from County Community College

22. What will the student most probably do now?

  (A) Return later in the day to see the woman in the admissions office
  (B) Go to the office for transfer students to be assigned an advisor
  (C) Enter information in the computer to complete the application process
  (D) See the woman's superior to get a provisional admission to State University

Listening 5 "Anthropology Class"

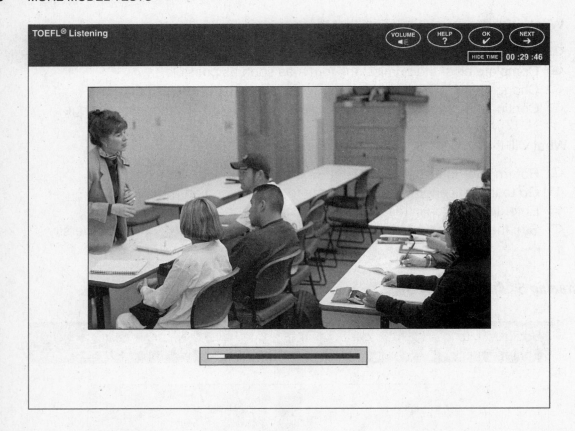

23. What is the main purpose of this lecture?

Ⓐ To discuss three types of authority
Ⓑ To distinguish between power and authority
Ⓒ To examine alternatives to Weber's model
Ⓓ To argue in favor of a legal rational system

24. Why does the professor mention Kennedy and Reagan?

Ⓐ They were founders of political movements.
Ⓑ They were examples of charismatic leaders.
Ⓒ They were attorneys who led by the law.
Ⓓ They had contrasting types of authority.

25. According to the professor, what two factors are associated with charismatic authority?

Click on 2 answer choices.

Ⓐ Sacred customs

Ⓑ An attractive leader

Ⓒ A social cause

Ⓓ Legal elections

26. Why does the professor say this:

  Ⓐ She is asking the students to answer a question.
  Ⓑ She is introducing the topic of the lecture.
  Ⓒ She is expressing an opinion about the subject.
  Ⓓ She is reminding students of a previous point.

27. In an evolutionary model, how is rational legal authority viewed?

  Ⓐ The most modern form of authority
  Ⓑ A common type of authority in the industrial age
  Ⓒ Authority used by traditional leaders
  Ⓓ A replacement for the three ideal types of authority

28. What does the professor imply about the three types of authority?

  Ⓐ There is only one legitimate type of authority in modern societies.
  Ⓑ Sociologists do not agree about the development of the types of authority.
  Ⓒ Societies tend to select and retain one type of authority indefinitely.
  Ⓓ Weber's model explains why the social structure rejects power over time.

Listening 6 "Geology Class"

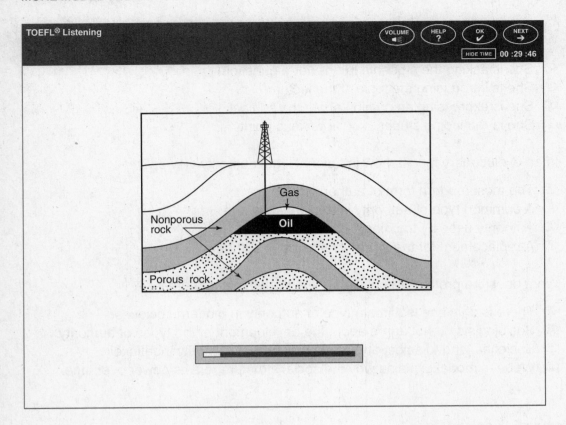

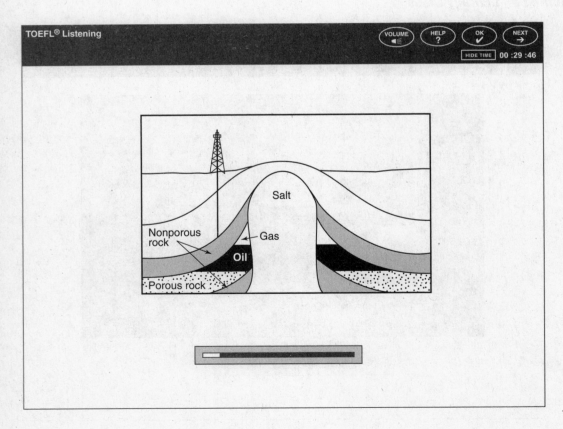

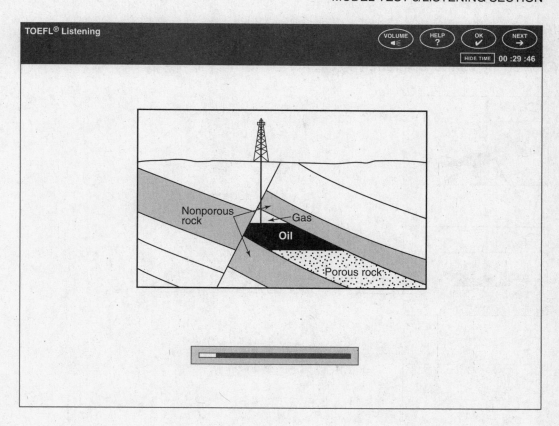

29. What is the lecture mainly about?

    Ⓐ The process of photosynthesis
    Ⓑ The major types of oil traps
    Ⓒ A method for collecting gas
    Ⓓ A comparison of gas and oil

30. Why does the professor begin by talking about the process that transforms organic material into oil and gas?

    Ⓐ He is introducing the main topic by providing background information.
    Ⓑ He is not very organized and he digresses a lot in the lecture.
    Ⓒ He wants the class to understand why hydrocarbons remain on the surface.
    Ⓓ He has to define a large number of terms before proceeding.

31. Why does the professor say this:

    Ⓐ He wants the class to participate more.
    Ⓑ He thinks that the reason is not logical.
    Ⓒ He wants all of the students to reply.
    Ⓓ He plans to answer the question.

32. Select the diagram of the anticline trap that was described in the lecture.

    Click on the correct diagram.

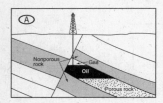

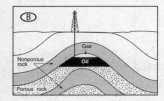

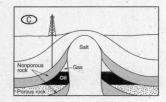

33. Identify the nonporous rock in the diagram.

    Click on the correct letter.

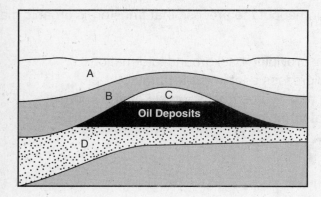

34. According to the professor, what do geologists look for when they are trying to locate a salt dome?

    Ⓐ A bulge in an otherwise flat area
    Ⓑ Underground rocks shaped like an arch
    Ⓒ Salt on the surface of a large area
    Ⓓ A deep crack in the Earth

PART III

Listening 7 "Library"

35. What does the man need from the librarian?

    Ⓐ A DVD player
    Ⓑ Material for a class
    Ⓒ Research by Dr. Parsons
    Ⓓ His student ID

36. What is the man's problem?

    Ⓐ He has to study for an important exam.
    Ⓑ He needs to prepare for a class discussion.
    Ⓒ He owes a fine at the library.
    Ⓓ He does not own a DVD player.

37. What does the man feel when he says this: 🎧

    Ⓐ Amused
    Ⓑ Worried
    Ⓒ Confused
    Ⓓ Interested

38. What is the policy for materials on reserve?

    Ⓐ The materials cannot leave the library without exception.
    Ⓑ There is a ten-dollar fine for each hour the materials are late.
    Ⓒ Students must show the professor's signature to use the materials.
    Ⓓ Materials may be checked out overnight two hours before closing.

39. What does the librarian imply when she tells the man to return at nine o'clock?

    Ⓐ She will see the man after work.
    Ⓑ The library probably closes at eleven.
    Ⓒ She is too busy to help the man now.
    Ⓓ Her supervisor will be there at that time.

Listening 8 "Literature Class"

40. What does this lecturer mainly discuss?

    Ⓐ Transcendentalism
    Ⓑ Puritanism
    Ⓒ Ralph Waldo Emerson
    Ⓓ Nature

41. Why does the professor say this:

    Ⓐ She is joking with the students.
    Ⓑ She is drawing a conclusion.
    Ⓒ She is correcting the students' behavior.
    Ⓓ She is reasoning aloud.

42. According to the professor, what was true about the Puritans?

    Ⓐ They stressed the essential importance of the individual.
    Ⓑ They supported the ideals of the Transcendental Club.
    Ⓒ They believed that society should be respected above persons.
    Ⓓ They thought that people should live in communes like Brook Farm.

43. Why did the church oppose the Transcendental movement?

    Ⓐ The authority of the church would be challenged by a code of personal ethics.
    Ⓑ The leaders of the Transcendentalists were not as well educated as the clergy.
    Ⓒ Church members were competing with Transcendentalists for teaching positions.
    Ⓓ Professors at Harvard College convinced the church to support their position.

44. Why did the professor mention *Walden*?

    Ⓐ It is probably well-known to many of the students in the class.
    Ⓑ It is considered an excellent example of Transcendental literature.
    Ⓒ It is required reading for the course that she is teaching.
    Ⓓ It is her personal favorite of nineteenth-century essays.

45. According to the professor, what was the most lasting contribution of Transcendentalism?

    Ⓐ Educational reorganization
    Ⓑ Religious reformation
    Ⓒ Experimental communities
    Ⓓ Political changes

Listening 9 "General Science Class"

46. What is this discussion mainly about?

    Ⓐ A model of the universe
    Ⓑ Interpretations of facts
    Ⓒ A definition of a hypothesis
    Ⓓ The scientific method

47. Why did the professor give the example of the ancient Egyptians?

    Ⓐ To explain the rotation of the Earth and the Sun
    Ⓑ To prove that facts may be interpreted differently
    Ⓒ To present a fact that can be verified by the students
    Ⓓ To discard a model that was widely accepted

48. Why did the professor say this:

    Ⓐ He is asking whether students need repetition.
    Ⓑ He is beginning a review of the process.
    Ⓒ He is complaining because students don't understand.
    Ⓓ He is making a suggestion before he proceeds.

49. According to the professor, what did Kepler do to verify his theory of planetary motion?

    Ⓐ He made predictions based on the model.
    Ⓑ He asked other scientists to make predictions.
    Ⓒ He used prior observations to test the model.
    Ⓓ He relied on insight to verify the theory.

50. What can be concluded from information in this discussion?

    Ⓐ A model does not always reflect observations.
    Ⓑ A model is not subject to change like a theory is.
    Ⓒ A model is considered true without doubt.
    Ⓓ A model does not require further experimentation.

51. What technique does the professor use to explain the practical application of the scientific method?

    Ⓐ A summary
    Ⓑ An example
    Ⓒ A prediction
    Ⓓ A formula

 **Please turn off the audio. There is a 10-minute break
between the Listening section and the Speaking section.**

SPEAKING SECTION

 Model Test 3, Speaking Section, CD 6, Track 1

The Speaking section tests your ability to communicate in English in an academic setting. During the test, you will be presented with six speaking questions. The questions ask for a response to a single question, a conversation, a talk, or a lecture.

You may take notes as you listen, but notes are not graded. You may use your notes to answer the questions. Some of the questions ask for a response to a reading passage and a talk or a lecture. The reading passages and the questions are written, but most of the directions will be spoken.

Your speaking will be evaluated on both the fluency of the language and the accuracy of the content. You will have 15–20 seconds to prepare and 45–60 seconds to respond to each question. Typically, a good response will require all of the response time, but the answer will be complete by the end of the response time.

The time for the Speaking section is about 20 minutes. A clock on the screen will show you how much time you have to prepare your answer and how much time you have to record it.

Independent Speaking Question 1 "A Prized Possession"

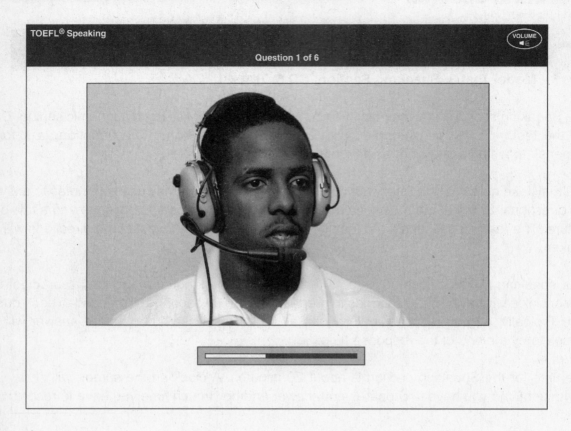

 Listen for a question about a familiar topic.

Question

A possession is an object that you own. If you were asked to choose one possession that you prize highly, which one would you choose? Why? What makes this possession especially valuable to you? Use specific reasons and details to explain your choice.

Preparation Time: 15 seconds
Recording Time: 45 seconds

Independent Speaking Question 2 "Climate"

 Listen for a question that asks your opinion about a familiar topic.

Question
Some people enjoy living in a location that has a warm climate all year. Other people like to live in a place where the seasons change. Which type of climate do you prefer and why? Use specific reasons and examples to support your opinion.

Preparation Time: 15 seconds
Recording Time: 45 seconds

Integrated Speaking Question 3 "Withdrawal from Classes"

Read a short passage and listen to a talk on the same topic.

Reading Time: 45 seconds

Withdrawal from Classes

In order to qualify for a refund of 100 percent at any time during the semester, you must first establish eligibility. Serious illness or injury must be verified by a written statement signed by a doctor or a psychologist. The death of a family member must be verified by a death certificate. Military duty must be verified by a copy of the orders. Students who wish to withdraw without submitting official documentation may do so before the end of the drop-add period without penalty. After the end of the second week of classes, students may petition for a 90 percent reimbursement. After the end of the fourth week, students are eligible for a 50 percent refund.

 Now listen to the students discuss the policy with each other.

Question

The student expresses her opinion of the policy for reimbursement. Report her opinion and explain the reasons that she gives for having that opinion.

Preparation Time: 30 seconds
Recording Time: 60 seconds

Integrated Speaking Question 4 "Ballads"

Read a short passage and listen to part of a lecture on the same topic.

Reading Time: 45 seconds

Ballads

A ballad is a poem that tells a story and is sung to music. Usually the story is of unknown origin, and a number of versions may be found for one song, a characteristic that stems from the oral tradition. As the song is passed on from one singer to another, a word is added or changed, or a slight alteration is made in the tune. In short, ballads represent a living tradition that evolves as the song is performed and passed to the next musician. A collection of ballads has been preserved in written form in the volume *English and Scottish Popular Ballads* by Francis James Child, and many ballads are still referred to by their "Child number."

Now listen to part of a lecture in a music appreciation class. The professor is talking about the ballad of "Barbara Allen."

Question

Define a ballad, and then explain why "Barbara Allen" can be classified as a ballad.

Preparation Time: 30 seconds
Recording Time: 60 seconds

Integrated Speaking Question 5 "The Assignment"

   Now listen to a conversation between a student and her friend.

Question

Describe the woman's problem and the two suggestions that her friend makes about how to handle it. What do you think the woman should do, and why?

Preparation Time: 20 seconds
Recording Time: 60 seconds

Integrated Speaking Question 6 "Ultrasound"

 Now listen to part of a lecture in a general science class. The professor is discussing the way that ultrasound works.

Question

Using the main points and examples from the lecture, describe the kind of information that ultrasound can provide, and then explain the way that ultrasound is used in medical diagnosis.

Preparation Time: 20 seconds
Recording Time: 60 seconds

WRITING SECTION

The Writing section tests your ability to write essays in English similar to those that you would write in college courses.

During the test, you will write two essays. The integrated essay asks for your response to an academic reading passage and a lecture on the same topic. You may take notes as you read and listen, but notes are not graded. You may use your notes to write the essay. The lecture will be spoken, but the directions and the questions will be written. You will have 20 minutes to plan, write, and revise your response. Typically, a good essay for the integrated topic will require that you write 150–225 words.

The independent essay usually asks for your opinion about a familiar topic. You will have 30 minutes to plan, write, and revise your response. Typically, a good essay for the independent topic will require that you write 300–350 words.

A clock on the screen will show you how much time you have to complete each essay.

Integrated Essay "Sydney Opera House"

You have 20 minutes to plan, write, and revise your response to a reading passage and a lecture on the same topic. First, read the passage and take notes. Then, listen to the lecture and take notes. Finally, write your response to the writing question. Typically, a good response will require that you write 150–225 words.

Reading Passage
Time: 3 minutes

The design for the Sydney Opera House was selected from entries in an international competition held in 1956. From more than 230 designs submitted by major architectural firms worldwide, the committee selected a dramatic concept by Jorn Utzon, a Danish architect who was virtually unknown outside of Denmark. He described his work as more like a sculpture than a building because it appeared to change shape depending on the direction from which it was viewed. He was also very committed to organic principles, which dictated that the structure must fit in with the environment. Situated in Bennelong Point, a promontory that stretches into the harbor, Utzon drafted the curved roofs of the opera house to look like a sailing ship at full sail on the water.

Clearly, the roof is the most revolutionary part of the design, which was so far ahead of the capabilities of engineering at the time that Utzon had to spend several years reworking the details for the construction of the roof sails in order to help the engineers solve the problems associated with actually building them. For example, stabilizing the shells that rose almost 200 feet high presented a serious challenge. Prestressed concrete was very new in building construction at the time that it was used to make the ribbed shells for the roof. In addition, computer technology was just catching up with the complex structural calculations and models that the architect needed for his vision to be realized.

By 1966, a decade after the design was chosen, the opera house was not even near completion. It was over budget, there were problems with the engineers and the contractors, and the fate of the structure was the object of political debate; Jorn Utzon resigned from the project. Eventually completed by others, by the time that it opened in 1973, it had been under construction for 17 years. The roof alone had required almost 2200 precast concrete sections, some of which weighed 15 tons, held together by 220 miles of tensioned steel cable and covered by more than a million white glazed ceramic tiles.

 Model Test 3, Writing Section, CD 6, Track 2

 Now listen to a lecture on the same topic as the passage that you have just read.

Question
Referring to the main points in the reading, describe the Sydney Opera House. Then, using information from both the reading and the lecture, explain why the professor classifies the building as unique.

Independent Essay "The College Years"

Question
Read and think about the following statement:

The college years are the best time in a person's life.

Do you agree or disagree with this statement?
Give reasons to support your opinion.

This is the end of Model Test 3.
To check your answers, refer to "Explanatory or Example Answers and
Audio Scripts for Model Tests: Model Test 3," Chapter 7, pages 617–648.

MODEL TEST 4: PROGRESS TEST

READING SECTION

The Reading section tests your ability to understand reading passages like those in college textbooks. The passages are about 700 words in length.

This is the long format for the Reading section. On the long format, you will respond to five passages. After each passage, you will answer 12–14 questions about it. Only three passages will be graded. The other passages are part of an exerimental section for future tests. Because you will not know which passages will be graded, you must try to do your best on all of them.

Most questions are worth 1 point, but the last question in each passage is worth more than 1 point.

You will have 100 minutes to read all of the passages and answer the questions. You may take notes while you read, but notes are not graded. You may use your notes to answer the questions. Some passages may include a word or phrase that is underlined in blue. Click on the word or phrase to see a glossary definition or explanation.

Choose the best answer for multiple-choice questions. Follow the directions on the page or on the screen for computer-assisted questions. Click on **Next** to go to the next question. Click on **Back** to return to the previous question. You may return to previous questions for all of the passages in the same reading part, but after you go to the next part, you will not be able to return to passages in a previous part. Be sure that you have answered all of the questions for the passages in each part before you click on **Next** at the end of the passage to move to the next part.

You can click on **Review** to see a chart of the questions you have answered and the questions you have not answered in each part. From this screen, you can return to the question you want to answer in the part that is open.

A clock on the screen will show you how much time you have to complete the Reading section.

PART I

Reading 1 "Layers of Social Class"

Taken together, income, occupation, and education are good measures of people's social standing. Using a layered model of stratification, most sociologists describe the class system in the United States as divided into several classes: upper, upper middle, middle, lower middle, and lower class. Each class is defined by characteristics such as income, occupational prestige, and educational attainment. The different groups are arrayed along a continuum with those with the most money, education, and prestige at the top and those with the least at the bottom.

In the United States, the upper class owns the major share of corporate and personal wealth; it includes those who have held wealth for generations as well as those who have recently become rich. Only a very small proportion of people actually constitute the upper class, but they control vast amounts of wealth and power in the United States. They exercise enormous control throughout society. Most of their wealth is inherited.

→ Despite social myths to the contrary, the best predictor of future wealth is the family into which you are born. Each year, the business magazine *Forbes* publishes a list of the "Forbes 400"—the four hundred wealthiest families and individuals in the country. Of all the wealth represented on the Forbes 400 list, more than half is inherited. Those on the list who could be called "self-made" were not typically of modest origins; most inherited significant assets (Forbes, 1997; Sklar and Collins,1997). Those in the upper class with newly acquired wealth are known as the *nouveau riche*. Although they may have vast amounts of money, they are often not accepted into "old rich" circles.

→ The *upper middle class* includes those with high incomes and high social prestige. They tend to be well-educated professionals or business executives. Their earnings can be quite high indeed—successful business executives can earn millions of dollars a year. It is difficult to estimate exactly how many people fall into this group because of the difficulty of drawing lines between the upper, upper middle, and middle class. Indeed, the upper middle class is often thought of as "middle class" because their lifestyle sets the standard to which many aspire, but this lifestyle is simply beyond the means of a majority of people in the United States.

→ The *middle class* is hard to define; in part, being "middle class" is more than just economic position. By far the majority of Americans identify themselves as middle class even though they vary widely in lifestyle and in resources at their disposal. But the idea that the United States is an open-class system leads many to think that the majority have a middle-class lifestyle because, in general, people tend not to want to recognize class distinctions in the United States. Thus, the middle class becomes the ubiquitous norm even though many who call themselves middle class have a tenuous hold on this class position.

In the hierarchy of social class, the *lower middle class* includes workers in the skilled trades and low-income bureaucratic workers, many of whom may actually define themselves as middle class. Examples are blue-collar workers (those in skilled trades who do manual labor) and many service workers, such as secretaries, hairdressers, waitresses, police, and firefighters. Medium to low income, education, and occupational prestige define the lower middle class relative to the class groups above it. The term "lower" in this class designation refers to the relative position of the group in the stratification system, but it has a pejorative sound to many people, especially to people who are members of this class.

→ The *lower class* is composed primarily of the displaced and poor. People in this class have little formal education and are often unemployed or working in minimum-wage jobs. A Forty percent of the poor work; 10 percent work year-round and full time—a proportion that has generally increased over time. Recently, the concept of the *underclass* has been added to the lower class. B The underclass includes those who have been left behind by contemporary economic developments. C Rejected from the economic system, those in the underclass may become dependent on public assistance or illegal activities. D

31

1. The word <u>those</u> in the passage refers to

    Ⓐ characteristics
    Ⓑ groups
    Ⓒ classes
    Ⓓ continuum

32

2. The word <u>enormous</u> in the passage is closest in meaning to

    Ⓐ very large
    Ⓑ very new
    Ⓒ very early
    Ⓓ very good

3. Which of the sentences below best expresses the information in the highlighted statement in the passage? The other choices change the meaning or leave out important information.

Ⓐ Although it is not generally accepted, your family provides the best prediction of your future wealth.

Ⓑ You can achieve great future wealth in spite of the family in which you may have been born.

Ⓒ It is not true that your family will restrict the acquisition of your future wealth and level of social status.

Ⓓ Social myths are contrary to the facts about the future wealth and social status of your family.

33

4. Why does the author mention the "Forbes 400" in paragraph 3?

Ⓐ To explain the meaning of the listing that appears every year

Ⓑ To support the statement that most wealthy people inherit their money

Ⓒ To cast doubt on the claim that family income predicts individual wealth

Ⓓ To give examples of successful people who have modest family connections

Paragraph 3 is marked with an arrow [➡].

34

5. In paragraph 4, the author states that business and professional people with educational advantages are most often members of the

Ⓐ lower middle class

Ⓑ upper middle class

Ⓒ *nouveau riche*

Ⓓ upper class

Paragraph 4 is marked with an arrow [➡].

35

6. The word <u>primarily</u> in the passage is closest in meaning to

Ⓐ mostly

Ⓑ somewhat

Ⓒ finally

Ⓓ always

36

7. The word <u>contemporary</u> in the passage is closest in meaning to

Ⓐ unexpected

Ⓑ modern

Ⓒ strategic

Ⓓ reliable

37

8. According to paragraph 5, why do most people identify themselves as middle class in the United States?

   Ⓐ They have about the same lifestyle as everyone else in the country.
   Ⓑ They prefer not to admit that there are class distinctions in the United States.
   Ⓒ They don't really know how to define their status because it is unclear.
   Ⓓ They identify themselves with the majority who have normal lifestyles.

Paragraph 5 is marked with an arrow [➔].

38

9. What can be inferred about poor people in the United States?

   Ⓐ They are not able to find entry-level jobs.
   Ⓑ They work in jobs that require little education.
   Ⓒ They are service workers and manual laborers.
   Ⓓ They do not try to find employment.

39

10. According to paragraph 7, why has the underclass emerged?

   Ⓐ The new term was necessary because the lower class enjoyed a higher lifestyle than it had previously.
   Ⓑ The increase in crime has supported a new class of people who live by engaging in illegal activities.
   Ⓒ Changes in the economy have caused an entire class of people to survive by welfare or crime.
   Ⓓ Minimum-wage jobs no longer support a class of people at a standard level in the economic system.

Paragraph 7 is marked with an arrow [➔].

40

11. All of the following are indicators of prestige in the United States EXCEPT

   Ⓐ the level of education that a person has achieved
   Ⓑ the amount of money that an individual has acquired
   Ⓒ the type of employment that someone pursues
   Ⓓ the hard work that a person does on a consistent basis

12. Look at the four squares [■] that show where the following sentence could be inserted in the passage.

The working poor constitute a large portion of those who are poor.

Where could the sentence best be added?

Click on a square [■] to insert the sentence in the passage.

13. **Directions:** An introduction for a short summary of the passage appears below. Complete the summary by selecting the THREE answer choices that mention the most important points in the passage. Some sentences do not belong in the summary because they express ideas that are not included in the passage or are minor points from the passage. *This question is worth 2 points.*

The levels of education, the acquisition of wealth, and occupational prestige determine social status in the United States.

- •

- •

- •

Answer Choices

Ⓐ People who have made their money more recently tend not to be accepted by those who have inherited their wealth from family holdings.

Ⓑ The lower class includes working people with low incomes and a new underclass of people who are dependent on welfare or engage in crime.

Ⓒ The upper class tends to acquire wealth through inheritance, whereas the upper middle class has a high income that they earn in their professions.

Ⓓ Although the lifestyle of the upper middle class is the goal for the majority, it is difficult for many people to maintain this standard of living.

Ⓔ Most people identify themselves as middle class, including blue-collar workers and service workers as well as bureaucratic employees.

Ⓕ It is still possible to move from one social class to another in the United States by working your way up the ladder in a corporate environment.

PART II

Reading 2 "Weather and Chaotic Systems"

Scientists today have a very good understanding of the physical laws and mathematical equations that govern the behavior and motion of atoms in the air, oceans, and land. Why, then, do we have so much trouble predicting the weather? For a long time, most scientists assumed that the difficulty of weather prediction would go away once we had enough weather stations to collect data from around the world and sufficiently powerful computers to deal with all the data. However, we now know that weather is fundamentally unpredictable on time scales longer than a few weeks. To understand why, we must look at the nature of scientific prediction.

→ Suppose you want to predict the location of a car on a road 1 minute from now. You need two basic pieces of information: where the car is now, and how fast it is moving. If the car is now passing Smith Road and heading north at 1 mile per minute, it will be 1 mile north of Smith Road in 1 minute.

Now, suppose you want to predict the weather. Again, you need two basic types of information: (1) the current weather and (2) how weather changes from one moment to the next. You could attempt to predict the weather by creating a "model world." For example, you could overlay a globe of the Earth with graph paper and then specify the current temperature, pressure, cloud cover, and wind within each square. These are your starting points, or initial conditions. Next, you could input all the initial conditions into a computer, along with a set of equations (physical laws) that describe the processes that can change weather from one moment to the next.

→ Suppose the initial conditions represent the weather around the Earth at this very moment and you run your computer model to predict the weather for the next month in New York City. The model might tell you that tomorrow will be warm and sunny, with cooling during the next week and a major storm passing through a month from now. Now suppose you run the model again but make one minor change in the initial conditions—say, a small change in the wind speed somewhere over Brazil. A For tomorrow's weather, this slightly different initial condition will not change the weather prediction for New York City. B But for next month's weather, the two predictions may not agree at all! C

The disagreement between the two predictions arises because the laws governing weather can cause very tiny changes in initial conditions to be greatly magnified over time. D This extreme sensitivity to initial conditions is sometimes called the *butterfly effect:* If initial conditions change by as much as the flap of a butterfly's wings, the resulting prediction may be very different.

→ The butterfly effect is a hallmark of *chaotic systems*. Simple systems are described by linear equations in which, for example, increasing a cause produces a proportional increase in an effect. In contrast, chaotic systems are described by nonlinear equations, which allow for subtler and more intricate interactions. For example, the economy is nonlinear because a rise in interest rates does not automatically produce a corresponding change in consumer spending. Weather is nonlinear because a change in the wind speed in one location does not automatically produce a corresponding change in another location. Many (but not all) nonlinear systems exhibit chaotic behavior.

→ Despite their name, chaotic systems are not completely random. In fact, many chaotic systems have a kind of underlying order that explains the general features of their behavior even while details at any particular moment remain unpredictable. In a sense, many chaotic systems are "predictably unpredictable." Our understanding of chaotic systems is increasing at a tremendous rate, but much remains to be learned about them.

41

14. According to the passage, it will be difficult to predict weather

   Ⓐ unless we learn more about chaotic systems
   Ⓑ because we don't have enough weather stations
   Ⓒ without more powerful computers
   Ⓓ until we understand the physical laws of atoms

42

15. The word <u>assumed</u> in the passage is closest in meaning to

   Ⓐ agreed
   Ⓑ supposed
   Ⓒ revealed
   Ⓓ expressed

43

16. The word <u>fundamentally</u> in the passage is closest in meaning to

   Ⓐ typically
   Ⓑ historically
   Ⓒ presently
   Ⓓ basically

44

17. Why does the author mention a car in paragraph 2?

   Ⓐ The car is an example of how conditions are used to make predictions.
   Ⓑ The author digresses in order to tell a story about a car.
   Ⓒ The car introduces the concept of computer models.
   Ⓓ The mathematical equations for the car are very simple to understand.

   Paragraph 2 is marked with an arrow [➔].

45

18. Why do the predictions disagree for the computer model described in paragraph 4?

   Ⓐ The conditions at the beginning were very different.
   Ⓑ The model was not accurately programmed.
   Ⓒ Computer models cannot predict weather.
   Ⓓ Over time models are less reliable.

   Paragraph 4 is marked with an arrow [➔].

46

19. Why is weather considered a chaotic system?

   Ⓐ Because it is made up of random features
   Ⓑ Because it is not yet very well understood
   Ⓒ Because it is described by nonlinear equations
   Ⓓ Because it does not have an orderly structure

47

20. Based on information in paragraph 6, which of the following best explains the term "butterfly effect"?

    Ⓐ Slight variations in initial conditions can cause very different results.
    Ⓑ A butterfly's wings can be used to predict different conditions in various locations.
    Ⓒ The weather is as difficult to predict as the rate of a butterfly's wings when it flaps them.
    Ⓓ A butterfly flaps its wings in one location, which automatically produces a result in another place.

Paragraph 6 is marked with an arrow [➜].

48

21. The phrase <u>in which</u> in the passage refers to

    Ⓐ the butterfly effect
    Ⓑ chaotic systems
    Ⓒ simple systems
    Ⓓ linear equations

49

22. Why does the author mention the economy in paragraph 6?

    Ⓐ To contrast a simple system with a chaotic system
    Ⓑ To provide an example of another chaotic system
    Ⓒ To compare nonlinear equations with linear equations
    Ⓓ To prove that all nonlinear systems are not chaotic

Paragraph 6 is marked with an arrow [➜].

50

23. The word <u>features</u> in the passage is closest in meaning to

    Ⓐ problems
    Ⓑ exceptions
    Ⓒ characteristics
    Ⓓ benefits

24. In paragraph 7, the author suggests that our knowledge of chaotic systems

    Ⓐ will never allow us to make accurate predictions
    Ⓑ has not improved very much over the years
    Ⓒ reveals details that can be predicted quite accurately
    Ⓓ requires more research by the scientific community

Paragraph 7 is marked with an arrow [➜].

25. Look at the four squares [■] that show where the following sentence could be inserted in the passage.

For next week's weather, the new model may yield a slightly different prediction.

Where could the sentence best be added?

Click on a square [■] to insert the sentence in the passage.

26. **Directions:** An introduction for a short summary of the passage appears below. Complete the summary by selecting the THREE answer choices that mention the most important points in the passage. Some sentences do not belong in the summary because they express ideas that are not included in the passage or are minor points from the passage. *This question is worth 2 points.*

Because weather is a chaotic system, it is very difficult to predict.

-
-
-

Answer Choices

A The accuracy of weather prediction will improve as we make progress in the application of computers to equations.

B It is very easy to make predictions about the location of a car when you know where it is and how fast it is going.

C A slight variation in initial conditions will cause a very different prediction for weather over the long term.

D Because weather is chaotic but not random, it may be described by nonlinear equations that provide for sensitive interactions.

E The economic system demonstrates chaotic behavior, and it must be represented by a nonlinear equation.

F Weather is predictable only within a time frame of a few weeks because of the nature of scientific prediction.

Reading 3 "Building with Arches"

Round Arch and Vault

→ Although the round arch was used by the ancient peoples of Mesopotamia several centuries before our common era, it was most fully developed by the Romans, who perfected the form in the 2nd century B.C.E. The arch has many virtues. In addition to being an attractive form, it enables the architect to open up fairly large spaces in a wall without risking the building's structural soundness. These spaces admit light, reduce the weight of the walls, and decrease the amount of material needed. As utilized by the Romans, the arch is a perfect semicircle, although it may seem elongated if it rests on columns. It is constructed from wedge-shaped pieces of stone that meet at an angle always perpendicular to the curve of the arch. Because of tensions and compressions inherent in the form, the arch is stable only when it is complete, when the topmost stone, the **keystone**, has been set in place. For this reason an arch under construction must be supported from below, usually by a wooden framework.

→ Among the most elegant and enduring of Roman structures based on the arch is the Pont du Gard at Nimes, France, built about 15 C.E. when the empire was nearing its farthest expansion. At this time, industry, commerce, and agriculture were at their peak. Roman engineering was applied to an ambitious system of public-works projects, not just in Italy but in the outlying areas as well. The Pont du Gard functioned as an aqueduct, a structure meant to transport water, and its lower level served as a footbridge across the river. That it stands today virtually intact after nearly two thousand years (and is crossed by cyclists on the route of the famous Tour de France bicycle race) testifies to the Romans' brilliant engineering skills. Visually, the Pont du Gard exemplifies the best qualities of arch construction. Solid and heavy, obviously durable, it is shot through with open spaces that make it seem light and its weight-bearing capabilities effortless.

→ When the arch is extended in depth—when it is, in reality, many arches placed flush one behind the other—the result is called a **barrel vault**. This vault construction makes it possible to create large interior spaces. The Romans made great use of the barrel vault, but for its finest expression we look many hundreds of years later, to the churches of the Middle Ages.

→ The church of Sainte-Foy, in the French city of Conques, is an example of the style prevalent throughout Western Europe from about 1050 to 1200—a style known as **Romanesque**. Romanesque builders adopted the old Roman forms of round arch and barrel vault so as to add height to their churches. Until this period most churches had beamed wooden roofs, which not only posed a threat of fire but also limited the height to which architects could aspire. With the stone barrel vault, they could achieve the soaring, majestic space we see in the <u>nave</u> of Sainte-Foy.

Pointed Arch and Vault
→ While the round arch and vault of the Romanesque era solved many problems and made many things possible, they nevertheless had certain drawbacks. For one thing, a round arch, to be stable, must be a semicircle; therefore, the height of the arch is limited by its width. Two other difficulties were weight and darkness. Barrel vaults are both literally and visually heavy, calling for huge masses of stone to maintain their structural stability. Also, the builders who constructed them dared not make light-admitting openings in or around them, for fear the arches and vaults would collapse, and so the interiors of Romanesque buildings tend to be dark. The **Gothic** period in Europe, which followed the Romanesque, solved these problems with the pointed arch. Ⓐ

The pointed arch, while seemingly not very different from the round one, offers many advantages. Ⓑ Because the sides arc up to a point, weight is channeled down to the ground at a steeper angle, and therefore the arch can be taller. The vault constructed from such an arch also can be much taller than a barrel vault. C Architects of the Gothic period found they did not need heavy masses of material throughout the curve of the vault, as long as the major points of intersection were reinforced. D

Glossary
nave: the long central area in a church with aisles on each side

27. Why does the author mention the keystone in paragraph 1?

   Ⓐ To explain the engineering of an arch
   Ⓑ To provide historical background on arches
   Ⓒ To point out one of the virtues of arches
   Ⓓ To suggest an alternative to the arch

   Paragraph 1 is marked with an arrow [→].

28. The word <u>inherent</u> in the passage is closest in meaning to

   Ⓐ uncertain
   Ⓑ unsatisfactory
   Ⓒ expansive
   Ⓓ essential

29. The Pont du Gard mentioned in paragraph 2 has all of the following characteristics EXCEPT

   Ⓐ It was an aqueduct.
   Ⓑ It is still being used.
   Ⓒ It was built 2000 years ago.
   Ⓓ It was repaired recently.

   Paragraph 2 is marked with an arrow [→].

30. According to paragraph 3, what is the advantage of a barrel vault?

   Ⓐ It was used in the Middle Ages.
   Ⓑ Many arches were joined.
   Ⓒ The space was larger.
   Ⓓ It was a typical Roman look.

   Paragraph 3 is marked with an arrow [→].

31. The word <u>virtually</u> in the passage is closest in meaning to

   Ⓐ obviously
   Ⓑ accurately
   Ⓒ routinely
   Ⓓ practically

6

32. What can be inferred from paragraph 4 about Romanesque architecture?

Ⓒ Arches and barrel vaults were used in the designs.
Ⓓ Wood beams characterized the buildings.
Ⓔ The structures were smaller than those of Roman style.
Ⓕ The architecture was popular during the Roman occupation.

Paragraph 4 is marked with an arrow [➞].

33. Which of the sentences below best expresses the information in the highlighted statement in the passage? The other choices change the meaning or leave out important information.

Ⓒ Architects wanted to build higher ceilings in churches, but they were limited because of the fire hazard caused by wooden beams in the roofs.
Ⓓ The majority of the churches prior to this time were constructed with wooden roofs that caused a considerable fire hazard because of their height.
Ⓔ The wood beams in the roofs of most churches before this period were a concern because of fire and the constraints they imposed on the height of the ceiling.
Ⓕ The limitations on the architecture of the churches were a result of the construction materials and the limited vision of the architects.

7

34. The word <u>achieve</u> in the passage is closest in meaning to

Ⓒ retain
Ⓓ accomplish
Ⓔ decorate
Ⓕ finance

8

35. Gothic architects extended the height of their arches by

Ⓒ using barrel vaults
Ⓓ designing pointed arches
Ⓔ including a nave
Ⓕ adding windows

9

36. The word <u>their</u> in the passage refers to

Ⓒ masses
Ⓓ builders
Ⓔ stone
Ⓕ vaults

10

37. According to paragraph 5, why are Romanesque churches so dark?

Ⓒ It was a characteristic of construction with pointed arches.
Ⓓ It was too difficult to make windows in the heavy materials.
Ⓔ Openings for light could have compromised the structure.
Ⓕ Reinforcements covered the areas where light could shine in.

Paragraph 5 is marked with an arrow [➞].

38. Look at the four squares [■] that show where the following sentence could be inserted in the passage.

   These reinforcements, called ribs, are visible in the nave ceiling of Reims Cathedral.

   Where could the sentence best be added?

   Click on a square [■] to insert the sentence in the passage.

39. **Directions:** Complete the table by matching the phrases on the left with the headings on the right. Select the appropriate answer choices and drag them to the type of architecture to which they relate. TWO of the answer choices will NOT be used. *This question is worth 4 points.*

   To delete an answer choice, click on it. To see the passage, click on **View Text**.

Answer Choices	Round Arch
Ⓐ Allowed architects to create a taller arch	•
Ⓑ Used in fortresses so that the soldiers could see out	•
Ⓒ Represented the Romanesque style of architecture	•
Ⓓ Similar to arches constructed in the ancient world	•
Ⓔ Popular in many structures of the Gothic period	**Pointed Arch**
Ⓕ Required special building materials for construction	•
Ⓖ Prevalent in churches during the Middle Ages	•
Ⓗ Associated with structures that include barrel vaults	•
Ⓘ Permitted openings in or around them for light	

PART III

Reading 4 "The Digital Divide"

The Challenge of Technology and Equity

Information technology is influencing the way many of us live and work today. We use the Internet to look and apply for jobs, shop, conduct research, make airline reservations, and explore areas of interest. We use e-mail and the Internet to communicate instantaneously with friends and business associates around the world. Computers are commonplace in homes and the workplace.

→ Although the number of Internet users is growing exponentially each year, most of the world's population does not have access to computers or the Internet. Only 6 percent of the population in developing countries are connected to telephones. Although more than 94 percent of U.S. households have a telephone, only 42 percent have personal computers at home and 26 percent have Internet access. The lack of what most of us would consider a basic communications necessity—the telephone—does not occur just in developing nations. On some Native American reservations only 60 percent of the residents have a telephone. The move to wireless connections may eliminate the need for telephone lines, but it does not remove the barrier to equipment costs.

→ Who has Internet access? Fifty percent of the children in urban households with an income over $75,000 have Internet access, compared with 2 percent of the children in low-income, rural households. Nearly half of college-educated people have Internet access, compared to 6 percent of those with only some high school education. Forty percent of households with two parents have access; 15 percent of female, single-parent households do. Thirty percent of white households, 11 percent of black households, and 13 percent of Hispanic households have access. Teens and children are the two fastest-growing segments of Internet users. The digital divide between the populations who have access to the Internet and information technology tools is based on income, race, education, household type, and geographic location. Only 16 percent of the rural poor, rural and central city minorities, young householders, and single-parent female households are connected.

→ Another problem that exacerbates these disparities is that African-Americans, Hispanics, and Native Americans hold few of the jobs in information technology. Women hold about 20 percent of these jobs and are receiving fewer than 30 percent of the computer science degrees. The result is that women and members of the most oppressed ethnic groups are not eligible for the jobs with the highest salaries at graduation. Baccalaureate candidates with degrees in computer science were offered the highest salaries of all new college graduates in 1998 at $44,949.

Do similar disparities exist in schools? Ⓐ More than 90 percent of all schools in the country are wired with at least one Internet connection. Ⓑ The number of classrooms with Internet connections differs by the income level of students. Using the percentage of students who are eligible for free lunches at a school to determine income level, we see that nearly twice as many of the schools with more affluent students have wired classrooms as those with high concentrations of low-income students. Ⓒ

→ Access to computers and the Internet will be important in reducing disparities between groups. Ⓓ It will require greater equality across diverse groups whose members develop knowledge and skills in computer and information technologies. If computers and the Internet are to be used to promote equality, they will have to become accessible to populations that cannot currently afford the equipment which needs to be updated every three years or so. However, access alone is not enough. Students will have to be interacting with the technology in authentic settings. As technology becomes a tool for learning in almost all courses taken by students, it will be seen as a means to an end rather than an end in itself. If it is used in culturally relevant ways, all students can benefit from its power.

40. Why does the author mention the telephone in paragraph 2?

    Ⓐ To demonstrate that even technology like the telephone is not available to all
    Ⓑ To argue that basic telephone service is a first step to using the Internet
    Ⓒ To contrast the absence of telephone usage with that of Internet usage
    Ⓓ To describe the development of communications from telephone to Internet

    Paragraph 2 is marked with an arrow [→].

41. Which of the sentences below best expresses the information in the highlighted statement in the passage? The other choices change the meaning or leave out important information.

    Ⓐ Most of the people in the world use the Internet now because the number of computers has been increasing every year.
    Ⓑ The number of people who use computers and the Internet is increasing every year, but most people in the world still do not have connections.
    Ⓒ The number of computers that can make the Internet available to most of the people in the world is not increasing fast enough.
    Ⓓ The Internet is available to most of the people in the world, even though they don't have their own computer terminals.

42. The word <u>residents</u> in the passage is closest in meaning to

    Ⓐ homes
    Ⓑ towns
    Ⓒ people
    Ⓓ locations

13

43. The word <u>eliminate</u> in the passage is closest in meaning to

    Ⓐ accept
    Ⓑ dispute
    Ⓒ define
14   Ⓓ remove

44. Based on information in paragraph 3, which of the following best explains the term "digital divide?"

    Ⓐ The number of Internet users in developing nations
    Ⓑ The disparity in the opportunity to use the Internet
    Ⓒ Differences in socioeconomic levels among Internet users
    Ⓓ Segments of the population with Internet access

Paragraph 3 is marked with an arrow [➔].

15

45. Why does the author give details about the percentages of Internet users in paragraph 3?

    Ⓐ To prove that there are differences in opportunities among social groups
    Ⓑ To argue for more Internet connections at all levels of society
    Ⓒ To suggest that improvements in Internet access are beginning to take place
    Ⓓ To explain why many people have Internet connections now

Paragraph 3 is marked with an arrow [➔].

16

46. According to paragraph 3, which of the following households would be least likely to have access to the Internet?

    Ⓐ A household with one parent
    Ⓑ A black household
    Ⓒ A Hispanic household
    Ⓓ A household with both parents

Paragraph 3 is marked with an arrow [➔].

17

47. The word <u>those</u> in the passage refers to

    Ⓐ classrooms
    Ⓑ students
    Ⓒ schools
    Ⓓ concentrations

48. According to paragraph 4, why are fewer women and minorities employed in the field of computer technology?

   Ⓐ They are not admitted to the degree programs.
   Ⓑ They do not possess the educational qualifications.
   Ⓒ They do not have an interest in technology.
   Ⓓ They prefer training for jobs with higher salaries.

Paragraph 4 is marked with an arrow [➔].

49. The word <u>concentrations</u> in the passage is closest in meaning to

   Ⓐ protections
   Ⓑ numbers
   Ⓒ confidence
   Ⓓ support

50. What can be inferred from paragraph 6 about Internet access?

   Ⓐ Better computers need to be designed.
   Ⓑ Schools should provide newer computers for students.
   Ⓒ The cost of replacing equipment is a problem.
   Ⓓ Technology will be more helpful in three years.

Paragraph 6 is marked with an arrow [➔].

51. Look at the four squares [■] that show where the following sentence could be inserted in the passage.

Thus, the students who are most unlikely to have access at home also do not have access in their schools, increasing the divide between groups even further.

Where could the sentence best be added?

Click on a square [■] to insert the sentence in the passage.

52. **Directions:** An introduction for a short summary of the passage appears below. Complete the summary by selecting the THREE answer choices that mention the most important points in the passage. Some sentences do not belong in the summary because they express ideas that are not included in the passage or are minor points from the passage. *This question is worth 2 points.*

The availability of technology is unequal throughout the world.

-

-

-

Answer Choices

A Currently, only about 10 percent of all the schools in the United States are not wired for Internet access.

B Less affluent schools have fewer Internet connections, and minorities as well as women hold fewer computer science degrees.

C Children and teenagers are the two fastest growing segments of the population gaining access to the Internet.

D Internet access is limited by education, income, geographic location, race, and the age and marital status of the head of household.

E Computer science graduates can earn almost $50,000.

F Access to the Internet is one way to encourage equality among diverse groups

Reading 5 "The Evolution of Birds"

Birds Began as Feathered Reptiles

Birds evolved during the great reptilian radiation of the Mesozoic era. Amniotic eggs and scales on the legs are just two of the reptilian features we see in birds. But modern birds look quite different from modern reptiles because of their feathers and other distinctive flight equipment.

Characteristics of Birds

→ Almost every part of a typical bird's anatomy is modified in some way that enhances flight. The bones have an internal structure that is honeycombed, making them strong but light. The skeleton of a frigate bird, for instance, has a wingspan of more than 2 meters but weighs only about 113 grams. Another adaptation reducing the weight of birds is the absence of some organs. Females, for instance, have only one ovary. Also, modern birds are toothless, an adaptation that trims the weight of the head. Food is not chewed in the mouth but ground in the gizzard, a digestive organ near the stomach. (Crocodiles also have gizzards, as did some dinosaurs.) The bird's beak, made of keratin, has proven to be very adaptable during avian evolution, taking on a great variety of shapes suitable for different diets.

Flying requires a great expenditure of energy from an active metabolism. Birds are endothermic; they use their own metabolic heat to maintain a warm, constant body temperature. Feathers and, in some species, layers of fat provide insulation that enables birds to retain their metabolically generated heat. An efficient respiratory system and a circulatory system with a four-chambered heart keep tissues well supplied with oxygen and nutrients, supporting a high rate of metabolism. The lungs have tiny tubes leading to and from elastic air sacs that help dissipate heat and reduce the density of the body.

For safe flight, senses, especially vision, must be acute. Birds have excellent eyes, perhaps the best of all the vertebrates. The visual areas of the brains are well developed, as are the motor areas; flight also requires excellent coordination.

With brains proportionately larger than those of reptiles and amphibians, birds generally display very complex behavior. Avian behavior is particularly intricate during breeding season, when birds engage in elaborate rituals of courtship. Because eggs are shelled when laid, fertilization must be internal. Copulation involves contact between the mates' vents, the openings to their cloacas. After eggs are laid, the avian embryo must be kept warm through brooding by the mother, father, or both, depending on the species.

→ A bird's most obvious adaptation for flight is its wings. Bird wings are airfoils that illustrate the same principles of aerodynamics as the wings of an airplane. Providing power for flight, birds flap their wings by contractions of large pectoral (breast) muscles anchored to a keel on the sternum (breastbone). Some birds, such as eagles and hawks, have wings adapted for soaring on air currents and flap their wings only occasionally; other birds, including hummingbirds, must flap continuously to stay aloft. In either case, it is the shape and arrangement of the feathers that form the wings into an airfoil. The fastest birds are the appropriately named swifts, which can fly 170 km/hr.

→ In being both extremely light and strong, feathers are among the most remarkable of vertebrate adaptations. Feathers are made of keratin, the same protein that forms our hair and fingernails and the scales of reptiles. Feathers may have functioned first as insulation during the evolution of endothermy, only later being co-opted as flight equipment.

The evolution of flight required radical alteration in body form, but flight provides many benefits. [A] It enhances hunting and scavenging: many birds exploit flying insects, an abundant, highly nutritious food resource. [B] Flight also provides ready escape from earthbound predators and enables some birds to migrate great distances to utilize different food resources and seasonal breeding areas. ⒞ The bird that travels farthest in its annual migration is the arctic tern, which flies round-trip between the North Pole and South Pole each year. ⒟

→ Analyses of fossilized skeletons support the hypothesis that the closest reptilian relatives of birds were the **theropods**, a group of relatively small, bipedal carnivorous dinosaurs. Most researchers agree that the ancestor of birds was a feathered theropod. However, some scientists place the origin of birds much earlier, from an ancestor common to both birds and dinosaurs. The intense current interest in the origin of birds will undoubtedly bring us closer to understanding how these masters of the sky evolved from nonflying reptiles.

Glossary
brooding: to hatch eggs by sitting on the nest
cloacas: the opening to the reproductive and intestinal tract

21

53. According to paragraph 2, how did birds adapt to achieve efficient flight?

  Ⓐ They developed a skeleton with fewer bones.
  Ⓑ Their organs became smaller over time.
  Ⓒ Most of their weight was distributed in their heads.
  Ⓓ Teeth were replaced by a beak made of keratin.

Paragraph 2 is marked with an arrow [→].

22

54. The word modified in the passage is closest in meaning to

  Ⓐ made different
  Ⓑ made better
  Ⓒ made smaller
  Ⓓ made modern

23

55 The word their in the passage refers to

  Ⓐ feathers
  Ⓑ species
  Ⓒ layers
  Ⓓ birds

24

56. The word elaborate in the passage is *opposite* in meaning to

  Ⓐ simple
  Ⓑ quiet
  Ⓒ sad
  Ⓓ short

57. According to paragraph 6, which of the following is true about the wings of birds?

    Ⓐ All birds flap their wings constantly by using breast muscles.
    Ⓑ Eagles and hawks have wings that propel them at 170 km/hr.
    Ⓒ The airfoils of birds function like the wings on airplanes.
    Ⓓ Wings are attached to airfoils in the bird's skeletal structure.

    Paragraph 6 is marked with an arrow [➜].

58. In paragraph 7, the author explains the term *keratin* by

    Ⓐ identifying it in hair and fingernails
    Ⓑ comparing it to bird feathers
    Ⓒ providing a definition in the text
    Ⓓ describing the way that it looks

    Paragraph 7 is marked with an arrow [➜].

59. The word radical in the passage is closest in meaning to

    Ⓐ very clear
    Ⓑ very wide
    Ⓒ very fast
    Ⓓ very new

60. According to the passage, which characteristic do birds share with reptiles?

    Ⓐ They defend themselves with claws.
    Ⓑ They reproduce by laying eggs.
    Ⓒ They have a similar skeletal structure.
    Ⓓ They utilize a two-chambered heart.

61. Which of the sentences below best expresses the information in the highlighted statement in the passage? The other choices change the meaning or leave out important information.

    Ⓐ Very early birds appeared after the dinosaurs.
    Ⓑ Birds and dinosaurs may share a mutual ancestor.
    Ⓒ Birds and dinosaurs were probably very common.
    Ⓓ The origin of birds and dinosaurs is very early.

62. According to paragraph 9, what can be inferred about research on the evolution of birds?

    Ⓐ The research is not very recent.
    Ⓑ The subject is popular.
    Ⓒ Many researchers are working on it.
    Ⓓ There are some definitive conclusions.

    Paragraph 9 is marked with an arrow [➜].

63. All of the following are mentioned as adaptations to the bird's anatomy to accommodate flight EXCEPT

    Ⓐ a covering of feathers
    Ⓑ relatively large brains
    Ⓒ very sharp eyes
    Ⓓ small legs and feet

64. Look at the four squares [■] that show where the following sentence could be inserted in the passage.

Furthermore, migration allows birds to avoid climates that are too hot or too cold during certain seasons.

Where could the sentence best be added?

Click on a square [■] to insert the sentence in the passage.

65. **Directions:** An introduction for a short summary of the passage appears below. Complete the summary by selecting the THREE answer choices that mention the most important points in the passage. Some sentences do not belong in the summary because they express ideas that are not included in the passage or are minor points from the passage. *This question is worth 2 points.*

Birds evolved during the reptilian radiation of the Mesozoic era.

-
-
-

Answer Choices

Ⓐ Birds and reptiles are most probably related.

Ⓑ Feathers are among the most unusual evolutionary changes.

Ⓒ Many structural adaptations were required for birds to fly.

Ⓓ Therapods are relatively small, meat-eating dinosaurs.

Ⓔ There are a number of advantages for creatures that fly.

Ⓕ Migration patterns are typical of many species of birds.

LISTENING SECTION

 Model Test 4, Listening Section, CD 6, Track 4

The Listening section tests your ability to understand spoken English that is typical of interactions and academic speech on college campuses. During the test, you will respond to conversations and lectures.

This is the short format for the Listening section. On the short format, you will respond to two conversations and four lectures. After each listening passage, you will answer 5–6 questions about it.

You will hear each conversation or lecture one time. You may take notes while you listen, but notes are not graded. You may use your notes to answer the questions.

Choose the best answer for multiple-choice questions. Follow the directions on the page or on the screen for computer-assisted questions. Click on **Next** and **OK** to go to the next question. You cannot return to previous questions. You have 20–30 minutes to answer all of the questions. A clock on the screen will show you how much time you have to complete your answers for the section. The clock does not count the time you are listening to the conversations and lectures.

PART I

Listening 1 "Professor's Office"

1. Why does the man go to see his professor?

   Ⓐ To take a makeup test for a class that he missed
   Ⓑ To explain why he has been absent from class
   Ⓒ To turn in an extra credit project to the professor
   Ⓓ To ask the professor how to bring up his grade

2. Why did Ernie get a low grade on the last test?

   Ⓐ He does not understand the material.
   Ⓑ He is not a very good student.
   Ⓒ He did not have time to finish it.
   Ⓓ He was in a hurry to leave the class.

3. What do we know about the test?

   Ⓐ There were 100 questions on it.
   Ⓑ It was worth 25 percent of the final grade.
   Ⓒ The test was an extra credit assignment.
   Ⓓ The questions were very difficult.

4. Why does the professor say this:

    &Ⓐ Because she doesn't understand what the man wants her to do
    Ⓑ Because she has finished the discussion about the man's problem
    Ⓒ Because she wants the man to be more specific about his plan
    Ⓓ Because she does not want to do what the man suggests

5. What can be inferred about the professor?

    Ⓐ She tries to be fair to all of her students.
    Ⓑ She is not very flexible about her policies.
    Ⓒ She does not have very many students.
    Ⓓ She is not sure what she wants to do.

Listening 2 "Anthropology Class"

6. Which of the following is the main topic of the lecture?

     Ⓐ A progressive view of agriculture
     Ⓑ The conditions for the development of agriculture
     Ⓒ A comparison of hunter-gatherers and farmers
     Ⓓ The negative effects of agriculture on early farmers

7. What are two key characteristics of hunter-gatherers mentioned in the lecture?

    Click on 2 answer choices.

    Ⓐ They were taller than farmers.

    Ⓑ They ate less well than farmers.

    Ⓒ They lived longer than farmers.

    Ⓓ They were less physically fit than farmers.

8. Why does the professor say this:

     Ⓐ To emphasize the point that he has just made
     Ⓑ To indicate that another point will be made
     Ⓒ To demonstrate that the point is his opinion
     Ⓓ To regain the students' attention for the next point

9. How does the professor organize his lecture?

     Ⓐ He contrasts older theories of agriculture with newer ones.
     Ⓑ He makes an argument for the revisionist view of agriculture.
     Ⓒ He defines revisionism by giving examples of early farmers.
     Ⓓ He provides a chronological account of early farmers.

10. Which of the following statements best summarizes the position of the revisionists?

     Ⓐ The agricultural revolution affected all human activity.
     Ⓑ The development of agriculture had a positive influence on nutrition.
     Ⓒ Agriculture contributed to the health risks for early farmers.
     Ⓓ Agricultural people had to move from place to place to plant crops.

11. In the lecture, the professor describes the relationship between health and agriculture. Indicate whether each of the following is true or false. Click in the correct box for each phrase.

		Yes	No
A	Epidemics were spread by crowded towns and trade.		
B	Crop failures threatened the entire population.		
C	Wars with invading hunter-gatherers devastated them.		
D	Unbalanced diets contributed to malnutrition.		
E	Hard labor damaged their bones.		

Listening 3 "Business Class"

12. What is the lecture mainly about?

    Ⓐ Commercials on television
    Ⓑ Marketing brand-name products
    Ⓒ A book by Rob Frankel
    Ⓓ Selling Aunt Ruby's chicken

13. Why does the professor say this:

    Ⓐ To emphasize the importance of commercials
    Ⓑ To correct something that he said earlier
    Ⓒ To identify the time limits for most commercials
    Ⓓ To relate new information to a previous example

14. According to the professor, why do consumers develop brand loyalty?

    Ⓐ They have a relationship with the personality that the product projects.
    Ⓑ They are able to recognize the brand easily when they see it.
    Ⓒ They tend to make decisions based on recommendations by friends.
    Ⓓ They find a product that they like and continue to buy it.

15. How does the professor emphasize his point about branding?

    Ⓐ He uses Aunt Ruby's chicken as an example.
    Ⓑ He defines it by contrasting it with related concepts.
    Ⓒ He refers to a book that he has written.
    Ⓓ He shows a familiar commercial in class.

16. Why does the professor mention laundry detergent?

    Ⓐ To give an example of price wars
    Ⓑ To show that consumers buy different brands
    Ⓒ To name an industry that introduces new brands
    Ⓓ To explain the concept of brand loyalty

17. According to the professor, what would be a good way to sell a product?

    Ⓐ Design a good logo to present the product to the public
    Ⓑ Hire a celebrity that customers like and relate to
    Ⓒ Make it easy for consumers to recognize the packaging
    Ⓓ Increase the customer service for the product

PART II

Listening 4 "Students on Campus"

18. What is the purpose of this conversation?

    Ⓐ The man wants to borrow the woman's lab notes.
    Ⓑ The woman is helping the man to write a report.
    Ⓒ The man asks the woman to study for their test with him.
    Ⓓ The woman and the man are performing an experiment.

19. What is the study about?

    Ⓐ Reaction times for drivers drinking alcohol in comparison with those of nondrinkers
    Ⓑ The effects of drinking beer as compared with those of drinking gin and tonic
    Ⓒ The time that it takes to stop a car going 35 miles per hour when the brakes are applied
    Ⓓ The problems of riding bicycles on college campuses that have 35 mile-per-hour speed limits

20. According to the man, why is it important to mention that the subjects were randomly selected?

   Ⓐ The random selection explains why the results were so general.
   Ⓑ This information allows another researcher to repeat the experiment.
   Ⓒ The lab assistant included it in the example that the students received.
   Ⓓ Randomly selected subjects assure researchers of an accurate outcome.

21. Why does the woman say this:

   Ⓐ She is not sure about her observation.
   Ⓑ She is insulting the man with this comment.
   Ⓒ She is certain the man agrees with her.
   Ⓓ She is asking for the man's opinion.

22. Which section includes the conclusions?

   Ⓐ Discussion
   Ⓑ Results
   Ⓒ Chart
   Ⓓ Introduction

Listening 5 "Biology Class"

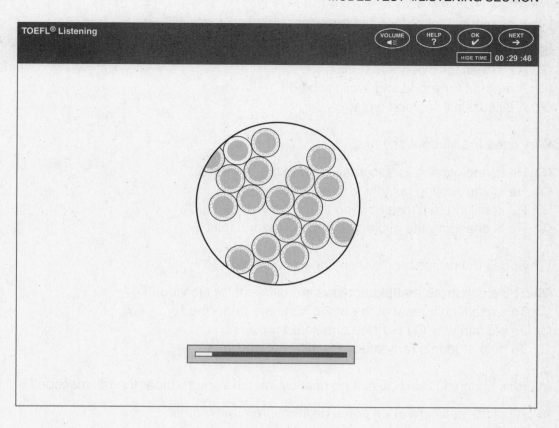

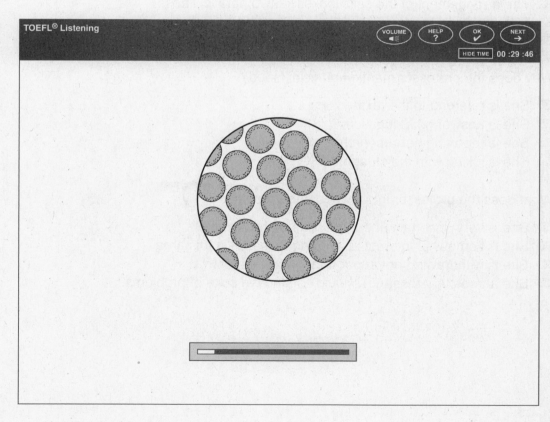

23. What aspect of blood does the professor mainly discuss?

   Ⓐ An explanation of stem cells
   Ⓑ A process for blood transfusion
   Ⓒ A method for producing artificial blood
   Ⓓ A discussion of blood typing

24. Why does the student say this:

   Ⓐ He is apologizing for disagreeing with the professor.
   Ⓑ He is interrupting politely to ask a question.
   Ⓒ He is talking to himself during the lecture.
   Ⓓ He is changing the subject of the professor's talk.

25. Why does the professor mention fingerprints?

   Ⓐ To demonstrate that blood types are different for individuals
   Ⓑ To explain how most of the blood tests are performed
   Ⓒ To explain why O blood is considered universal
   Ⓓ To help students remember the different antigens

26. In cross matching, how does a compatible match appear under the microscope?

   Ⓐ All of the cells are at an equal distance from each other.
   Ⓑ The arrangement of the cells looks like two parallel lines.
   Ⓒ The cells tend to group together in a large clump.
   Ⓓ The red cells and the plasma separate in an irregular pattern.

27. Why does the professor mention artificial blood?

   Ⓐ She is referring to the textbook.
   Ⓑ She is answering a question.
   Ⓒ She is reporting her research.
   Ⓓ She is joking with the students.

28. What does the professor imply when she says this:

   Ⓐ She is very uncertain about the risks of the research.
   Ⓑ She is somewhat interested in doing research in this area.
   Ⓒ She is withdrawing her support for future research.
   Ⓓ She agrees that research should continue in spite of problems.

Listening 6 "Orientation Session"

29. What is this discussion mainly about?

  Ⓐ Success in college
  Ⓑ How to read faster
  Ⓒ Academic study skills
  Ⓓ Research on college students

30. How does the professor organize the discussion?

  Ⓐ She cites research to support her arguments.
  Ⓑ She gives a demonstration of her theory.
  Ⓒ She debates the issues with her students.
  Ⓓ She shares strategies that she developed.

31. Why does the professor mention running?

  Ⓐ To digress from the topic with a personal story
  Ⓑ To make a comparison between reading and running
  Ⓒ To show that reading requires physical effort
  Ⓓ To clarify the times two rule

32. Why does the professor say this:

  Ⓐ She doesn't think the point is very important.
  Ⓑ She is trying to finish the lecture on time.
  Ⓒ She thinks the idea will fit in better later on.
  Ⓓ She doesn't want the student to interrupt her.

33. The professor mentions several negative habits. Match these habits to the explanations. Click on the habit and drag it to the correct explanation.

Habit	Explanation
	Pauses that the eye makes
	Reading the same words more than once
	Moving your lips while reading

  Ⓐ Fixating
  Ⓑ Auditory reading
  Ⓒ Regressing

34. What would the professor probably like the students to do?

    Ⓐ Spend more time studying outside of class
    Ⓑ Use their dictionaries when they are reading
    Ⓒ Take one of her classes at the college
    Ⓓ Get help at the Learning Center

**Please turn off the audio. There is a 10-minute break
between the Listening section and the Speaking section.**

SPEAKING SECTION

 Model Test 4, Speaking Section, CD 7, Track 1

The Speaking section tests your ability to communicate in English in an academic setting. During the test, you will be presented with six speaking questions. The questions ask for a response to a single question, a conversation, a talk, or a lecture.

You may take notes as you listen, but notes are not graded. You may use your notes to answer the questions. Some of the questions ask for a response to a reading passage and a talk or a lecture. The reading passages and the questions are written, but most of the directions will be spoken.

Your speaking will be evaluated on both the fluency of the language and the accuracy of the content. You will have 15–20 seconds to prepare and 45–60 seconds to respond to each question. Typically, a good response will require all of the response time, but the answer will be complete by the end of the response time.

The time for the Speaking section is about 20 minutes. A clock on the screen will show you how much time you have to prepare your answer and how much time you have to record it.

Independent Speaking Question 1 "A City"

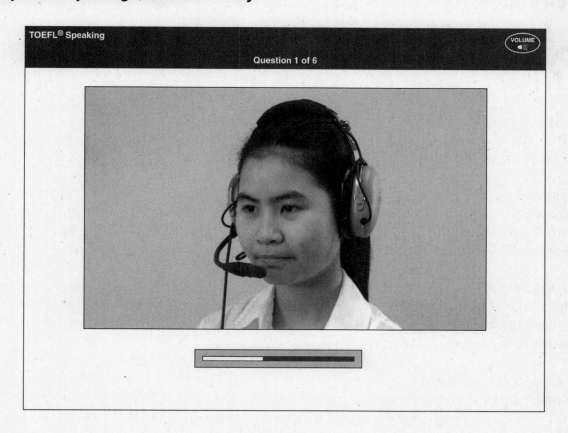

 Listen for a question about a familiar topic.

Question
Which city in the world would you like to visit? Use specific reasons and details to explain your choice.

Preparation Time: 15 seconds
Recording Time: 45 seconds

Independent Speaking Question 2 "Schools"

 Listen for a question that asks your opinion about a familiar topic.

Question
Some students prefer to attend a school that provides education for women only or men only. Other students prefer to attend a coeducational school for both women and men. Which environment do you think is better and why? Use specific reasons and examples to support your opinion.

Preparation Time: 15 seconds
Recording Time: 45 seconds

Integrated Speaking Question 3 "English Requirements"

Read a short passage and listen to a talk on the same topic.

Reading Time: 45 seconds

> Notice concerning proposed changes in language requirements
> All international students at Community College are currently required to submit a TOEFL score of 80 in order to be admitted to credit classes. Students who score lower than 80 are referred to the English Language Institute for additional language instruction. The college is considering a proposal that would allow students with a score of 75 to take at least one credit class while they continue to study part time in the English Language Institute. The students would be assigned to an academic advisor who would help them select an appropriate course. This proposal will be discussed at a public meeting in the student union at 7 P.M. on December 1.

TOEFL® Speaking

Question 3 of 6

 Now listen to a student who is speaking at the meeting. She is expressing her opinion about the policy for international students.

Question
The student expresses her opinion of the policy for international students. Report her opinion and explain the reasons that she gives for having that opinion.

Preparation Time: 30 seconds
Recording Time: 60 seconds

Integrated Speaking Question 4 "Myths and Legends"

Read a short passage and then listen to part of a lecture on the same topic.

Reading Time: 45 seconds

Myths and Legends
Myths are stories that explain the origin of events from the distant past, as, for example, how the universe was created, how human beings and animals populated the Earth, the reason that death exists, and the nature of the afterlife. Myths are usually tied to religious beliefs and involve beings with supernatural powers. In contrast, legends usually refer to stories about a more recent period of time, and the characters are often real people with heroic qualities that reflect the values of their society and culture. Because the heroes in legends often become larger than life as the legend is retold and embellished, they may actually be attributed with supernatural powers like their mythological counterparts. This blurs the distinction between mythology and legends.

 Now listen to part of a lecture in an anthropology class. The professor is talking about the legend of Paul Bunyan.

Question
Using the main points and examples from the reading, explain the differences between myths and legends. Then refer to the lecture to explain why Paul Bunyan would be considered a legend.

Preparation Time: 30 seconds
Recording Time: 60 seconds

Integrated Speaking Question 5 "Roommate"

 Now listen to a short conversation between a student and her advisor.

Question

Describe the woman's problem and the two suggestions that her advisor makes about how to handle it. What do you think the woman should do, and why?

Preparation Time: 20 seconds
Recording Time: 60 seconds

Integrated Speaking Question 6 "Urban Wildlife"

 Now listen to part of a lecture in a biology class. The professor is discussing the types of habitats for wildlife found in cities.

Question
Using the main points and examples from the lecture, describe the two general types of habitats for wildlife found in urban areas.

Preparation Time: 20 seconds
Recording Time: 60 seconds

WRITING SECTION

The Writing section tests your ability to write essays in English similar to those that you would write in college courses.

During the test, you will write two essays. The integrated essay asks for your response to an academic reading passage and a lecture on the same topic. You may take notes as you read and listen, but notes are not graded. You may use your notes to write the essay. The lecture will be spoken, but the directions and the questions will be written. You will have 20 minutes to plan, write, and revise your response. Typically, a good essay for the integrated topic will require that you write 150–225 words.

The independent essay usually asks for your opinion about a familiar topic. You will have 30 minutes to plan, write, and revise your response. Typically, a good essay for the independent topic will require that you write 300–350 words.

A clock on the screen will show you how much time you have to complete each essay.

Integrated Essay "Jet Streams"

You have 20 minutes to plan, write, and revise your response to a reading passage and a lecture on the same topic. First, read the passage and take notes. Then, listen to the lecture and take notes. Finally, write your response to the writing question. Typically, a good response will require that you write 150–225 words.

Reading Passage
Time: 3 minutes

    The jet stream is an irregular band of wind that occurs in high altitudes at about 20,000 feet, that is, between 6 and 9 miles above the surface of the Earth. Consequently, the jet stream wanders near the top of the Earth's troposphere, and, coincidentally, that is exactly where most of the Earth's weather patterns occur. It is helpful to think of the jet stream like a river of air that occurs at several different locations, but in general flows from west to east over the middle latitudes. Technically, to be called a jet stream, the winds should be moving faster than 57 miles an hour, but it can have average core speeds of 190 miles per hour, and in the winter, when the jet stream is strongest, winds have been clocked at 300 miles an hour. For the most part, the winds are stronger in the winter because during the winter months the surface temperature contrasts more with the temperature in the troposphere. To put that another way, the greater the contrast in the temperature of the Earth and the atmosphere, the stronger the jet stream winds will blow.

    In general, there are two jet streams between the equator and the North Pole. The subtropical jet stream tends to hover around the southern border of the continental United States, whereas the polar jet stream blows over Idaho and Montana. The condition that causes these two streams is the difference in the temperature between the tropic and the arctic regions of the Earth, which tends to concentrate in small zones called fronts. It is along these fronts that storms tend to develop. The jet streams blow the storms along their path. When the jet stream is over an area, strong storms may move into it, but when the jet stream has dipped out of the area, calm, dry weather will probably be forecast.

Model Test 4, Writing Section, CD 7, Track 2

TOEFL® Writing   VOLUME   HELP ?   NEXT →

Now listen to a lecture on the same topic as the passage that you have just read.

Question

Describe *jet streams* by using the information in the reading, and provide examples of the way that they affect air travel by drawing on the material that you heard in the lecture.

Independent Essay "Lifestyle"

Question

Many people believe that it is very important to make large amounts of money, while others are satisfied to earn a comfortable living. Analyze each viewpoint and take a stand. Give specific reasons for your position.

 This is the end of Model Test 4.
To check your answers, refer to "Explanatory or Example Answers and Audio Scripts for Model Tests: Model Test 4," Chapter 7, pages 649–676.

MODEL TEST 5: PROGRESS TEST

READING SECTION

The Reading section tests your ability to understand reading passages like those in college textbooks. The passages are about 700 words in length.

This is the short format for the Reading section. On the short format, you will respond to three passages. After each passage, you will answer 12–14 questions about it.

Most questions are worth 1 point, but the last question in each passage is worth more than 1 point.

You will have 60 minutes to read all of the passages and answer the questions. You may take notes while you read, but notes are not graded. You may use your notes to answer the questions. Some passages may include a word or phrase that is underlined in blue. Click on the word or phrase to see a glossary definition or explanation.

Choose the best answer for multiple-choice questions. Follow the directions on the page or on the screen for computer-assisted questions. Click on **Next** to go to the next question. Click on **Back** to return to the previous question. You may return to previous questions for all of the passages in the same reading part, but after you go to the next part, you will not be able to return to passages in a previous part. Be sure that you have answered all of the questions for the passages in each part before you click on **Next** at the end of the passage to move to the next part.

You can click on **Review** to see a chart of the questions you have answered and the questions you have not answered in each part. From this screen, you can return to the question you want to answer in the part that is open.

A clock on the screen will show you how much time you have to complete the Reading section.

PART I

Reading 1 "Rising Sea Levels"

Perhaps the most pervasive climatic effect of global warming is rapid escalation of ice melt. Mount Kilimanjaro in Africa, portions of the South American Andes, and the Himalayas will very likely lose most of their glacial ice within the next two decades, affecting local water resources. Glacial ice continues its retreat in Alaska. NASA scientists determined that Greenland's ice sheet is thinning by about 1 m per year. The additional meltwater, especially from continental ice masses and glaciers, is adding to a rise in sea level worldwide. Satellite remote sensing is monitoring global sea level, sea ice, and continental ice. Worldwide measurements confirm that sea level rose during the last century.

Surrounding the margins of Antarctica, and constituting about 11% of its surface area, are numerous ice shelves, especially where sheltering inlets or bays exist. Covering many thousands of square kilometers, these ice shelves extend over the sea while still attached to continental ice. The loss of these ice shelves does not significantly raise sea level, for they already displace seawater. The concern is for the possible surge of grounded continental ice that the ice shelves hold back from the sea.

Although ice shelves constantly break up to produce icebergs, some large sections have recently broken free. In 1998 an iceberg (150 km by 35 km) broke off the Ronne Ice Shelf, southeast of the Antarctic Peninsula. In March 2000 an iceberg tagged B-15 broke off the Ross Ice Shelf (some 90° longitude west of the Antarctic Peninsula), measuring 300 km by 40 km. Since 1993, six ice shelves have disintegrated in Antarctica. About 8000 km of ice shelf are gone, changing maps, freeing up islands to circumnavigation, and creating thousands of icebergs. The Larsen Ice Shelf, along the east coast of the Antarctic Peninsula, has been retreating slowly for years. Larsen-A suddenly disintegrated in 1995. In only 35 days in early 2002, Larsen-B collapsed into icebergs. This ice loss is likely a result of the 2.5°C temperature increase in the region in the last 50 years. In response to the increasing warmth, the Antarctic Peninsula is sporting new vegetation growth, previously not seen there.

→ A loss of polar ice mass, augmented by melting of alpine and mountain glaciers (which experienced more than a 30% decrease in overall ice mass during the last century) will affect sea-level rise. The IPCC assessment states that "between one-third to one-half of the existing mountain glacier mass could disappear over the next hundred years." Also, "there is conclusive evidence for a worldwide recession of mountain glaciers . . . This is among the clearest and best evidence for a change in energy balance at the Earth's surface since the end of the 19th century."

A Sea-level rise must be expressed as a range of values that are under constant reassessment. B The 2001 IPCC forecast for global mean sea-level rise this century, given regional variations, is from 0.11–0.88 m. C The median value of 0.48 m is two to four times the rate of previous increase. These increases would continue beyond 2100 even if greenhouse gas concentrations are stabilized. D

→ The Scripps Institute of Oceanography in La Jolla, California, has kept ocean temperature records since 1916. Significant temperature increases are being recorded to depths of more than 300 m as ocean temperature records are set. Even the warming of the ocean itself will contribute about 25% of sea-level rise, simply because of *thermal expansion* of the water. In addition, any change in ocean temperature has a profound effect on weather and, indirectly, on agriculture and soil moisture. In fact the ocean system appears to have delayed some surface global warming during the past century through absorption of excess atmospheric heat.

→ A quick survey of world coastlines shows that even a moderate rise could bring changes of unparalleled proportions. At stake are the river deltas, lowland coastal farming valleys, and low-lying mainland areas, all contending with high water, high tides, and higher storm surges. Particularly tragic social and economic consequences will affect small island states—being able to adjust within their present country boundaries, disruption of biological systems, loss of biodiversity, reduction in water resources, among the impacts. There could be both internal and international migration of affected human populations, spread over decades, as people move away from coastal flooding from the sea-level rise.

1. The word <u>confirm</u> in the passage is closest in meaning to

   Ⓐ clarify
   Ⓑ prove
   Ⓒ assume
   Ⓓ predict

2. There is more new plant life in Antarctica recently because

   Ⓐ the mountain glaciers have melted
   Ⓑ the land masses have split into islands
   Ⓒ the icebergs have broken into smaller pieces
   Ⓓ the temperature has risen by a few degrees

3. It may be inferred from this passage that icebergs are formed

   Ⓐ by a drop in ocean temperatures
   Ⓑ when an ice shelf breaks free
   Ⓓ from intensely cold islands
   Ⓒ if mountain glaciers melt

34

4. The word <u>there</u> in the passage refers to

    Ⓐ polar ice mass in the last 50 years
    Ⓑ the temperature increase
    Ⓒ new vegetation growth
    Ⓓ in the Antarctic Peninsula

35

5. In paragraph 4, the author explains the loss of polar and glacial ice by

    Ⓐ stating an educated opinion
    Ⓑ referring to data in a study
    Ⓒ comparing sea levels worldwide
    Ⓓ presenting his research

Paragraph 4 is marked with an arrow [➔].

36

6. The word <u>conclusive</u> in the passage is closest in meaning to

    Ⓐ definite
    Ⓑ independent
    Ⓒ unique
    Ⓓ valuable

37

7. The word <u>range</u> in the passage is closest in meaning to

    Ⓐ function
    Ⓑ scale
    Ⓒ version
    Ⓓ lack

38

8. Why does the author mention the Scripps Institute of Oceanography in paragraph 6?

    Ⓐ The location near the coast endangers the Scripps facility.
    Ⓑ Research at Scripps indicates that the ocean is getting warmer.
    Ⓒ One quarter of the rising sea levels has been recorded at Scripps.
    Ⓓ Records at Scripps have been kept for nearly one hundred years.

Paragraph 6 is marked with an arrow [➔].

9. Which of the sentences below best expresses the information in the highlighted statement in the passage? The other choices change the meaning or leave out important information.

Ⓐ Global warming on the surface of the planet may have been retarded during the last hundred years because heat in the atmosphere was absorbed by the oceans.

Ⓑ Global warming on the surface of the ocean was greater than it was on the rest of the planet during the past century because of heat in the atmosphere.

Ⓒ Too much heat in the atmosphere has caused global warming on the surface of the planet for the past hundred years in spite of the moderation caused by the oceans.

Ⓓ There is less heat being absorbed by the oceans now than there was a hundred years ago before the atmosphere began to experience global warming.

39

10. According to paragraph 7, why will people move away from the coastlines in the future?

Ⓐ It will be too warm for them to live there.

Ⓑ The coastlines will have too much vegetation.

Ⓒ Flooding will destroy the coastal areas.

Ⓓ No agricultural crops will be grown on the coasts.

Paragraph 7 is marked with an arrow [➜].

40

11. Which of the following statements most accurately reflects the author's opinion about rising sea levels?

Ⓐ Sea levels would rise without global warming.

Ⓑ Rising sea levels can be reversed.

Ⓒ The results of rising sea levels will be serious.

Ⓓ Sea levels are rising because of new glaciers.

12. Look at the four squares [■] that show where the following sentence could be inserted in the passage.

During the last century, sea level rose 10–20 cm, a rate 10 times higher than the average rate during the last 3000 years.

Where could the sentence best be added?

Click on a square [■] to insert the sentence in the passage.

13. **Directions:** An introduction for a short summary of the passage appears below. Complete the summary by selecting the THREE answer choices that mention the most important points in the passage. Some sentences do not belong in the summary because they express ideas that are not included in the passage or are minor points from the passage. *This question is worth 2 points.*

Global warming is causing a rise in sea levels, with accompanying changes in coastal boundaries as well as social and economic ramifications.

-
-
-

Answer Choices

Ⓐ The ice shelf called Larsen-A suddenly disintegrated in 1995.

Ⓑ Thermal expansion due to the warming of ocean water will cause about one quarter of the rise in sea level.

Ⓒ Continental ice shelves and grounded ice sheets from Antarctica to the Polar cap are melting into the oceans.

Ⓓ Beginning in 1916, the Scripps Institute of Oceanography in California has documented ocean temperatures.

Ⓔ The melting of glacial ice on high mountain ranges will affect regional water resources worldwide.

Ⓕ Scientists at NASA have concluded that the ice sheet in Greenland is melting at a rate of about 1 meter every year.

PART II

Reading 2 "Organic Architecture"

One of the most striking personalities in the development of early-twentieth-century architecture was Frank Lloyd Wright (1867–1959). Wright attended the University of Wisconsin in Madison before moving to Chicago, where he eventually joined the firm headed by Louis Sullivan. Wright set out to create "architecture of democracy." Early influences were the volumetric shapes in a set of educational blocks the German educator Friedrich Froebel designed, the organic unity of a Japanese building Wright saw at the Columbian Exposition in Chicago in 1893, and a Jeffersonian belief in individualism and populism. Always a believer in architecture as "natural" and "organic," Wright saw it as serving free individuals who have the right to move within a "free" space, envisioned as a nonsymmetrical design interacting spatially with its natural surroundings. He sought to develop an organic unity of planning, structure, materials, and site. Wright identified the principle of continuity as fundamental to understanding his view of organic unity: "Classic architecture was all fixation. . . . Now why not let walls, ceilings, floors become seen as component parts of each other? . . . This ideal, profound in its architectural implications . . . I called . . . continuity."

Wright manifested his vigorous originality early, and by 1900 he had arrived at a style entirely his own. In his work during the first decade of the twentieth century, his cross-axial plan and his fabric of continuous roof planes and screens defined a new domestic architecture.

→ Wright fully expressed these elements and concepts in Robie House, built between 1907 and 1909. Like other buildings in the Chicago area he designed at about the same time, this was called a "prairie house." Wright conceived the long, sweeping ground-hugging lines, unconfined by abrupt wall limits, as reaching out toward and capturing the expansiveness of the Midwest's great flatlands. Abandoning all symmetry, the architect eliminated a façade, extended the roofs far beyond the walls, and all but concealed the entrance. Wright filled the "wandering" plan of the Robie House with intricately joined spaces (some large and open, others closed), grouped freely around a great central fireplace. A (He believed strongly in the hearth's age-old domestic significance.) Wright designed enclosed patios, overhanging roofs, and strip windows to provide unexpected light sources and glimpses of the outdoors as people move through the interior space. These elements, together with the open ground plan, create a sense of space-in-motion inside and out. B He set masses and voids in equilibrium; the flow of interior space determined the exterior wall placement. C The exterior's sharp angular planes meet at apparently odd angles, matching the complex play of interior solids, which function not as inert containing surfaces but as elements equivalent in role to the design's spaces. D

The Robie House is a good example of Wright's "naturalism," his adjusting of a building to its site. However, in this particular case, the confines of the city lot constrained the building-to-site relationship more than did the sites of some of Wright's more expansive suburban and country homes. The Kaufmann House, nicknamed "Fallingwater" and designed as a weekend retreat at Bear Run near Pittsburgh, is a prime example of the latter. Perched on a rocky hillside over a small waterfall, this structure extends the Robie House's blocky masses in all four directions. The contrast in textures between concrete, painted metal, and natural stones in its walls enliven its shapes, as does Wright's use of full-length strip windows to create a stunning interweaving of interior and exterior space.

→ The implied message of Wright's new architecture was space, not mass—a space designed to fit the patron's life and enclosed and divided as required. Wright took special pains to meet his client's requirements, often designing all the accessories of a house. In the late 1930s, he acted on a cherished dream to provide good architectural design for less prosperous people by adapting the ideas of his prairie house to plans for smaller, less expensive dwellings. The publication of Wright's plans brought him a measure of fame in Europe, especially in Holland and Germany. The issuance in Berlin in 1910 of a portfolio of his work and an exhibition of his designs the following year stimulated younger architects to adopt some of his ideas about open plans. Some forty years before his career ended, his work was already of revolutionary significance.

14. Frank Lloyd Wright took inspiration for his work from

   Ⓐ the designs in classical architecture
   Ⓑ Jefferson's home near Washington
   Ⓒ educational blocks by Friedrich Froebel
   Ⓓ a trip to Japan when he was a young man

15. What did Wright mean by the term "organic?"

   Ⓐ Fixation
   Ⓑ Ideal
   Ⓒ Continuity
   Ⓓ Classic

16. The phrase <u>his own</u> in the passage refers to

   Ⓐ style
   Ⓑ originality
   Ⓒ work
   Ⓓ plan

17. The word <u>conceived</u> in the passage is closest in meaning to

   Ⓐ utilized
   Ⓑ noticed
   Ⓒ created
   Ⓓ examined

18. The word <u>Abandoning</u> in the passage is closest in meaning to

   Ⓐ Influencing
   Ⓑ Modifying
   Ⓒ Perfecting
   Ⓓ Discontinuing

19. It can be inferred from paragraph 3 that the author gives details for the design of the Robie House because

Ⓐ the design included both indoor and outdoor plans
Ⓑ Robie House included many of Wright's original ideas
Ⓒ all of the accessories of the house were included in the design
Ⓓ Wright lived in Robie House between 1907 and 1909

Paragraph 3 is marked with an arrow [➜].

20. The word prime in the passage is closest in meaning to

Ⓐ most important
Ⓑ most numerous
Ⓒ most common
Ⓓ most accepted

21. How was "Fallingwater" different from the "Robie House"?

Ⓐ "Fallingwater" was an earlier example of naturalism than "Robie House."
Ⓑ "Fallingwater" was much smaller than "Robie House" because it was a retreat.
Ⓒ "Fallingwater" was better suited to the site with views through huge windows.
Ⓓ "Fallingwater" was built with an open floor plan, unlike "Robie House."

22. According to paragraph 5, why did Wright begin to build smaller versions of his prairie designs?

Ⓐ To publish his plans in Europe
Ⓑ To give the middle class a good design
Ⓒ To help younger architects with their work
Ⓓ To begin a revolution in architecture

Paragraph 5 is marked with an arrow [➜].

23. According to paragraph 5, Wright's work became well known in Europe because

Ⓐ his plans were published and he held exhibitions
Ⓑ he visited several universities and gave lectures
Ⓒ his revolutionary ideas appealed to younger architects
Ⓓ he was already very famous in the United States

Paragraph 5 is marked with an arrow [➜].

24. According to the passage, a prairie house has all of the following features EXCEPT

Ⓐ a central fireplace
Ⓑ enclosed patios
Ⓒ an inviting entrance
Ⓓ strip windows

25. Look at the four squares [■] that show where the following sentence could be inserted in the passage.

    Wright matched his new and fundamental interior spatial arrangement in his exterior treatment.

    Where could the sentence best be added?

    Click on a square [■] to insert the sentence in the passage.

26. **Directions:** An introduction for a short summary of the passage appears below. Complete the summary by selecting the THREE answer choices that mention the most important points in the passage. Some sentences do not belong in the summary because they express ideas that are not included in the passage or are minor points from the passage. *This question is worth 2 points.*

    By 1900, Frank Lloyd Wright had developed a unique style of architecture.

    -
    -
    -

Answer Choices

A Wright spent a few years extending his influence to Europe where he was well known.

B Frank Lloyd Wright had attended the University of Wisconsin prior to taking a position with a Chicago firm.

C Wright became famous for spaces that were true to their organic functions.

D "Fallingwater," like other suburban and country homes that Wright built, joined the structure to the natural setting.

E Wright was interested in the design of German building blocks for children created by Friedrich Froebel.

F Robie House and other buildings in Chicago were examples of an organic structure called a "prairie house."

Reading 3 "New Women of the Ice Age"

The status of women in a society depends in large measure on their role in the economy. The reinterpretation of the Paleolithic past centers on new views of the role of women in the food-foraging economy. Amassing critical and previously overlooked evidence from Dolní Věstonice and the neighboring site of Pavlov, researchers Olga Soffer, James Adovasio, and David Hyland now propose that human survival there had little to do with men hurling spears at big-game animals. Instead, observes Soffer, one of the world's leading authorities on Ice Age hunters and gatherers and an archeologist at the University of Illinois in Champaign-Urbana, it depended largely on women, plants, and a technique of hunting previously invisible in the archeological evidence—net hunting. "This is not the image we've always had of Upper Paleolithic macho guys out killing animals up close and personal," Soffer explains. "Net hunting is communal, and it involves the labor of children and women. And this has lots of implications."

→ Many of these implications make her conservative colleagues cringe because they raise serious questions about the focus of previous studies. European archeologists have long concentrated on analyzing broken stone tools and butchered big-game bones, the most plentiful and best preserved relics of the Upper Paleolithic era (which stretched from 40,000 to 12,000 years ago). From these analyses, researchers have developed theories about how these societies once hunted and gathered food. Most researchers ruled out the possibility of women hunters for biological reasons. Adult females, they reasoned, had to devote themselves to breast-feeding and tending infants. "Human babies have always been immature and dependent," says Soffer. "If women are the people who are always involved with biological reproduction and the rearing of the young, then that is going to constrain their behavior. They have to provision that child. For fathers, provisioning is optional."

→ To test theories about Upper Paleolithic life, researchers looked to ethnography, the scientific description of modern and historical cultural groups. While the lives of modern hunters do not exactly duplicate those of ancient hunters, they supply valuable clues to universal human behavior. In many historical societies, Soffer observes, women played a key part in net hunting, since the technique did not call for brute strength nor did it place young mothers in physical peril. Among Australian aborigines, for example. Women as well as men knotted the mesh, laboring for as much as two or three years on a fine net. Among Native American groups, they helped lay out their handiwork on poles across a valley floor. Then the entire camp joined forces as beaters. Fanning out across the valley, men, women, and children alike shouted and screamed, flushing out game and driving it in the direction of the net. "Everybody and their mother could participate," says Soffer. "Some people were beating, others were screaming or holding the net. And once you got the net on these animals, they were immobilized. You didn't need brute force. You could club them, hit them any old way."

→ People seldom returned home empty-handed. Researchers living among the net hunting Mbuti in the forests of the Congo report that they capture game every time they lay out their woven traps, scooping up 50 percent of the animals encountered. "Nets are a far more valued item in their panoply of food-producing things than bows and arrows are," says Adovasio. So lethal are these traps that the Mbuti generally rack up more meat than they can consume, trading the surplus with neighbors. Other net hunters traditionally smoked or dried their catch and stored it for leaner times.

→ Ⓐ Soffer doubts that the inhabitants of Dolní Věstonice and Pavlov were the only net makers in Ice Age Europe. Ⓑ Camps stretching from Germany to Russia are littered with a notable abundance of small-game bones, from hares to birds like ptarmigan. And at least some of their inhabitants whittled bone tools that look much like the awls and net spacers favored by historical net makers. Ⓒ

Although the full range of their activities is unlikely ever to be known for certain, there is good reason to believe that Ice Age women played a host of powerful roles. Ⓓ And the research that suggests those roles is rapidly changing our mental images of the past. For Soffer and others, these are exciting times.

27. How do Soffer's theories compare with those of more conservative researchers?

   Ⓐ They are in agreement for the most part regarding the activities that women performed.
   Ⓑ Soffer has based her theories on archeological evidence that her colleagues had not considered.
   Ⓒ Conservative researchers are doubtful about the studies of stone tools and big-game bones.
   Ⓓ Her theories are much more difficult to prove because she relies on modern cultural evidence.

28. The word it in the passage refers to

   Ⓐ evidence
   Ⓑ survival
   Ⓒ site
   Ⓓ technique

29. The word implications in the passage is closest in meaning to

   Ⓐ defects
   Ⓑ advantages
   Ⓒ suggestions
   Ⓓ controversies

30. What can be inferred about Dr. Soffer from paragraph 2?

   Ⓐ She does not agree that women should be the primary caretakers for children.
   Ⓑ She is probably not as conservative in her views as many of her colleagues.
   Ⓒ She is most likely a biologist who is doing research on European women.
   Ⓓ She has recently begun studying hunting and gathering in the Upper Paleolithic era.

   Paragraph 2 is marked with an arrow [→].

31. The word constrain in the passage is closest in meaning to

   Ⓐ limit
   Ⓑ plan
   Ⓒ notice
   Ⓓ improve

32. Which of the sentences below best expresses the information in the highlighted statement in the passage? The other choices change the meaning or leave out important information.

   Ⓐ Historically, net hunting was considered too dangerous for women because it required physical strength that they did not possess.
   Ⓑ Women throughout history have participated in societies by teaching their children how to use net hunting.
   Ⓒ In many societies, the women did not participate in net hunting because hunting was an exception to historical traditions.
   Ⓓ Because, historically, net hunting was not perilous and did not require great strength, women have been important participants in it.

33. Based on the information in paragraph 3, which of the following best explains the term "net hunting"?

   Ⓐ An approach to hunting developed by Australian fishermen
   Ⓑ A very dangerous method of hunting large animals
   Ⓒ A way for the camp to protect women and children from wild animals
   Ⓓ A hunting technique that includes the entire community

   Paragraph 3 is marked with an arrow [➜].

34. Why does the author mention Native American and Aborigine groups in paragraph 3?

   Ⓐ To give examples of modern groups in which women participate in net hunting
   Ⓑ To demonstrate how net hunting should be carried out in modern societies
   Ⓒ To describe net hunting techniques that protect the women in the group
   Ⓓ To contrast their net hunting techniques with those of the people in the Congo

   Paragraph 3 is marked with an arrow [➜].

35. According to paragraph 4, which of the following is true about hunting in the Congo?

   Ⓐ The Mbuti value their nets almost as much as their bows and arrows.
   Ⓑ Trade with other tribes is limited because all food must be stored.
   Ⓒ Net hunters are successful in capturing half of their prey.
   Ⓓ Vegetables are the staple part of the diet for the Mbuti people.

   Paragraph 4 is marked with an arrow [➜].

36. According to paragraph 5, why does Soffer conclude that net hunting was widespread in Europe during the Ice Age?

   Ⓐ Because there are a lot of small game still living in Europe
   Ⓑ Because tools to make nets have been found in camps throughout Europe
   Ⓒ Because the bones of small animals were found in Dolní Věstonice and Pavlov
   Ⓓ Because German and Russian researchers have verified her data

   Paragraph 5 is marked with an arrow [➜].

37. The word <u>roles</u> in the passage is closest in meaning to

   Ⓐ problems
   Ⓑ developments
   Ⓒ locations
   Ⓓ functions

38. Look at the four squares [■] that show where the following sentence could be inserted in the passage.

   Such findings, agree Soffer and Adovasio, reveal just how shaky the most widely accepted reconstructions of Upper Paleolithic life are.

   Where could the sentence best be added?

   Click on a square [■] to insert the sentence in the passage.

39. **Directions**: Complete the table by matching the phrases on the left with the headings on the right. Select the appropriate answer choices and drag them to the theory to which they relate. TWO of the answer choices will NOT be used. *This question is worth 4 points.*

   To delete an answer choice, click on it. To see the passage, click on **View Text**.

   Answer Choices   **Previous Theories**

   Ⓐ The introduction of farming   •
      methods changed the status of women.

   Ⓑ Finding big game bones is a major   •
      purpose of archaeological digs.

   Ⓒ Stone tools prove that large animals   •
      were used for provisions.

   Ⓓ Caring for babies limited women to   **Soffer's Theory**
      gathering food instead of hunting.

   Ⓔ Big game hunting was not as important   •
      as net hunting in the Ice Age.

   Ⓕ Bows and arrows are considered   •
      less important than traps.

   Ⓖ The responsibilities of women in the   •
      Paleolithic period included net hunting.

   Ⓗ Paleolithic women participated in big   •
      game hunting expeditions.

   Ⓘ Bone tools such as spacers and awls
      provide evidence for the theory.

LISTENING SECTION

 Model Test 5, Listening Section, CD 7, Track 4, continued on CD 8, Track 1

The Listening section tests your ability to understand spoken English that is typical of interactions and academic speech on college campuses. During the test, you will respond to conversations and lectures.

This is the long format for the Listening section. On the long format, you will respond to three conversations and six lectures. After each listening passage, you will answer 5–6 questions about it. Only two conversations and four lectures will be graded. The other conversation and lectures are part of an experimental section for future tests. Because you will not know which conversations and lectures will be graded, you must try to do your best on all of them.

You will hear each conversation or lecture one time. You may take notes while you listen, but notes are not graded. You may use your notes to answer the questions.

Choose the best answer for multiple-choice questions. Follow the directions on the page or on the screen for computer-assisted questions. Click on **Next** and **OK** to go to the next question. You cannot return to previous questions. You have 20–30 minutes to answer all of the questions. A clock on the screen will show you how much time you have to complete your answers for the section. The clock does not count the time you are listening to the conversations and lectures.

PART I

Listening 1 "Professor's Office"

1. Why does the woman go to see her professor?

   Ⓐ To get advice about memorizing information
   Ⓑ To clarify several terms that she doesn't understand
   Ⓒ To get permission to bring her children to class
   Ⓓ To ask a question about classroom procedures

2. What do semantic memory and episodic memory have in common?

   Ⓐ They are both included in short-term memory.
   Ⓑ They do not concentrate on each step in the process.
   Ⓒ They are subcategories of declarative memory.
   Ⓓ They are the two major types of long-term memory.

3. When the professor gives the example of riding a bicycle, what kind of memory is he referring to?

   Ⓐ Declarative memory
   Ⓑ Episodic memory
   Ⓒ Procedural memory
   Ⓓ Semantic memory

4. What does the student mean when she says this:

Ⓐ She wants confirmation that the professor understands.
Ⓑ She is worried that the professor may not be able to remember.
Ⓒ She remembers something else that she needs to say.
Ⓓ She disagrees with the professor's example about vocabulary.

5. What does the professor suggest?

Ⓐ He wants the woman to come back to his office again.
Ⓑ He expects the woman to ask questions in writing.
Ⓒ He offers to respond to additional questions by e-mail.
Ⓓ He does not think that the woman will have more questions.

Listening 2 "Literature Class"

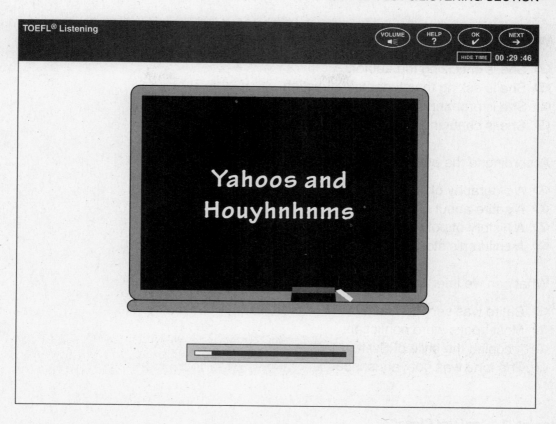

6. What is the discussion mainly about?

    Ⓐ The life of author Jonathan Swift
    Ⓑ A narrative of the fourth voyage of Gulliver
    Ⓒ A description of the Houyhnhnms
    Ⓓ The literature of the 1700s

7. What does Gulliver learn about himself?

    Ⓐ He is like the Yahoos in many ways.
    Ⓑ He does not want to return to England.
    Ⓒ He wants to write about his experience.
    Ⓓ He is afraid of the Houyhnhnm.

8. In the discussion, the professor describes the characteristics of the Yahoos. Indicate whether each of the following is one of their characteristics. Click in the correct box for each sentence.

		Yes	No
A	They eat flowers.		
B	They have a foul odor.		
C	They engage in an immoral lifestyle.		
D	They are satirical caricatures of humans.		
E	They live in trees.		

9. Why does the professor say this: 🎧

  Ⓐ She is criticizing the author.
  Ⓑ She is asking the students a question.
  Ⓒ She is preparing to draw a conclusion.
  Ⓓ She is changing the subject.

10. According to the professor, what kind of book is *Gulliver's Travels*?

  Ⓐ A biography of Jonathan Swift
  Ⓑ A satire about mankind
  Ⓒ A history of politics in England
  Ⓓ A children's story about animals

11. What can we infer about the literature of the period?

  Ⓐ Satire was very popular.
  Ⓑ Most books were nonfiction.
  Ⓒ It copied the style of Swift.
  Ⓓ The tone was not very serious.

Listening 3 "Geology Class"

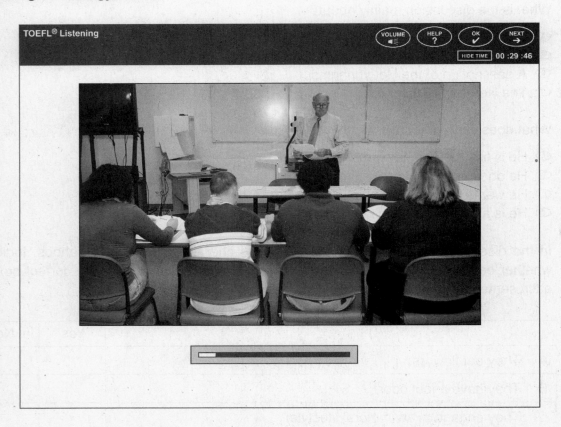

12. What is this discussion mainly about?

Ⓐ How to exploit nonrenewable mineral resources
Ⓑ The exploitation of minerals in protected environments
Ⓒ Pollution as a by-product of mineral exploitation
Ⓓ The economic and environmental costs of exploiting minerals

13. According to the professor, what are two problems that can be anticipated when roads are cut into an area for mining?

Click on 2 answer choices.

Ⓐ The labor is difficult to retain.

Ⓑ The natural landscape is damaged.

Ⓒ The roadbeds create waste piles.

Ⓓ The ecosystem is disturbed.

14. Why does the professor say this:

Ⓐ As encouragement for a more complete answer
Ⓑ Because he doesn't understand the student's answer
Ⓒ To give another student an opportunity to speak
Ⓓ For positive reinforcement of a correct answer

15. What option is proposed as an alternative when all of the mineral resources in easily accessible locations have been depleted?

    Ⓐ Converting to nonrenewable resources
    Ⓑ Concentrating on conservation of the resources
    Ⓒ Developing synthetic resources to replace minerals
    Ⓓ Using new technology to search the area again

16. What does the professor imply about the environmental costs of mineral exploitation?

    Ⓐ He thinks that the environmental costs are less than the economic costs.
    Ⓑ He regrets that the environment is damaged during mineral exploitation.
    Ⓒ He opposes mineral exploitation when it is done close to urban areas.
    Ⓓ He believes in exploiting the resources in national parks and historic reserves.

17. What does the professor want the students to do in this class session?

    Ⓐ Listen carefully and take notes
    Ⓑ Bring in alternative ideas to present
    Ⓒ Ask questions and draw conclusions
    Ⓓ Prepare for a quiz at the end

PART II

Listening 4 "Professor's Office"

18. Why does the student go to the professor's office?

    Ⓐ To change his schedule
    Ⓑ To apply for a job
    Ⓒ To introduce himself
    Ⓓ To help the professor

19. What does the professor mean when she says this:

    Ⓐ She does not want the man to be uncomfortable.
    Ⓑ She thinks that the responsibilities are too difficult.
    Ⓒ She is concerned that the man will be bored.
    Ⓓ She is worried that the man will not try to help her.

20. What experience does the man have that may be helpful?

    Ⓐ He knows how to operate the grading machine.
    Ⓑ He has answered the telephone in a law office.
    Ⓒ He has used computer programs for office work.
    Ⓓ He has been a work-study student in another office.

21. What is the pay for the work-study position?

    Ⓐ An hourly rate for sixteen hours per week regardless of the activity.
    Ⓑ An hourly rate for the time spent working but not for studying.
    Ⓒ A higher rate for working and a lower rate for studying.
    Ⓓ A weekly rate depending on the number of hours worked.

22. What can we assume about the meeting?

    Ⓐ The professor was impressed with the student.
    Ⓑ The student is not interested in the opportunity.
    Ⓒ The secretary will not need to interview the student.
    Ⓓ The work is very difficult to accomplish.

Listening 5 "Music Appreciation Class"

23. What is the main purpose of the lecture?

    Ⓐ To explain chamber music
    Ⓑ To give examples of composers
    Ⓒ To congratulate the University Quartet
    Ⓓ To introduce madrigal singing

24. What is the origin of the term *chamber music*?

    Ⓐ A medieval musical instrument
    Ⓑ An old word that means "small group"
    Ⓒ A place where the music was played
    Ⓓ A name of one of the original musicians

25. Which of the following are the key characteristics of chamber music in the Classical Period?

    Click on 2 answer choices.

    Ⓐ Baroque style

    Ⓑ Complex melodies

    Ⓒ Longer pieces

    Ⓓ Amateur musicians

26. What does the professor mean when she says this about Beethoven:

     ⓐ She doubts that Beethoven could have written the quartets.
     ⓑ She is in admiration of Beethoven's exceptional talent.
     ⓒ She thinks that the later quartets could have been improved.
     ⓓ She is inviting the students to question her information.

27. Why does the professor mention Impressionism?

     ⓐ She is comparing the experimentation in art with that in music.
     ⓑ She is making a transition into a discussion of art in the Modern Period.
     ⓒ She is giving an example of the work of the Romantics.
     ⓓ She is telling a story that includes some of the Impressionist painters.

28. How did the professor organize the lecture?

     ⓐ She compared different types of musical compositions.
     ⓑ She arranged the information in chronological order.
     ⓒ She argued the advantages and disadvantages.
     ⓓ She responded to questions that the students asked.

Listening 6 "Botany Class"

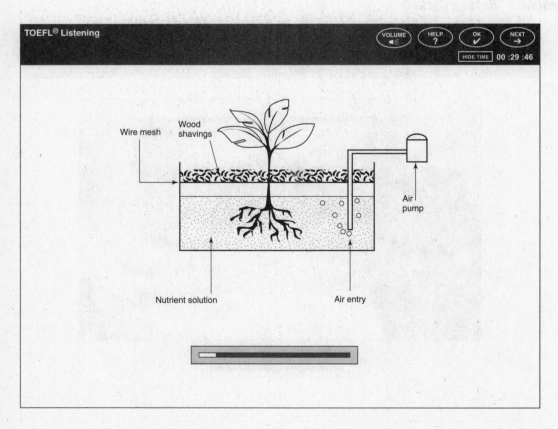

29. What is this discussion mainly about?

   Ⓐ Growing plants without soil
   Ⓑ Mixing nutrients in water
   Ⓒ Identifying chemicals in soil
   Ⓓ Solving problems in the water

30. Why does the professor talk about the history of hydroponics?

   Ⓐ She wants to put the modern method in historical context.
   Ⓑ She is trying to prove that hydroponics is a new idea.
   Ⓒ She is following the information in the textbook very closely.
   Ⓓ She digressed from the subject for a long time.

31. According to the professor, what is the greatest advantage of hydroponics?

   Ⓐ The plants are less likely to develop soil-borne diseases.
   Ⓑ The cultivation requires much less labor than traditional methods.
   Ⓒ The water can be recycled in a hydroponic environment.
   Ⓓ Less space is needed to produce a large number of plants.

32. Why does the professor say this:

   Ⓐ She is making a statement to generate further discussion.
   Ⓑ She is drawing a conclusion to end the point about soil.
   Ⓒ She is answering the question that was posed about regions.
   Ⓓ She is trying to understand what the student just said.

33. Why does the professor suggest that the students refer to their lab workbook?

   Ⓐ To see the diagram of the experiment
   Ⓑ To read more about plant growth
   Ⓒ To find a list of important plant nutrients
   Ⓓ To locate the instructions for building a tank

34. According to the professor, why are roots important to plants?

   Click on 2 answer choices.

   Ⓐ To absorb water and nutrients

   Ⓑ To take in enough oxygen

   Ⓒ To suspend the plants in the solution

   Ⓓ To filter out toxic substances

PART III

Listening 7 "Library"

35. Why does the man approach the librarian?

   Ⓐ He needs an explanation of his assignment.
   Ⓑ He is looking for an encyclopedia.
   Ⓒ He needs help finding some data.
   Ⓓ He is trying to find the reference section.

36. What does the woman mean when she says this:

   Ⓐ She is showing comprehension.
   Ⓑ She is expressing surprise.
   Ⓒ She is talking to herself.
   Ⓓ She is dismissing the man.

37. What does the librarian imply?

   Ⓐ The man can find a chart in an encyclopedia.
   Ⓑ The professor has explained the assignment clearly.
   Ⓒ The library has a very good reference section.
   Ⓓ The man should not change the assignment.

38. What example does the librarian give for the assignment?

     Ⓐ A relative comparison of home prices
     Ⓑ Average family income in several countries
     Ⓒ International business around the world
     Ⓓ Global economic patterns in this decade

39. What will the man do with the information?

     Ⓐ Show it to the librarian
     Ⓑ Write a report for class
     Ⓒ Draw a chart or a graph
     Ⓓ Decide where to live

Listening 8 "Art History Class"

TOEFL® Listening

Photo of Jackson Pollock painting
Photograph by Hans Namuth
Courtesy Center for Creative Photography, University of Arizona
© 1991 Hans Namuth Estate

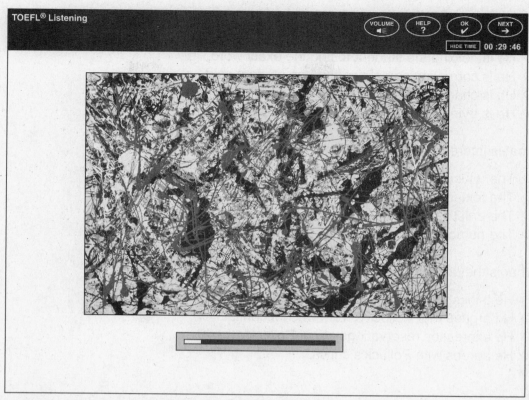

40. What is this discussion mainly about?

Ⓐ Artists in New York
Ⓑ Post Impressionists
Ⓒ Abstract Expressionism
Ⓓ The Guggenheim collection

41. To what did some critics compare Pollock's work?

Ⓐ Nature
Ⓑ Dancing
Ⓒ Chaos
Ⓓ Houses

42. According to the professor, what defines action art?

Click on 2 answer choices.

Ⓐ Control

Ⓑ Design

Ⓒ Coincidence

Ⓓ Imbalance

43. Why does the professor say this:

   Ⓐ He is helping the student to find the exact word.
   Ⓑ He is correcting something that the student said.
   Ⓒ He is changing the topic of the discussion.
   Ⓓ He is trying to regain the floor to continue.

44. What is interesting about the painting, "Lavender Mist?"

   Ⓐ The unusual color
   Ⓑ The texture of the paint
   Ⓒ The artist's handprints
   Ⓓ The number of copies

45. What is the professor's opinion of Pollock?

   Ⓐ He thinks that Pollock was an excellent illustrator.
   Ⓑ He argues that Pollock's work was influential.
   Ⓒ He expresses reservations about Pollock's work.
   Ⓓ He agrees with Pollock's critics.

Listening 9 "Engineering Class"

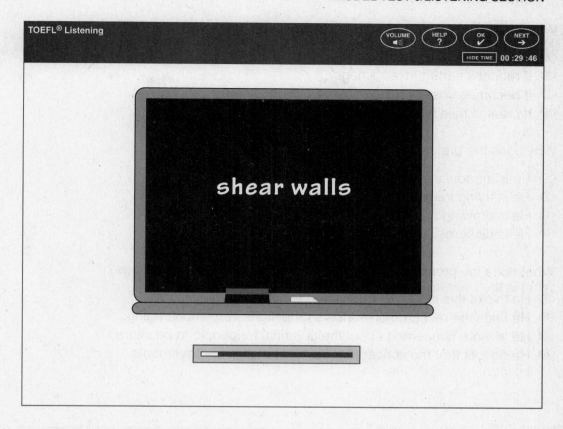

46. What is this lecture mainly about?

   Ⓐ Reinforced concrete in buildings
   Ⓑ The stresses caused by earthquakes
   Ⓒ Earthquake-resistant structures
   Ⓓ Understanding construction sites

47. Which technique is used to reinforce walls?

   Ⓐ Cross-bracing
   Ⓑ Shear cores
   Ⓒ Bolting
   Ⓓ Base isolators

48. Which two materials are used in base isolators?

   Click on 2 answer choices.

   Ａ Rubber

   Ｂ Steel

   Ｃ Concrete

   Ｄ Soil

49. What happens to fill dirt during an earthquake?

   Ⓐ It allows the building to sway.
   Ⓑ It reduces earthquake damage.
   Ⓒ It becomes unstable and collapses.
   Ⓓ It creates mild shock waves.

50. Why does the professor say this:

   Ⓐ He is introducing a new major point.
   Ⓑ He is trying to get the students to participate.
   Ⓒ He is drawing a conclusion about engineering.
   Ⓓ He is disagreeing with his previous comment.

51. What does the professor think about computer sensors for buildings?

   Ⓐ He thinks this is a superior method for preserving buildings.
   Ⓑ He finds the research on sensors for pistons very encouraging.
   Ⓒ He is more concerned about the potential for people to be injured.
   Ⓓ He doubts that the concept will result in design improvements.

STOP   **Please turn off the audio. There is a 10-minute break between the Listening section and the Speaking section.**

SPEAKING SECTION

 Model Test 5, Speaking Section, CD 8, Track 2

The Speaking section tests your ability to communicate in English in an academic setting. During the test, you will be presented with six speaking questions. The questions ask for a response to a single question, a conversation, a talk, or a lecture.

You may take notes as you listen, but notes are not graded. You may use your notes to answer the questions. Some of the questions ask for a response to a reading passage and a talk or a lecture. The reading passages and the questions are written, but most of the directions will be spoken.

Your speaking will be evaluated on both the fluency of the language and the accuracy of the content. You will have 15–20 seconds to prepare and 45–60 seconds to respond to each question. Typically, a good response will require all of the response time but the answer will be complete by the end of the response time.

The time for the Speaking section is about 20 minutes. A clock on the screen will show you how much time you have to prepare your answer and how much time you have to record it.

Independent Speaking Question 1 "A Tourist Attraction"

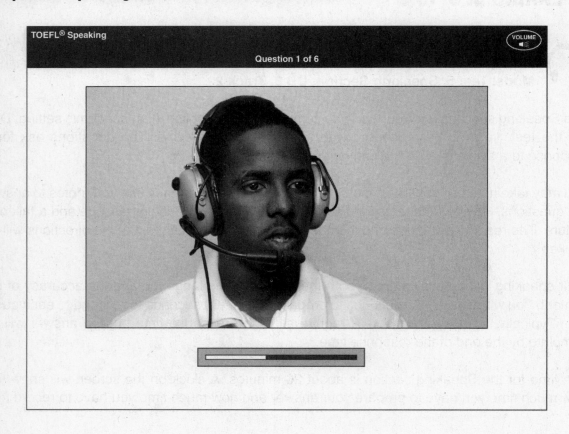

    Listen for a question about a familiar topic.

Question

If you were asked to choose one place in your country where you would take a tourist, which one would you choose? Why? What is especially impressive about the place? Use specific reasons and details to explain your choice.

Preparation Time: 15 seconds
Recording Time: 45 seconds

Independent Speaking Question 2 "Success"

 Listen for a question that asks your opinion about a familiar topic.

Question

Some people believe that the best way to succeed is to set goals and work hard to achieve them. Other people think that hard work is not as important as good luck. Which point of view do you think is true and why? Use specific reasons and examples to support your opinion.

Preparation Time: 15 seconds
Recording Time: 45 seconds

Integrated Speaking Question 3 "Auto Registration"

Read a short passage and listen to a talk on the same topic.

Reading Time: 45 seconds

> Policy for Vehicles on Campus
> Vehicles parked on campus by students, faculty, or staff must be registered with the Campus Police Department. Parking permits are required for both part-time and full-time students. Permits may be purchased at the Campus Police Department, which is located at the south entrance to the campus or at the Business Office in the Administration Building. The fee per vehicle is $20. Please be advised that you must have a permit for every vehicle that you park in campus lots. Parking enforcement will begin one week after the first day of each semester.

 Now listen to a student who is speaking at the meeting. She is expressing her opinion about the policy.

Question
The student expresses her opinion of the policy for vehicle registration. Report her opinion and explain the reasons that she gives for having that opinion.

Preparation Time: 30 seconds
Recording Time: 60 seconds

Integrated Speaking Question 4 "Stress"

Read a short passage and then listen to part of a lecture on the same topic.

Reading Time: 45 seconds

Stress

Stress is defined as a mental and physical condition that occurs when an adjustment or adaptation must be made to the environment. Unpleasant conditions or events cause stress, as, for example, financial problems, a divorce, health issues, or pressure at work. However, a certain amount of stress occurs even when the adjustment is to a condition that is perceived as desirable. Exercise, dating, moving to a new home, or taking a trip are all stressful situations. Although short-term stress is usually harmless, the consequences of long-term stress can be dangerous to health. Factors that decrease the consequences of stress are the ability to predict stressful situations and the level of control over them that can be achieved.

TOEFL® Speaking

Question 4 of 6

VOLUME

 Now listen to part of a lecture in a psychology class. The professor is talking about an experiment.

Question
Explain the causes of stress and relate them to the experiment with rats.

Preparation Time: 30 seconds
Recording Time: 60 seconds

Integrated Speaking Question 5 "Art Project"

  Now listen to a short conversation between a student and her friend.

Question

Describe the woman's problem and the two suggestions that her friend makes about how to handle it. What do you think the woman should do, and why?

Preparation Time: 20 seconds
Recording Time: 60 seconds

Integrated Speaking Question 6 "Caverns"

 Now listen to part of a lecture in a geology class. The professor is discussing caverns.

Question

Using the main points and examples from the lecture, describe the two kinds of rock formations in a cavern, and explain how the professor helps his students remember the difference between the two.

Preparation Time: 20 seconds
Recording Time: 60 seconds

WRITING SECTION

The Writing section tests your ability to write essays in English similar to those that you would write in college courses.

During the test, you will write two essays. The integrated essay asks for your response to an academic reading passage and a lecture on the same topic. You may take notes as you read and listen, but notes are not graded. You may use your notes to write the essay. The lecture will be spoken, but the directions and the questions will be written. You will have 20 minutes to plan, write, and revise your response. Typically, a good essay for the integrated topic will require that you write 150–225 words.

The independent essay usually asks for your opinion about a familiar topic. You will have 30 minutes to plan, write, and revise your response. Typically, a good essay for the independent topic will require that you write 300–350 words.

A clock on the screen will show you how much time you have to complete each essay.

Integrated Essay "Effective Discipline"

You have 20 minutes to plan, write, and revise your response to a reading passage and a lecture on the same topic. First, read the passage and take notes. Then, listen to the lecture and take notes. Finally, write your response to the writing question. Typically, a good response will require that you write 150–225 words.

Reading Passage
Time: 3 minutes

According to the most recent research on parenting, caretakers tend to use three strategies for disciplining children. Power includes the use of physical punishment such as a spanking or the threat of physical punishment, but parents can also demonstrate power by taking away a privilege such as using the car, attending a sporting event, or, in the case of a very young child, playing with a favorite toy. In spite of the fact that power strategies, especially severe physical punishment, can cause children to fear or even hate parents, it's surprising that power remains the strategy used most often in disciplining children. It's also worth noting that children who are harshly disciplined in this way tend to be hostile, defiant, and aggressive socially. Second in popularity after power is the withholding of affection. This can take the form of refusal to communicate with a child, threatening to abandon or reject the child, or otherwise treating children as though they were unworthy of love. Interesting enough, children disciplined in this way appear on the surface to be very self-disciplined, even model children who are seldom in trouble, but underneath, these same children are generally very nervous, insecure, and dependent on others to approve of and guide their evaluation of behavior. Finally, management techniques are employed for discipline. These begin with a set of rules that are clearly expressed at an age-appropriate level. To enforce the rules, parents use a combination of praise and approval with explanation and reasoning, always referring back to the rules.

But regardless of the strategy, the behavior that has precipitated punishment should be clearly understood, and the consequences should be consistent. Key to any kind of discipline is a pattern of consistency so that children understand the relationship between the rules, their behavior, and the consequences.

 Model Test 5, Writing Section, CD 8, Track 3

 Now listen to a lecture on the same topic as the passage that you have just read.

Question

Referring to the main points in the lecture, summarize the professor's views on effective discipline and contrast them with the options that parents tend to use, as outlined in the reading passage.

Independent Essay "Technological Innovations"

Question
Advances in transportation and communication like the airplane and the telephone have changed the way that nations interact with each other in a global society. Choose another technological innovation that you think is important. Give specific reasons for your choice.

This is the end of Model Test 5.
To check your answers, refer to "Explanatory or Example Answers and Audio Scripts for Model Tests: Model Test 5," Chapter 7, pages 677–710.

MODEL TEST 6: PROGRESS TEST

READING SECTION

The Reading section tests your ability to understand reading passages like those in college textbooks. The passages are about 700 words in length.

This is the long format for the Reading section. On the long format, you will respond to five passages. After each passage, you will answer 12–14 questions about it. Only three passages will be graded. The other passages are part of an exerimental section for future tests. Because you will not know which passages will be graded, you must try to do your best on all of them.

Most questions are worth 1 point, but the last question in each passage is worth more than 1 point.

You will have 100 minutes to read all of the passages and answer the questions. You may take notes while you read, but notes are not graded. You may use your notes to answer the questions. Some passages may include a word or phrase that is underlined in blue. Click on the word or phrase to see a glossary definition or explanation.

Choose the best answer for multiple-choice questions. Follow the directions on the page or on the screen for computer-assisted questions. Click on **Next** to go to the next question. Click on **Back** to return to the previous question. You may return to previous questions for all of the passages in the same reading part, but after you go to the next part, you will not be able to return to passages in a previous part. Be sure that you have answered all of the questions for the passages in each part before you click on **Next** at the end of the passage to move to the next part.

You can click on **Review** to see a chart of the questions you have answered and the questions you have not answered in each part. From this screen, you can return to the question you want to answer in the part that is open.

A clock on the screen will show you how much time you have to complete the Reading section.

PART I

Reading 1 "Exotic and Endangered Species"

→ When you hear someone bubbling enthusiastically about an **exotic species**, you can safely bet the speaker isn't an ecologist. This is a name for a resident of an established community that was deliberately or accidentally moved from its home range and became established elsewhere. Unlike most imports, which can't take hold outside their home range, an exotic species permanently insinuates itself into a new community.

Sometimes the additions are harmless and even have beneficial effects. More often, they make native species **endangered species**, which by definition are extremely vulnerable to extinction. Of all species on the rare or endangered lists or that recently became extinct, *close to 70 percent owe their precarious existence or demise to displacement by exotic species.* Two examples are included here to illustrate the problem.

During the 1800s, British settlers in Australia just couldn't bond with the koalas and kangaroos, so they started to import familiar animals from their homeland. In 1859, in what would be the start of a wholesale disaster, a northern Australian landowner imported and then released two dozen wild European rabbits *(Oryctolagus cuniculus).* Good food and good sport hunting—that was the idea. An ideal rabbit habitat with no natural predators was the reality.

Six years later, the landowner had killed 20,000 rabbits and was besieged by 20,000 more. The rabbits displaced livestock, even kangaroos. Now Australia has 200 to 300 million hippityhopping through the southern half of the country. They overgraze perennial grasses in good times and strip bark from shrubs and trees during droughts. You know where they've been; they transform grasslands and shrublands into eroded deserts. They have been shot and poisoned. Their warrens have been plowed under, fumigated, and dynamited. Even when all-out assaults reduced their population size by 70 percent, the rapidly reproducing imports made a comeback in less than a year. Did the construction of a 2,000-mile-long fence protect western Australia? No. Rabbits made it to the other side before workers finished the fence.

→ In 1951, government workers introduced a myxoma virus by way of mildly infected South American rabbits, its normal hosts. This virus causes *myxomatosis.* The disease has mild effects on South American rabbits that coevolved with the virus but nearly always had lethal effects on *O. cuniculus.* Biting insects, mainly mosquitoes and fleas, quickly transmit the virus from host to host. Having no coevolved defenses against the novel virus, the European rabbits died in droves. But, as you might expect, natural selection has since favored rapid growth of populations of *O. cuniculus* resistant to the virus.

➜ In 1991, on an uninhabited island in Spencer Gulf, Australian researchers released a population of rabbits that they had injected with a calcivirus. The rabbits died quickly and relatively painlessly from blood clots in their lungs, hearts, and kidneys. In 1995, the test virus escaped from the island, possibly on insect vectors. It has been killing 80 to 95 percent of the adult rabbits in Australian regions. At this writing, researchers are now questioning whether the calcivirus should be used on a widespread scale, whether it can jump boundaries and infect animals other than rabbits (such as humans), and what the long-term consequences will be.

A vine called kudzu *(Pueraria lobata)* was deliberately imported from Japan to the United States, where it faces no serious threats from herbivores, pathogens, or competitor plants. In temperate parts of Asia, it is a well-behaved legume with a well-developed root system. It *seemed* like a good idea to use it to control erosion on hills and highway embankments in the southeastern United States. Ⓐ With nothing to stop it, though, kudzu's shoots grew a third of a meter per day. Vines now blanket streambanks, trees, telephone poles, houses, and almost everything else in their path. Attempts to dig up or burn kudzu are futile. Grazing goats and herbicides help, but goats eat other plants, too, and herbicides contaminate water supplies. Ⓑ Kudzu could reach the Great Lakes by the year 2040.

➜ On the bright side, a Japanese firm is constructing a kudzu farm and processing plant in Alabama. The idea is to export the starch to Asia, where the demand currently exceeds the supply. Ⓒ Also, kudzu may eventually help reduce logging operations. Ⓓ At the Georgia Institute of Technology, researchers report that kudzu might become an alternative source for paper.

1. Based on the information in paragraph 1, which of the following best explains the term "exotic species"?

   Ⓐ Animals or plants on the rare species list
   Ⓑ A permanent resident in an established community
   Ⓒ A species that has been moved to a different community
   Ⓓ An import that fails to thrive outside of its home range

   Paragraph 1 is marked with an arrow [➜].

2. The word itself in the passage refers to

   Ⓐ most imports
   Ⓑ new community
   Ⓒ home range
   Ⓓ exotic species

3. The word <u>bond</u> in the passage is closest in meaning to

 Ⓐ move
 Ⓑ connect
 Ⓒ live
 Ⓓ fight

4. According to the author, why did the plan to introduce rabbits in Australia fail?

 Ⓐ The rabbits were infected with a contagious virus.
 Ⓑ Most Australians did not like the rabbits.
 Ⓒ No natural predators controlled the rabbit population.
 Ⓓ Hunters killed the rabbits for sport and for food.

5. All of the following methods were used to control the rabbit population in Australia EXCEPT

 Ⓐ They were poisoned.
 Ⓑ Their habitats were buried.
 Ⓒ They were moved to deserts.
 Ⓓ They were surrounded by fences.

6. Why does the author mention mosquitoes and fleas in paragraph 5?

 Ⓐ Because they are the origin of the myxoma virus
 Ⓑ Because they carry the myxoma virus to other animals
 Ⓒ Because they die when they are infected by myxoma
 Ⓓ Because they have an immunity to the myxoma virus

Paragraph 5 is marked with an arrow [➜].

7. According to paragraph 6, the Spencer Gulf experiment was dangerous because

 Ⓐ insect populations were exposed to a virus
 Ⓑ rabbits on the island died from a virus
 Ⓒ the virus may be a threat to humans
 Ⓓ some animals are immune to the virus

Paragraph 6 is marked with an arrow [➜].

8. The word <u>consequences</u> in the passage is closest in meaning to

 Ⓐ stages
 Ⓑ advantages
 Ⓒ results
 Ⓓ increases

19 9. Why does the author give details about the kudzu farm and processing plant in paragraph 8?

    Ⓐ To explain why kudzu was imported from abroad
    Ⓑ To argue that the decision to plant kudzu was a good one
    Ⓒ To give a reason for kudzu to be planted in Asia
    Ⓓ To offer partial solutions to the kudzu problem

Paragraph 8 is marked with an arrow [➜].

20 10. The word <u>exceeds</u> in the passage is closest in meaning to

    Ⓐ surpasses
    Ⓑ destroys
    Ⓒ estimates
    Ⓓ causes

21 11. Which of the following statements most accurately reflects the author's opinion about exotic species?

    Ⓐ Exotic species should be protected by ecologists.
    Ⓑ Importing an exotic species can solve many problems.
    Ⓒ Ecologists should make the decision to import an exotic species.
    Ⓓ Exotic species are often disruptive to the ecology.

12. Look at the four squares [■] that show where the following sentence could be inserted in the passage.

Asians use a starch extract from kudzu in drinks, herbal medicines, and candy.

Where could the sentence best be added?

Click on a square [■] to insert the sentence in the passage.

13. **Directions:** An introduction for a short summary of the passage appears below. Complete the summary by selecting the THREE answer choices that mention the most important points in the passage. Some sentences do not belong in the summary because they express ideas that are not included in the passage or are minor points from the passage. *This question is worth 2 points.*

Exotic species often require containment because they displace other species when they become established in a new environment.

-
-
-

Answer Choices

A Rabbits were able to cross a fence 2,000 miles long that was constructed to keep them out of western Australia.

B Methods to control exotic species include fences, viruses, burning, herbicides, natural predators, and harvesting.

C Rabbits that were introduced in Australia and kudzu which was introduced in the United States, are examples of species that caused problems.

D Researchers may be able to develop material from the kudzu vine that will be an alternative to wood pulp paper.

E The problem is that exotic species make native species vulnerable to extinction.

F A virus that is deadly to rabbits may have serious effects for other animals.

PART II

Reading 2 "Paleolithic Art"

→ The several millennia following 30,000 B.C. saw a powerful outburst of artistic creativity. The artworks produced range from simple shell necklaces to human and animal forms in ivory, clay, and stone to monumental paintings, engravings, and relief sculptures covering the huge wall surfaces of caves. From the moment in 1879 that cave paintings were discovered at Altamira, scholars have wondered why the hunter-artists of the Old Stone Age decided to cover the walls of dark caverns with animal images. Various answers have been given, including that they were mere decoration, but this theory cannot explain the narrow range of subjects or the inaccessibility of many of the paintings. In fact, the remoteness and difficulty of access of many of the cave paintings and the fact they appear to have been used for centuries are precisely what have led many scholars to suggest that the prehistoric hunters attributed magical properties to the images they painted. According to this argument, by confining animals to the surfaces of their cave walls, the artists believed they were bringing the beasts under their control. Some have even hypothesized that rituals or dances were performed in front of the images and that these rites served to improve the hunters' luck. Still others have stated that the painted animals may have served as teaching tools to instruct new hunters about the character of the various species they would encounter or even to serve as targets for spears!

By contrast, some scholars have argued that the magical purpose of the paintings was not to facilitate the *destruction* of bison and other species. Instead, they believe prehistoric painters created animal images to assure the *survival* of the herds. Paleolithic peoples depended on for their food supply and for their clothing. Ⓐ A central problem for both the hunting-magic and food-creation theories is that the animals that seem to have been diet staples of Old Stone Age peoples are not those most frequently portrayed. Ⓑ

Other scholars have sought to reconstruct an elaborate mythology based on the cave paintings, suggesting that Paleolithic humans believed they had animal ancestors. Still others have equated certain species with men and others with women and also found sexual symbolism in the abstract signs that sometimes accompany the images. Ⓒ Almost all of these theories have been discredited over time, and art historians must admit that no one knows the intent of these paintings. Ⓓ In fact, a single explanation for all Paleolithic murals, even paintings similar in subject, style, and *composition* (how the motifs are arranged on the surface), is unlikely to apply universally. For now, the paintings remain an enigma.

→ That the paintings did have meaning to the Paleolithic peoples who made and observed them cannot, however, be doubted. In fact, signs consisting of checks, dots, squares, or other arrangements of lines often accompany the pictures of animals. Several observers have seen a primitive writing form in these representations of nonliving things, but the signs, too, may have had some other significance. Some look like traps and arrows and, according to the hunting-magic theory, may have been drawn to insure success in capturing or killing animals with these devices. At Pech-Merle in France, the "spotted horses" painted on the cave wall may not have spots. Some scholars have argued that the "spots," which appear both within and without the horses' outlines, are painted rocks thrown at the animals.

→ Representations of human hands also are common. Those around the Pech-Merle horses, and the majority of painted hands at other sites, are "negative," that is, the artist placed one hand against the wall and then painted or blew pigment around it. Occasionally, the artist dipped a hand in paint and then pressed it against the wall, leaving a "positive" imprint. These handprints, too, must have had a purpose. Some scholars have considered them "signatures" of cult or community members or, less likely, of individual artists.

14. According to paragraph 1, the cave art was difficult to find because the artists

    Ⓐ were probably trying to keep their work a secret from their tribe
    Ⓑ could have begun their painting while they were confined in the caves
    Ⓒ may have chosen a location deep in the caves to hold ceremonies
    Ⓓ had to practice before they made images that more people could see

    Paragraph 1 is marked with an arrow [➔].

15. According to paragraph 1, Paleolithic people may have used cave art for all of the following purposes EXCEPT

    Ⓐ People may have danced in front of the images.
    Ⓑ Hunters could have used the figures for target practice.
    Ⓒ Shamans might have performed magical rituals in the caves.
    Ⓓ Animals may have been kept in the caves near the drawings.

    Paragraph 1 is marked with an arrow [➔].

16. The word access in the passage is closest in meaning to

    Ⓐ admission
    Ⓑ meaning
    Ⓒ site
    Ⓓ research

17. The word facilitate in the passage is closest in meaning to

    Ⓐ specify
    Ⓑ permit
    Ⓒ assist
    Ⓓ discover

18. The word those in the passage refers to

    Ⓐ peoples
    Ⓑ staples
    Ⓒ animals
    Ⓓ theories

19. The word discredited in the passage is closest in meaning to

    Ⓐ not attentive
    Ⓑ not believed
    Ⓒ not hopeful
    Ⓓ not organized

28 20. Which of the sentences below best expresses the information in the highlighted statement in the passage? The other choices change the meaning or leave out important information.

    Ⓐ It is true that the paintings were meaningful to the Paleolithic peoples.
    Ⓑ Doubtless, the Paleolithic peoples were the ones who made the paintings.
    Ⓒ There is no doubt about the meaning of the Paleolithic paintings.
    Ⓓ Paintings that had meaning for the Paleolithic peoples are doubtful.

29 21. How have some scholars interpreted the arrangement of lines into geometric shapes near the animal paintings?

    Ⓐ They are probably more pictures of animals.
    Ⓑ They may be an early writing system.
    Ⓒ It is possible that they have no significance.
    Ⓓ Probably most of the lines are scratches from age.

30 22. According to paragraph 4, why do scholars believe that the spots on the horses may represent a hunting scene?

    Ⓐ Other cave paintings near this one include hunting scenes.
    Ⓑ The spots are made of rocks that were attached to the wall.
    Ⓒ The spots are painted outside the horses' forms as well as inside them.
    Ⓓ The primitive writing is interpreted as an accounting of a hunt.

Paragraph 4 is marked with an arrow [➜].

31 23. According to paragraph 5, why did artists leave a positive imprint of their hands on cave paintings?

    Ⓐ It represents human beings in the cave paintings.
    Ⓑ It could have been a way for them to sign their work.
    Ⓒ It was a hunter's handprint among the herd of animals.
    Ⓓ It might have been a pleasing image without much meaning.

Paragraph 5 is marked with an arrow [➜].

32 24. Which of the following statements most accurately reflects the author's opinion about the purpose of cave paintings?

    Ⓐ The cave paintings were part of a hunting ritual.
    Ⓑ Artists were honoring their animal ancestors in cave paintings.
    Ⓒ The exact purpose of cave paintings is not known.
    Ⓓ Decoration was probably the main reason for painting in caves.

25. Look at the four squares [■] that show where the following sentence could be inserted in the passage.

At Altamira, for example, faunal remains show that red deer, not bison, were eaten.

Where could the sentence best be added?

Click on a square [■] to insert the sentence in the passage.

26. **Directions:** An introduction for a short summary of the passage appears below. Complete the summary by selecting the THREE answer choices that mention the most important points in the passage. Some sentences do not belong in the summary because they express ideas that are not included in the passage or are minor points from the passage. *This question is worth 2 points.*

The purpose of the art discovered on cave walls is a topic of discussion among scholars.

- •
- •
- •

Answer Choices

A Some of the lines and the geometrical figures beside the drawings could be a very early form of a writing system.

B It is possible that the paintings were created as part of a magical ritual either to guarantee a good hunt or an abundance of animals.

C At Altamira, excavations indicate that the protein diet of the inhabitants was probably deer rather than bison.

D Perhaps the artists were paying homage to their animal ancestors by recreating their mythology in the pictures.

E The art may be more recent than first assumed when the caves were originally discovered in the late 1800s.

F There are a number of human handprints arranged around the Pech-Merle horses that could have been pressed there by the artists.

Reading 3 "Group Decision Making"

Advantages of Group Decision Making

→ Committees, task forces, and ad hoc groups are frequently assigned to identify and recommend decision alternatives or, in some cases, to actually make important decisions. In essence, a group is a tool that can focus the experience and expertise of several people on a particular problem or situation. Thus, a group offers the advantage of greater total knowledge. Groups accumulate more information, knowledge, and facts than individuals and often consider more alternatives. Each person in the group is able to draw on his or her unique education, experience, insights, and other resources and contribute those to the group. The varied backgrounds, training levels, and expertise of group members also help overcome tunnel vision by enabling the group to view the problem in more than one way.

→ Participation in group decision making usually leads to higher member satisfaction. People tend to accept a decision more readily and to be better satisfied with it when they have participated in making that decision. In addition, people will better understand and be more committed to a decision in which they have had a say than to a decision made for them. As a result, such a decision is more likely to be implemented successfully.

Disadvantages of Group Decision Making

→ While groups have many potential benefits, we all know that they can also be frustrating. Ⓐ One obvious disadvantage of group decision making is the time required to make a decision. Ⓑ The time needed for group discussion and the associated compromising and selecting of a decision alternative can be considerable. Ⓒ Time costs money, so a waste of time becomes a disadvantage if a decision made by a group could have been made just as effectively by an individual working alone. Ⓓ Consequently, group decisions should be avoided when speed and efficiency are the primary considerations.

A second disadvantage is that the group discussion may be dominated by an individual or subgroup. Effectiveness can be reduced if one individual, such as the group leader, dominates the discussion by talking too much or being closed to other points of view. Some group leaders try to control the group and provide the major input. Such dominance can stifle other group members' willingness to participate and could cause decision alternatives to be ignored or overlooked. All group members need to be encouraged and permitted to contribute.

→ Another disadvantage of group decision making is that members may be less concerned with the group's goals than with their own personal goals. They may become so sidetracked in trying to win an argument that they forget about group performance. On the other hand, a group may try too hard to compromise and consequently may not make optimal decisions. Sometimes this stems from the desire to maintain friendships and avoid disagreements. Often groups exert tremendous social pressure on individuals to conform to established or expected patterns of behavior. Especially when they are dealing with important and controversial issues, interacting groups may be prone to a phenomenon called groupthink.

→ Groupthink is an agreement-at-any-cost mentality that results in ineffective group decision making. It occurs when groups are highly cohesive, have highly directive leaders, are insulated so they have no clear ways to get objective information, and—because they lack outside information—have little hope that a better solution might be found than the one proposed by the leader or other influential group members. These conditions foster the illusion that the group is invulnerable, right, and more moral than outsiders. They also encourage the development of self-appointed "mind guards" who bring pressure on dissenters. In such situations, decisions—often important decisions—are made without consideration of alternative frames or alternative options. It is difficult to imagine conditions more conducive to poor decision making and wrong decisions.

Recent research indicates that groupthink may also result when group members have preconceived ideas about how a problem should be solved. Under these conditions, the team may not examine a full range of decision alternatives, or it may discount or avoid information that threatens its preconceived choice.

27. In paragraph 1, the author states that groups frequently

   Ⓐ generate more options than individuals
   Ⓑ agree on the way that the problem should be approached
   Ⓒ make recommendations instead of decisions
   Ⓓ are chosen to participate because of their experience

Paragraph 1 is marked with an arrow [→].

28. According to paragraph 2, why do group decisions tend to be more successful?

   Ⓐ When more people are involved, there are more ideas from which to choose.
   Ⓑ People are more accepting of decisions when they have been involved in them.
   Ⓒ Implementing ideas is easier with a large number of people to help.
   Ⓓ People like to be participants in decisions that are successful.

Paragraph 2 is marked with an arrow [→].

29. The word <u>considerable</u> in the passage is closest in meaning to

    Ⓐ valuable
    Ⓑ significant
    Ⓒ predictable
    Ⓓ unusual

30. The word <u>Consequently</u> in the passage is closest in meaning to

    Ⓐ About now
    Ⓑ Without doubt
    Ⓒ Before long
    Ⓓ As a result

31. According to paragraph 3, group discussion can be problematic because

    Ⓐ individual decisions are always more effective
    Ⓑ it takes more time for a group to arrive at a decision
    Ⓒ it costs more to pay all of the group members
    Ⓓ interaction among group members can be a problem

Paragraph 3 is marked with an arrow [→].

32. What can be inferred about a group leader?

    Ⓐ A good leader will provide goals for the group to consider and vote on.
    Ⓑ The purpose of the leader is to facilitate the participation of all of the members.
    Ⓒ A group leader should be the dominant member of the group.
    Ⓓ Expectations for group behavior must be presented by the group leader.

33. The word <u>controversial</u> in the passage is closest in meaning to

    Ⓐ accepted
    Ⓑ debatable
    Ⓒ recent
    Ⓓ complicated

34. The phrase <u>the one</u> in the passage refers to

    Ⓐ solution
    Ⓑ information
    Ⓒ hope
    Ⓓ leader

35. According to paragraph 5, how does the author explain compromise in a group?

Ⓐ The group may try to make a better decision by compromising.
Ⓑ A compromise may be the best way to encourage groupthink.
Ⓒ Compromising may allow the group members to remain friends.
Ⓓ To compromise can help one member to reach a personal goal.

Paragraph 5 is marked with an arrow [➔].

36. What does the term "mind guards" refer to?

Ⓐ People who conform to the group opinion without thinking
Ⓑ Group members who try to force others to agree with the group
Ⓒ Members of the group who are the most ethical and influential
Ⓓ Those people who disagree without offering an alternative view

37. According to paragraph 6, why are alternative solutions often rejected in groupthink?

Ⓐ Dissenters exert pressure on the group.
Ⓑ Group leaders are not very creative.
Ⓒ Information is not made available.
Ⓓ The group is usually right.

Paragraph 6 is marked with an arrow [➔].

38. Look at the four squares [■] that show where the following sentence could be inserted in the passage.

In fact, the traditional group is prone to a variety of difficulties.

Where could the sentence best be added?

Click on a square [■] to insert the sentence in the passage.

39. **Directions**: Complete the table by matching the phrases on the left with the headings on the right. Select the appropriate answer choices and drag them to the advantages or disadvantages of group decision making. TWO of the answer choices will NOT be used. ***This question is worth 4 points.***

To delete an answer choice, click on it. To see the passage, click on **View Text**.

Answer Choices

Ⓐ Sometimes a strong leader will dominate the group.

Ⓑ Sometimes personal objectives dictate the outcome.

Ⓒ Most of the time people are happier with the decision.

Ⓓ It is usually possible to gather more data.

Ⓔ It will probably take much longer to arrive at a decision.

Ⓕ The group may tend to make decisions based on friendship.

Ⓖ Discussion is required before a decision is made.

Ⓗ Implementation is often much easier after the decision.

Ⓘ A group member may disagree with the majority opinion.

Advantages

•

•

•

Disadvantages

•

•

•

•

PART III

Reading 4 "Four Stages of Planetary Development"

Planetary Development

→ In our study of the planet Earth, we will find a four-stage history of planetary development. The moon and all the terrestrial planets have passed through these stages, although differences in the way the planets were altered by these stages have produced dramatically different worlds. The moon, for example, is much like Earth, but its evolution has been dramatically altered by its smaller size. As we explore the solar system, we will discover not entirely new processes but rather familiar effects working in slightly different ways.

The Four Stages

The first stage of planetary evolution is *differentiation*, the separation of material according to density. Earth now has a dense core and a lower-density crust, and that structure must have originated very early.

Differentiation would have occurred easily if Earth were molten when it was young. Two sources of heat could have heated Earth. First, heat of formation would be created by in-falling material. A meteorite hitting Earth at high velocity converts most of its energy of motion into heat, and the in-falling of a large number of meteorites could release tremendous heat. If Earth formed rapidly, this heat would have accumulated much more rapidly than it could leak away, and Earth may have been molten when it formed. A second source of heat requires more time to develop. The decay of radioactive elements trapped in the Earth releases heat gradually; but, as soon as Earth formed, that heat would have begun to accumulate and could have helped melt Earth to facilitate differentiation. Most of Earth's radioactive elements are now concentrated in the crust, where they continue to warm and soften the rock layers.

Earth formed by material falling together, but meteorites could have left no trace until a crust solidified. Once Earth had a hard surface, the meteorites could form craters. This second stage in planetary evolution, *cratering*, was violent. The heavy bombardment was intense because the solar nebula was filled with rocky and icy debris, and the young Earth was battered by meteorites that pulverized the newly forming crust. The largest meteorites blasted out crater basins hundreds of kilometers in diameter. As the solar nebula cleared, the amount of debris decreased, and the level of cratering fell to its present low level. Although meteorites still occasionally strike Earth and dig craters, cratering is no longer the dominant influence on Earth's geology. As we compare other worlds with Earth, we will discover traces of this intense period of cratering, the heavy bombardment, on every old surface in the solar system.

→ The third stage, *flooding*, no doubt began while cratering was still intense. The fracturing of the crust and the heating caused by radioactive decay allowed molten rock just below the crust to well up through fissures and flood the deeper basins. We will discuss such flooded basins on other worlds, such as the moon, but all traces of this early lava flooding have been destroyed by later geological activity in Earth's crust. On Earth, flooding continued as the atmosphere cooled and water fell as rain, filling the deepest basins to produce the first oceans. [A] Notice that on Earth flooding involves both lava and water, a circumstance that we will not find on most worlds. [B]

The fourth stage, *slow surface evolution*, has continued for the last 3.5 billion years or more. [C] Earth's surface is constantly changing as sections of crust slide over each other, push up mountains, and shift continents. [D] Almost all traces of the first billion years of Earth's geology have been destroyed by the active crust and erosion.

Earth as a Planet

All terrestrial planets pass through these four stages, so in that respect, Earth is a good basic reference planet for comparative planetology. Some planets have emphasized one stage over another, and some planets have failed to progress fully through the four stages. Nevertheless, Earth is a good standard of comparison. Every major process on any rocky world in our solar system is represented in some form on Earth.

On the other hand, Earth is peculiar in two ways. First, it has large amounts of liquid water on its surface. Fully 75 percent of its surface is covered by this liquid and no other planet in our solar system is known to have such extensive liquid water on its surface. Furthermore, some of the matter on the surface of this world is alive, and a small part of that living matter is aware. We do not know how the presence of living matter has affected the evolution of Earth, but this process seems to be totally missing from other worlds in our solar system.

Glossary

meteorite: a mass that falls to the surface of a planet from space
planetology: the study of planets

40. Why does the author mention the moon in paragraph 1?

    (A) To explain the stages in planetary development for the Earth
    (B) To contrast the evolution of the moon with that of the Earth
    (C) To demonstrate that the moon passed through different stages
    (D) To give an example of exploration in the solar system

    Paragraph 1 is marked with an arrow [→].

41. The word <u>its</u> in the passage refers to

   Ⓐ meteorite
   Ⓑ Earth
   Ⓒ velocity
   Ⓓ motion

42. Which of the sentences below best expresses the information in the highlighted statement in the passage? The other choices change the meaning or leave out important information.

   Ⓐ The Earth was probably liquid because the heat collected faster than it dissipated if the formation took place quickly.
   Ⓑ Because of the rapid formation of the Earth, the crust took a long time to cool before it became a solid.
   Ⓒ The liquid core of the Earth was created when the planet first formed because the heat was so high and there was little cooling.
   Ⓓ The cooling caused the Earth to form much more quickly as it met with the intense heat of the new planet.

43. The word <u>pulverized</u> in the passage is closest in meaning to

   Ⓐ melted into liquid
   Ⓑ broken into small parts
   Ⓒ frozen very hard
   Ⓓ washed very clean

44. What can be inferred about radioactive matter?

   Ⓐ It is revealed by later activity.
   Ⓑ It generates intense heat.
   Ⓒ It is an important stage.
   Ⓓ It fractures the planet's crust.

45. The word <u>dominant</u> in the passage is closest in meaning to

   Ⓐ most limited
   Ⓑ most likely
   Ⓒ most rapid
   Ⓓ most important

46. According to paragraph 5, how were the oceans formed?

    Ⓐ Ice gouged out depressions in the Earth.
    Ⓑ Rain filled the craters made by meteorites.
    Ⓒ Earthquakes shifted the continents.
    Ⓓ Molten rock and lava flooded the basins.

Paragraph 5 is marked with an arrow [➔].

47. What is the author's opinion of life on other planets?

    Ⓐ She does not know whether life is present on other planets.
    Ⓑ She is certain that no life exists on any planet except Earth.
    Ⓒ She does not express an opinion about life on other planets.
    Ⓓ She thinks that there is probably life on other planets.

48. According to the passage, which stage occurs after cratering?

    Ⓐ Flooding
    Ⓑ Slow surface evolution
    Ⓒ Differentiation
    Ⓓ Erosion

49. All of the following are reasons why the Earth is a good model of planetary development for purposes of comparison with other planets EXCEPT

    Ⓐ The Earth has gone through all four stages of planetary evolution.
    Ⓑ Life on Earth has affected the evolution in a number of important ways.
    Ⓒ All of the fundamental processes on terrestrial planets have occurred on Earth.
    Ⓓ There is evidence of extensive cratering both on Earth and on all other planets.

50. Look at the four squares [■] that show where the following sentence could be inserted in the passage.

Also, moving air and water erode the surface and wear away geological features.

Where could the sentence best be added?

Click on a square [■] to insert the sentence in the passage.

51. The word <u>peculiar</u> in the passage is closest in meaning to

    Ⓐ different
    Ⓑ better
    Ⓒ interesting
    Ⓓ new

52. **Directions:** An introduction for a short summary of the passage appears below. Complete the summary by selecting the THREE answer choices that mention the most important points in the passage. Some sentences do not belong in the summary because they express ideas that are not included in the passage or are minor points from the passage. *This question is worth 2 points.*

There are four stages of development for the terrestrial planets.

-
-
-

Answer Choices

A All rocky planets go through different stages in their evolution because of variations in composition.

B In spite of several unique features, the Earth is a good example of how a planet proceeds through the stages.

C Fewer meteorites fall to Earth now than in the earlier stages of the planet's evolutionary history.

D About three quarters of the surface of the Earth is submerged by the water in its oceans.

E Differentiation and cratering are early stages that are influenced by in-falling meteorites.

F Flooding includes both lava and water, while slow surface evolution causes shifting in the crust.

Reading 5 "Speech and Writing"

It is a widely held misconception that writing is more perfect than speech. To many people, writing somehow seems more correct and more stable, whereas speech can be careless, corrupted, and susceptible to change. Some people even go so far as to identify language with writing and to regard speech as a secondary form of language used imperfectly to approximate the ideals of the written language.

➜ One of the basic assumptions of modern linguistics, however, is that speech is primary and writing is secondary. The most immediate manifestation of language is speech and not writing. Writing is simply the representation of speech in another physical medium. Spoken language encodes thought into a physically transmittable form, while writing, in turn, encodes spoken language into a physically preservable form. Writing is a two-stage process. All units of writing, whether letters or characters, are based on units of speech, i.e., words, sounds, or syllables. When linguists study language, they take the spoken language as their best source of data and their object of description (except in instances of languages like Latin for which there are no longer any speakers).

There are several reasons for maintaining that speech is primary and writing is secondary. Ⓐ First, writing is a later historical development than spoken language. Ⓑ Current archeological evidence indicates that writing was first utilized in Sumer, that is, modern-day Iraq, about 6,000 years ago. Ⓒ As far as physical and cultural anthropologists can tell, spoken language has probably been used by humans for hundreds of thousands of years. Ⓓ

→ Second, writing does not exist everywhere that spoken language exists. This seems hard to imagine in our highly literate society, but the fact is that there are still many communities in the world where a written form of language is not used, and even in those cultures using a writing system, there are individuals who fail to learn the written form of their language. In fact, the majority of the Earth's inhabitants are illiterate, though quite capable of spoken communication. However, no society uses only a written language with no spoken form.

Third, writing must be taught, whereas spoken language is acquired automatically. All children, except children with serious learning disabilities, naturally learn to speak the language of the community in which they are brought up. They acquire the basics of their native language before they enter school, and even if they never attend school, they become fully competent speakers. Writing systems vary in complexity, but regardless of their level of sophistication, they must all be taught.

Finally, neurolinguistic evidence (studies of the brain in action during language use) demonstrates that the processing and production of written language is overlaid on the spoken language centers in the brain. Spoken language involves several distinct areas of the brain; writing uses these areas and others as well.

→ So what gives rise to the misconception that writing is more perfect than speech? There are several reasons. For one thing, the product of writing is usually more aptly worded and better organized, containing fewer errors, hesitations, and incomplete sentences than are found in speech. This perfection of writing can be explained by the fact that writing is the result of deliberation, correction, and revision, while speech is the spontaneous and simultaneous formulation of ideas; writing is therefore less subject to the constraint of time than speech is. In addition, writing is ultimately associated with education and educated speech. Since the speech of the educated is more often than not set up as the "standard language," writing is associated indirectly with the varieties of language that people tend to view as "correct." However, the association of writing with the standard variety is not a necessary one, as evidenced by the attempts of writers to transcribe faithfully the speech of their characters. Mark Twain's *Huckleberry Finn* and John Steinbeck's *Of Mice and Men* contain examples of this. Furthermore, because spoken language is physically no more than sound waves through the air, it is transient, but writing tends to last, because of its physical medium (characters on some surface), and can be preserved for a very long time. Spelling does not seem to vary from individual to individual or from place to place as easily as pronunciation does. Thus, writing has the appearance of being more stable. Spelling does vary, however, as exemplified by the differences between the American ways of spelling *gray* and words with the suffixes *-ize* and *-ization* as compared with the British spelling of *grey* and *-ise* and *-isation*. Writing could also change if it were made to follow the changes of speech. The fact that people at various times try to carry out spelling reforms amply illustrates this possibility.

53. The word <u>approximate</u> in the passage is closest in meaning to

Ⓐ make better than
Ⓑ come close to
Ⓒ take out of
Ⓓ get on with

54. According to paragraph 2, what can be inferred about linguistic research?

Ⓐ Linguists do not usually study Latin.
Ⓑ Research on writing is much easier.
Ⓒ Studies always require several sources.
Ⓓ Researchers prefer speech samples.

Paragraph 2 is marked with an arrow [→].

55. According to paragraph 4, what is true about literacy?

Ⓐ Only a minority of the world's population can read and write.
Ⓑ Literate populations are more capable than other groups.
Ⓒ The modern world has a very highly literate population.
Ⓓ Many people fail to become literate because it is difficult.

Paragraph 4 is marked with an arrow [→].

56. Which of the sentences below best expresses the information in the highlighted statement in the passage? The other choices change the meaning or leave out important information.

Ⓐ Writing that has a very complex system must be learned.
Ⓑ All writing has to be taught because the systems are variable.
Ⓒ In spite of complex features in writing systems, people can learn them.
Ⓓ Both simple and complex writing systems require direct instruction.

57. The word <u>deliberation</u> in the passage is closest in meaning to

    Ⓐ work
    Ⓑ thought
    Ⓒ time
    Ⓓ intelligence

58. Why does the author mention Mark Twain and John Steinbeck in paragraph 7?

    Ⓐ To demonstrate that speech cannot be transcribed
    Ⓑ To provide examples of two good writing styles
    Ⓒ To prove that a nonstandard variety can be written
    Ⓓ To contrast varieties of speech for their characters

    Paragraph 7 is marked with an arrow [➜].

59. The word <u>transient</u> in the passage is closest in meaning to

    Ⓐ unimportant
    Ⓑ temporary
    Ⓒ interesting
    Ⓓ clear

60. According to paragraph 7, what is true about spelling?

    Ⓐ Spelling does not change from one geographical region to another.
    Ⓑ British and American spellings are more similar than pronunciation.
    Ⓒ Pronunciation in English is not related to spelling changes.
    Ⓓ Changes in spelling are occasionally initiated because of speech.

    Paragraph 7 is marked with an arrow [➜].

61. The phrase <u>this possibility</u> in the passage refers to

    Ⓐ writing could also change
    Ⓑ the changes of speech
    Ⓒ people try to carry out
    Ⓓ spelling reforms illustrate

62. Which of the following statements most closely represents the author's opinion?

    Ⓐ Speech and writing have historical similarities.
    Ⓑ Standard speech is the best model for writing.
    Ⓒ Writing is not more perfect than speech.
    Ⓓ Writing should not change like speech does.

13 63. How does the author organize the passage?

    Ⓐ Cause and effect
    Ⓑ Chronological narrative
    Ⓒ Persuasive argument
    Ⓓ Contrastive analysis

64. Look at the four squares [■] that show where the following sentence could be inserted in the passage.

The Sumerians probably devised written characters for the purpose of maintaining inventories of livestock and merchandise.

Where could the sentence best be added?

Click on a square [■] to insert the sentence in the passage.

65. **Directions**: Complete the table by matching the phrases on the left with the headings on the right. Select the appropriate answer choices and drag them to the type of language to which they relate. TWO of the answer choices will NOT be used. *This question is worth 4 points.*

To delete an answer choice, click on it. To see the passage, click on **View Text**.

Answer Choices

    Ⓐ Not observable in brain activity

    Ⓑ A primary form of language

    Ⓒ Direct representation of thought

    Ⓓ A two-stage process

    Ⓔ An earlier development

    Ⓕ Associated with education

    Ⓖ Contains fewer errors

    Ⓗ No regional variations

    Ⓘ Acquired naturally

Speech

•

•

•

•

Writing

•

•

•

•

LISTENING SECTION

 Model Test 6, Listening Section, CD 8, Track 5, continued on CD 9, Track 1

The Listening section tests your ability to understand spoken English that is typical of interactions and academic speech on college campuses. During the test, you will respond to conversations and lectures.

This is the short format for the Listening section. On the short format, you will respond to two conversations and four lectures. After each listening passage, you will answer 5–6 questions about it.

You will hear each conversation or lecture one time. You may take notes while you listen, but notes are not graded. You may use your notes to answer the questions.

Choose the best answer for multiple-choice questions. Follow the directions on the page or on the screen for computer-assisted questions. Click on **Next** and **OK** to go to the next question. You cannot return to previous questions. You have 20–30 minutes to answer all of the questions. A clock on the screen will show you how much time you have to complete your answers for the section. The clock does not count the time you are listening to the conversations and lectures.

PART I

Listening 1 "Professor's Office"

1. Why does the man go to see his professor?

   Ⓐ To borrow some books for his project
   Ⓑ To hand in the first book report
   Ⓒ To ask about the professor's requirements
   Ⓓ To talk about literary movements

2. How is the second part of the reading list different from the first part?

   Ⓐ More minority authors are represented.
   Ⓑ All of the writers are from North America.
   Ⓒ It includes books from the Post Modern Period.
   Ⓓ In addition to novels, some plays are on the list.

3. What does the man mean when he says this:

   Ⓐ He does not understand the term.
   Ⓑ He is interested in the idea.
   Ⓒ He is not sure how to pronounce it.
   Ⓓ He thinks that the word is humorous.

4. What will the man probably do before the next meeting?

    Ⓐ Write a synopsis of each book on the list
    Ⓑ Make a list of books that he wants to read
    Ⓒ Finish the art project on his computer
    Ⓓ Prepare to talk with the professor

5. What can be inferred about the professor?

    Ⓐ She does not have regular office hours.
    Ⓑ She is willing to help her students.
    Ⓒ She is not very flexible with assignments.
    Ⓓ She teaches British literature.

Listening 2 "Environmental Science Class"

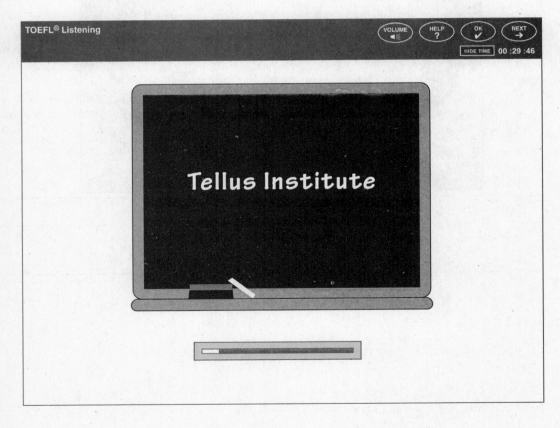

6. What aspect of wind power is the lecture mainly about?

   Ⓐ Electrical power in California
   Ⓑ Alternative energy sources
   Ⓒ Problems associated with turbines
   Ⓓ Wind as a renewable energy option

7. Which two regions of the United States have the greatest potential for supplying wind power?

   Click on 2 answer choices.

   Ⓐ The Eastern Seaboard

   Ⓑ The Midwestern Plains

   Ⓒ The Desert Southwest

   Ⓓ The Pacific Northwest

8. Why does the professor say this:

   Ⓐ He is disagreeing with the figures.
   Ⓑ He is expressing surprise at the statistics.
   Ⓒ He is correcting a previous statement.
   Ⓓ He is trying to maintain the students' interest.

9. In the lecture, the professor identifies several problems associated with wind power. Indicate whether each of the following is one of the problems mentioned. Click in the correct box for each phrase.

		Yes	No
A	Poor television reception		
B	Noisy turbines		
C	Expensive operating costs		
D	Remote areas		
E	Dangerous blades for birds		

10. How did the Tellus Institute solve the problem of intermittent wind?

   Ⓐ By building twice as many wind farms in problem areas
   Ⓑ By moving wind farms into areas of steady winds
   Ⓒ By using more wind turbines on each wind farm
   Ⓓ By separating one wind farm into two locations

11. What is the professor's opinion about the future of wind power?

    Ⓐ He thinks that wind power will require more research before it becomes practical.
    Ⓑ He supports the use of wind power only as a secondary source of energy.
    Ⓒ He feels that most of the world's energy problems will be solved by wind power.
    Ⓓ He believes that there are too many problems associated with wind power.

Listening 3 "Philosophy Class"

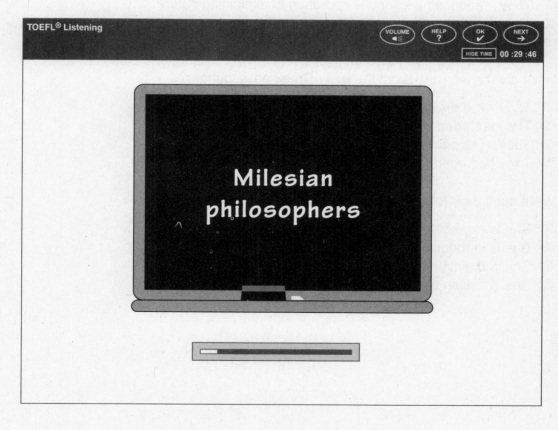

12. What is the discussion mainly about?

    Ⓐ The laws of motion
    Ⓑ The origin of water
    Ⓒ The nature of the universe
    Ⓓ The spirit of the world

13. Why does the student mention evolutionary theory?

    Ⓐ He is digressing from the main topic.
    Ⓑ He is trying to embarrass the professor.
    Ⓒ He is expressing doubt about Greek philosophy.
    Ⓓ He is comparing evolution to Anaximander's theory.

14. Why does the professor say this:

    Ⓐ She is not happy with the student's response.
    Ⓑ She is introducing an alternative view.
    Ⓒ She is going to expand on the comment.
    Ⓓ She is ending the discussion.

15. What view did the three Milesian philosophers share?

    Ⓐ They all believed that the mythology had a basis in fact.
    Ⓑ They introduced a scientific approach to explaining nature.
    Ⓒ They thought that water was the original element.
    Ⓓ They all agreed with the teachings of Socrates.

16. What can be inferred about the early Greek philosophers?

    Ⓐ They were exploring the physical sciences.
    Ⓑ They recorded many of the Greek myths.
    Ⓒ They were primarily interested in religion.
    Ⓓ They had contact with other European scholars.

17. What does the professor mean when she says this:

    Ⓐ She is expressing strong agreement.
    Ⓑ She is introducing doubt.
    Ⓒ She is maintaining a neutral position.
    Ⓓ She is asking the students to agree.

PART II

Listening 4 "Professor's Office"

18. Why does the woman want to talk with her professor?

    Ⓐ She wants to make an appointment outside of office hours.
    Ⓑ She needs to get him to approve the topic for her research.
    Ⓒ She has some questions about the report she is writing.
    Ⓓ She would like a recommendation for a job in the lab.

19. What advice does the professor give the woman?

    Ⓐ Have some friends read the research
    Ⓑ Refer to the explanation in the textbook
    Ⓒ Ask a chemistry major to help her
    Ⓓ Include more references in the report

20. What does the professor offer to do?

    Ⓐ Read a draft of the report before she submits it
    Ⓑ Help her find some better references
    Ⓒ Show her how to complete the experiment
    Ⓓ Give her a job in the laboratory

21. Why does the professor say this:

   Ⓐ He realizes that she won't have time to revise the report.
   Ⓑ He is concerned that she will not complete the research.
   Ⓒ He recalls that he will not be available to help her.
   Ⓓ He wants her to get an extension to finish the project.

22. What is the professor's opinion of the woman?

   Ⓐ He assumes that she is too busy to work.
   Ⓑ He is very impressed with her attitude.
   Ⓒ He thinks that she is not a serious student.
   Ⓓ He wants her to change her major to chemistry.

Listening 5 "Biology Class"

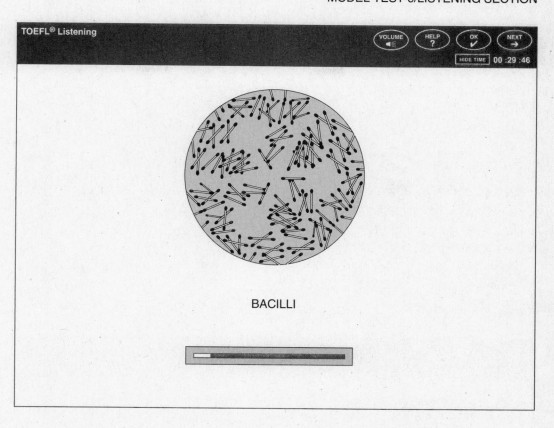

BACILLI

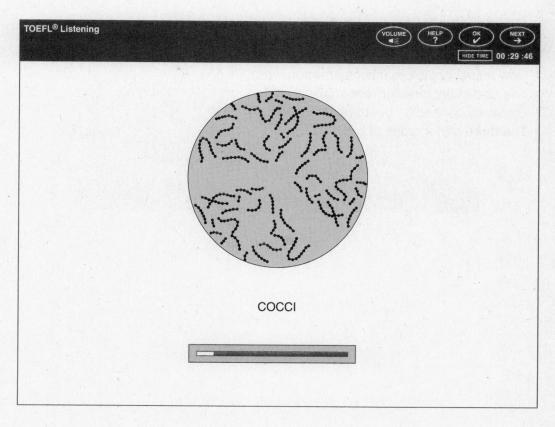

COCCI

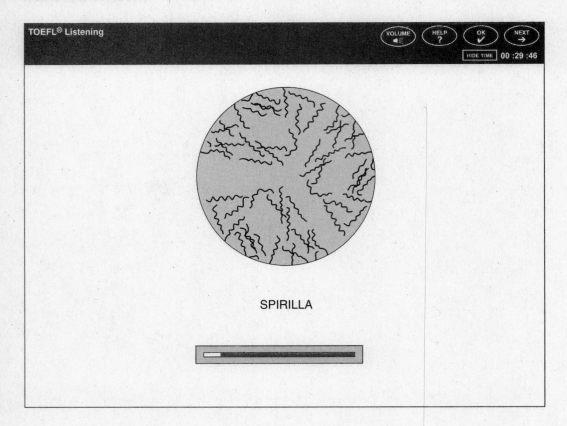

SPIRILLA

23. What aspect of bacteria is this lecture mainly about?

Ⓐ How microscopic organisms are measured
Ⓑ The use of bacteria for research in genetics
Ⓒ Diseases caused by bacterial infections
Ⓓ The three major types of bacteria

24. Which of the following slides contain cocci bacteria?

Click on the correct diagram.

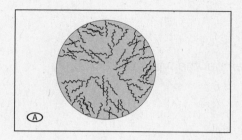

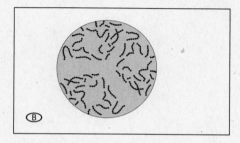

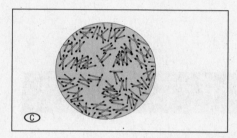

25. Which two characteristics are common in bacteria?

Click on 2 answer choices.

A They have one cell.

B They are harmful to humans.

C They reproduce quickly.

D They die when exposed to air.

26. Why are bacteria being used in the research study at the university?

    Ⓐ Bacteria have unusual cell formations.
    Ⓑ Bacteria live harmlessly on the skin.
    Ⓒ Bacteria are similar to other life forms.
    Ⓓ Bacteria cause many diseases in humans.

27. How does the professor help the students to remember the types of bacteria?

    Ⓐ He shows them many examples of slides.
    Ⓑ He tells them to look at specimens in the lab.
    Ⓒ He uses the first letter to represent the shape.
    Ⓓ He explains the various DNA structures.

28. Why does the professor say this:

    Ⓐ He is showing the students some slides.
    Ⓑ He does not want the students to ask questions.
    Ⓒ He wants the students to pay attention.
    Ⓓ He thinks that the information is very clear.

Listening 6 "History Class"

29. What is the lecture mainly about?

    Ⓐ Provisions of the Homestead Act
    Ⓑ How to construct a log cabin
    Ⓒ Frontier homes in the West
    Ⓓ Early construction materials

30. How does the professor organize his lecture?

    Ⓐ He makes a persuasive argument in favor of sod homes.
    Ⓑ He narrates stories about life on the Western frontier.
    Ⓒ He explains the process for becoming a homesteader.
    Ⓓ He contrasts several types of homes in the West.

31. What does the professor imply about construction materials for early homes?

    Ⓐ Settlers used the materials from the natural environment.
    Ⓑ Not many of the materials from that era have survived.
    Ⓒ Most of the supplies had to be shipped in by railroad.
    Ⓓ Wagons and tents were used in constructing homes.

32. What is the evidence for the inexpensive price of a sod home?

    Ⓐ Short stories and novels
    Ⓑ Letters written to relatives
    Ⓒ Newspaper advertisements
    Ⓓ Personal records and accounts

33. Why does the professor say this:

Ⓐ To criticize the sod house
Ⓑ To demonstrate uncertainty
Ⓒ To draw a conclusion
Ⓓ To uphold an opinion

34. In the lecture, the professor identifies attributes for different frontier homes. Indicate whether each attribute refers to a sod house or a log cabin. Click in the correct box for each phrase.

		Sod House	Log Cabin
A	A mud roof		
B	A rock foundation		
C	Chinked walls		
D	Notching techniques		
E	Thick brick insulation		

STOP   **Please turn off the audio. There is a 10-minute break between the Listening section and the Speaking section.**

SPEAKING SECTION

 Model Test 6, Speaking Section, CD 9, Track 2

The Speaking section tests your ability to communicate in English in an academic setting. During the test, you will be presented with six speaking questions. The questions ask for a response to a single question, a conversation, a talk, or a lecture.

You may take notes as you listen, but notes are not graded. You may use your notes to answer the questions. Some of the questions ask for a response to a reading passage and a talk or a lecture. The reading passages and the questions are written, but most of the directions will be spoken.

Your speaking will be evaluated on both the fluency of the language and the accuracy of the content. You will have 15–20 seconds to prepare and 45–60 seconds to respond to each question. Typically, a good response will require all of the response time but the answer will be complete by the end of the response time.

The time for the Speaking section is about 20 minutes. A clock on the screen will show you how much time you have to prepare your answer and how much time you have to record it.

Independent Speaking Question 1 "A Good Son or Daughter"

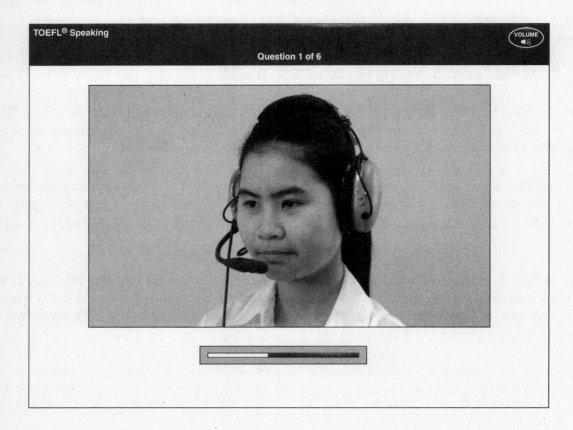

    Listen for a question about a familiar topic.

Question

In your opinion, what are the characteristics of a good son or daughter in a family? Use specific examples and details to explain your answer.

Preparation Time: 15 seconds
Recording Time: 45 seconds

Independent Speaking Question 2 "Job Opportunities"

 Listen for a question that asks your opinion about a familiar topic.

Question

Some people are attracted to jobs that include a great deal of travel. Other people prefer jobs that allow them to return to their homes every evening. Which type of job opportunity would you prefer and why? Use specific reasons and examples to support your opinion.

Preparation Time: 15 seconds
Recording Time: 45 seconds

Integrated Speaking Question 3 "Excused Absence"

Read a short passage and listen to a talk on the same topic.

Reading Time: 45 seconds

Policy for Excused Absence

You may request an excused absence once per semester without explanation. Just e-mail me and specify the date that you will be absent from class. If you plan to be absent on the day of a test or an exam, however, you must provide an explanation and make arrangements for a makeup test or exam. Please see me in my office for an excused absence from a test or exam. If you must be absent for more than one session, your grade may be affected. Your grade may be lowered one letter for each additional absence after the excused absence.

 Now listen to a student who is talking with friends about the policy.

Question

The student expresses his opinion of the professor's policy for excused absences. Report his opinion and explain the reasons that he gives for having that opinion.

Preparation Time: 30 seconds
Recording Time: 60 seconds

Integrated Speaking Question 4 "Insects"

Read a short passage and then listen to part of a lecture on the same topic.

Reading Time: 45 seconds

Insects

An insect belongs to the class of invertebrates called arthropods. Regardless of size, all adult insects have a similar body structure, which includes a head, a thorax, and an abdomen. The head contains not only the brain and mouth but also the sensory organs, usually a pair of eyes and a pair of antennae. The thorax is the central part of the insect's body where the wings and legs are attached, allowing the insect to move in the air and on feeding surfaces. Typically, insects have three pairs of legs and two pairs of wings. The third part of the insect's body structure consists of an abdomen where food is processed and also where the reproductive organs are found.

 Now listen to part of a lecture in a biology class. The professor is talking about insects.

Question

Describe the structure of an insect and explain why a spider is not strictly considered an insect.

Preparation Time: 30 seconds
Recording Time: 60 seconds

Integrated Speaking Question 5 "Meeting People"

  Now listen to a short conversation between a student and his friend.

Question
Describe the man's problem, and the two suggestions that his friend makes about how to handle it. What do you think the man should do, and why?

Preparation Time: 20 seconds
Recording Time: 60 seconds

Integrated Speaking Question 6 "Skinner Box"

 Now listen to part of a lecture in a psychology class. The professor is discussing the Skinner Box.

Question
Using the main points and examples from the lecture, describe the Skinner Box, and then explain how the device is used in psychology experiments.

Preparation Time: 20 seconds
Recording Time: 60 seconds

WRITING SECTION

The Writing section tests your ability to write essays in English similar to those that you would write in college courses.

During the test, you will write two essays. The integrated essay asks for your response to an academic reading passage and a lecture on the same topic. You may take notes as you read and listen, but notes are not graded. You may use your notes to write the essay. The lecture will be spoken, but the directions and the questions will be written. You will have 20 minutes to plan, write, and revise your response. Typically, a good essay for the integrated topic will require that you write 150–225 words.

The independent essay usually asks for your opinion about a familiar topic. You will have 30 minutes to plan, write, and revise your response. Typically, a good essay for the independent topic will require that you write 300–350 words.

A clock on the screen will show you how much time you have to complete each essay.

Integrated Essay "Primordial Soup"

You have 20 minutes to plan, write, and revise your response to a reading passage and a lecture on the same topic. First, read the passage and take notes. Then, listen to the lecture and take notes. Finally, write your response to the writing question. Typically, a good response will require that you write 150–225 words.

Reading Passage
Time: 3 minutes

The origin of life was highly speculative until a graduate student at the University of Chicago, Stanley Miller designed and conducted an empirical research project under the guidance of his graduate advisor, Harold Urey. In this classic experiment, the researchers tried to simulate the chemical evolution process that generated life. Miller and Urey took a five-liter flask half filled with water and connected it with glass tubing to another flask into which they inserted tungsten electrodes. They then mixed methane, hydrogen, and ammonia into the water in the lower flask and heated it to induce evaporation, while at the same time subjecting it to continuous electrical charges that jumped across the space between the electrodes in the upper flask. The atmosphere was cooled again so that the water could condense and trickle back into the first flask in a continuous cycle. In this way, they sought to recreate the conditions in the early atmosphere of Earth, which they speculated was probably subjected to powerful electrical storms. In about an hour, the water turned orange. At the end of the first week, they observed that almost 15 percent of the carbon was converted into organic compounds. After several weeks, the liquid in the flask clouded and then gradually turned a dark brown. When they analyzed it, Miller and Urey found that it contained a large number of amino acids, which form one of the basic structures of living organisms. They then hypothesized that the amino acids that they had created in the laboratory might be typical of the chemical mixture of the early oceans on Earth, and further, that additional amino acids could have been added to the mixture in the early oceans by carbon enriched meteorites or comets.

When the scientific results were popularized, the mixture became known as "primordial soup." However, much was still unknown about the process that caused the first cell to develop within the soup. The molecules produced were relatively simple organic molecules, not a complete living biochemical system. Nevertheless, the experiment established that natural processes could produce the building blocks of life without requiring life to synthesize them in the first place. The experiment served as inspiration for a large number of further investigations.

 Model Test 6, Writing Section, CD 9, Track 3

 Now listen to a lecture on the same topic as the passage that you have just read.

Question
Summarize the main points in the reading passage, explaining how the lecture casts doubt on the ideas.

Independent Essay "Learning a Foreign Language"

Question

Many people have learned a foreign language in their own country; others have learned a foreign language in the country in which it is spoken. Which is better? Give the advantages of each and support your viewpoint.

This is the end of Model Test 6.
To check your answers, refer to "Explanatory or Example Answers and Audio Scripts for Model Tests: Model Test 6," Chapter 7, pages 711–740.

MODEL TEST 7: PROGRESS TEST

READING SECTION

The Reading section tests your ability to understand reading passages like those in college textbooks. The passages are about 700 words in length.

This is the short format for the Reading section. On the short format, you will respond to three passages. After each passage, you will answer 12–14 questions about it.

Most questions are worth 1 point, but the last question in each passage is worth more than 1 point.

You will have 60 minutes to read all of the passages and answer the questions. You may take notes while you read, but notes are not graded. You may use your notes to answer the questions. Some passages may include a word or phrase that is underlined in blue. Click on the word or phrase to see a glossary definition or explanation.

Choose the best answer for multiple-choice questions. Follow the directions on the page or on the screen for computer-assisted questions. Click on **Next** to go to the next question. Click on **Back** to return to the previous question. You may return to previous questions for all of the passages in the same reading part, but after you go to the next part, you will not be able to return to passages in a previous part. Be sure that you have answered all of the questions for the passages in each part before you click on **Next** at the end of the passage to move to the next part.

You can click on **Review** to see a chart of the questions you have answered and the questions you have not answered in each part. From this screen, you can return to the question you want to answer in the part that is open.

A clock on the screen will show you how much time you have to complete the Reading section.

PART I

Reading 1 "The Hydrologic Cycle"

→ The hydrologic cycle is the transfer of water from the oceans to the atmosphere to the land and back to the oceans. The processes involved include evaporation of water from the oceans; precipitation on land; evaporation from land; and runoff from streams, rivers, and subsurface groundwater. The hydrologic cycle is driven by solar energy, which evaporates water from oceans, freshwater bodies, soils, and vegetation. Of the total 1.3 billion km water on Earth, about 97% is in oceans, and about 2% is in glaciers and ice caps. The rest is in freshwater on land and in the atmosphere. Although it represents only a small fraction of the water on Earth, the water on land is important in moving chemicals, sculpturing landscape, weathering rocks, transporting sediments, and providing our water resources. The water in the atmosphere—only 0.001% of the total on Earth—cycles quickly to produce rain and runoff for our water resources.

Especially important from an environmental perspective is that rates of transfer on land are small relative to what's happening in the ocean. For example, most of the water that evaporates from the ocean falls again as precipitation into the ocean. On land, most of the water that falls as precipitation comes from evaporation of water from land. This means that regional land-use changes, such as the building of large dams and reservoirs, can change the amount of water evaporated into the atmosphere and change the location and amount of precipitation on land—water we depend on to raise our crops and supply water for our urban environments. Furthermore, as we pave over large areas of land in cities, storm water runs off quicker and in greater volume, thereby increasing flood hazards. Bringing water into semi-arid cities by pumping groundwater or transporting water from distant mountains through aqueducts may increase evaporation, thereby increasing humidity and precipitation in a region.

Approximately 60% of water that falls by precipitation on land each year evaporates to the atmosphere. A smaller component (about 40%) returns to the ocean surface and subsurface runoff. Ⓐ This small annual transfer of water supplies resources for rivers and urban and agricultural lands. Ⓑ Unfortunately, distribution of water on land is far from uniform. Ⓒ As human population increases, water shortages will become more frequent in arid and semi-arid regions, where water is naturally nonabundant. Ⓓ

→ At the regional and local level, the fundamental hydrological unit of the landscape is the drainage basin (also called a watershed or catchment). A drainage basin is the area that contributes surface runoff to a particular stream or river. The term *drainage basin* is usually used in evaluating the hydrology of an area, such as the stream flow or runoff from hill slopes. Drainage basins vary greatly in size, from less than a hectare (2.5 acres) to millions of square kilometers. A drainage basin is usually named for its main stream or river, such as the Mississippi River drainage basin.

→ The main process in the cycle is the global transfer of water from the atmosphere to the land and oceans and back to the atmosphere. Together, the oceans, ice caps and glaciers account for more than 99% of the total water, and both are generally unsuitable for human use because of salinity (seawater) and location (ice caps and glaciers). Only about 0.001% of the total water on Earth is in the atmosphere at any one time. However, this relatively small amount of water in the global water cycle, with an average atmospheric residence time of only about 9 days, produces all our freshwater resources through the process of precipitation.

→ On a global scale, then, total water abundance is not the problem; the problem is water's availability in the right place at the right time in the right form. Water can be found in either liquid, solid, or gaseous form at a number of locations at or near Earth's surface. Depending on the specific location, the residence time may vary from a few days to many thousands of years. However, as mentioned, more than 99% of Earth's water in its natural state is unavailable or unsuitable for beneficial human use. Thus, the amount of water for which all the people, plants, and animals on Earth compete is much less than 1% of the total.

As the world's population and industrial production of goods increase, the use of water will also accelerate. The world per capita use of water in 1975 was about 185,000 gal/yr. And the total human use of water was about 10^{15} gal/yr. Today, world use of water is about 6,000, which is a significant fraction of the naturally available freshwater.

1. Which of the sentences below best expresses the information in the highlighted statement in the passage? The other choices change the meaning or leave out important information.

   Ⓐ It is the hydrologic cycle that causes water to evaporate from plants, soil, and bodies of water inland as well as from the oceans.

   Ⓑ Solar energy is the source of power for the hydrologic cycle, which begins by evaporating water from plants, soil, oceans, and freshwater sources.

   Ⓒ The evaporation of water from the oceans, freshwater sources, plants, and soils is the natural process, which we call the hydrologic cycle.

   Ⓓ Energy from the sun and the hydrologic cycle are power sources for plants that require water from the oceans and freshwater sources.

2. Based on information in paragraph 1, which of the following best explains the term "hydro-logic cycle"?

Ⓐ The movement of water from freshwater bodies into the oceans
Ⓑ Solar energy in the atmosphere that produces rain over land and oceans
Ⓒ Water resources from oceans and freshwater sources inland
Ⓓ Transportation of water from oceans into the atmosphere and onto the land

Paragraph 1 is marked with an arrow [➜].

3. The phrase <u>The rest</u> in the passage refers to

Ⓐ oceans
Ⓑ ice caps
Ⓒ glaciers
Ⓓ water

4. How do man-made water resources such as reservoirs and lakes affect the water cycle?

Ⓐ They increase the danger of flooding in the areas surrounding them.
Ⓑ They cause changes in the patterns of rainfall in the immediate area.
Ⓒ They provide water sources for agricultural purposes in dry areas.
Ⓓ They improve the natural flow of water into the oceans.

5. Freshwater is considered important because

Ⓐ it evaporates more quickly than water in the ocean
Ⓑ it is the largest source of water on Earth
Ⓒ it determines the landscape of rocks and sediment
Ⓓ it is the runoff that empties into the oceans

6. The word <u>component</u> in the passage is closest in meaning to

Ⓐ error
Ⓑ part
Ⓒ estimate
Ⓓ source

7. The word <u>fundamental</u> in the passage is closest in meaning to

Ⓐ diverse
Ⓑ common
Ⓒ basic
Ⓓ attractive

8. Why does the author mention the Mississippi River in paragraph 4?

   Ⓐ The Mississippi River is an example of a drainage basin.
   Ⓑ The Mississippi River is one of the largest rivers in the region.
   Ⓒ The Mississippi River is used in evaluating the runoff from hills.
   Ⓓ The Mississippi River is named for the area surrounding it.

   Paragraph 4 is marked with an arrow [➔].

9. According to paragraph 5, which of the following is true about the global transfer of water?

   Ⓐ Most rainwater stays in the atmosphere for less than a week.
   Ⓑ Glaciers are a better source of water than the oceans.
   Ⓒ Most of the water in the world is currently in the water cycle.
   Ⓓ Less than 1 percent of the water can be used for human consumption.

   Paragraph 5 is marked with an arrow [➔].

10. According to paragraph 6, why is water a problem?

    Ⓐ There is not enough water available in the world.
    Ⓑ Plants and animals are using the water that humans require.
    Ⓒ Distribution of water where it is needed can be difficult.
    Ⓓ Most of the water is too old to be used safely.

    Paragraph 6 is marked with an arrow [➔].

11. The word significant in the passage is closest in meaning to

    Ⓐ rare
    Ⓑ small
    Ⓒ important
    Ⓓ regular

12. Look at the four squares [■] that show where the following sentence could be inserted in the passage.

    As a result, water shortages occur in some areas.

    Where could the sentence best be added?

    Click on a square [■] to insert the sentence in the passage.

13. **Directions:** An introduction for a short summary of the passage appears below. Complete the summary by selecting the THREE answer choices that mention the most important points in the passage. Some sentences do not belong in the summary because they express ideas that are not included in the passage or are minor points from the passage. *This question is worth 2 points.*

The hydrologic cycle transfers water from the oceans to the atmosphere, from the atmosphere to the land, and back to the oceans.

-

-

-

Answer Choices

A The global problem is the availability of water that is suitable for human use where and when it is needed.

B Only about 0.001% of the total water on Earth is in the atmosphere at a particular point in time.

C Solar energy causes the evaporation of oceans and freshwater lakes and rivers into the atmosphere.

D Water shortages will probably become more common as more people begin to live in desert regions.

E Precipitation in the form of rainfall replenishes the water in the ocean and in drainage basins on land.

F Desalination is a key solution to the problem of adequate water supplies for human use.

PART II

Reading 2 "Piaget's Cognitive Development Theory"

The famous Swiss psychologist Jean Piaget (1896–1980) proposed an important theory of cognitive development. **Piaget's theory** *states that children actively construct their understanding of the world and go through four stages of cognitive development.* Two processes underlie this cognitive construction of the world: organization and adaptation. To make sense of our world, we organize our experiences. For example, we separate important ideas from less important ideas. We connect one idea to another. But not only do we organize our observations and experiences, we also *adapt* our thinking to include new ideas because additional information furthers understanding. Piaget (1954) believed that we adapt in two ways: assimilation and accommodation.

→ **Assimilation** *occurs when individuals incorporate new information into their existing knowledge.* **Accommodation** *occurs when individuals adjust to new information.* Consider a circumstance in which a 9-year-old girl is given a hammer and nails to hang a picture on the wall. She has never used a hammer, but from observation and vicarious experience she realizes that a hammer is an object to be held, that it is swung by the handle to hit the nail, and that it is usually swung a number of times. Recognizing each of these things, she fits her behavior into the information she already has (assimilation). However, the hammer is heavy, so she holds it near the top. She swings too hard and the nail bends, so she adjusts the pressure of her strikes. These adjustments reveal her ability to alter slightly her conception of the world (accommodation).

Piaget thought that assimilation and accommodation operate even in the very young infant's life. Newborns reflexively suck everything that touches their lips (assimilation), but, after several months of experience, they construct their understanding of the world differently. Some objects, such as fingers and the mother's breast, can be sucked, but others, such as fuzzy blankets, should not be sucked (accommodation).

Piaget also believed that we go through four stages in understanding the world. Each of the stages is age-related and consists of distinct ways of thinking. Remember, it is the *different* way of understanding the world that makes one stage more advanced than another; knowing *more* information does not make the child's thinking more advanced, in the Piagetian view. This is what Piaget meant when he said the child's cognition is *qualitatively* different in one stage compared to another (Vidal, 2000). Ⓐ What are Piaget's four stages of cognitive development like?

Ⓑ The *sensorimotor stage,* which lasts from birth to about 2 years of age, is the first Piagetian stage. In this stage, infants construct an understanding of the world by coordinating sensory experiences (such as seeing and hearing) with physical, motoric actions—hence the term *sensorimotor.* Ⓒ At the end of the stage, 2-year-olds have sophisticated sensorimotor patterns and are beginning to operate with primitive symbols. Ⓓ

→ The *preoperational stage,* which lasts from approximately 2 to 7 years of age, is the second Piagetian stage. In this stage, children begin to represent the world with words, images, and drawings. Symbolic thought goes beyond simple connections of sensory information and physical action. However, although preschool children can symbolically represent the world, according to Piaget, they still lack the ability to perform *operations,* the Piagetian term for internalized mental actions that allow children to do mentally what they previously did physically.

→ The *concrete operational stage,* which lasts from approximately 7 to 11 years of age, is the third Piagetian stage. In this stage, children can perform operations, and logical reasoning replaces intuitive thought as long as reasoning can be applied to specific or concrete examples. For instance, concrete operational thinkers cannot imagine the steps necessary to complete an algebraic equation, which is too abstract for thinking at this stage of development.

→ The *formal operational stage,* which appears between the ages of 11 and 15, is the fourth and final Piagetian stage. In this stage, individuals move beyond concrete experiences and think in abstract and more logical terms. As part of thinking more abstractly, adolescents develop images of ideal circumstances. They might think about what an ideal parent is like and compare their parents to this ideal standard. They begin to entertain possibilities for the future and are fascinated with what they can be. In solving problems, formal operational thinkers are more systematic, developing hypotheses about why something is happening the way it is, then testing these hypotheses in a deductive manner.

14. Which of the sentences below best expresses the information in the highlighted statement in the passage? The other choices change the meaning or leave out important information.

   Ⓐ Our new experiences require that we adjust in order to understand information that we have never seen.
   Ⓑ Understanding new ideas is easier if we include observations and personal experiences.
   Ⓒ We engage in both organization of what we see and experience and adaptation of novel ideas.
   Ⓓ Thinking must include direct observation and experiences in order to organize the information.

15. Why does the author mention a hammer in paragraph 2?

   Ⓐ To explain the concepts of assimilation and accommodation
   Ⓑ To demonstrate how a 9-year-old girl responds to a new experience
   Ⓒ To prove that a young child cannot engage in problem solving
   Ⓓ To provide an example of the first stage of cognitive development

   Paragraph 2 is marked with an arrow [→].

16. The word <u>alter</u> in the passage is closest in meaning to

    Ⓐ change
    Ⓑ improve
    Ⓒ hide
    Ⓓ find

17. The word <u>others</u> in the passage refers to

    Ⓐ months
    Ⓑ objects
    Ⓒ fingers
    Ⓓ blankets

18. The word <u>distinct</u> in the passage is closest in meaning to

    Ⓐ new
    Ⓑ simple
    Ⓒ different
    Ⓓ exact

19. The word <u>sophisticated</u> in the passage is closest in meaning to

    Ⓐ limited
    Ⓑ complex
    Ⓒ useful
    Ⓓ necessary

20. Based on the information in paragraph 6, which of the following best explains the term "operations"?

    Ⓐ Symbolic thought
    Ⓑ Mental actions
    Ⓒ Physical activity
    Ⓓ Abstract reasoning

Paragraph 6 is marked with an arrow [➔].

21. According to paragraph 7, why would a 10-year-old be unable to solve algebra problems?

    Ⓐ Algebra requires concrete operational thinking.
    Ⓑ A 10-year-old has not reached the formal operational stage.
    Ⓒ A child of 10 does not have logical reasoning abilities.
    Ⓓ An algebra problem has too many steps in order to solve it.

Paragraph 7 is marked with an arrow [➔].

22. In paragraph 8, the author mentions parents because

Ⓐ teenagers are already thinking about their roles in the future
Ⓑ parents are very important teachers during the final stage of development
Ⓒ the comparison of real and ideal parents is an example of abstract thinking
Ⓓ adolescents tend to be critical of their parents as part of their development

Paragraph 8 is marked with an arrow [➜].

23. What can be inferred from the passage about people who are older than 15 years of age?

Ⓐ They must have completed all of Piaget's stages of cognitive development.
Ⓑ They are probably in the formal operational state of development.
Ⓒ They have mastered deductive reasoning and are beginning to learn intuitively.
Ⓓ They may still not be able to solve problems systematically.

24. All of the following refer to Piaget's theory EXCEPT

Ⓐ Even very young infants may engage in constructing the way that they understand the world.
Ⓑ Both assimilation and accommodation are processes that we can use to help us adapt to new information.
Ⓒ When children learn more information, then their thinking is at a higher stage of development.
Ⓓ Operations require a more advanced stage of development than symbolic representation.

25. Look at the four squares [■] that show where the following sentence could be inserted in the passage.

At the beginning of this stage, newborns have little more than reflexive patterns with which to work.

Where could the sentence best be added?

Click on a square [■] to insert the sentence in the passage.

26. **Directions**: Complete the table by matching the phrases on the left with the headings on the right. Select the appropriate answer choices and drag them to the operational stages proposed by Piaget. TWO of the answer choices, which refer to the earlier stages, will NOT be used. *This question is worth 4 points.*

To delete an answer choice, click on it. To see the passage, click on **View Text**.

Answer Choices

Ⓐ Intuitive thought in images and drawings

Ⓑ Imagination of ideal situations or relationships

Ⓒ Logical reasoning for specific examples

Ⓓ Applied reasoning that requires little abstract thought

Ⓔ Abstract thinking that includes hypotheses

Ⓕ Complex coordination of the five senses

Ⓖ Successful solution of tangible problems

Ⓗ Thinking about potential situations for the future

Ⓘ Methodical trials to determine the reason for events

Concrete Operational Stage

•

•

•

Formal Operational Stage

•

•

•

•

Reading 3 "Conquest by Patents"

→ Patents are a form of <u>intellectual property</u> rights often touted as a means to give 'incentive and reward' to inventors. But they're also a cause for massive protests by farmers, numerous lawsuits by transnational corporations and indigenous peoples, and countless rallies and declarations by members of civil society. It is impossible to understand why they can have all these effects unless you first recognize that patents are about the control of technology and the protection of competitive advantage.

Lessons from History

In the 1760s, the Englishman Richard Arkwright invented the water-powered spinning frame, a machine destined to bring cotton-spinning out of the home and into the factory. It was an invention which made Britain a world-class power in the manufacture of cloth. To protect its competitive advantage and ensure the market for manufactured cloth in British colonies, Parliament enacted a series of restrictive measures including the prohibition of the export of Arkwright machinery or the emigration of any workers who had worked in factories using it. From 1774 on, those caught sending Arkwright machines or workers abroad from England were subject to fines and 12 years in jail.

→ In 1790, Samuel Slater, who had worked for years in the Arkwright mills, left England for the New World disguised as a farmer. A He thereby enabled the production of commercial-grade cotton cloth in the New World and put the U.S. firmly on the road to the Industrial Revolution and economic independence. B Slater was highly rewarded for his achievement. C He is still deemed the 'father of American manufacturing'. D To the English, however, he was an intellectual property thief.

Interestingly, patent protection was a part of U.S. law at the time of Slater's deed. But that protection would only extend to U.S. innovations. It is worth remembering that until the 1970s it was understood, even accepted, that countries only enforced those patent protections that served their national interest. When the young United States pirated the intellectual property of Europe—and Slater wasn't the only infringer—people in the US saw the theft as a justifiable response to England's refusal to transfer its technology.

By the early 1970s, the situation had changed. U.S. industry demanded greater protection for its idea-based products—such as computers and biotechnology—for which it still held the worldwide lead. Together with its like-minded industrial allies, the U.S. pushed for the inclusion of intellectual property clauses, including standards for patents, in international trade agreements.

When U.S. business groups explained the 'need' for patents and trademarks in trade agreements, they alleged $40–60 billion losses due to intellectual property piracy; they blamed the losses on Third World pirates; they discussed how piracy undermined the incentive to invest; and they claimed that the quality of pirated products was lower than the real thing and was costing lives.

→ The opposition pointed out that many of the products made in the industrial world, almost all its food crops and a high percentage of its medicines had originated in plant and animal germplasm taken from the developing world. First, knowledge of the material and how to use it was stolen, and later the material itself was taken. For all this, they said, barely a cent of royalties had been paid. Such unacknowledged and uncompensated appropriation they named 'biopiracy' and they reasoned that trade agreement patent rules were likely to facilitate more theft of their genetic materials. Their claim that materials 'collected' in the developing world were stolen, elicited a counterclaim that these were 'natural' or 'raw' materials and therefore did not qualify for patents. This in turn induced a counter-explanation that such materials were not 'raw' but rather the result of millennia of study, selection, protection, conservation, development and refinement by communities of Majority World and indigenous peoples.

Others pointed out that trade agreements which forced the adoption of unsuitable notions of property and creativity—not to mention an intolerable commercial relationship to nature—were not only insulting but also exceedingly costly. To a developing world whose creations might not qualify for patents and royalties, there was first of all the cost of unrealized profit. Secondly, there was the cost of added expense for goods from the industrialized world. For most of the people on the planet, the whole patenting process would lead to greater and greater indebtedness; for them, the trade agreements would amount to 'conquest by patents'—no matter what the purported commercial benefits.

Glossary

intellectual property: an invention or composition that belongs to the person who created it

27. According to paragraph 1, what is the real reason for patents to exist?

   Ⓐ Protests
   Ⓑ Lawsuits
   Ⓒ Prizes
   Ⓓ Control

Paragraph 1 is marked with an arrow [➜].

28. The word It in the passage refers to

   Ⓐ factory
   Ⓑ home
   Ⓒ cotton-spinning
   Ⓓ machine

29. Which of the sentences below best expresses the information in the highlighted statement in the passage? The other choices change the meaning or leave out important information.

   Ⓐ Among the laws to protect Britain from competition in the textile industry was a ban on exporting Arkwright equipment and on emigration of former employees.
   Ⓑ Former employees of Arkwright could not leave the country because they might provide information about the company to competing factories.
   Ⓒ The reason that Britain passed laws to prevent emigration was to keep employees in the textile mills from leaving their jobs to work in other countries.
   Ⓓ Parliament passed laws to ensure that the price of textiles was kept high in spite of competition from the former British colonies who were exporting cloth.

30. In paragraph 3, how does the author explain the concept of technological transfer?

   Ⓐ By recounting how Samuel Slater, an American farmer, established a successful textile mill in Great Britain
   Ⓑ By describing how Samuel Slater used workers from Britain to develop the textile industry in the United States
   Ⓒ By exposing how Samuel Slater stole ideas and technology from one nation to introduce them in another
   Ⓓ By demonstrating how Samuel Slater used the laws to his advantage in order to transfer technology

Paragraph 3 is marked with an arrow [➜].

31. The word <u>innovations</u> in the passage is closest in meaning to

    Ⓐ discoveries
    Ⓑ exceptions
    Ⓒ disputes
    Ⓓ territories

32. How did the perspective of industrialists in the United States change in the 1970s?

    Ⓐ They favored free exchange of technology.
    Ⓑ They supported the protection of patents.
    Ⓒ They refused to sign international trade agreements.
    Ⓓ They began to collaborate with Third World nations.

33. How did industrialized nations justify using plants and animals from the developing world for food and medicine products?

    Ⓐ They claimed that the plant and animal sources were raw materials that could not be patented.
    Ⓑ They asserted that the original plant and animal materials were found in their own nations.
    Ⓒ They paid a large royalty for the use of plants and animals that were not original to their countries.
    Ⓓ They stated that they had manufactured a higher quality of products than the competition.

34. Based on information in paragraph 7, which of the following best explains the term "biopiracy"?

    Ⓐ A conspiracy by farmers
    Ⓑ The theft of plants and animals
    Ⓒ Secret trade agreements
    Ⓓ Natural resources in the biosphere

Paragraph 7 is marked with an arrow [➔].

35. The word <u>facilitate</u> in the passage is closest in meaning to

    Ⓐ permit
    Ⓑ assist
    Ⓒ require
    Ⓓ delay

36. The word <u>notions</u> in the passage is closest in meaning to

    Ⓐ customs
    Ⓑ records
    Ⓒ property
    Ⓓ ideas

42 37. Why does the author call this article "Conquest by Patents"?

    Ⓐ Because most trade agreements are unfair to developing nations
    Ⓑ Because patents cost too much money for developing nations
    Ⓒ Because industrialized countries do not pay their debts to developing nations
    Ⓓ Because natural resources are a source of power for developing nations

38. Look at the four squares [■] that show where the following sentence could be inserted in the passage.

Arriving in the U.S., he sought financing and recreated from memory an entire Arkwright factory and all its equipment.

Where could the sentence best be added?

Click on a square [■] to insert the sentence in the passage.

39. **Directions:** An introduction for a short summary of the passage appears below. Complete the summary by selecting the THREE answer choices that mention the most important points in the passage. Some sentences do not belong in the summary because they express ideas that are not included in the passage or are minor points from the passage. ***This question is worth 2 points.***

Patents are used to protect the competitive interests of nations and control the ownership of technology.

-
-
-

Answer Choices

Ⓐ The purpose of patents is to protect the originator from competition and control of the technology.

Ⓑ In 1790, Samuel Slater, an English citizen who smuggled plans for a textile mill into the United States, was considered a thief.

Ⓒ Anyone who conspired to send machines or workers at the Arkwright factory overseas could suffer fines or even a jail term of 12 years.

Ⓓ The United States, along with other industrialized nations, pushed for more protection of intellectual property in trade agreements negotiated in the 1970s.

Ⓔ U.S.-based businesses claimed that the infringement of intellectual property rights by pirates cost them $40–60 billion in lost profits.

Ⓕ The developing world has opposed trade agreements that favor the industrialized nations and ignore the origin of the plant and animal products used.

LISTENING SECTION

 Model Test 7, Listening Section, CD 9, Track 5, continued on CD 10, Track 1

The Listening section tests your ability to understand spoken English that is typical of interactions and academic speech on college campuses. During the test, you will respond to conversations and lectures.

This is the long format for the Listening section. On the long format, you will respond to three conversations and six lectures. After each listening passage, you will answer 5–6 questions about it. Only two conversations and four lectures will be graded. The other conversation and lectures are part of an experimental section for future tests. Because you will not know which conversations and lectures will be graded, you must try to do your best on all of them.

You will hear each conversation or lecture one time. You may take notes while you listen, but notes are not graded. You may use your notes to answer the questions.

Choose the best answer for multiple-choice questions. Follow the directions on the page or on the screen for computer-assisted questions. Click on **Next** and **OK** to go to the next question. You cannot return to previous questions. You have 20–30 minutes to answer all of the questions. A clock on the screen will show you how much time you have to complete your answers for the section. The clock does not count the time you are listening to the conversations and lectures.

PART I

Listening 1 "Professor's Office"

1. Why does the man go to see his professor?

    Ⓐ He wants to withdraw from the class.
    Ⓑ He needs to ask the professor a question.
    Ⓒ His professor promised to give him a tape.
    Ⓓ His professor asked him to come to the office.

2. Why does the student say this:

    Ⓐ He is disrespectful.
    Ⓑ He is surprised.
    Ⓒ He is sorry.
    Ⓓ He is happy.

3. What does the professor mean when she says this:

    Ⓐ She is warning the student that she could take more serious action.
    Ⓑ She is indicating that she is not sure what she wants to do.
    Ⓒ She is asking the man to come up with a solution for the situation.
    Ⓓ She is forgiving the man for causing a problem in her class.

4. How does the professor feel about questions in class?

    Ⓐ She would rather answer questions during her office hours.
    Ⓑ She thinks that students who ask questions are showing interest.
    Ⓒ She does not like students to be disrespectful by asking questions.
    Ⓓ She wants her students to help each other instead of asking questions.

5. What will the man probably do during the next class?

    Ⓐ He will ask fewer questions.
    Ⓑ He will tape record the lecture.
    Ⓒ He will refer to the outline in the book.
    Ⓓ He will participate more in the discussion.

Listening 2 "Art Class"

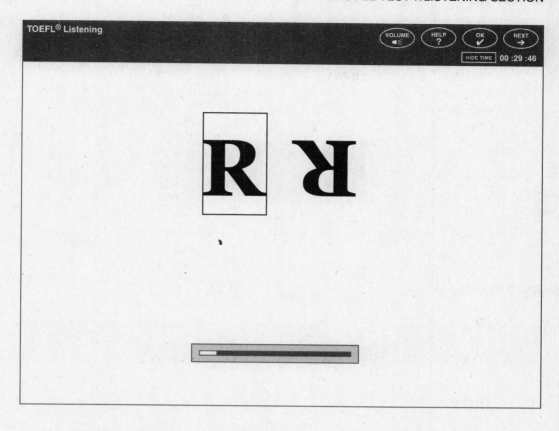

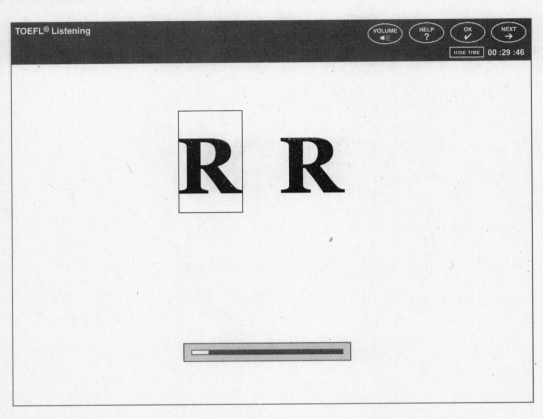

6. What is this lecture mainly about?

    Ⓐ Symmetry in the visual arts
    Ⓑ The characteristics of patterns
    Ⓒ How the brain organizes information
    Ⓓ A definition of beauty

7. What does the professor mean when he says this:

    Ⓐ He plans to give others an opportunity to speak.
    Ⓑ He is talking too fast and intends to slow down.
    Ⓒ He needs to correct something that he has said.
    Ⓓ He wants to talk about that subject later.

8. Which of the following slides represents reflection symmetry?

    Click on the correct diagram.

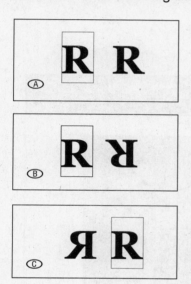

9. How is it possible to recognize an object when only part of it is visible?

    Ⓐ The brain recognizes symmetry and visualizes the whole.
    Ⓑ The object is often familiar enough to be recognized.
    Ⓒ The pieces are large even though some are missing.
    Ⓓ The principles for identification can be learned.

10. In addition to a system for organization, what characteristics define a pattern?

    Click on 2 answer choices.

    Ⓐ A basic unit

    Ⓑ An image

    Ⓒ Repetition

    Ⓓ Rotation

11. What assignment does the professor give his students?

    Ⓐ They are supposed to identify patterns in the classroom.
    Ⓑ They should be prepared for a quiz on this lecture.
    Ⓒ They need to go to the lab to complete an experiment.
    Ⓓ They have to design a pattern that includes symmetry.

Listening 3 "Biology Class"

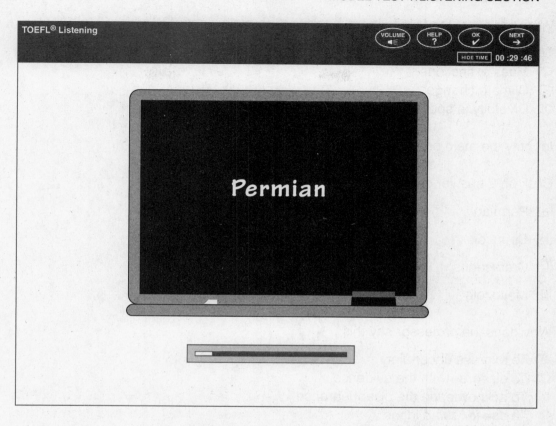

12. What aspect of the fossil record is this lecture mainly about?

   Ⓐ .The impact hypothesis
   Ⓑ Mass extinctions
   Ⓒ Climate change
   Ⓓ Diversity in species

13. Identify the main periods of mass extinction.

   Click on 2 answer choices.

   Ａ Permian

   Ｂ Cenozoic

   Ｃ Cretaceous

   Ｄ Mesozoic

14. Why does the professor say this:

   Ⓐ To express uncertainty
   Ⓑ To disagree with the evidence
   Ⓒ To acknowledge the disappearance
   Ⓓ To ask for some ideas

15. What is the impact hypothesis?

   Ⓐ The theory that the continents drifted and collided with each other
   Ⓑ The idea that volcanic eruptions disrupted the climate worldwide
   Ⓒ The view that a lightening storm caused a global fire
   Ⓓ The premise that an asteroid crashed, blocking the sunlight on Earth

16. What is the evidence for the impact hypothesis?

   Ⓐ The clay from the Cretaceous Period contains an element that is rare on Earth.
   Ⓑ Both hemispheres suffered the same amount of damage and extinction.
   Ⓒ Acidic precipitation is still not evenly distributed across the Earth.
   Ⓓ Rocks that may have been part of an asteroid have been identified.

17. What can be inferred about the professor's opinion?

   Ⓐ He is strongly in favor of the impact hypothesis.
   Ⓑ He does not believe that mass extinctions happened.
   Ⓒ He thinks that mass extinctions were important to evolution.
   Ⓓ He views mass extinction as a preventable occurrence.

PART II

Listening 4 "Students on Campus"

18. What are the students discussing?

Ⓐ The T.A. in their class
Ⓑ The woman's presentation
Ⓒ PowerPoint handouts
Ⓓ The woman's class

19. Which strategy does the woman use for her presentation?

Ⓐ Read the information on the handouts
Ⓑ Ask volunteers to participate
Ⓒ Show visuals to explain the points
Ⓓ Respond to questions from the group

20. Why did the woman make overhead copies of the slides?

Ⓐ She was very nervous about going first.
Ⓑ She was afraid that the computer program would fail.
Ⓒ She took the man's advice about making them.
Ⓓ She wanted to show them to the man.

21. What does the man mean when he says this:

    Ⓐ He does not appreciate the woman's comment.
    Ⓑ He has difficulty hearing the woman.
    Ⓒ He wants the woman to continue.
    Ⓓ He understands the woman's point of view.

22. Why didn't the class ask questions after the presentation?

    Ⓐ The material was presented very clearly.
    Ⓑ The presentation was not interesting to them.
    Ⓒ There wasn't enough time for questions.
    Ⓓ They were anxious to make their presentations.

Listening 5 "Sociology Class"

23. How does the professor organize the discussion?

    Ⓐ By defining gang activity, using information from articles
    Ⓑ By contrasting gang activity with noncriminal organizations
    Ⓒ By reading part of an article on gang activity to the class
    Ⓓ By reporting her research on gang activity in the local area

24. What was surprising about Thrasher's study?

    Ⓐ The size of the study, which included 1300 gangs
    Ⓑ The excellent summary by the student who located the research
    Ⓒ The changes that were reported in the history of gangs
    Ⓓ The fact that gang activity has been prevalent for so long

25. According to the study by Moore, what causes gang activity?

    Ⓐ Cliques that form in high school
    Ⓑ Normal feelings of insecurity in teens
    Ⓒ Abusive family members in the home
    Ⓓ Loyalty to family already in the gang

26. Why does the professor say this:

    Ⓐ To show that she does not agree with the response
    Ⓑ To encourage the student to give an example
    Ⓒ To indicate that she does not understand
    Ⓓ To praise the student for his answer

27. What is the role of women in gangs?

    Ⓐ They are full members of the gangs.
    Ⓑ They are protected by the gangs.
    Ⓒ They are a support system for the gangs.
    Ⓓ They have little contact with gangs.

28. In the discussion, the students identify aspects of gang activity. Indicate whether each of the following is one of the aspects. Click in the correct box for each phrase.

		Yes	No
A	A replacement for high school cliques		
B	A group socialized on the streets		
C	A peer group that is 14–20 years old		
D	Young people who have dropped out of school		
E	A group that makes careful plans		

Listening 6 "Anthropology Class"

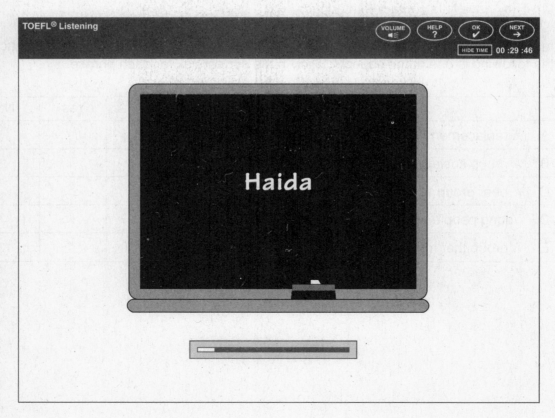

29. Which of the following is an important reason the Haida people carve totem poles?

   Ⓐ To frighten away spirits
   Ⓑ To decorate the village
   Ⓒ To recall traditional stories
   Ⓓ To worship the animals

30. What does the professor mean when he says this:

   Ⓐ This fact does not directly relate to the topic.
   Ⓑ He expects the students to write down the definition.
   Ⓒ He is expressing uncertainty about the information.
   Ⓓ The professor should not be talking about this tradition.

31. Why does the professor mention the coat of arms of Canada?

   Ⓐ To compare the symbolism to that of a totem pole
   Ⓑ To prove that the Haida live in Canada
   Ⓒ To argue that the Haida symbols are superior
   Ⓓ To place the events in chronological order

32. What does the saying *low man on the totem pole* mean?

    Ⓐ A very good representative member of the group
    Ⓑ A person who begins to tell an important story
    Ⓒ A person who has the least status among the members
    Ⓓ A member of the community who is not accepted

33. Why do the master carvers work on the bottom figures?

    Ⓐ Master carvers are usually too old to work at the top of the pole.
    Ⓑ The figures near the bottom are more visible to the public.
    Ⓒ The totem pole is too large for just one carver to complete.
    Ⓓ The last carving is an honor reserved for the masters.

34. What does the professor mean when he says this:

    Ⓐ He is indicating that the information to follow is very reliable.
    Ⓑ He is showing the class that he knows a great deal about the information.
    Ⓒ He is signaling that the students should learn this information.
    Ⓓ He is informing the students that there may be more information.

PART III

Listening 7 "Professor's Office"

35. Why does the man go to see his professor?

    Ⓐ He is worried about the professor's class.
    Ⓑ He wants to bring up the grade in her class.
    Ⓒ He would like some advice about his classes.
    Ⓓ He needs to get the woman's signature.

36. Why does the man say this:

    Ⓐ He is apologizing for the problem.
    Ⓑ He is asking the woman to explain.
    Ⓒ He is thinking of what to say next.
    Ⓓ He is correcting the professor politely.

37. What is the man's problem?

    Ⓐ He is taking too many classes this semester.
    Ⓑ He is failing one of his required courses.
    Ⓒ He has a problem with his academic advisor.
    Ⓓ He took classes with heavy reading assignments.

38. What does the professor suggest?

    Ⓐ Registration for a course in how to read faster
    Ⓑ Extra help sessions to bring up the grade in her class
    Ⓒ Immediate withdrawal from one of the courses
    Ⓓ Intensive study until the end of the semester

39. What can we infer about the situation?

    Ⓐ The student will probably talk with his advisor before registration next term.
    Ⓑ The professor believes that the student will probably not take her advice.
    Ⓒ The date for changing the student's schedule has probably passed already.
    Ⓓ The professor is probably the student's academic program advisor.

Listening 8 *"Psychology Class"*

40. What is the lecture mainly about?

    Ⓐ Neurotransmitters
    Ⓑ Seasonal affective disorder
    Ⓒ Genetic research
    Ⓓ The National Institute of Mental Health

41. What are neurotransmitters?

    Ⓐ Chemical imbalances
    Ⓑ Chemicals in the brain
    Ⓒ Images of the brain
    Ⓓ Genetic triggers

42. What happens when there is a reduction of light during the winter months?

    Ⓐ A decrease in melatonin may cause a chemical imbalance.
    Ⓑ The pineal gland begins functioning to compensate.
    Ⓒ The retina of the eye opens to receive more light.
    Ⓓ The mental processes in the brain are slower.

43. Why does the professor think that the acronym S.A.D. is unsuitable?

    Ⓐ She did not participate in creating the acronym.
    Ⓑ It does not reflect the seriousness of the problem.
    Ⓒ Some of her patients object to the acronym.
    Ⓓ The acronym is not an abbreviation for the words.

44. What does the professor mean when she says this:

    Ⓐ She is reminding the students of previous facts.
    Ⓑ She is disagreeing with the statistics.
    Ⓒ She is indicating that the example is unimportant.
    Ⓓ She is expressing uncertainty about the information.

45. In the lecture, the professor reports the preliminary results of her research. Indicate whether each of the following is one of the findings. Click in the correct box for each sentence.

		Yes	No
A	Morning exposure for the treatment is superior.		
B	A regular sleep schedule supports therapy.		
C	Eye damage occurs in only a few subjects.		
D	Sessions of less than two hours are preferable.		
E	Fluorescent lighting cannot be used for therapy.		

Listening 9 "Physics Class"

46. What is the discussion mainly about?

    (A) The theory of everything
    (B) Einstein's unified field theory
    (C) Advances in brain theory
    (D) Theoretical mathematics

47. How does the professor explain the closed string?

    (A) He refers the students to a web site.
    (B) He rewords the definition in the book.
    (C) He compares it with a thin rubber band.
    (D) He contrasts it with an open string.

48. Why does the professor say this:

    (A) He does not expect the student to answer the question.
    (B) He does not know the answer to the question.
    (C) He does not want to continue the debate in class.
    (D) He does not want to influence the woman's thinking.

49. According to the discussion, what reason does the man give for rejecting string theory?

    (A) There may have been errors in the mathematical calculations.
    (B) Strings have not been observed in a laboratory.
    (C) String theory does not prove the theory of everything.
    (D) The experiments were not performed correctly.

50. What can be inferred about the students?

    Ⓐ They have not formed opinions about the theory.
    Ⓑ They do not agree with the professor's point of view.
    Ⓒ They have reached different conclusions about the theory.
    Ⓓ They have changed their minds during the discussion.

51. Why does the professor suggest that the students visit a web site?

    Ⓐ The textbook does not have the latest information about the topic that they will debate.
    Ⓑ The web site should provide objective data, which they can use for the next discussion.
    Ⓒ The professor wants the students to understand the history of the theory they are studying.
    Ⓓ The site will prepare the students to complete mathematical calculations before the next class.

 Please turn off the audio. There is a 10-minute break between the Listening section and the Speaking section.

SPEAKING SECTION

 Model Test 7, Speaking Section, CD 10, Track 2

The Speaking section tests your ability to communicate in English in an academic setting. During the test, you will be presented with six speaking questions. The questions ask for a response to a single question, a conversation, a talk, or a lecture.

You may take notes as you listen, but notes are not graded. You may use your notes to answer the questions. Some of the questions ask for a response to a reading passage and a talk or a lecture. The reading passages and the questions are written, but most of the directions will be spoken.

Your speaking will be evaluated on both the fluency of the language and the accuracy of the content. You will have 15–20 seconds to prepare and 45–60 seconds to respond to each question. Typically, a good response will require all of the response time but the answer will be complete by the end of the response time.

The time for the Speaking section is about 20 minutes. A clock on the screen will show you how much time you have to prepare your answer and how much time you have to record it.

Independent Speaking Question 1 "A Book"

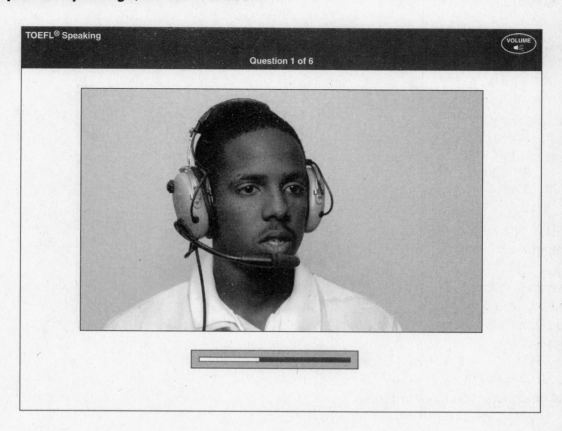

 Listen for a question about a familiar topic.

Question
Think about a book that you have enjoyed reading. Why did you like it? What was especially interesting about the book? Use specific details and examples to support your response.

Preparation Time: 15 seconds
Recording Time: 45 seconds

Independent Speaking Question 2 "Foreign Travel"

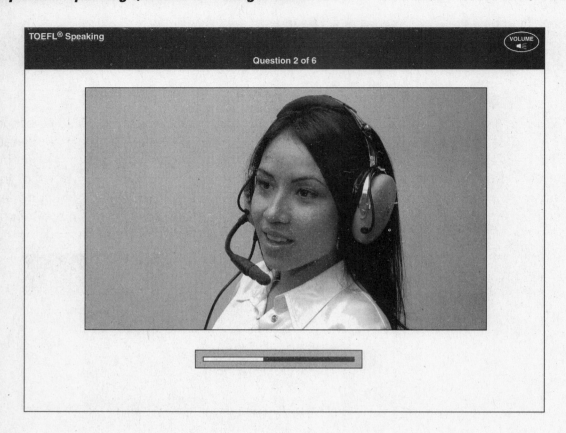

 Listen for a question that asks your opinion about a familiar topic.

Question

Some people think that it is better to travel as part of a tour group when they are visiting a foreign country. Other people prefer to make their own travel plans so that they can travel independently. Which approach do you think is better and why? Use specific reasons and examples to support your opinion.

Preparation Time: 15 seconds
Recording Time: 45 seconds

Integrated Speaking Question 3 "Old Main"

Read a short passage and listen to a talk on the same topic.

Reading Time: 45 seconds

Notice Concerning Old Main

The college will be celebrating the one-hundredth anniversary of the founding of the school by renovating Old Main, the original building. Two alternative plans are being considered. One plan would leave the outer structure intact and concentrate on electrical and plumbing upgrades as well as minor structural support. The other plan would demolish all of the building except the clock tower, which would form the centerpiece of a new structure. An open meeting is scheduled for Friday afternoon at three o'clock in the Old Main auditorium.

 Now listen to a professor who is speaking at a meeting. She is expressing her opinion about the proposals.

Question

The professor expresses her opinion of the plan for the renovation of Old Main. Report her opinion and explain the reasons that she gives for having that opinion.

Preparation Time: 30 seconds
Recording Time: 60 seconds

Integrated Speaking Question 4 "Pangea"

Read a short passage and then listen to part of a lecture on the same topic.

Reading Time: 45 seconds

<u>Pangea</u>
Plate tectonics assumes that the Earth's rigid outer layer is comprised of a number of slabs called plates, which are constantly in motion, changing the position of land masses and seascapes relative to each other throughout history. The plates move slowly but continuously at about the rate of 2 inches every year. The movement of the plates themselves may be caused by the unequal distribution of heat and pressure below them. Very hot material deep within the mantle, that is, the layer of rock inside the Earth, moves upward while the cooler layer descends into the mantle, putting the outer crust of the continents in motion. Several large plates include an entire continent with its surrounding seafloor; however, the boundaries of the plates do not correspond precisely with the seven continents that we recognize today.

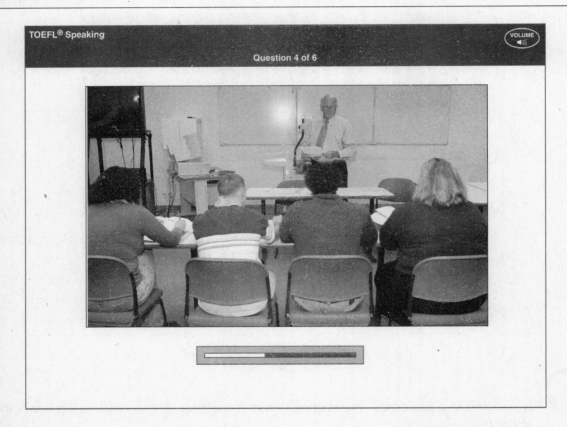

 Now listen to part of a lecture in a geography class. The professor is talking about Pangea.

Question
Explain how plate tectonics relates to the theory of *continental drift.*

Preparation Time: 30 seconds
Recording Time: 60 seconds

Integrated Speaking Question 5 "Headaches"

 Now listen to a short conversation between a student and her friend.

Question
Describe the woman's problem and the two suggestions that her friend makes about how to handle it. What do you think the woman should do, and why?

Preparation Time: 20 seconds
Recording Time: 60 seconds

Integrated Speaking Question 6 "Fax Machines"

 Now listen to part of a lecture in a business class. The professor is discussing the way that a fax machine transmits and receives data.

Question

Using the main points and examples from the lecture, describe the three parts of a fax machine and then explain how the fax process works.

Preparation Time: 20 seconds
Recording Time: 60 seconds

WRITING SECTION

The Writing section tests your ability to write essays in English similar to those that you would write in college courses.

During the test, you will write two essays. The integrated essay asks for your response to an academic reading passage and a lecture on the same topic. You may take notes as you read and listen, but notes are not graded. You may use your notes to write the essay. The lecture will be spoken, but the directions and the questions will be written. You will have 20 minutes to plan, write, and revise your response. Typically, a good essay for the integrated topic will require that you write 150–225 words.

The independent essay usually asks for your opinion about a familiar topic. You will have 30 minutes to plan, write, and revise your response. Typically, a good essay for the independent topic will require that you write 300–350 words.

A clock on the screen will show you how much time you have to complete each essay.

Integrated Essay "Problem Solving"

You have 20 minutes to plan, write, and revise your response to a reading passage and a lecture on the same topic. First, read the passage and take notes. Then, listen to the lecture and take notes. Finally, write your response to the writing question. Typically, a good response will require that you write 150–225 words.

Reading Passage
Time: 3 minutes

Solving a problem can be broken down into several steps. First, the problem must be identified correctly. Psychologists refer to this step as *problem representation*. For many problems, figuring out which information is relevant and which is extraneous can be difficult and can interfere with arriving at a good solution. Clearly, before a problem can be solved, it must be obvious what the problem is; however, this is not as easy as it might seem. One obstacle to efficient problem representation is *functional fixedness*, that is, allowing preconceived notions and even prejudices to color the facts. Most people tend to see objects and events in certain fixed ways, and by being inflexible in viewing the problem, they may be unable to notice the tools for the solution. Once the problem is identified accurately, however, the second step consists of considering the alternatives for a solution. A common way to evaluate alternatives is to write them down and then make a list of advantages and disadvantages for each solution. Here again, people may be limited by prior experiences. Often people adopt *mental sets* that lead them to the same problem-solving strategies that were successful for problems in the past. Although that can be helpful most of the time, sometimes a new situation requires a different strategy. In that case, the mental set must be abandoned, and new alternatives must be explored. This can be a difficult adjustment for some people.

After the alternatives have been compared, a strategy must be selected from among them. One way to avoid becoming mired in the options is to try the best options with a view to abandoning it for another if the results are unfavorable. This attitude allows many people to move on expeditiously to the next step—action. The strategy selected must be implemented and tested. If it solves the problem, no further action is necessary, but if not, then an unsuccessful solution may actually lead to a more successful option. If the solution is still not apparent, then the cycle begins again, starting with problem identification. By continuing to review the problem and repeat the problem-solving steps, the solution can be improved upon and refined.

Model Test 7, Writing Section, CD 10, Track 3

 Now listen to a lecture on the same topic as the passage that you have just read.

Question

Summarize the main points in the lecture, referring to the way that they relate to the reading passage.

Independent Essay "Study Abroad"

Question

You are planning to study abroad. What do you think you will like and dislike about this experience? Why? Use specific reasons and details to support your answer.

This is the end of Model Test 7.
To check your answers, refer to "Explanatory or Example Answers and Audio Scripts for Model Tests: Model Test 7," Chapter 7, pages 741–774.

7

ANSWERS AND AUDIO SCRIPTS FOR ACTIVITIES, QUIZZES, AND MODEL TESTS

ANSWERS AND AUDIO SCRIPTS FOR PRACTICE ACTIVITIES IN CHAPTER 3

PRACTICE ACTIVITY 1

1. Settlement Patterns	classification *or* comparison and contrast
2. The Functions of Art	classification
3. Language Development	sequence
4. How Important Is Relativity?	persuasion *or* evaluation
5. Causes of Schizophrenia	cause and effect
6. Evaluating Kohlberg's Theory	persuasion *or* evaluation
7. Types of Financial Services	classification
8. A History of Plate Tectonics	sequence
9. Estimating Population	cause and effect *or* problem and solution
10. Black Holes	definition *or* description

PRACTICE ACTIVITY 2

 Activity 2, CD 2, Track 4. Listen to part of a lecture in an astronomy class.

1. Listen to part of a lecture in a business class.
2. Listen to part of a lecture in a music appreciation class.
3. Listen to part of a lecture in a biology class.
4. Listen to part of a lecture in an anthropology class.
5. Listen to part of a lecture in an engineering class.
6. Listen to part of a lecture in a linguistics class.
7. Listen to part of a lecture in an art history class.
8. Listen to part of a lecture in a psychology class.

9. Listen to part of a lecture in a geology class.
10. Listen to part of a lecture in a history class.

PRACTICE ACTIVITY 3

 Activity 3, CD 2, Track 5

1. I have several slides of *mosaic art*, mostly from the fifth century.
2. Right. So last time we were discussing uh, multinational companies. Today we're going to look at *global companies*.
3. Well, today's lecture is about *light years*.
4. So, if you read the chapter in your textbook, the one about *insurance*, then you have some background for today's lecture.
5. Although Malthus's theory of population is still important, I'm going to share a different approach with you today called *demographic transition*.
6. Okay then, let's begin our discussion of *marshland habitats*.
7. Sorry about the mixup with our classroom on the schedule. I'm glad you found us. So this will be the room we'll be using for the rest of the semester. Okay, then, let's get on with our discussion of *igneous rocks*.
8. From your syllabus, you know that today we're talking about *adobe construction*, specifically, how it can be adapted to modern architecture.
9. Let's ask ourselves this simple question: how does an *antibiotic* make you well?
10. All right. We've been talking about *reptiles*. Now let's turn our attention to *amphibians*.

PRACTICE ACTIVITY 4

There are three arguments in support of protecting endangered species.

Aesthetic justification Various forms of nature influence the life experience of human beings in a positive way.	uniquely beautiful appreciated universally in art and literature important to the religious community
Ecological self-interest assumes that a balance of nature benefits all species.	perform essential functions ex. unique carrier of a cure for a human disease to protect ourselves, we must protect other species
Moral justification asserts that the creatures themselves have rights.	United Nations World Charter for Nature— all species have the right to exist human beings have the responsibility to preserve all species

The professor does not directly promote any argument, but advocacy for the protection of endangered species is implied in the lecture.

PRACTICE ACTIVITY 5

1. According to Mead, the self has two sides: the "I" and the "me."

The "I" represents the individuality of a person.	For instance, a spontaneous reaction might reveal the "I." This part of the self is less predictable because it is unique.
The "me" represents the expectations and attitudes of others.	This part of the self is formed through socialization by others. It is predictable because social conformity is expected.

2. The mystery of pulsars was resolved in the 1960s.

We know that pulsars are neutron stars, like lighthouses left by supernova explosions.	Like a lighthouse, the neutron star revolves. We see pulses of light each time the beam sweeps past the Earth.
We also know that pulsars are not perfectly timed because each revolution of a pulsar takes a little longer.	The pulsar in the Crab Nebula, for example, currently spins about thirty times per second. It will probably spin about half as fast two thousand years from now.

3. Britain transported convicts to Australia in an effort to solve the problems of overcrowding in prisons.

In 1787, the first fleet left for Botany Bay in New South Wales.	There were 11 ships with 750 prisoners aboard. Four companies of marines sailed with them as guards. They took enough supplies for two years.
Shortly after arriving in 1788, the colony was moved to Sydney Cove.	In Sydney, the water supply and soil were better. Although Sydney was the new site, for many years it was called Botany Bay.

4. Frederick Carl Frieseke was an American impressionist.

Born in Michigan, he went to Paris in 1897.	He studied with Whistler in the late 1800s. From Whistler, he learned the academic style of the salons.
In 1905, Frieseke moved to Giverney where he lived until 1920.	At Giverney, Frieseke was influenced by Monet. Monet was experimenting with the effects of sunlight. The style of Monet and his school is known as impressionism.
By 1920, Frieseke had left Giverney for Normandy.	In Normandy, he began to paint indoor settings. In his later work, he began to use a darker palette.

5. Two types of weathering will break down rock masses into smaller particles.

Interaction between surface or ground water and chemicals causes chemical weathering.	With increased precipitation or temperature, chemicals tend to break down faster. The weathering of feldspar in granite can be caused by a reaction to acids in rain. A common example is the wearing away of granite facades on buildings.
Mechanical weathering occurs when force and pressure grind rocks down.	Pressure from freezing and thawing causes rocks to expand and contract. When a rock is broken in two by physical forces, it is more vulnerable to weathering.

PRACTICE ACTIVITY 6

1. There are two <u>types</u> of mixtures—heterogeneous and homogeneous. *Classification*
2. <u>As a result</u>, the litmus paper turns blue when the solution is a base. *Cause and Effect*
3. <u>In contrast</u>, a counterculture exhibits behavior that is contrary to the dominant culture. *Contrast*
4. The first <u>stage</u> of sleep produces alpha waves. *Sequence*
5. The main <u>properties</u> of soil include color, texture, and structure. *Description and Example*
6. Community service <u>should</u> be a requirement for graduation from the College of Education. *Persuasion and Evaluation*
7. <u>For example</u>, the Navajo create sacred images in colored sand in order to restore the spiritual and physical health of the sick. *Description and Example*
8. The maximum amount of water that air can hold at a given temperature and pressure <u>is known as</u> saturation. *Definition*
9. <u>Whereas</u> an objective is specific and measurable, a goal is broader and is usually not time specific. *Comparison and Contrast*
10. Dutch explorers in the early <u>seventeenth century</u> called the west coast of Australia "New Holland," a name that was used to describe the continent until the beginning of the <u>nineteenth century</u>. *Sequence*

PRACTICE ACTIVITY 7

 Activity 7, CD 2, Track 6. Listen to the beginning of a lecture in a linguistics class.

Good morning. Well, we have a lot to do today, so let's get going. If you're caught up with your . . . your reading assignments, you've already read the article on the three types of language, but before we go on with the discussion, I, uh, want to take a few minutes to compare them. Okay, standard language first. That's language that's comprehended, used, and considered, uh, acceptable by most speakers, I mean, native speakers. So definitions of words and phrases in standard language . . . they're found in the dictionary. They can be used in both formal and informal, uh, situations . . . settings. And this is important—standard language is appropriate in both speech and writing. I'd say that all of these characteristics combine to make standard language, well, let's just say that it's the permanent core of a language.

That brings us to colloquial language, which is . . . is . . . uh, included in dictionaries but, uh, colloquial language is marked, and usually it's a colloquial idiom. So these patterns of colloquial language are understood and used and accepted in informal exchanges and in, well people use them in informal situations, but they're not really considered appropiate in formal settings. Did I say that colloquial language is more prevalent in speech than in writing? That's important and the key point in the article was that colloquial language becomes so much a part of the culture that at some point, it often . . . uh . . . evolves . . . into standard language. So you can compare an earlier dictionary with a recent dictionary and that will . . . you can see how some phrases that are marked as colloquial language lose that designation in later editions of the same dictionary.

Okay, so you can see that colloquial idioms last a long time, either uh . . . um remaining popular in colloquial speech or, as I said, it can evolve into standard language and become a permanent part of the language. But that's very different from slang expressions because . . . and this is the key point . . . slang is usually a temporary phenomenon. It's used by some speakers or groups in informal situations and they're much more common in speech than they are in writing. Sometimes they're included in a dictionary but, uh, they're always clearly marked as slang, and when you check later editions of the dictionary, quite often, the . . . the slang expression is no longer included because it's out of style.

Now, let's consider the three types of language together and uh . . . I want you to think of them on a continuum from most to least formal. So, if we do that, colloquial language would have to go between standard and slang. So the slang is often relegated to a temporary fad, and standard language contains the stable elements of the language and colloquial language has the potential to become a permanent part of a language, but . . . it might not.

I think it's interesting that most native speakers will use all three types of language and they'll use them all appropriately without thinking about it. In fact, only a few speakers will be able to analyze their speech and writing using the labels that the author identified in the article.

That said, let's get out the article for today's discussion and . . .

Notes

Definition + comparison = three types of language

Standard usage *Permanent core	definitions of words + phrases found in dictionary *used formal + informal situations appropriate speech + writing
Colloquial language *Often evolves into standard	included in dictionary marked as colloquial idioms understood + used in informal situations, not formal more common in speech
Slang expressions *Temporary phenomenon	sometimes in dictionary marked as slang used by some speakers in informal situations more common in speech

PRACTICE ACTIVITY 8

 Activity 8, CD 2, Track 7. Listen to the beginning of a lecture in a sociology class as you read the transcript. The professor is discussing status and roles.

Status refers to, uh, a position in society or . . . or in a group. But there are really two types of status—ascribed status and achieved status. Okay, in ascribed status, the status is automatic so you don't have a choice. In other words, it's an involuntary status. And some examples that come to mind are status because of race or sex. Not much you can do about that. On the other hand, achieved status requires some effort, and there's a choice involved. For instance, a marriage partner, or the type of education, or, for that matter, uh, the length of time in school. Well, these are choices, uh, achievements, and so they fall under the category of achieved status. So, that brings us to the status set. A status set is the combination of all statuses that an individual has. Me, for example. I'm a professor, but I'm also a husband and a father, and, uh, uh, a son, since my mother is still living.

So, in each of these statuses, I, I have certain behaviors that are expected, uh, because of the status. Okay, all of the behaviors are roles, I mean, a role is the behavior expected because of status. Okay, back to status set. All of the statuses—husband, father, son, professor combine to form the status set, and each of the statuses have certain expectations. Let me use that professor status again. So, as a professor, I have a teaching role, and I have to prepare classes. That's expected. I also advise students, grade assignments, and evaluate my students. But this role has very different expectations. Uh, as a researcher, I, I have to design studies, raise funds for grants, and uh, then perform the research, and, and, finally, I write articles and reports. So, I think you see what I mean.

But, one more thing, and this is important, sometimes role conflict can occur. Let me say that again, role conflict. And that means that meeting the expectations for one role will cause problems for an individual who is trying to meet other expectations in a different role. Okay, let's say that one of my students is dating my daughter. I don't recommend this. But anyway, I may have role strain that could even develop into role conflict because it will be difficult for me to meet the expectations for my role as teacher and, uh, when the student comes to my house, I'll have to remember my status as father and my role that requires me to welcome a guest into my home, and well, form an opinion about someone who wants to take my daughter out on a date. The textbook actually . . .

Notes

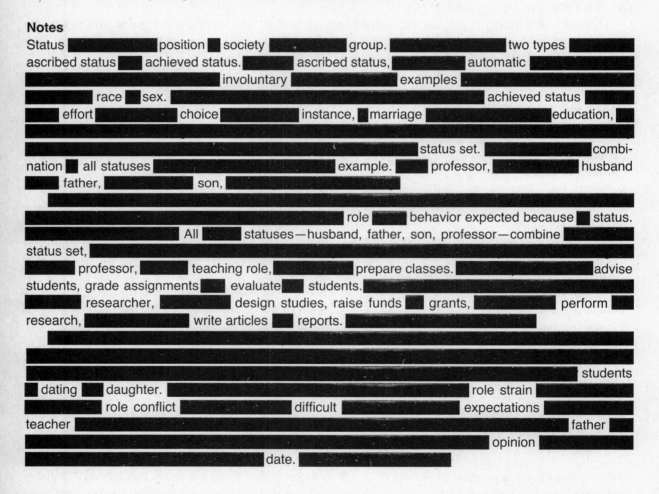

Status ▮▮▮▮▮▮ position ▮ society ▮▮▮▮▮ group. ▮▮▮▮▮▮▮▮▮ two types ▮▮▮▮▮ ascribed status ▮▮ achieved status. ▮▮▮▮▮ ascribed status, ▮▮▮▮▮▮ automatic ▮▮▮▮▮▮▮ ▮▮▮▮▮▮▮▮▮▮ involuntary ▮▮▮▮▮▮▮ examples ▮. ▮▮▮▮▮▮ race ▮ sex. ▮▮▮▮▮▮▮▮▮▮▮▮▮ achieved status ▮▮▮▮ ▮▮ effort ▮▮▮▮▮▮▮ choice ▮▮▮▮▮▮ instance, ▮ marriage ▮▮▮▮▮▮▮▮ education, ▮▮ ▮▮▮▮▮▮▮▮▮▮▮▮▮▮▮▮▮▮▮▮ ▮▮▮▮▮▮▮▮▮▮▮▮▮ status set. ▮▮▮▮▮▮▮▮ combination ▮ all statuses ▮▮▮▮▮▮▮▮▮▮▮▮ example. ▮▮▮ professor, ▮▮▮▮▮▮▮ husband ▮▮▮ father, ▮▮▮▮▮▮▮▮ son, ▮▮▮▮▮▮▮▮▮▮▮▮▮ ▮▮▮▮▮▮▮▮▮▮▮▮▮▮▮▮▮▮▮▮▮▮▮ role ▮▮▮ behavior expected because ▮ status. ▮▮▮▮▮▮▮▮▮▮▮ All ▮▮▮▮ statuses—husband, father, son, professor—combine ▮▮▮▮▮▮ status set, ▮▮▮▮▮▮▮▮▮▮▮▮▮▮▮▮▮▮▮ ▮▮▮▮▮ professor, ▮▮▮▮ teaching role, ▮▮▮▮▮▮▮ prepare classes. ▮▮▮▮▮▮▮▮▮▮▮ advise students, grade assignments ▮▮ evaluate ▮▮ students. ▮▮▮▮▮▮▮▮▮▮▮ ▮▮▮▮▮▮ researcher, ▮▮▮▮▮▮▮ design studies, raise funds ▮▮ grants, ▮▮▮▮▮▮▮ perform ▮▮ research, ▮▮▮▮▮▮▮▮▮ write articles ▮▮ reports. ▮▮▮▮▮▮▮▮▮ ▮▮▮▮▮▮▮▮▮▮▮▮▮▮▮▮▮▮▮▮▮▮▮▮▮ ▮▮▮▮▮▮▮▮▮▮▮▮▮▮▮▮▮▮▮▮▮▮▮ students ▮ dating ▮ daughter. ▮▮▮▮▮▮▮▮▮▮▮▮ role strain ▮▮▮▮▮▮ role conflict ▮▮▮▮▮▮ difficult ▮▮▮▮▮▮ expectations teacher ▮▮▮▮▮▮▮▮▮▮▮▮▮▮▮▮▮ father ▮▮ ▮▮▮▮▮▮▮▮▮▮▮▮▮▮▮▮ opinion ▮▮▮▮▮▮▮ ▮▮▮▮▮▮▮▮▮▮ date. ▮▮▮▮▮▮▮▮▮

PRACTICE ACTIVITY 9

 Activity 9, CD 2, Track 8. Listen to some sentences from college lectures. Take notes as quickly as you can.

1. The Nineteenth Amendment to the U.S. Constitution gave women the right to vote, beginning with the elections of 1920.
   19 → women vote/1920

2. In a suspension bridge, there are two towers with one or more flexible cables firmly attached at each end.
   suspension = 2 towers w/flex cables @ ends

3. A perennial is any plant that continues to grow for more than two years, as for example, trees and shrubs.
   perennial = plant 2+ yrs ex. trees, shrubs

4. Famous for innovations in punctuation, typography, and language, Edward Estlin Cummings, known to us as e.e. cummings, published his collected poems in 1954.
   ee. cummings → innovations punctuation, typo, language 1954 poems

5. Absolute zero, the temperature at which all substances have zero thermal energy, and thus the lowest possible temperatures, is unattainable in practice.
   absolute zero = temp. all substances 0 thermal energy → lowest temps

6. Because Columbus, Ohio, is considered a typical metropolitan area, it is often used for market research to test new products.
   Columbus, O = typical metro → market research new products

7. The cacao bean was cultivated by the Aztecs not only to drink but also as currency in their society.
   cocao bean ← Aztecs = currency

8. The blue whale is the largest known animal, reaching a length of more than one hundred feet, which is five times its size at birth.
   blue whale = largest animal 100′ = 5× birth size

9. Ontario is the heartland of Canada, both geographically, and, I would say, historically as well.
   Ontario = heartland Canada geograph + hist

10. Nuclear particles called hadrons, which include the proton and neutron, are made from quarks—very odd particles that have a slight electrical charge but that cannot exist alone in nature.
    nuclear particles = hadrons = proton + neutron ← quarks = particles slight electric charge Ø nature

PRACTICE ACTIVITY 10

 Activity 10, CD 2, Track 9. Listen to some sentences from college lectures. Take notes by drawing diagrams.

Notes

1. A *filament* is the stalk of a stamen.

   filament = stalk /stamen

2. There are three factors that determine whether a credit applicant is a good risk—character, capacity, and capital.

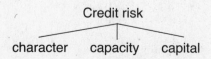

3. In photosynthesis, the chloroplasts in the leaf absorb energy from the Sun and then convert carbon dioxide from the atmosphere and water into carbohydrates.

$$\text{photosynthesis} = \text{chloroplasts} \leftarrow \text{energy/ Sun} \rightarrow CO_2 \rightarrow \text{carbohydrates}$$

4. It was in the Cenozoic Era that *Homo sapiens* first appeared, which was only about 1.8 million years ago, long after the Mesozoic Era, perhaps 200 million years ago, when the dinosaurs were roaming the Earth, and even earlier, approximately 540 million years ago, well, that was the Paleozoic Era when there was an explosive evolution of marine life.

   - Cenozoic 1.8 m/yrs   *Homo sapiens*
   - Mesozoic 200   dinosaurs
   - Paleozoic 540   marine life

5. In the sense that it is used among sociologists, the overwhelming feeling or need to escape a situation immediately is known as *panic*.

   Feeling/need to escape = panic

6. The difference between slate and phyllite is the coarseness of the grain and the color—slate being much more fine, often gray and easily split along the cleavage, whereas phyllite tends to be more coarsely grained, rather lustrous in appearance and feel, and, oh yes, it can be gray, green, or even red.

Slate	Phyllite
fine	coarse
split/cleavage	lustrous
gray	gray, green, red

7. Regulatory genes called homeotic genes cause the body parts of animals to develop appropriately.

   homeotic genes → body parts/animals develop

8. There were two types of decorations on Renaissance structures—the *cartouche*, which was an ornamental panel in the form of a scroll or some type of document, and the *graffito*, which was a white surface with a black undercoating, and uh, the . . . the design was made by scraping the white to reveal the black.

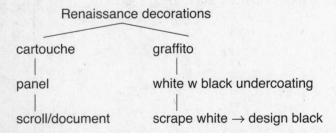

Renaissance decorations

cartouche   graffito
  | |
panel   white w black undercoating
  | |
scroll/document   scrape white → design black

9. Ptolemy, a Greek living in Alexandria in the second century A.D. . . . Ptolemy assumed that the Earth was at the center of the universe, a theory that was accepted until 1543 when Copernicus, a Polish cleric, proposed that the Sun was at the center and the planets, including the Earth, revolved around it.

Ptolemy/Greek in Alexandria	Copernicus/Polish cleric
2 Cent A.D.	1543
Earth center	Sun center

10. The brain consistently sends out electrical waves during sleep, and there are two basic types—slow waves, which are larger and more often occur at the beginning of the sleep cycle and . . . and may be more important for physical recuperation . . . as compared with REM or "rapid eye movement" waves that are faster and probably occur three to five times in an eight-hour period, usually later in the sleep cycle and we think that REM may be more effective in resting the brain than slow waves.

Slow waves	REM
larger	rapid eye movement
beginning sleep	later 3–5/8 hrs
physical recuperation	rests brain

PRACTICE ACTIVITY 11

1. The copperhead, a snake that <u>attacks</u> without warning, is <u>regarded</u> as much more <u>treacherous</u> than the rattlesnake.
2. Because J. P. Morgan was known as a <u>trustworthy</u> and <u>careful</u> businessman, he was able to <u>convince</u> others to <u>stay</u> in the market even after the crash had <u>started</u>.
3. Phosphorus is <u>employed</u> in paint on highway signs and markers because it is <u>luminous in the dark</u>.
4. Rain forests are <u>frequently</u> <u>situated</u> <u>close to</u> the equator.
5. By the mid-<u>1900s</u>, land was so <u>costly</u> in <u>big</u> cities that architects <u>started</u> <u>to save</u> space by <u>constructing</u> skyscrapers.
6. <u>Investigations</u> of vertebrates <u>demonstrate</u> <u>evolution</u> from a very <u>basic</u> heart in fish to a <u>complicated</u> four-chamber heart in humans.
7. When two products are <u>essentially</u> <u>identical</u>, advertising can <u>affect</u> the <u>decision</u> that the public makes.
8. <u>In general</u>, in birds, the male of the species is <u>more vividly</u> colored.
9. The <u>value</u> of gold on the world market <u>depends on</u> several <u>factors</u>, including but not <u>restricted to</u> supply and demand.
10. The <u>concept</u> of a submarine is not <u>new</u>, dating from the <u>fifteenth century</u> when Drebbel and da Vinci <u>made</u> <u>preliminary</u> <u>drawings</u>.

PRACTICE ACTIVITY 12

 Activity 12, CD 2, Track 10

1. Because light travels faster than sound, lightning appears to <u>go before</u> thunder.
2. Congress <u>looked up to</u> Jefferson because of his intelligence and creativity.
3. The lower teeth in crocodiles <u>stick out</u> when their mouths are closed.
4. Some sponges <u>look like</u> plants.
5. The first census was <u>carried out</u> in Great Britain in 1801.
6. People who have <u>gone through</u> a traumatic event may have recurring images of it.
7. In algebra, letters and other symbols <u>stand for</u> numbers

8. During periods of stress or excitement, the heart rate <u>goes up</u> and airways to the lungs become dilated.
9. Theories of prehistory and early humans are constantly changing as we <u>take into account</u> the new evidence from archeological finds.
10. Dreams may have been the inspiration for the Surrealists to <u>come up with</u> their works of art.

PRACTICE ACTIVITY 13

 Activity 13, CD 2, Track 11

ADJECTIVES
1. The temperature in many desert regions is <u>not hot</u> at night.
2. Facial expressions may <u>not</u> be <u>unique</u> across cultures.
3. Obsidian is <u>not dull</u> because it cools too quickly for crystals to form.
4. <u>Not many</u> musical instruments play louder than 100 decibels or softer than 20 decibels.
5. The people who have adapted to life at very high altitudes are usually <u>not tall</u>.

NOUNS
1. In many cities, <u>people who are trying to sell their goods</u> must have a license to set up their booths in public areas.
2. Studies show that small <u>animals that live indoors</u> are a positive influence in elderly people's lives.
3. Staircases were an important feature of the <u>palaces where the aristocracy lived</u> constructed during the Baroque period.
4. Global wind patterns are affected by the <u>way that the Earth turns</u>.
5. <u>Education that includes two languages</u> is more common in regions where language minorities live.

VERBS
1. Unlike cast iron, pure wrought iron <u>has</u> no carbon.
2. Hypnosis <u>causes</u> a heightened state of suggestibility in a willing participant.
3. Productivity increases when fewer employees are required to <u>do</u> the work.
4. Normally, the plasma in human blood <u>is</u> 50–60 percent of the total blood volume.
5. Three fourths of the goods <u>made</u> in Canada for export are sold to the United States.

PRACTICE ACTIVITY 14

CHRONOLOGY
1. The first primitive mammals appeared in the Triassic Period.
2. Before the late Middle Ages, glass was not a major construction material.
3. Hydrogen was used as a power source for dirigibles before helium, which was safer.
4. The Europeans arrived in 1791, long after the Moriori people settled the Chatham Islands off the coast of New Zealand.
5. Store your test tubes and pipettes in the lab cabinets after you rinse them with a small amount of distilled water.

COORDINATION
1. Not only genes but also viruses are made of essential chemicals called nucleoproteins.
2. Successful managers don't proceed without a plan, but they don't ignore opportunities that arise either.

3. Technically, both glass and water are considered minerals.
4. Corn and winter wheat are not native to the Americas.
5. Ethnicity is usually based on race, religion, and national origin.

CAUSE

1. According to psychologists, workers increase productivity because of incentives.
2. Anthropologists conclude that flakes were used as tools for cutting and scraping since many of them have been found in excavations of Stone Age settlements.
3. Plants can turn brown on the edges because of too much water.
4. Increasing the consumption of salt can cause higher blood pressure.
5. Most of the roads in the interstate highway system linking roads across the country need to be repaired because they were built in the 1930s.

COMPARISON

1. Viruses have a structure that is like that of the first life forms that appeared on Earth thousands of years ago.
2. The oxygen concentration in the blood is lower than that in the lungs.
3. The Atlantic Ocean is larger but it is not deeper than the Indian Ocean.
4. Picasso's works during various artistic periods differ quite a lot from each other.
5. The weight of one object cannot be the same as that of another because the gravitational attraction differs from place to place on the surface of the Earth.

CONCESSION

1. Even though insulin levels are close to or above normal in type 2 diabetes, target cells cannot respond adequately.
2. The idea of an English language academy is regularly proposed, but the response has never been very positive.
3. The Jovian planets are grouped together; however, each one has had a very different evolutionary history.
4. Even though young people enjoy an advantage for recall in vocabulary studies, older people appear to be better at word recognition.
5. Although interviews are the most common strategy for assessing job applicants, they tend to have low validity.

NEGATIVE

1. The geyser known as Old Faithful has never failed to erupt on time.
2. Only standard dialects are used as educational models in schools.
3. There has never been such wide access to news from so many media.
4. The construction of a city on the ruins of a previous settlement is common.
5. The first primitive mammals did not develop until the Triassic Period.

PASSIVE

1. It is interesting that fewer mental health disorders are experienced by people over the age of 65.
2. In the stringed instruments, the tones are produced by a bow when it is played across a set of strings made of wire or gut.
3. Gases in the ionosphere are partly ionized by high-frequency radiation from the Sun and other sources.
4. A domed roof can be used by architects to conserve floor space.
5. Papyrus was used by the Egyptians to make paper, sails, baskets, and clothing.

PRACTICE ACTIVITY 15

1. **D**   An animal learns how to get food by hitting a bar.
2. **A**   Poe is remembered more for a poem than for his short stories.
3. **C**   Everything in the universe was reduced to pure energy in one atom.
4. **C**   During the winter, the bear's temperature is normal and its respiration is regular, but it does not require food.
5. **B**   The board will assume control only if they lose confidence in the CEO.
6. **A**   Fluctuations in the air pressure are a result of changes in temperature.
7. **C**   Metabolism and exercise are ways to stabilize consumption and production of energy for a healthy weight.
8. **D**   The child's interest in playing with language is encouraged by the nursery rhyme.
9. **B**   It does not matter where employees work at their computers.
10. **A**   The Firbolgs arrived in Ireland from the Mediterranean after the Scottish people had already settled there.

PRACTICE ACTIVITY 16

1. Problem: The paraphrase is too much like the original. Only the subject and complement have been reversed in this alternative grammatical structure.

   Edited
   Paraphrase: Molecules that function as regulators in the transmission of substances across cell walls are known as proteins.

   Why is this better? Because synonyms have been substituted for all the nontechnical vocabulary and the subject and complement are reversed in an alternative grammatical structure.

2. Problem: The paraphrase is not complete. Information about the factory system and the cotton industry are not included.

   Edited
   Paraphrase: The factory system spread across a large number of enterprises in addition to cotton manufacturing as a result of the introduction of steam engines.

   Why is this better? Because the relationship between cause and effect has been retained using different vocabulary and grammar.

3. Problem: The paraphrase is not correct. The meaning has been changed.
   Edited
   Paraphrase: Small enterprises are frequently using bloggers to compete effectively with large businesses that are still employing more conventional marketing strategies as well as some of the more recent options.

   Why is this better? Because the meaning of the original sentence has been retained.

4. Problem: The paraphrase is too much like the original. Too many words and phrases are the same, and the grammatical structure is too similar.

   Edited
   Paraphrase: Although fossilized bones may look like stone, minerals from sedimentary material fill the spaces.

   Why is this better? Because synonyms have been substituted for all the nontechnical vocabulary, and the subject and complement are reversed in an alternative grammatical structure.

5. Problem: The paraphrase is incomplete. The dates are important here.
    Edited
    Paraphrase: About 3500 B.C., two thousand years after written symbols were introduced in 1500 B.C., the first pictographic writing system appeared simultaneously in various regions of the known world.

Why is this better? Because the chronology is not clear without a time frame. The date solves this problem.

6. Problem: This is not a paraphrase. It is copied directly from the original.
    Edited
    Paraphrase: In all likelihood, the Earth's current atmosphere was preceded by three earlier atmospheres.

Why is this better? Because copying directly from a source is the worst kind of plagiarism. Even when you are in a hurry, be sure that you are not copying.

7. Problem: This is not a paraphrase. It is too general.
    Edited
    Paraphrase: Alcohol depresses the central nervous system, but coffee increases neural transmission.

Why is this better? Because details are necessary for a paraphrase to be specific. A general statement does not include enough information.

8. Problem: This paraphrase changes the meaning of the original statement.
    Edited
    Paraphrase: Australia and the islands of Oceania comprise the Pacific Basin, an area that encompasses about 33 percent of the Earth's surface.

Why is this better? Because this paraphrase retains the original meaning. The area is one third of the surface of the Earth, not one third of the Pacific Ocean.

9. Problem: The paraphrase is incomplete. It does not identify the process as fresco painting.
    Edited
    Paraphrase: The lime in wet plaster bonds with the colors on the surface when the paints are mixed for frescos.

Why is this better? Because the process described in the paraphrase is identified as fresco painting.

10. Problem: The paraphrase is too much like the original. Too many words and phrases are repeated.
    Edited
    Paraphrase: The Linnaean chart used to classify all biological species was initially created to categorize each specimen in conformity with its resemblance to other organisms.

Why is this better? Because the edited paraphrase retains the meaning of the original, but the words and phrases are different, and the grammatical structure is changed.

Practice Activity 17

1. According to the professor, "A stock is equity in a company, and, therefore, it represents ownership."

2. According to the professor, "The desalination of the ocean is going to be a crucial aspect of water management."

3. According to the professor, "The theme of a world-wide flood is found in the mythology of many cultures."

4. According to the professor, "Psychology focuses on the individual, whereas sociology focuses on social groups."

5. According to the professor, "The ethics of science will become more important in this decade."

6. According to the professor, her idea is called "the simplification principle."

7. According to the professor, "The three-domain system is superior to the five-domain system of classification in biology."

8. According to the professor, "The term *relief* describes any printing method with a raised image."

9. According to the professor, "Training programs must address the issue of technology in the workplace."

10. According to the professor, "Quasars are difficult to study because they are so far away."

PRACTICE ACTIVITY 18

 Activity 18, CD 2, Track 12

1. Written: According to a study by Professor Carter, "patients can lower their blood pressure by losing weight and decreasing their intake of salt."

   Spoken: According to a study by Professor Carter, and I quote, "patients can lower their blood pressure by losing weight and decreasing their intake of salt." End quote.

2. Written: According to Professor Jones, "over fourteen billion Euros were introduced into the world economy in January, 2002."

   Spoken: According to Professor Jones, and I am quoting here, "over fourteen billion euros were introduced into the world economy in January, 2002." End quote.

3. Written: To quote a study in the *Journal of Psychology*, "many people who have achieved their career ambitions by midlife are afflicted by depression."

   Spoken: To quote a study in the *Journal of Psychology*, "many people who have achieved their career ambitions by midlife are afflicted by depression." End quote.

4. Written: According to the textbook, "an organ is a group of tissues capable of performing some special function."

   Spoken: According to the textbook, and I am quoting here, "an organ is a group of tissues capable of performing some special function." End quote.

5. Written: According to Professor Stephens, "John Philip Sousa was the greatest composer of marches for bands."

   Spoken: According to Professor Stephens, and I quote, "John Philip Sousa was the greatest composer of marches for bands." End Quote.

6. Written: In Professor Davison's opinion, "Ben Johnson may be the author of several plays attributed to William Shakespeare."

   Spoken: In Professor Davison's opinion, and I quote, "Ben Johnson may be the author of several plays attributed to William Shakespeare." End quote.

7. Written: Professor Davis said that, "statistical data can be very difficult to interpret because correlations are not causes."

   Spoken: Professor Davis said that, and I am quoting here, "statistical data can be very difficult to interpret because correlations are not causes." End quote.

8. Written: As Professor Gray puts it, "the prime minister serves at the pleasure of the parliament."

   Spoken: As Professor Gray puts it, and I quote, "the prime minister serves at the pleasure of the parliament." End quote.

9. Written: According to the reading passage, "moving water is the single most important factor in determining the surface features of the Earth."

   Spoken: According to the reading passage, and I quote, "moving water is the single most important factor in determining the surface features of the Earth." End quote.

10. Written: In Professor Russell's opinion, "the most important quality for a scientist is the ability to make careful observations."

   Spoken: In Professor Russell's opinion, and I am quoting here, "the most important quality for a scientist is the ability to make careful observations." End quote.

PRACTICE ACTIVITY 19

1. <u>Neutral report</u>: Sociologist Lee Clark <u>observed</u> that when danger <u>arose</u>, the rule <u>was</u> for people to help those next to them before they helped themselves.
2. <u>Doubtful report</u>: Biological Anthropologist Barry Bogin <u>claimed</u> that we <u>could</u> use the average height of any group of people as a barometer of the health of their society.
3. <u>Certain report</u>: Physician Stanley Joel Reiser <u>maintained</u> that machines <u>directed</u> the attention of both doctor and patient to the measurable aspect of illness, but away from the human factors that are at least equally important.
4. <u>Certain report</u>: Educator Harry Wong <u>concluded</u> that there <u>was</u> but one correlation with success, and that <u>was</u> attitude.
5. <u>Doubtful report</u>: Choreographer Martha Graham <u>suggested</u> that technique and training <u>had</u> never been a substitutes for that condition of awareness which was talent.
6. <u>Doubtful report</u>: Psychologist Carl Jung <u>believed</u> that the collective unconscious <u>seemed</u> to be something like an unceasing stream or perhaps an ocean of images and figures which drifted into consciousness in our dreams.
7. <u>Neutral report</u>: Computer entrepreneur Bill Gates <u>indicated</u> that the key for Microsoft™ <u>had</u> always been hiring very smart people.
8. <u>Doubtful report</u>: Geneticists James Watson and Francis Crick <u>proposed</u> that DNA structure <u>had</u> two helical chains each coiled around the same axis.
9. <u>Neutral report</u>: Environmentalist John Sinclair <u>pointed out</u> that many politicians <u>were</u> hostile to the environmental movement because they <u>saw</u> it in conflict with the economic model they <u>supported</u>.
10. <u>Certain report</u>: Astrophysicist Carl Sagan <u>argued</u> that even a relatively small nuclear war <u>might</u> be capable of producing a global climatic catastrophe.

PRACTICE ACTIVITY 20

 Activity 20, CD 2, Track 13

1. In his book, *The Making of the President,* <u>Theodore White</u> noted that the 1960 presidential debate was more like a press conference. According to <u>White</u>, Nixon proceeded as though he were engaged in a personal debate. In contrast, Kennedy spoke directly to the TV viewers. <u>He</u> estimated that Kennedy gained two million votes as a result.
2. <u>Paul Cezanne</u> believed that all forms in nature were based on geometric shapes. <u>Cezanne</u> identified the cone, sphere, and cylinder as the primary forms. <u>He</u> used outlining to emphasize these shapes.
3. Along with her husband, <u>Marie Curie</u> won the Nobel prize for physics in 1903 for the discovery of radium. <u>Curie</u> then received the Nobel prize for chemistry in 1911 for the isolation of pure radium. <u>She</u> was the first person to be awarded two Nobel prizes.
4. Psychologist <u>Erik Erikson</u> proposed eight stages of personal development. <u>Erikson</u> claimed that psychological crises at each stage shaped the sense of self. <u>He</u> believed that development was a lifelong process.

5. Margaret Mead did her first fieldwork in Samoa in 1925. Mead's book, *Coming of Age in Samoa*, was a best seller that was translated into many languages. She is still one of the most well-known anthropologists in the world. Mead believed that people in simple societies could provide valuable lessons for the industrialized world.

6. Leonardo da Vinci was the quintessential Renaissance man. A brilliant painter, da Vinci was perhaps best remembered for his art. But he was also interested in mechanics, and his understanding of mathematics is clear in his use of perspective.

7. Author Peter Drucker wrote *Management Challenges for the 21st Century*. In this book, Drucker proposed five transforming forces. He predicted that these trends will have major implications for the long-term strategies of companies.

8. Freidrich Mohs devised a scale of hardness for ten minerals. By assigning 10 to diamond, the hardest known mineral, Mohs was able to attribute relative values to all the other minerals. His scale is still useful in the study of minerals today.

9. Maria Montessori proposed an educational model that has become known as the Montessori method. Montessori insisted that education should not be merely the transmission of knowledge but the freedom to develop as a person. She felt her greatest success was achieved when a child began working independently.

10. In collaboration with Louis Leaky, Jane Goodall spent years living with chimpanzees on the Gombe Reserve. Goodall imitated their behaviors and discovered that chimpanzees lived within a complex social organization. She was the first to document chimpanzees making and using tools, and she also identified twenty different sounds that were part of a communication system.

PRACTICE ACTIVITY 21

1. Reading

Step 1: Examples Deleted

Although speech is the most advanced form of communication, there are many ways of communicating without using speech. Signals, signs, and symbols may be found in every known culture. The basic function of a signal is to impinge upon the environment in such a way that it attracts attention. Unlike signals, which are coded to refer to speech, signs contain meaning in and of themselves. Finally, gestures are actions, which are more difficult to describe because of their relationship with cultural perceptions.

Step 2: Paraphrased Summary

Found in every culture, signals, signs, and symbols are examples of alternatives to speech communication. A signal, which is referenced to speech, intrudes upon the environment so that it is noticed. In contrast, a sign does not refer to speech because it displays a general message. Last, gestures, which are culturally defined, consist of actions.

2. Lecture

 Activity 21, CD 2, Track 14. Listen to part of a lecture in a botany class.

The *Acacia* is a genus of trees and shrubs of the Mimosa family that originated in Australia and has long been used in building simple mud and stick structures there. The acacia is called a *wattle* in Australia, and the structures are made of wattle stuck together with daub, which is a kind of mud adobe. Now this is interesting—the acacia is related to the family of plants known as legumes, and I'm sure you remember that legumes include peas, beans, lentils, peanuts, and pods with beanlike seeds. Some acacias actually produce edible crops. But other acacia varieties are valued for the sticky resin, called gum Arabic or gum acacia, and that is used widely in medicines, foods, and perfumes. A few varieties are grown for the dark, dense wood, which is just excellent for making pianos, or for the bark that is very rich in tannin, a dark, acidic substance used to cure the hides of animals to make leather.

Let's see. Nearly five hundred species of *Acacia* have been identified and categorized and proven capable of survival in hot and generally arid parts of the world, but only a dozen of the three hundred Australian varieties seem to thrive in the southern United States. Most acacia imports are low, spreading trees, but of these, only three flower. The Bailey Acacia has fernlike silver leaves and small, fragrant flowers arranged in, uh, in sort of rounded clusters. The Silver Wattle is similar to the Bailey Acacia, but it grows about twice as high, and the Sydney Golden Wattle is bushy with broad, flat leaves, and it's the Golden Wattle with the showy bright yellow blossoms. Okay. The Black Acacia is also called the Blackwood. It has dark green foliage and the blossoms are rather ordinary, but besides being a popular ornamental tree, the Black Acacia is considered valuable for its dark wood, which is used in making furniture and musical instruments. I think I mentioned that acacias are used to make pianos. Well, a piano made of Black Acacia is highly prized in the musical world.

Now, some of you may have heard that the acacia's unique custom of blossoming in February in the United States has something to do with its Australian origins, but that just isn't so. It isn't the date. It's the quality of light that makes the difference for the flowering cycle of a tree. As you know, in the Southern Hemisphere, the seasons are reversed, and February, which is wintertime in the United States, is summertime in Australia. Actually, however, the pale, yellow blossoms appear in August in Australia. So, whether it grows in the Northern or the Southern Hemisphere, the acacia blossoms in winter.

Step 1: Examples Deleted

The *Acacia*, a genus of trees and shrubs of the Mimosa family that originated in Australia, is called a *wattle* in Australia. The acacia is related to the family of plants known as legumes. Some acacias actually produce edible crops. Other acacia varieties are valued for the sticky resin, dense wood, or bark. Nearly five hundred species of *Acacia* are capable of survival in hot and generally arid parts of the world. A dozen of the three hundred Australian varieties survive in the southern United States. Whether it grows in the Northern or Southern Hemisphere, the acacia blossoms in winter.

Step 2: Paraphrased Summary

The *Acacia*, called a *wattle* in its native Australia, is a member of the Mimosa family and a relative of the family of plants that includes legumes. Acacias are valuable for wood, resin, and even food crops. Of the five hundred species of *Acacia* that grow in hot, dry climates, three hundred are found in Australia, but only twelve flourish in the southern United States. One of its unusual characteristics is that it typically flowers in the winter, whether it is planted in the Northern or Southern Hemisphere.

PRACTICE ACTIVITY 22

1. Charlie Chaplin was a comedian who was best known for his work in silent movies.
2. Water becomes steam when it is heated to 212 degrees F.
3. Quasars, which are relatively small objects, emit an enormous amount of energy.
4. The Earth moves into the shadow of the Moon during a total eclipse. *or*
   During a total eclipse, the Earth moves into the shadow of the Moon.
5. Founded by John Smith, Jamestown became the first successful English colony in America.
6. Many of the names of cities in California are adapted from the Spanish language since early missionaries and settlers from Spain had extended their influence in the area. *or*
   Since early missionaries and settlers from Spain had extended their influence in the area, many of the names of cities in California are adapted from the Spanish language. *or*
   Many of the names of cities in California are adapted from the Spanish language because early missionaries and settlers from Spain had extended their influence in the area. *or*

Because early missionaries and settlers from Spain had extended their influence in the area, many of the names of cities in California are adapted from the Spanish language. *or*

Many of the names of cities in California are adapted from the Spanish language because of the influence in the area of early missionaries and settlers from Spain.

7. The oceans, which cover two thirds of the Earth's surface, are the object of study for oceanographers. *or*

The oceans, which are the object of study for oceanographers, cover two thirds of the Earth's surface.

8. A chameleon is a tree lizard that can change colors to conceal itself in vegetation.

9. Cultural nationalism arose among people with similar languages and traditions before political nationalism threatened the existing order. *or*

Before political nationalism threatened the existing order, cultural nationalism arose among people with similar languages and traditions. *or*

Political nationalism threatened the existing order after cultural nationalism arose among people with similar languages and traditions. *or*

After cultural nationalism arose among people with similar languages and tradition, political nationalism threatened the existing order.

10. Empowerment increases the autonomy of employees in organizations and improves communication between workers and management. *or*

Empowerment increases the autonomy of employees in organizations; moreover, it improves communication between workers and management.

11. Monogamy means being married to one spouse, whereas serial monogamy involves marriage to one spouse, divorce, and remarriage to another spouse. *or*

Whereas serial monogamy involves marriage to one spouse, divorce, and remarriage to another spouse, monogamy means being married to one spouse.

12. Humor is associated with fun, but it is also used as a coping strategy to relieve stress. *or*

Humor is associated with fun; however, it is also used as a coping strategy to relieve stress.

13. Although solar panels can convert sunlight into electricity, they are still not being exploited fully. *or*

Solar panels are still not being exploited fully, although they can convert sunlight into electricity.

Even though solar panels can convert sunlight into electricity, they are still not being exploited fully. *or*

Solar panels are still not being exploited fully, even though they can convert sunlight into electricity.

14. The root system of the alfalfa plant allows it to survive despite drought conditions. *or*

The root system of the alfalfa plant allows it to survive in spite of drought conditions.

15. Pain warns the victim before further damage is done; therefore, pain has a positive function. *or*

Pain warns the victim before further damage is done; thus, pain has a positive function.

PRACTICE ACTIVITY 23

1. Reading

Summary

Whereas one third of the population consists of the traditional nuclear family of two parents and their children, most Americans are either married couples with no children at home, single people, or single-parent households, many of whom have developed close friendships to replace extended family living at a distance.

2. Lecture

 Activity 23, CD 2, Track 15. Listen to part of a lecture in a chemistry class.

Although the purpose and techniques were often magical, alchemy was, in many ways, the predecessor of the modern science of chemistry. The fundamental premise of alchemy derived from the best philosophical dogma and scientific practice of the time, and the majority of educated persons between 1400 and 1600 believed that alchemy had great merit.

The earliest authentic works on European alchemy are those of the English monk Roger Bacon and the German philosopher St. Albertus Magnus. In their treatises, they maintained that gold was the perfect metal and that inferior metals such as lead and mercury were removed by various degrees of imperfection from gold. They further asserted that these base metals could be transmuted to gold by blending them with a substance more perfect than gold. This elusive substance was referred to as the "Philosopher's Stone." The process was called transmutation.

Most of the early alchemists were artisans who were accustomed to keeping trade secrets and often resorted to cryptic terminology to record the progress of their work. The term Sun was used for gold, Moon for silver, and the five known planets for the base metals. This convention of substituting symbolic language attracted some mystical philosophers who compared the search for the perfect metal with the struggle of humankind for the perfection of the soul. The philosophers began to use the artisan's terms in the mystical literature that they produced. Thus, by the fourteenth century, alchemy had developed two distinct groups of practitioners—the laboratory alchemist and the literary alchemist. Both groups of alchemists continued to work throughout the history of alchemy, but, of course, it was the literary alchemist who was more likely to produce a written record; therefore, much of what is known about the science of alchemy is derived from philosophers rather than from the alchemists who labored in laboratories.

Despite centuries of experimentation, laboratory alchemists failed to produce gold from other materials. However, they gained wide knowledge of chemical substances, discovered chemical properties, and invented many of the tools and techniques that are used by chemists today. Many laboratory chemists earnestly devoted themselves to the scientific discovery of new compounds and reactions and, therefore, must be considered the legitimate forefathers of modern chemistry. They continued to call themselves alchemists, but they were becoming true chemists.

Summary

Laboratory alchemists failed to refine base metals to produce gold, but they discovered chemical substances, properties, compounds, reactions, tools, and techniques that helped to establish the field of modern chemistry.

PRACTICE ACTIVITY 24

1. Reading

Choice A is a major point because the paragraph that follows includes details about each section.

Choice B is a detail that describes one of the types of mouth parts. It refers to the major point about how insects are classified.

Choice C is a detail that describes one of the adaptations of mouth parts. It refers to the major point about how insects are classified.

Choice D is a major point because several types of mouth parts are explained in reference to this point.

Choice E is true but it is not mentioned in the passage.

Choice F is a detail that defines the term *proboscis*. It refers to the major point about how insects are classified.

Choice G is a detail that refers to one of the body parts in the major point about the three-section body.

Choice H is a detail that explains the purpose of one of the adaptations of mouth parts. It refers to the major point about how insects are classified.

2. Lecture

 Activity 24, CD 2, Track 16. Listen to part of a lecture in an English class.

Few have influenced the development of American English to the extent that Noah Webster did. After a short career in law, he turned to teaching, but he discovered how inadequate the available schoolbooks were for the children of a new and independent nation.

In response to the need for truly American textbooks, Webster published *A Grammatical Institute of the English Language*, a three-volume work that consisted of a speller, a grammar, and a reader. The first volume, which was generally known as *The American Spelling Book*, was so popular that eventually it sold more than eighty million copies and provided him with a considerable income for the rest of his life. Can you imagine that?

Anyway, in 1807, Noah Webster began his greatest work, *An American Dictionary of the English Language.* In preparing the manuscript, he devoted ten years to the study of English and its relationship to other languages, and seven more years to the writing itself. Published in two volumes in 1828, *An American Dictionary of the English Language* has become the recognized authority for usage in the United States. Webster's purpose in writing it was to demonstrate that the American language was developing distinct meanings, pronunciations, and spellings from those of British English. He is responsible for advancing many of the simplified spelling forms that distinguish American English from British.

Webster was the first author to gain copyright protection in the United States by being awarded a copyright for *The American Spelling Book* and he continued to lobby over the next fifty years for the protection of intellectual properties, that is, for author's rights. By the time that Webster brought out the second edition of his dictionary, which included 70,000 entries instead of the original 38,000, the name Webster had become synonymous with American dictionaries. It was this second edition that served as the basis for the many revisions that have been produced by others, ironically, under the uncopyrighted Webster name.

Summary

The American Spelling Book, Webster's first successful textbook, afforded him an income while he was writing his dictionary. *An American Dictionary of the English Language* was written to demonstrate the unique usage of English in the United States. Although he had a copyright for *The American Spelling Book*, ironically, Webster did not have a copyright for the original dictionary and subsequent editions that bear his name.

Choice A is a detail that refers to Webster's life before he began to write.

Choice B is a major point because the spelling book allowed Webster to continue his writing career.

Choice C is a major point because several examples refer to the unique usage.

Choice D is a detail because the revisions refer to the major point about copyrights.

Choice E is probably true but it is not mentioned in the lecture.

Choice F is a major point because about one third of the lecture is on the topic of copyright protection.

Choice G is a detail that relates to Webster's early life.

PRACTICE ACTIVITY 25

1. Reading

Both oil paints and canvas were artistic improvements introduced in the fifteenth century. Canvas was superior to the wood panels that predated it because it could be stretched to accommodate the huge works that were then popular, and then rolled up to ship. When it arrived, it was light enough to be easily framed and hung and, unlike wood, it didn't crack. Oil paints were preferable because they dried slowly, allowing the artist to rework on top of a previously painted section. Furthermore, it was possible to mix the oils to either a thin or thick consistency from a glaze to a paste.

2. Lecture

 Activity 25, CD 2, Track 17. Listen to part of a lecture in an engineering class.

The question has often been posed: Why were the Wright brothers able to succeed in an effort at which so many others had failed? Well, many explanations have been mentioned, but, uh, three reasons are most often cited, and I tend to agree with them. First, the Wright brothers were a team. Both men worked congenially and cooperatively, read the same books, located and shared information, talked incessantly about the possibility of manned flight, and, uh, . . . and served as consistent sources of inspiration and, uh, and encouragement to each other. So, to put it quite simply, two geniuses are better than one genius.

Second, both the brothers were glider pilots. So, unlike some other engineers who experimented with the theories of flight, Orville and Wilbur Wright experienced the practical aspects of aerodynamics by building and flying gliders, and this may surprise you, they even flew in kites. Now, each craft they built was slightly superior to the last because they incorporated the knowledge that they had gained from previous failures to adjust the next design. They had realized fairly early on from their experiments that the most serious challenge in manned flight would be stabilizing and maneuvering the aircraft once it was airborne. So, um, while others concentrated their efforts on the problem of achieving lift for take-off, the Wright brothers were focusing on developing a three-axis control for guiding their aircraft. By the time that the brothers started to build an airplane, they were already among the world's best glider pilots and they knew about the problems of riding the air firsthand.

In addition, the Wright brothers had designed more effective wings for their airplane than anyone else had been able to engineer. Using a wind tunnel, they tested more than two hundred different wing designs, recording the effects of slight variations in shape on the pressure of air on the wings. The data from these experiments allowed the Wright brothers to construct a superior wing for their aircraft.

But, you know, in spite of these advantages, the Wright brothers still might not have succeeded if they hadn't been born at precisely the right time in history. Attempts to achieve manned flight in the early nineteenth century were doomed because the steam engines that powered the aircrafts were just too heavy in proportion to the power that they produced. But by the end of the nineteenth century, when the brothers were experimenting with engineering options, a relatively light internal combustion engine had already been invented, and they were able to bring the ratio of weight to power within acceptable limits for flight.

Summary

The Wright brothers were successful in achieving the first manned flight because they worked collaboratively; they were both glider pilots who recognized the importance of stabilization and control in an aircraft; they were able to design, test, and engineer the best wings for the plane; and they were able to take advantage of the relatively light internal combustion engine.

PRACTICE ACTIVITY 26

1. Reading

1. **B**   The first opera in Italy
2. **C**   The growth of opera throughout Europe
3. **A**   Three types of musical pieces in opera

2. Lecture

 Activity 26, CD 2, Track 18. Listen to part of a lecture in a biology class.

The protozoans, minute aquatic creatures, each of which consists of a single cell of protoplasm, constitute a classification of the most primitive forms of animal life. The very name protozoan indicates the scientific understanding of the animals. *Proto* means "first" or "primitive" and *zoa* refers to the animal.

They are fantastically diverse, but three major groups may be identified on the basis of their motility. The Mastigophora have one or more long tails that they use to propel themselves forward. The Ciliata, which use the same basic means for locomotion as the Mastigophora, have a larger number of short tails. The Sarcodina, which include amoebae, float or row themselves about on their crusted bodies.

In addition to their form of movement, several other features discriminate among the three groups of protozoans. For example, at least two nuclei per cell have been identified in the Ciliata, usually a large nucleus that regulates growth but decomposes during reproduction, and a smaller one that contains the genetic code necessary to generate the large nucleus.

So all of this seems very straightforward to this point, but now we are going to complicate the picture. Chlorophyll, which is the green substance in plants, is also found in the bodies of some protozoans, enabling them to make at least some of their own food from water and carbon dioxide. Sounds like photosynthesis, doesn't it? But protozoans are animals, right? And plants are the life forms that use photosynthesis. Okay. Well protozoans are not considered plants because, unlike pigmented plants to which some protozoans are otherwise almost identical, they do not live on simple organic compounds. Their cells demonstrate all of the major characteristics of the cells of higher animals, such as eating, breathing, and reproducing.

Now many species of protozoans collect into colonies, physically connected to one another and responding uniformly to outside stimuli. Current research into this phenomenon along with investigations carried out with advanced microscopes may necessitate a redefinition of what constitutes protozoans, even calling into question the basic premise that they have only one cell. Nevertheless, with the current data available, almost 40,000 species of protozoans have been identified. No doubt, as technology improves methods of observation, better models of classification of these simple single cells will be proposed.

1. **D**   A definition of protozoans—single cell
2. **A**   A method of classification for protozoans—the three types motility
3. **C**   Similarity to plants—make food from water + CO_2
4. **E**   Considered animals—eating, breathing, reproducing
5. **B**   Current research—questions, redefinitions

PRACTICE ACTIVITY 27

1. Reading

1. **A**
2. **B**
3. **B**
4. **A**
5. **C**
6. **B**
7. **B**
8. **C**

Summary

The author's main purpose in the passage is to describe the nature of sunspots. Sunspots are solar particles that are hurled into space by disturbances of wind on the Sun. Matter from the Sun that enters the Earth's atmosphere affects changes in the weather patterns on Earth. Most sunspots appear as a shadow encircled by bright and dark lines extending out like spokes in a wheel. Sunspots usually occur in a configuration of two spots. The color of sunspots could be affected by their temperature. Sunspots may be related to magnetic fields that follow longitudinal lines on the Sun. The sunspot theory is subject to debate, however.

2. Lecture

 Activity 27, CD 2, Track 19. Listen to part of a lecture in an anthropology class.

The development of the horse has been recorded from the beginning, through all of its evolutionary stages, to the modern form. It is, perhaps, one of the most complete and well-documented chapters of paleontological history. Fossil finds provide us not only with detailed information about the horse itself but also with valuable insights into the migration of herds and even evidence for the speculation about the climatic conditions that could have instigated their migratory behavior.

Now geologists believe that the first horses appeared on Earth about sixty million years ago as compared with only two million years ago for the appearance of human beings. There is evidence of early horses on both the American and European continents, but it has been documented that, almost twelve million years ago at the beginning of the Pliocene Age, a horse about midway through its evolutionary development crossed a land bridge where the Bering Strait is now located. It traveled from Alaska into the grasslands of Asia and all the way to Europe. So, this early horse was a hipparion, about the size of a modern-day pony with three toes and specialized cheek teeth for grazing. In Europe, the hipparion encountered another less advanced horse called the anchitheres, which had previously invaded Europe by the same route, probably during the Miocene Period. Less developed and smaller than the hipparion, the anchitheres was eventually completely replaced by it.

By the end of the Pleistocene Age, both the anchitheres and the hipparion had become extinct in North America where they originated, as fossil evidence clearly demonstrates. In Europe, they evolved into the larger and stronger animal that is very similar to the horse as we know it today. For many years, this horse was probably hunted for food by early tribes of human beings. Then the qualities of the horse that would have made it a good servant were recognized—mainly its strength and speed. It was time for the horse to be tamed, used as a draft animal at the dawning of agriculture, and then ridden as need for transportation increased. It was the descendant of this domesticated horse that was brought back across the ocean to the Americas by European colonists.

1. **D**
2. **A**
3. **B**
4. **A**
5. **C**
6. **B**
7. **A**
8. **C**

Summary

According to the lecturer, fossils document the evolution of the horse, providing information about the climate and migration patterns. Geologists claim that horses appeared on Earth millions of years before human beings. A horse known as the anchitheres had migrated to Europe in the Miocene from North America. Following the same route, the hipparion migrated to Europe later in the Pliocene. When the hipparion invaded Europe, the anchitheres did not survive. In contrast, the hipparion developed into a sturdy animal, like modern breeds of horses. Ironically, horses were already extinct in North America by the Pleistocene, and Europeans returned the horse to the American colonies on ships.

PRACTICE ACTIVITY 28

1. Reading

50%   The function and responsibilities of the Fed
40%   The composition of the Fed
10%   A comparison of the Fed to a fourth branch of government

Although the summary below is actually closer to 50%, 30%, 20%, it still maintains a reasonably accurate emphasis.

Summary

The function of the Federal Reserve System is to regulate money and credit by buying and selling government securities, thereby influencing periods of recession and inflation. Moreover, the Fed cooperates with the Department of the Treasury to issue new coins and paper notes to banks and participates in international financial policies through member banks overseas.

The Fed includes twelve district reserve banks and branches, all national commercial banks and credit unions, as well as several committees and councils, including the powerful board of governors appointed by the President.

Because of its powerful membership, the Fed has been compared to a fourth branch of government, but the President's policies are usually implemented.

2. Lecture

 Activity 28, CD 2, Track 20. Listen to part of a lecture in a psychology class.

Okay then, let's talk about human memory, which was formerly believed to be rather inefficient as compared with, for example, computers. But we are finding that we probably have a much more sophisticated mechanism than we had originally assumed. Researchers approaching the problem from a variety of points of view have all concluded that there is a great deal more stored in our minds than has been generally supposed. Here's what I mean—Dr. Wilder Penfield, a Canadian neurosurgeon, proved that by stimulating their brains electrically, he could elicit the total recall of complex events in his subjects' lives. Even dreams and other minor events supposedly forgotten for many years suddenly emerged in detail.

The *memory trace* is the term for whatever forms the internal representation of the specific information about an event stored in the memory. So, the trace is probably made by structural changes in the brain, but the problem is that the memory trace isn't really subject to direct observation because it's . . . it's . . . more a theoretical construct that we use to speculate about how information presented at a particular time can cause performance at a later time. So most theories include the strength of the memory trace as a variable in the degree of learning, retention, and retrieval possible for a memory. One theory is that the fantastic capacity for storage in the brain is the result of an almost unlimited combination of interconnections between brain cells, stimulated by patterns of activity. And repeated references to the same information supports recall. Or, to say that another way, improved performance is the result of strengthening the chemical bonds in the memory.

Now here's the interesting part. Psychologists generally divide memory into at least two types—short-term memory and long-term memory, which combine to form what we call *working memory*. Short-term memory contains what we are actively focusing on at any particular time but items are not retained longer than twenty or thirty seconds without verbal rehearsal. We use short-term memory when we look up a telephone number and repeat it to ourselves until we can place the call. In contrast, long-term memory can store facts, concepts, and experiences after we stop thinking about them. All conscious processing of information, as in problem solving, for example, involves both short-term and long-term memory. As we repeat, rehearse, and recycle information, the memory trace is strengthened, allowing that information to move from short-term memory to long-term memory.

25%	The level of sophistication for human memory
40%	The memory trace
35%	Working memory

Although the summary below is actually closer to 25%, 35%, 40%, it still maintains a reasonably accurate emphasis.

Summary

Human memory is more highly developed than previously thought. Penfield's experiments prove that detailed memories can be recalled when the brain is stimulated electrically. Using the memory trace, a theoretical model, we can conjecture how facts are retrieved and used at a later time. Current thinking assumes that chemical bonds can be improved by repeated exposure to the same information. The concept of working memory includes both short-term memory, which includes recall for twenty or thirty seconds, and long-term memory, which stores facts and experiences more permanently. Information is transferred from short-term to long-term memory when the memory trace is reinforced.

PRACTICE ACTIVITY 29

1. Reading

Summary

Charles Ives started his musical career as a member of his father's band and received a degree from Yale University in music, but he became a businessman instead because he was afraid that his music would not be well accepted. His music was very different from the popular songs of his era because he used small phrases from well-known music with unusual rhythms and tones. Fifty years after he wrote his *Second Symphony*, it was performed by the New York Philharmonic, and he was awarded the Pulitzer Prize. I think that Charles Ives was wrong not to pursue his musical career from the beginning. If he had continued writing music instead of selling insurance, we would have more pieces now.

2. Lecture

 Activity 29, CD 3, Track 1. Listen to part of a lecture in a geology class.

A geyser is the result of underground water under the combined conditions of high temperatures and increased pressure beneath the surface of the Earth. Now, temperature rises about maybe 1 degree Fahrenheit for every 60 feet under the Earth's surface, and we know that pressure also increases with depth, water that seeps down in cracks and fissures, so when the water, uh, when the water reaches very hot rocks in the Earth's interior, it becomes heated to the temperature of, let's say, 290 degrees.

Okay, then, water under pressure can remain liquid at temperatures above the normal boiling point, but in a geyser, the weight of the water nearer the surface exerts so much pressure on the deeper water that the water at the bottom of the geyser reaches much higher temperatures than the water at the top. And as the deep water becomes hotter, and consequently lighter, it suddenly rises to the surface and shoots out of the ground in the form of steam and hot water. In turn, the explosion agitates all of the water in the geyser reservoir, and what do you think happens then? More explosions. So immediately afterward, the water goes back into the underground reservoir, it starts to heat up again, and the whole process repeats itself.

So, in order to function, then, a geyser must have a source of heat, a reservoir where water can be stored until the temperature rises to an unstable point, an opening through which the hot water and steam can escape, and underground channels for resupplying water after an eruption.

Now, favorable conditions for geysers exist in regions of geologically recent volcanic activity, especially in areas of more than average precipitation. For the most part, geysers are located in three regions of the world—New Zealand, Iceland, and the Yellowstone park area of the United States. I'd say that the most famous geyser in the world is Old Faithful in Yellowstone. It erupts every hour, rising to a height of 125 to 170 feet and expelling more than ten thousand gallons of hot water during each eruption. Old Faithful earned its name, because, un- unlike most geysers, it has never failed to erupt on schedule even once in eighty years of observation.

Summary

In my opinion, geysers are interesting. They happen when underground water gets hot and pressure from above causes the water to get hotter and lighter so it goes up to the surface and explodes out. Then, the water runs back into the ground and starts all over again. Geysers have to have heat, a place to store water, an opening where the water can shoot up, and cracks in the ground for the water to go back down into a pool. Geysers are in New Zealand, Iceland, and the United States. Old Faithful in Yellowstone is the most famous geyser, but the best place to see geysers is in New Zealand. I saw the Pohutu Geyser there on my vacation two years ago, and it was awesome.

Practice Activity 30

Summary 1

This is a good summary. The content is accurate, and all the major points are included. The problem here is that the writer did not follow the order in the original so the points are not in the same sequence and they are difficult to follow.

Summary 2

This is a good summary because it is brief, uses the same organization as the original, includes the major points, reports the content accurately, paraphrases using the summarizer's own words, and maintains an objective point of view that does not include the opinions of the person summarizing the original.

Summary 3

This is not really a summary of the original passage. Instead of a factual report, this paragraph includes opinions and judgments that the original author did not express.

Summary 4

This summary is not paraphrased. Sentences are copied from the original. The summary would not be scored, and no credit would be assigned. This is the most serious problem in summarizing.

Summary 5

The problem in this summary is the emphasis. Too much attention is given to information in the first paragraph of the original reading, whereas points from the second paragraph are not included. Facts from the third and fourth paragraphs are only briefly mentioned.

Practice Activity 31

1. Summarize the points in the <u>lecture</u>, explaining how they support the data in the reading.
2. Explain the model described in the <u>reading</u>, and then show how the lecture contradicts it.
3. Explaining how they provide evidence for the information in the reading, summarize the points made in the <u>lecture</u> you have just heard.
4. Summarize the hypothesis outlined in the <u>reading</u>, explaining how the lecture supports it.
5. Summarize the major points in the <u>reading</u>, explaining how the lecture contradicts them.
6. Explain how the lecturer's view substantiates the opinions expressed in the <u>reading</u>.
7. Summarize the points made in the <u>lecture</u> you have just heard, explaining how they differ from the points made in the reading.
8. Summarize the points from the <u>lecture</u>, explaining how they cast doubt on the reading.

9. Referring to the main points in the <u>lecture</u>, summarize the professor's opinion, contrasting it with the views expressed in the reading.
10. Summarize the concept in the <u>reading</u>, referring to the examples provided in the lecture you have just heard.

PRACTICE ACTIVITY 32

1. Summarize the points that the lecturer makes, explaining how they <u>support</u> the information in the reading.
   Agreement
2. Explain the theory proposed in the reading, and then <u>contrast</u> the ideas in the theory with the views expressed in the lecture.
   Disagreement
3. Summarize the points made in the lecture you have just heard, explaining how they <u>support</u> the information in the reading.
   Agreement
4. Referring to the main points in the lecture, summarize the professor's views, <u>contrasting</u> them with the opinion expressed in the reading.
   Disagreement
5. Summarize the hypothesis outlined in the lecture, explaining how the reading <u>casts doubt</u> on its validity.
   Disagreement
6. Summarize the points in the lecture you have just heard, referring to the <u>examples provided</u> in the reading.
   Agreement
7. Summarize the major points in the reading, explaining how the lecture <u>contradicts</u> them.
   Disagreement
8. Explain how the lecturer's ideas <u>differ from</u> those in the reading.
   Disagreement
9. Summarize the points made in the lecture you have just heard, explaining how they <u>reinforce</u> the points made in the reading.
   Agreement
10. Summarize the points from the lecture, explaining how they <u>cast doubt</u> on the reading.
    Disagreement

PRACTICE ACTIVITY 33

1. Primary source: The advantages of cooperative learning in schools
   Advantages
   Secondary source: The disadvantages of cooperative learning in schools
   Disadvantages

2. Primary source: An explanation of theoretical linguistics
   Explanation
   Secondary source: An explanation of applied linguistics
   Contrast

3. Primary source: The eradication of diseases on a world-wide basis
   Issue/Situation/Problem
   Secondary source: The World Health Organization's campaign against smallpox
   Solution/Example

4. Primary source: The problem of noise pollution in a technological society
   Problem
   Secondary source: European noise ordinances that limit noise pollution
   Solution/Example

5. Primary source: Advertising products abroad
   Concept
   Secondary source: The marketing plan for Toyota in the United States
   Case Study

6. Primary source: The theory of flow
   Theory
   Secondary source: A Harvard University study on flow
   Research Study

7. Primary source: The impact of a large meteor on Earth
   Cause
   Secondary source: The disappearance of dinosaurs after the meteor
   Result

8. Primary source: Nuclear power plants are dangerous
   Opinion
   Secondary source: Nuclear power is a good source of energy
   Contrasting opinion

9. Primary source: Qualitative research designs in the social sciences
   Theory/Concept
   Secondary source: The Hawthorne effect as a limiting factor in qualitative research
   Research Study/
   Example/Disadvantage

10. Primary source: The size, price, and power of early computers
   Issue/Situation
   Secondary source: The size, price, and power of modern computers
   Comparison/Contrast

PRACTICE ACTIVITY 34

 Activity 34, CD 3, Track 2. Listen to part of a lecture in a biology class.

People call it a bear, but the koala is really a marsupial. So, it is much more like a kangaroo than it is like a bear. Here's what I mean. First, the koala has a gestation period of only about 35 days before it is born. Then a tiny pink, furless creature about 19 millimeters long makes its way from the birth canal into the mother's pouch where it attaches itself to one of two nipples. So it stays in the pouch to complete it's development, and six to seven months later, it pokes its head out and explores a short distance from the mother, jumping back into the pouch until it reaches eight months when it is too big to fit, and for another four months it rides on the mother's back or hangs from her stomach until it finally becomes independent at about one year old. By then, it is about the same size as a Teddy Bear and looks remarkably like one, with a furry coat, rounded ears and a large nose to support its keen senses of smell and hearing. Native to Australia, the koala lives in trees and is a skillful climber. It sleeps in the branches during the day, and at night, it combs the trees for its favorite meal—eucalyptus leaves.

1. What is the primary source? The reading about marsupials.
2. What is the secondary source? The lecture about koalas.
3. What is the task? A synthesis for extension or for contrast? Extension.
4. What is the specific relationship between the primary and secondary sources? A definition and an example.

PRACTICE ACTIVITY 35

Summary

Marsupials are mammals that are distinguished by the way that they complete their embryonic development. Marsupials emerge after a short gestation and find their way from the birth canal to the mother's pouch, where they attach themselves to one of the nipples to nurse until they are fully developed. Marsupials are not prone to family groupings, but the young stay with the mother for a year or longer.

Although marsupials were once abundant on several continents, today there are few outside of New Zealand and Australia where more than 250 species may still be found. Some of the characteristics that they share are a keen sense of smell and hearing, which are important to their nocturnal nature, and additional pelvic bones that support the pouch.

PRACTICE ACTIVITY 36

1. Transition sentence to connect one concept with another concept in a comparison. <u>In comparison,</u> a biome is a major regional ecosystem. According to the lecturer, . . .
2. Transition sentence to connect a concept with an example. <u>An example</u> of an innovation in industrial production in the 19th century <u>is</u> Henry Ford's assembly line. According to the lecturer, . . .
3. Transition sentence to connect the advantages with the disadvantages. <u>On the other hand</u>, stone has several disadvantages. According to the reading, . . .
4. Transition sentence to connect one concept with another in a contrast. <u>In contrast</u>, agrarian societies cultivate crops with draft animals and plows. According to the lecturer, . . .
5. Transition sentence to connect a cause (El Nino) with an effect (changes in climate). El Nino <u>may have caused</u> the changes in the climate of the North American coastline. According to the lecturer, . . .
6. Transition sentence to connect a business concept with a case study of a restaurant franchise. The Kentucky Fried Chicken chain <u>is a case study of</u> franchises. According to the lecturer, . . .
7. Transition sentence to connect a concept with a research study. <u>A research study on</u> risks for heart problems <u>was carried out with</u> Type A and Type B personalities. According to the study, . . .
8. Transition sentence to connect one opinion with an opposing opinion. The case that the United States should convert to metrics is strong. <u>However, a case may be made for the opposing view that</u> the United States should retain the English system. According to the reading, . . .
9. Transition sentence to connect a concept with an example. <u>An example of</u> South Africa's natural resources <u>is</u> gold. According to the lecturer, gold mining . . .
10. Transition sentence to connect a problem (commuting) with a solution (home offices). Home offices <u>may offer a solution for</u> the problems associated with commuting to work. According to the lecture, . . .

PRACTICE ACTIVITY 37

Activity 37, CD 3, Track 3. Now that you have read the explanation of human migration patterns in the reading, listen to part of a lecture on a similar topic.

Okay, today I want to talk to you about a hypothesis that explains where humans might have evolved and how they might have migrated around the world. It's an alternative hypothesis to the *replacement hypothesis* that you read about earlier. It's called the *multiregional hypothesis* but I've also heard it referred to as the *continuity hypothesis*. Now, according to the scientists who support this view, modern humans spread throughout Eurasia about a million years ago and regional populations retained some unique anatomical features for hundreds of thousands of years, but they also exchanged some inherited traits with neighboring populations when they mated with them. And we call this exchange of traits *gene flow*.

So through this gene flow, certain characteristics that we consider crucial to modern mankind were inherited, as, for example, an increase in brain size with an accompanying change in the skull. And . . . and this gene flow resulted in the evolution of the early humans whose remains are found throughout Europe and Asia as well as Africa.

Now, scientists who support this theory contend that the populations that migrated were linked by gene flow so that the features that all people have in common spread throughout the world. The relatively slight differences among modern people would have been caused by hundreds of thousands of years of regional evolution. But actually, researchers who support the *continuity hypothesis* tend to focus on the genetic similarities among human populations world-wide, not the differences. We're really amazingly similar as a species. And the fossils of archaic and modern humans in some regions do suggest a continuous evolution in regional traits, like the cheekbone structure, for example, which is further evidence that modern humans may have evolved over a broad area among multiple groups of human ancestors.

Synthesis

Summarize the major points in the reading and explain how the lecturer casts doubt on those points.

According to the replacement hypothesis, also called the Out of Africa hypothesis, modern humans evolved from a common ancestor in Africa. As they migrated to Asia and Europe, and finally spread throughout the world, they replaced the less evolved populations that they encountered. Proof for this hypothesis comes from both genetic and paleontological research. The large number of genetic traits that human populations have in common are confirmed by DNA investigations in mitochondria structures. In addition, the oldest fossils identified as modern human remains have been discovered in Africa.

Nevertheless, the lecturer casts doubt on the replacement theory, offering the continuity hypothesis as an alternative. Also known as the multiregional hypothesis, the continuity hypothesis proposes that advanced human populations migrated and mated with less advanced regional populations, introducing new traits into these populations. Because the regional populations were not replaced, they retained some of their unique characteristics. The exchange of traits, referred to as gene flow, accounts for the genetic similarity of modern human beings. The retention of regional genetic material explains why some traits, such as cheekbone structure, are limited to discrete populations, and casts doubt on the replacement hypothesis. The fact that modern human remains are found in widespread sites also supports the alternative hypothesis that the lecturer presents.

PRACTICE ACTIVITY 38

🎧   **Activity 38, CD 3, Track 4.** Now that you have read the explanation of population in the reading, listen to part of a lecture on a similar topic.

Well, it is certainly true that Malthus has had an enormous impact on the study of population, and in fact, many of his predictions about limitations on population appeared to be true for a time, but right now the major debate in economic population theory is between a group who believes that population growth has reached a critical mass and can no longer be controlled through the events and forces that Malthus predicted and, on the other side of the debate, a group that views birth control as part of a larger demographic transition. Here's what I mean. Demographic transition is a model in which large populations move from Stage 1, with very high birth and death rates like Malthus predicted, to Stage 2 in which the birth rates remain high but the death rates begin to decline, mostly because of progress in food production, sanitation methods, and medical treatment, all of these modern advances that could not have been predicted when Malthus was developing his theory. So, the population grows very rapidly in Stage 2. Okay, in Stage 3, population continues to increase because, although the birth rate decreases, the death rate also decreases, so fewer people are born, but they tend to live longer. Now Stage 4 is the point at which the population increases very slowly, or it may even start to decline because both the birth rate and death rates are even lower than in the previous stage. So we see this in Japan, Europe, and North America. In fact, in Europe, we see something that appears to be a Stage 5. In Europe, the decline in the birth rate has dropped to a level of 1.7, which is below the 2.0 replacement level for a couple. So, unless immigration rates increase, Europe's population may be an indication of future demographics for other industrialized regions.

Synthesis

Summarize the major points in the lecture that you have just heard, explaining how they cast doubt on the ideas in the reading passage.

According to the lecturer, one modern view asserts that world population has reached a "critical mass," and the limiting forces Malthus had proposed to control population, such as war, starvation, disease, and disasters, can no longer stem the growth. In contrast, another group of economists argues that population control is part of a five-stage demographic transition model. From Stage 1, in which large birth rates and death rates interact somewhat like Malthus predicted, populations move into Stage 2, characterized by very rapid growth as a result of improvements in sanitation, agriculture, and medicine. By Stage 3, both the birth and death rates decrease, a trend that continues in Stage 4 as the population growth slows or even declines. At Stage 5, birth rates fall below replacement levels, and even with declining death rates, the population begins to decrease. The lecturer notes that the industrialized areas of Japan and North America are in Stage 4, whereas Europe appears to be moving from Stage 4 to Stage 5.

Since Malthus pointed out that populations at the highest level of the economy exercise controls as a result of education and a desire to preserve their standard of living, he did, in a way, predict the trends for the industrialized world; however, he certainly did not foresee advances in agriculture, public health, and medicine that would influence population. According to the lecturer, his predictions are not valid for the critical mass model and are accurate only for the beginning stages of the demographic transition model.

PRACTICE ACTIVITY 39

🎧 **Activity 39, CD 3, Track 5.** Now that you have read the explanation of crop circles in the reading, listen to part of a lecture on a similar topic.

Okay, let's look at the scientific data on crop circles. Serious scientists have catalogued photographs of crop circles that are strikingly similar to computer fractals, that is, geometric patterns that are smaller than traditional geometry, and even mirror processes in quantum physics. And Professor Gerald Hawkins has used principles of Euclidean geometry to prove four theorems that can be derived from the relationships of elements in crop circles, as well as an additional fifth theorem from which he derived the other four. In spite of a challenge to the scientific community, no one has been able to create that mysterious fifth theorem, although Euclid alluded to it. So it was a shock when its equilateral version appeared in a barley field in Britain.

Another interesting scientific theory also originates in ancient writing. The Egyptians referred to geometry as frozen music, and, in fact, modern investigations of sound vibration confirm that sound frequencies can create circles at low frequencies and more complex forms at higher frequencies. And direct observation of the crop circles also provides some interesting data along those lines. In most of the cases, the stems of the grain are not broken but bent. The biophysical evidence seems to indicate that the plant's nodes have become hugely extended, the seed embryos have been distorted, and the crystalline structure appears to have been reorganized. Nevertheless, the plants do not appear to be damaged, and will continue to mature and ripen. Further laboratory investigations suggest that the plants may have been subjected to a very high intensity heat in a short burst similar to the results of infrasound, which is measured at below twenty hertz. In experiments with infrasound, water in plant stems has come to a boil in less than one nanosecond. This would be consistent with the reports by witnesses that the process takes place within seconds and that there appears to be steam within the newly created crop circles. In addition, soil samples from inside the circles themselves display characteristic crystalline structures that would suggest their having been subjected to temperatures of almost 1500 degrees C.

Synthesis

Summarize the major points in the lecture that you have just heard, explaining how they cast doubt on the ideas in the reading passage.

The lecturer provides scientific evidence from quantum physics and computer-generated patterns to support the legitimacy of crop circles. In one experiment, Hawkins uses crop circles to prove four geometrical theorems and derive a fifth that has eluded mathematicians since Euclid first hinted at its existence. Furthermore, research on sound vibrations demonstrates that certain frequencies can create geometrical shapes, just as the ancient Egyptians suggested when they called geometry "frozen music." Finally, biophysical studies establish that the crystalline structures in crops are reorganized when crop circles appear, although there is insufficient injury to prevent later growth. Extreme temperatures produced by short surges of infrasound appear to produce similar results.

The research presented in the lecture calls into question the information in the reading. Pointing out that hoaxers have been responsible for some complex crop circles around the world, the writer relies heavily on the demonstration sponsored by the Discovery Channel in New Zealand to make the case against the authenticity of crop circles. Despite the fact that a team was able to create 100 crop circles in about four hours, the writer concedes that the secluded location and the lighting were problematic to critics.

In short, the anecdotal information in the reading seems inferior to the data provided in the lecture which casts serious doubt on the veracity of the reading.

PRACTICE ACTIVITY 40

Activity 40, CD 3, Track 6. Now that you have read the explanation of strategic business alliances in the reading, listen to part of a lecture on a similar topic.

Okay, now I want you to think about two companies that have historically been in competition for the package delivery service in the United States. Well, the first to come to mind has to be the U.S. Postal Service, right? But now think *fast* delivery. For that, Federal Express is at the top of the list. But, instead of viewing their relationship as totally competitive, these two companies struck an unprecedented strategic alliance several years ago. The U.S. Postal Service agreed to let Federal Express place package collection boxes at thousands of post offices throughout the United States, which was great for Fed Ex because they achieved an immediate national presence. But in exchange, Fed Ex allowed the Postal Service to buy unused space on the Federal Express airplanes in order to carry first-class, priority, and, most importantly, express mail envelopes and packages, increasing the speed with which they could deliver the mail without purchasing aircraft. Moreover, by sharing web sites to track their deliveries, both companies have been able to create a larger Internet presence.

So why would these companies be willing to help each other? Probably the most commonly espoused explanation is that they both are battling fax, e-mail, and other emerging messaging technologies and their combined resources may result in survival and success for both of them against a common threat. And that fits in nicely with the whole concept of strategic alliances. But, besides that, many countries—New Zealand, Sweden, Germany, and the Netherlands, to name only a few—these countries have ended the special government status that postal services have traditionally enjoyed, with all the benefits, including tax advantages and subsidies. So, it may be that the U.S. Postal Service is trying to find alternatives to show progress before privatization ends its chance of survival. And Federal Express might be positioning itself to be the really big winner if the Postal Service goes up on the auction block at some time in the future. In other words, the real purpose of strategic alliances may be to serve competing interests in the long term.

Synthesis

Summarize the major points in the reading, explaining how the lecture supports these ideas.

According to the reading, a global economy may necessitate strategic alliances. Unlike a merger or a joint venture that creates a separate business, a strategic alliance permits companies to retain their individual identities while they collaborate in achieving their goals. In general, the agreement allows companies to share resources, as in the case of a business that exchanges technical experience for financial support or a business that allows another company to use its brand advantage in exchange for a product with a large market. An international agreement benefits businesses with products to sell overseas when they ally with foreign advertising companies. The primary advantage of strategic alliances is that they are not difficult either to organize or to terminate, a benefit when business conditions are shifting.

An example of a strategic alliance is the agreement between the U.S. Postal Service and Federal Express in which the Postal Service allowed Fed Ex to place its depositories in a large number of post offices in exchange for the opportunity to buy space on Fed Ex airplanes. Both companies retained their identities and the alliance created mutual benefit. On the one hand, the Postal Service obtained transportation for their first class, priority, and express mail without purchasing aircraft, and on the other hand, Fed Ex secured a national presence for their brand. Moreover, by sharing web sites, both companies increased their Internet exposure. In spite of speculation about long-term self-interest, the Fed Ex-USPS case study is an excellent example of a strategic alliance.

ANSWERS AND AUDIO SCRIPTS FOR QUIZZES IN CHAPTER 5

READING

➤ Progress Chart for the Reading Quiz

The chart below will help you evaluate your progress and determine what you need to read again. First, use the Correct Answer column to grade the quiz. Next, check the Problem Types to locate which ones you answered incorrectly. Review the Referral Pages that correspond to the Reading Problem for each question that you missed. Finally, review the Academic Skills in Chapter 3.

Quiz Question	Problem Types	Correct Answer	Academic Skill	Referral Pages
1	True-False	B	Paraphrasing	Problem 1, page 204
2	Paraphrase	A	Paraphrasing	Problem 6, page 206
3	Vocabulary	D	Paraphrasing	Problem 2, page 204
4	Purpose	B	Paraphrasing	Problem 5, page 205
5	Inference	A		Problem 4, page 205
6	Cause	B	Paraphrasing	Problem 8, page 206
7	Reference	C		Problem 9, page 207
8	Terms	A	Paraphrasing	Problem 3, page 205
9	Detail	D	Paraphrasing	Problem 7, page 206
10	Exception	D	Taking Notes	Problem 12, page 208
11	Opinion	C		Problem 10, page 207
12	Insert	B		Problem 11, page 207
13	Classification: Hereditarian Environmentalist	D E I B F G H	Summarizing	Problem 13, page 208
14	Summary	D B F	Summarizing	Problem 14, page 209

LISTENING

➤ Script for the Listening Quiz

This is a quiz for the Listening section of the Next Generation TOEFL. This section tests your ability to understand campus conversations and academic lectures. During the quiz, you will listen to one conversation and one lecture. You will hear each conversation or lecture one time and respond to twelve questions about them. You may take notes while you listen. You may use your notes to answer the questions. Once you begin, do not pause the audio. To check your answers, refer to the question number in the margin beside the shaded area in the script to which that question refers.

CONVERSATION

 Questions 1–4, Conversation, CD 4, Track 6. Listen to a conversation on campus between a professor and a student.

Student:	Hi Professor Taylor.
Professor:	Hi Jack.
Student:	I was hoping that I could talk with you for a few minutes. It's about the test. [Q1]
Professor:	Oh, okay.
Student:	Well, I've never taken an open-book test, and I just don't know what to expect. Does that mean I can use my book during the test . . . as a reference?
Professor:	Exactly. And you can use your notes and the handouts, too.
Student:	Really?
Professor:	Yes, but Jack, since you've never taken an open-book test, I should warn you. It isn't as easy as it seems. [Q2]
Student:	Because?
Professor:	Because you don't have enough time to look up every answer and still finish the test.
Student:	Oh.
Professor:	That's the mistake that most students make. You see, the purpose of an open-book test is to allow you to look up a detail or make a citation. But the students who are looking up every answer spend too much time on the first few questions, and then they have to leave some of the questions at the end blank.
Student:	So it's important to pace yourself.
Professor:	It is. The test is one hour long and there are twenty questions so you have to be working on question ten in half an hour.
Student:	Right. That's clear enough. So, how do I prepare for an open-book test?
Professor:	Well, the first thing to do is to organize your notes into subject categories, so you can refer easily to topics that might appear in the test questions. And then study your book, just like you would for any other test. Well, some people mark passages in the book with flags to make it easier to locate certain facts, but other than that, just prepare for a test like you usually do. [Q3]
Student:	Right . . . Uh, Professor Taylor, could I ask you . . . um . . . why are you making this test open-book? I mean, we have to study for it like always, so . . . . I hope you don't mind that I asked. I'm just curious.
Professor:	I don't mind at all. Jack, I think an open-book test provides an opportunity for real learning. Too many of my students used to memorize small facts for a test and then forget all about the broad concepts. I want you to study the concepts so you will leave my class with a general perspective that you won't forget. [Q4]
Student:	Wow. I can relate to that.
Professor:	Most people can. But, the way I see it, this is a psychology class, not a memory class.
Student:	Well, thanks for taking the time to explain everything, Dr. Taylor.
Professor:	You're welcome, Jack. See you next week then.
Student:	Okay. Have a nice weekend.
Professor:	You, too.

Audio Answer	1. Why does the man go to see his professor? **C** To get advice about studying for the test

Audio Replay	2. Listen again to part of the conversation. Then answer the following question. Yes, but Jack, since you've never taken an open-book test, I should warn you. It isn't as easy as it seems. Because? Because you don't have enough time to look up every answer and still finish the test.

Audio Replay Answer	Why does the student say this: Because? **B** To encourage the professor to explain. When it is asked in a neutral tone, this one-word question invites further explanation.

Audio Answer	3. How should Jack prepare for the test? **C** He should organize his notes by topic.

Audio Answer	4. Why does the professor give open-book tests? **D** Because she thinks it provides a better learning experience.

LECTURE

Questions 5–14, Lecture, CD 4, Track 6 continued. Listen to part of a lecture in an economics class. The professor is talking about supply-side economics.

Q5

Q13

The fundamental concept in supply-side economics is that tax cuts will spur economic growth because these tax cuts will allow entrepreneurs to invest their tax savings, thereby creating more jobs and profits, which ultimately allow the entrepreneur and the additional employees to pay more taxes, even though the rates are lower. Let's go through that again, step by step. First, taxes are lowered. Then business owners use their tax savings to hire more workers. This increases profits so the business owner pays more taxes at a lower rate, and in addition, the newly hired workers all pay taxes as well. So there's more income flowing into the government through taxes.

Q6

Q7

Historically in the United States, several presidents have championed tax cuts to get the economy moving. Although this top-down economic theory is more popular among Republicans who have traditionally been aligned with business interests, in 1960, John Fitzgerald Kennedy, a Democratic president, also used tax cuts to improve economic conditions. He probably wouldn't qualify as a true supply-sider, but he *did* understand and capitalize on the basic concept. But it's perhaps Ronald Reagan who is most closely associated with supply-side economics. So much so that his policies in the 1980s were referred to as Reaganomics. During his term of office, Reagan cut taxes, but actually, the huge increases in spending, especially for the military budget, caused supply-siders to debate with their conservative cousins.

You see, *conservative* and *supply-side* are not the same thing. Traditional conservative economists insist that tax cuts should be accompanied by fiscal responsibility, that is, spending cuts by government. But supply-side economists aren't concerned with spending. They rely on tax cuts to do the job. Period. Back to the supply-side policies under Reagan, well, the supply-siders believed that the economic growth resulting from tax cuts would be so great and the total increase in taxes so high that the United States economy would grow beyond its deficit spending. When this didn't happen, some economists distanced themselves from the label *supply-side* while advocating tax cuts with greater attention to spending.

Even Milton Friedman, Nobel laureate and an influential member of the Chicago School of Economics—even Friedman is now pointing out that the problem is how to hold down government spending, which accounts for about half of the national income. But he still looks to tax cuts as a solution.

So, a more recent problem for supply-siders, in addition to the fiscal responsibility issue, is that corporate business tends to move their investment and jobs overseas, which critics say eventually will lead to high unemployment in the United States. But Friedman insists that by moving jobs abroad, incomes and dollars are created that sooner or later will be used to purchase goods that are made in the United States and produce jobs in the United States. It's supply-side economics with a global perspective. `Q8`

In fact, conservatives and supply-siders alike argue that progress in the American economy has been made from technological changes and increased productivity—producing different goods or more goods with fewer workers. Dr. Barry Asmus cites the example of the millions of tons of copper wire that had to be produced for us to communicate by telephone across country. Now, a few satellites will do the job. Clearly, the people who were employed in the copper wire industry suffered unemployment when the change in technology occurred. Or, another example, in the case of manufacturing, thirty years ago, `Q11` a General Electric plant required 3000 workers to produce one dishwasher every minute. Now, the same plant needs 300 people to produce one dishwasher every six seconds. So, you might focus on the `Q12` fact that many workers will be without jobs making dishwashers, but what do you suppose supply-siders would say? Think this through. They would counter with the argument that the dishwasher will be cheaper as a result of the increased productivity, so more people can buy dishwashers and still have some money left. Again Asmus reasons that if the consumers spend money on more goods, they create `Q9` jobs because workers are needed to produce the goods they buy. If they invest their money, they also create more jobs by supporting the economy.

So some people do lose jobs because of technology, productivity, and the shift of manufacturing overseas, and only 70 percent find better-paying jobs when they transition to another job. Yes, that's true, and it's a personally painful transition for those involved. But the argument by supply-siders and many conservatives as well is that this is temporary unemployment and the important word here is *temporary*. So the temporary unemployment occurs in the process of shifting people not just from one job to another but from one segment of the economy to another. To use an analogy, it would be like the shift from farming to manufacturing that's occurred worldwide as better methods allowed fewer farmers to `Q10` produce food and resulted in the movement of farmers from the country to the cities where they became employed in manufacturing. And now there's a shift from manufacturing to technology, which, if supply-siders and conservative economists are to be believed, will result in an even higher standard of living in the United States and globally. But, of course, the success of the United States within the global economy will largely depend on a favorable balance of trade—how much we can produce in this country in the new segments of the economy and how much we can sell abroad.

Audio 5. What is the lecture mainly about?
Answer **C** Supply-side economics

Audio 6. How does the professor organize the lecture?
Answer **B** By taking an historical perspective

Audio 7. According to the lecturer, what did Kennedy and Reagan have in common?
Answer **B** They cut taxes to spur the economy during their administrations.

Audio 8. What would Milton Freidman most likely say about moving a manufacturing plant from the United States to a site abroad?
Answer **C** He would view it as a natural process in the shift to technology.

Audio   9. According to Barry Asmus, what are two key ways that consumers contribute to the creation of new jobs?

Answer   **A** By investing their tax savings
                   D By spending more money

Audio   10. How does the professor explain the shift from manufacturing to technology?

Answer   **C** He compares it with the change from agriculture to manufacturing.

Audio   11. Why does the professor mention the General Electric plant?

Answer   **A** Because the plant is a good example of increased productivity

Audio   12. Listen again to part of the lecture. Then answer the following question.

Replay   Now, the same plant needs 300 people to produce one dishwasher every six seconds. So, you might focus on the fact that many workers will be without jobs making dishwashers, but what do you suppose supply-siders would say? Think this through.

Audio   Why does the professor say this:

Replay   Think this through.

Answer   **C** He wants the students to follow his logical answer.

Audio   13. In the lecture, the professor explains supply-side economics. Indicate whether each of the following strategies supports the theory.

Answer

	Yes	No
A Reduce tax rates	✔	
B Cut government spending		✔
C Increase productivity	✔	
D Tolerate temporary unemployment	✔	
E Discourage consumer spending		✔

Audio   14. Put the following events in the correct order.

Answer   **B** The government works to affect a reduction in taxes.
                   A Businesses hire more employees with the tax savings.
                   D Profits increase because of the growth in businesses.
                   C The businesses and their employees pay more taxes.

➤ Progress Chart for the Listening Quiz

The chart below will help you evaluate your progress and determine what you need to read again. First use the Correct Answer column to grade the quiz. Next, check the Problem Types to locate which ones you answered incorrectly and review the Referral Pages that correspond to the Listening Problem for each question that you missed. Finally, review the Academic Skills in Chapter 3.

Quiz Question	Problem Types	Correct Answer	Academic Skill	Referral Pages
1	Purpose	C	Taking Notes Summarizing	Problem 15, page 221
2	Pragmatics	B		Problem 18, page 222
3	Inference	C		Problem 17, page 222
4	Detail	D	Taking Notes Paraphrasing	Problem 16, page 221
5	Main Idea	C	Summarizing	Problem 19, page 225
6	Organization	B	Taking Notes	Problem 20, page 225
7	Detail	B	Taking Notes Paraphrasing	Problem 16, page 221
8	Inference	C		Problem 17, page 222
9	Details	A D	Taking Notes Paraphrasing	Problem 21, page 225
10	Technique	C		Problem 22, page 226
11	Inference	A		Problem 17, page 222
12	Pragmatics	C		Problem 18, page 222
13	Yes-No	A C D Yes B E No	Taking Notes Paraphrasing	Problem 23, page 226
14	Connections	B A D C	Summarizing	Problem 24, page 227

SPEAKING

➤ Script for the Speaking Quiz

This is a quiz for the Speaking section of the Next Generation TOEFL. This section tests your ability to communicate in English in an academic context. During the quiz, you will respond to six speaking questions. You may take notes as you listen. You may use your notes to answer the questions. The reading passages and the questions are printed in the book, but most of the directions will be spoken. Once you begin, do not pause the audio.

 Speaking Quiz, CD 4, Track 13

Narrator 2: Number 1. Listen for a question about a familiar topic. After you hear the question, you have 15 seconds to prepare and 45 seconds to record your answer.

Narrator 1: If you were asked to choose one movie that has influenced your thinking, which one would you choose? Why? What was especially impressive about the movie? Use specific reasons and details to explain your choice.

Narrator 2: Please prepare your answer after the beep.

Beep

[Preparation time: 15 seconds]

Narrator 2: Please begin speaking after the beep.

Beep

[Recording time: 45 seconds]

Beep

Narrator 2: Number 2. Listen for a question that asks your opinion about a familiar topic. After you hear the question, you have 15 seconds to prepare and 45 seconds to record your answer.

Narrator 1: Some people think that teachers should be evaluated by the performance of their students on standardized tests at the end of the term. Other people maintain that teachers should be judged by their own performance in the classroom, and not by the scores that their students achieve on tests. Which approach do you think is better and why? Use specific reasons and examples to support your opinion.

Narrator 2: Please prepare your answer after the beep.

Beep

[Preparation time: 15 seconds]

Narrator 2: Please begin speaking after the beep.

Beep

[Recording time: 45 seconds]

Beep

Narrator 2: Number 3. Read a short passage and listen to a talk on the same topic. Then listen for a question about them. After you hear the question, you have 30 seconds to prepare and 60 seconds to record your answer.

Narrator 1: A meeting is planned to explain the residence requirements for instate tuition. Read the policy in the college catalogue printed on page 251. You have 45 seconds to complete it. Please begin reading now.

[Reading time: 45 seconds]

Narrator 1: Now listen to a student who is speaking at the meeting. He is expressing his opinion about the policy.

Student:
Well, I agree with most of the policy, but what I don't understand is why I have to use my parents' address as my permanent address. This is my third year in a dorm on campus, and I've gone to school every summer, so I've lived in this state for three consecutive years. I don't pay state taxes because I don't earn enough as a full-time student to, uh, to pay taxes, but I don't receive support from my parents either. I have a small grant and a student loan that I'm responsible for, and . . . and I plan to live and work in this state after I graduate, so, um, I think students like me should be eligible for a waiver.

Narrator 1: The student expresses his opinion of the policy for instate tuition. Report his opinion and explain the reasons that he gives for having that opinion.

Narrator 2: Please prepare your answer after the beep.

Beep

[Preparation time: 30 seconds]

Narrator 2: Please begin speaking after the beep.

Beep

[Recording time: 60 seconds]

Beep

Narrator 2: Number 4. Read a short passage and listen to a lecture on the same topic. Then listen for a question about them. After you hear the question, you have 30 seconds to prepare and 60 seconds to record your answer.

Narrator 1: Now read the passage about communication with primates printed on page 252. You have 45 seconds to complete it. Please begin reading now.

[Reading time: 45 seconds]

Narrator 1: Now listen to part of a lecture in a zoology class. The professor is talking about a primate experiment.

Professor:
Let me tell you about an experiment that didn't turn out quite like the researcher had expected. Dr. Sue Savage-Rumbaugh had been trying to train a chimpanzee to use a keyboard adapted with symbols. But no luck. What is interesting about the experiment is that the chimpanzee's adopted son Kanzi, also a bonobo Chimpanzee, well, Kanzi had been observing the lessons and had acquired a rather impressive vocabulary. After that, Kanzi was not given structured training, but he was taught language while walking through the forest or in other informal settings with his trainers. By six years of age, Kanzi had acquired a vocabulary of more than 200 words and was able to form sentences by combining words with gestures or with other words. So, the question is this: should we proceed by trying to teach language to primates in a classroom environment, or should we simply live with them and interact informally like we do with beginning learners of language in our own species? I tend to side with those who elect to support language acquisition in natural settings.

Narrator 1: Explain the importance of the Kanzi experiment in the context of research in primate communication.

Narrator 2: Please prepare your answer after the beep.

Beep

[Preparation time: 30 seconds]

Narrator 2: Please begin speaking after the beep.

Beep

[Recording time: 60 seconds]

Beep

Narrator 2: Number 5. Listen to a short conversation. Then listen for a question about it. After you hear the question, you have 20 seconds to prepare and 60 seconds to record your answer.

Narrator 1: Now listen to a conversation between a student and her friend.

Friend:	Did you decide to take Johnson's class?
Student:	Yeah. I'm going to work it out somehow. Yesterday I walked from the chemistry lab to Hamilton Hall—that's where Johnson's class is.
Friend:	And?
Student:	And it took me twenty minutes.
Friend:	Uh-oh. You only have fifteen minutes between classes, so that means you'll be five minutes late. Listen, why don't you buy a bike? I'm sure you could cut at least five minutes off your time if you took the bike trail.
Student:	I thought about that. But then I'd have to get a license, and I'd have to find somewhere to store it at night. I thought it might be a hassle.
Friend:	Oh, it's not so bad. I have a bike. The license is only ten dollars, and I just park my bike on the deck outside my apartment when the weather's good. And the weather should be okay for most of spring semester.
Student:	That's true.
Friend:	Well, your other option is to talk with Dr. Johnson. Maybe he'll give you permission to be five minutes late to his class because of the distance from your lab. Actually, I've had several classes with him, and he seems very approachable. Anyway, it's an alternative to the bike, if you don't want to do that.

Narrator 1: Describe the woman's problem, and the two suggestions that her friend makes about how to handle it. What do you think the woman should do, and why?

Narrator 2: Please prepare your answer after the beep.

Beep

[Preparation time: 20 seconds]

Narrator 2: Please begin speaking after the beep.

Beep

[Recording time: 60 seconds]

Beep

Narrator 2: Number 6. Listen to part of a lecture. Then listen for a question about it. After you hear the question, you have 20 seconds to prepare, and 60 seconds to record your answer.

Narrator 1: Now listen to part of a lecture in an astronomy class. The professor is discussing the habitable zone.

Professor:
Of course, stars are too hot to support life, but the light from a star warms orbiting planets or moons, supplying the energy needed for life to develop. Besides energy, a liquid, let's say, a chemical solvent of some kind, is also necessary. On Earth, the solvent in which life developed was water, but others such as ammonia, hydrogen fluoride, or methane might also be appropriate. So, in order for the solvent to remain in liquid form, the planet or moon must lie within a certain range of distances from the star. Why is this so? Well, think about it. If the planet is too close to the star, the solvent will change into a gas, boiling and evaporating. If it is too far from the star, the solvent will freeze, transforming into a solid. For our

sun and life as we know it, the habitable zone appears to lie between the orbits of Venus and Mars. Within this range, water remains liquid. And until recently, this area was indeed the accepted scientific definition of the habitable zone for our solar system. But now scientists have postulated that the habitable zone may be larger than originally supposed. They speculate that the strong gravitational pull caused by larger planets may produce enough energy to heat the cores of orbiting moons. So that means that these moons may support life. There may be habitable zones far beyond Venus!

Narrator 1: Using the main points and examples from the lecture, describe the habitable zone, and then explain how the definition has been expanded by modern scientists.

Narrator 2: Please prepare your answer after the beep.

Beep

[Preparation time: 20 seconds]

Narrator 2: Please begin speaking after the beep.

Beep

[Recording time: 60 seconds]

Beep

Progress Chart for the Speaking Quiz

The chart below will help you evaluate your progress and determine what you need to practice again. First, compare your answers on the quiz with the Example Answers. Use the Checklists in the Review to evaluate specific features of your speech. Next, check the Problem Types to locate which ones were most difficult for you. Review the Referral Pages that correspond to the Speaking Problem for each question that you missed. Finally, review the Academic Skills in Chapter 3.

Quiz Question	Problem Types	Correct Answer	Academic Skill	Referral Pages
1	Experiences	1	Summarizing Taking Notes	Problem 25, pages 235–236
2	Preferences	2	Summarizing Taking Notes	Problem 26, pages 236–237
3	Reports	3	Synthesizing Taking Notes	Problem 27, pages 237–239
4	Examples	4	Synthesizing Taking Notes	Problem 28, pages 239–241
5	Problems	5	Summarizing Taking Notes	Problem 29, pages 241–243
6	Summaries	6	Summarizing Taking Notes	Problem 30, pages 243–245

Example Answers, CD 5, Track 1

QUESTION 1: EXAMPLE ANSWER

The movie that has influenced my thinking the most is *Fantasia* because it's my first memory of classical music and ballet. One reason the movie was so impressive is, um, I was at a very impressionable age when I saw it—five years old. Besides that, it was made using the latest technology. In the 1950s, it was amazing to see detailed animation and . . . and hear high quality sound. But what really influenced me was the music and the dance scenes. I especially remember Mickey Mouse dancing with the brooms and I'm sure I took ballet lessons because of it. The coordination of the storm scene with the music from *The Hall of the Mountain King* still impresses me when I see it today and, thanks to Walt Disney, classical music is still my favorite music.

QUESTION 2: EXAMPLE ANSWER

I think it's good to evaluate teachers by their student's performace on standardized tests because when teachers and students are judged by the same criteria, they'll work efficiently toward the same goals. Now some teachers argue that tests aren't important but still, students need good scores for admission to universities so the tests are important to them. If teachers were evaluated on the same basis, then they would pay more attention to the criteria on tests to design their lessons so both students and teachers would benefit. Another reason to use this evaluation is to compare teachers from different schools on a standardized scale. And this system would be more fair, too, because the possibility of a teacher getting a high evaluation because of friendship with the supervisor is also eliminated.

QUESTION 3: EXAMPLE ANSWER

The student said that he mostly agreed with the policy for instate tuition but he disagreed with a couple of requirements. For one thing, you can't use a campus address as a permanent address, but he's a dorm student, and he explained that he's lived in the dorm for three years because he's gone to school every summer without returning to his parent's home to live so the dorm really is his permanent address right now. He doesn't think he should have to use his parent's out-of-state address. Besides that, he hasn't been subsidized by his parents. In the policy, the most recent taxes must be filed in the state of residence but, uh, he didn't make enough money to pay taxes. He didn't mention in which state he had his voter's registration or car registration and driver's licenses, but he said that he plans to continue living and working in the state after graduation, and he thought that he should be eligible for a waiver of the out-of-state fees.

QUESTION 4: EXAMPLE ANSWER

The experiment with Kanzi is important because it supports the theory that language should be acquired in natural settings instead of in a formal classroom. Previous research to teach primates to communicate included direct instruction in American Sign Language and, uh, also plastic shapes that could be arranged on a magnetic board. Earlier research . . . I think it was with Kanzi's mother . . . it replicated this formal approach. But when Kanzi learned vocabulary by observing the lessons, the direction of the experiment changed. In informal settings with trainers, Kanzi acquired a vocabulary of about 200 words, and began to create sentences with words and gestures to . . . to communicate with human, uh, companions. Children of our own species learn by informal interaction with adults. The Kanzi experiment suggests that this may be a better way to teach language to primates.

Question 5: Example Answer

The problem is that the woman has only fifteen minutes between classes but it takes twenty minutes to walk from the chemistry lab to Hamilton Hall where Professor Johnson's class is held. So she would like to take the class with Johnson but she would be late. Um, her friend suggests that she buy a bike but her concern is that she would need a license and would have to store the bike somewhere at night. The other, uh, recommendation is . . . is to ask Dr. Johnson for permission to enter the class five minutes late. So . . . I think the woman should talk with the professor first. Her friend says he's approachable and he might give her permission to be late for class. The first five minutes in a class is usually just business anyway—taking attendance and handing back papers—so she wouldn't miss much. And, if he refuses, then she can always resort to the other alternative. She can buy a bike and a license, and she can find a place to store it.

Question 6: Example Answer

The habitable zone is an area in which life can develop. There are several requirements, including an energy source and a chemical solvent that retains its liquid form. Okay, that means that the moon or the planet where life may develop has to be close enough to the energy source—probably a star—close enough that the solvent will remain a liquid. Outside the habitable zone, it would freeze or boil, depending on whether it was far way or too close to the star. In the case of Earth, the Sun supplied the energy and water was the chemical solvent. So, for life to evolve in ways similar to our own, the habitable zone would have to fall between Venus and Mars. But, modern scientists are questioning whether the forces of gravity on larger planets might not generate enough energy to heat up the cores of the moons that orbit them. Now, if that's the case, then there could be habitable zones at a great distance from Venus, which was the previously determined limit for a habitable zone in our solar system.

WRITING

➤ Script for the Writing Quiz

This is a quiz for the Writing section of the Next Generation TOEFL (iBT). This section tests your ability to write essays in English. During the quiz, you will respond to two writing questions. You may take notes as you read and listen to academic information. You may use your notes to write the essays. Once you begin, you have 20 minutes to write the first essay and 30 minutes to write the second essay.

 Question 1, CD 5, Track 4

Now listen to a lecture on the same topic as the passage you have just read.

Professor: Let me tell you about a case study that is often used as an example of how a win-win situation can be negotiated by both parties. Tony was a computer software designer who had come up with a great idea for a computer game, but his problem was that he couldn't afford to quit his job while he worked on the game because he had to make a living for his family. He thought it would probably take him about a year to actually complete the programming for the game if he worked in his spare time. Okay. Well, he put together a proposal, and took it to a multinational company that had launched several successful computer games. But the problem was that the company made him a very low offer—just a thousand dollars a month for twelve months. And although that would have paid his bills during the time that he would have been working on the program, he knew that the game had a huge potential for return on the company's investment. So he felt like he would be taking all the risk without having the opportunity to share in the reward. But when the company refused to give him any additional upfront money, then, instead of getting angry, Tony went back with a counteroffer. He agreed to accept the $12,000 as an advance on the profits that he expected the game to generate. And he suggested that they share the future revenues in a ratio of 40:60—40 percent for Tony and 60 percent for the company. The company was interested, but explained to Tony that they would be investing over a million dollars in order to produce and market the game and would need a larger share in order to proceed. So they agreed on a 30:70 split. And, as it happened, the game was a big success, the company made a huge profit and Tony was able to quit his regular job and start his own game design company. So—everybody won. They were both able to minimize their risk and increase their profits.

➤ Progress Chart for the Writing Quiz

The chart below will help you to evaluate your progress and determine what you need to practice again. First, compare your answers on the quiz with the Example Essays. Use the Checklists in the Review to evaluate specific features of your writing. Next, check the Problem Types to locate which was most difficult for you. Read the Referral Pages that correspond to the Writing Problem for the question that you found most difficult. Finally, review the Academic Skills in Chapter 3.

Quiz Question	Problem Types	Checklists	Academic Skill	Referral Pages
1	Integrated	Content	Paraphrasing Summarizing Synthesizing	Problems 31, 32, pages 254–260
2	Independent	Opinion		Problems 33, 34, pages 260–264

QUESTION 1: EXAMPLE ESSAY

A win-win negotiation is a successful compromise in which both sides improve their situation through mutual cooperation. The key is for one party to offer the other party something that they will perceive as valuable but which does not harm the party conceding it. This, in turn, provides an incentive for the other side to make a similar offer. In this way, both sides will win. Unlike traditional negotiations in which the negotiators have an adversarial relationship, in a win-win negotiation, they view each other as collaborators who are working toward a mutual goal. After the terms have been agreed upon, it is much more likely that the relationship will continue to develop with a view to cooperating with each other to insure the continuing success of both parties.

One case study of a win-win negotiation is often cited as an example. Tony had an idea for a computer game but was unable to develop it because of constraints on his time and limitations in funding. In the negotiations with a large company to produce the game, Tony and the company made several offers and counteroffers in order to arrive at a mutually beneficial agreement. Although Tony could have become angry about the original offer of $12,000, he made a counteroffer. He agreed to accept their offer if they would concede an additional share of the future revenues. When the company reviewed his counteroffer, they conceded that he should receive a share and offered slightly less than Tony had proposed. Because they continued to negotiate toward a win-win situation, both parties were able to decrease their risk and increase their revenues, sharing in the success of the game. The company was very pleased with their return on investment, and Tony was able to launch his own game design company. In short, both parties won.

QUESTION 2: EXAMPLE ESSAY

Although it can be argued that voice mail and e-mail are more efficient, and in many ways, more convenient, I still prefer to communicate in person, or if that is not possible, by telephone. In my experience, face-to-face interactions are best for a number of reasons. In the first place, when you hear the speaker's tone of voice, you are better able to judge the attitude and emotions that can be easily hidden in a written reply. In addition, the exchange is more immediate. Even instant messaging isn't as fast as a verbal interaction in person or by phone. E-mail seems efficient; however, sometimes multiple messages over several days are required to clarify the information that a short phone call would have taken care of in one communication. We have all tried to return a voice mail only to hear a recording on the original caller's voice mail. Clearly, no real communication is possible in a situation that allows only one person to talk. Moreover, the body language and the expression on the speaker's face often communicate more than the words themselves. Research indicates that more than 80 percent of a message is nonverbal. The way that a speaker stands or sits can indicate interest or disagreement. The eye contact and the movement of the eyebrows and the mouth can actually communicate the opposite of the words that the speaker is saying. Finally, no technology has succeeded in duplicating a firm handshake to close a deal, a hug to encourage a friend, or a kiss goodbye. Until e-mail and voice mail can provide the subtle communication, the immediate interaction, and the emotional satisfaction of a face-to-face conversation, complete with facial expressions and gestures, I will prefer to talk instead of to type.

EXPLANATORY OR EXAMPLE ANSWERS AND AUDIO SCRIPTS FOR MODEL TESTS

MODEL TEST 1: PRETEST

➤ Reading

READING 1 "BEOWULF"

1. **C** "...*Beowulf* was written by an anonymous [author unknown] Englishman in Old English." Choice A is not correct because it is one of four surviving manuscripts. Choice B is not correct because it was written in old English about Germanic characters. Choice D is not correct because scholars do not know if it is the sole surviving epic from about A.D. 1000.

2. **B** "Although *Beowulf* was written by an anonymous Englishman in Old English, the tale takes place in that part of Scandinavia from which [that part of Scandinavia] Germanic tribes emigrated to England."

3. **A** "Iron was accessible everywhere in Scandinavia, usually in the form of 'bog iron' found in the layers of peat in peat bogs." Choice B is not correct because the author had already stated that the best swords had iron or iron-edged blades. Choice C is not correct because the Celts taught the Northmen how to use the materials, but they did not provide the bog iron. Choice D is not correct because the bog iron does not relate to the date, although 500 B.C. is mentioned as the time when the Northmen learned how to forge iron.

4. **A** *Society in Anglo-Saxon England* paraphrases "Anglo-Saxon society." . . . *both advanced* paraphrases "neither primitive," and *cultured* paraphrases "nor uncultured." Two negatives [*nor* and *–un*] produce an affirmative meaning.

5. **B** In this passage, *rare* is a synonym for "unique." Context comes from the reference to the "sole surviving epic" in the beginning of the same sentence.

6. **B** ". . . the original manuscript was probably lost during the ninth century . . ., in which the Danes destroyed the Anglo-Saxon monasteries and their great libraries." Choice A is true but it is not the reason that scholars believe the original manuscript was lost. Choice C is not correct because the Danes were invaders, not poets. Choice D is not correct because the location of the discovery is not mentioned, although the author may have been a monk.

7. **D** "Although the *Beowulf* manuscript was written in about A.D. 1000, it was not discovered until the seventeenth century." Choice A is not correct because the first century was the date the manuscript was written, not discovered. Choice B is not correct because the ninth century was the date when the original manuscript may have been lost. Choice C is not correct because some scholars think that the manuscript was written in the eleventh century.

8. **A** Because the word "apparently" means "appearing to be so," the author is expressing doubt about the information that follows, ". . . [the *Beowulf* poet] was a Christian." Choice B is not correct because the word "obviously" would be used. Choice C is not correct because the phrases "for example" or "for instance" would signal an example. Choice D is not correct because evidence would not be presented as "appearing to be so."

9. **A** ". . . Beowulf is a very appealing hero . . . Like Hercules." Choice B is not correct because a fight with a dragon is mentioned in reference to Beowulf but not to Hercules. Choice C is not correct because the Danish hero's welcome is the only reference to a speech, and it was jealous, not inspiring. Choice D is not correct because the time period for the life of Hercules is not mentioned.

10. **B** In this passage, *demonstrates* is a synonym for "exhibits."

11. **C**   In this passage, *refuse* is a synonym for "reject." Context comes from the contrast with "accept" in the previous sentence.

12. **B**   Addition is a transitional device that connects the insert sentence with the previous sentence. *Moreover* signals that additional, related information will follow. ". . . they [scholars] disagree" refers to "Scholars do not know" in the previous sentence.

13. **E, D, F**   summarize the passage. Choice A is true, but it is a minor point that establishes the time period for the poem and refers to major point D. Choice B is true, but it is a detail that refers to major point E and explains why there may be only one manuscript. Choice C is not clear from the information in the passage.

READING 2 "THERMOREGULATION"

14. **A**   "The most basic mechanism [for maintenance of warm body temperature] is the high metabolic rate." Choices B, C, and D are all ways to maintain body temperature, but they are not the most fundamental adaptation.

15. **D**   "In some mammals, certain hormones can cause mitochondria to increase their metabolic activity and produce heat instead of ATP. This **nonshivering thermogenesis (NST).** . . ." Choice A is not correct because thermogenesis is the activity that generates heat, not the heat loss. Choice B is not correct because brown fat is one example of a more generalized process. Choice C is not correct because thermogenesis is a response to the environment to maintain the health of the animal, not a process that maintains the environment.

16. **B**   A passive grammatical structure in the passage is paraphrased by an active grammatical structure in the answer choice.

17. **D**   In this passage, *smallest* is a synonym for "minimal."

18. **B**   "For example, heat loss from a human is reduced when arms and legs cool." Choice A is not correct because goose bumps, not heat loss in the extremities, is a vestige of our evolution. Choice C is not correct because no direct comparisons of these processes are made in the paragraph. Choice D is not correct because the types of insulation are mentioned before the concept of vasodilatation and vasoconstriction are introduced.

19. **D**   In this passage, *control* is a synonym for "regulate." Context comes from the reference to "temperature differences" at the end of the same sentence.

20. **B**   "The loss of heat to water occurs 50 to 100 times more rapidly than heat loss to air." Choice A is not correct because hair loses insulating power when wet, but the evolution of marine animals is not mentioned. Choice C is not correct because dry hair insulates better than wet hair. Choice D is not correct because there are land animals that are of similar size.

21. **D**   ". . . marine mammals maintain body core temperatures of about 36–38°C with metabolic rates about the same as those [metabolic rates] of land mammals of similar size."

22. **A**   ". . . capable of astonishing feats of thermoregulation. For example, small birds called chickadees . . . hold body temperature nearly constant." Choice B is not correct because the food supply supports thermoregulation, which is the main point of the example. Choice C is not correct because chickadees are capable of astonishing feats of thermoregulation. Choice D is not correct because the reason for heat production in animals is explained before the example of the chickadee.

23. **D**   Choice A is mentioned in paragraph 6, sentence 7. Choice B is mentioned in paragraph 6, sentence 8. Choice C is mentioned in paragraph 6, sentences 3 and 4.

24. **B**   In this passage, *improve* is a synonym for "enhance." Context comes from the reference to "promote" in the previous sentence.

25. **A**   Reference is a transitional device that connects the insert sentence with the previous sentence. ". . . a layer of fur or feathers" and "how much still air the layer [of fur or feathers] traps" in the insert sentence refers to ". . . fur or feathers" and "a thicker layer of air" in the previous sentence.

26. **E, C, F** summarize the passage. Choice A is a minor point that supports major point C. Choice B is true but it is not mentioned in the passage. Choice D is a minor point that supports major point F.

READING 3 "SOCIAL READJUSTMENT SCALES"

27. **D**   "Overall, these studies have shown that people with higher scores on the SRRS tend to be more vulnerable to many kinds of physical illness." Choice A is not correct because a person with a higher score will experience more, not less, stress. Choice B is not correct because the numerical values for major problems are not identified, and a score of 30 does not have meaning unless it is compared with a higher or lower score. Choice C is not correct because the effects of positive or negative change are not mentioned in the first two paragraphs.

28. **C**   ". . . the desirability of events affects adaptational outcomes more than the amount of change that they [events] require."

29. **D**   In this passage, *different* is a synonym for "diverse."

30. **C**   ". . . divorce may deserve a stress value of 73 for *most* people, a particular person's divorce might generate much less stress and merit a value of only 25." Choice A is not correct because a particular person is compared with most people. Choice B is not correct because the serious nature of divorce is not mentioned. Choice D is not correct because the numerical value of 73 for most people is questioned.

31. **A**   ". . . what qualifies as 'trouble with the boss'? Should you check that because you're sick and tired of your supervisor? What constitutes a 'change in living conditions'? Does your purchase of a great new sound system qualify?" Choice B is not correct because the author does not offer examples of responses to the questions posed. Choice C is not correct because options for scores are not provided in paragraph 5. Choice D is not correct because the author suggests that people do not respond consistently but whether they respond carefully is not mentioned.

32. **B**   ". . . subjects' neuroticism affects both their responses to stress scales and their self-reports of health problems." Choice A is not correct because they recall more symptoms, but they are not ill more often. Choice C is not correct because they recall more stress, but they do not necessarily suffer more actual stress. Choice D is not correct because the effects of neuroticism obscures the meaning of the scores that are recorded.

33. **C**   In this passage, *arranged* is a synonym for "assembled."

34. **C**   In this passage, *related* is a synonym for "relevant."

35. **B**   ". . . dropping the normative weights and replacing them with personally assigned weightings." Choice A is not correct because long-term consequences are not included in positive, negative, and total change scores. Choice C is not correct because the differences in people reflect their appraisal of stress, not how they handle stress. Choice D is not correct because normative weighting is replaced by personally assigned weightings.

36. **C**   In paragraph 1, the authors state that the SRRS ". . . assigns numerical values." Choices A and B are not correct because they are mentioned in paragraph 10 in reference to the LES, not the SRRS. Choice D is not correct because recalling events from one year ago is a problem on the SRRS.

37. **A**   "The LES deals with the failure of the SRRS to sample the full domain of stressful events." Choice B is not correct because the author explains several ways that the LES deals with the failure of the SRRS. Choice C is not correct because it has been used in thousands of studies by researchers all over the world. Choice D is not correct because the LES, not the SRRS, has a special section for students.

38. **B**   Reference is a transitional device that connects the insert sentence with the previous sentence. "This sum" in the insert sentence refers to the phrase "adds up the numbers" in the previous sentence.

39.   SRRS: **A, H, I**   LES: **B, D, E**   Not used: **C, F, G**

➤ **Listening**

 Model Test 1, Listening Section, CD 1, Track 1

LISTENING 1 "LEARNING CENTER"

Audio Conversation

Narrator:	Listen to a conversation on campus between two students.
Man:	Hi. Are you Paula?
Woman:	Jim?
Man:	Hi. Nice to meet you.
Woman:	Glad to meet you.
Q1 Man:	So, you need some tutoring in English?
Woman:	Yeah. I'm taking English composition, and I'm not doing very well on my essays.
Man:	Right. Um, well, first let's see if we can figure out a time to meet . . . that we're both free.
Woman:	Okay.
Man:	How about Mondays? Maybe in the morning? I don't have any classes until eleven on Mondays.
Woman:	That would work, but I was hoping we could, you know, meet more than once a week.
Man:	Oh. Well, Tuesdays are out. I've got classes and, uh, I work at the library part time on Tuesdays and Thursdays. But I could get together on Wednesdays.
Woman:	In the morning?
Man:	Probably nine-thirty would be best. That way we'd have an hour to work before I'd have to get ready for my eleven o'clock.
Woman:	So that would be two hours a week then?
Man:	I could do that.
Q2 Woman:	Oh, but, would that be extra? You know, would I need to pay you for the extra session?
Q3 Man:	No. Um, just so you meet me here at the Learning Center, and we both sign in, then I'll get paid. Tutoring is free, to you, I mean. The school pays me. But we both have to show up. If you don't show up and sign in for a session, then I don't get paid. So . . .
Woman:	Oh, don't worry about that. I really need the help. I won't miss any sessions unless I'm sick or something.
Man:	Okay then. So you want me to help you with your essays?
Woman:	Right. I could bring you some that have, you know, comments on them. I'm getting C's and . . .
Man:	Well, that's not too bad. Once I see some of your writing, we should be able to pull that up to a B.
Woman:	You think so?
Q4 Man:	Sure. But I need to explain something. Some of my students in the past . . . they expected me to write their essays for them. But that's not what a tutor is supposed to do. My job is to help you be a better writer.
Woman:	Oh, I understand that. But you'll read my essays, right?
Man:	Oh yeah. No problem. We'll read them together, and I'll make suggestions.
Woman:	Great. I think part of the problem is I just don't understand the teacher's comments. Maybe you can help me figure them out.
Man:	Sure. Who's the teacher?
Woman:	Simpson.

Man:	No problem. I've tutored a couple of her students, so I know more or less where she's coming from. Okay, then. I guess we'll meet here on Monday.	Q5
Woman:	I'll be here. Nine-thirty you said.	
Man:	Just sign in when you get here.	

| Audio | 1. | What does the woman need? |
| Answer | C | An appointment for tutoring |

Audio	2.	Listen again to part of the conversation and then answer the following question.
Replay		"Oh, but, would that be extra? You know, would I need to pay you for the extra session?"
Audio		Why does the woman say this:
Replay		"Oh, but would that be extra?"
Answer	A	Her tone indicates that she is worried.

| Audio | 3. | Why is the man concerned about the woman's attendance? |
| Answer | B | He will not get a paycheck if she is absent. |

| Audio | 4. | What does the man agree to do? |
| Answer | D | He will show the woman how to improve her writing. |

| Audio | 5. | What does the man imply about the woman's teacher? |
| Answer | D | ". . . know . . . where she's coming from" means "to understand her." |

LISTENING 2 "GEOLOGY CLASS"

Audio Lecture
Narrator: Listen to part of a lecture in a geology class.

Professor:
Okay, today we're going to discuss the four major types of drainage patterns. I trust you've already read the chapter so you'll recall that a drainage pattern is the arrangement of channels that carry water in an area. And these patterns can be very distinctive since they're determined by the climate, the topography, and the composition of the rock that underlies the formations. So, consequently, we can see that a drainage pattern is really a good visual summary of the characteristics of a particular region, both geologically and climactically. In other words, when we look at drainage patterns, we can draw conclusions about the structural formation and relief of the land as well as the climate.

Q6
Q7

Now all drainage systems are composed of an interconnected network of streams, and, when we view them together, they form distinctive patterns. Although there are at least seven identifiable kinds of drainage patterns, for our purposes, we're going to limit our study to the four major types. Probably the most familiar pattern is the dendritic drainage pattern.

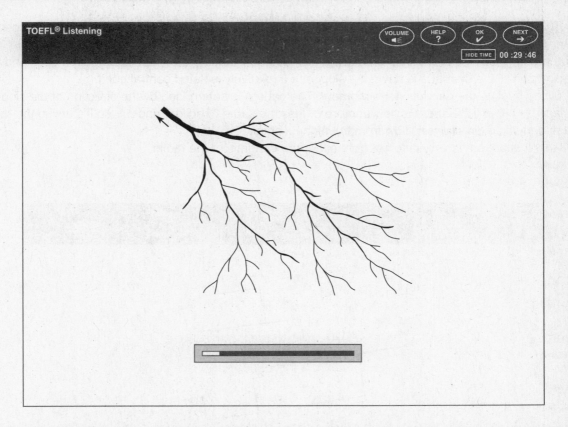

Q8 This is a stream that looks like the branches of a tree. Here's an example of a dendritic pattern. As you can see, it's similar to many systems in nature. In addition to the structure of a tree, it also resembles the human circulation system. This is a very efficient drainage system because the overall length of any one branch is fairly short, and there are many branches, so that allows the water to flow quickly and efficiently from the source or sources.

Okay, let's look at the next example.

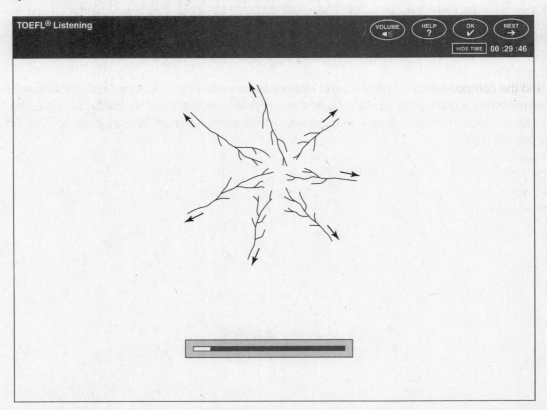

This drainage pattern is referred to as a radial pattern. Notice how the streams flow from a central point. This is usually a high mountain, or a volcano. It kind of looks like the spokes that radiate out from the hub of a wheel. When we see a radial pattern, we know that the area has experienced uplift and that the direction of the drainage is down the slopes of a relatively isolated central point.

Q9

Going back to the dendritic for a moment. The pattern is determined by the direction of the slope of the land, but it, uh, the streams flow in more or less the same direction, and . . . so it's unlike the radial that had multiple directions of flow from the highest point.

Now this pattern is very different from either the dendritic or the radial.

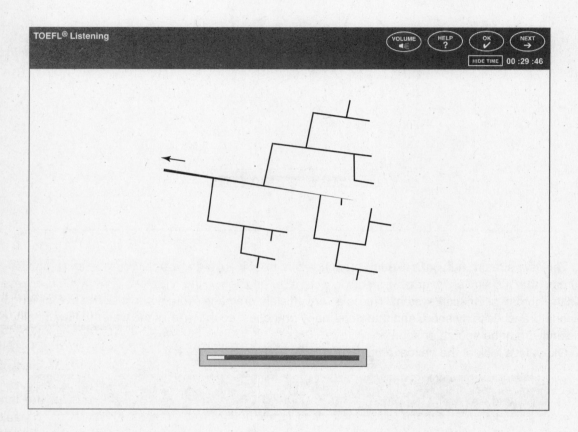

This is called a rectangular pattern, and I think you can see why. Just look at all of those right-angle turns. The rectangle pattern is typical of a landscape that's been formed by fractured joints and faults. And because this broken rock is eroded more easily than unbroken rock, stream beds are carved along the jointed bedrock.

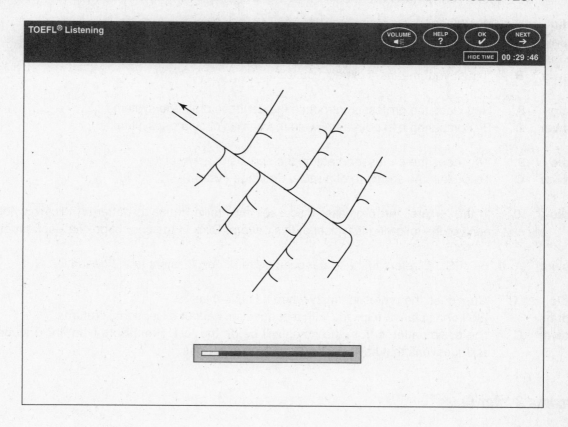

Finally we have the trellis pattern. And here in this example, you can see quite clearly how the tributaries of an almost parallel structure drain into valleys and . . . and form the appearance of a garden

Q10 trellis. This pattern forms in areas where there are alternating bands of variable resistance, and by that I mean that the bands of rock that are very strong and resistant to erosion alternate with bands of rock that are weak and easily eroded. This often happens when a horizontal plain folds and outcroppings appear.

So, as I said, as a whole, these patterns are dictated by the structure and relief of the land. The kinds of rocks on which the streams are developed, the structural pattern of the folds, uh, faults, and . . . uplift will usually determine a drainage system. However, I should also mention that drainage patterns can occasionally appear to be, well, out of sync with the landscape. And this can happen when a stream flows over older structures that have been uncovered by erosion or . . . or when a stream keeps its original drainage system when rocks are uplifted. So when that happens, the pattern appears

Q11 to be contrary to the expected course of the stream. But I'm interested in your understanding the basic drainage systems. So I don't plan to trick you with test questions about exceptional patterns, but I expect you to know that exceptions to the patterns can occur when geological events influence them.

Audio   6.   What is this lecture mainly about?
Answer **B**   A comparison of different types of drainage systems

Audio   7.   Listen again to part of the lecture and then answer the following question.
Replay   "Okay, today we're going to discuss the four major types of drainage patterns. I trust you've already read the chapter so you'll recall that a drainage pattern is the arrangement of channels that carry water in an area."

Audio   Why does the professor say this:
Replay   "I trust you've already read the chapter so you'll recall that a drainage pattern is the arrangement of channels that carry water in an area."
Answer **B**   "I trust you" means "I expect you to."

Audio 8.   How does the professor introduce the dendritic drainage system?
Answer **B**   By comparing it to both a tree and the human circulatory system

Audio 9.   Why does the professor mention the spokes of a wheel?
Answer **C**   To explain the structure of a radial drainage system

Audio 10. In the lecture, the professor discusses the trellis drainage pattern. Indicate whether each of the following is typical of this pattern. Click in the correct box for each phrase.

Answer **A, D, E:** YES   **B** refers to the rectangular pattern, and **C** refers to the dendritic.

Audio 11. What does the professor imply when he says this:
Replay   "So I don't plan to trick you with test questions about exceptional patterns."
Answer **C**   The basic patterns from the notes will be on the test. Professors who "trick" students ask questions that have not been discussed in class.

LISTENING 3 "ART CLASS"

Audio Lecture
Narrator: Listen to part of a lecture in an art class. The professor is discussing drawing.

Professor:
Drawing is a very basic art form. It's appealing because it can be used to make a very quick record of the ideas that an artist may be envisioning, so, a drawing can serve as a visual aid for the artist to remember a certain moment of inspiration and maybe use it for a more detailed work later on. Okay, usually such sketches allow the artist to visualize the proportions and the shapes without much attention to details so these images can be used by painters, architects, sculptors—any artist really. And large renderings, sketches of parts of the whole . . . these can be helpful in the creative process when a . . . a huge image might be more difficult to conceive of in its entirety. Or, a sketch of just one face in a crowd can allow the artist to . . . focus on creating just that part of the image. So, in many artists' studios, countless drawings are strewn about as the final painting or sculpture takes form. And this gives us insight into the creative process, as well the opportunity to see changes from the images at the beginning in the images of the finished work. It's rare, in fact, for an artist to use permanent materials to begin a piece of art. And some painters, for example, even sketch onto the surface of the canvas before applying the pigments. Now, architects are especially prone to sketches because, of course, their buildings are so large that an image in smaller scale is necessary to the imagination and implementation of such projects. So, uh, these studies become the basis for future works. And again, this is very interesting as a record of the creative process. Okay so far?   Q13 Q14

  Okay, drawing has several other functions besides as a temporary reference. For centuries, artists Q12 have used drawing as a traditional method of education. By copying the great works, especially of the Old Masters, aspiring artists could learn a lot about proportion, how to capture light and shadow and . . . and so forth. In fact, some artists who later achieve recognition, still continue to use this practice to hone their skills or . . . or simply to pay homage to another artist, as is often the case when a work of art originally created in another medium like a sculpture . . . when it's recreated in the form of a drawing. Many examples of drawings of Michelangelo's sculptures were re-created by well-known artists. One that comes to mind is the *Study of Michelangelo's Bound Slave* by Edgar Degas. The original by Michelangelo was a marble sculpture that was, oh, about seven feet in height, but the small drawing was made in a sketchpad. In any case, the study is also considered a masterpiece, on a small scale, of course.

Q12   So . . . what additional purposes might be served by the medium of drawing? Well, let's remember that photography is a relatively new art form, so prior to the use of photographs to record historical events, a quick drawing by an artist was about the only way to preserve a real-time visual account of an important moment. Although a more permanent visual impression might be rendered later, it would be

Q15   based on memory and not on the artist's actual observation. Probably the most often cited example of a sketch that preserved an historical record would be the small drawing of Marie Antoinette as she was taken to the guillotine in a cart through the streets of Paris. Jacques-Louis David sketched this famous drawing on a piece of paper about the size of the palm of his hand. And the artist, the artist reporter, is still important even in modern times, when photography isn't possible, for example, when judges won't permit cameras in the courtroom.

Q17   Okay, to review, we've talked about three functions for drawing—as a visual aid for the artist to complete a future work, as a method of education for aspiring artists or even practiced artists, and as a way to report an event. But the sketchbook has . . . other possibilities. Sometimes a drawing is the final execution of the art. Picasso produced hundreds of drawings in, well, every conceivable medium, but especially in pencil and crayon. I find it very interesting that Picasso did so much of this kind of work . . . drawing, I mean, in his last years. Some critics have argued that he was just laughing at the art world, which was willing to pay outrageous sums for anything with his name on it, and clearly, a drawing can be executed in a short period of time. But others, other critics, they feel as I do that Picasso was draw-

Q16   ing because it was so basic, and because it was so spontaneous and so much fun. And also, think about how difficult it really is to produce a quick drawing with a few lines and, uh, no opportunity to . . . to recreate the original, either by painting it out or remodeling the clay or changing the building materials, or . . . or any of the other methods for revision of a finished artistic work that artists have at their disposal. So, what I'm saying is that drawing when it's elevated to a finished piece, it must be done with confidence and it must show a high degree of creativity and mastery of the art form. In a way, it harkens back to the beginnings of art itself, when some unknown artist must have stuck a finger in the earth to draw an image or . . . maybe he picked up a stone and made a drawing on the wall of a cave.

Okay, so, as a first assignment, I want you to make a couple of sketches yourself. I'm not going to grade them. This isn't a studio art class. I just want you to use a few basic strokes to capture an image. You can do the first one in pencil, crayon, ink, chalk, or even charcoal . . . whatever you like. Then, I want you to sketch the same image in a different medium. So, if you do a face in pencil, I want you to do the same face but in chalk or crayon. Bring them to class next week and we'll continue our discussion of drawing, but we'll talk more about the materials artists use to produce drawings, and, uh, we'll refer to your sketches as examples.

Audio   12.   What is the lecture mainly about?
Answer   **C**   The distinct purposes of drawing

Audio   13.   According to the professor, why do architects use sketches?
Answer   **B**   To design large buildings, architects must work in a smaller scale.

Audio   14.   Listen again to part of the lecture and then answer the following question.
Replay   "So, uh, these studies become the basis for future works. And again, this is very interesting as a record of the creative process. Okay so far?"
Audio   What does the professor mean when she says this:
Replay   "Okay so far?"
Answer   **A**   Professors sometimes pause for a comprehension check by asking if everything is okay. This gives students an opportunity to answer questions.

Audio   15.   Why does the professor mention the drawing of Marie Antoinette?
Answer   C   The sketch was an historical account of an important event.

Audio   16.   What is the professor's opinion of Picasso?
Answer   C   Picasso's drawings required the confidence and skill of a master artist.

Audio   17.   According to the lecture, what are the major functions of drawing?
Answer   A   A technique to remember parts of a large work
                B   A method to preserve an historical record
                D   An educational approach to train artists

LISTENING 4 "PROFESSOR'S OFFICE"

Audio Conversation

Narrator: Listen to a conversation on campus between a student and a professor.

Student: Thanks for seeing me, Professor Williams.
Professor: Glad to, Alice. What do you have on your mind?
Student: Well, I got a little mixed up when I started to go over my notes from the last class, so I   `Q18`
                   had a few questions.
Professor: Shoot.
Student: Okay. I understand the three basic sources of personnel for multinational companies.
                   That's fairly self-explanatory.
Professor: Host country, home country, and third country.
Student: Right. But then you started talking about staffing patterns that . . . let me see . . . okay
                   . . . you said, "staffing patterns may vary depending on the length of time that the multi-   `Q19`
                   national company has been operating," and you gave some examples, but I got con-
                   fused and now I can't read my notes.
Professor: Okay. Well, one pattern is to rely on home country managers to staff the key positions
                   when the company opens, but gradually moving more host country nationals into upper
                   management as the company grows.
Student: So, for example, if a French company opened a factory in Canada, then French man-
                   agement would gradually replace themselves with Canadian managers. Is that what
                   you mean?
Professor: Right. I think I used that very example in class. So do you want to try to explain the sec-
                   ond pattern to me?
Student: Sure. I think it's the one where home country nationals are put in charge of the com-
                   pany if it's located in a developed country, but in a developing country, then home
                   country nationals manage the company sort of indefinitely.
Professor: Right again. And an example of that would be . . .   `Q20`
Student: . . . maybe using German management for a Swiss company in Germany, but, uh, they
                   might send Swiss management to provide leadership for a Swiss company in . . . in . . .
Professor: How about Zimbabwe?
Student: This is one of the confusing parts. Zimbabwe has a very old and highly developed cul-
                   ture, so...
Professor: . . . but it's still defined as a developing country because of the economic base—which
                   is being developed now.
Student: Oh, okay. I guess that makes sense. Then the example of the American company with   `Q21`
                   British management . . . when the company is in India . . . that would be a third-country
                   pattern.

Professor: Yes. In fact, this pattern is fairly prevalent among multinational companies in the United States. Many Scottish or English managers have been hired for top management positions at United States subsidiaries in the former British colonies—India, Jamaica, the West Indies, some parts of Africa . . .

Student: Okay. So I've got all the examples right now.

Professor: Anything else?

Student: Just one thing. There were some typical patterns for certain countries.

Professor: Like the last example.

Student: No. This came later in the lecture. Something about Japan and Europe.

Q22 Professor: Oh. Right. I probably said that both Japanese multinational companies and European companies tend to assign senior-level home country managers to overseas locations for their entire careers, whereas multinational companies in the United States view overseas assignments as temporary, so they may actually find themselves reporting to a senior-level manager from the host country who has more experience.

Student: So, for example, a Japanese company in the United States would most probably have senior-level Japanese managers with mid-level managers maybe from the United States. But in Japan, the senior-level Japanese managers at an American company would probably have mid-level American managers reporting to them?

Professor: Well, generalities are always a little tricky, but for the most part, that would be a typical scenario. Because living as a permanent expatriate is a career move in Japan, but a temporary strategy in the United States.

Student: Okay. That's interesting.

Professor: And important for you to know as a business major with an interest in international business. You're still on that track, aren't you?

Student: I sure am. But, you know, I wasn't thinking in terms of living abroad for my entire career. That really is a huge commitment, and something to ask about going in. Anyway, like you say, most American companies view overseas assignments as temporary. That's more what I have in mind, for myself, I mean.

Audio 18. Why does the woman go to see her professor?
Answer B To clarify some of the information from a lecture

Audio 19. According to the professor, which factor causes staffing patterns to vary?
Answer D The number of years that a company has been in business

Audio 20. Listen again to part of the conversation and then answer the following question.
Replay "I think it's the one where home country nationals are put in charge of the company if it's located in a developed country, but in a developing country, then home country nationals manage the company sort of indefinitely."
"Right again. And an example of that would be . . ."
Audio Why does the professor say this:
Replay "And an example of that would be . . ."
Answer B Sometimes professors begin a statement and pause to allow the student to continue.

Audio 21. Which of the following would be an example of a third-country pattern?
Answer A A Scottish manager in an American company in Africa
C A British manager in an American company in India

Audio 22. According to the professor, how do senior-level Japanese managers view their assignments abroad?
Answer A They consider them to be permanent career opportunities.

LISTENING 5 "ASTRONOMY CLASS"

Audio Discussion

Narrator: Listen to part of a discussion in an astronomy class. The professor is talking about the solar system.

Professor:

Okay, let's get started. Um, as you know today I promised to take you on a walk through the solar system, so let's start here with the central object of our solar system—the Sun. As you can see, the Sun is about five inches in diameter and that's about the size of a large grapefruit, which is exactly what I've used to represent it here in our model. So, I'm going to take two steps and that will bring me to the planet closest to the Sun. That would be Mercury. Two more steps to Venus. And one step from Venus to Earth. Let's continue walking three steps from Earth to Mars. And that's as far as I can go here in the classroom, but we can visualize the rest of the journey. Don't bother writing this down. Just stay with me on this. So, to go from Mars to Jupiter, we'd have to walk a little over half the length of a football field, so that would put us about at the library here on campus, and then to get from Jupiter to Saturn, we'd have to walk another 75 yards, so by then we'd be at Harmon Hall. From Saturn to Uranus, we'd have to walk again as far as we'd gone in our journey from the Sun to Saturn, and so we'd probably be at the Student Union. From Uranus to Neptune we'd have to walk the same distance again, which would take us all the way to the graduate dormitory towers. From Neptune to Pluto, another 125 yards. So, we'd end up about one third of a mile from this classroom at the entrance to the campus. | Q24

Okay. That's interesting, but now I want you to think about the orbits of the planets in those locations. Clearly, the first four planets could orbit fairly comfortably in this room, but to include the others, we'd have to occupy an area of more than six-tenths of a mile, which is all the way from College Avenue to Campus Drive. Remember that for this scale, the Sun is five inches, and most of the planets are smaller than the lead on a sharpened pencil. Okay, with that in mind, I want you to think about space. Sure, there are some moons around a few planets, and a scattering of asteroids and comets, but really, there isn't a lot out there in such a vast area. It's, well, it's pretty empty. And that's what I really want to demonstrate with this exercise.

Now, it would really be even more impressive if you could actually make that walk, and actually you can, if you visit Washington, D.C., where a scale model is set up on the National Mall, starting at the National Air and Space Museum and ending up at the Arts and Industries Museum. I did that a couple of years ago, and it was, well amazing. Even though I knew the distances intellectually, there's nothing like the experience. Has anybody else done that walk?

Student 1:

I have. And you're right. It's an eye-opener. It took me about twenty minutes to go from the Sun to Pluto because I stopped to read the information at each planet, but when I made the return trip, it was about ten minutes.

Professor: Did you take pictures?

Student 1:   I didn't. But, you know, I don't think it would have captured it anyway.

Professor:

I think you're right. What impressed me about doing it was to see what was not there. I mean, how much space was between the bodies in the solar system. And a photograph wouldn't have shown that. | Q25

So back to our model. Here's another thought for you. The scale for our model is 1 to 10 billion. Now, let's suppose that we want to go to the nearest star system, the neighbor to our solar system. That would be the Alpha Centauri system, which is a little less than four and a half light years away. Okay. Let's walk it on our model. Here we are on the East Coast of the United States. So if we want to make it all the way to Alpha Centauri, we have to hike all the way to the West Coast, roughly a distance of 2,700 miles. And that's just the closest one. To make a model of the Milky Way Galaxy would require a completely different scale because . . . because the surface of the Earth wouldn't be large enough to accommodate a model at the scale of 1 to 10 billion.

Now, let's stop here for a minute because I just want to be sure that we're all together on the terms *solar system* and *galaxy*. Remember that our solar system is a single star, the Sun, with various bodies orbiting around it—nine planets and their moons, and asteroids, comets, meteors. But the galaxy has a lot of star systems—probably 100 billion of them. Okay? This is important because you can be off by almost 100 billion if you get confused by these terms. Not a good idea.

Q26

Okay, then, even if we could figure out a different scale that would let us make a model of the Milky Way Galaxy, even then, it would be challenging to make 100 billion stars, which is what you'd have to do to complete the model. How many would that be exactly? Well, just try to count all the grains of sand on all the beaches on Earth. That would be about 100 billion. But of course, you couldn't even count them in your lifetime, could you? If you'd started counting in 1000 B.C.E. you'd be finishing just about now, with the counting, I mean. But of course, that assumes that you wouldn't sleep or take any breaks.

Q27

So, what am I hoping for from this lecture? What do you think I want you to remember?

Q23   Student 2:   Well, for one thing, the enormous distances . . .

Student 3:   . . . and the vast emptiness in space.

Professor:
That's good. I hope that you'll also begin to appreciate the fact that the Earth isn't the center of the universe. Our planet, although it's very beautiful and unique, it's still just one planet, orbiting around just one star in just one galaxy.

Audio   23.   What is the discussion mainly about?
Answer   C   The vast expanse of the universe around us.

Audio   24.   Listen again to part of the lecture and then answer the following question.
Replay   "And that's as far as I can go here in the classroom, but we can visualize the rest of the journey. Don't bother writing this down. Just stay with me on this."
Audio   Why does the professor say this:
Replay   "Don't bother writing this down. Just stay with me on this."
Answer   B   Sometimes a professor will tell students to stop taking notes, which usually means that the information is not a main point or, in this case, the professor wants the students to concentrate on listening.

Audio   25.   Why wouldn't a photograph capture a true picture of the solar system walk?
Answer   A   It would not show the distances between the bodies in space.

Audio   26.   How does the professor explain the term *solar system*?
Answer   D   He contrasts a solar system with a galaxy.

Audio   27.   Listen again to part of the lecture and then answer the following question.
Replay   "So, what am I hoping for from this lecture? What do you think I want you to remember?"
          "Well, for one thing, the enormous distances . . . "
          ". . . and the vast emptiness in space."
          "That's good. I hope that you'll also begin to appreciate the fact that the Earth isn't the center of the universe."

Audio		Why does the professor say this:
Replay		"So, what am I hoping for from this lecture? What do you think I want you to remember?"
Answer	**C**	When professors ask their students to think about what they might want them to remember, this usually signals the beginning of a summary of the important points.

Audio	28.	What can be inferred about the professor?
Answer	**B**	The professor likes his students to participate in the discussion.

LISTENING 6 "PSYCHOLOGY CLASS"

Audio Discussion

Narrator: Listen to part of a discussion in a psychology class. The professor is discussing defense mechanisms.

Professor:

Okay, we know from our earlier study of Freud that defense mechanisms protect us from bringing painful thoughts or feelings to the surface of our consciousness. We do this because our minds simply can't tolerate these thoughts. So, defense mechanisms help us to express these painful thoughts or feelings in another way, while we repress the real problem. The function of defense mechanisms is to keep from being overwhelmed. Of course, the avoidance of problems can result in additional emotional issues. And there's a huge distinction between repression and suppression. Anybody want to explain the difference? `Q29`

Student 1:

I'll try it. I think *repression* is an unconscious response to serious events or images but *suppression* is more conscious and deals with something unpleasant but not usually, well, terrible experiences. `Q30`

Professor:

I couldn't have said it better. Now remember that the thoughts or feelings that we're trying to *repress* may include, just to mention a few, anger, depression, competition, uh . . . fear, envy, hate, and so on. For instance, let's suppose that you're very angry with your professor. Not me, of course. I'm referring to another professor. So, you're very angry because he's treated you unfairly in some way that . . . that could cause you to lose your scholarship. Maybe he failed you on an examination that didn't really cover the material that he'd gone over in class, and an F grade in the course is going to be unacceptable to your sponsors. So, this would be very painful, as I'm sure you'd agree. And I'd say it would qualify as a serious event. `Q34` `Q35`

So let's take a look at several different types of defense mechanisms that you might employ to repress the feelings of disappointment, rage perhaps, and . . . and even violence that you'd feel toward the professor. Most of them are named so the mechanism is fairly obvious and one of the most common mechanisms is *denial*, which is . . . `Q29`

Student 2:   If I want to deny something, I'll just say I'm not angry with the professor.

Professor:

Exactly. You may even extend the denial to include the sponsors, and you could tell your friends that they'd never revoke your scholarship. And this mechanism would allow you to deny the problem, even in the face of direct evidence to the contrary. Let's say, a letter from the sponsor indicating that you won't receive a scholarship for the next term. . . . Okay on that one? Okay. How about *rationalization*?

Student 2:   Well, in rationalization, you come up with some reasons *why* the professor might have given an unfair test.

Professor: And how would you do that?

Student 2:   Well, you might defend him. You could say that he gave the test to encourage students to learn information on their own. Is that what you mean?

Professor:
Sure. Because you'd be rationalizing . . . providing a reason that justifies an otherwise mentally intolerable situation. Okay, another example of rationalizing is to excuse the sponsor for refusing to hear your side of the situation. You might say that sponsors are too busy to investigate why students are having problems in their classes. And you might do that while you deny your true feelings that sponsors really should be more open to hearing you out.

Student 3:   So when you deny something, I mean when you use denial, you're refusing to acknowledge a situation, but . . . when you use rationalization, you're excusing the behavior?

Professor:
Excellent summary. So, now let me give you another option. If you use a *reaction formation* as a defense mechanism, you'll proclaim the *opposite* of your feelings. In this case, what would you say about the professor?

Student 4:   I'd say that I like the professor when, in fact, I hate him for destroy . . . depriving me of my opportunity.

Professor:
And you might insist that you have no hard feelings and even go so far as to tell your friends that he's an excellent teacher. You see, a reaction formation turns the expression of your feelings into the opposite reaction, that is, on the surface.

And that brings us to *projection*, which is a defense mechanism that tricks your mind into believing that someone else is guilty of the negative thought or feeling that *you* have.

Student 1:   Can you give us an example of that one?

Professor:
Okay. Feelings of hate for the professor might be expressed by telling classmates about *another* student who hates the professor, or, uh, . . . or even suggesting that the professor has strong feelings of hate for *you* but you really like the professor yourself. So you would project, um, . . . attribute your feelings . . . to someone else. Get it?

Student 1:   So if I hate someone, I'd believe that another person hates him or that he hates me.

Professor: But you wouldn't admit that *you* hate him yourself.

Student: Okay. That's projection.

Professor:
Q32 Now *displacement* serves as a defense mechanism when a less threatening person or object is substituted for the person or object that's really the cause of your anxiety. So, instead of confronting the professor about the unfair test, well, you might direct your anger toward the friend who studied for the test with you, and you could blame him for wasting your time on the material that was in the book and notes.

Of course, there are several other defense mechanisms like *fantasy*, which includes daydreaming or watching television maybe to escape the problems at school. Or *regression,* which includes immature behaviors that are no longer appropriate, like, uh, maybe expressing temper in the same way that a preschooler might respond to having a toy snatched away. And your textbook contains a few more that we haven't touched on in class.

Just one more thing, it's good to understand that the notion of unconscious thoughts and the mechanisms that allow us to manage them, that this is a concept that goes in and out of fashion. Many psychologists rejected defense mechanisms altogether during the 70s and 80s, and then in the 90s, cognitive psychologists showed a renewed interest in research in this area. But I must warn you, that although they found similar responses, they tended to give them different names. For instance, *denial* might appear in a more recent study as *positive illusion*, or *scapegoating* might be referred to instead of *displacement*. But when you get right down to it, the same categories of behavior for defense mechanisms still exist in the research even if they're labeled differently. And, uh, in my view, if you compare Freud's traditional defense mechanisms with those that are being presented by more modern researchers, you'll find that Freud is easier to understand and gives us a broader perspective. And, if you understand Freud's categories, well, you'll certainly be able to get a handle on the newer terms. What is exciting about the modern studies is the focus on coping skills and what's being referred to as healthy defenses. So next time, we'll take a look at some of these processes.

Audio	29.	What is the discussion mainly about?
Answer	**C**	Some of the more common types of defense mechanisms

Audio	30.	How does the student explain the term *repression*?
Answer	**A**	He contrasts it with suppression.

Audio	31.	Listen again to part of the discussion and then answer the following question.
Replay		"For instance, let's suppose that you're very angry with your professor. Not me, of course. I'm referring to another professor. So, you're very angry because he's treated you unfairly in some way that . . . that could cause you to lose your scholarship."
Audio		Why does the professor say this:
Replay		"Not me, of course. I'm referring to another professor."
Answer	**B**	The professor's tone is not serious. She is joking.

Audio	32.	Which of the following is an example of *displacement* that was used in the lecture?
Answer	**C**	Blaming someone in your study group instead of blaming the professor

Audio	33.	According to the professor, what happened in the 1990s?
Answer	**B**	New terms were introduced for the same mechanisms.

Audio	34.	How does the professor organize the lecture?
Answer	**B**	She uses a scenario that students can relate to. She talks about the way that a student might respond to a professor by using defense mechanisms.

LISTENING 7 "BOOKSTORE"

Audio Conversation

Narrator: Listen to part of a conversation in the bookstore.

Student: Excuse me. I'm looking for someone who can help me with the textbook reservation program.

Manager: Oh, well, I can do that. What do you need?

	Student:	Okay. Um, my friend told me that I could get used books if I order, I mean, preorder them now.
	Manager:	That's right. Do you want to do that?
Q35	Student:	I think so, but I'm not sure how it works.
	Manager:	Actually, it's fairly straightforward. We have a short form for you to fill out. Do you know what you're going to take next semester?
	Student:	Yeah, I do.
	Manager:	And you have the course names and the schedule numbers for all your classes?
	Student:	Unhuh.
	Manager:	Okay, then, just put that information down on the form and, uh, make a checkmark in the box if you want recommended books as well as required books. And you said you were interested in used books, right?
	Student:	Right.
	Manager:	So mark the box for used books, sign the form and bring it back to me.
	Student:	Do I have to pay now? Or, do you want a deposit?
	Manager:	No, you can pay when you pick up the books.
	Student:	And when can I do that?
	Manager:	The week before classes begin.
	Student:	That's good, but, um, what if I change my schedule? I mean, I don't plan to but . . .
Q36	Manager:	. . . it happens. Don't worry. If you change classes, you can just bring the books back any time two weeks from the first day of class to get a full refund. Of course, you'll need the original cash register receipt and a photo ID and, if it's a new book, you can't have any marks in it. But you said you wanted used books, so it won't matter.
	Student:	Yeah, that's the main reason why I want to do this—because I'll have a better chance to get used books.
	Manager:	If there are used books available and you marked the form, that's what we'll pull for you.
	Student:	Okay, thanks a lot. I'll just fill this out and bring it back to you later today. I don't have all the numbers with me, the section numbers for the classes.
	Manager:	Fine. We need those numbers because when different professors are teaching the same class, they don't always order the same books.
	Student:	Right. So, will you be here this afternoon?
Q37	Manager:	I probably will, but if I'm not, just give the form to the person in this office. Don't give it to one of the student employees, though. They're usually very good about getting the forms back to the office, but sometimes it gets really busy and . . . you know how it is.
	Student:	Sure. Well, I'll bring it back to the office myself.
Q38	Manager:	That's probably a good idea. And, oh, uh, one more thing. I should tell you that the used books tend to go first, so, if you want to be sure that you get used books . . .
Q39	Student:	You know what? I'm going to go right back to the dorm to get those numbers now, while you're still here.
	Manager:	Okay. That's good.

Audio 35. What does the man need from the bookstore?
Answer **B** A form to order books

Audio 36. What does the man need if he wants a full refund?
Answer **A** Identification
      C A receipt for the purchase

Audio 37. Listen again to part of the conversation and then answer the following question.
Replay "Don't give it to one of the student employees, though. They're usually very good about getting the forms back to the office, but sometimes it gets really busy and . . . you know how it is."

Audio   What does the woman mean when she says this:
Replay   ". . . sometimes it gets really busy and . . . you know how it is."
Answer   A   She is not sure that the student employee will give her the form. The phrase "you know how it is" implies that the man will be able to make a logical conclusion. If the student employees are very busy, they might forget to take the forms to the office.

Audio   38.   What does the woman imply about the used books she sells?
Answer   A   They are purchased before new books.

Audio   39.   What does the man need to do now?
Answer   D   Locate the schedule numbers for his classes. They are in his room at the dorm.

LISTENING 8 "ENVIRONMENTAL SCIENCE CLASS"

Audio Lecture
Narrator: Listen to part of a lecture in an environmental science class.

Professor:
Hydrogen is the most recent and, I'd say, one of the most promising, in a long list of alternatives to petroleum. Some of the possibilities include batteries, methanol, natural gas, and, well, you name it. But hydrogen fuel cells have a couple of advantages over some of the other options. First of all, they're really quiet, and they don't pollute the atmosphere. Besides that, hydrogen is the most abundant element in the universe, and it can be produced from a number of sources, including ammonia, or . . . or even water. So, it's renewable, and there's an almost unlimited supply.

Q40

Q41

Okay. Now fuel cells represent a radical departure from the conventional internal combustion engine and even a fairly fundamental change from electric battery power. Like batteries, fuel cells run on electric motors; however, batteries use electricity from an external source and store it for use in the battery while the fuel cells create their own electricity through a chemical process that uses hydrogen and oxygen from the air. Are you with me? Look, by producing energy in a chemical reaction rather than through combustion, a fuel cell can convert, say 40–60 percent of the energy from the hydrogen into electricity. And when this ratio is compared with that of a combustion engine that runs at about half the efficiency of a fuel cell, well, it's obvious that fuel cell technology has the potential to revolutionize the energy industry.

So, fuel cells have the potential to generate power for almost any kind of machinery or equipment that fossil fuels run, but, the most important, um, let's say goal, the goal of fuel cell technology is the introduction of fuel cell powered vehicles. Internationally, the competition is fierce to commercialize fuel cell cars. I guess all of the leading automobile manufacturers worldwide have concept cars that use fuel cells, and some of them can reach speeds of as high as 90 miles per hour. Even more impressive is the per tank storage capacity. Can you believe this? Some of those cars can run for 220 miles between refills. But many of those cars were designed decades ago, so . . . what's the holdup?

Well, the problem in introducing fuel cell technology is really twofold. In the first place, industries will have to invest millions, maybe even billions of dollars to refine the technology—and here's the real cost—the infrastructure to, uh, support the fueling of the cars. And by infrastructure, I mean basic facilities and services like hydrogen stations to refuel cars and mechanics who know how to repair them. I think you get the picture. And then, consumers will have to accept and use the new products powered by fuel cells. So, we're going to need educational programs to inform the public about the safety and . . . and convenience of fuel cells, if we're going to achieve a successful transition to fuel cell products. But, unfortunately, major funding efforts get interrupted. Here's what I mean. When oil prices are high, then there seems to be more funding and greater interest in basic research and development, and more public awareness of fuel cells, and then the price of oil goes down a little and the funding dries up and people just go back to using their fossil fueled products. And this has been going on for more than thirty years.

Q44

Q42   Some government sponsored initiatives have created incentives for fuel cell powered vehicles but probably one of the most successful programs, at least in my opinion, is, uh, the STEP program, which is an acronym for the Sustainable Transportation Energy Program. STEP is a demonstration project sponsored by the government of Western Australia. Now, in this project, gasoline driven buses have been replaced with fuel cell buses on regular transportation routes. I think that British Petroleum is the supplier of the hydrogen fuel, which is produced at an oil refinery in Kwinana, south of Perth. So we need to watch this carefully. Another collaborative research effort is being undertaken by the European Union and the United States. Scientists and engineers are trying to develop a fuel cell that's effectively

Q43   engineered and attractive to the commercial market. Now, under an agreement signed in about 2000, if memory serves, it was 2003, but anyway, the joint projects include the writing of codes and standards, the design of fueling infrastructures, the refinement of fuel cell models, and the demonstration of fuel cell vehicles. In Europe, the private sector will combine efforts with government agencies in the public sector to, uh, to create a long-term plan for the introduction of fuel cells throughout the E.U. And the World Bank is providing funding to promote the development and manufacture of fuel cell buses for public transportation in China, Egypt, Mexico, and India, and we're starting to see some really interesting projects in these areas. So, uh, clearly, fuel cell technology is an international effort.

Okay, at the present time, Japan leads the way in addressing the issues of modifying the infrastructure. Several fueling stations that dispense hydrogen by the cubic meter are already in place, with plans for more. But even when a nationwide system is completed, decisions about how and where to produce the hydrogen and how to transport it will still have to be figured out. Most countries share the view that fleets of vehicles have significant advantages for the introduction of fuel cell powered transportation because, well obviously they can be fueled at a limited number of central locations. And, uh, and other benefits of a fleet are the opportunity to provide training for a maintenance crew and for the drivers. As for consumer education, no one country seems to have made the advances there that . . . that would serve as a model for the rest of us. But perhaps when the demonstration projects have concluded and

Q45   a few model cars are available to the public, well, more attention will be directed to public information programs.

Audio	40.	What is this lecture mainly about?
Answer	**A**	An overview of fuel cell technology. The professor discusses the process for producing energy, the efficiency of the cells, the problems, and some model programs.
Audio	41.	Listen again to part of the lecture and then answer the following question.
Replay		"Hydrogen is the most recent and, I'd say, one of the most promising, in a long list of alternatives to petroleum. Some of the possibilities include batteries, methanol, natural gas, and, well, you name it."
Audio		What does the professor mean when he says this:
Replay		"Some of the possibilities include batteries, methanol, natural gas, and, well, you name it."
Answer	**D**	He does not plan to talk about the alternatives. The comment "you name it" implies that there are a large number of alternatives and that he is not interested in them.
Audio	42.	Why does the professor mention the STEP program in Australia?
Answer	**D**	He thinks it is a very good example of a project.
Audio	43.	Listen again to part of the conversation and then answer the following question.
Replay		"Now, under an agreement signed in about 2000, if memory serves, it was 2003, but anyway, the joint projects include the writing of codes and standards, the design of fueling infrastructures, the refinement of fuel cell models, and the demonstration of fuel cell vehicles."

Audio		Why does the professor say this:
Replay		" . . . if memory serves, it was 2003 . . . "
Answer	**D**	To show that he is uncertain about the date

Audio	44.	What are some of the problems associated with fuel cell technology?
Answer	**B**	Public acceptance
	D	Investment in infrastructures

Audio	45.	What is the professor's attitude toward fuel cells?
Answer	**B**	He is hopeful about their development in the future. He would like more attention to be directed to public information programs, which would solve one of the major problems for fuel cell technology.

LISTENING 9 "PHILOSOPHY CLASS"

Audio Discussion

Narrator: Listen to part of a discussion in a philosophy class.

Professor:

Humanism is a philosophical position that places the dignity of the individual at the center of its movement. A primary principle of humanism—I don't need to spell that for you, do I? Okay, a primary principle of humanism is that human beings are rational and have an innate predisposition for good. Although humanism is associated with the beginning of the Reformation, the humanist philosophy was not new when it became popular in Italy during the Middle Ages. In fact, according to the ancient Greek philosopher, Protagoras, mankind was "the measure of all things." And this idea was echoed by Sophocles when he said, "Many are the wonders of the world, and none so wonderful as mankind." This is classical humanism. Man as the ideal at the center of all creation. Even the ancient Greek gods were viewed as resembling man both physically and psychologically. And, in a sense, isn't this personification of the deity just another way to exalt human beings? But that aside, it was precisely the rediscovery and translation of classical manuscripts that coincided with the invention of printing presses around the mid-15th century, which, uh, . . . which provided a catalyst for the humanistic movement throughout Europe. As the clergy and upper classes participated in the rediscovery and dissemination of classical literature, humanism became popular among theologians and scholars, and soon set the stage for the Renaissance. This one, I'll spell. Does anybody remember the meaning of the word *renaissance*?

Q46

Q47

Student 1:   Rebirth, renewal.

Professor:

Right you are. *Renaissance* literally means "rebirth," and it refers to the return to ancient Greek and Roman art and literature, which, like all things in the humanistic tradition, they were measured by human standards. Art returned to the classical principles of harmony and balance. In the field of architecture, we see both religious and secular buildings styled after ancient Roman designs, with mathematical proportions and . . . a human scale, a scale that contrasted with the Medieval Gothic buildings of the previous era. Public works such as bridges and aqueducts from the Roman occupation were repaired, restored, or rebuilt. In the sculptures of the period, nude figures were modeled in life-sized images, with true proportions, and it was also at this point that realism became the standard for painting, with a preference for naturalistic settings and the placement of figures in . . . realistic proportion to those settings. It was also evident that the portraits tended to be more personal and authentic. And artists even produced self-portraits at this time. Remember, the figures in the paintings of the previous era tended to be of another world, but Renaissance painters placed recognizable human beings in *this* world. In music, there was an effort to create harmonies that were pleasing to the human ear and melodies that were compatible with the human voice. In addition, music lessons became more widespread as a source of education and enjoyment. Dancing increased in popularity with a concurrent trend toward music that had rhythm and invited movement as a pleasurable activity.

Student 2:   Wasn't that why Latin became so important?

Professor:
Yes. Both Greek and Latin became important as tools for scholarship, and classical Latin became the basis for an international language of the intellectuals throughout Europe. To be true to humanism, and all it represented, it was necessary to be knowledgeable about, and, uh, . . . and faithful to the ancient philosophies as expressed in their writing, and how best to express them than in the original languages? **Q49** By the way, Latin as a universal language for clerics and the aristocracy, this encouraged the exchange of ideas on a wider scale than ever before, and legitimized in a sense the presumption that mankind was at the center of all things. It also made it possible for individual scholars to make a name for themselves and establish their place in the history of mankind.

Q48 Well, it was at this time that a close association, almost a partnership was forged between art and science. In their efforts to be precise, sculptors and painters studied the human form. In effect, they became anatomists. You may recall the drawing in your textbook, the one by Leonardo da Vinci which demonstrates the geometrical proportions of the human body. And, of course, Alberti, in his many books on architecture, sculpture, and painting . . . he emphasized the study of mathematics as the underlying principle of all the arts. Whereas artists had considered themselves craftsmen in the Middle Ages, the great Renaissance artists viewed themselves as intellectuals, philosophers, if you will, of humanism. They were designing a world for human beings to live in and enjoy. One that was in proportion and in harmony with mankind. So, perhaps you can see why the so-called Renaissance man emerged.

Student 1:   Okay. But exactly what is the definition of a Renaissance man? I know it means a very talented person, but . . .

Professor:
Q50 Good question. Sometimes we use these terms without really defining them. So I would say that a Renaissance man would be talented, as you said, but would also have to demonstrate broad interests . . . in both the arts and the sciences. The quality that was most admired in the Renaissance was the extraordinary, maybe even . . . universality of talents . . . in diverse fields of endeavor. After all, this quality proved that mankind was capable of reason and creation, that humanism was justified in placing man in the center of the world, as the measure of all things in it. With the humanistic philosophy as a justification, scholars would interpret the ancient classics and some of them would argue to a reasonable conclusion a very new and more secular society built on individual, human effort. It was not difficult for the Renaissance man to make the leap of logic from classical humanism to political humanism, which encouraged freedom of thought, and indeed even democracy, within both the church and the state. But that is a topic for another day.

Audio	46.	What is the main focus of this discussion?
Answer	**C**	The other topics are mentioned in the discussion as they relate to the main focus: Humanism.

Audio	47.	Listen again to part of the discussion and then answer the following question.
Replay		"A primary principle of humanism—I don't need to spell that for you, do I? Okay, a primary principle of humanism is that human beings are rational and have an innate predisposition for good."
Audio		Why does the professor say this:
Replay		"I don't need to spell that for you, do I?"
Answer	**B**	Her tone indicates that she assumes that the students know how to spell the term. Later, she spells a more difficult term.

Audio   48.   Why does the professor mention the drawing by Leonardo da Vinci?
Answer   B   She uses it as an example of the union of art and science.

Audio   49.   According to the professor, what was the effect of using Latin as a universal language of scholarship?
Answer   A   It facilitated communication among intellectuals in many countries.

Audio   50.   According to the professor, what can be inferred about a Renaissance man?
Answer   B   He would have an aptitude for both art and science.

Audio   51.   All of the following characteristics are true of humanism EXCEPT
Answer   B   Scholars must serve society.

➤ Speaking

Model Test 1, Speaking Section, CD 1, Track 2

INDEPENDENT SPEAKING QUESTION 1 "MARRIAGE PARTNER"

Narrator 2: Number 1. Listen for a question about a familiar topic. After you hear the question, you have 15 seconds to prepare and 45 seconds to record your answer.

Narrator 1: Describe an ideal marriage partner. What qualities do you think are most important for a husband or wife? Use specific reasons and details to explain your choices.

Narrator 2: Please prepare your answer after the beep.

Beep

[Preparation time: 15 seconds]

Narrator 2: Please begin speaking after the beep.

Beep

[Recording time: 45 seconds]

Beep

INDEPENDENT SPEAKING QUESTION 2 "NEWS"

Narrator 2: Number 2. Listen for a question that asks your opinion about a familiar topic. After you hear the question, you have 15 seconds to prepare and 45 seconds to record your answer.

Narrator 1: Some people like to watch the news on television. Other people prefer to read the news in a newspaper. Still others use their computers to get the news. How do you prefer to be informed about the news and why? Use specific reasons and examples to support your choice.

Narrator 2: Please prepare your answer after the beep.

Beep

[Preparation time: 15 seconds]

Narrator 2: Please begin speaking after the beep.

Beep

[Recording time: 45 seconds]

Beep

INTEGRATED SPEAKING QUESTION 3 *"MEAL PLAN"*

Narrator 2: Number 3. Read a short passage and listen to a talk on the same topic. Then listen for a question about them. After you hear the question, you have 30 seconds to prepare and 60 seconds to record your answer.

Narrator 1: A new meal plan is being offered by the college. Read the plan in the college newspaper printed on page 60. You have 45 seconds to complete it. Please begin reading now.

[Reading time: 45 seconds]

Narrator 1: Now listen to two students who are talking about the plan.

Man:	I don't like to cook, but I don't like to eat in the cafeteria every day either.
Woman:	True. The food does get kind of . . . same old same old.
Man:	My point exactly. And besides, I go home about every other weekend, so paying for my meals when I'm not there doesn't make a lot of sense.
Woman:	Right. So you'll probably sign up for the five-day plan next semester.
Man:	I already did. If I want to eat in the cafeteria some weekend, I can just buy a meal, but I'd probably go out somewhere with my friends if I'm here over the weekend.
Woman:	Well, I don't go home on the weekends as much as you do, but I still eat out a lot on the weekends.
Man:	So the five-day plan might work out better for you, too. I'm really glad to have the option.

Narrator 1: The man expresses his opinion of the new meal plan. Report his opinion, and explain the reasons that he gives for having that opinion.

Narrator 2: Please prepare your answer after the beep.

Beep

[Preparation time: 30 seconds]

Narrator 2: Please begin speaking after the beep.

Beep

[Recording time: 60 seconds]

Beep

 Model Test 1, Speaking Section, CD 2, Track 1

INTEGRATED SPEAKING QUESTION 4 "ABORIGINAL PEOPLE"

Narrator 2: Number 4. Read a short passage and listen to a lecture on the same topic. Then listen for a question about them. After you hear the question, you have 30 seconds to prepare and 60 seconds to record your answer.

Narrator 1: Now read the passage about Aboriginal People printed on page 61. You have 45 seconds to complete it. Please begin reading now.

[Reading time: 45 seconds]

Narrator 1: Now listen to part of a lecture in an anthropology class. The professor is talking about Aboriginal People.

Professor:
According to your textbook, the Aboriginal People are very diverse, and, I would agree with that; however, there are certain beliefs that unite the groups, and in fact, allow them to identify themselves and others as members of the diverse Aboriginal societies. For one thing, unlike the anthropologists who believe that tribes arrived in eastern Australia from Tasmania about 40,000 years ago, the Aboriginal People believe that they have always been in Australia, and that they have sprung from the land. Evidence for this resides in the oral history that has been recorded in stories and passed down for at least fifty generations. This history is referred to as the "Dreaming." The stories teach moral and spiritual values and provide each member of the group with an identity that reflects the landscape where the person's mother first becomes aware of the unborn baby, or to put it in terms of the "Dreaming," where the spirit enters the mother's body. So, I am saying that the way that the Aboriginal People identify themselves and each other, even across groups, is by their membership in the oral history that they share.

Narrator 1: Explain how the Aboriginal People are identified. Draw upon information in both the reading and the lecture.

Narrator 2: Please prepare your answer after the beep.

Beep

[Preparation time: 30 seconds]

Narrator 2: Please begin speaking after the beep.

Beep

[Recording time: 60 seconds]

Beep

INTEGRATED SPEAKING QUESTION 5 "SCHEDULING CONFLICT"

Narrator 2: Number 5. Listen to a short conversation. Then listen for a question about it. After you hear the question, you have 20 seconds to prepare and 60 seconds to record your answer.

Narrator 1: Now listen to a conversation between a student and his friend.

Friend:	So what time should we pick you up on Friday? Can you be ready by noon or do you need another hour or so?
Student:	I really wanted to spend the weekend with my family, and the ride with you would have made it even more fun, but . . .
Friend:	You mean you aren't going?
Student:	I can't. I'm not doing too well in my economics class, and I have a lecture Friday afternoon. I don't think I should miss it.
Friend:	Well, why don't you borrow the notes from someone? Isn't your roommate in that class?
Student:	Yeah, he is. But I've already asked to borrow his notes once this semester. He didn't seem to mind though.
Friend:	Well, there you are. Unless you want to go to class on Thursday. I'm fairly sure that Dr. Collins teaches the same class Thursday night.
Student:	Really? She probably wouldn't mind if I sat in on the Thursday class, but I wonder if she'll give the same lecture. You know, maybe they're one week behind or one week ahead of us.
Friend:	I suppose that's possible, but it would be easy enough to find out. You could just tell her that you'd like to attend the Thursday session this week because you need to go out of town. Then you can ride home with us. If there's a problem, you can still borrow your roommate's notes on Sunday when we get back.

Narrator 1: Describe the man's problem and the two suggestions that his friend makes about how to handle it. What do you think the man should do, and why?

Narrator 2: Please prepare your answer after the beep.

Beep

[Preparation time: 20 seconds]

Narrator 2: Please begin speaking after the beep.

Beep

[Recording time: 60 seconds]

Beep

INTEGRATED SPEAKING QUESTION 6 "LABORATORY MICROSCOPE"

Narrator 2: Number 6. Listen to part of a talk. Then listen for a question about it. After you hear the question, you have 20 seconds to prepare and 60 seconds to record your answer.

Narrator 1: Now listen to part of a talk in a biology laboratory. The teaching assistant is explaining how to use the microscope.

Teaching Assistant:
All right, now that you all have microscopes at your tables, I want to explain how they work and how to use them. First of all, you should know that they are compound microscopes so they can magnify objects up to 1000 times their size. These microscopes have two systems—an illuminating system and an imaging system. You'll see that the illuminating system has a light source built in, and you can control it by adjusting the lever on the side. Why is this important? Well, the specimen must be pretty thin, or let's say, transparent enough to let light pass through it. So the light source controls the amount of light that passes through the specimen. Okay. The other system provides magnification. Use this lever to switch powers. So, when you switch to a higher power, you see a larger image, and when you switch to a lower power, you see a smaller image. But, I should remind you that the field of view is smaller at a higher power. In other words, at a higher magnification, you see a larger image of a smaller area. Okay. So what about the focus? Well, these microscopes are parfocal, and that means you usually don't have to refocus when you switch to a higher or lower power of magnification. But there are two adjustment knobs—the larger one for coarse adjustment and the smaller one for fine adjustment just in case.

Narrator 1: Using the main points and examples from the talk, describe the two major systems of the laboratory microscope, and then explain how to use it.

Narrator 2: Please prepare your answer after the beep.

Beep

[Preparation time: 20 seconds]

Narrator 2: Please begin speaking after the beep.

Beep

[Recording time: 60 seconds]

Beep

➤ Writing

INTEGRATED ESSAY "SCHOOL ORGANIZATION"

First, read the passage on page 64 and take notes.

    Model Test 1, Writing Section, CD 2, Track 2

Narrator: Now listen to a lecture on the same topic as the passage that you have just read.

Professor:
So what are the problems associated with the graded school system? Well, for one thing, graded schools don't take into account the . . . the differences in academic readiness on the part of individual learners. And by that I mean that some six-year-olds are simply not socially, mentally, or even physically mature enough to begin school, but others are ready in all of those important ways by their fifth or even fourth birthdays. And uh . . . by the time that girls and boys are in their early teens, we can see that there's a significant difference in maturity, in . . . in physical and social maturity but . . . they're still grouped together in intermediate grades in a graded school system.

Okay, besides the obvious differences in individual readiness and maturity, the . . . the whole issue of promotion needs to be reviewed. Grade-level requirements don't really deal with the actual learning that has occurred, uh, in a positive way. Many research studies confirm that repeating an entire year because some of the material is not learned contributes to . . . to boredom, poor self-concept, and . . . and eventually to higher drop-out rates. And since graded schools are using group expectations as measured by performance on standardized tests, this is another way to evaluate the group rather than the individual. So, what happens is that individual differences in how long it takes to learn a concept or . . . or the partial achievement of a grade-level curriculum . . . that is never addressed by the graded school system. Students who need more time to learn have to repeat material that they already know. Students who can learn at a faster rate have to wait for the new material to be presented. So, as you can see, it's not ideal.

➤ Example Answers and Checklists for Speaking and Writing

 Model Test 1, Example Answers, CD 2, Track 3

EXAMPLE ANSWER FOR INDEPENDENT SPEAKING QUESTION 1 "MARRIAGE PARTNER"

In my view, three characteristics are essential for a marriage partner. Compatibility is very important because spending the rest of your life with someone is a huge commitment, and without compatibility in values and interests, and goals, it could be a struggle rather than a partnership. Um, I also think that a good marriage partner should fit into your family. Without acceptance and affection for you as a couple, you could risk the relationships you have with family members. And attraction is another factor. Since fidelity is part of the marriage contract, the expression of love will be limited to your partner, so it should be a person you're attracted to.

Checklist 1

✔ The talk answers the topic question.
✔ The point of view or position is clear.
✔ The talk is direct and well-organized.
✔ The sentences are logically connected.
✔ Details and examples support the main idea.
✔ The speaker expresses complete thoughts.
✔ The meaning is easy to comprehend.
✔ A wide range of vocabulary is used.
✔ There are only minor errors in grammar.
✔ The talk is within a range of 125–150 words.

EXAMPLE ANSWER FOR INDEPENDENT SPEAKING QUESTION 2 "NEWS"

Although newspapers contain some information that's limited to local interests and I like to turn to those pages, for the most part, I prefer to get my news on TV and on my computer. The problem with printed news is it takes so long to produce it that the stories could have changed or more important news could have happened minutes after the newspaper is delivered. So, I scan the local stories in the paper when I get home from work, then I watch the international news on TV at night for the most current information, and the following morning, I click on one of the web sites that offer the most recent updates of the lead stories. That way, I'm taking advantage of the best aspects of all the news media, and I stay current locally and internationally.

Checklist 2

✔ The talk answers the topic question.
✔ The point of view or position is clear.
✔ The talk is direct and well-organized.
✔ The sentences are logically connected.
✔ Details and examples support the main idea.
✔ The speaker expresses complete thoughts.
✔ The meaning is easy to comprehend.
✔ A wide range of vocabulary is used.
✔ There are only minor errors in grammar.
✔ The talk is within a range of 125–150 words.

EXAMPLE ANSWER FOR INTEGRATED SPEAKING QUESTION 3 "MEAL PLAN"

The man is glad that an alternative to the seven-day meal plan is now available for students who live in the dorms. He'll purchase the five-day meal plan, which provides three meals on weekdays and the option to buy meals on the weekends for $3 each. The new five-day meal plan is better for him because he likes to go home every other weekend, and when he's on campus, he likes to go out with his friends. So he wasn't taking advantage of the cafeteria on the weekends even though he was paying for it. The Student Union has fast-food as well as booths in the food court for Chinese or Mexican food or even a salad bar. Besides, if he wants to eat in the cafeteria on a weekend, he can buy a meal. He should save about $48 a month by using the new plan, and he can use that money to eat out.

Checklist 3

✔ The talk summarizes the situation and opinion.
✔ The point of view or position is clear.
✔ The talk is direct and well-organized.
✔ The sentences are logically connected.
✔ Details and examples support the opinion.
✔ The speaker expresses complete thoughts.
✔ The meaning is easy to comprehend.
✔ A wide range of vocabulary is used.
✔ Errors in grammar are minor.
✔ The talk is within a range of 125–150 words.

EXAMPLE ANSWER FOR INTEGRATED SPEAKING QUESTION 4 "ABORIGINAL PEOPLE"

The Aboriginal People are culturally and linguistically diverse, in part because the geography dictated both limitations and opportunities for their communities. So the establishment of identity as a member of the Aboriginal People because of appearance, language, culture, or geographical location is not considered accurate. The Department of Education suggests that the best means of identification is to be recognized and accepted by other members of the Aboriginal society. Um, according to the lecturer, even diverse groups have certain unifying beliefs that are passed down as oral tradition, called the "Dreaming." The stories associated with this tradition are used to teach ethical principles and spiritual lessons. It would probably be through knowledge of this shared oral history that Aborigines would identify each other.

Checklist 4

✔ The talk relates an example to a concept.
✔ Inaccuracies in the content are minor.
✔ The talk is direct and well-organized.
✔ The sentences are logically connected.
✔ Details and examples support the opinion.
✔ The speaker expresses complete thoughts.
✔ The meaning is easy to comprehend.
✔ A wide range of vocabulary is used.
✔ The speaker paraphrases in his/her own words.
✔ The speaker credits the lecturer with wording.
✔ Errors in grammar are minor.
✔ The talk is within a range of 125–150 words.

EXAMPLE ANSWER FOR INTEGRATED SPEAKING QUESTION 5 "SCHEDULING CONFLICT"

The man would like to visit his family over the weekend, but his friends are leaving before his economics class on Friday. He doesn't want to miss the class because he needs to bring his grade up. His friend suggests that he borrow the notes from the class. His roommate didn't have a problem lending him notes from that class earlier in the semester, but he's reluctant to do that. The other possibility that his friend mentions is for him to attend another section of the same class on Thursday night, but he isn't sure that the professor will give the same lecture. To find out, he would have to ask the professor. In my opinion, the man should stay for his economics class and take notes. It's hard to read someone else's notes, and besides, if he's in the class, he can ask questions. If he wants to visit his family, he should try to find a ride on Saturday or on Friday after the class.

Checklist 5

✔ The talk summarizes the problem and recommendations.
✔ The speaker's point of view or position is clear.
✔ The talk is direct and well-organized.
✔ The sentences are logically connected.
✔ Details and examples support the opinion.
✔ The speaker expresses complete thoughts.
✔ The meaning is easy to comprehend.
✔ A wide range of vocabulary is used.
✔ Errors in grammar are minor.
✔ The talk is within a range of 125–150 words.

EXAMPLE ANSWER FOR INTEGRATED SPEAKING QUESTION 6 "LABORATORY MICROSCOPE"

The two major systems of the laboratory microscope are the illuminating system and the imaging system. The illuminating system has a light source that can be controlled to let more or less light pass through the specimen you're viewing when you move a lever on the side of the microscope. The imaging system is actually a magnification feature, which can be calibrated by using the other lever to change powers. When you look through a higher power, the image appears to be larger, and conversely, when you look through a lower power, it appears to be smaller. What that really means is when you use a higher magnification, the image actually shows you a smaller part of the specimen because it's enlarged. Now when you switch powers, the lenses will focus automatically, but the big knob will allow you to make a rough adjustment, and the small knob will let you make a more detailed adjustment, if you want.

Checklist 6

✔ The talk summarizes a short lecture.
✔ Inaccuracies in the content are minor.
✔ The talk is direct and well-organized.
✔ The sentences are logically connected.
✔ Details and examples support the opinion.
✔ The speaker expresses complete thoughts.
✔ The meaning is easy to comprehend.
✔ A wide range of vocabulary is used.
✔ The speaker paraphrases in his/her own words.
✔ The speaker credits the lecturer with wording.
✔ Errors in grammar are minor.
✔ The talk is within a range of 125–150 words.

EXAMPLE RESPONSE FOR INTEGRATED ESSAY "SCHOOL ORGANIZATION"

Some writers begin with an outline and others begin with a map of their ideas. Only the essay will be scored.

Outline

Graded school system
Disadvantages

- Maturity
    First grade
        6 yrs old
    Intermediate
        Boys, girls
- Progress
    Standardized test
        Repeat concepts
        Penalizes capable
- Dropout rate
    Repeat all
    Learned part

Map

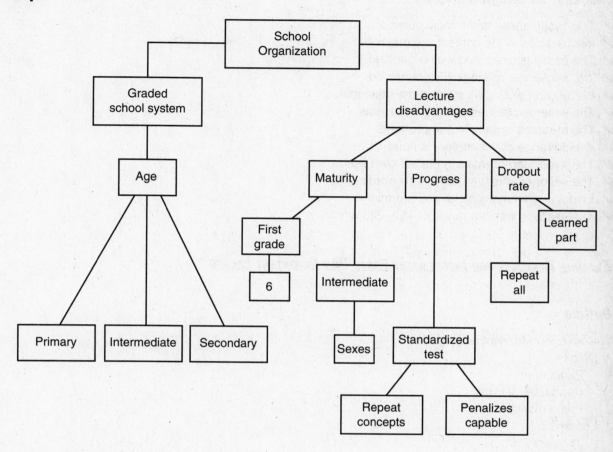

Example Essay

The graded school system, which groups students by age, is usually divided into primary, intermediate, and secondary grades. However, according to the lecture, there are several disadvantages to this type of system. In the first place, maturity is not considered. All students begin the first grade at six years old; however, many children are not mature enough to go to school at that age. In contrast, some younger children are ready for school before their sixth birthdays but are denied the opportunity to begin until they reach the required age of six. In addition, the disparity in the maturity of girls and boys is marked in the intermediate grades. Nevertheless, they are still scheduled for classes according to age, not maturity. Even more concerning is the problem of grade-level standards, which rely on testing to evaluate progress by age instead of by actual mastery on the part of individuals. The grade-level system is inefficient because it requires some learners to repeat concepts that they have already learned in order to master those that they still need to know. It also penalizes students who are capable of learning more material than the grade-level curriculum allows. Furthermore, research shows a correlation between low self-esteem and drop-out rates with the requirement that students repeat a calendar year because they have not learned part of the material for their grade.

Checklist for Integrated Essay

✔ The essay answers the topic question.
✔ Inaccuracies in the content are minor.
✔ The essay is direct and well-organized.
✔ The sentences are logically connected.
✔ Details and examples support the main idea.
✔ The writer expresses complete thoughts.
✔ The meaning is easy to comprehend.
✔ A wide range of vocabulary is used.
✔ The writer paraphrases in his/her own words.
✔ The writer credits the author with wording.
✔ Errors in grammar and idioms are minor.
✔ The essay is within a range of 150–225 words.

EXAMPLE RESPONSE FOR INDEPENDENT ESSAY "AN IMPORTANT LEADER"

Outline

William Lyon Mackenzie King
* Offices
    Parliament
    Head Liberal Party
    Prime minister
* Longevity
    21 years P.M.
    50 years public service
* Accomplishments
    Unity French + English provinces
    Represented all Canadians

Map

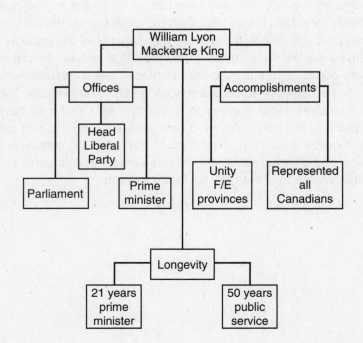

Example Essay

William Lyon Mackenzie King was a member of the Canadian parliament and head of the Liberal Party in the first half of the twentieth century. He held the office of prime minister for a total of twenty-one years, which is a longer period of time than that of any public servant in the history of Canada. Because his terms of office as prime minister were not consecutive, he held other positions of public service in many appointed and elected offices as well over a period of fifty years. Although it could be argued that he was an important world leader on the basis of longevity alone, I admire him because of his qualities of leadership. He was active in government during two world wars and the Great Depression and played a key role in guiding Canada during those very difficult years. He understood the importance of a unified nation and worked to bring various partisan groups together for the higher good of the country. Under his tenure in office, Canada became a participant in world affairs.

His three terms of office as prime minister were marked by compromise and often criticism, but he earned the respect of most Canadians for his political astuteness and his determination to unify Canada. In part because of his friendship with Wilfrid Laurier, he was able to preserve the unity between the French-speaking and English-speaking provinces, a negotiation that must be considered his greatest achievement. One biographer, John Moir of the University of Toronto, has identified a quality in King called "essential Canadianness." I understand this to mean that he was able to understand and represent all of the people of Canada.

King's methods were frustrating to some, but he was able to extend Canadian autonomy and maintain unity while acting within a difficult federal system. He did so for a very long time, even representing Canada in the international arena in his elder years. In my view, William Lyon Mackenzie King is worthy of being named in the company of John F. Kennedy and Martin Luther King as a world leader who made an important contribution to humanity.

Checklist for Independent Essay

✔ The essay answers the topic question.
✔ The point of view or position is clear.
✔ The essay is direct and well-organized.
✔ The sentences are logically connected.
✔ Details and examples support the main idea.
✔ The writer expresses complete thoughts.
✔ The meaning is easy to comprehend.
✔ A wide range of vocabulary is used.
✔ Various types of sentences are included.
✔ Errors in grammar and idioms are minor.
✔ The essay is within a range of 300–350 words.

MODEL TEST 2: PROGRESS TEST

➤ Reading

READING 1 "RESOURCES AND INDUSTRIALISM IN CANADA"

1. **B** "The building of the Temiskaming and Northern Ontario Railway led to the discovery of rich silver deposits." Choices A, C, and D are true, but they do not relate to the main point in paragraph 1, the resources in the western frontier.

2. **C** ". . . Sudbury became the world's largest nickel producer." Choice A is not correct because it is not mentioned directly in the paragraph. Choice B is not correct because Sudbury was a supplier, not a market for metals. Choice D is not correct because Sudbury is in Ontario, not in the Klondike.

3. **D** In this passage, *improve* is a synonym for "enhance." Context comes from the word "treasury" in the following sentence.

4. **B** ". . . the federal government created the Yukon Territory . . . in an effort to ward off the prospect of annexation to Alaska." Choice A is not correct because fortune-seekers were flocking there already. Choice C is not correct because the tales of lawlessness were told in popular fiction, but no effort to establish law and order was mentioned. Choice D is not correct because the legality of the mining claims was not mentioned.

5. **D** In this passage, *formerly* is a synonym for "previously." Context comes from the reference to "unsettled" for an area that was increasing in population.

6. **A** ". . . the tales [of the Klondike strike] . . . were immortalized through . . . the poetic verses of Robert W. Service." Choices B and C may have been true, but they were not mentioned in connection with the poetry of Robert Service. Choice D is not correct because the creation of the Yukon Territory, not the poetry, prevented the Klondike's annexation to Alaska.

7. **B** Choice A is mentioned in paragraph 3, sentence 2. Choice C is mentioned in paragraph 3, sentence 5. Choice D is mentioned in paragraph 3, sentence 4.

8. **D** In this passage, *Moreover* is a synonym for "Furthermore." Context comes from the addition of another way that the forest and water resources were exploited.

9. **C** *Federal taxes* paraphrases "the high tariff policies" and *cheaper imported goods* paraphrases "lower-priced foreign manufactured goods." . . . *protecting domestic industries* paraphrases "protecting existing industries" and *supporting new businesses* paraphrases "encouraging the creation of new enterprises."

10. **C** "To climb the tariff wall, large American industrial firms opened branches in Canada, and the governments of Ontario and Quebec aggressively urged them [American industrial firms] on by offering bonuses, subsidies, and guarantees to locate new plants." The pronoun "them" does not refer to Choices A, B, or D.

11. **A** ". . . the governments of Ontario and Quebec . . . [offered] bonuses, subsidies, and guarantees to locate new plants within their borders." Choice B is true, but it is not the reason why British and American businesses opened affiliates. Choice C is not correct because the consumers in western Canada were eager to buy goods from eastern and central Canada, not from abroad. Choice D is not correct because British investors contributed to the construction of urban infrastructure.

12. **C** Vocabulary reference is a transitional device that connects the insert sentence with the previous sentence. The connection is "Railway construction" and "discoveries of gold, silver, copper, lead, and zinc" to "The building of the . . . Railway" and "rich silver deposits."

13. **C, E, F** summarize the passage. Choices A and B are minor points that support major point C. Choice D is a minor point that supports major point E.

READING 2 "LOOKING AT THEATRE HISTORY"

14. **C** ". . . the buildings in later periods became sources of stone for other projects and what remains is usually broken and scattered." Choice A is not correct because other theatres have been identified and many of them have been excavated. Choice B is not correct because the archeologists were not the ones who broke the stones. Choice D is not correct because concrete was not mentioned as construction material during early periods. The word "concrete" in the passage means "true" or "verifiable" in reference to "evidence."

15. **B** ". . . many pieces are irrevocably lost." Choice A is not correct because drawings are conjectural. Choice C is not correct because the number of skenes that archeologists have excavated is not specified. Choice D is not correct because excavations did not begin until the late 1800s, not the early 1800s.

16. **B** In this passage, *important* is a synonym for "primary." Context comes from the phrase, "most concrete evidence."

17. **D** In this passage, *exact* is a synonym for "precise." Context comes from the contrast with the word "conjectural" in the same sentence.

18. **A** ". . . the myths on which dramatists drew were known to everyone, including vase painters, who might well depict the same subjects as dramatists." Choice B is not correct because reproductions were not mentioned. Choice C is not correct because the qualifications of scholars were not discussed. Choice D is not correct because thousands of vases have survived.

19. **B** In this passage, *debated* is a synonym for "controversial." Context comes from the phrases "easy to misinterpret" and "questionable assumption" in later sentences.

20. **D** ". . . these characters [women] often seem victims of their own powerlessness." Choice A is not correct because many plays featured strong female characters. Choice B is not correct because some critics have seen these plays [with women as victims] as rationalizations by the male-dominated culture and other critics have seen them as an attempt to examine this aspect of the culture. Choice C is not correct because plays featured numerous choruses of women.

21. **B** ". . . copies of plays had to be made by hand, and therefore the possibility of textual errors . . . was magnified." Choice A is not correct because the problem of sources was identified for archeological findings, not written evidence. Choices C and D are not mentioned as problems for written evidence.

22. **B** ". . . the majority of written references to Greek theatre date from several hundred years after the events they report. The writers seldom mention their sources of evidence, and thus we do not know what credence to give them [the sources]." The pronoun "them" does not refer to Choices A, C, or D.

23. **A** ". . . historical treatment of Greek theatre is something like assembling a jigsaw puzzle of which many pieces are missing." The reference to "missing pieces" is an analogy to the partial evidence for Greek theatre. Choice B is not correct because no comparison is made between written references and the paintings in paragraph 4. Choice C is not correct because the author does not use words and phrases that suggest justification. Choice D is not correct because the last sentence is a summary of the reading passage, not an opening sentence for a new topic.

24. **D** Because the author refers to the archeological evidence in vase paintings as "controversial," it must be concluded that there is disagreement among scholars. Choice A is not correct because the oldest surviving manuscripts date from 1500 years after they were first performed. Choice B is not correct because they are easy to misinterpret. Choice C is not correct because the author does not mention the condition of the vases.

25. **C** Vocabulary reference and contrast are two transitional devices that connect the previous and following sentences to the insert sentence. The connection is "theatres . . . have been excavated" in the previous sentence and "These excavations" in the insert sentence as well as the contrast with "Nevertheless, they" [the theatres or excavations of theatres] in the following sentence.

26. **B, D, C** summarize the passage. Choice A is a minor point that supports major point D. Choice E is a minor point that supports major point C. Choice F is reasonable, but it is not mentioned in the passage.

READING 3 "GEOTHERMAL ENERGY"

27. **A**   The author mentions geothermal power in 1904 in Italy, and then lists a number of countries worldwide that are using geothermal energy. Choice B is not correct because only successful production is mentioned. Choices C and D are discussed later in the passage.

28. **D**   ". . . at the global level, geothermal energy supplies less than 0.15% of the total energy supply." Choice A is not correct because geothermal energy was used as early as 1904. Choice B is not correct because Russia, Iceland, Mexico, and the United States are in the Northern Hemisphere. Choice C is not correct because several advantages of using geothermal power are noted, but the comparative cost was not mentioned.

29. **C**   In this passage *nearly* is a synonym for "approaching." Context comes from the number after the word.

30. **B**   "Some 40 million people today receive their electricity from geothermal energy at a cost competitive with that [the cost] of other energy sources." The pronoun "that" does not refer to Choices A, C, or D.

31. **D**   ". . . considered a nonrenewable energy source when rates of extraction are greater than rates of natural replenishment." Choices A, B, and C are true, but they do not explain the term "nonrenewable."

32. **A**   *High heat is the source of most of the geothermal energy* paraphrases ". . . most geothermal energy production involves the tapping of high heat sources," and *low heat groundwater is also used sometimes* paraphrases "people are also using the low-temperature geothermal energy of groundwater in some applications."

33. **B**   ". . . areas of high heat flow are associated with plate tectonic boundaries." Choice A is not correct because geothermal heat flow is very low compared with solar heat. Choice C is not correct because, in some areas, heat flow is sufficiently high. Choice D is not correct because geothermal energy is very practical along plate boundaries.

34. **A**   In this passage, *large* is a synonym for "considerable." Context comes from the contrast with the phrase "not be as extensive" in the first part of the same sentence.

35. **B**   ". . . geothermal energy does not produce the atmospheric pollutants associated with burning fossil fuels." Choice A is not correct because the pollution caused by geothermal energy was introduced before the discussion on atmospheric pollution. Choice C is not correct because environmental problems caused by geothermal energy are mentioned. Choice D is not correct because the author points out the problem of pollution, but does not suggest that the use of raw materials and chemicals be discontinued.

36. **A**   Choice B is mentioned in paragraph 6, sentence 4. Choices C and D are mentioned in paragraph 6, sentences 5 and 6.

37. **C**   ". . . known geothermal resources . . . could produce . . . 10% of the electricity . . . for the western states. . . . Geohydrothermal resources not yet discovered could . . . provide . . . [the] equivalent [of] the electricity produced from water power today." Choice A is not correct because the author points out the disadvantages but argues in favor of using geothermal energy. Choice B is not correct because the author does not mention exploration as a prerequisite to further production. Choice D is not correct because the author cites the potential for geothermal energy to equal the production of water power, not to replace water power.

38. **C** Vocabulary reference is a transitional device that connects the insert sentence with the previous sentence. "One such region" is a phrase in the insert sentence that refers to "Oceanic ridge systems" in the previous sentence.

39. Fossil fuels: **C, H, I** Geothermal energy: **B, D, E, F** Not used: **A, G**

READING 4 "MIGRATION FROM ASIA"

40. **D** In this passage, *particular* is a synonym for "distinctive."

41. **C** ". . . Stone Age hunter-gatherers were attracted by these animal populations [large animals]." Choice A is not mentioned. Choice B is not correct because the tools were made from the animals, not traded with other tribes. Choice D is not correct because the dogs accompanied them.

42. **B** In this passage, the phrase *Joined by* is a synonym for "Accompanied by." Context comes from the word part, "company."

43. **B** "Because modern Asian populations include all three blood types, however, the migrations must have begun before the evolution of type B, which [evolution] geneticists believe occurred." The pronoun "which" does not refer to Choices A, C, or D.

44. **D** ". . . the migrations must have begun before the evolution of type B." Choice A is not correct because the time frame was the same as the settlement of Scandinavia, but the origin of the migration was not Scandinavian. Choice B is not correct because almost no Native Americans have type B. Choice C is not correct because the blood typing was done with Native Americans and Asians, not Scandinavians.

45. **D** ". . . glacial melting created an ice-free corridor along the eastern front range of the Rocky Mountains. Soon hunters . . . had reached the Great Plains." Choices A and C are not correct because the corridor was ice-free. Choice B is not correct because the hunters were looking for big game, but the game did not leave a migration path.

46. **B** "The most spectacular find, at Monte Verde in southern Chile, produced striking evidence of tool making, house building . . . before the highway had been cleared of ice." Choice A is not correct because archeologists believe that migration in boats may have occurred, but no boats were found. Choice C is not correct because the footprints found there were human, not those of large animals. Choice D is not correct because no conclusions were made about the intelligence of the early humans.

47. **A** In this passage, *In the end* is a synonym for "Eventually." Context comes from the phrase "The final migration" in the following sentence.

48. **A** *Beringia was under water* paraphrases "Beringia had been submerged" and *the last people* paraphrases "The final migration."

49. **D** Choice A is mentioned in paragraph 6, sentence 3. Choices B and C are mentioned in paragraph 6, sentence 5. Choice D is not true because the Yuptiks settled the coast of Alaska, not the Great Plains.

50. **D** ". . . the most compelling support [for migration] . . . comes from genetic research." Choice A is not correct because oral traditions include a long journey from a distant place to a new homeland. Choice B is not correct because the author presents the evidence without commenting on the authenticity. Choice C is not correct because the author states that the Asian migration hypothesis is supported by most of the scientific evidence.

51. **C** Chronological order and place reference are transitional devices that connect the insert sentence with the previous sentence. The date, 13,000 B.C.E. in the previous paragraph is a date that precedes 11,000 to 12,000 years old in the insert sentence. In addition, Washington State, California, and Peru in the insert sentence refer to the Pacific coast of North and South America in the previous sentence.

52. **E, D, C** summarize the passage. Choice A is a concluding point that is not developed with examples and details. Choice B is a minor point that supports major point E. Choice F is a minor point that supports major point D.

READING 5 "PHYSICAL AND CHEMICAL PROPERTIES AND CHANGES"

53. **C**   "They [characteristic properties] are subdivided into two categories: physical properties and chemical properties." Choice A is not correct because they are used to identify or characterize a substance, not to create a substance. Choice B is not correct because sugar and water are substances, but the physical and chemical properties of them are not identified in the paragraph. Choice D is not correct because the properties do not depend on the quantity of the substance.

54. **B**   In this passage, *relate* is a synonym for "pertain." Context comes from the word "relate" in the previous sentence.

55. **C**   ". . . some intensive physical properties include the tendency to dissolve in water, electrical conductivity, and density, which [density] is the ratio of mass to volume." The pronoun "which" does not refer to Choices A, B, or D.

56. **C**   ". . . to act as a poison or carcinogen (cancer-causing agent)." An explanation of a word or phrase often appears immediately after it in parentheses. Choices A, B, and D are not correct because they are intensive chemical properties that are mentioned before the reference to a carcinogen.

57. **B**   *The quantity of a substance* paraphrases "the amount present" in reference to extensive properties and *the characteristics of the substance* paraphrases "characterize a particular kind of matter" in reference to intensive properties.

58. **D**   "When a candle is burned, there are both physical and chemical changes." Choice A is not correct because only the example of the candle is mentioned. Choice B is not correct because the meaning is explained by example, not by definition. Choice C is not correct because the common characteristics were mentioned in previous paragraphs.

59. **A**   In this passage, *distinctive* is a synonym for "unique."

60. **B**   "This is a phase change (liquid to gas) which is a physical change." Because this example of a physical change is provided, it must be concluded that phase changes are sometimes physical changes. Choice A is not correct because the example is a physical change, not a chemical change. Choice C is not correct because the quantity of a substance (extensive properties) is not mentioned in the discussion on phase changes. Choice D is not correct because in a physical change the fundamental composition of a substance has not changed.

61. **B**   In this passage, *important* is a synonym for "critical."

62. **A**   "Has the fundamental composition of the substance changed? In a chemical change . . . it has, but in a physical change, it has not." Choice B is not correct because the quantity refers to extensive properties, not to the difference between physical or chemical properties. Choice C is not correct because both physical and chemical properties are intensive properties. Choice D is not correct because the apparent disappearance of a substance is not necessarily a sign that we are observing a chemical change.

63. **D**   "The following questions pertain to the chemical properties of a substance: '. . . Does it decompose . . . when heated?'" Choices A and B are mentioned as characteristic physical properties in paragraph 4. Choice C is mentioned as a characteristic physical property in paragraph 2 in the discussion of "viscosity."

64. **B**   Pronoun reference is a transitional device that connects the insert sentence with the previous sentence. The pronoun "It" in the insert sentence refers to "aluminum" in the previous sentence. The description of aluminum as "ductile" and "malleable" in the previous sentence means that this metal can be made into wire or shaped into flexible sheets as stated in the insert sentence.

65.   Physical properties: **A, D, E** Chemical properties: **B, C, F, H** Not used: **G, I**

➤ Listening

 Model Test 2, Listening Section, CD 3, Track 7

LISTENING 1 "PROFESSOR'S OFFICE"

Audio Conversation

Narrator: Listen to part of a conversation between a student and a professor.

Student: Professor James. Do you have a minute?
Professor: Sure. Come on in. What can I do for you?
Student: Well, I did pretty well on the midterm . . .
Professor: You sure did. One of the best grades, as I recall.
Q1 Student: But I missed a question, and I'd appreciate it if you could help me understand what I did wrong. I have the test right here, and I just can't figure it out.
Professor: Okay. Fire away.
Student: It's question 7 . . . the one on biotic provinces and biomes.
Professor: Oh, that one. Um, quite a few people missed it. I was thinking that we should go over it again in class. But anyway, let's look at your answer.
Q2 Student: Thanks. Here's the thing. I said that a biotic province was a region with similar life, but with boundaries that prevent plants and animals from spreading to other regions. So an animal, for example, a mammal . . . it may have a genetic ancestor in common with another mammal. But a biome is a similar environment, an ecosystem really, like a desert or a tropical rainforest. So, in the case of a biome, well, the similar climate causes the plants and animals to evolve . . . to adapt to the climate, and that's why they look alike.
Q3 Professor: That's good, very good . . . as far as you went. But there's a second part to the question. Look, right here. "Include an explanation of convergent and divergent evolution." So . . . I was looking for a more complete answer. Next time, be sure to include both parts of a question . . . when there are two parts like this one. . . . Do you know how to explain convergent and divergent evolution?
Q4 Student: I think so. Isn't it . . . like when a group of plants or animals . . . when they're separated by mountains or a large body of water . . . then subpopulations evolve from a common ancestor and they have similar characteristics but their development diverges because of the separation, so that's why we call it divergent evolution.
Professor: Right. Even when the habitat is similar, if they're separated, then they diverge. . . . How about convergent evolution then?
Student: Well, that would be a situation where a similar environment . . . a habitat . . . it may cause plants and animals to evolve in order to adapt to the conditions. So a species that isn't really related can evolve with similar characteristics because . . . it can look like a species in another geographic region because of adaptation . . . and that would be convergent evolution?
Professor: Right again. So temperature and rainfall, proximity to water, latitude and longitude all combine to determine the climate, and if we know the climate of an area, then we can actually predict what kind of life will inhabit it.
Student: Okay. And I really did know that. I just didn't put it down. To tell the truth, I didn't see the second part. Not until you pointed it out to me.

Professor:	That's what I thought. Well, Jerry, it's a good idea to double-check all the questions on a test . . . not just my test . . . any test . . . to make sure you've answered each part of the question completely. Otherwise, you won't get full credit.
Student:	I see that. Well, live and learn.
Professor:	Jerry, you're one of my best students.
Student:	Thanks. I really like biology. In fact, I'm thinking of majoring in it.
Professor:	Good. That means you'll be in some of my upper-level classes.
Student:	And I'll be watching out for those two-part questions on your exams.
Professor:	And all the rest of your exams. I'll be honest with you. My questions usually have two parts so the students will have an insight into the grading system . . . and a lot of professors do that. In an essay question, it's difficult to know what to include and how much to write. Just read the question carefully, and be sure to include all the parts. There may be three or four in some essay questions. This is the way that the professor helps you organize your answer. I'm giving my students a hint about what I'm looking for by including several parts to the question. But if you miss one of the parts, then it lowers your score.
Student:	That makes sense. I think I was just trying to finish within the time limit, and I didn't read as carefully as I should have. On the final, I'll spend more time reading the questions before I start to answer them.
Professor:	Good plan.

Q5

Audio	1.	Why does the man go to see his professor?
Answer	**B**	To clarify a question from the midterm

Audio Replay	2.	Listen again to part of the conversation and then answer the following question.
		"Thanks. Here's the thing. I said that a biotic province was a region with similar life, but with boundaries that prevent plants and animals from spreading to other regions."
Audio Replay		Why does the man say this:
		"Thanks. Here's the thing."
Answer	**D**	He is signaling that he will explain his problem.

Audio	3.	What did the man do wrong?
Answer	**C**	He did not answer one question completely. He did not see the second part.

Audio	4.	According to the student, what is *divergent evolution*?
Answer	**C**	A similar group that is separated may develop different characteristics.

Audio	5.	What will Jerry probably do on the next test?
Answer	**A**	To avoid the same problem that he had on the midterm, he will look for questions with several parts.

LISTENING 2 "ART HISTORY CLASS"

Audio Discussion
Narrator: Listen to part of a discussion in an art history class.

Professor:
Sorry about the tests. I don't have them finished. They just took longer to grade than I thought they would. So . . . I'll have them for you next time. Okay then. Let's begin our discussion of the ballet. . . . If you read the chapter in your text, you already know that uh . . . in 1489, a performance that was something like a dinner theater was organized to celebrate the marriage of the Duke of Milan, and . . . a dance

Q6

Q7

representing Jason and the Argonauts was performed just before the roasted lamb was served. By the way, it's interesting that the dance was called an *entree* and that name has been retained for courses in meals. Anyway, about the same time, outdoor entertainment, you know . . . parades and equestrian events . . . they were becoming more popular, and uh . . . we have evidence that they were referred to as "horse ballets."

Student 1:
So this . . . the horse ballet . . . was it the first time the term "ballet" was used?

Professor:

Q8

Right. The actual term in Italian was *balletti*, which meant "a dance done in figures." And it was characterized by the arrangement of the performers in various patterns. Actually, the balletti were staged versions of the social dances that were popular at court, and the steps . . . the basic movements . . . they were walking, swaying, and turning . . . so they combined in a variety of . . . of . . . sequences, each of which was named so that, uh, they could be referred to in the directions for individual dances. In fact, specific instructions for the placement of the dancer's feet probably provided the first, uh . . . the first record of the five positions of classical ballet. Question?

Student 2:
Sorry. I'm trying to get clear on the dancers. Um . . . could you explain what the book means about court dancing and, uh . . . I'm not saying this very well.

Professor:
I think I know where you're going. You see, the directions that were written down were intended as a reference for social dancing, but they were, uh . . . important in the history of ballet because uh . . . the theatrical dances or entertainments that preceded ballet were . . . not performed by professional dancers. Members of the court danced for the entertainment of society, and in general, the performances were in the central halls of castles and palaces with the audience seated in galleries above so that, uh, the floor figures could . . . could be seen when the people looked down. But back to your question . . . because of

Q9

the limitations of the performers and the arrangement of the staging, well, the best way to impress the audience was to keep the steps simple enough for the amateur dancers but the geometrical patterns had to be, uh, . . . intricate and . . . and fresh . . . so the spectators would go away pleased because they'd seen something new.

Student 2:
Oh, I get it now. That makes sense, too, because everyone would be looking down at the dancers.

Professor:
Exactly. Now to continue that thought for a moment . . . by the middle of the sixteenth century, variety shows were being presented on a grand scale in Northern Italy. They included both indoor and outdoor entertainment, and most people called them *spectaculi*. And, uh . . . France had begun to make a significant contribution to the dance form that evolved into modern ballet.

But, to be precise, it was Catherine de Medici who used dance as part of her court entertainments and is, uh . . . credited with the use of the term *ballet*. In 1573 . . . I think it was 1573 . . . anyway, she organized a huge celebration to welcome the ambassadors from Poland who had arrived to, uh . . . to offer their country's throne to her son Henri. So she called it the *Polish Ballet*, and the production was staged on a landing at the top of a grand staircase. Sixteen ladies . . . and these would not have been dancers . . . just members of court . . . so they represented the sixteen provinces of France, and they performed a choreographed dance with a variety of floor figures. Afterward, the audience joined in court dances, similar to the ballroom dancing that evolved later. . . . So that's a long answer to your original question.

Student 1:   Now *I* have a question.   Q11

Professor: Okay.

Student 1:
You said that the *Polish Ballet* was the first ballet, but I thought that the book said the first ballet was *Queen Louise's Ballet.*

Professor:
Good question. Well, I said the *Polish Ballet* was the first use of the term *ballet* for a dance performance, but *Queen Louise's Ballet* is generally considered the first modern ballet. As you'll remember, from the book, the ballet was performed before ten thousand guests, and it was five hours long. When I was doing   Q10
the research for this lecture, I saw several references to the time, so . . . so I know that this is accurate, but I kept thinking, no one would watch a ballet for five hours. But it must be correct. I can only assume that other activities were going on simultaneously, like a banquet and conversation. Don't you think?
        Anyway, what makes *Queen Louise's Ballet* so unique, besides the length, and why it's the first modern ballet, is that it was connected by a story line or, in technical terms, uh, it's called *dramatic cohesion*. Each scene was related to the tales of Circe, a Greek enchantress, who used her powers to battle with man and the gods. The triumph of good, portrayed by Jupiter, over evil, portrayed by Circe, was told in a . . . let's call it a unified production.

Audio	6.	What is the discussion mainly about?
Answer	C	All of the other choices are mentioned in relationship to the main topic: the development of the ballet.

Audio	7.	Listen again to part of the lecture and then answer the following question.
Replay		"So . . . I'll have them for you next time. Okay then. Let's begin our discussion of the ballet. . . . "
Audio		Why does the professor say this:
Replay		"Okay then."
Answer	A	To end his explanation and begin the lecture. Professors often use the word "Okay" as a transition from classroom management activities before the class to the beginning of their lectures.

| Audio | 8. | According to the professor, what does the term *balletti* mean? |
| Answer | C | A dance done in figures |

| Audio | 9. | How did the early choreographers accommodate the abilities of amateur performers? |
| Answer | A | The steps were quite simple. |

| Audio | 10. | Why does the professor mention that he checked several references about the length of *Queen Louise's Ballet*? |
| Answer | C | He wasn't sure that it was accurate. |

| Audio | 11. | What can be inferred about the professor? |
| Answer | B | He encourages the students to participate. |

LISTENING 3 "LINGUISTICS CLASS"

Audio Discussion

Narrator: Listen to part of a discussion in a linguistics class.

Professor: What comes to mind when I say the word *grammar*?

Student 1:   That's easy. English class and lots of rules.

Student 2:   Memorizing parts of speech . . . like nouns and verbs.

Student 3:   Diagramming sentences.

Professor:

Q12 Well, yes, that's fairly typical. But today we're going to look at grammar from the point of view of the linguist, and to do that, we really have to consider three distinct grammars for every language.

The first grammar is referred to as a *mental grammar*. And that's what a speaker of a language knows, often implicitly, about the grammar of that language. This has also been called *linguistic competence* and from that term *competence grammar* has become popular. I like to think of it, of mental or competence grammar, I mean . . . I like to think of it as an incredibly complex system that allows a speaker to produce language that other speakers can understand. It includes the sounds, the vocabulary, the order of words in sentences and . . . even the appropriateness of a topic or a word in a particular social situation. And what's so amazing is that most of us carry this knowledge around in our heads and use it without much reflection.

Q13 One way to clarify mental or competence grammar is to ask a friend a question about a sentence. Your friend probably won't know *why* it's correct, but that friend will know *if* it's correct. So one of the features of mental or competence grammar is this incredible sense of correctness and the ability to hear something that "sounds odd" in a language. Haven't you had the experience of hearing a sentence, and it stood out to you? It just wasn't quite right? For native speakers we can call this ability *native intuition*, but even language learners who've achieved a high level of competence in a second language will be able to give similar intuitive responses even if they can't explain the rules. So that's mental grammar or competence grammar.

Okay then, that brings us to the second type of grammar, and this is what linguists are most concerned about. This is *descriptive grammar*, which is a description of what the speakers know intuitively about a language. Linguists try to discover the underlying rules of mental or competence grammar and describe them objectively. So descriptive grammar is a *model* of competence grammar, and as such, it has to be based on the best effort of a linguist, and consequently, subject to criticism and even disagreement from *other* linguists. Because no matter how skilled a linguist is, describing grammar is an enormous task. In the first place, the knowledge is incredibly vast and complex; in the second place, the
Q14 language itself is changing even while it's being described; and finally, the same data can be organized in different but equally correct ways in order to arrive at generalizations. And the ultimate goal of a descriptive grammar is to formulate generalizations about a language that accurately reflect the mental rules that speakers have in their heads.

But, getting back to what most people think of as grammar—the grammar that we may have learned in school. That's very different from either competence grammar or descriptive grammar because the rules aren't meant to describe language at all. They're meant to prescribe and judge language as good or bad. And this kind of grammar is called, not surprisingly, *prescriptive grammar* because of its judgmental perspective. Again, to contrast prescriptive grammar with descriptive grammar, just think of descriptive generalizations as accepting the language that a speaker uses in an effort to describe it and recognizing that there may be several dialects that are used by various groups of speakers and that any one speaker will probably choose to use different language depending on the formality, for example, of the situation. On the other hand, prescriptive rules are rigid and subject to enforcement. Prescriptivists want to make all speakers conform to one standard in all situations, and that tends to be a very formal level of language all the time.

Now which of these types of grammar do you think you were learning in school when you had to memorize parts of speech and rules and diagram sentences?

Student 2:   Sounds like prescriptive grammar to me.

Professor:
Precisely. But how did prescriptive rules get to be accepted, at least in the schools? And probably even more important, why are so many of these rules disregarded even by well-educated speakers in normal situations?

Student 1:   Did you say *disregarded*?   Q15

Professor:
I did. Some of you may recall that during the seventeenth and eighteenth centuries in Europe, Latin was considered the perfect language and was used by the educated classes. The argument for the perfec-   Q16
tion of Latin was reinforced by the fact that Latin had become a written language and, consequently . . . Latin had stopped changing in the normal ways that spoken languages do, so the rules were also fixed, and for many writers of English during that period, the rules of Latin were held as a standard for *all* languages, including English. But the problem was that English had a different origin and very different constructions. For example, how many times have you heard the prescriptive rule, "never end a sen-   Q17
tence with a preposition?" This is a Latin rule, but it doesn't apply to English, so it sounds very formal and even strange when this Latin rule is enforced. Now, how many of you would say, "What are we wait-ing for?" I think most of us would prefer it to "For what are we waiting?" But as you see, this breaks the rule—the Latin rule, that is.

Student 2:
So we're really learning Latin rules in English classes. No wonder I was confused. But wouldn't you think that . . . well, that things would change? I mean, Latin hasn't been recognized as a world language for a long time.

Professor:
You're right. But the reason that prescriptive rules survive is the school system. Teachers promote the prescriptive grammar as the standard for the school, and consequently for the educated class. And "good" language is a requisite for social mobility, even when it's very dissimilar to the mental grammar or the descriptive grammar of a language.

Audio   12.   What is the discussion mainly about?
Answer   **B**   Different types of grammar

Audio   13.   How does the professor make his point about *native intuition*?
Answer   **A**   He explains how to perform an easy experiment. By asking a friend about a sentence, the students will understand the concept.

Audio   14.   What are two key problems for descriptive grammar?
Answer   **A**   The information is very complicated and subject to change.
             C   The language can be organized correctly in more than one way.

Audio Replay	15.	Listen again to part of the lecture and then answer the following question.
		"But how did prescriptive rules get to be accepted, at least in the schools? And probably even more important, why are so many of these rules disregarded even by well-educated speakers in normal situations?"
		"Did you say *disregarded*?"
Audio Replay		Why does the student say this:
		"Did you say *disregarded*?"
Answer	**B**	She is confirming that she has understood. Her tone is confused, not challenging.

| **Audio** | 16. | According to the professor, why were Latin rules used for English grammar? |
| **Answer** | **A** | Latin was a written language with rules that did not change. |

| **Audio** | 17. | Why does the professor discuss the rule to avoid ending a sentence with a preposition? |
| **Answer** | **D** | It demonstrates the problem in using Latin rules for English. |

LISTENING 4 "COLLEGE CAMPUS"

Audio Conversation

Narrator: Listen to part of a conversation on campus between two students.

Man: I didn't see you at the International Talent Show.
Woman: No time for that kind of thing.
Man: You mean you don't belong to the ISA?
Woman: The ISA?
Man: International Student Association.
Woman: Oh, no. I don't belong to any clubs.
Man: But this isn't like a regular club.
Woman: How so?
Man: Well, we have a house. You know, the brick house on fraternity row and . . .
Woman: You live there, right?
Man: Yeah. I moved in last year. It's really inexpensive because we take care of the house ourselves and we cook our own meals.
Woman: That sounds like it would take a lot of time.
Man: Not really. There's a list of chores posted every week, and you can choose something you like to do, so I usually put my name down for yard work. I like being outside so it's fun for me.
Woman: But you have to cook too, right?
Man: Okay, it's like this: twenty of us live there so every night two of the guys cook and two of the guys clean up, so you only have to cook about once a week and clean up once.
Woman: What about breakfast and lunch?
Man: Oh, well, you're on your own for that, but the dinners are just fantastic. It's like eating in a different ethnic restaurant every night. You know, because the guys are from different countries.
Woman: That sounds good.
Q19 Man: And it costs about half what it did to live in the dorm. But really, I'm doing it because it's a great experience living with people from so many different countries. My best friend in the house is from Korea. My roommate's from Brazil. And I've got friends from . . . well, Q20 just about everywhere.
Woman: But you don't have to live in the house to belong to the club.
Man: No, no. There are about a hundred members in the International Student Association. Only guys live in the house, but there are a lot of women in the association.

| Woman: | I wish I had time to do it. It really sounds interesting. |
| Man: | You've got to relax sometimes. Anyway, we meet at the house the first Friday of the month from seven to ten. We have a buffet dinner and after that, we have a short meeting. That's when we plan our activities, like the talent show and picnics and dances. Then a lot of the people stay for music and a party, but some people leave after the meeting. |

Q21

| Woman: | So it's only a couple hours a month. |
| Man: | Right. Listen, why don't you come over next Friday for the meeting, as my guest, I mean. You have to eat anyway. And if you have a good time, you can think about joining. |

Q18

| Woman: | Next Friday? Well, I don't know . . . I usually study on Friday night, but . . . I could take a break . . . Sure I'll come over . . . but I might have to leave early. |

Q22

| Man: | Great. |

| Audio | 18. | What is the purpose of this conversation? |
| Answer | C | The man is convincing the woman to join the International Student Association. He invites the woman to attend a meeting as his guest. |

| Audio | 19. | What does the man imply about the house where he is living? |
| Answer | A | He is saving money by living at the house, but he prefers the house to the dorm because it is a great experience. |

| Audio | 20. | How does the man feel about the International Student Association? |
| Answer | B | He enjoys meeting people with different backgrounds. |

Audio	21.	Listen again to part of the conversation and then answer the following question.
Replay		"Then a lot of the people stay for music and a party, but some people leave after the meeting."
		"So it's only a couple hours a month."
Audio		What does the woman mean when she says this:
Replay		"So it's only a couple hours a month."
Answer	D	Her tone indicates indecision. She is changing her mind about going.

| Audio | 22. | What does the woman agree to do? |
| Answer | C | Go to a meeting |

LISTENING 5 "ZOOLOGY CLASS"

Audio Lecture

Narrator: Listen to part of a lecture in a zoology class. The professor is discussing coral reefs.

Professor:
Every ecosystem on Earth is unique, but the coral reef is perhaps the most unusual of all because it's the only ecosystem made by and made *of*—animals. All coral reefs are constructed by coral polyps, which are generally small, about the size of this pencil eraser. But, the structures themselves are, well, enormous. Astronauts have been able to identify the Great Barrier Reef in Australia from space. Can you believe that? And the diversity of species in large coral reefs is second only to the rainforest habitats. In fact, we estimate that for every species we've identified on a coral reef, there are probably a hundred times that number that remain to be classified and studied.

But how do these little polyps build such impressive reefs? Well, hard coral secrete a shell of calcium carbonate around their bodies. The polyp *isn't* hard, you see, but the shell *is*. And these shells are the material that forms a coral reef. So a coral reef is just a colony—millions and millions of coral animals whose shells are connected. And reproduction is really the basis for the construction of a large reef. You see, as each polyp matures, it converts the calcium and other minerals in ocean water to a hard limestone exoskeleton called a *corallite*. And this is fascinating. Although the polyps themselves don't appreciably increase in size, they continue to build new shells periodically, um, connecting them with . . . with partitions.

Now coral can reproduce sexually through an activity called mass spawning. During one night in the spring when the moon is full, coral polyps release egg bundles that contain both eggs and sperm. Most polyps have both male and female reproductive cells. The egg bundles are round, about half the size of marbles, I would say. They're brightly colored in orange or red or pink, and they float up to the surface to form a thick layer of, uh . . . well think of them as rather fragrant beads. So with the water so saturated with them, predators will only be able to devour a small number compared with the huge number that will survive and break open. The sperm cells swim away to fertilize the eggs from another bundle. So . . . once fertilized, the little egg begins to mature from a coral larva to a planulae, which can swim for a few hours, days, or even a few weeks. Ultimately it locates a hard surface on which to attach itself and from which it will *not* move for the rest of its life, except for the movement involved in the process of building a new, neighboring shell as . . . as it continues to mature.

But actually sexual reproduction isn't the way that coral reefs are really constructed. When a polyp matures on the site it's selected, the habitat is identified as being conducive to reef building. So the mature polyp doesn't just grow bigger, it actually replicates itself in a process called *budding*. After the genetic material is duplicated, then the polyp divides itself in half, and each half becomes a completely mature polyp. This budding process repeats itself, eventually producing thousands of asexually budded coral polyps connected by a tissue that grows over the limestone shells between the polyps. So, as you can imagine, budding will produce a large number of individual polyps, but they'll all have exactly the same genetic code as the first polyp. And this creates the beginning of a coral reef, but without the diversity that eventually populates the habitat. Wherever a coral reef is constructed, abundant sea life congregates. In fact, it's been estimated that about 25 percent of all ocean species can be found within the coral reefs.

Now most coral polyps eat plankton—single-celled microscopic organisms that float or swim very slowly in the ocean water in their habitat. But, um, a coral reef has such a high concentration of polyps, they can't rely solely on plankton to survive. So coral polyps have developed a symbiotic relationship with a single-celled algae called zooxanthella. Remember that to qualify as symbiotic, a relationship must be, um, mutually beneficial. So the zooxanthella produces food for the coral through the by-products of photosynthesis, and the coral provides a safe home for the zooxanthella, because it's hidden from predators that inhabit the coral reef.

Every species of coral grows at a different rate, some as much as six inches a year. But faster growing colonies are more prone to breaking apart either from their own weight or from the continuous force of the ocean waves. Some species tend to grow more slowly, but they may live as long as a thousand years. Even so, only the top portion of any reef is actually alive and growing and the lower structure is comprised of the skeletal remains . . . that's limestone corallite from coral that has died.

And what I find incredibly interesting about coral reefs is that each is a unique structure. But, of course, scientists need to classify, and so there's a classification system for coral reefs. A *fringing reef* grows around islands and the shorelines of continents and extends out from the shore. In order to flourish, fringing reefs must have clean water, lots of sunshine, and a moderately high concentration of salt. Some good examples of fringing reefs can be found around the Hawaiian Islands. Oh, yes, these are the most common and also the most recently formed class of coral reefs. Here's a drawing of a fringing reef.

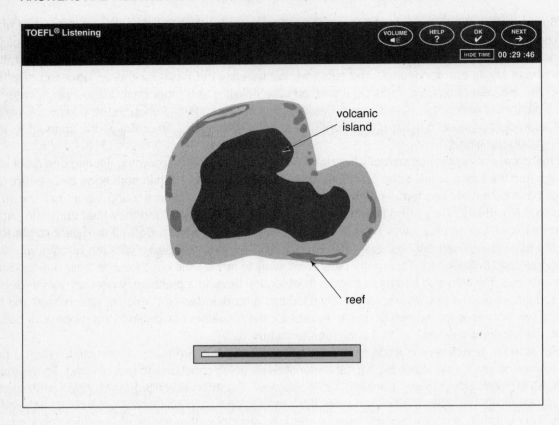

I think this is actually one of the Hawaiian reefs.

Now, *barrier reefs*—they're found further from shore, and they're usually separated from the shoreline by a shallow body of water, maybe a lagoon. As in the case of the Great Barrier Reef off the shore of Australia, the body of water can be miles wide, so the reef is miles away from the shoreline. And there may actually be a collection of coral reefs fused together. This is a drawing of a reef in the Great Barrier chain.

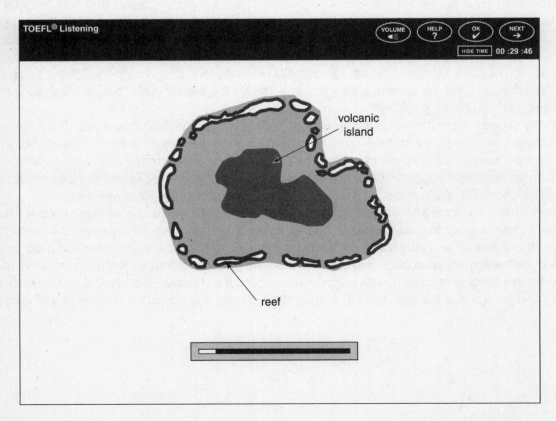

As I recall there are about twenty-five, or maybe even more individual coral reefs connected to form the Great Barrier Reef. As a general rule, barrier reefs are larger and older than fringing reefs.

Q27 But the oldest class of coral reef is the *atoll*, which is a ring-shaped reef with a lagoon in the middle and deep water surrounding the ring. These are scattered throughout the South Pacific, kind of like oasis settlements in the desert. And they abound with a diversity of sea life. This is one of the South Pacific atolls.

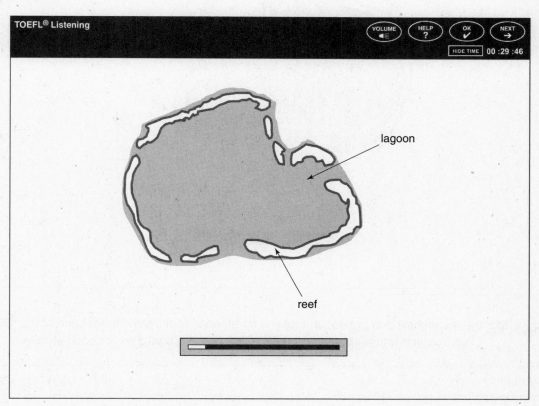

Q28 So, as we reflect on everything we've said about coral, we know that it's a relatively simple organism with a body ending in a mouth and tentacles. It reproduces both sexually and asexually by budding, and, um . . . it survives by forming a symbiotic relationship with zooxanthella. But none of this is very extraordinary. What is unique about coral in the animal kingdom is its ability to construct a variety of reefs, creating habitats that are absolutely unlike any others on Earth.

Audio	23.	According to the professor, how do coral reefs grow?
Answer	**B**	They connect corallite shells to build structures.

Audio	24.	Why are so many egg bundles released during mass spawning?
Answer	**C**	A number of the egg bundles will be eaten [by predators].

Audio	25.	According to the professor, what is *budding*?
Answer	**A**	The division of a polyp in half to reproduce itself.

Audio	26.	What is the relationship between zooxanthella and coral polyps?
Answer	**B**	The zooxanthella uses the coral for a shelter from enemies.
	C	The coral eats food produced by the zooxanthella.
		The relationship is symbiotic.

Audio	27.	Which of the following reefs is probably an atoll?
Answer	**C**	A ring-shaped reef with a lagoon in the middle and deep water surrounding the ring.

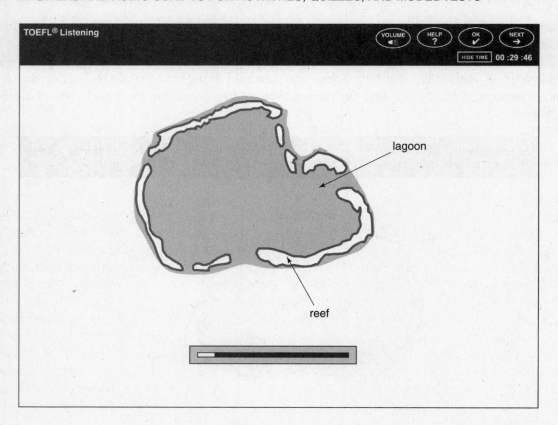

Audio 28. In the lecture, the professor explains coral reefs. Indicate whether each of the following is a true statement about coral reefs. Click in the correct box for each phrase.

		Yes	No
A	In general, the organism is quite simple.	✔	
B	The structure of a reef can be very large.	✔	
C	The living coral grows on top of dead shells.	✔	
D	Mass spawning is not very effective.		✔

LISTENING 6 "BUSINESS CLASS"

Audio Discussion
Narrator: Listen to part of a discussion in a business class.

Professor:
Industry analysts report that multinational food companies are trying to use the same types of strategies that automobile and electronics manufacturers have found to be successful in the global marketplace. The problem is that general rules for products that tend to be traditional for national or even regional tastes . . . these products are very difficult to identify and sales aren't easy to project. But, the companies that tend to do best are those that are the most responsive to local tastes. And they spend development dollars on taste testing in the local markets before they formulate the final product. Can anyone recall any examples from the case studies in the text? Sandy?

Q29

Q30

Student 1:
McDonald's Big Mac has more mustard in the special sauce in Paris than it does in New York.

Professor: Because?

Student 1:
Because taste tests verified that people in the United States liked sweeter condiments than people did in France. In fact, I think the . . . the sugar content for export foods in general usually has to be modified when American products are taste tested overseas.

Professor:
Right you are. Probably the company that's adapted most to local tastes is Nestle. Can you believe that they produce more than 200 slightly different blends of Nescafe for export to different countries? Amazing but true. But sometimes taste is less a problem of ingredients and more a matter of the way a food product looks or feels. One case study that comes to mind is the one about the soft cookies that just don't sell as well in England as crisp cookies. So, you can see that taste extends way beyond just flavor. It's really a combination of flavor preferences and local expectations.

Look, here's another example of accommodation that had more to do with the expectation for a process than the flavor of the product. In this case study, it was cake. Remember when Betty Crocker cake mixes were introduced in England, they weren't accepted because the English homemaker felt more comfortable with convenience foods that required more than water to prepare them. Go figure. But that was the problem uncovered by extensive market research. So when the mix was reformulated without an egg, and the preparation included adding an egg with the water before mixing it, well, Betty Crocker cake mixes became very popular in England.
Q31 Any other examples come to mind? They don't have to be from the case studies in the book.

Student 2:   How about serving sizes?

Professor: Go on.

Student 2:
Well soft drinks for one. Just compare the serving sizes in the United States and many foreign markets where soft drinks are sold. The cans in foreign markets are much smaller because consumers expect it. But, uh, in the United States, well, super sizing is probably a consideration when a foreign company is trying to crack the American market.

Professor:
Q32 That's a great example. So the taste can be acceptable, but the packaging has to compare favorably with the competing brands and the public's expectations.

Student 3:
Yeah, but that makes products more expensive, doesn't it? I mean because you can't standardize the product or the packaging so that would make it more . . . more costly to produce, wouldn't it?

Professor:
Right you are, Chris. In fact, you've really gone to the heart of the issue. A compromise has to occur between the requirement that products be adapted to please the taste and the expectations of local consumers and the pressure to standardize products for maximum cost effectiveness. Now, let's complicate that even further. Even the experts don't agree on the importance of how far to go in adapting products for local markets. A few years ago, Ted Levitt—he's the editor of the *Harvard Business*
Q33 *Review*—Levitt predicted what he called a "pluralization of consumption." What he means is that at least in some areas, tastes are likely to converge, which makes sense when you think about the increased

opportunities for travel and sampling of foods, as well as the continued global marketing efforts by multi-national corporations. So logically, it's smarter to simply identify the areas in which tastes are most likely to be the same, and concentrate efforts on those food products.

But there's also the issue of global marketing. How about the potential to create taste? I mean, selling the image that surrounds using a product. If consumers want to associate themselves with that image, won't they develop a taste for the product that does that for them? For example, there's some ⟦Q34⟧ evidence that the popularity of products seen in movies and television spills into the foreign market-place. This subtle brand association with the movie or the celebrities in it translates into high dollar deals for certain brands to be visibly displayed in widely distributed films.

Student 3:
Oh, right. I was reading about that. It was in a couple of the case studies. The bottle, a can, or . . . or a package appears as part of the character's persona, and if it's a character that audiences choose to identify with, then the taste for the product may follow, or at least that's what the marketing experts are betting on.

Professor:
And that includes foreign audiences. Anyone drink Starbucks coffee? Well, Starbucks began as a regional coffee in Seattle, Washington, and made the global leap in 2000, opening shops in China, a huge market surely, but also a traditionally *tea-drinking* society. So what's the attraction? Starbucks is marketing to the cosmopolitan consumer, the young trendy set looking for a modern image as well as a different taste.

Still, there have been some real surprises in the multinational dinner party. No one has really figured out why the Italians, Germans, and British love Kraft's Philadelphia cream cheese, and the Greeks simply don't buy it. And why did Perrier, a mineral water from France . . . why did Perrier take America by storm while other imported mineral waters . . . didn't? In short, success in the food export industry is probably a combination of the real taste . . . the flavor of the product, with some adaptation for the local markets, the satisfaction of certain expectations for the preparation and packaging, and the taste for the product created by images in the global marketing plan. Add to this mix the potential for a short shelf life or even perishable products and, well, you have a very challenging problem for the multinational food industry.

Audio	29.	What is the discussion mainly about?
Answer	**A**	The other choices relate to the main topic: the global marketing of food products.
Audio	30.	How does the professor organize the lecture?
Answer	**C**	He refers to case studies from the textbook.
Audio	31.	Listen again to part of the lecture and then answer the following question.
Replay		"Any other examples come to mind? They don't have to be from the case studies in the book."
		"How about serving sizes?"
Audio		Why does the student say this:
Replay		"How about serving sizes?"
Answer	**B**	She is offering a possible answer to the professor's question. "How about" is a polite way to offer a possibility.
Audio	32.	What technique does the professor use to encourage student discussion?
Answer	**A**	He gives students positive reinforcement by praising their efforts.

Audio   33.   What did Ted Levitt mean by "the pluralization of consumption"?
Answer **D**   More people will want the same products.

Audio   34.   What does the professor say about television and movie companies?
Answer **D**   He points out that they are paid to display brand-name products.

➤ Speaking

   Model Test 2, Speaking Section, CD 3, Track 8, continued on CD 4, Track 1

INDEPENDENT SPEAKING QUESTION 1 "A BIRTHDAY"

Narrator 2: Number 1. Listen for a question about a familiar topic. After you hear the question, you have 15 seconds to prepare and 45 seconds to record your answer.

Narrator 1: Explain how birthdays are celebrated in your country. Use specific examples and details in your explanation.

Narrator 2: Please prepare your answer after the beep.

Beep

[Preparation time: 15 seconds]

Narrator 2: Please begin speaking after the beep.

Beep

[Recording time: 45 seconds]

Beep

INDEPENDENT SPEAKING QUESTION 2 "COURSE REQUIREMENTS"

Narrator 2: Number 2. Listen for a question that asks your opinion about a familiar topic. After you hear the question, you have 15 seconds to prepare and 45 seconds to record your answer.

Narrator 1: Some students would rather write a paper than take a test. Other students would rather take a test instead of writing a paper. Which option do you prefer and why? Use specific reasons and examples to support your opinion.

Narrator 2: Please prepare your answer after the beep.

Beep

[Preparation time: 15 seconds]

Narrator 2: Please begin speaking after the beep.

Beep

[Recording time: 45 seconds]

Beep

INTEGRATED SPEAKING QUESTION 3 "HEALTH INSURANCE"

Narrator 2: Number 3. Read a short passage and listen to a talk on the same topic. Then listen for a question about them. After you hear the question, you have 30 seconds to prepare and 60 seconds to record your answer.

Narrator 1: A student is discussing the university's health insurance policy with the foreign student advisor. Read the policy in the college schedule printed on page 195. You have 45 seconds to complete it. Please begin reading now.

[Reading time: 45 seconds]

Narrator 1: Now listen to the foreign student advisor. He is explaining the policy and expressing his opinion about it.

Advisor:
I think it's very important for you to know that this policy wasn't instituted in order to increase fees for international students. In fact, the university doesn't make a profit from the sale of health insurance. The problem is that health care costs in this country are so high that it could be financially disastrous for the family of an international student who needed more than just a simple visit to the doctor's office. A trip to the emergency room at the hospital could cost thousands of dollars without health insurance! Most families abroad just don't realize how costly it is. As for foreign health insurance providers—well, it was just too difficult to validate their coverage for medical services, and the local doctors and hospitals simply stopped accepting them. So . . . to be sure that our students are protected, we're offering low-cost health insurance through the school.

Narrator 1: The foreign student advisor expresses his opinion of the policy for health insurance. Report his opinion and explain the reasons that he gives for having that opinion.

Narrator 2: Please prepare your answer after the beep.

Beep

[Preparation time: 30 seconds]

Narrator 2: Please begin speaking after the beep.

Beep

[Recording time: 60 seconds]

Beep

INTEGRATED SPEAKING QUESTION 4 "ANTARCTICA"

Narrator 2: Number 4. Read a short passage and listen to part of a lecture on the same topic. Then listen for a question about them. After you hear the question, you have 30 seconds to prepare and 60 seconds to record your answer.

Narrator 1: Now read the passage about Antarctica printed on page 196. You have 45 seconds to complete it. Please begin reading now.

[Reading time: 45 seconds]

Narrator 1: Now listen to part of a lecture in a geography class. The professor is talking about Antarctica.

Professor:
With the increasing pressure to replace raw materials that are being consumed in other parts of the world, Antarctica and the waters offshore could become a stage for international conflict in the future. During the eighteenth and nineteenth centuries, hunters decimated huge populations of whales and seals, and the race to reach the South Pole resulted in national claims by explorers from a variety of countries, which finally resulted in the partitioning of pie-shaped sectors radiating away from the center at the pole. So today several claims overlap, and only one sector remains unclaimed. Virtually all of these claims are covered by an ice sheet about two miles thick, but the question is, what's beneath the ice? Scientific experiments indicate that proteins, fuels, and minerals exist in abundance, and that means that in spite of the difficulties and challenges involved in the exploitation of these natural resources, the countries with claims haven't demonstrated an intention to relinquish their stake in the area. While resources are available in more convenient sites, the remote areas in Antarctica appear to be relatively safe from exploitation. In addition, as the reading passage suggests, global self-interest may engender international cooperation in this crucial environmental system.

Narrator 1: Explain why many countries have staked claims in Antarctica, and why national interests have not been pursued.

Narrator 2: Please prepare your answer after the beep.

Beep

[Preparation time: 30 seconds]

Narrator 2: Please begin speaking after the beep.

Beep

[Recording time: 60 seconds]

Beep

INTEGRATED SPEAKING QUESTION 5 "EXTRA MONEY"

Narrator 2: Number 5. Listen to a short conversation. Then listen for a question about it. After you hear the question, you have 20 seconds to prepare and 60 seconds to record your answer.

Narrator 1: Now listen to a conversation between a student and her friend.

Student:	I need to earn some extra money. My budget's just out of control.
Friend:	I hear you. I had the same problem last semester.
Student:	So what did you do?
Friend:	I got a job at the cafeteria. I don't really like the work, but the good thing is that you get free meals.
Student:	Really? Are they hiring?
Friend:	I don't know, but I could ask. The pay isn't great though. See, the meals are the thing.
Student:	Oh. Still, that would cut down on the grocery bill.
Friend:	Yeah . . . Or, you know what? You could rent that extra room in your apartment. I'll bet you could get $250 a month, at least.
Student:	I've been thinking about that. It would help with the rent and the utilities, and I wouldn't have to work so I could use my time for my classes, but, I keep thinking, what if my roommate doesn't pay on time, or what if there's a lot of noise.
Friend:	Well, you'd have to have a deposit and a contract . . . something in writing so you could keep the deposit if there were problems, and you could break the contract if it didn't work out.

Narrator 1: Describe the woman's problem, and the two suggestions that her friend makes about how to handle it. What do you think the woman should do, and why?

Narrator 2: Please prepare your answer after the beep.

Beep

[Preparation time: 20 seconds]

Narrator 2: Please begin speaking after the beep.

Beep

[Recording time: 60 seconds]

Beep

INTEGRATED SPEAKING QUESTION 6 "RESEARCH REFERENCES"

Narrator 2: Number 6. Listen to part of a lecture. Then listen for a question about it. After you hear the question, you have 20 seconds to prepare, and 60 seconds to record your answer.

Narrator 1: Now listen to part of a lecture in a sociology class. The professor is discussing the criteria for using older research references.

Professor:

Well, first of all you have to understand that there's no hard and fast rule for deciding when a research reference is too old. But that doesn't help you much. So, I'll try to give you a couple of guidelines, and then you'll just have to use good judgment. Okay, let's just say for our purposes, that the research is thirty years old. Then the next thing to think about is whether any changes have occurred in society to call the data into question. For example, in a study that looks at diet, we know logically that many changes have occurred in eating patterns over the past thirty years, so this study would probably be out of date. But a study of, say, uh, language development may be okay because the way that babies learn their native language hasn't changed much in the same period of time. So, what I'm saying is . . . the date is less important than the potential for change. Okay, then the second criteria to consider is whether the citation is a *finding* or an *opinion*. If you have a study that indicates, uh, for example, that college students are drinking more, that's a *finding*, but if you have a statement by the researcher that drinking is the most serious problem on campus, then you have an *opinion*. And opinions are accurate over the years as long as they're attributed to the person and the date is cited. But the finding for an older study may be too old. In that case, it's probably better to use a more recent study.

Narrator 1: Using the main points and examples from the lecture, describe the two criteria for using an older research reference presented by the professor.

Narrator 2: Please prepare your answer after the beep.

Beep

[Preparation time: 20 seconds]

Narrator 2: Please begin speaking after the beep.

Beep

[Recording time: 60 seconds]

Beep

➤ Writing

INTEGRATED ESSAY "THE TURING TEST"

First, read the passage on page 199 and take notes.

   Model Test 2, Writing Section, CD 4, Track 2

Narrator: Now listen to a lecture on the same topic as the passage that you have just read.

Professor:

Philosopher John Searle has challenged the validity of the Turing Test because it's premised on behavior rather than on thought. To prove his argument, he's suggested a paradox, which he refers to as the Chinese Room. If a monolingual English-speaking person receives questions on a computer terminal from a Chinese person in another room, naturally the English-speaking person won't understand the questions. However, if there's a large reference that can be accessed, and if the reference is detailed and comprehensible, then the English speaker could, conceivably, break the code. For example, if a sequence of Chinese characters are received, the reference could indicate which sequence of Chinese characters would be expected in response. In other words, the behavior would be correct, although the English speaker wouldn't be thinking at a level that included meaning. The person would be manipulating symbols without understanding them, or, as Searle suggests, the person would be *acting* intelligent without *being* intelligent, which is exactly what a computer could be programmed to do.

Therefore, at least theoretically, a computer could be designed with complex input that would allow it to provide adequate behavioral output without being aware of what it's doing. If so, then it could pass the Turing Test. But the test itself would be meaningless because it doesn't really answer the most basic question about artificial intelligence, which is, can the computer think?

➤ Example Answers and Checklists for Speaking and Writing

 Model Test 2, Example Answers, CD 4, Track 3

EXAMPLE ANSWER FOR INDEPENDENT SPEAKING QUESTION 1 "A BIRTHDAY"

In my country, birthdays are celebrated every year but the most important birthday for a young girl is the *quinceañera*, the birthday when she's fifteen. This is celebrated with a church service. The girl wears a white dress, kind of like a wedding dress, and several attendants accompany her to the altar where the priest talks with her about becoming an adult woman. After the service, the whole family celebrates with friends. And there's music and dancing and food. Traditionally, only relatives and close friends are invited to the church service, but many more people attend the party afterward. Um, in the old days, the ceremony presented the girl to society for marriage proposals . . . but now she's considered the appropriate age to begin dating.

Checklist 1

✔ The talk answers the topic question.
✔ The point of view or position is clear.
✔ The talk is direct and well-organized.
✔ The sentences are logically connected.
✔ Details and examples support the main idea.
✔ The speaker expresses complete thoughts.
✔ The meaning is easy to comprehend.
✔ A wide range of vocabulary is used.
✔ There are only minor errors in grammar.
✔ The talk is within a range of 125–150 words.

EXAMPLE ANSWER FOR INDEPENDENT SPEAKING QUESTION 2 "COURSE REQUIREMENTS"

I prefer to write a paper instead of taking a test because I know exactly what the topic is when I'm researching a paper, but there are a large number of possibilities for questions on a test and that makes it much more difficult to prepare for. Besides, in my experience, some teachers aren't very straightforward about their tests, and even though I've studied and understand the subject, well, sometimes the questions that you would expect to see aren't on the test and some obscure information is tested instead. But probably the most important reason for my preference is that I get very nervous when I'm taking a test, and that can affect my performance. Writing a paper doesn't cause me the same level of anxiety.

Checklist 2

✔ The talk answers the topic question.
✔ The point of view or position is clear.
✔ The talk is direct and well-organized.
✔ The sentences are logically connected.
✔ Details and examples support the main idea.
✔ The speaker expresses complete thoughts.
✔ The meaning is easy to comprehend.
✔ A wide range of vocabulary is used.
✔ There are only minor errors in grammar.
✔ The talk is within a range of 125–150 words.

EXAMPLE ANSWER FOR INTEGRATED SPEAKING QUESTION 3 "HEALTH INSURANCE"

The foreign student advisor agrees with the policy that requires international students to purchase health insurance from the university at registration. He assures students that the university isn't trying to increase fees for international students by doing this. He explains that health care is very expensive. For example, a visit to the emergency room can be a financial burden to a family who doesn't have medical insurance. He says that most families of international students don't expect the costs to be so excessive. And the reason that the university doesn't allow students to substitute other health care providers is because the local medical community has had problems with validation for health insurance plans from abroad and now refuses to accept them. So, um, in order to protect the students, the school doesn't make any exceptions to the policy.

Checklist 3

✔ The talk summarizes the situation and opinion.
✔ The point of view or position is clear.
✔ The talk is direct and well-organized.
✔ The sentences are logically connected.
✔ Details and examples support the opinion.
✔ The speaker expresses complete thoughts.
✔ The meaning is easy to comprehend.
✔ A wide range of vocabulary is used.
✔ Errors in grammar are minor.
✔ The talk is within a range of 125–150 words.

EXAMPLE ANSWER FOR INTEGRATED SPEAKING QUESTION 4 "ANTARCTICA"

Many countries have staked claims in Antarctica because the natural resources in other areas are being depleted and, uh, research indicates that minerals, fuels, and even some sources of protein are probably under the ice in large quantities. So, the implication is that as raw materials are exploited in areas that are relatively easy to reach, nations will think about taking advantage of their claims. For the time being, the location and climate have discouraged exploitation, and so have the treaties that protect the environment and encourage scientists to collaborate. It's also worth mentioning that Antarctica is vitally important to the balance that's maintained in the environment worldwide. So, in addition to all the difficulties that would have to be overcome to take advantage of the resources in their claims, individual nations also recognize the danger to the global environment and, at least for now, they're not pursuing their national interests.

Checklist 4

✔ The talk relates an example to a concept.
✔ Inaccuracies in the content are minor.
✔ The talk is direct and well-organized.
✔ The sentences are logically connected.
✔ Details and examples support the opinion.
✔ The speaker expresses complete thoughts.
✔ The meaning is easy to comprehend.
✔ A wide range of vocabulary is used.
✔ The speaker paraphrases in his/her own words.
✔ The speaker credits the lecturer with wording.
✔ Errors in grammar are minor.
✔ The talk is within a range of 125–150 words.

EXAMPLE ANSWER FOR INTEGRATED SPEAKING QUESTION 5 "EXTRA MONEY"

The woman needs additional income to meet her expenses so her friend suggests that she get a job at the cafeteria. Even though the salary isn't very high, the free meals are helpful. He isn't sure whether there's a job available but he agrees to find out. He also recommends that she rent the second bedroom in her apartment for a minimum of $250 a month, which would subsidize the rent and utilities. The problem she points out is that roommates can be disruptive, and sometimes they aren't financially responsible. But, she would have more time to study if she didn't have to work and her friend reminds her that she could require an agreement in writing, along with a deposit. Okay, in my opinion, she should try to get a job either in the cafeteria or someplace else on campus because if she lives alone, she can maintain a quiet environment for study, and she won't have to worry about a contract that could be difficult to enforce.

Checklist 5

✔ The talk summarizes the problem and recommendations.
✔ The speaker's point of view or position is clear.
✔ The talk is direct and well-organized.
✔ The sentences are logically connected.
✔ Details and examples support the opinion.
✔ The speaker expresses complete thoughts.
✔ The meaning is easy to comprehend.
✔ A wide range of vocabulary is used.
✔ Errors in grammar are minor.
✔ The talk is within a range of 125–150 words.

EXAMPLE ANSWER FOR INTEGRATED SPEAKING QUESTION 6 "RESEARCH REFERENCES"

According to the lecturer, there are two major criteria for using an older research reference. First, she mentions, and I'm quoting here, the "potential for change." For example, research on diet may be too old after thirty years because many changes have occurred in dietary practices during that time, but research on language development may be okay because fewer changes have taken place in language acquisition in the same number of years. The other criteria requires that you first identify the research as a conclusion or an opinion. Because, uh, in general, a conclusion may be outdated when a newer study is published, but an opinion credited to a person with the date of the opinion in the citation, um, that's correct over time. In other words, there's no exact number of years to decide whether a reference is acceptable so the date isn't as significant as the criteria. So, an older study can be used if changes in the research haven't taken place or if the results are worded as opinions with the dates cited.

Checklist 6

✔ The talk summarizes a short lecture.
✔ Inaccuracies in the content are minor.
✔ The talk is direct and well-organized.
✔ The sentences are logically connected.
✔ Details and examples support the opinion.
✔ The speaker expresses complete thoughts.
✔ The meaning is easy to comprehend.
✔ A wide range of vocabulary is used.
✔ The speaker paraphrases in his/her own words.
✔ The speaker credits the lecturer with wording.
✔ Errors in grammar are minor.
✔ The talk is within a range of 125–150 words.

EXAMPLE RESPONSE FOR INTEGRATED ESSAY "THE TURING TEST"

Some writers begin with an outline and others begin with a map of their ideas. Only the essay will be scored.

Outline

Turing Test—1950

* People interact w/ something
    In another room
    Questions microphone or computer
    Response voice synthesizer or text
* Evaluate
    Person or computer
    Wrong or can't decide →
    Machine passed Turing Test

Lecturer
* Premised on behavior, not thought
* Chinese Room—John Searle
    Questions in Chinese
    Reference
    Correct behavior
    Symbols w/o comprehension

Map

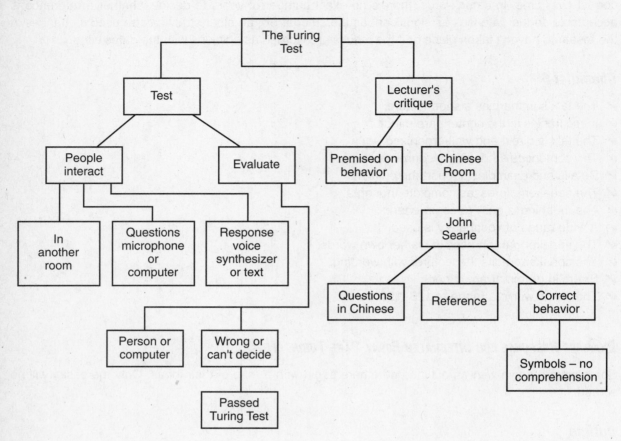

Example Essay

The Turing Test, developed in 1950, allows subjects to interact with a person or a computer in another room by speaking into a microphone or typing questions onto a computer. When they receive an answer by voice synthesizer or by text on their computer screens, subjects must determine whether they have been communicating with a computer or with a human being. If they think that they have been interacting with a person or they are unable to decide, then the computer has passed the Turing Test, proving that the machine is actually capable of higher-level thought processes similar to those of a human brain.

According to the lecture, however, a machine can be programmed to produce responses that appear to be intelligent without the awareness required for thought. In John Searle's Chinese Room, an English-speaking person is able to respond to questions in Chinese by referring to source material that allows him or her to break the code without comprehending the underlying meaning of the symbols. The person can behave correctly without the higher-level thought required to process the meaning. Therefore, a computer could pass the Turing Test if it were programmed to generate behavioral output but the Turing Test itself would be flawed. The experiment would not prove that a computer can think.

Checklist for Integrated Essay

✔ The essay answers the topic question.
✔ Inaccuracies in the content are minor.
✔ The essay is direct and well-organized.
✔ The sentences are logically connected.
✔ Details and examples support the main idea.

✔ The writer expresses complete thoughts.
✔ The meaning is easy to comprehend.
✔ A wide range of vocabulary is used.
✔ The writer paraphrases in his/her own words.
✔ The writer credits the author with wording.
✔ Errors in grammar and idioms are minor.
✔ The essay is within a range of 150–225 words.

EXAMPLE RESPONSE FOR INDEPENDENT ESSAY "FAMILY PETS"

Outline

Outline
Agree that pets should be treated like family members
* Children—learn how to care for brother, sister
* Couple—substitute for babies
* Disabled, elderly—help, caring like family members
* Every stage in life

Map

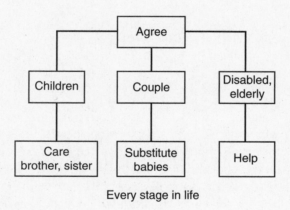

Every stage in life

Example Essay

Although the argument has been made that money spent on pets could better be directed to programs that provide assistance for needy people, I agree that pets should be treated like family members because they live in our homes and interact with us like family members do. Often parents allow children to have pets in order to teach them to be responsible. By feeding, walking, and grooming a dog, children learn to be dependable and kind. Parents expect their children to take care of the pets as if they were members of the family in order to learn these valuable lessons. For many children, a dog or a kitten is also a best friend and a wonderful way to learn how to treat a new brother or sister when the family expands.

Besides the friendship that children enjoy with animals, pets can substitute for the absence of other family members. Sometimes a couple who is unable to have children will adopt pets and treat them like babies. They shower the love on their cats that they might have provided a child, and receive affection and companionship in return. Many people who are living alone enjoy the companionship of a pet instead of loved ones who are at a distance or have passed away. The pet becomes a family member for these people and deserves the same kind of treatment that a family member would receive.

Many articles have appeared in the popular press citing the benefits of pets to the disabled and the elderly. In addition to the usual services that pets may provide, such as bringing objects to their owners or helping a vision-impaired owner to walk in unfamiliar surroundings, there is evidence that pets actually extend the life expectancy of their owners. In a real sense, these pets are caring for their owners like family members would, and for this reason, they should be treated like family.

At every stage in life we interact with our pets in the same ways that we interact with family. Children, young married couples, and elderly people have reason to treat their pets like family members.

Checklist for Independent Essay

✔ The essay answers the topic question.
✔ The point of view or position is clear.
✔ The essay is direct and well-organized.
✔ The sentences are logically connected.
✔ Details and examples support the main idea.
✔ The writer expresses complete thoughts.
✔ The meaning is easy to comprehend.
✔ A wide range of vocabulary is used.
✔ Various types of sentences are included.
✔ Errors in grammar and idioms are minor.
✔ The essay is within a range of 300–350 words.

MODEL TEST 3: PROGRESS TEST

➤ Reading

READING 1 "SYMBIOTIC RELATIONSHIPS"

1. **C**   In this passage, *obtains* is a synonym for "derives." Context comes from the close association with the word "benefit."

2. **C**   "Parasitism is a relationship in which one organism, known as the parasite, lives in or on another organism, known as the host, from which it [the parasite] derives nourishment." The pronoun "it" does not refer to Choices A, B, or D.

3. **A**   In this passage, *comparatively* is a synonym for "relatively." Context comes from the phrase "not killed immediately" in the same sentence.

4. **C**   . . . *when the parasite first invades* paraphrases "Newly established" and *the most destructive phase* paraphrases "more destructive."

5. **A**   In this passage, *permit* is a synonym for "tolerate." Context comes from the phrase "reducing the harm" in the same sentence.

6. **D**   "Parasites that live on the surface of their hosts are known as **ectoparasites**." . . . *surface* means "outside." Choice A is not correct because "mold and mildew" are ectoparasites, not ways that ectoparasites survive. Choices B and C refer to endoparasites, not to ectoparasites.

7. **A**   "There are many examples of commensal relationships. Orchids often use trees as a surface upon which to grow." Choices B and D are mentioned as examples of parasites. Choice C is not correct because ants are mentioned with the Acacia as an example of mutualism, not a commensal relationship.

8. **C**   In this passage, *really* is a synonym for "actually."

9. **B**   The author uses the example of the Acacia to explain how two species can benefit from contact. "Some species of Acacia, a thorny tree, provide food in the form of sugar . . . Certain species of ants . . . receive food and a place to live, and the [Acacia] tree is protected from animals. . . " Both organisms benefit.

10. **C**   "The bacteria do not cause disease but provide the plants with nitrogen-containing molecules." Choice A is not correct because the bacteria do not cause disease. Choice B is not correct because the bacteria is used for growth. Choice D is not correct because the nodules supply nitrogen, which is beneficial.

11. **A**   Pronoun reference is a transitional device that connects the insert sentence with the previous sentence. "Fleas, lice and some molds and mildews are examples of ectoparasites. They [fleas, lice and some molds] live on the feathers of birds or the fur of animals." Choices B, C, and D are not correct because the pronoun does not refer to endoparasites, which live inside the host and are explained later in the passage.

12. **A**   Because the text explains the types of relationships between species, it must be concluded that the passage would be found in a chapter about the environment and organisms. Choices B, C, and D are not correct because they are not as closely associated with the main idea.

13.   Parasitic: **D, E, H**   Commensal: **A**   Mutualistic: **B, G, I**   Not used: **C, F**

READING 2 "CIVILIZATION"

14. **B**   ". . . Neolithic settlements were hardly more than villages. But as their inhabitants mastered the art of farming, they gradually began to give birth to more complex human societies [civilizations]." Choice A is not correct because the Neolithic settlements preceded civilizations. Choice C is not correct because agriculture is mentioned as a cause of the rise in complex

cultures, not as a definition of civilization. Choice D is not correct because the population centers increased in size as civilizations grew, but other basic characteristics had to be present as well.

15. **B**   "Although copper was the first metal to be utilized in producing tools, after 4000 B.C., crafts-people in western Asia discovered that a combination of copper and tin produced bronze, a much harder and more durable metal than copper. Its [bronze's] widespread use has led historians to speak of a Bronze Age." The pronoun "its" does not refer to Choices A, C, or D.

16. **B**   "As wealth increased, such societies began to develop armies and to build walled cities." Choices A, C, and D may be logical, but they are not mentioned and may not be concluded from information in the passage.

17. **C**   In this passage, *hardly* is a synonym for "barely."

18. **D**   Because the author states that Neolithic towns gave "birth to more complex human societies," it may be concluded that they are mentioned to contrast them with the civilizations that evolved. Choice A is not correct because a Neolithic town does not qualify as a civilization. Choice B is not correct because writing systems were not part of Neolithic settlements. Choice C is not correct because Neolithic settlements were referred to as villages, and no argument was made for the classification.

19. **B**   ". . . a new social structure . . . [included] kings and an upper class . . . free people . . . and a class of slaves." Choice A is not correct because it does not include free people. Choice C is not correct because it does not include free people. Choice D is not mentioned and may not be concluded from information in the passage. The new structure described is based on economics, not on education.

20. **A**   . . . *the majority* paraphrases "most of which."

21. **A**   In this passage, *fundamental* is a synonym for "crucial."

22. **B**   In this passage, *important* is a synonym for "prominent." Context comes from the word "monumental" in the same sentence.

23. **B**   "A number of possible explanations of the beginning of civilization have been suggested." Choice A is not correct because scholars do not agree on one explanation. Choice C is not correct because trade routes are not mentioned in paragraph 4. Choice D is not correct because coincidence is not mentioned as one of the possible explanations.

24. **C**   Choice A is mentioned in paragraph 4, sentence 9. Choice B is mentioned in paragraph 4, sentence 8. Choice D is mentioned in paragraph 4, sentence 6.

25. **B**   A rhetorical question is a question that is asked and answered by the same speaker. Response is a transitional device that connects the insert sentence with the previous rhetorical question. Choices A, C, and D are not correct because the pronoun "they" in the insert sentence does not refer to plural nouns in the previous sentence.

26. **B, E, F** summarize the passage. Choice A is true, but it is a minor point that is mentioned as an example of the characteristics of a class structure. Choice C may be one of the architectural structures built, but it is not specified. Choice D is true of Mesopotamia and Egypt, but is not developed as a major point.

READING 3 "LIFE IN OUR SOLAR SYSTEM"

27. **D**   In this passage, *naturally* is a synonym for "automatically." Context comes from the prefix *auto*, which means "self" and the root *matic*, which is found in many words that refer to "machines."

28. **C**   "The moon is airless, and although some data suggest ice frozen in the soil at its poles, it [the moon] has never had liquid water on its surface." The pronoun "it" does not refer to Choices A, B, or D.

29. **A**   "Venus has some traces of water vapor in its atmosphere, but it is much too hot for liquid water to survive." Choice B is not correct because the water transformed to vapor, not ice. Ice refers to our moon, not to Venus. Choice C is not correct because the lakes or oceans evaporated quickly. Choice D is not correct because the airless atmosphere refers to Mercury, not to Venus.

24 30. **C**   In this passage, *constant* is a synonym for "stable." Context comes from the contrast with "evolve" later in the sentence.

25 31. **B**   Because Jupiter's moon is used as an example of satellites of Jovian planets, it must be concluded that Jupiter is a Jovian planet. Choice A is not correct because the satellites, not the planets, have conditions that support life. Choice C is not correct because the size of Europa is not mentioned. Choice D is not correct because the author draws no conclusion about the change of orbits. If orbits were modified, then a conclusion could be drawn about whether Europa was frozen.

26 32. **C**   ". . . life there may be unlikely because of the temperature. The surface of Titan is a deadly −179°C." Choice A is not correct because there are oceans of liquid methane and ethane. Choice B is true, but it is not the reason why life would be improbable. Choice D is not correct because it is the temperature, not the atmosphere, that is low.

33. **B**   . . . *the evidence did not demonstrate* paraphrases "the results did not confirm."

27 34. **C**   In this passage, *begun* is a synonym for "originated." Context comes from the root *origin*, which means "beginning."

28 35. **C**   "ALH84001 is important because a team of scientists studied it and announced in 1996 that it contained chemical and physical traces of ancient life on Mars." Choice A is not correct because the meteorite was found closer to twenty years ago. Choice B is not correct because the impact on Mars was not recent. Choice D is true, but it is not the reason why the author mentions the meteorite.

29 36. **B**   ". . . conclusive evidence [of life] may have to wait until a geologist in a space suit can . . . open rocks . . . searching for fossils." Choice A is not correct because a geologist will travel in the spacecraft. Choice C is not correct because pictures are not mentioned as a way to confirm the existence of life on Mars. Choice D is not correct because the present conditions could be studied in a variety of ways, but conclusive evidence depends on a manned flight that will allow a geologist to study the physical evidence.

30 37. **C**   "We are left to conclude that, so far as we know, our solar system is bare of life except for Earth." Choice A is not correct because the author states that our solar system is bare of life. Choice B is not correct because the evidence is not encouraging. Choice D is not correct because the search takes us to other planetary systems.

38. **C**   Reference is a transitional device that connects the insert sentence with the previous sentence. *Such periods* refers to "some points in history." Choices A, B, and D are not correct because *such periods* does not refer to phrases in the sentences that precede the insert options.

39. **F, D, B** summarize the passage. Choice A is a minor point that supports the major point in Choice B. Choice C is a minor point that supports the major point in Choice D. Choice E is not true because the author entertains the possibility of life based on something other than carbon chemistry.

➤ Listening

 Model Test 3, Listening Section, CD 5, Track 5

LISTENING 1 "STUDENTS ON CAMPUS"

Audio Conversation
Narrator: Listen to part of a conversation on campus between two students.

Q2   Man: I wish I were as sure about my future as you seem to be. I . . . I really don't know what I want to do after I graduate.

Woman:	Well, have you talked with a counselor over at the Office of Career Development?
Man:	No. . . . I talked to my academic advisor, though.
Woman:	That's good, but it's really better to see someone who specializes in helping people make career decisions. You see, an academic advisor is there to help you work out your academic program. You know, figure out what your major is going to be and which courses to take and all that. But a career counselor has a lot of experience and resources to help you decide what you want to do in the work world.
Man:	Did you see a career counselor?
Woman:	I sure did. Last semester. I was . . . well, I didn't even know what I would be good at, for a career, I mean. So I made an appointment at the Office of Career Development, and I talked with a counselor.
Man:	Do you remember who it was?
Woman:	Sure. It was Ruth Jackson.
Man:	Oh, but since I'm interested in careers for math majors, probably I should see someone else.
Woman:	Not really. Any of the counselors can help you. Look, first I took some aptitude tests and something called a . . . uh . . . I think it was called a *career inventory*. Anyway, I took several tests, and then the counselor gave me some ideas about different careers. I even went to some group sessions with some other students for a few weeks. Mrs. Jackson was the group leader, so, um, that's how I met her, and then I just sort of naturally started making my appointments with her when I needed some advice.
Man:	It sounds like it took a lot of time. I'm so busy already.
Woman:	Well, it did take time. Probably three hours for the tests, and I think I went to maybe four group sessions, and then I saw Ruth a couple of times. I guess about nine or ten hours probably. But it was worth it.
Man:	So, is that why you decided to go into library science? Because of the tests and everything?
Woman:	In part. But, mostly it was because of the internship. You see, I also got my internship through the Office of Career Development. And when I was working as an intern in the public library, it all sort of came together for me. I really liked what I was doing, and I realized that I didn't want the internship to end.
Man:	And you get paid for working there in the library too, don't you?
Woman:	I get paid, and I get credit toward my degree. But even better, I have a job offer from the library where I'm doing my internship.
Man:	Wow! Are you going to take it?
Woman:	I think so. I have to let them know next week. If I do take the job, I'll have to go to graduate school to get a degree in library science, but I can do that part-time while I'm working, and I had thought about graduate school anyway. So, I'm leaning toward taking the job.
Man:	That's great, Anne. I'm glad for you. So, uh, I guess I'd better make an appointment with Ruth Jackson. Maybe she can find me an internship.
Woman:	Maybe.

Audio	1.	What are the students mainly discussing?
Answer	**B**	Choices A and C are mentioned in reference to the main topic: the advantages of career counseling for the man.
Audio	2.	What is the man's problem?
Answer	**C**	He does not know which career to choose.
Audio	3.	Why does the woman tell the man about her experience?
Answer	**A**	Because the woman's experience was positive, she probably told the man about it in order to demonstrate the benefits.

Audio   4.   What is the woman's attitude toward her internship?

Answer   C   She thinks that it is a very positive experience.

Audio   5.   What will the man probably do?

Answer   B   He will go to the Office of Career Development [to see Ruth Jackson].

LISTENING 2 "SOCIOLOGY CLASS"

Audio Lecture

Narrator: Listen to part of a lecture in a sociology class.

Professor:

Q6   Social influence involves the changes in behavior influenced by the actions of other people. Social influence can come about for a variety of reasons, on a continuum from mere suggestion to, in the more severe form, well, to torture. How does social influence work? Well, first we must become aware of a difference between ourselves and the values or behaviors of other people. There are a great many studies of social influence that demonstrate how the presence of others can cause us to change our attitudes or actions. Studies show that people eat more when dining with others than, and I'm talking about dining out here, so they eat more in the company of others than they do when they're alone. They also run faster when others are running with them. There's even some interesting research on social influence among animals with similar results to . . . to those of human studies.

Probably one of the most interesting aspects of social influence is the pressure for conformity. Conformity is a process by which an individual's opinion or behavior moves toward the norms of the group. In a classic study by Solomon Asch, seven people were shown cards with three lines drawn on them. Here's an example:

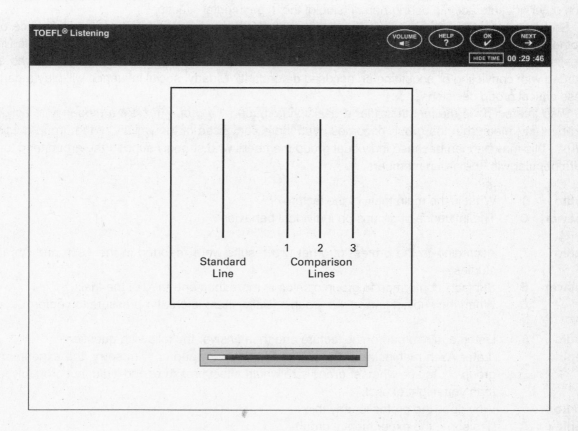

So, they were shown the lines, and then they were asked to select the line among the three that matched the, uh . . . the . . . standard line. Here's the standard. So there's no question as to the comparison. This has to be easy, right? Wrong. You see, Asch enlisted the cooperation of six of the seven participants in the experiment. On the first card, the six respond correctly—they . . . they identify the lines of the same length—so the seventh person, who is the only real subject in the experiment, well, the seventh person answers correctly, in agreement with the others. But on the next card, four of the cooperating participants choose an incorrect answer, but they're in agreement, so the problem for the subject is whether to conform to the opinion of the peer group, even though the answer, uh, is in conflict with the answer that the subject knows to be correct.

Q10

So what do you think happened? Well, subjects who were tested alone made errors in answers fewer than 1 percent of the time. This was the control group. But of those tested in groups of seven, let's see, uh, 75 percent yielded at least once to conform to a group answer that was clearly incorrect, and on average, subjects conformed to the group in about 37 percent of the critical trials. This means that they were bringing their behavior into agreement with group norms in . . . in spite of what they were seeing.

Q7

Later Asch manipulated the size of the control group . . . I'm sorry, the experimental group . . . to see whether group size would affect pressure, and it did, but probably less than you might expect. Um . . . groups of four demonstrated about the same results as groups of eight. Interestingly enough, a unanimous agreement by the group was more important than the number. In other words, a unanimous opinion by three exerted more pressure to conform than a majority of seven with a dissenting opinion in a group of eight.

Q8

Similar experiments have been performed in various countries, among diverse cultural groups, with, um, comparable results. Of course, people in cultures that emphasize group cooperation tended to be more willing to conform, but remember that many of the original studies were done in the United States where there's a high value placed on individualism. In an interesting variation on the study, Abrams found that conformity is especially strong when the group is selected from among those people that the subject clearly identifies with, either because, um . . . they have characteristics in common or . . . or they know each other and interact in a peer group outside of the experimental situation.

Q7

So what does all of this mean in the real world? Well, since group members can influence one another to conform to the opinion of the group, the group . . . decisions of a group, uh, may be called into question. What about decisions by political committees or parliaments? What about juries who are charged with convicting or acquitting an accused defendant? Clearly, social influence will play a part in these critical group decisions.

Also interesting is the fact that after a decision is made by a group, there's a tendency to solidify, and by that I mean that the group becomes even more convinced of the validity of the group opinion. Um . . . this may happen because individual group members who strongly support the group tend to be more popular with the group members.

Q9

Q11

Audio	6.	What is the main topic of the lecture?
Answer	C	The influence of groups on individual behavior

Audio	7.	According to the professor, what two results were reported in the Asch and Abrams studies?
Answer	B	Subjects conformed to group opinion in more than one-third of the trials.
	C	When the subject knows the group socially, there is greater pressure to conform.

Audio	8.	Listen again to part of the lecture and then answer the following question.
Replay		"Later Asch manipulated the size of the control group . . . I'm sorry, the experimental group . . . to see whether group size would affect pressure, and it did, but probably less than you might expect."
Audio		Why does the professor say this:
Replay		"I'm sorry, the experimental group . . . "

Answer   C   She needed to correct what she had said in a previous statement. Professors occasionally misspeak, apologize briefly, and provide the correct information.

Audio   9.   What generally happens after a group makes a decision?
Answer   C   As a whole, the group is even more united in its judgment.

Audio   10.   Based on information in the lecture, indicate whether the statements describe the Asch study. For each sentence, click in the YES or NO column.
Answer

		Yes	No
A	Only one subject is being tested.	✔	
B	The cards can be interpreted several ways.		✔
C	Some of the group collaborate with the experimenter.	✔	

Audio   11.   What is the professor's attitude about the studies on social influence?
Answer   B   She appears to be very interested in them. Her tone indicates interest and she cites some of the facts as "interesting."

LISTENING 3 "ART HISTORY CLASS"

Audio Lecture
Narrator: Listen to part of a lecture in an art history class.

Professor:

Q12 We know that the Chinese had been aware of basic photographic principles as early as the fifth century B.C., and Leonardo da Vinci had experimented with a dark room in the 1500s, but it was a number of discoveries in chemistry during the eighteenth century that, uh, accelerated the development of modern photography. The discovery that silver salts were light sensitive led to . . . experimentation with images of light on a . . . a surface that had been coated with silver. Often glass was used in the early images. But the problem was that these images were ephemeral—fading after only a short time. Some of the chemists who worked with them called them fairy pictures, and considered them, uh, that they were only momentary creations, uh, that they would disappear.

Okay. How to fix the image permanently was one of the most important, uh, challenges . . . of the early photographer chemists. In France, in about 1820, Nicephore Niepce discovered a method for fixing the image after a long exposure time, oh, probably eight hours. So, although his work was considered interesting, it was, uh, uh, largely dismissed for . . . as impractical. Nevertheless, one of his associates, Louis Daguerre, managed to find a way to, uh, reduce . . . the exposure time to less than twenty minutes. So the story goes, in 1835, Daguerre was experimenting with some exposed plates, and he put a couple of them into his chemical cupboard, so a few days later, he opened the cupboard,

Q14 and, uh, to his surprise, the latent images on the plates had developed. At first, he couldn't figure out why, but eventually, he concluded that this must have occurred as a result of mercury vapor . . . from a broken thermometer that was also in the, uh, enclosed in the cupboard. Supposedly, from this fortunate accident, he was able to invent a process for developing latent images on . . . on exposed plates.

The process itself was somewhat complicated. First, he exposed copper plates to iodine which released fumes of, uh, of light-sensitive silver iodide. These copper plates were used to capture the image, and by the way, they had to be used almost immediately after their exposure to the iodine. So, the image on the plate was then exposed to light for ten to twenty minutes. The plate was developed over mercury heated to about 75 degrees centigrade, which . . . that caused the mercury to amalgamate with the silver. Now here's the ingenious part—he then fixed the image in a warm solution of common salt, but later he began using sodium sulphite. Anyway, after he rinsed the plate in hot distilled water, a white image was left permanently on the plate. And the quality was really quite amazing. `Q15`

But, um . . . the process had its limitations. First, the images couldn't be reproduced, so each one was a unique piece, and that, uh, greatly increased the cost of photography. Second, the image was reversed, so the subjects would actually see themselves as though they were looking in a mirror, although, uh, in the case of portraits, the fact that people were accustomed to seeing themselves in a mirror made this less . . . this problem less urgent than some of the others. Nevertheless, some photographers did point their cameras at a mirrored reflection of the image that they wanted to capture so that the reflection would be reversed, and a true image could be produced. Okay. Third, the chemicals and the fumes that they released were highly toxic, so photography was a very dangerous occupation. Fourth, the surface of the image was extremely fragile and . . . had to be protected, often under glass, so they didn't disintegrate from being . . . from handling. The beautiful cases that were made to hold the early images became popular not only for aesthetic purposes but, uh, but also for very practical reasons. And finally, although the exposure time had been radically reduced, it was still . . . inconveniently long . . . at twenty minutes, especially for portraits, since people would have to sit still in the sun for that length of time. Elaborate headrests were constructed to keep the subjects from moving so that the image wouldn't be ruined, and, uh, many people simply didn't want to endure the discomfort. `Q13` `Q16` `Q13`

But, by the mid 1800s, improvements in chemistry and optics had resolved most of these issues. Bromide as well as iodine sensitized the plates, and some photographers were even using chlorine in an effort to decrease exposure time. The . . . the portrait lens was also improved by reducing the size of the opening, and limiting the amount of light that could enter, so the exposure time was about twenty seconds instead of twenty minutes. And negative film had been introduced in France, sorry, in England, and negatives permitted the production of multiple copies from a single image. So, photography was on its way to becoming a popular profession and pastime. `Q17`

Audio	12.	What is the main topic of this lecture?
Answer	**D**	The other choices are all mentioned in order to develop the main topic: the history of early photography.

Audio	13.	According to the professor, what two limitations were noted in Daguerre's process for developing and fixing latent images?
Answer	**B**	The images were very delicate and easily fell apart.
	C	Multiple images could not be made from the plate.

Audio	14.	Listen again to part of the lecture and then answer the following question.
Replay		" At first, he couldn't figure out why, but eventually, he concluded that this must have occurred as a result of mercury vapor . . . from a broken thermometer that was also in the, uh, enclosed in the cupboard. Supposedly, from this fortunate accident, he was able to invent a process for developing latent images on . . . on exposed plates."
Audio		Why does the professor say this:
Replay		"Supposedly, from this fortunate accident, he was able to invent a process for developing latent images on . . . on exposed plates."
Answer	**C**	The word "supposedly" implies that the speaker is not sure whether the information is accurate.

Audio	15.	What substance was first used to fix the images?
Answer	**B**	Table salt

Audio	16.	What can we assume about photographers in the 1800s?
Answer	**D**	Some of them must have experienced health problems as a result of their laboratory work because the chemicals and the fumes that they released were highly toxic.

Audio   17.   In what order does the professor explain photographic principles?
Answer   **B**   In a chronological sequence of events, beginning with the fifth century B.C. and ending with the mid-1800s

LISTENING 4 "ADMISSIONS OFFICE"

Audio Conversation

Narrator: Listen to part of a conversation between a student and an admissions assistant.

Student: Excuse me, but the secretary referred me to your office.
Assistant: Yes?

Q18   Student: I'm a new student . . . well, actually, I'm not enrolled yet, but I'm trying to get all my admissions applications turned in today.

Assistant: What's your name?
Student: Robert Franklin.
Assistant: Middle initial?
Student: T.
Assistant: Oh, I see. Wait a minute and we'll find out what you have to do. . . . Well, according to the records here, you have your admissions form, a financial aid application, three let-

Q19   ters of recommendation, transcripts from Regional College . . . so that's everything you need except a transcript from County Community College.

Student: That's what I thought. You see, I took a couple of courses there during the summer because it's close to my parent's house. Anyway, almost all of my first two years is from Regional College, and, uh, that's where I'm transferring from. In fact, the credit for the community college courses appears on the transcript from Regional College as transfer credit, but, uh, it doesn't show my final grades in the courses.

Q20   Assistant: Oh, and you haven't been able to register for your courses here at State University because the computer shows that you are missing some of your application materials. Is that it?

Student: Exactly. What I was wondering is whether you have, like a policy for this kind of situation so I could go ahead and register for this first semester while we wait for the transcript to get here. It should be here now. I requested it the same time that I requested a transcript from Regional College, but they're just slow at County Community.

Assistant: That happens sometimes. . . . Do you have a copy of your transcript from County Community College?

Student: Yes, I do. It's right here. Of course, it isn't an official copy. It's stamped "unofficial copy."

Assistant: But I can use this one until the official copy gets here. Here's the best way to handle this. We can give you a provisional admission. That means that you're admitted contingent upon the receipt of your official transcript. That will allow you to register for your courses this semester. When County Community College sends us your official transcript, then I can change your status from provisional admission to regular admission.

Student: Oh, that's great!
Assistant: Is this the only copy you have of your transcript?
Student: No. I have another one.
Assistant: Good. Then I'll just keep this in your file.
Student: Okay.

Q21   Assistant: Now the only problem is you can't register for next semester without regular admission status, and you need the official transcript for me to do that, so you still need to keep after them to get everything sent to us as soon as possible.

Student: Right. Well, I'll do that. But at least I have some time to get it done. . . . Um . . . what do I need to do now . . . to get registered, I mean.

Assistant: Just wait here while I enter everything into the computer, and then you can take a copy   `Q22`
              of your provisional admission along with you to the office for transfer students. They'll
              assign you an advisor and help you get registered later today.

Audio   18.   Why does the student go to the admissions office?
Answer **D**   He is trying to enroll in classes.

Audio   19.   What is missing from the student's file?
Answer **B**   A transcript from County Community College

Audio   20.   Listen again to part of the conversation and then answer the following question.
Replay   "Oh, and you haven't been able to register for your courses here at State University
                  because the computer shows that you are missing some of your application materials.
                  Is that it?"
Audio   Why does the woman say this:
Replay   "Is that it?"
Answer **B**   The admissions assistant paraphrases the problem and then asks for confirmation that
                  she has understood it. "Is that it?" means "Is that correct?"

Audio   21.   What does the woman suggest that the man do?
Answer **D**   Continue to request an official transcript from County Community College

Audio   22.   What will the student most probably do now?
Answer **B**   Go to the office for transfer students to be assigned an advisor

LISTENING 5 "ANTHROPOLOGY CLASS"

Audio Lecture
Narrator: Listen to part of a lecture in an anthropology class.

Professor:
The concepts of power and authority are related, but they're not the same. Power is the ability to
exercise influence . . . and control over others. And this can be observed on every level of society, from,
well . . . the relationships within a family to the relationships among nations. Power is usually structured
by customs and . . . and social institutions or laws and tends to be exerted by persuasive arguments or
coercion or . . . or even brute force. In general, groups with the greatest, uh, resources tend to have the
advantage in power struggles. So, is power always legitimate? Is it viewed by members of society as
justified? Well, no. Power can be realized by individuals or groups . . . even when it involves the resistance of others if . . . as long as . . . as long as they're in a position to impose their will. But what about   `Q23`
power that is accepted by members of society as right and just, that is, legitimate power? Now we're
talking about authority. And that's what I want to focus on today.   `Q26`

   Okay. When individuals or institutions possess authority, they have, um, a recognized and established right . . . to determine policies, with the acceptance of those over . . . over whom they exercise control. Max Weber, the German classical sociologist, proposed three types of authority in society:
traditional, charismatic, and rational or legal authority. In all three types, he, uh, he acknowledged the
right of those in positions of power to lead . . . with the consent of the governed. So, how did Weber dif-   `Q23`
ferentiate among the three types of authority? Well, he divided them according to how the right to lead
and the duty to follow are, uh, interpreted. In traditional authority, power resides in customs and conven-
tions that provide certain people or groups with legitimate power in their societies. Often their origin is
found in sacred traditions. The example that most often comes to mind is a monarchy in which kings or

queens rule . . . by . . . by birthright, not because of any particular . . . quality of leadership or political election, just because they have a claim to authority, based on traditional acceptance of their position, and in some cases, their, uh, their, uh, unique relationship with and, uh, responsibility in religious practices. The royal families in Europe or the emperors in Asia are . . . come to mind as examples of traditional authority.

Q25   Okay. This contrasts sharply with charismatic authority, which is . . . um . . . derived . . . because of personal attributes that inspire admiration, loyalty . . . and even devotion. Leaders who exercise this type of authority may be the founders of religious movements or political parties, but it's not their traditional right to lead. What's important here is that their followers are mobilized more by . . .

Q24   uh, by the force of the leader's personality than by the tradition or the law. So when we think of "charismatic" leaders in the United States, perhaps John Kennedy would be an example because he was able to project a youthful and energetic image that people were proud to identify with, or, if you prefer Republicans, you may argue that Ronald Reagan was able to exercise authority by virtue of his charismatic appeal. In any case, going back to Weber, to qualify for charismatic authority, a leader must be able to enlist others in the service of a . . . a cause that transforms the social structure in some way.

Which leaves us with legal rational authority, or power that is legitimized by rules, uh, laws, and procedures. In such a system, leaders gain authority not by traditional birthrights or by charismatic appeal but . . . but rather because they're elected or appointed in accordance with the law, and power is delegated to layers of officials who owe their allegiance to the, uh, principles that are agreed upon rationally, and because they accept the ideal that the law is supreme. In a legal rational society, people accept the legitimacy of authority as a government of laws, not of leaders. So, an example of this type of authority might be a president, like Richard Nixon, who was threatened with, uh, impeachment because he was perceived as not governing within the law.

Some sociologists have postulated that the three types of authority represent stages of evolution in society. That preindustrial societies tend to respect traditional authority, but, uh, as societies move into an industrial age, the importance of tradition . . . wanes . . . in favor of charismatic authority, with a nat-

Q27   ural rise of charismatic leaders. Then, as . . . as the modern era evolves, the rational legal authority, embodied by rules and regulations, replaces the loyalty to leaders in favor of . . . a respect for law. Of

Q28   course, other sociologists argue that in practice, authority may be represented by a combination of several of these ideal types at any one time.

Audio   23.   What is the main purpose of this lecture?
Answer   A   The distinction between power and authority is made in the introduction, but the main purpose of the lecture is to discuss three types of authority.

Audio   24.   Why does the professor mention Kennedy and Reagan?
Answer   B   They were examples of charismatic leaders.

Audio   25.   According to the professor, what two factors are associated with charismatic authority?
Answer   B   An attractive leader
        C   A social cause

Audio   26.   Listen again to part of the lecture and then answer the following question.
Replay   "But what about power that is accepted by members of society as right and just, that is, legitimate power? Now we're talking about authority. And that's what I want to focus on today."
Audio   Why does the professor say this:
Replay   "But what about power that is accepted by members of society as right and just, that is, legitimate power?"
Answer   B   Professors often ask questions to introduce a topic. After the question, she continues, "And that's what I want to focus on today" [authority].

Audio 27. In an evolutionary model, how is rational legal authority viewed?
Answer **A**   The most modern form of authority

Audio 28. What does the professor imply about the three types of authority?
Answer **B**   Because the professor presents both an evolutionary model and an argument for an inclusive model that combines several types of authority, it must be concluded that sociologists do not agree about the development of the types of authority.

LISTENING 6 "GEOLOGY CLASS"

Audio Lecture
Narrator: Listen to part of a lecture in a geology class.

Professor:
The original source of energy is what? The Sun. Then plants use the Sun's energy during photosynthesis to convert water and carbon dioxide into sugar and oxygen, and they store the energy in the chemicals that the plant produces. When animals eat plants, the energy is transferred to their bodies. So then, the plants and animals die and decay, and they sink to the bottom of the sea or . . . or disintegrate into the soil and then they're covered by more and more sediment as rivers deposit mud and sand into the sea or the seas advance and retreat. Of course, it's a very gradual process . . . one that takes place over, well, millions of years. But finally, the organic material begins to transform into the hydrocarbons, and the hydrocarbons eventually become oil and gas deposits. So how does this happen? Well, at first, the oil and gas are mixed with sand and sediment but . . . as the layers on top increase, then so does the pressure. And under pressure, mixtures of oil and sand and water . . . they seep down through the layers of porous rock . . . that's usually sandstone or limestone . . . so they sink down until they reach a layer of nonporous rock, and that's where they pool because they can't pass through the nonporous rock.

Okay. Sometimes there are breaks in the layers of rocks and the breaks allow oil and gas to bubble up and . . . and eventually they reach the surface of the Earth again. So, when this happens, the gas and some oil evaporate into the air . . . but they leave a sticky black tar that appears in pools or pits on the surface. But most crude oil is found in underground formations, which we call traps. So today, I want to talk about the major types of oil traps. In all the different types of traps, the oil collects in porous rocks, along with gas and water. And, over time, the oil moves up toward the surface of the Earth through cracks and holes in the porous rock . . . until it reaches a nonporous rock deposit . . . and the nonporous rock, remember, it won't allow the oil to continue moving. So the oil becomes trapped under the nonporous rock deposit. `Q29`

Now think for a moment. While oil was forming and moving, the Earth was also undergoing changes. In fact, there were enormous movements of the crust as the center began to cool. When *folding* happened, well, it was like the Earth fell back onto itself. And when *faulting* happened, it was . . . well, one layer was forced by rocks above down through the layers below. So, you can see that the . . . the . . . repositioning of porous and nonporous rock . . . this repositioning would have affected the movement of oil. When the Earth shifted, cracks would have been opened, and nonporous layers would have been . . . dropped . . . dropped over channels that had previously been used as . . . as pathways for the transfer of oil and gas to the surface.

Okay, as geologists, we're interested in locating the traps. Now why would that be so? Because that's where we'll find the oil and gas reserves. And that's what I really want to talk about today. So, there are several different types of traps, but today we're going to talk about the three most common ones—the anticline trap, the salt dome trap, and the fault trap. `Q30` `Q31`

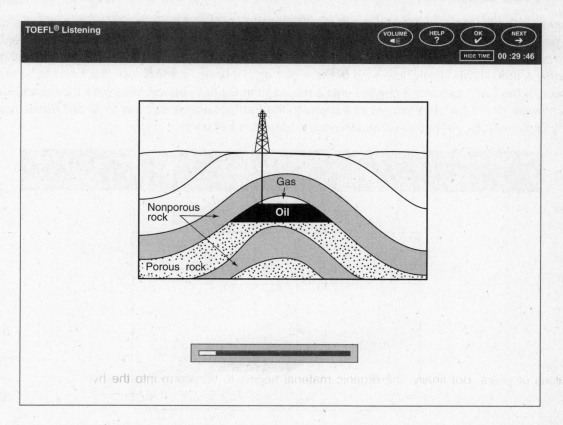

Q32   Look at this diagram. Here's an example of an anticline. As you can see, the oil is trapped under a formation of rock that resembles an arch. That's because the arch was bent from a previously flat formation by uplifting. In this anticline, the petroleum is trapped under a formation of nonporous rock with a gas deposit directly over it. This is fairly typical of an anticline. Because gas isn't as dense as oil, it rises above it. The dome over the top can be rock as in this example, or it could be a layer of clay. The important thing
Q33   is that the cap of nonporous material won't let the oil or gas pass upwards or sideways around it.

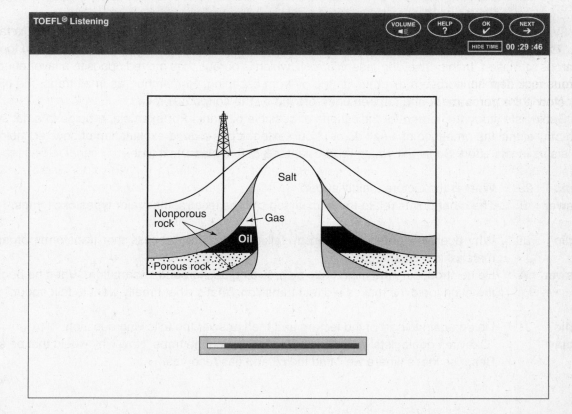

Now let's look at a diagram of a salt dome. This salt dome shows how a cylinder-shaped salt deposit has pushed up through a layer of sedimentary rocks, causing them to arch and fracture. The oil deposits have collected along the sides of the salt dome. Salt is a unique substance. With enough heat and pressure on it, the salt will slowly flow, kind of like a glacier, but unlike glaciers, salt that's buried below the surface of the Earth can move upward until it reaches the Earth's surface, where it's then dissolved by groundwater or . . . rain. Well, to get all the way to the Earth's surface, salt has to lift and break through many layers of rock. And that's what ultimately creates the salt dome.

Q34

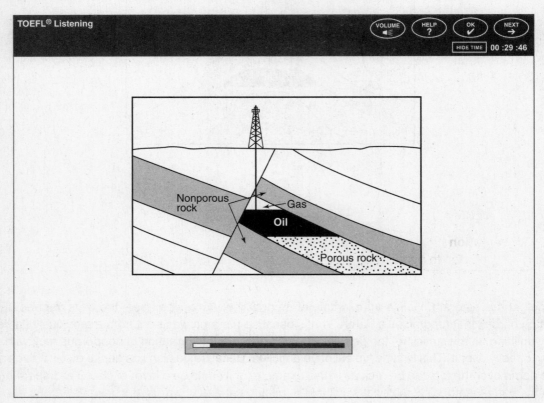

Finally, I want to show you a fault trap. Fault traps are formed by the movement of rock along a fault line. This diagram represents a fracture in the Earth that's shifted a nonporous rock formation on top of a porous formation. In this case, the reservoir rock, which is porous, has moved opposite a layer of nonporous rock. The nonporous rock prevents the oil from escaping. Remember, as in all traps, the oil is collected in the porous rock and trapped underground by the nonporous rock.

Geologists study the terrain for indications of possible oil traps. For example, a bulge in a flat surface may signal the presence of a salt dome. Your textbook has a good explanation of how technology assists us in this effort. So I want you to read Chapter 3 before class next time.

Audio 29. What is the lecture mainly about?

Answer B The other points relate to the main topic of the lecture: the major types of oil traps.

Audio 30. Why does the professor begin by talking about the process that transforms organic material into oil and gas?

Answer A He is introducing the main topic by providing background information. When he begins the main topic, he makes a direct transition: "that's what I really want to talk about."

Audio 31. Listen again to part of the lecture and then answer the following question.
Replay "Okay, as geologists, we're interested in locating the traps. Now why would that be so? Because that's where we'll find the oil and gas reserves."

Audio		Why does the professor say this:
Replay		"Now why would that be so?"
Answer	**D**	He plans to answer the question. Professors often use rhetorical questions in their lectures. By posing a question that they plan to answer, they help students follow the main points.

Audio	32.	Select the diagram of the anticline trap that was described in the lecture. Click on the correct diagram.
Answer	**B**	An anticline trap is shown in diagram B.

Audio	33.	Identify the nonporous rock in the diagram. Click on the correct letter.
Answer	**B**	In all traps, the oil is collected in the porous rock and trapped underground by the nonporous rock.

Audio	34.	According to the professor, what do geologists look for when they are trying to locate a salt dome?
Answer	**A**	A bulge in an otherwise flat area

LISTENING 7 "LIBRARY"

Audio Conversation

Narrator: Listen to part of a conversation between a student and a librarian.

Librarian: Hi, how can I help you?

Q35 Student: Hi, I'm looking for some material on reserve for Business 210.

Librarian: Okay. Well, who's the professor? You see, we keep the files under the professor's name because there are a couple of sections and the requirements are a little different . . .

Student: Oh, okay. It's, uh, Dr. Parsons.

Librarian: Umhum. Parsons? I don't see any books . . .

Student: I think it's a DVD.

Librarian: Oh, yes. Here it is . . . Oh, wait, actually, there are two of them. But that's all right. Now all I need is your student ID.

Student: No problem.

Librarian: There you go. Now, these will be due back at the desk in two hours.

Student: Two hours? But that won't even give me time to go home and . . .

Librarian: Oh, you can't leave the library with reserve materials. You have to use them here. But we have some DVD players in the booths behind the reference section. I think there are several free now.

Student: But I have to take notes and, uh, uh, I don't think I can get everything done in two hours.

Librarian: Well, you can't take materials out again until someone else has used them because the professor only left one copy of each. Sorry. Look, maybe two hours will be enough.

Q36 Student: I don't think so. These are case studies, and we're supposed to be able to discuss them.

Librarian: Oh, I see. Well, when do you have class?

Student: Tomorrow morning. I know I should have come in earlier, but this isn't my only class. I had an exam earlier today, and I was just waiting to get that out of the way.

Librarian: I see. Well, look, why don't you . . .

Student: Isn't there any way to get an exception to the policy?

Librarian: I'm afraid not.

Student: Oh. Okay then, let me just check out one of the DVDs. That way, if I finish it, I can check out the other one for two hours, right?

Librarian:	Sure. That's perfectly fine. And, here's a thought. I don't know if it will work for you since you have a morning class, but if you check out reserve material less than two hours before the library closes, then you can have it overnight . . .	Q37
Student:	Overnight?	Q38
Librarian:	Yes, but you have to have it back when the library opens the next day and . . .
Student:	But I could do that. Oh, I'm sorry, you were going to say . . .
Librarian:	Well, if you don't return the material to the reserve desk when the library opens, then there's a ten-dollar fine for the first hour and a five-dollar fine for every hour after that . . . that it's late, I mean. The usual fee is one dollar for every hour but when it's an overnight . . .
Student:	Ouch.
Librarian:	It's a stiff fine because we need students to take the privilege seriously. Otherwise, other students who need to use the reserve materials wouldn't have access to them.
Student:	Oh, I understand.
Librarian:	And another thing. Sometimes more than one person is trying to use the overnight privilege so . . . so sometimes when you wait until the end of the day . . .
Student:	Oh. And there isn't any way to put your name on a list or anything?
Librarian:	No, not really. It's first come, first served.
Student:	Okay. Okay. Then, I think I'll go ahead and take the one DVD out now because I can still try to get the second one tonight overnight, can't I?
Librarian:	Sure. I tell you what. Come back a little before nine.	Q39
Student:	Okay. Will you be here? I mean, I'd rather come back to you.
Librarian:	I'll be here until the library closes.
Student:	Well, then.
Librarian:	Do you still want to take out one of the DVDs?
Student:	Yeah. I might as well get one of them out of the way so I'll only have one left to watch.
Librarian:	Wait a minute. Your ID.
Student:	Oh, I'm sorry, I thought I showed it to you.
Librarian:	You did, but I need to keep it here at the desk until you return the materials.

Audio   35.   What does the man need from the librarian?
Answer   B   Material for a class—Business 210, taught by Dr. Parsons.

Audio   36.   What is the man's problem?
Answer   B   He needs to prepare for a class discussion.

Audio   37.   Listen again to part of a conversation and then answer the following question.
Replay   "I don't know if it will work for you since you have a morning class, but if you check out reserve material less than two hours before the library closes, then you can have it overnight . . . "
"Overnight?"

Audio   What does the man feel when he says this:
Replay   "Overnight?"
Answer   D   His tone expresses surprise and interest.

Audio   38.   What is the policy for materials on reserve?
Answer   D   Materials may be checked out overnight two hours before closing.

Audio   39.   What does the librarian imply when she tells the man to return at nine o'clock?
Answer   B   Because reserve materials can be checked out two hours before the library closes, and the librarian tells the man to come back at nine o'clock, she implies that the library will close two hours later, or eleven o'clock.

LISTENING 8 "LITERATURE CLASS"

Audio Lecture

Narrator: Listen to part of a lecture in a literature class.

Professor:

Q40 Today we'll discuss Transcendentalism . . .Transcendentalism . . .which is a philosophical and literary movement that developed in New England in the early nineteenth century. Transcendentalism began with the formation in 1836 of the Transcendental Club in Boston, Massachusetts, by a group of artists and writers. There's evidence that the group was involved in somewhat of a protest against the intellectual climate of Harvard. Interestingly enough, many of the Transcendentalists were actually Harvard educated, but they never met in Cambridge. Remember, at this time Harvard had only eleven professors, and at least eleven members could be expected to attend a meeting of the Transcendental Club. So their intellectual community was large enough to rival the Harvard faculty.

Q41 All right then. Their criticism of Harvard was that the professors were too conservative and old fashioned. Which, come to think of it, isn't an unusual attitude for students when they talk about their professors. But, in fairness, the classroom method of recitation that was popular at Harvard required the repetition of a lesson without any operational understanding of it. In contrast, the Transcendentalists considered themselves modern and liberal because they preferred a more operational approach to education. Bronson Alcott translated Transcendentalism into pedagogy by encouraging the students to think, using dialogues and journals to develop and record their ideas. Language was viewed as the connection between the individual and society. In 1834, Alcott established the Temple School near Boston Commons and later founded a form of adult education, which he referred to as *Conversation*. This was really a process whereby the give and take in a conversation became more important than the doctrine that a teacher might have been inclined to pass on to students, an approach that stood in diametric opposition to the tradition at Harvard that encouraged students to memorize their lessons.

Q42 The Transcendental group also advanced a reaction against the rigid Puritanism of the period, especially insofar as it emphasized society at the expense of the individual—the Puritans, I mean. According to the Transcendentalists, the justification of all social organizations is the improvement of the individual. So, in the literature of the time, the Transcendentalists insisted that it was basic human nature to engage in self-expression, and many interpreted this as encouragement for them to write essays and other opinion pieces. One of the most distinguished members of the club was Ralph Waldo Emerson, who served as editor of the Transcendentalist's literary magazine, the *Dial*. His writing stressed the importance of the individual. In one of his best-known essays, "Self-Reliance," he appealed to intuition as a source of ethics, asserting that people should be the judge of their own actions, without the rigid restrictions of society. You can imagine the reaction of the church, in particular, the Unitarian
Q43 Church, in which many of the intellectuals held membership. If individuals were responsible for their own code of ethics, then the clergy, and the entire church organization was threatened.

Perhaps because they were encouraged to think for themselves, the Transcendentalists came up with several options for living out their philosophies. Many were devoted to the idea of a Utopian society or at least to a pastoral retreat without class distinctions, where everyone would be responsible for tending the gardens and maintaining the buildings, preparing the food, and so forth. And quite a few were involved in some sort of communal living. Brook Farm was probably the most successful of these cooperatives, although it lasted only six years. Brook Farm and some of the other experimental communities brought to the surface the problem that the Transcendentalists faced when they tried to reconcile a cooperative society and individual freedom. Both Emerson and Thoreau declined to participate in Brook Farm because they maintained that improvement had to begin with an individual, not a group.

From 1841 to 1843, Emerson and Thoreau lived and worked together in Emerson's home, exchanging ideas, developing their philosophies, and writing. Upon leaving Emerson's home, Thoreau built a small cabin along the shores of Walden Pond near Concord, Massachusetts, where he lived alone for
Q44 two years. Devoting himself to the study of nature and to writing, he published an account of his experiences in *Walden*, a book that's generally acknowledged as the most original and sincere contribution to literature by the Transcendentalists.

But I'm getting ahead of myself. Transcendentalism didn't change the educational system, and it certainly didn't reform the church in any significant way, but it did, in a sense, change the direction of American social and political culture because Transcendentalism evolved from its initial literary roots into a force that shaped the way a democratic society was interpreted on the North American continent.   Q45

Audio   40.   What does this lecturer mainly discuss?
Answer **A**   Transcendentalism

Audio   41.   Listen again to part of the lecture and then answer the following question.
Replay   "All right then. Their criticism of Harvard was that the professors were too conservative and old fashioned. Which, come to think of it, isn't an unusual attitude for students when they talk about their professors."
Audio   Why does the professor say this:
Replay   "Which, come to think of it, isn't an unusual attitude for students when they talk about their professors."
Answer **A**   Her tone implies that she is joking with the students.

Audio   42.   According to the professor, what was true about the Puritans?
Answer **C**   They believed that society should be respected above persons.

Audio   43.   Why did the church oppose the Transcendental movement?
Answer **A**   The authority of the church would be challenged by a code of personal ethics.

Audio   44.   Why did the professor mention *Walden*?
Answer **B**   It is considered an excellent example of Transcendental literature.

Audio   45.   According to the professor, what was the most lasting contribution of Transcendentalism?
Answer **D**   Political changes

LISTENING 9 "GENERAL SCIENCE CLASS"

Audio Discussion
Narrator: Listen to part of a discussion in a general science class.

Professor:
Okay. This is a general science course, and as such, the first thing I want you to understand is the scientific method. In your book, the definition of the scientific method is "an organized approach to explaining observed facts, with a model of nature that must be tested, and then modified or discarded if it fails to pass the tests." So let's take that apart and talk about it. What are observed facts? Anyone?   Q46

Student 1:   I'll try.

Professor: Okay.

Student 1:   Isn't a fact supposed to be a statement that everyone agrees on?

Professor: So you would say that a fact is objectively true.

Student 1:   Yeah. That's what I mean.

Professor:
Okay. That sounds good, but what about this . . . we consider it a fact that the Sun rises each morning and the Earth rotates. But facts like that are not always agreed upon. Look, when we say that the Sun rises each morning, we assume that it is the same Sun day after day—an idea that might not have been accepted by ancient Egyptians, whose mythology taught them that the Sun died with every sunset and was reborn with every sunrise. Now, let's consider the case of the Earth's rotation. Well, for most of human history, the Earth was assumed to be stationary at the center of the universe. So, as you can see, our interpretations of facts often are based on beliefs about the world that others might not share. Still, facts are the raw material that scientific models seek to explain, so it's important that scientists agree on the facts. How can we do that?

Student 2:
How about this . . . a fact has to be verified, I mean, that's where the testing comes in, so we have to be able to test a model, but we have to be able to test a fact, too, right?

Professor:
Now you're on the right track. In the context of science, a fact must therefore be something that anyone can verify for himself or herself, at least in principle. So, even though the interpretation may be different, some interpretation of the Sun is there every morning, and that can be verified. Then, a model is proposed to explain the facts. And a model is...

Student 3:   . . . an explanation of the facts.

Professor:
Right. Once the facts have been observed, a model can be proposed to explain them and not only explain what is obvious but also make predictions that can be tested through further observations or experiments. Let's go back to Ptolemy's model of the universe, which assumed that the Earth was the center of everything. Okay, that was a useful model because it predicted future locations of the Sun, Moon, and planets in the sky. However, although the Ptolemaic model remained in use for nearly 1500 years, eventually it became clear that its predictions didn't quite match actual observations—a key reason why the Earth-centered model of the universe finally was discarded.

Student 2:   So models are discarded when they don't match the observations.

Professor:
Exactly. And new models are proposed to explain the facts in a better or more inclusive way. Okay, how does a model achieve the status of a theory?

Student 1:
Well, I guess sometimes the model doesn't fail, you know, it gets repeated by many experiments and the, uh, the uh . . . pre- um, predictions are verified.

Professor:
So, when a prediction is verified . . . repeated, then we start to assume that the model is a valid representation of nature, and when that happens with many experiments and a number of different researchers, then the model achieves the status of a scientific theory.

Student 2:   But . . .

Professor: Yes? Jerry?

Student 2:   Well, the problem is that theories get discarded, too, don't they?

Professor:
Absolutely. Because it isn't really possible to prove that a theory is true beyond all shadow of a doubt. And that's good because doubt is a cornerstone of science. Even a well-researched and presented theory should undergo continuous challenges from the scientific community, with further observations and experiments.

Student 3:
I'm sorry. Did we mention the term *hypothesis*? Does that fit in with a model or a theory?

Professor:
Glad you brought that up. A proposed model is often called a hypothesis, and that just means that the scientist is making an educated guess that the model's predictions will bear up under testing.

Student 3:   So a hypothesis is a proposed model.   Q48

Professor:
Right. But let's put this all together, shall we? Step 1 is *observation*, the collection of data, that is, observations. Step 2 is *hypothesis* or a model to explain the facts and to make predictions. Step 3 is *additional observations* and *experiments*. And here's the important part, when the predictions fail, then we recognize that the model is flawed, and we have to revise or discard it, but when the predictions are verified on a consistent basis, then we consider the possibility that we have a true representation of nature and we elevate the model to the status of a theory.

Student: So step 4 is the *theory*?

Professor:
Right. But, even then, the theory must undergo step 5 . . . that's *further observations, experiments*, and challenges. Okay so far? . . . Okay. Now for a reality check. In the real world of science, discoveries are rarely made by a process as . . . as mechanical as the idealized scientific method outlined in your textbook . . . the one that we just summarized. For example, anyone recognize the name Johannes Kepler?

Student 2:   Sure. Didn't he propose the laws of planetary motion?

Professor:
He did, in about 1600. But instead of verifying new predictions on the basis of his model, he tested the   Q49
model against observations that had been made previously. And . . . and . . . like most scientific discoveries, Kepler's work involved intuition, collaboration with others, moments of insight, and luck. And   Q51
eventually, other scientists made a lot of observations to, uh . . . verify the planetary positions predicted
by his model.

Student 1:   Student 2:
So the . . .   . . . Then

Student 2:   Go ahead.

Student 1:   So the scientific method in the book . . . that's not really the way it happens a lot of the
                time?

Professor:

Okay, let's put it this way . . . the scientific method is a process that we need to keep in mind as we do the work of scientists, but we should also understand that it's an idealized process for making objective judgments about whether a proposed model of nature is close to the truth. And we should also keep in mind that in the work of scientists, other factors are also brought to bear on those ideal steps in the process.

Audio   46.   What is this discussion mainly about?
Answer   **D**   The scientific method

Audio   47.   Why did the professor give the example of the ancient Egyptians?
Answer   **B**   To prove that facts may be interpreted differently

Audio   48.   Listen again to part of the discussion and then answer the following question.
Replay   "So a hypothesis is a proposed model."
                    "Right. But let's put this all together, shall we?"

Audio   Why did the professor say this:
Replay   "But let's put this all together, shall we?"
Answer   **B**   He is beginning a review of the process. Professors often use the phrase "put it together" when they are summarizing, restating, and clarifying several parts of a concept.

Audio   49.   According to the professor, what did Kepler do to verify his theory of planetary motion?
Answer   **C**   He used prior observations to test the model.

Audio   50.   What can be concluded from information in this discussion?
Answer   **A**   A model does not always reflect observations.

Audio   51.   What technique does the professor use to explain the practical application of the scientific method?
Answer   **B**   An example of Kepler's work, which included intuition and luck.

➤ Speaking

  Model Test 3, Speaking Section, CD 6, Track 1

Independent Speaking Question 1 "A Prized Possession"

Narrator 2: Number 1. Listen for a question about a familiar topic. After you hear the question, you have 15 seconds to prepare and 45 seconds to record your answer.

Narrator 1: A possession is an object that you own. If you were asked to choose one possession that you prize highly, which one would you choose? Why? What makes this possession especially valuable to you? Use specific reasons and details to explain your choice.

Narrator 2: Please prepare your answer after the beep.

Beep

[Preparation time: 15 seconds]

Narrator 2: Please begin speaking after the beep.

Beep

[Recording time: 45 seconds]

Beep

INDEPENDENT SPEAKING QUESTION 2 "CLIMATE"

Narrator 2: Number 2. Listen for a question that asks your opinion about a familiar topic. After you hear the question, you have 15 seconds to prepare and 45 seconds to record your answer.

Narrator 1: Some people enjoy living in a location that has a warm climate all year. Other people like to live in a place where the seasons change. Which type of climate do you prefer and why? Use specific reasons and examples to support your opinion.

Narrator 2: Please prepare your answer after the beep.

Beep

[Preparation time: 15 seconds]

Narrator 2: Please begin speaking after the beep.

Beep

[Recording time: 45 seconds]

Beep

INTEGRATED SPEAKING QUESTION 3 "WITHDRAWAL FROM CLASSES"

Narrator 2: Number 3. Read a short passage and listen to a talk on the same topic. Then listen for a question about them. After you hear the question, you have 30 seconds to prepare and 60 seconds to record your answer.

Narrator 1: A new policy for withdrawal from classes at the university has been established. Read the policy in the college catalogue printed on page 310. You have 45 seconds to complete it. Please begin reading now.

[Reading time: 45 seconds]

Narrator 1: Now listen to the students discuss the policy with each other.

Woman: The difference in this policy from the old policy is . . . now you only have three reasons to request a full refund after the first week . . . illness, death in the family, or military service.

Man: Right, but that about covers it, don't you think?

Woman:	Not really. In the old policy, you could drop out to help your family. Look, let's say that your mother's sick. She's not dying but she needs care. Then what? If you drop out to help her, you just lose your tuition.
Man:	Oh, I see. So you think that there should be more flexibility.
Woman:	Yeah. I think every case should be decided on its own merits. This policy is too . . . too . . .
Man:	Too narrow?
Woman:	Too rigid. I think at least some students will have other good reasons to withdraw and they'll just have to take a partial reimbursement because they won't be able to document their eligibility. I'd like to see a procedure, you know, a way to petition for eligibility. . . . I'd like to see that added to the policy.

Narrator 1: The student expresses her opinion of the policy for reimbursement. Report her opinion and explain the reasons that she gives for having that opinion.

Narrator 2: Please prepare your answer after the beep.

Beep

[Preparation time: 30 seconds]

Narrator 2: Please begin speaking after the beep.

Beep

[Recording time: 60 seconds]

Beep

INTEGRATED SPEAKING QUESTION 4 "BALLADS"

Narrator 2: Number 4. Read a short passage and listen to part of a lecture on the same topic. Then listen for a question about them. After you hear the question, you have 30 seconds to prepare and 60 seconds to record your answer.

Narrator 1: Now read the passage about Ballads printed on page 311. You have 45 seconds to complete it. Please begin reading now.

[Reading time: 45 seconds]

Narrator 1: Now listen to part of a lecture in a music appreciation class. The professor is talking about the ballad of "Barbara Allen."

Professor:
There are countless versions of the ballad of "Barbara Allen," and although it probably originated in the British Isles, versions are found not only in the British colonies but also in many other countries, including Italy and several countries in Scandanavia. In fact, there are almost 100 versions in the United States alone. But, uh, the version that I'm going to play for you today is the traditional Child Ballad number 84 from the reference *English and Scottish Popular Ballads.* In it, the narrative tells the story of Barbara Allen and the young man who fell in love with her. After Barbara Allen rejects him, he dies of unrequited love. And the day after his funeral, Barbara Allen dies of regret. They are buried beside each

other in the churchyard, and a red rose grows from his grave. A briar grows from her grave . . . uh, that's a thorny bush . . . and as they twine around each other . . . the rose and the thorn . . . they form a lover's knot. So we see that the lovers who were not united in life are together in death. The music is repetitive, like most ballads, and also important to identifying it as a ballad, the second and the fourth lines of each four-line stanza rhyme.

Narrator 1: Define a ballad, and then explain why "Barbara Allen" can be classified as a ballad.

Narrator 2: Please prepare your answer after the beep.

Beep

[Preparation time: 30 seconds]

Narrator 2: Please begin speaking after the beep.

Beep

[Recording time: 60 seconds]

Beep

INTEGRATED SPEAKING QUESTION 5 "THE ASSIGNMENT"

Narrator 2: Number 5. Listen to a short conversation. Then listen for a question about it. After you hear the question, you have 20 seconds to prepare and 60 seconds to record your answer.

Narrator 1:   Now listen to a conversation between a student and her friend.

Friend: I thought you liked your history class.
Student: I do. I mean, it's a lot of reading and everything, but I enjoy that, even though it takes a lot of time.
Friend: So what's the deal?
Student: Okay, last week Dr. Norman assigned a paper.
Friend: Well, I think that's fairly standard for a history class.
Student: Sure. It's on the syllabus, but . . . but it isn't very clear what he wants us to do. And he didn't really clarify it when he talked about it in class. So, I don't know how to start.
Friend: Hmmn. When's the paper due?
Student: At midterm, so I have time, but still, I'd like to get going on it.
Friend: Yeah, but like you say, you have time. Just wait until next week and ask about it again in class.
Student: I could, but won't he be . . . insulted? After all, he already explained it once.
Friend: Oh, I don't think he'd mind. He'd probably be glad that you want to do it correctly.
Student: I don't know. Maybe he would.
Friend: But anyway, if you don't want to do that, you could just make an appointment to talk about your ideas for the paper, you know, to get some direction about the topic. That way the conversation will just naturally lead into an explanation of how he wants you to do it.

Narrator 1: Describe the woman's problem and the two suggestions that her friend makes about how to handle it. What do you think the woman should do, and why?

Narrator 2: Please prepare your answer after the beep.

Beep

[Preparation time: 20 seconds]

Narrator 2: Please begin speaking after the beep.

Beep

[Recording time: 60 seconds]

Beep

INTEGRATED SPEAKING QUESTION 6 "ULTRASOUND"

Narrator 2: Number 6. Listen to part of a lecture. Then listen for a question about it. After you hear the question, you have 20 seconds to prepare and 60 seconds to record your answer.

Narrator 1: Now listen to part of a lecture in a general science class. The professor is discussing the way that ultrasound works.

Professor:
Okay, let's talk about how ultrasound works, and how it's used in medical diagnosis. To make a long story short, ultrasound is very similar to the sonar devices we discussed last week. Remember the system that emits ultrasonic pulses and listens for reflected pulses from objects in the ocean? Well, ultrasound is really just another type of sonar. The sound waves used in the ultrasound are created by a crystal that moves rapidly back and forth, creating a sound, but you can't hear it because the frequency is so high. The doctor places the device, the transmitter that sends out the sound waves . . . the doctor puts that on the surface of the skin so the sound waves are transmitted inside the body. And when this high-frequency sound is directed to a particular area, then the tissue and organs reflect the sound. The patterns of sound that are reflected are processed by a computer, and an image appears on the screen. And that tells the doctor whether there is something unusual there or not. This is very important in the diagnosis of cancer . . . to know whether a tumor is present . . . and also as a noninvasive way to monitor the growth of a fetus during pregnancy.

Narrator 1: Using the main points and examples from the lecture, describe the kind of information that ultrasound can provide, and then explain the way that ultrasound is used in medical diagnosis.

Narrator 2: Please prepare your answer after the beep.

Beep

[Preparation time: 20 seconds]

Narrator 2: Please begin speaking after the beep.

Beep

[Recording time: 60 seconds]

Beep

➤ Writing

INTEGRATED ESSAY "SYDNEY OPERA HOUSE"

First, read the passage on pages 314–315 and take notes.

 Model Test 3, Writing Section, CD 6, Track 2

Narrator: Now listen to a lecture on the same topic as the passage that you have just read.

Professor:
There was only a small reference in your textbook to the Sydney Opera House, so let me make a few more remarks about it. Personally, I think it's the masterwork of architecture in the modern period for any number of reasons, but primarily because it's totally unique. I mean it doesn't really fit into any category. Sure, it's modern, but it isn't really part of that whole International School that was so popular at the time. Although he did take advantage of advances in structural engineering and the newer materials that had replaced masonry in the International Style buildings, and yes, even the clean geometric lines that were stripped of the ornamentation of an earlier period, but the Opera House isn't strictly International because it's so imaginative and the shape completely breaks out of the skyscraper mold associated with the International Style. So is it an example of Organic architecture then? Again, I would say not. True, it has elements of the Organic School, which makes sense because Utson worked under the supervision of Frank Lloyd Wright for a time and there's no doubt that the design fits into the surrounding environment. It's a ship in the harbor. But then, the function that Wright insisted upon didn't dictate the form as much as the aesthetic shape. The purpose of the sails is to please the eye, not to contribute to the function of the spaces inside them. There's the High Tech aspect of the project that pointed the way for architects and engineers to collaborate in the creation of fantastic structures. So in that sense, it's a creature of the computer age, and might be considered part of the High Tech revolution among architects. But no. It's a blend of art and architecture, engineering and technology. It's one of the most widely recognized buildings in the world, and is still considered one of the most extraordinary and beautiful structures built in the twentieth century. I simply cannot categorize it as representative of any one school of architecture. To me, the Sydney Opera House is one of a kind.

➤ Example Answers and Checklists for Speaking and Writing

 Model Test 3, Example Answers, CD 6, Track 3

EXAMPLE ANSWER FOR INDEPENDENT SPEAKING QUESTION 1 "A PRIZED POSSESSION"

My most prized possession is my good reputation. My grandfather taught me to value it above material things. When I was a child, I was attracted to my grandfather's watch, and he explained that if the watch failed to keep accurate time, he'd get a new watch. Later, I begged to drive my grandfather's car because it was a much better car than my parents had. He let me drive it occasionally, and he always asked me to be careful. He also made me understand that the car could be replaced but . . . but I could never be replaced. And he told me that his most prized possession was his good reputation and that was why he had good friends and a successful business . . . I'd like to be like my grandfather someday so that's why I need to guard my reputation as my most prized possession.

Checklist 1

✔ The talk answers the topic question.
✔ The point of view or position is clear.
✔ The talk is direct and well-organized.
✔ The sentences are logically connected.
✔ Details and examples support the main idea.
✔ The speaker expresses complete thoughts.
✔ The meaning is easy to comprehend.
✔ A wide range of vocabulary is used.
✔ There are only minor errors in grammar.
✔ The talk is within a range of 125–150 words.

EXAMPLE ANSWER FOR INDEPENDENT SPEAKING QUESTION 2 "CLIMATE"

I've lived in a place with a warm climate all year for most of my life, but one year my family moved to England where the seasons change. I thought it was a beautiful place, and I enjoyed the experience, but I was glad to be home again. In the fall, we don't have to rake leaves; in the winter, we don't have to shovel snow; and in the spring, we don't have to drive in the rain. So a warm climate is a lot less work. And I can wear the same clothes all year in a warm climate, but in a place where the seasons change, you can't. I remember putting my coats and heavy clothes away when the weather got warmer in England. Best of all, I'd like to see the sun shine every day. So, maybe I'm just used to a warm climate, but for now, that's my choice.

Checklist 2

✔ The talk answers the topic question.
✔ The point of view or position is clear.
✔ The talk is direct and well-organized.
✔ The sentences are logically connected.
✔ Details and examples support the main idea.
✔ The speaker expresses complete thoughts.
✔ The meaning is easy to comprehend.
✔ A wide range of vocabulary is used.
✔ There are only minor errors in grammar.
✔ The talk is within a range of 125–150 words.

EXAMPLE ANSWER FOR INTEGRATED SPEAKING QUESTION 3 "WITHDRAWAL FROM CLASSES"

The woman thinks that the eligibility requirement for a 100 percent refund after the second week of classes should be changed. Right now, to qualify, you have to show documentation of serious illness, injury, death of a family member, or military duty. She points out that there could be a case when a student's family might need help but, uh, the . . . the circumstances would not be covered by the policy. Um, she suggests that there should be a way to petition for full reimbursement by explaining the situation, and, uh, each case should be decided based on the circumstances, not on such a limited number of possibilities. So . . . her solution to the problem would be to add the option of petitioning for full refund . . . by explaining the reason for requesting an exception.

Checklist 3

✔ The talk summarizes the situation and opinion.
✔ The point of view or position is clear.
✔ The talk is direct and well-organized.
✔ The sentences are logically connected.
✔ Details and examples support the opinion.
✔ The speaker expresses complete thoughts.
✔ The meaning is easy to comprehend.
✔ A wide range of vocabulary is used.
✔ Errors in grammar are minor.
✔ The talk is within a range of 125–150 words.

EXAMPLE ANSWER FOR INTEGRATED SPEAKING QUESTION 4 "BALLADS"

A ballad is, and I am quoting here, "a poem that tells a story and is sung to music." Characteristic of most ballads is the rhyming of the second and fourth lines. And usually ballads are part of an oral tradition, which, uh, it means that over the years, the song is revised as it's passed down from one musician to another. Some popular ballads have been written down and uh, assigned a . . . assigned a number in a reference book by . . . Child. Now, "Barbara Allen" is classified as a ballad because it tells a story about lovers who were not united in life but are joined symbolically in death by the rose and the thorn on their graves. The second and fourth lines of the song rhyme, and many versions of it are found around the world. One version is listed in the Child reference as number 84. So you see, "Barbara Allen" is not only a ballad. It's a very popular one.

Checklist 4

✔ The talk relates an example to a concept.
✔ Inaccuracies in the content are minor.
✔ The talk is direct and well-organized.
✔ The sentences are logically connected.
✔ Details and examples support the opinion.
✔ The speaker expresses complete thoughts.
✔ The meaning is easy to comprehend.
✔ A wide range of vocabulary is used.
✔ The speaker paraphrases in his/her own words.
✔ The speaker credits the lecturer with wording.
✔ Errors in grammar are minor.
✔ The talk is within a range of 125–150 words.

EXAMPLE ANSWER FOR INTEGRATED SPEAKING QUESTION 5 "THE ASSIGNMENT"

The woman's problem is that she doesn't understand the assignment in her history class. She knows that she's supposed to write a paper, but she isn't sure what the professor wants her to do. Um . . . her friend suggests that she ask about the requirements for the paper in her class next week, but she's concerned that the professor will be offended because he's already explained it once. His other recommendation is to make an appointment to talk about the topic for her paper because, during the consultation, she could ask questions. I think the woman should make an appointment to see the professor in his office as soon as possible so she'll have more time to work on the paper after she understands the assignment better. I also think it'd be best to be direct about asking how to complete the requirement because most professors are willing to help students who show an interest in the class.

Checklist 5

✔ The talk summarizes the problem and recommendations.
✔ The speaker's point of view or position is clear.
✔ The talk is direct and well-organized.
✔ The sentences are logically connected.
✔ Details and examples support the opinion.
✔ The speaker expresses complete thoughts.
✔ The meaning is easy to comprehend.
✔ A wide range of vocabulary is used.
✔ Errors in grammar are minor.
✔ The talk is within a range of 125–150 words.

EXAMPLE ANSWER FOR INTEGRATED SPEAKING QUESTION 6 "ULTRASOUND"

Ultrasound is like sonar because it sends out ultrasonic, uh, ultrasonic pulses, and then it picks up the reflections of the pulses. In the case of ultrasound, a crystal creates sound waves at such a high frequency that you can't hear them, but when the device that transmits the waves is placed on some part of your body, it sends the waves inside to the part that's being tested, and the organs reflect the sound waves. So that informs the doctor if you have anything suspicious there. Um, ultrasound is very useful in locating cancer and other growths, but it's also used in prenatal care to examine the baby in the months before it's born. In fact, it's fairly standard to produce images of babies to check their patterns of growth, using ultrasound. So ultrasound is very useful for medical diagnosis because it can provide accurate information without surgery or surgical procedures.

Checklist 6

✔ The talk summarizes a short lecture.
✔ Inaccuracies in the content are minor.
✔ The talk is direct and well-organized.
✔ The sentences are logically connected.
✔ Details and examples support the opinion.
✔ The speaker expresses complete thoughts.
✔ The meaning is easy to comprehend.
✔ A wide range of vocabulary is used.
✔ The speaker paraphrases in his/her own words.
✔ The speaker credits the lecturer with wording.
✔ Errors in grammar are minor.
✔ The talk is within a range of 125–150 words.

EXAMPLE RESPONSE FOR INTEGRATED ESSAY "SYDNEY OPERA HOUSE"

Outline

Sydney Opera House

Describe

• Danish architect—Jorn Utzon
• Plan
    Sculpture—sailing ship
    Curved roof
    17 yrs

Explain—why unique—no representative arch. movement

- International School
     modern geometrical lines
     prestressed concrete
     structure not typical skyscraper
- Organic arch
     fits environment
     not functional—more artistic
- High Tech
     roof design
- Multiple influences

Map

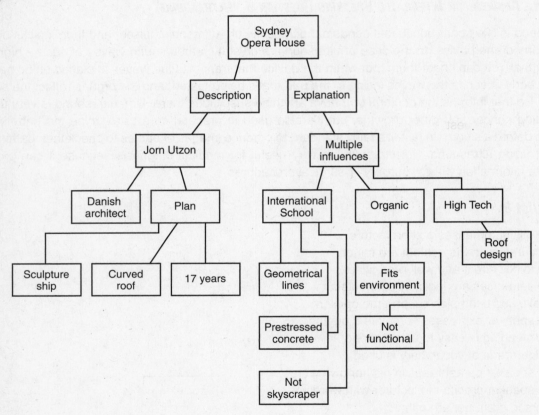

Example Essay

Designed by Danish architect Jorn Utzon, the Sydney Opera House has been portrayed as a piece of sculpture. Located on a promontory that extends into the harbor, it appears to be a large sailing ship among other ships on the water. Because of the complicated technology for the curved roof, it took 17 years to complete the project.

According to the professor, the Sydney Opera House is not representative of any one architectural movement. Its modern geometrical lines and the use of prestressed concrete was very new; however, the structure is not typical of the International School because the shape is unlike the skyscrapers that defined that style. Furthermore, although it is at home in the environment, which is a hallmark of Organic architecture, the form of a ship in the harbor does not serve a functional purpose as much as an artistic purpose. Finally, the computer technology required to create the design of the roof is somewhat like that of High Tech architecture, but not quite a part of that revolution. Perhaps because its creation occurred over several decades, the opportunity for multiple influences was greater.

Checklist for Integrated Essay

✔ The essay answers the topic question.
✔ Inaccuracies in the content are minor.
✔ The essay is direct and well-organized.
✔ The sentences are logically connected.
✔ Details and examples support the main idea.
✔ The writer expresses complete thoughts.
✔ The meaning is easy to comprehend.
✔ A wide range of vocabulary is used.
✔ The writer paraphrases in his/her own words.
✔ The writer credits the author with wording.
✔ Errors in grammar and idioms are minor.
✔ The essay is within a range of 150–225 words.

EXAMPLE RESPONSE FOR INDEPENDENT ESSAY "COLLEGE YEARS"

Outline

College years not best

- Stress
    Decisions—career, job, marriage
    Competition
- Dependence
    Family
    Debts

The best is yet to be

Map

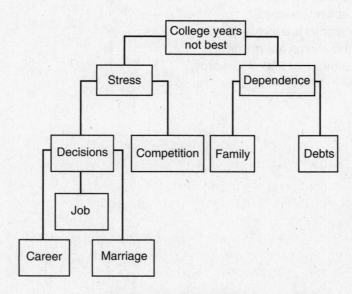

The best is yet to be

Example Essay

I disagree that the college years are the best time in a person's life. Admittedly, college often corresponds with a time when people are young, healthy, and physically strong, and those attributes are highly regarded in Western cultures; however, the college years must also be viewed as a period of high stress and a certain uncomfortable dependence.

Stress converges on college students from many directions. First, there is the pressure to choose a major field of study and, ultimately, to select a career, choices that will affect the rest of their lives. These choices often coincide with another life choice—the selection of a marriage partner. In combination, the stress associated with such important decisions can be very high. Second, there is the daily stress from competition in the classroom, exacerbated by staying up too late studying for tests, preparing papers, and reading assignments. It is well documented that college students tend to gain weight and suffer from many stress-related illnesses.

In addition to the stressful environment, most college students are not financially independent. Many rely on their families for funding, a circumstance that is often uncomfortable for young adults. Asking for money usually requires an explanation of why it is needed. In other words, financial dependence for college results in dependence in other areas of life at a time when young people are beginning to think for themselves and are old enough to be independent. Besides the embarrassment involved in negotiating for necessities, there is often a strict budget. For some students, there is also a debt to repay.

As a college student myself, I view this time of life as an opportunity to prepare for the next, and more important, stage of life, when I am independent and productive. I am eager to begin working and earning my own way. I look forward to the years after college with the hope that the best is yet to be.

Checklist for Independent Essay

✔ The essay answers the topic question.
✔ The point of view or position is clear.
✔ The essay is direct and well-organized.
✔ The sentences are logically connected.
✔ Details and examples support the main idea.
✔ The writer expresses complete thoughts.
✔ The meaning is easy to comprehend.
✔ A wide range of vocabulary is used.
✔ Various types of sentences are included.
✔ Errors in grammar and idioms are minor.
✔ The essay is within a range of 300–350 words.

MODEL TEST 4: PROGRESS TEST

➤ Reading

READING 1 "LAYERS OF SOCIAL CLASS"

1. **B** "Each class is defined by characteristics such as income, occupational prestige, and educational attainment. The different groups are arrayed along a continuum with those [groups] with the most money, education, and prestige at the top." The pronoun "those" does not refer to choices A, C, or D.

2. **A** In this passage, *very large* describes "enormous." ". . . a very small proportion of people" contrasts with very large control. ". . . vast amounts of wealth" also provides context.

3. **A** *Although it is not generally accepted* paraphrases "Despite social myths to the contrary." . . . *your family provides the best prediction of your future wealth* paraphrases ". . . the best predictor of future wealth is the family into which you are born."

4. **B** The author uses the example of the Forbes 400 to support the statement that most wealthy people inherit their money. ". . . most inherited significant assets."

5. **B** "The upper middle class . . . tend to be well-educated professionals or business executives." Choice A is not correct because the lower class is composed of the displaced and poor. Choice C is not correct because the term *nouveau riche* refers to the upper class that has recently acquired money. Choice D is not correct because the upper class is typically a group that has inherited wealth.

6. **A** In this passage, *mostly* is a synonym for "primarily." Context comes from the root *prime*, which means "first."

7. **B** In this passage, *modern* is a synonym for "contemporary." Context comes from the reference to "Recently" in the previous sentence.

8. **B** ". . . an open-class system leads many to think that the majority have a middle-class lifestyle because . . . people tend not to want to recognize class distinctions in the United States." Choice A is not correct because they vary widely in lifestyle and in resources. Choice C is not correct because, although the status may be unclear, people do not have a problem defining themselves as middle class. Choice D is not correct because "norm" refers to *average*, not *normal*.

9. **B** "People in this class have little formal education and are often unemployed or working in minimum-wage jobs." Choice A is not correct because 40 percent of the poor work. Choice C is not correct because service workers and manual laborers are part of the lower middle class. Choice D is not correct because the underclass that does not try to find employment is a special segment of the poor, not all poor people.

10. **C** "The underclass includes those who have been left behind by contemporary economic developments . . . the underclass may become dependent on public assistance or illegal activities." Choices A and D may be true, but they are not mentioned in the passage. Choice B is not correct because the illegal activities cause the increase in crime, not the opposite.

11. **D** Choices A, B, and C are mentioned for the first time in paragraph 1, sentence 1.

12. **A** Generalization and example is a transitional device that connects the insert sentence with the following sentence. "The working poor constitute a large portion of those who are poor" provides a general statement which is followed by an example, "Forty percent of the poor work." Choices B, C, and D are not correct because they are not examples of the generalization.

13. **C, E, B** summarize the passage. Choice A is a minor point that supports the major point in Choice C. Choice D is a minor point that supports the major point in Choice E. Choice F is true, but it is not developed as a major point.

READING 2 "WEATHER AND CHAOTIC SYSTEMS"

14. **A**   "Our understanding of chaotic systems is increasing at a tremendous rate, but much remains to be learned about them." Choice B is not correct because it was an incorrect assumption. Choice C is not correct because it was also an incorrect assumption. Choice D is not correct because today we have a very good understanding of the physical laws of atoms.

15. **B**   In this passage, *supposed* is a synonym for "assumed."

16. **D**   In this passage, *basically* is a synonym for "fundamentally."

17. **A**   The author uses the example of the car to explain how conditions are used to make predictions. The prediction of the location of the car is compared with the prediction of the weather.

18. **D**   "For tomorrow's weather, this slightly different initial condition will not change the weather prediction . . . But for next month's weather, the two predictions may not agree at all!" Choice A is not correct because the change in the initial conditions was minor. Choice B is not correct because it is not mentioned in the passage. Choice C is not correct because computer models are used to deal with all the data for weather prediction on time scales shorter than a few weeks.

19. **C**   ". . . chaotic systems are described by nonlinear equations." Choice A is not correct because chaotic systems [like weather] "are not completely random." Choice B is true, but it is not the reason why weather is considered a chaotic system. Choice D is not correct because many chaotic systems are "'predictably unpredictable.'"

20. **A**   "This extreme sensitivity to initial conditions is sometimes called the *butterfly effect*." Choice B is not correct because the flap of a butterfly's wings is used to describe the sensitivity, not to predict conditions. Choice C is not correct because the rate of the wings is not mentioned. Choice D is not correct because the cause and result do not refer to different locations. They refer to changes over time.

21. **D**   "Simple systems are described by linear equations in which, [in the linear equations] for example, increasing a cause produces a proportional increase in an effect." The phrase "in which" does not refer to Choices A, B, or C.

22. **B**   The author mentions the economy to provide an example of another chaotic system. "For example, the economy is nonlinear because a rise in interest rates does not automatically produce a corresponding change in consumer spending."

23. **C**   In this passage, *characteristics* is a synonym for "features." Context comes from the contrast with "details" later in the sentence.

24. **D**   "Our understanding of chaotic systems is increasing at a tremendous rate, but much remains to be learned about them." Choice A is not correct because "many chaotic systems have a kind of underlying order." Choice B is not correct because "Our understanding of chaotic systems is increasing at a tremendous rate." Choice C is not correct because "details . . . remain unpredictable."

25. **B**   Chronological order is a transitional device that connects the insert sentence in sequence within the text. ". . . tomorrow" should precede "next week" and "next month" should follow "next week."

26. **D, F, C** summarize the passage. Choice A may be true, but it is not directly stated in the passage. Choice B is a minor point because it is an example. Choice E is a minor point because it is an example.

READING 3 "BUILDING WITH ARCHES"

27. **A**   ". . . the arch is stable only when it is complete, when the topmost stone, the **keystone**, has been set in place." Choice B is not correct because the historical background was provided at the beginning of the passage. Choice C is not correct because the virtues are pointed out before the keystone is mentioned. Choice D is not correct because the passage is about arches, and no alternatives are suggested.

28. **D** In this passage, *essential* is a synonym for "inherent."

29. **D** Choice A is mentioned in paragraph 2, sentence 4. Choice B is mentioned in paragraph 2, sentence 5. Choice C is mentioned in paragraph 2, sentence 5.

30. **C** "This vault construction makes it possible to create large interior spaces." Choices A, B, and D are true, but they are not advantages of the arch.

31. **D** In this passage, *practically* is a synonym for "virtually."

32. **A** "Romanesque builders adopted the old Roman forms of round arch and barrel vault so as to add height to their churches." Choice B is not correct because wooden beams characterized buildings before the Romanesque style. Choice C is not correct because the Romanesque buildings added height. Choice D is not correct because the Romanesque style was many hundreds of years later.

33. **C** *. . . a concern because of fire* paraphrases "a threat of fire" and *constraints they imposed on the height of the ceiling* paraphrases "limited the height to which architects could aspire."

34. **B** In this passage, *accomplish* is a synonym for "achieve." Context comes from the contrast with "limited" in the previous sentence.

35. **B** "The pointed arch . . . offers many advantages . . . and . . . the arch can be taller." Choice A is not correct because such an arch [pointed] can be much taller than a barrel vault. Choice C is not correct because the nave added space but not height. Choice D is not correct because windows were an additional advantage of pointed arch construction, but they did not extend the height.

36. **D** "Barrel vaults are both literally and visually heavy, calling for huge masses of stone to maintain their [the vaults] structural stability." The pronoun "their" does not refer to Choices A, B, or C.

37. **C** ". . . the builders . . . dared not make light-admitting openings . . . for fear the arches and vaults would collapse, and so the interiors of Romanesque buildings tend to be dark." Choice A is not correct because the Gothic period, which followed the Romanesque, solved the problem with pointed arches that allowed for windows. Choice B is not correct because the author does not mention that windows were difficult to make. Choice D is not correct because the reference to reinforcement at the major points of intersection was characteristic of Gothic, not Romanesque, architecture.

38. **D** Vocabulary reference is a transitional device that connects the insert sentence with the previous sentence. The connection is the reference to "reinforced" in the first sentence and "These reinforcements" in the second sentence. Choices A, B, and C are not correct because there are no vocabulary references to connect them with the insert sentence.

39.   Round Arch: **C, D, G, H**   Pointed Arch: **A, E, I**   Not used: **B, F**

READING 4 "THE DIGITAL DIVIDE"

40. **A** The author mentions the telephone to demonstrate that even technology like the telephone is not available to all. "Only 6 percent of the population in developing countries are connected to telephones."

41. **B** *The number of people who use computers and the Internet is increasing* paraphrases "the number of Internet users is growing" and *most people in the world still do not have connections* paraphrases "most of the world's population does not have access to computers or the Internet."

42. **C** In this passage, *people* refers to "residents." Context comes from the previous reference to a place, "some Native American reservations," in the same sentence. Choices A, B, and D are not correct because they are not capable of being residents [living in a place].

43. **D** In this passage, *remove* is a synonym for "eliminate." Context comes from the word "remove" later in the same sentence.

44. **B** "The digital divide between the populations who have access to the Internet and information technology tools is based on income, race, education, household type, and geographic location." Choice A is not correct because the divide is not limited to developing nations. Choice C is not correct because socioeconomic level is only one of the factors. Choice D is not correct because the divide is between those with access and without access, not between different groups with access.

45. **A** The author gives details about the percentages of Internet users to prove that there are differences in opportunities among social groups. Choice B is not correct because the author is presenting facts and statistics, not a persuasive argument. Choice C is not correct because no improvements are mentioned. Choice D is not correct because no explanation is provided with the facts.

46. **B** ". . . 11 percent of black households." Choice A is not correct because 15 percent of households with one parent have access. Choice C is not correct because 13 percent of Hispanic households have access. Choice D is not correct because 40 percent of households with two parents have access.

47. **C** ". . . twice as many of the schools with more affluent students have wired classrooms as those [schools] with high concentrations of low-income students." The pronoun "those" does not refer to Choices A, B, or D.

48. **B** "Women . . . are receiving fewer than 30 percent of the computer science degrees. The result [of receiving fewer degrees] is that women and members of the most oppressed ethnic groups are not eligible for the jobs." Choice A is not correct because information about admission is not included in the passage. Choice C is not correct because we do not know whether they are interested. Choice D is not correct because the jobs with the highest salaries are in computer science.

49. **B** In this passage, *numbers* is a synonym for "concentrations." Context comes from the references in previous sentences to "percentage" and "number."

50. **C** Because "populations . . . cannot currently afford the equipment which needs to be updated every three years," it must be concluded that the cost of replacing equipment is a problem. Choice A is not correct because the quality of the computers is not mentioned. Choices B and D are not correct because no judgments are made.

51. **C** Conclusion from evidence is the transitional device that connects the insert sentence with the previous sentence. ". . . twice as many of the schools with more affluent students have wired classrooms . . . Thus, the students who are most unlikely to have access at home also do not have access in their schools." Choices A, B, and D are not correct because they do not provide the evidence for the conclusion in the insert sentence that follows them.

52. **D, B, F** summarize the passage. Choice A is a detail that is not developed in the passage. Choice C is a minor point that supports major point D. Choice E is a minor point that supports major point B.

READING 5 "THE EVOLUTION OF BIRDS"

53. **D** ". . . birds are toothless, an adaptation that trims the weight of the head . . . The bird's beak, made of keratin, has proven to be very adaptable." Choice A is not correct because the skeleton is honeycombed, which makes it strong and light, but it does not have fewer bones. Choice B is not correct because the organs are fewer, not smaller. Choice C is not correct because the head is lighter, not heavier.

54. **A** In this passage, the phrase *made different* describes "modified." Context comes from the examples in the sentences that follow and from the reference to "adaptation."

55. **D** "Feathers, and in some species, layers of fat provide insulation that enables birds to retain their [birds] metabolically generated heat." The pronoun "their" does not refer to Choices A, B, or C.

56. **A** In this passage, *simple* is an antonym for "elaborate." Context comes from the references to "complex" in the previous sentence and "intricate" in the same sentence.

25 57. **C** "Bird wings are airfoils that illustrate the same principles of aerodynamics as the wings of an airplane." Choice A is not correct because some birds flap their wings only occasionally. Choice B is not correct because swifts, not eagles and hawks, can fly 170 km/hr. Choice D is not correct because the wings are the airfoils, and they are attached to the sternum (breast-bone).

26 58. **A** "Feathers are made of keratin, the same protein that forms our hair and fingernails and the scales of reptiles." Choice B is not correct because feathers are made of keratin, not compared with keratin. Choice C is not correct because the author does not refer to the text. Choice D is not correct because the only description is the comparison with hair, fingernails, and scales.

27 59. **B** In this passage, *very wide* describes "radical." Context comes from the examples of alterations in the previous two paragraphs.

28 60. **B** "Amniotic eggs and scales on the legs are just two of the reptilian features we see in birds." Choice A is true, but it is not mentioned in the passage. Choice C is not correct because the adaptations for the skeleton are described in paragraph 2. Choice D is not correct because birds have a four-chambered heart.

61. **B** . . . *a mutual ancestor* paraphrases "an ancestor common to both birds and dinosaurs."

29 62. **B** "The intense current interest" implies that the subject is popular. Choice A is not correct because the interest is current. Choice C is not correct because the number of researchers is not mentioned. Choice D is not correct because a "closer understanding" implies that the research is not definitive.

30 63. **D** Choice A is mentioned in paragraph 1, sentence 3. Choice B is mentioned in paragraph 5, sentence 1. Choice C is mentioned in paragraph 4, sentences 1 and 2.

64. **C** Addition is a transitional device that connects the insert sentence with previous sentences. Several benefits of flight are explained before the insert sentence. The sentence after the insert expands on the benefit of migrating to avoid extreme climates.

65. **A, C, E** summarize the passage. Choice B is an example of major point C. Choice D is a minor point that refers to major point A. Choice F is an example of major point E.

➤ Listening

  Model Test 4, Listening Section, CD 6, Track 4

LISTENING 1 "PROFESSOR'S OFFICE"

Audio Conversation

Narrator:	Listen to part of a conversation on campus between a student and a professor.

Q1

Professor:	So what did you want to see me about Ernie?
Student:	My grade. I'm not doing very well in this class.
Professor:	Well, that's not exactly true. You were doing very well until the last test.
Student:	I got a D. Professor Adams, I've never gotten a D in my life . . . before this, I mean. So that's why I'm here. I hope you can give me some advice.
Professor:	Well, from my class book, I see that your attendance is excellent. No absences, so that's not the problem.
Student:	No, I never miss class. I'm a serious student. I just don't know what happened on that test.
Professor:	Did you bring it? The test?
Student:	Yes, I did. Here it is.

Professor:	Okay. I think I remember this, but there were almost a hundred tests to grade, so let's have a look at it.
Student:	Thanks.
Professor:	Well, Ernie . . . let's see . . . Here it is. Yes, I do recall this test. You didn't finish it. You stopped after question 15. So you had 5 questions that were counted wrong because they . . . because you didn't complete the test.
Student:	I know. I didn't watch the time, and I just couldn't believe it when you asked us to hand in the tests.
Professor:	Yes, I see. But you did a good job on the questions that you *did* respond to.
Student:	Professor Adams, maybe you won't believe me, but I know the answers to the questions that I . . . that . . . that . . .
Professor:	The ones that you left blank at the end.
Student:	Yeah. So now I need some advice about how to bring up my grade because a D is going to make a big difference.
Professor:	This test counts 25 percent so, uh, . . . you're right. It will bring it down at least a letter.
Student:	I know.
Professor:	Okay then. The first thing is to learn something from this. You have to find a way to pace yourself through tests or you're going to have this problem again.
Student:	I know, and believe me, I learned that already.
Professor:	Okay. That's good. Now, uh, what about the grade for this class?
Student:	I was hoping you might give me a chance to . . . to maybe do an extra credit assignment.
Professor:	Hummm. I don't know about that.
Student:	Oh.
Professor:	But here's what we *can* do. If you want to finish the test right now, and your answers are satisfactory, then I'll add some points to your grade.
Student:	You will? I know the answers. Really I . . .
Professor:	. . . I can't give you full credit for your answers. That wouldn't be fair to the other students, but I can add some points, and that should help you somewhat.
Student:	Wow. This is great.
Professor:	Okay. Just take your test over there and finish it. You had about an hour to complete 20 questions, so, uh, . . . that would be 15 minutes to finish the 5 questions you left blank. And Ernie . . . pace yourself.
Student:	I will! Thanks. Thanks a lot.

Q2

Q3

Q4

Q5

Audio 1. Why does the man go to see his professor?
Answer **D** To ask the professor how to bring up his grade

Audio 2. Why did Ernie get a low grade on the last test?
Answer **C** He did not have time to finish it.

Audio 3. What do we know about the test?
Answer **B** It was worth 25 percent of the final grade.

Audio 4. Listen again to part of the conversation and then answer the following question.
Replay " I was hoping you might give me a chance to . . . to maybe do an extra credit assignment."
"Hummm. I don't know about that."

Audio Why does the professor say this:
Replay "Hummm. I don't know about that."
Answer **D** Her tone indicates that she does not want to do what the man suggests. "I don't know about that" is an indirect way to say no.

Audio   5.   What can be inferred about the professor?
Answer   **A**   She tries to be fair to all of her students.

Listening 2 "Anthropology Class"

Audio Lecture
Narrator: Listen to part of a lecture in an anthropology class. The professor is discussing agriculture.

Professor:
Let's just pick up where we left off last week. Okay, as you'll recall, earlier theories about the development of agriculture tended to view it as a progressive event, or even as a catalyst for everything from art to industry, but I'm going to share a rather different view with you. From a revisionist perspective, the development of agriculture about 10,000 years ago didn't improve the lives of early farmers. On the contrary, when hunter-gatherers abandoned the age-old method of foraging for food and began to cultivate crops, they put their health at risk. Now I know it's just the opposite of . . . it's quite a different viewpoint let's say, so . . . why would this be so . . . why would their health decline when agriculture provided people with an efficient way to get more food for less work?

Clearly, cultivated fields yield more food per acre than uncultivated land with undomesticated patches of berries and nuts. Well, first let's consider the conditions that are necessary for agriculture to flourish. In order to have enough labor to plant, tend, and harvest crops, a larger number of people must well, . . . they have to cooperate. That means that the density of the population must increase in the area surrounding the cultivated farms. And, as we know, crowding contributes to the transmission of infectious diseases. So when hunter-gatherers were wandering in small bands, the likelihood of an epidemic was slight, but after the agricultural revolution, tuberculosis . . . and diseases of the intestinal tract . . . these began to reach epidemic proportions in the crowded agricultural communities. And in addition, because the population was no longer mobile and . . . and relied on trade to inject variety into the lives and diets of the farmers, that meant that disease was also transmitted through the exchange of goods.

Now, the revisionists also argue that the content of the diet for early farmers was inferior to that of the hunter-gatherers. You'll recall that hunter-gatherers enjoyed a variety of foods selected from wild plants and game, and in studies of modern tribes that have continued the tradition of hunting and gathering food, it appears that those . . . the hunters and gatherers . . . they have a better balance of nutrients and even more protein than tribes that have adopted agricultural lifestyles. Today, three grain crops . . . wheat, corn, and rice . . . these account for the bulk of calories consumed by farming societies. So, consider the implications. Extrapolating from this and from evidence that early farmers raised only one or two crops, we can conclude that a disproportionate amount of carbohydrates formed the basis of their diets.

Now another interesting series of studies involve the skeletal remains of hunter-gatherers as compared with their agricultural relatives. And one such study from Greece and Turkey . . . it indicates that the average height of hunter-gatherers at the end of the Ice Age was . . . let me check my notes . . . yes, it was 5′9″ for men and 5′5″ for women. And their bones were strong, healthy, and athletic. But, after the agricultural revolution, skeletal remains revealed that height had diminished to a shocking 5′3″ for men and 5′ for women. And evidence from bone samples suggests that they suffered from diseases caused by malnutrition, like anemia. And this is interesting. Further studies from paleontologists at the University of Massachusetts project life expectancies for hunter-gatherers at about twenty-six years, but post agricultural life expectancies were less than twenty years. Let me just read you something from one of the studies by George Armelagos, and I quote, "episodes of nutritional stress and infectious disease were seriously affecting their ability to survive." And he's referring to early farmers here.

So, let's see where we are. Oh, yes. Consider that hunter-gatherers had the advantage of mobility. So if food wasn't plentiful, they broke camp and moved on in search of an area with a larger food supply. And, if one type of food were in short supply, for example . . . well, berries, then they wouldn't eat berries but there would probably be a good supply of another type of food, like nuts. Or hunting might compensate for a bad year for plant foods. But farmers were very vulnerable to crop failures. Remember, most early farmers cultivated only one or two crops. If there was a drought and the grain harvest failed, they didn't have other resources and that's why they were subject to malnutrition or even starvation. So, as you see, revisionists have made a rather convincing case. To sum it up, according to the revisionists, the development of agriculture put the health of early farmers at risk.

Q11

Q9

| **Audio** | 6. | Which of the following is the main topic of the lecture? |
| **Answer** | **D** | The negative effects of agriculture on early farmers |

Audio	7.	What are two key characteristics of hunter-gatherers mentioned in the lecture?
Answer	**A**	They were taller than farmers.
	C	They lived longer than farmers.

Audio	8.	Listen again to part of the lecture and then answer the following question.
Replay		"So, let's see where we are. Oh, yes. Consider that hunter-gatherers had the advantage of mobility."
Audio		Why does the professor say this:
Replay		"Oh yes."
Answer	**B**	To indicate that another point will be made. Professors may use the phrase "Oh yes" when it is something that they have just remembered to add.

| **Audio** | 9. | How does the professor organize his lecture? |
| **Answer** | **B** | He makes an argument for the revisionist point of view. |

| **Audio** | 10. | Which of the following statements best summarizes the position of the revisionists? |
| **Answer** | **C** | Agriculture contributed to the health risks for early farmers. |

| **Audio** | 11. | In the lecture, the professor describes the relationship between health and agriculture. Indicate whether each of the following is true or false. Click in the correct box for each phrase. |

Answer

	Yes	No
A Epidemics were spread by crowded towns and trade.	✔	
B Crop failures threatened the entire population.	✔	
C Wars with invading hunter-gatherers devastated them.		✔
D Unbalanced diets contributed to malnutrition.	✔	
E Hard labor damaged their bones.		✔

LISTENING 3 "BUSINESS CLASS"

Audio Lecture

Narrator: Listen to part of a lecture in a business class.

Professor:

Q12 In your textbook, the author states that "companies sell products but companies market brands." And several of you have asked me about that distinction . . . between selling products and marketing brands. . . . I thought we ought to take some time to talk about it in class. So, let me give you an example. Suppose that we have a company, and the product is chicken. Then it's easy to understand that we're selling chicken. Maybe we're even selling a special preparation of chicken—barbecued chicken—and maybe we include lemonade and a hot roll free with our barbecued chicken. We may even have the best service. But, we're still selling chicken, even though it's a special preparation and even though we've provided an attractive package with free additional products and good service. All of that is still selling.

But what's marketing then? Well, when we market a product, we have to create meaning that attaches itself to the product . . . something that makes the product more unique and more desirable than other similar products. Maybe this chicken was a family recipe that was handed down from Aunt Ruby. So this isn't just chicken. It's Aunt Ruby's recipe. And eating it is special because she doesn't give the recipe to anyone but family, and being in the restaurant is just like being in Aunt Ruby's kitchen. How you interpret the *experience* is just as important as how you view the product. See what I mean?

Take a look at commercials on television if you really want to understand marketing because these commercials almost always represent the product as something else—success, sex, youth. All of these are important to the consumer. So, when a car is marketed, for example, it's shown in the context of a successful crowd of people in an upscale neighborhood, or the man who buys the car gets the woman, or the woman who buys the car is young, beautiful, and desirable while she's driving it. And marketing is what attaches that meaning to the product. You may not be able to buy youth, but you can buy products, and the message is that these products will get you what you really want.

Okay, so *marketing* is selling an image or a benefit . . . something that's really attractive and larger than the product itself, and by attaching it to the product, we can give that larger meaning to what we **Q13** want to sell. Go back to the car commercial for a minute. We want to sell cars, but we market them by selling something bigger first, and by association, we sell the cars.

This brings us to the term *branding*. Now branding is similar to marketing because the customer *perceives* the product as being valuable. So then, branding is more about the customer than it is about the product. It's the personality of the product that people relate to. Think Allstate Insurance, and you'll probably come up with "You're in good hands," and their competitor, State Farm will remind you, "Like a good neighbor, State Farm is there." This is an emotional relationship that customers have with the personality of the product. Rob Frankel is probably one of the most widely respected business consultants in the area of product branding. In his book, *The Revenge of Brand X*, he says, "business is about relationships, not about transactions." That's not an exact quote but it's close. And he's so right on. Brand- **Q14** ing isn't about the product or even about the customer service. It's about the customer's perception of the product and the relationship with the personality of the product. And that's how branding works.

Q15 So it's not a logo, it's not a name, although name recognition or the familiarity of a logo is helpful. It's not a commercial or even a string of commercials in a marketing plan. It's more about loyalty and confidence and all of the things that make a relationship good. Customers have to do more than recognize the brand. They have to be motivated to buy it . . . and . . . and continue to buy it, over time. In a way, it's a telegraphic marketing message that's easy to understand and speaks to the customer, and it has to be a consistent message. I mean that to build a brand, and more important, brand loyalty, you have to repeat that message over and over. Say it loud enough and long enough and it starts to sound right, and even more important, it starts to echo in your customers' heads when they think about making a purchase.

So what's the result that we're going for? It's when the customer will wait until the store gets more of it instead of buying a different brand, or if the price goes up, the customer will pay extra instead of buying a cheaper brand. And this is brand loyalty, which is especially important in an industry where there isn't very much difference in the competing products. Laundry detergent . . . now that's really a very similar product across brands . . . but people tend to buy the same one.   Q16

Okay then. How do we give our products a personality so we can develop a relationship with customers? Well, Aunt Ruby is someone that we can relate to when we think about chicken. But celebrity spokespersons are an even more obvious option. When kids think about Nike shoes, do they want a relationship with a shoe, with Nike, or with Michael Jordan? It's pretty obvious that Air Jordan shoes are all about the basketball player. That's taking branding to its logical conclusion.   Q17

Audio	12.	What is the lecture mainly about?
Answer	**B**	Marketing brand-name products

Audio	13.	Listen again to part of the lecture and then answer the following question.
Replay		"Go back to the car commercial for a minute. We want to sell cars, but we market them by selling something bigger first, and by association, we sell the cars."
Audio		Why does the professor say this:
Replay		"Go back to the car commercial for a minute."
Answer	**D**	To relate new information to a previous example. Professors often ask students to "go back to" something that was previously mentioned when it is relevant to the point they are currently discussing.

Audio	14.	According to the professor, why do consumers develop brand loyalty?
Answer	**A**	They have a relationship with the personality that the product projects.

Audio	15.	How does the professor emphasize his point about branding?
Answer	**B**	He defines it by contrasting it with related concepts. He explains what branding is *not* in order to clarify what branding *is*.

Audio	16.	Why does the professor mention laundry detergent?
Answer	**D**	To explain the concept of brand loyalty

Audio	17.	According to the professor, what would be a good way to sell a product?
Answer	**B**	Hire a celebrity that customers like and relate to

LISTENING 4 "STUDENTS ON CAMPUS"

Audio Conversation

Narrator: Listen to part of a conversation on campus between two students.

Woman: This is an interesting assignment.
Man: It is. I'm just having a problem figuring out how to write up the report.   Q18
Woman: Oh? How much have you done?
Man: Well, the introduction was easy. I just expanded on the information that the lab assistant provided, you know, about the effects of alcohol on reflexes, and I used the same references that he cited.   Q19
Woman: Me, too.
Man: Then I described the experiment in the second part . . . the methods and materials section.

Woman:		What did you include there? The lab assistant said that it was important to be specific when we did this part.
Man:		Yeah, he did. So I mentioned that there were ten subjects, and five were drinking gin and tonic, but the other five . . . that's the control group . . . they were drinking tonic only, and no one knew which group was which. Then they each had to drive in a computerized . . . what was it called? A . . . a simulator . . . a simulator of a car that was supposed to be moving at 35 miles an hour. And when they saw a bicycle, they were supposed to hit the brakes.
Woman:		So far so good. The only thing I can think of that you might want to add is maybe a little more about the subjects. I think they were college students, and they were selected at random to be in the experimental or control group.
Q20 Man:		Good idea. Especially the part about the random selection. That would be important information if someone wanted to duplicate the experiment, and didn't he say that this section had to be specific enough for another researcher to be able to repli . . . repli . . .
Woman:		replicate . . .
Man:		Yeah. Replicate the study.
Woman:		Okay, so what did you do with the results section?
Man:		That's the problem. I can't seem to figure out what to put in the results section and what to use for the discussion section. If I put the chart with the reaction times in the results, should I explain the chart in the discussion, or what?
Q21 Woman:		Oh, now I see the problem. The chart's fairly self-explanatory, isn't it? I mean, it's really a simple chart to read.
Man:		That's what I thought.
Woman:		But you still have to explain the chart in the results section.
Man:		You do?
Q19 Woman:		Yeah. Um, look, here's what I'd do. I'd look at the chart and try to come up with a few general statements. For example, um, well, all of the subjects who were drinking alcohol had longer reaction times. Then you can look at the range—1 second to 4 seconds for the subjects who were drinking only tonic, and that's compared with 3 seconds to 20 seconds for the subjects who were drinking gin with the tonic.
Man:		So, I'm really just repeating what's on the chart, but I'm explaining it in words.
Woman:		Right. But, here's the thing—you shouldn't draw any conclusions in the results section. Just the facts.
Man:		You mean, just what happened in the experiment.
Q22 Woman:		Right. You have to save the conclusions for the discussion section.
Man:		Okay. So in the conclusions, I might say that driving after having four drinks . . . if you have four drinks, you probably won't be in a position to avoid an accident.
Woman:		That's good. And you could also point out problems in the research, if there are any, or suggestions for future research.
Man:		Like doing the experiment with beer instead of hard liquor or repeating the same experiment with three drinks instead of four.
Woman:		Sure. That's the idea.

Audio	18.	What is the purpose of this conversation?
Answer	**B**	The woman is helping the man to write a report.

Audio	19.	What is the study about?
Answer	**A**	Reaction times for drivers drinking alcohol in comparison with those of nondrinkers

Audio   20.   According to the man, why is it important to mention that the subjects were randomly selected?

Answer   **B**   This information allows another researcher to repeat the experiment.

Audio   21.   Listen again to part of the conversation and then answer the following question.

Replay   "Oh, now I see the problem. The chart's fairly self-explanatory, isn't it? I mean, it's really a simple chart to read."

"That's what I thought."

Audio   Why does the woman say this:

Replay   "The chart is fairly self-explanatory, isn't it?"

Answer   **C**   She is certain the man agrees with her. A tag question with a falling intonation indicates that the speaker assumes agreement.

Audio   22.   Which section includes the conclusions?

Answer   **A**   Discussion

LISTENING 5 "BIOLOGY CLASS"

Audio Lecture

Narrator: Listen to part of a lecture in a biology class. The professor is discussing blood types.

Professor:

Before we begin our discussion of blood types, let's review what we know about blood. According to the   Q23
textbooks, about half of the volume of blood is made up of blood cells that begin as stem cells in bone marrow. And these stem cells can develop into any of the other kinds of cells found in blood, including red cells, white cells, and platelets. So . . . some stem cells become white cells or leukocytes and these are essential to the immune system. And when bacteria or germs invade the body, some of the white cells form antibodies to resist the infection directly while other white cells begin to work on the chemistry of the foreign substance itself . . . to fight the infection. Now, compared with red blood cells, there are relatively few white blood cells . . . only about one for every seven hundred red cells. And the smallest of the blood cells are called platelets, but what they don't have in size they make up for in numbers. Well, most of us have about two trillion of them and they work to help the blood to clot and . . . , uh, repair holes in the walls of blood vessels. But we need a way to transport the blood, right? Plasma is the liquid substance in blood that transports most of the chemicals . . . vitamins and minerals . . . hormones and enzymes.

But most stem cells become red blood cells, or erythocytes. They're the most numerous. As I mentioned before, there are about seven hundred to every one white blood cell. So the red cells give blood the color red, and they're important for what we call blood typing. And blood typing is what I want to get   Q23
going on today.

Now blood types are a classification of red blood cells according to the presence of specific substances . . . antigenic proteins and carbohydrates . . . and you can see them under the microscope on the surface of the cells. The four blood types are identified by letters . . . A, B, AB, and O. Blood type A contains red blood cells with the antigen A. Blood type B contains red blood cells with the antigen B. The AB blood type contains both antigens, and the O blood type contains no antigens, but the individual with this type can form antibodies containing either A or B antigens.

Student 1:

Excuse me. Is that why the O blood type is considered a universal blood type? Because it can form anti-   Q24
bodies with either A or B antigens?

Professor:

Q25
Right you are. But, in typing the blood, the antigens are really much more complex than this explanation might suggest. There are at least 300 different antigens. In fact, there are so many potential combinations that an individual's blood type is almost as unique as a fingerprint. But anyway, these basic types are used for determining compatibilities for blood transfusions. Before a transfusion is approved, hospitals always perform a procedure called a cross match which involves taking a sample of the donor's red blood cells and mixing them with a sample of the patient's plasma. You see, in almost every individual, the plasma contains antibodies that will react to antigens that are not found on their own red blood cells. So during a transfusion, antibodies in the patient's plasma can bind to antigens on the donor's red blood cells when the donor's blood is not similar to that of the patient. Well, many minor reactions can occur like fever or chills, but some reactions are so severe that they lead to a . . . a spontaneous destruction of the red blood cells from the donor and that can result in shock or even death. So you can understand why blood typing is so important. Cross matching lowers the risk of a serious reaction.

Okay. In cross matching, we take red cells from one person and plasma from the other person, and we watch to see whether there's a negative response. Take a look at this diagram. It's on page 112 in your textbook. Here's what you would be looking at with a reaction caused by incompatible blood. See how the cells clump together?

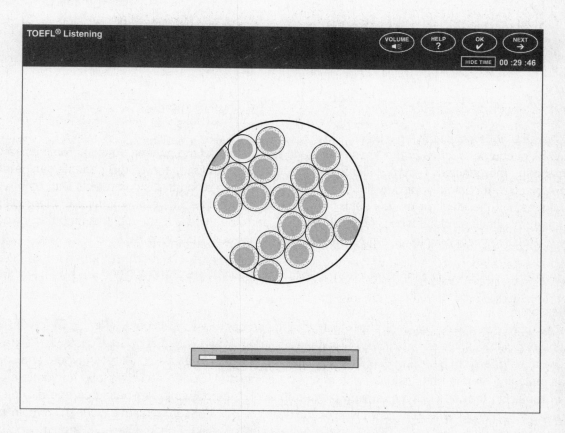

Q26
The reason that this is happening is because there's a chemical reaction between the protein molecules in the red cells of one person and the plasma of the other. Now look at this slide. This diagram is on the next page in your text and this shows a compatible match with no clumping.

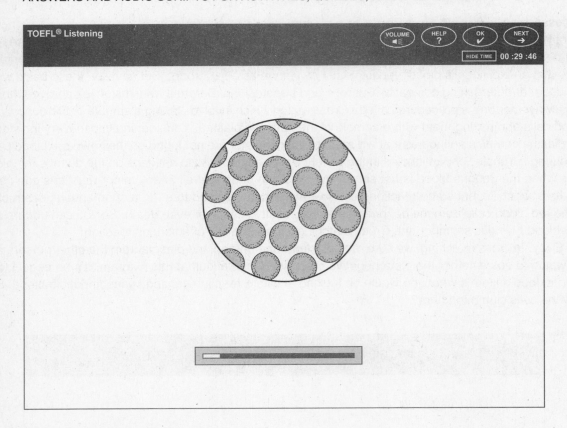

See how the cells are evenly spaced?

Well, of course, doctors prefer to use the same type as that of the patient, but compromises have to be made in emergencies. Type A patients can't receive type B blood, and type B patients can't receive type A blood, but back to your question; since an O donor has blood that's compatible with both A and B antigens, it's the ideal, or as you said, the universal donor. In an emergency, type O blood can be used for patients of all blood types. And fortunately, worldwide, type O is the most common, followed by type A. Relatively few people have type B blood, and the fewest have type AB.

Student 2: Professor Stephens, can you tell us anything about artificial blood? Q27

Professor:
Well actually, scientists developed artificial blood that's been used successfully in blood transfusions with human patients. It's a white fluid, chemically similar to Teflon, the material that coats cookware and prevents material from adhering to it. The fluid can be used as a match with all blood types, and so, the cross matching step in transfusions . . . that can be eliminated. So far, artificial blood has done a good job of replacing the red cells by carrying oxygen through the body and eliminating carbon dioxide, but there are no white cells present, no antibodies, no platelets. So, it doesn't clot, and it doesn't remain in the body very long. Still, continuing research along these lines should probably be encouraged. Um, even Q28 with cross matching and other precautions, transfusions with human blood involve risks.

Audio 23. What aspect of blood does the professor mainly discuss?
Answer **D** A discussion of blood typing

Audio 24. Listen again to part of the lecture and then answer the following question.
Replay "Excuse me. Is that why the O blood type is considered a universal blood type? Because it can form antibodies with either A or B antigens?"
"Right you are."

Audio		Why does the student say this:
Replay		"Excuse me."
Answer	**B**	She is interrupting politely to ask a question.

Audio	25.	Why does the professor mention fingerprints?
Answer	**A**	To demonstrate that blood types are different for individuals

Audio	26.	In cross matching, how does a compatible match appear under the microscope?
Answer	**A**	All of the cells are at an equal distance from each other.

Audio	27.	Why does the professor mention artificial blood?
Answer	**B**	She is answering a question.

Audio	28.	Listen again to part of the lecture and then answer the following question.
Replay		"Still, continuing research along these lines should probably be encouraged. Um, even with cross matching and other precautions, transfusions with human blood involve risks."
Audio		What does the professor imply when she says this:
Replay		"Still, continuing research along these lines should probably be encouraged."
Answer	**D**	She agrees that research should continue in spite of problems.

LISTENING 6 "ORIENTATION SESSION"

Audio Discussion
Narrator: Listen to part of a discussion in an orientation class.

Professor:

Q29 For the most part, college students don't read fast enough to keep up with the demands of their reading assignments. Let's just say that the typical college student reads 150 to 300 words per minute. Okay. The professor in the Western Civilization course uses the topics from Chapter 1 of the textbook for three lectures the first week of the semester. Each page has about 500 words on it, and that includes space for pictures and drawings. So, at 150 words per minute . . . let me see . . . each page will take more than three minutes to complete, and . . . if my figures are right . . . that's almost three hours just to read the textbook assignment once through. That doesn't even count what you need to do to think and connect the lectures with the book, and you can be sure that there will be additional reading or other assignments besides the lectures and the textbook. . . . Have you heard about the *times two rule*?

Student 1:

Isn't that . . . doesn't that mean a student should spend two hours of study time for every hour of class time in every subject?

Professor:

Exactly. Okay. I think you'll agree that reading faster is important to success in college. So it's only practical to learn to read faster. And, uh, that's why I'm going to talk with you about the human capacity for reading . . . and some habits that you may have that could be slowing you down. First, I want you to think about reading like you think about running. The more you run, the faster and farther you can go . . . and the more you read, the faster you're going to read. In fact, researchers hypothesize that our physical capacity to read surpasses our ability to turn the pages. In other words, our brains can take in the information faster than our hands can move. So reading 700 to 1000 words a minute should be a reasonable goal for almost everyone. That would be quite a time saver, wouldn't it?

Student 1:   Yeah. It sure would.

Professor:
Now, let's talk about why most of us probably aren't reading at that speed . . . at 1000 words a minute . . . why we're not doing that now. We know that we have the capacity—that our brains can take it in. But there are a few habits that prevent readers from reaching that target speed of 700 to 1000 words. In the first place, some people are auditory readers. That means that they hear every word in their minds. Some people even move their lips so they seem to be speaking while they're reading. This is a serious problem because we can only speak about 300 words per minute, but, uh, our capacity to read . . . it's many times faster. So if you're hearing the words in your head or moving your lips, you know that you're preventing your mind from processing as fast as it can. Can any of you relate to that?   `Q33`

Student 2:   I can. I hear every word.

Professor:
A lot of people do. Now, another problem is something called *fixations*. Fixations are the actual pauses that the eye makes. We can't see while the eye is moving so we have to stop to take in the text. Everyone has to fixate to see the print, but, uh, some people . . . they stop their eyes on every single word and that will really slow you down. So if you're looking at every word or even at every few words, that habit is something to work on. When you're not reading word by word, your mind has to connect and, uh, build associations and . . . and patterns. You can do this because so much of a written text is redundant—that means that there's a lot of repetition, so quite a few words can be skipped without losing the meaning.   `Q33`

Student 3:   So you're saying we should try to guess the meaning?

Professor:
I think I would use the term *predict* rather than *guess*, but basically the answer to your question is "yes." Now this may surprise you. Using a dictionary is a *good* habit. Right? Well, yes, in moderation. But stopping to look up *every* new word is a *bad* habit because you don't need to know every word in order to understand what you're reading. Remember what I just said about redundancy. So, uh, stopping to use the dictionary too often . . . that interrupts your train of thought and, uh, prevents you from reaching your potential reading speed.

Student 3:   I've heard that before and it makes sense but . . .

Professor: But you're afraid to try it?

Student 3:   That's probably true.

Professor:
Well, I'll come back to that in a minute. First I want to point out one more problem. A lot of readers go   `Q32`
back over the words they've already read to clarify the meaning. But this is probably the worst habit because, uh, when we're repeating twice or even more times, that causes our reading speed to drop and it goes to 50 or even 30 percent of our capacity. Did I mention that this is called *regression*? Okay,   `Q33`
well this regression not only slows us down, it also makes it more difficult to understand the meaning because, uh, the way that we comprehend . . . we understand by connecting with the next phrase, so going back all the time makes us lose the connections.
    And this is what's *really* important in all of this—research demonstrates a correlation between speed   `Q30`
and comprehension. In an overwhelming number of cases, when students increase their reading speed, they also increase their comprehension of the material. So how can *you* do this? First break the habits that are causing you to read slowly. Don't think the words in your head or move your lips to sound out

each word. Don't let your eyes pause on every word. Don't look up every new word in the dictionary. And try not to go back over paragraphs and, uh, sentences that you've already read. But, that's hard to do if you have these habits, isn't it? Especially if you're also trying to read in order to learn a new subject. That's why you're afraid to try it . . . because, uh, you have to learn the content in order to pass the course and . . . you don't want to try something new . . . to take a risk.

Student 3:   Yeah. That's about the size of it.

Professor:

Q34   Well, I understand that. But you *can* take a risk and try to change some of those habits, but it helps if you do it in a structured environment like the Learning Center. It's free and you'll more than make up for the time you spend in one of the reading courses they offer when you begin to read all of your assignments at twice the speed you're reading them now.

Audio   29.   What is this discussion mainly about?
Answer **B**   How to read faster

Audio   30.   How does the professor organize the discussion?
Answer **A**   She cites research to support her arguments. She does this at several points in the discussion.

Audio   31.   Why does the professor mention running?
Answer **B**   To make a comparison between reading and running

Audio   32.   Listen again to part of the discussion and then answer the following question.
Replay   "Well, I'll come back to that in a minute. First I want to point out one more problem."
Audio   Why does the professor say this:
Replay   "Well, I'll come back to that in a minute."
Answer **C**   She thinks the idea will fit in better later on. Professors often make a comment and then remark that they will "come back" or "get back" to it later. This is usually an indication that the information relates to points that will be made later in the lecture.

Audio   33.   The professor mentions several negative habits. Match these habits to the explanations. Click on the habit and drag it to the correct explanation.
Answer

Habit	Explanation
A Fixating	Pauses that the eye makes
C Regressing	Reading the same words more than once
B Auditory reading	Moving your lips while reading

Audio   34.   What would the professor probably like the students to do?
Answer **D**   Get help at the Learning Center

➤ Speaking

   Model Test 4, Speaking Section, CD 7, Track 1

INDEPENDENT SPEAKING QUESTION 1 "A CITY"

Narrator 2: Number 1. Listen for a question about a familiar topic. After you hear the question, you have 15 seconds to prepare and 45 seconds to record your answer.

Narrator 1: Which city in the world would you like to visit? Use specific reasons and details to explain your choice.

Narrator 2: Please prepare your answer after the beep.

Beep

[Preparation time: 15 seconds]

Narrator 2: Please begin speaking after the beep.

Beep

[Recording time: 45 seconds]

Beep

INDEPENDENT SPEAKING QUESTION 2 "SCHOOLS"

Narrator 2: Number 2. Listen for a question that asks your opinion about a familiar topic. After you hear the question, you have 15 seconds to prepare and 45 seconds to record your answer.

Narrator 1: Some students prefer to attend a school that provides education for women only or men only. Other students prefer to attend a coeducational school for both women and men. Which environment do you think is better and why? Use specific reasons and examples to support your opinion.

Narrator 2: Please prepare your answer after the beep.

Beep

[Preparation time: 15 seconds]

Narrator 2: Please begin speaking after the beep.

Beep

[Recording time: 45 seconds]

Beep

INTEGRATED SPEAKING QUESTION 3 "ENGLISH REQUIREMENTS"

Narrator 2: Number 3. Read a short passage and listen to a talk on the same topic. Then listen for a question about them. After you hear the question, you have 30 seconds to prepare and 60 seconds to record your answer.

Narrator 1: A meeting is planned to explain the proposal for a change in the English language requirements for Community College. Read the notice in the college newspaper printed on page 357. You have 45 seconds to complete it. Please begin reading now.

[Reading time: 45 seconds]

Narrator 1: Now listen to a student who is speaking at the meeting. She is expressing her opinion about the policy for international students.

Student:
I think that this is a good policy because sometimes international students don't do well on an English test but they're still good students in their major field. So, they can probably succeed with a lower score on the TOEFL. And besides that, um, it's a good idea to begin with one credit class instead of a full course load. I mean, studying part time while finishing the language classes will provide more of a . . . a transition into regular courses. Also, after several semesters in the English Language Institute, most international students become impatient . . . and this opportunity . . . to begin regular classes . . . it would increase their motivation toward the end of their language program.

Narrator 1: The student expresses her opinion of the policy for international students. Report her opinion and explain the reasons that she gives for having that opinion.

Narrator 2: Please prepare your answer after the beep.

Beep

[Preparation time: 30 seconds]

Narrator 2: Please begin speaking after the beep.

Beep

[Recording time: 60 seconds]

Beep

INTEGRATED SPEAKING QUESTION 4 "MYTHS AND LEGENDS"

Narrator 2: Number 4. Read a short passage and then listen to part of a lecture on the same topic. Then listen for a question about them. After you hear the question, you have 30 seconds to prepare and 60 seconds to record your answer.

Narrator 1: Now read the passage about Myths and Legends printed on page 358. You have 45 seconds to complete it. Please begin reading now.

[Reading time: 45 seconds]

Narrator 1: Now listen to part of a lecture in an anthropology class. The professor is talking about the legend of Paul Bunyan.

Professor:
Paul Bunyan is one of the more popular characters in American legends. A hero among the lumberjacks of the American Northwest, Paul Bunyan had the size, strength, and the frontier spirit of the North American continent that embraced the stories about him. According to legend, Paul Bunyan was a giant of a man who ate forty bowls of porridge for breakfast and used wagon wheels for the buttons on his shirts. His feet were so large that while he was walking west across Minnesota, his footprints created 10,000 lakes. He's also attributed with the creation of the Grand Canyon, Puget Sound, and the Black Hills. Some of my colleagues who specialize in folklore believe that the legend has a French-Canadian origin; however, they agree with me that the whole idea of the giant fits in well with the expansion of the frontier in both Canada and the United States. The legend was retold and embellished in the logging camps of Michigan, Wisconsin, and Minnesota. Some of the earliest publications are found in the *Detroit News-Tribune* in 1910.

Narrator 1: Using the main points and examples from the reading, explain the differences between myths and legends. Then refer to the lecture to explain why Paul Bunyan would be considered a legend.

Narrator 2: Please prepare your answer after the beep.

Beep

[Preparation time: 30 seconds]

Narrator 2: Please begin speaking after the beep.

Beep

[Recording time: 60 seconds]

Beep

INTEGRATED SPEAKING QUESTION 5 "ROOMMATE"

Narrator 2: Number 5. Listen to a short conversation. Then listen for a question about it. After you hear the question, you have 20 seconds to prepare and 60 seconds to record your answer.

Narrator 1:   Now listen to a conversation between a student and her advisor.

Student: So, I really like my roommate, I mean, we get along great, and she's a good student. We take a lot of the same classes, and we study together, but . . . well, I have a problem, and I just don't seem to be able to deal with it.
Advisor: Okay. What's the problem?
Student: You see, she has a boyfriend in Florida, and she calls him on my cell phone.
Advisor: Then you have a bill for the extra minutes at the end of the month.
Student: Exactly. And I really can't afford it.
Advisor: Have you talked with her about it?
Student: Not really. I just don't know what to say.

Advisor: Well, I think you have a couple of options. You can tell her that you can't let her use your cell phone anymore, and you can offer to go with her to buy her own cell phone. That way she'll see that you're trying to help.

Student: That might work, but she'll probably still be upset . . .

Advisor: Or another possibility is . . . you could let her use your cell phone if she pays you for the extra minutes that you have had to cover for her, and if she agrees to pay her share of all the bills from now on. Just tell her that you can't afford it.

Narrator 1: Describe the woman's problem and the two suggestions that her advisor makes about how to handle it. What do you think the woman should do, and why?

Narrator 2: Please prepare your answer after the beep.

Beep

[Preparation time: 20 seconds]

Narrator 2: Please begin speaking after the beep.

Beep

[Recording time: 60 seconds]

Beep

INTEGRATED SPEAKING QUESTION 6 "URBAN WILDLIFE"

Narrator 2: Number 6. Listen to part of a lecture. Then listen for a question about it. After you hear the question, you have 20 seconds to prepare, and 60 seconds to record your answer.

Narrator 1: Now listen to part of a lecture in a biology class. The professor is discussing the types of habitats for wildlife found in cities.

Professor:
Although cities have not generally been associated with wildlife, there are many species that have become so much a part of the urban landscape that they are, for the most part, unnoticed neighbors. For example, in New York's Central Park, almost 300 species of birds have been identified. Urban parks certainly provide some of the world's safest and in many ways, best wildlife habitats, and as the natural habitats shrink, well, these urban parks will become more and more important to the conservation of wildlife, including not only birds . . . but, uh . . . but also freshwater animals and, even small mammals. So, as you see, man-made areas are one important type of habitat in cities. But artificial structures in the urban landscape . . . these can also provide a home for animals that adapt to life in the city. For instance, chimney swifts are birds that originally lived in hollow trees, but now chimney swifts are commonly found in the long brick chimneys in factories or other vertical shafts in tall buildings. Think about it. A city has more chimneys than there are hollow trees in a forest of equal area. Consequently, these birds flock to the city. Another case of adaptation is the urban drainage system, which is usually made up of concrete ditches, and they naturally attract stream and marsh animals. Again, to use New York City as an example, probably 250 species of fish are found in the harbor, many of which make their way into the pools and ponds and ditches in the New York drainage system. In Boston, the Back Bay was actually designed to create habitats and attract marshland wildlife to the city.

Narrator 1: Using the main points and examples from the lecture, describe the two general types of habitats for wildlife found in urban areas.

Narrator 2: Please prepare your answer after the beep.

Beep

[Preparation time: 20 seconds]

Narrator 2: Please begin speaking after the beep.

Beep

[Recording time: 60 seconds]

Beep

➤ Writing

INTEGRATED ESSAY "JET STREAMS"

First, read the passage on pages 361–362 and take notes.

 Model Test 4, Writing Section, CD 7, Track 2

Narrator: Now listen to a lecture on the same topic as the passage that you have just read.

Professor:
In North America, the jet stream usually separates cold air from the polar region in the north from warmer air to the south, so it's called the polar jet stream. Okay, when it's cold in the United States, the polar jet stream often dips south into Texas or even as far as Mexico, and when it's hot, the jet stream retreats into Canada. Now, think about some of the trips you may have taken across country. Did you notice that the airline schedules factor in the effect of the jet stream on flight times? For example, if you were flying from Los Angeles to New York, the flight would be more than one hour shorter than your return trip from New York to Los Angeles. Why would this be so, do you think? Well, because a particularly strong jet stream can provide a strong tailwind that moves the plane along faster as it travels with the wind, but on the way back, the plane will encounter a headwind, and it will have to travel against the wind. So the flight will take longer. And the plane will also consume more fuel when it's traveling against the jet stream, and you'll probably also feel more turbulence. Besides that, the weather for your flight can also be affected by the jet stream because this strong current of air moves weather systems and storms around the world by pushing them forward, just like the tailwind that pushes your plane.

➤ Example Answers and Checklists for Speaking and Writing

Model Test 4, Example Answers, CD 7, Track 3

EXAMPLE ANSWER FOR INDEPENDENT SPEAKING QUESTION 1 "A CITY"

If I could visit any city in the world, I'd like to see Rome because I'm an architecture major, and it would be exciting to see the structures in the old city like the Colosseum and the Forum and, uh, temples. I'd also want to inspect the arches that define the perimeter of the old city. I think one of them is almost 2000 years old, but it's still supposed to be quite beautiful and strong. In a book about Rome, I read that the streets in the old city are made of the original cobblestones laid in ancient times. So besides seeing the architecture, it would be exciting to walk on the stones. I have a good imagination, and I'm sure I could visualize soldiers and philosophers even if I'm looking at a lot of other tourists.

Checklist 1

✔ The talk answers the topic question.
✔ The point of view or position is clear.
✔ The talk is direct and well-organized.
✔ The sentences are logically connected.
✔ Details and examples support the main idea.
✔ The speaker expresses complete thoughts.
✔ The meaning is easy to comprehend.
✔ A wide range of vocabulary is used.
✔ There are only minor errors in grammar.
✔ The talk is within a range of 125–150 words.

EXAMPLE ANSWER FOR INDEPENDENT SPEAKING QUESTION 2 "SCHOOLS"

I think a coeducational school is a better environment for both men and women because it's more representative of the . . . the, uh, world that they'll live in after they finish school. In modern society, men and women will compete for employment opportunities so it's good practice to compete in classes. And men and women need to learn how to interact socially, and a coeducational school provides activities and social events where they can associate with each other in a somewhat supervised environment. So I think if men and women are separated throughout their school life, it might be harder for them to work together and develop social relationships after they finish school.

Checklist 2

✔ The talk answers the topic question.
✔ The point of view or position is clear.
✔ The talk is direct and well-organized.
✔ The sentences are logically connected.
✔ Details and examples support the main idea.
✔ The speaker expresses complete thoughts.
✔ The meaning is easy to comprehend.
✔ A wide range of vocabulary is used.
✔ There are only minor errors in grammar.
✔ The talk is within a range of 125–150 words.

EXAMPLE ANSWER FOR INTEGRATED SPEAKING QUESTION 3 "ENGLISH REQUIREMENTS"

The college is considering a change in the TOEFL requirement. It would allow international students who score five points below the cut-off score of 80 to take a credit class while they're finishing their English courses in the English Language Institute. Um, the student thinks that the new policy is a good idea because . . . some students have problems taking a test but they still have the . . . the capacity . . . to succeed in their credit classes, especially in their major field. And students who qualify will have an academic advisor so they'll be more likely to take a class they can handle. So she also suggests that a part-time schedule would give students a smoother transition into a full-time academic schedule and, uh, it would also motivate students who have been in the Institute for a long time and they're getting tired of studying English.

Checklist 3

✔ The talk summarizes the situation and opinion.
✔ The point of view or position is clear.
✔ The talk is direct and well-organized.
✔ The sentences are logically connected.
✔ Details and examples support the opinion.
✔ The speaker expresses complete thoughts.
✔ The meaning is easy to comprehend.
✔ A wide range of vocabulary is used.
✔ Errors in grammar are minor.
✔ The talk is within a range of 125–150 words.

EXAMPLE ANSWER FOR INTEGRATED SPEAKING QUESTION 4 "MYTHS AND LEGENDS"

Myths are stories from ancient times that offer an explanation for why things happened and they often have their origin in religion, but legends are stories about more current heroes who really lived and they represent examples of the best values of their culture. So Paul Bunyan would be considered a legend because there was probably a big lumberjack, and as the stories about him were told, they got more and more exaggerated until he was a giant who used wagon wheels for buttons on his shirt and he could create lakes with his big footprints. The professor says that this legend was appropriate for Canada and the United States during the Westward expansion of these countries because the stories were about recent events and the territories were so vast, a hero would need to be a giant to represent the best values of such a time and place.

Checklist 4

✔ The talk relates an example to a concept.
✔ Inaccuracies in the content are minor.
✔ The talk is direct and well-organized.
✔ The sentences are logically connected.
✔ Details and examples support the opinion.
✔ The speaker expresses complete thoughts.
✔ The meaning is easy to comprehend.
✔ A wide range of vocabulary is used.
✔ The speaker paraphrases in his/her own words.
✔ The speaker credits the lecturer with wording.
✔ Errors in grammar are minor.
✔ The talk is within a range of 125–150 words.

EXAMPLE ANSWER FOR INTEGRATED SPEAKING QUESTION 5 "ROOMMATE"

The woman's problem is that she's friends with her roommate but the roommate's using her cell phone to call a boyfriend long distance and it's getting expensive and she can't afford the extra minutes on the bill. Her advisor suggests that she tell her roommate not to use her cell phone anymore and she could even offer to help buy her roommate a cell phone . . . or another idea was that she could ask her roommate to pay for the extra minutes from previous calls and any future calls. Well, I think the woman should reconsider the friendship because a real friend wouldn't take advantage of her like that. So, I don't think the advisor gave her very good advice. In my opinion, the woman should go back to the advisor and ask him to help her find a new roommate in the dorm.

Checklist 5

✔ The talk summarizes the problem and recommendations.
✔ The speaker's point of view or position is clear.
✔ The talk is direct and well-organized.
✔ The sentences are logically connected.
✔ Details and examples support the opinion.
✔ The speaker expresses complete thoughts.
✔ The meaning is easy to comprehend.
✔ A wide range of vocabulary is used.
✔ Errors in grammar are minor.
✔ The talk is within a range of 125–150 words.

EXAMPLE ANSWER FOR INTEGRATED SPEAKING QUESTION 6 "URBAN WILDLIFE"

Both man-made areas and artificial structures become habitats for wildlife in cities. One of the most impressive examples of a man-made area is Central Park in New York, which has become a safe haven for hundreds of species of birds, small mammals, and even freshwater animals that live in the streams and lakes. Back Bay in Boston is a marshland environment that was developed to provide habitats for wildlife. Um, artificial structures allow wildlife to adapt to city living by using a space that has similar advantages to those of a natural habitat. For example, the chimney swift is a small bird that makes its home in hollow trees but . . . it has adapted itself to the city by nesting in chimneys, and the fish that live in natural harbors often swim into the ditches that connect to urban drainage systems. So, even in cities, wildlife can survive and thrive.

Checklist 6

✔ The talk summarizes a short lecture.
✔ Inaccuracies in the content are minor.
✔ The talk is direct and well-organized.
✔ The sentences are logically connected.
✔ Details and examples support the opinion.
✔ The speaker expresses complete thoughts.
✔ The meaning is easy to comprehend.
✔ A wide range of vocabulary is used.
✔ The speaker paraphrases in his/her own words.
✔ The speaker credits the lecturer with wording.
✔ Errors in grammar are minor.
✔ The talk is within a range of 125–150 words.

EXAMPLE RESPONSE FOR INTEGRATED ESSAY "JET STREAMS"

Outline

Description

- Rivers of wind
- 20,000 feet
- Avg. 190 mph
- Difference temp Arctic/Tropics → storms

Airline travel

- Flying time W → E 1 hr less bc/tailwind
- More fuel + more turbulence for headwind
- Storms along current

Map

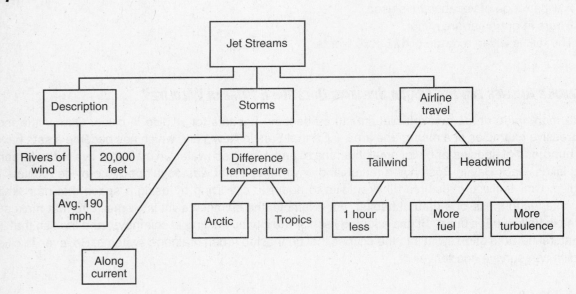

Example Essay

According to the reading, jet streams are "rivers of wind" that occur at altitudes of about 20,000 feet and travel at an average speed of 190 miles per hour. Two jet streams are affected by the difference in temperature between the arctic and the tropics, causing storms to develop along their paths. When the jet stream moves out of an area, the weather clears.

Airlines consider the conditions of the jet streams when they are calculating the flying times for their schedules. For example, on a round-trip flight across the United States, the flying time west to east could be as much as an hour less than the return trip east to west because of a strong tailwind that carries the plane with it, or, conversely, a strong headwind against which the plane has to push. In addition, more fuel is required for a headwind, and more turbulence will be experienced. Furthermore, weather conditions will be influenced by the position of the jet stream relative to the flight pattern because storms will tend to move along with the current of the jet stream.

Checklist for Integrated Essay

✔ The essay answers the topic question.
✔ Inaccuracies in the content are minor.
✔ The essay is direct and well-organized.
✔ The sentences are logically connected.
✔ Details and examples support the main idea.
✔ The writer expresses complete thoughts.
✔ The meaning is easy to comprehend.
✔ A wide range of vocabulary is used.
✔ The writer paraphrases in his/her own words.
✔ The writer credits the author with wording.
✔ Errors in grammar and idioms are minor.
✔ The essay is within a range of 150–225 words.

EXAMPLE RESPONSE FOR INDEPENDENT ESSAY "LIFESTYLE"

Outline

Comfortable living

* Healthy lifestyle—less pressured, less stress
* Time with family members

Large amounts of money

* Better standard of living for family
* More opportunities for charities

My experience

* Busy father
* Prefer time with my children

Map

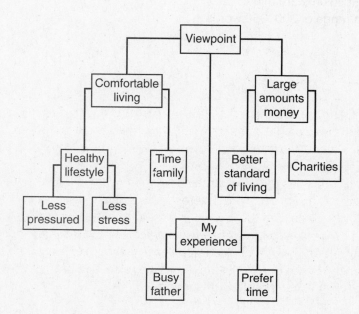

Example Essay

When we are considering options for a major field in college, the counselors often mention the amount of money that we can expect to earn if we make that career choice. Then it is up to us to decide whether it is important to make large amounts of money or whether we are satisfied to earn a comfortable living. Certainly, there are good reasons for both decisions.

If we make a lot of money, it will be possible to provide a better standard of living for our families. We can live in better homes, our children can go to more prestigious schools and participate in activities or take lessons, we can go on vacations and have experiences that would be impossible without the financial resources that a high-paying job produces. We can enjoy what the material world has to offer because we can pay for it. Besides supporting our personal lifestyles, we can afford to give generously to charities.

In contrast, if we make a comfortable living, the advantages are less visible but nonetheless important. We can participate in a healthy lifestyle because we will be less pressured. A job that pays less may have a slower pace and fewer responsibilities. Less stress may allow us to sleep better. There may be fewer demands on our time so we can exercise more and have more meals at home, contributing to good health. The extra time can also be spent with family members instead of at the office. We can be at the ball game when our child hits the home run.

In making a personal decision, I am opting for a comfortable living instead of the high-powered job with a larger salary. As the son of a successful executive, I remember expensive vacations that my father paid for but did not participate in because he was too busy at work. I prefer to spend time with my children instead of spending money on them. I plan to be at the ball game.

Checklist for Independent Essay

✔ The essay answers the topic question.
✔ The point of view or position is clear.
✔ The essay is direct and well-organized.
✔ The sentences are logically connected.
✔ Details and examples support the main idea.
✔ The writer expresses complete thoughts.
✔ The meaning is easy to comprehend.
✔ A wide range of vocabulary is used.
✔ Various types of sentences are included.
✔ Errors in grammar and idioms are minor.
✔ The essay is within a range of 300–350 words.

MODEL TEST 5: PROGRESS TEST

➤ Reading

READING 1 "RISING SEA LEVELS"

1. **B**   In this passage, *prove* is a synonym for "confirm."

2. **D**   "In response to the increasing warmth, the Antarctic Peninsula is sporting new vegetation growth." Choices A and C are true, but they are not the reason for the new plant life. Choice B is not correct because the islands have appeared because of ice melt, not because the land masses have split.

3. **B**   "About 8000 km of ice shelf are gone, changing maps, freeing up islands to circumnavigation, and creating thousands of icebergs." Choice A is not correct because a rise in temperature breaks an ice shelf into icebergs. Choice C is not correct because the reference to islands relates to warmer temperatures and melting ice. Choice D is not correct because mountain glaciers that melt will cause a rise in sea level, not the creation of icebergs.

4. **D**   "This ice loss is likely a result of the . . . temperature increase in the region in the last 50 years. In response to the increasing warmth, the Antarctic Peninsula is sporting new vegetation growth, previously not seen there [in the Antarctic Peninsula]." Choice A refers to a time, not a place. Choices B and C refer to what happened, not where it occurred.

5. **B**   Most of paragraph 4 is in quotation marks in reference to data in a study by the IPCC. Choice A is not correct because the author is quoting data from a source. Choice C is not correct because data on sea levels does not compare one area with another. Choice D is not correct because the author does not mention his studies when he is presenting the data.

6. **A**   In this passage, *definite* is a synonym for "conclusive." Context comes from the phrase "the clearest and best evidence" in the following sentence.

7. **B**   In this passage, *scale* is a synonym for "range." Context comes from the numbers in the following sentence, "from 0.11–0.88 m."

8. **B**   "Significant temperature increases are being recorded to depths of more than 300 m as ocean temperature records are set." Choice A is not correct because only a general location of Scripps in La Jolla, California, was provided. Choice C is not correct because 25% refers to the sea level rise, not to the percentage of rising sea levels recorded at Scripps. Choice D is true, but it is not the reason why the author mentions the Scripps Institute of Oceanography.

9. **A**   *Global warming on the surface of the planet* paraphrases "some surface global warming" and *may have been retarded* paraphrases "appears to have delayed." . . . *during the last hundred years* paraphrases "the past century" and *heat in the atmosphere was absorbed by the oceans* paraphrases "through absorption of excess atmospheric heat."

10. **C**   ". . . people move away from coastal flooding from the sea-level rise." Choice A is not correct because the temperature on land is not mentioned. Choice B is not correct because the vegetation along the coastlines will die as seawater floods it. Choice D is true, but it is not the reason why people will migrate.

11. **C**   The reference to "Particularly tragic social and economic consequences" in the last paragraph gives an insight into the author's opinion. Choices A and B are not correct because they are not directly expressed and cannot be concluded from information in the passage. Choice D is not correct because the breaking up of ice shelves and the melting of ice causes the sea levels to rise, not the new glaciers that are created when the ice shelves disintegrate.

12. **B**   Chronological order is a transitional device that connects the insert sentence with the previous sentence and the following sentence. *During the last century* precedes "2001" and "beyond 2100."

13. **C, B, E** summarize the passage. Choice A is an example that supports major point C. Choice D is a detail that supports major point B. Choice F is an example that supports major point C.

READING 2 "ORGANIC ARCHITECTURE"

14. **C** "Early influences were the volumetric shapes in a set of educational blocks . . . Friedrich Froebel designed." Choice A is not correct because Wright criticized classical architecture as "fixation." Choice B is not correct because it was not Jefferson's home, but Jefferson's philosophy, that inspired Wright. Choice D is not correct because Wright saw a Japanese building at the Columbian Exposition in Chicago, not on a trip to Japan.

15. **C** According to a quote by Wright, "This ideal [organic unity] . . . I called . . . continuity." Choice A is not correct because it refers to classical architecture, not to organic architecture. Choice B is not correct because, although he considered organic architecture his ideal, he referred to it as "continuity." Choice D is not correct because Wright rejected classic architecture.

16. **A** "Wright manifested his vigorous originality early, and by 1900 he had arrived at a style entirely his own [style]." The phrase "his own" does not refer to Choices B, C, or D.

17. **C** In this passage, *created* is a synonym for "conceived." Context comes from the word "designed" in the previous sentence.

18. **D** In this passage, *Discontinuing* is a synonym for "Abandoning." Context comes from the contrast of "symmetry" with the "spaces . . . grouped freely."

19. **B** "Wright fully expressed these elements and concepts in Robie House." Choice A is true but it is only one of the original ideas expressed. Choice C is not correct because, although it is often true of Wright's designs, the accessories for Robie House were not mentioned in the passage. Choice D is not correct because the house was built between 1907 and 1909, but Wright did not live there during the construction.

20. **A** In this passage, the phrase *most important* describes "prime." The word "prime" is often used with "example."

21. **C** Because "the city lot constrained the building-to-site relationship" at "Robie House," the description of "Fallingwater" implies that it was better suited to the site. Choice A is not correct because "Fallingwater" was built after "Robie House." Choice B is not correct because "Fallingwater" extended the "Robie House" design in all four directions. Choice D is not correct because "Robie House" had many large and open spaces in the "wandering" floor plan.

22. **B** ". . . he acted on a cherished dream to provide good architectural design for less prosperous people by adapting the ideas of his prairie house to plans for smaller, less expensive dwellings." Choice A is not correct because the smaller, prairie houses were not designed specifically for Europe. Choice C is not correct because many younger architects adopted his designs, but he did not build prairie houses to help architects. The revolution in architecture mentioned in Choice D occurred, but it was not Wright's purpose in building the smaller versions of his prairie designs.

23. **A** "The publication of Wright's plans brought him a measure of fame in Europe . . . and an exhibition of his designs [in Berlin] . . . stimulated younger architects to adopt some of his ideas." Choice B is not correct because lectures are not mentioned in the passage. Choices C and D are correct, but they are not the reasons that Wright's work became well known in Europe.

24. **C** The entrance in a prairie house was "all but concealed." Choice A is mentioned in paragraph 3, sentence 5. Choice B is mentioned in paragraph 3, sentence 7. Choice D is mentioned in paragraph 3, sentence 7.

25. **B** A general statement followed by examples is a transitional device that connects the insert sentence with the following sentences. The insert sentence introduces the examples of the relationship between interior and exterior spaces.

26. **C, F, D** summarize the passage. Choices A, B, and E are details of Wright's professional life that are not main points in the passage.

READING 3 "NEW WOMEN OF THE ICE AGE"

27. **B** "Amassing critical and previously overlooked evidence . . . Soffer [proposes] a technique of hunting previously invisible in the archaeological evidence." Choice A is not correct because

her theories "make her conservative colleagues cringe." Choice C is not correct because conservative researchers concentrated on studies of tools and bones and used them to support their theories. Choice D is not correct because she uses not only modern cultural evidence but also archeological evidence, including small game bones and tools that could have been used to make nets.

28. **B** "Amassing . . . evidence from Dolní Věstonice and the neighboring site of Pavlov, researchers . . . propose that human survival there had little to do with men hurling spears at big game animals. Instead . . . it [survival] depended largely on women, plants, and a technique of hunting previously invisible in the archeological evidence." The pronoun "it" does not refer to Choices A, C, or D.

29. **C** In this passage, *suggestions* is a synonym for "implications." Context comes from the clause "they raise serious questions" in the same sentence.

30. **B** Because her views "make her conservative colleagues cringe," it must be concluded that her views are not as conservative. Choice A is not correct because she disagrees about the role of women as hunters, not as caretakers. Choice C is not correct because she is identified as an authority on the Ice Age and as an archeologist, not as a biologist. Choice D is not correct because she is a leading authority on hunting and gathering in the Ice Age.

31. **A** In this passage, *limit* is a synonym for "constrain." Context comes from the logical supposition in the same sentence.

32. **D** . . . *historically* paraphrases "In many historical societies" and *not perilous* paraphrases "nor . . . in physical peril." . . . *did not require great strength* paraphrases "did not call for brute strength," and *women have been important participants* paraphrases "women played a key part."

33. **D** "'Everybody and their mother could participate [in net hunting].'" Choice A is not correct because the Australian hunters were not fishermen, and there is no evidence that they developed it. Choice B is not correct because net hunting did not place young mothers in physical peril. Choice C is not correct because net hunting was used to capture game, not to protect the camp.

34. **A** The author mentions Native American and Aborigine groups to give examples of modern groups in which women participate in net hunting. Choice B is not correct because the author presents facts, not opinions. Choice C is not correct because the techniques do not place women in peril but they do not protect them, either. Choice D is not correct because the example of the people in the Congo reinforces the information about the Native American and Aborigine groups.

35. **C** ". . . Mbuti in the forests of the Congo report that they capture game every time they lay out their woven traps, scooping up 50 percent of the animals encountered." Choice A is not correct because nets are valued more than bows and arrows. Choice B is not correct because they trade the surplus meat with neighbors. Choice D is not correct because vegetables are not mentioned.

36. **B** ". . . some of their inhabitants whittled bone tools that look much like the awls and net spacers . . ." Choice A is true but it is not mentioned as evidence. Choice C is not correct because Soffer believes that net hunting was more widespread than these two sites. Choice D is not correct because the camps stretched from Germany to Russia, but the researchers from those areas were not mentioned.

37. **D** In this passage, *functions* is a synonym for "roles." Context comes from the reference to "activities" in the same sentence.

38. **C** A conclusion based on evidence is a transitional device that connects the conclusion in the insert sentence to the evidence in the previous sentences. Choices A and B are not correct because the conclusion in the insert sentence would appear before the evidence. Choice D is not correct because the insert sentence would interrupt the relationship between the first and second sentences in the last paragraph.

39.   Previous Theories: **B, C, D**   Soffer's Theory: **E, F, G, I**   Not used: **A, H**

➤ Listening

Model Test 5, Listening Section, CD 7, Track 4, continued on CD 8, Track 1

LISTENING 1 "PROFESSOR'S OFFICE"

Audio Conversation

Narrator:	Listen to part of a conversation between a student and a professor.
Student:	Professor Collins. I'm really sorry. I mean . . . These are my daughters. They're twins. I wouldn't ordinarily bring them to an appointment, but the babysitter didn't show up, and I couldn't leave them. I didn't want to cancel. I hope it's okay.
Professor:	It's okay. I have three kids of my own, and I've been in the same situation.
Student:	Thanks. Well, this shouldn't take much of your time. I really just have one question.
Professor:	All right.
Student:	I'm having a problem understanding the difference between declarative memory and procedural memory. I think from my notes that they're both examples of . . . let me see . . . I have it down here . . . "Declarative and procedural memory are two broad types of memory circuits in long-term memory."
Professor:	That's right. But you need to distinguish between them.
Student:	Exactly.
Professor:	Okay, well, declarative memory is a memory that links us to a fact. Like a name or a date or even an experience.
Student:	So when I remember a professor's name when I see him, that's declarative memory?
Professor:	Yes, at its most basic level, it is. But declarative memory also includes problem solving. Like today, when you decided to bring your daughters to my office, you were using declarative memory to access previous experiences and facts that would allow you to make a decision.
Student:	Oh, right. I remember your example in class. That makes sense now. You were talking about problem solving by recalling experiences. But wasn't that episodic memory?
Professor:	Very good. Yes, it's called episodic memory. But declarative memory includes episodic memory, which is the ability to access prior experiences or personal episodes in our life, usually for the purpose of making a decision or solving a problem. So episodic memory is a subcategory of declarative memory, so to speak. And semantic memory is just the storehouse of facts that we have in our memory circuits . . .
Student:	. . . which is also a subcategory of declarative memory?
Professor:	Precisely.
Student:	Okay. Then procedural memory doesn't include facts or experiences.
Professor:	Not directly, no. Procedural memory refers to skills that we've learned and are now remembering in order to . . . to perform the skill without really thinking much about it. Like, for example, riding a bike or . . . or do you play a musical instrument?
Student:	Piano, sort of. Not really.
Professor:	Okay. Well, when you ride a bike then, you aren't thinking about the name of every part of the bike and how to use the handle bars or the pedals . . . or at least not consciously.
Student:	No.
Professor:	But at some level, you *are* remembering how to do these things, so you *are* using your memory.
Student:	And that would be procedural memory.

Q1

Q2

Q3

Professor:	Yes, it would.
Student:	Okay, then. That's why you said that declarative memory can be more rapidly learned, but it can also be more rapidly forgotten—because a fact can come and go in the memory. But procedural memory takes repetition and practice, so it's harder to unlearn. I'm not saying that very well.
Professor:	But you have the idea. Often with declarative memory, you're consciously trying to remember, but with procedural memory, you're performing a skill without consciously trying to recall how . . . without each step in the process.
Student:	That's what I mean. . . . But . . .
Professor:	Yes?
Student:	Well, I was thinking about language. When my girls were learning to talk . . .
Professor:	Oh, I see where you are going. You want to know whether language learning is declarative or procedural.
Student:	Yeah.
Professor:	What do you think?
Student:	I was thinking that maybe it's both? Because you have to memorize vocabulary, but eventually, it's more like a skill . . . like riding a bike . . . because you don't think about each individual word. It's more . . . more automatic. Um. Do you see what I mean?

Q4

Professor:	A very good analysis. I think you've got this.
Student:	Okay. Well, thanks a lot.
Professor:	And, uh, if you ever need to ask me a question and it's . . . hard to get in to see me, just drop me an e-mail.
Student:	I thought about that, but . . .

Q5

Professor:	Look, I'm always glad to see you, but I answer a lot of questions like this by e-mail every day and if it's easier for you, that's fine with me.
Student:	That's very kind of you. Thank you so much.

Audio	1.	Why does the woman go to see her professor?
Answer	B	To clarify several terms that she doesn't understand—declarative memory and procedural memory

Audio	2.	What do semantic memory and episodic memory have in common?
Answer	C	They are subcategories of declarative memory.

Audio	3.	When the professor gives the example of riding a bicycle, what kind of memory is he referring to?
Answer	C	Procedural memory

Audio	4.	Listen again to part of the conversation and then answer the following question.
Replay		"Um. Do you see what I mean?"
		"A very good analysis. I think you've got this."
		"Okay. Well, thanks a lot."
Audio		What does the student mean when she says this:
Replay		"Do you see what I mean?"
Answer	A	She wants confirmation that the professor understands.

Audio	5.	What does the professor suggest?
Answer	C	He offers to respond to additional questions by e-mail.

LISTENING 2 "LITERATURE CLASS"

Audio Discussion
Narrator: Listen to part of a discussion in a literature class.

Professor:
Today we're continuing our discussion of *Gulliver's Travels* by Jonathan Swift. We left off last session at the point where Gulliver began his fourth voyage as the captain of a merchant ship. As you'll recall, his crew had confined him and cast him ashore on an island. While making his way along a road, he was attacked by a herd of deformed beasts with brown skin and no tails, but suddenly the attack was interrupted by the appearance of a beautiful horse. And this is where we left off. So what happens next?   Q6

Student 1:
Well, another horse comes along, and they appear to be having a conversation, the two horses, I mean, and they keep using the words *Yahoo* and *Houyhnhnm* so Gulliver is able to understand that Yahoo refers to the animals that attacked him and Houyhnhnm refers to the horses. Then Gulliver goes home with the horses.

Professor:
And what is Gulliver thinking about while he's observing the Yahoos and the Houyhnhnms?

Student 2:
Oh, this was good. He starts to understand that the only difference between himself and the Yahoos is his clothing. But he's . . . he's horrified by this, so we see him trying to be more like the horses.   Q7

Professor: How do you know that he's striving to emulate the Houyhnhnms?

Student 2:   Well, he learns their language . . . so he can communicate with them.

Professor:
Right. So this brings us to the most important part of the narrative—the comparison between the Yahoos and the Houyhnhnms. First tell us how the Yahoos are portrayed. What do they eat? How do they look?

Student 3:
Well, I think the author used the word *depraved* several times. They eat dog and donkey meat and even garbage, and they drink, um, they drink . . . too much. And he says they're filthy, and they stink.   Q8

Professor:
So their behavior . . . the Yahoos' behavior . . . is neither rational nor moral. Now take a look at the description of the Yahoos that Gulliver has known in England. Let me refer to the book here. Okay, Gulliver explains that Yahoos in England fight wars for religious reasons, that lawyers use reason to argue for the wrong side, that the wealthy live to acquire more luxuries, and that greed makes them ill. By this, we assume that he's referring to the rich gourmet diet that causes gout and other health problems among the upper classes. So this is in contrast with the Houyhnhnms, right? How so?

Student 1   Student 2:
Well . . .   Yes . . .

Student 1:   Sorry, go ahead.

Student 2:
I was just going to say that they eat oats, bread, and honey, but not meat, not other animals. And they don't drink.

Student 1:
I think it's important that they don't even understand the concept of a lie. That proves that they are . . . that they have a very innocent nature.

Professor:
Good point. You're referring to the fact that they failed to grasp how the crew was able to initiate the mutiny that brought Gulliver to their island.

Student 1:   Umhum.

Professor:
Okay, so what do the Houyhnhnms think about Gulliver? And what does Gulliver conclude about himself?

Student 2:
Well, Gulliver isn't really a Yahoo and he isn't really a Houyhnhnm either. I'd say he's kind of in the middle. But, he's trying to become a Houyhnhnm. When he goes back to England, he's actually afraid of other humans . . . I mean . . . Yahoos.

Q8

Professor:
But he can't quite achieve his transformation, can he? Even though his pride motivates him to continue the impossible pursuit of perfection. . . . So, what does this all mean?

Q9

Student 1:
I think it's like the other chapters. The fourth voyage is . . . it's another critique of the weaknesses in human nature.

Professor:
Then Swift is making the point that although humankind is capable of rational behavior, we seldom choose to exercise it. The very meaning of the word *Yahoo* in the Houyhnhnm language is "evil." So Swift is very satirical then. And when we consider the time period for the book, the early 1700s, we must appreciate the exceptional departure from the literature of the era, which was mostly written to flatter or entertain. Swift used satire to provide the reader with a perspective that's very different from that of other writers in an age of science and reason.

Q10

Q11

Audio   6.   What is the discussion mainly about?
Answer   **B**   A narrative of the fourth voyage of Gulliver

Audio   7.   What does Gulliver learn about himself?
Answer   **A**   He is like the Yahoos in many ways.

Audio   8.   In the discussion, the professor describes the characteristics of the Yahoos. Indicate whether each of the following is one of their characteristics. Click in the correct box for each sentence.

Answer

	Yes	No
A They eat flowers.		✔
B They have a foul odor.	✔	
C They engage in an immoral lifestyle.	✔	
D They are satirical caricatures of humans.	✔	
E They live in trees.		✔

Audio   9.   Listen again to part of the discussion and then answer the following question.
Replay   "But he can't quite achieve his transformation, can he? Even though his pride motivates him to continue the impossible pursuit of perfection. . . . So, what does this all mean?"
Audio   Why does the professor say this:
Replay   "So what does this all mean?"
Answer   B   She is asking the students a question. Sometimes professors ask rhetorical questions that they intend to answer as they continue the lecture, but, in this case, the professor pauses long enough to indicate that he is waiting for a student to respond.

Audio   10.   According to the professor, what kind of book is *Gulliver's Travels*?
Answer   B   A satire about mankind.

Audio   11.   What can we infer about the literature of the period?
Answer   D   The tone was not very serious. It was meant to entertain.

LISTENING 3 "GEOLOGY CLASS"

Audio Discussion
Narrator: Listen to part of a discussion in a geology class.

Professor: The exploitation of minerals involves five steps. First, you have to explore and locate the mineral deposits, then you set up a mining operation, next, you must refine the raw minerals and transport the refined minerals to the manufacturer.
Student 1:   Excuse me. Sorry. I only have four steps. Could you . . . ?
Professor: Sure. That's exploration, mining, refining, transportation, and manufacturing.
Student 1:   Thanks.
Professor: So, each of these activities involves costs, there are costs associated with them, and the costs can be economic, but not necessarily so. Mineral exploitation also has environmental costs associated with it. For example, the exploration stage will clearly have a high economic cost because of . . . of personnel and technology, but the environmental cost will probably be quite low. Why would that be, do you think?   Q12
Student 2:   Because you aren't actually disturbing the environment. You're just looking, I mean, after you find a mineral deposit, you don't do anything about it at that stage.
Professor: Right. So the environmental costs would be low. But what happens when you use up all the resources that are easy to find? Then what?   Q17

	Student 2:	Then the costs go up for exploration.
Q17	Professor:	Which costs?
	Student 2:	Well, probably both of them, but I can see where the economic costs would increase.
	Professor:	Okay. Let's say, for example, that some areas such as national parks or historic reserves have been . . . off-limits to exploration. What will happen when we use up the minerals outside of these areas? Remember now that these are, uh . . . nonrenewable resources that we're looking for.
	Student 1:	Then there will be a lot of pressure . . . you know . . . to open up these areas to exploration and exploitation.
Q17	Professor:	Probably so. And that means that there could be a high environmental cost. Any other options?
	Student 1:	Find an alternative.
	Professor:	Yes. You're on the right track.
Q15	Student 1:	Okay. Find an alternative, I mean a substitute, something that will substitute for the mineral. Maybe something man-made?
	Professor:	Good. That will involve a different kind of exploration, again with economic costs. I'm talking about basic research here to find synthetics. But, uh, let's go on to the other steps, and we'll see if we can pull this all together. How about mining? Now, we're looking at high environmental costs because of the destruction of the landscape and . . . and the accumulation . . . of waste products that have to be dealt with. Air and water pollution is almost always a problem. . . . Any ideas on refining?
	Student 2:	Wouldn't it be the same as mining? I mean, you would have high costs because of labor and equipment, and there would be problems of waste and pollution, like you said.
	Professor:	True. True. And in refining, well that often involves the separation of a small amount of a valuable mineral from a large amount of surrounding rock. So that means that . . . that, uh, refining also carries the additional cost of cleanup. And don't forget that it's often difficult to get vegetation to grow on piles of waste. In fact, some of it, the waste piles I mean, they can even be dangerous to living creatures, including people. Not to mention the appearance of the area. So the environmental costs can be extremely
Q16		high. Isn't it sad and ironic that so much of the mining and refining must take place in areas of great natural beauty?
	Student 1:	So you're saying that both mining and refining have heavy costs . . . heavy economic and environmental costs.
	Professor:	Right. And in both mining and refining, you would need transportation to support the movement of supplies, equipment, and personnel. But, after the minerals are mined and refined, then transportation becomes even more essential.
Q14	Student 2:	And I was just thinking that in addition to the economic costs of the transportation for trucks and fuel and labor and everything, there could be, there might be some construction too, if there aren't any roads in and out of the area.
	Professor:	And that would mean . . .
Q13	Student 2:	That would mean that the landscape and even the ecosystem for the plants and animal life could be altered, so . . . so that's an environmental cost.
	Professor:	It is indeed. Good point. That leaves us with manufacturing. After we find it, mine it, refine it, and transport it, we still have to manufacture it. What are the costs associated with that? Well, construction again, for factories, then there would be energy costs, technology, and labor.
	Student 1:	So all that's economic. No environmental costs in manufacturing then.
	Professor:	Well, yes there are actually. Pollution is often a costly problem for, uh, manufacturing plants.

Student 1:	Oh right. I was thinking of the natural landscape, and the manufacturing is often positioned near cities to take advantage of the labor pool. But, um . . . cities have the environmental problems associated with pollution. So, every step has both economic and environmental costs then.
Professor:	Right.

Q12

Audio   12.   What is this discussion mainly about?
Answer   D   The economic and environmental costs of exploiting minerals

Audio   13.   According to the professor, what are two problems that can be anticipated when roads are cut into an area for mining?
Answer   B   The natural landscape is damaged.
        D   The ecosytem is disturbed.

Audio   14.   Listen again to part of the discussion and then answer the following question.
Replay   "And I was just thinking that in addition to the economic costs of the transportation for trucks and fuel and labor and everything, there could be, there might be some construction, too, if there aren't any roads in and out of the area."
        "And that would mean . . ."

Audio   Why does the professor say this:
Replay   "And that would mean . . ."
Answer   A   Professors often begin a sentence and then wait for a student to complete it. In this case, the professor is encouraging the student to continue by adding information to the answer that he gave initially.

Audio   15.   What option is proposed as an alternative when all of the mineral resources in easily accessible locations have been depleted?
Answer   C   Developing synthetic resources [man-made] to replace [natural] minerals

Audio   16.   What does the professor imply about the environmental costs of mineral exploitation?
Answer   B   Because the professor comments that it is "sad and ironic that so much of the mining and refining must take place in areas of great natural beauty," it may be concluded that he regrets that the environment is damaged.

Audio   17.   What does the professor want the students to do in this class session?
Answer   C   Because the professor encourages student questions and asks questions that will generate participation, he must want the students to ask questions and draw conclusions.

LISTENING 4 "PROFESSOR'S OFFICE"

Audio Conversation
Narrator: Listen to part of a conversation on campus between a student and a professor.

Student:	Hi. I'm Ron Watson. I'm here to apply for the work-study job.
Professor:	Oh, good. Um, have you ever had a work-study position?
Student:	Not really. To tell the truth, I'm not exactly sure how it works.
Professor:	Well, it's like this: on work-study, you have regular hours and assigned responsibilities, but, if you get everything done, you can study. You can't leave because there may be something else to do later, during your hours. But you should always bring your books and, oh, I'd guess that probably about 25 percent of the time, you should be able to study.

Q18

Q19	Student:	This is even better than I thought. What kind of assignments would I have, I mean, if I get this opportunity.
	Professor:	Clerical mostly, I'm afraid. Nothing too demanding, but it isn't the most interesting work either. Filing, copying, delivering mail, uh, some grading, but only multiple-choice tests, and we use a grading machine for that.
	Student:	Would someone show me how to operate the grading machine? I'm sure I could do it if someone showed me once or twice.
	Professor:	No problem. We have a secretary here in the department, and she'll be the main person you'd report to. She'd show you how to do everything.
	Student:	Okay. Great.
	Professor:	Now, let's see whether your hours will fit in with the hours we need. Could you work Monday through Thursday from ten to two?
	Student:	That's sixteen hours a week?
	Professor:	To start. We may actually want to extend that to Fridays, so, if that happens, it would be twenty hours. You'll notice that the hours include the usual lunch break. That would let Nancy . . . she's the secretary . . . so she could get you started on the work, and then take her lunch from noon to one, and be back for the last hour of your day, in case you had any questions.
	Student:	Okay.
	Professor:	Oh, and I should tell you about the phone. While Nancy's gone for lunch, we'll want you to answer the phone.
Q20	Student:	Sure. I can do that. Uh, will there be any work on the computer? I'm familiar with most of the basic office programs. I used to help my Dad in his office when I was in high school. He's a lawyer.
	Professor:	Oh. Well, we hadn't planned to include anything like that in the job, but it's a plus.
	Student:	Sorry to ask, but . . . how does the pay work? Do I get paid for the time I work minus the study time or . . .
Q21	Professor:	Oh no. You get paid for sixteen hours a week whether you're working or studying. This is a special program for students.
	Student:	It seems too good to be true.
	Professor:	Well, you need to have an interview with Nancy. Since you'll be working closely with her, she'll make the final decision.
	Student:	Okay. Should I make an appointment or . . .
	Professor:	No. Just go over to her desk and tell her who you are. She's expecting you. We want to get the position filled as soon as possible.
	Student:	Well, thank you for seeing me. I hope I'll be working here.
Q22	Professor:	Good luck. . . . Oh, yes, be sure to tell Nancy about the computer experience.
	Student:	I will.
	Professor:	And let her know I've already interviewed you, and I referred you to her.
	Student:	Thanks again. I really appreciate your taking the time to explain everything to me.
	Professor:	You're welcome.

| **Audio** | 18. | Why does the student go to the professor's office? |
| **Answer** | **B** | To apply for a job |

Audio	19.	Listen again to part of the conversation and then answer the following question.
Replay		"What kind of assignments would I have, I mean, if I get this opportunity."
		"Clerical mostly, I'm afraid. Nothing too demanding, but it isn't the most interesting work either."
Audio		What does the professor mean when she says this:
Replay		"Clerical mostly, I'm afraid."
Answer	**C**	She is concerned that the man will be bored.

Audio   20.   What experience does the man have that may be helpful?
Answer   C   He has used computer programs for office work.

Audio   21.   What is the pay for the work-study position?
Answer   A   An hourly rate for sixteen hours per week regardless of the activity.

Audio   22.   What can we assume about the meeting?
Answer   A   Because she sent him to the secretary for an interview and she wanted the student to tell the secretary that she referred him, it may be concluded that the professor was impressed with the student.

LISTENING 5 "MUSIC APPRECIATION CLASS"

Audio Lecture
Narrator: Listen to part of a lecture in a music appreciation class.

Professor:
As you know, tonight's the concert that I want you to attend so I'll keep the class short today. Let me tell [Q23] you a little bit about the history of chamber music so you'll be prepared to appreciate the music that you hear tonight. The University Quartet is one of the best in the region so you'll be hearing an excellent example . . . anyway . . . about chamber music. From medieval times through the eighteenth century, musicians in Europe had basically two options for employment—the church or the nobility. So . . . when they weren't creating pieces for religious occasions and performing at church functions . . . musicians were playing in the chambers of stately homes. Now a *chamber* is the name for a room where guests [Q24] may be assembled, kind of like a *hall.* And because of their association with this room, this chamber, the musicians who played for the wealthy patrons came to be known as *chamber players.*

Chamber music is written to be performed by a relatively small group . . . more than one, but fewer than a dozen musicians. I should tell you that pieces for more than eight players are unusual though, and it's very rare to see a conductor. It may surprise you to know that any combination of instruments can be used for chamber music. The strings, woodwinds, and piano are so often associated with chamber music and . . . uh . . . they remain the most popular, even today, but chamber music has been written for other instruments as well.

Well, the history of chamber music is usually divided into three distinct periods. In the Classical [Q28] Period . . . and that extends from the mid seventeen hundreds to around 1820 . . . so in the classical [Q25] period, chamber music, like many other expressions of the arts . . . it reacted to the extravagant Baroque style by creating new structures, and these structures expressed simplicity, balance, and order. It was the age of the Enlightenment with the ideals of logic and reason. So this translated into compositions with one melodic line. Uh, the line . . . the melody . . . it was usually written for the violin and all other instruments provided an accompaniment. Early chamber music in the Classical tradition often included the recorder, the harpsichord, and the viola.

Vienna was a . . . a . . . hub . . . of activity . . . for chamber music, and three composers dominated the artistic scene. Franz Joseph Haydn is generally credited with organizing the string quartet, and he produced more than 80 pieces for it . . . the quartet. Wolfgang Amadeus Mozart also composed chamber music, including not only quartets but also quintets, and trios with clarinet, and even piano sonatas. Since the music was relatively simple, many amateurs played for their own enjoyment. This was new, [Q25] but by then, music was being printed and more people had access to it. So music rooms became popular and people played chamber music as a social activity.

Well, it was Ludwig Von Beethoven who probably bridged between the Classical Period and the Romantic Period, and I say that because his works were longer and . . . and perhaps more complex than [Q26] his predecessors. And I find this amazing since the later quartets were all created when he was totally deaf. In any case, composers and performers were beginning to . . . to break free of the formal confines of the Classical Period. Their works became increasingly more difficult, expressing some of the high emotions of the nineteenth century, which, as you will recall the backdrop of that century . . . the French and the American revolutions . . . they were defining moments. So Chopin, Liszt, and Wagner wrote very little chamber music . . . because they preferred the emotional power of the full orchestra . . . or, uh, the personal expression in a piano solo. It was also at about this time that Franz Schubert, Johannes Brahms, Felix Mendelssohn, and Antonin Dvorak made their contributions, and they wrote melodic, passionate compositions for chamber players. But now the music was more difficult to play, and the patronage system was declining anyway, so . . . so most chamber music moved from the great homes of the wealthy and into the concert halls, which were frequented by a growing middle class. And it was a very creative period for chamber music, and professional chamber groups emerged during this time. The composers probably felt a new freedom because they weren't so much pressed to please their patrons and they could explore their art.

Well, at the turn of the century, the Modern Period ushered in an opportunity for even greater experimentation. Painters were bringing Impressionism to the forefront of the artistic consciousness, and this was reflected musically in the work of Claude Debussy and Maurice Ravel. Their chamber music was considered revolutionary . . . Debussy and Ravel . . . because, unlike previous composers, their compositions had recurring themes instead of a continuous melody. And there are a number of other composers who wrote chamber music in the Modern Period but . . . but whether they'll be remembered is, well, a question to be answered by future historians. What we *do* know is that the Modernists gave chamber music new combinations of instruments and arrangements. And as the music became more . . . more . . . unexpected, often with unusual tonality, well, it also became even more difficult to play and that meant that the scores for modern chamber music had to be played by very skilled ensemble musicians.

This evening, at the concert, the University Quartet will perform one of the Classical pieces by Hayden. You'll hear the *Quartet in D Minor, Opus 76, Number 2, Third Movement*. There are two violins, one cello, and one viola. So, that said . . . I'll see you tonight.

Audio	23.	What is the main purpose of the lecture?
Answer	**A**	To explain chamber music
Audio	24.	What is the origin of the term *chamber music*?
Answer	**C**	A place where the music was played
Audio	25.	Which of the following are the key characteristics of chamber music in the Classical Period?
Answer	**A**	Baroque style
	D	Amateur musicians
Audio	26.	Listen again to part of the lecture and then answer the following question.
Replay		"Well, it was Ludwig Von Beethoven who probably bridged between the Classical Period and the Romantic Period, and I say that because his works were longer and . . . and perhaps more complex than his predecessors. And I find this amazing since the later quartets were all created when he was totally deaf."
Audio		What does the professor mean when she says this about Beethoven:
Replay		"And I find this amazing since the later quartets were all created when he was totally deaf."
Answer	**B**	Her positive tone indicates that she is in admiration of Beethoven's exceptional talent.
Audio	27.	Why does the professor mention Impressionism?
Answer	**A**	She is comparing the experimentation in art with that in music.
Audio	28.	How did the professor organize the lecture?
Answer	**B**	She arranged the information in chronological order.

Q27

LISTENING 6 "BOTANY CLASS"

Audio Discussion

Narrator: Listen to part of a discussion in a botany class. The professor is talking about hydroponics.

Professor:

Although the recent interest in hydroponics may lead you to believe that it's a relatively new idea, the process probably originated in ancient times. In fact, the famous Hanging Gardens of Babylon may well have been one of the first successful attempts to grow plants in water, that is, hydroponically. Early agriculture in Pakistan and India as well as other areas throughout the Middle East included water crops, and we also have evidence that the Egyptians were growing plants in water along the Nile . . . and that was without soil. Asia and the South Pacific were prime locations for early hydroponic gardens. And, in the Western Hemisphere, we know that the Aztecs had developed an advanced system of water agriculture along the marshlands of Lake Tenochtitlan in the Central Valley of Mexico because, when the Spanish arrived, they made drawings in their journals of "floating islands of trees and vegetation," in other words, hydroponic agriculture.   `Q29`

Okay, well, this isn't a history class. It's a botany class. But I think it's important when we're talking about scientific discoveries that we understand how science works. Sometimes we're rediscovering and refining methods that have been used for a very long time, and that's certainly the case of hydroponics. Through the years, it's been called *nutriculture, chemiculture*, *acquiculture*, *soilless* culture, but the current term is *hydroponics*, and that encompasses the modern science of growing plants without soil by using an inert medium such as sand, peat, gravel, or . . . or even sawdust or Styrofoam. Of course, you have to add a solution of nutrients.   `Q30`

Clearly, good soil has the nutrients necessary for plant growth, but when plants are grown without soil, all the nutrients must be provided in another way. So, why do you think that we would go to all of this additional effort to replace soil?

Student 1:

Well, I think the book mentioned something about keeping the growing medium more sterile.

Professor:

Umhum. Soil-borne diseases and pests and even weeds can be . . . virtually eliminated . . . by using a soil alternative.

Student 1:

So I was thinking probably you wouldn't require as much labor, to get rid of the pests and weeds.

Professor:

Good thought. Now tell me what you know about fertilizer and water.

Student 2:

Oh, right. Less fertilizer and water are required per plant since they're constantly reused, and aren't the results more uniform because of the highly controlled conditions?

Professor:

Right on both counts. But probably the most important advantage is the ability to cultivate a larger number of plants in a limited space. . . . Where would this be important do you think?   `Q31`

Student 1:

Well, small or isolated environments or very arid climates with limited fresh water supplies probably.

Student 2:

Or regions with poor soils, for instance, in developing countries where the weather conditions aren't dependable and . . . and famine might . . . could happen.   `Q32`

Student 1:　　Or the area may have a dense population.

Professor:　　So hydroponics is limited to developing regions then.

Student 3:

I'm not sure about that. Even in highly industrialized nations, populations are growing and . . . and isn't the total acreage in cultivation dropping to accommodate the expansion of urban areas?

Professor:

Well stated. As agricultural land is sold for development, hydroponics has become a viable option for, well, for almost every country in the world.

Now earlier, I said that we're often rediscovering ancient methods in science, but we're also adapting them by using improvements from other scientific research. In the case of hydroponics, there are probably two modern discoveries that have supported progress in hydroponics. Okay. First, the development of plastics . . . that allowed growers to abandon the old concrete beds, which were costly to construct and problematic because . . . because they leached into the nutrient solution. But, plastic beds are cheap, they're light, and sterile . . . an ideal replacement for concrete. And many of the greenhouses themselves are even built of plastic panels. Okay. The other important advancement is the knowledge we've accumulated about plant nutrition. Of course, like I said, good soil has the nutrients necessary for plant growth, but when plants are grown without soil, all the nutrients must be provided in another way. And now we have a much better idea of what we need to use in the solution to obtain the best results.

So . . . all of that said, let's talk about the lab experiment that we've set up here. This solution contains potassium nitrate, ammonium sulfate, magnesium sulfate, monocalcium phosphate, and calcium sulfate. Don't try to write down all of that now. You can refer to your lab workbook for the list of substances and the proportions needed for proper plant growth.

Q33

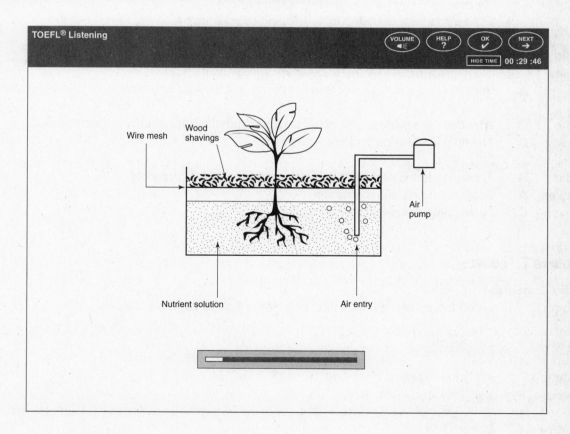

For now, just look at this diagram. The drawing in your lab workbook should look more or less like this one. As you know, for plants grown in soil, the roots absorb water and nutrients, but they also serve to anchor the plant. That's why the roots of our hydroponic plants aren't placed directly in the water and nutrient solution. We used sterile gravel held in place by wire mesh to anchor the plants and that allowed us to suspend the roots in the tank below. Remember, the tank contains the water and nutrient solution. So . . . because oxygen is also taken in by the roots, we had to attach an air pump to mix oxygen into the solution. Remember, a constant source of oxygen is one of the major problems with hydroponics tanks of this kind. And you can see the way that the pump is attached to the tank. `Q34`

Okay, it's almost time for our break this morning, so I'd like you to come over to the hydroponics area and examine the experiment close up. I'd also like you to take a closer look at this specimen of nutrient solution. What do you notice about this? Can you draw any conclusions? Today is Day 1 for you to record your observations on the chart in your workbook.

Audio	29.	What is this discussion mainly about?
Answer	**A**	Growing plants without soil

Audio	30.	Why does the professor talk about the history of hydroponics?
Answer	**A**	She wants to put the modern method in historical context.

Audio	31.	According to the professor, what is the greatest advantage of hydroponics?
Answer	**D**	Less space is needed to produce a large number of plants.

Audio	32.	Listen again to part of the discussion and then answer the following question.
Replay		"Or regions with poor soils, for instance, in developing countries where the weather conditions aren't dependable and . . . and famine might . . . could happen."
		"Or the area may have a dense population."
		"So hydroponics is limited to developing regions then."
		"I'm not sure about that."
Audio		Why does the professor say this:
Replay		"So hydroponics is limited to developing regions then."
Answer	**A**	Her tone is not conclusive. She is making a statement to generate further discussion.

Audio	33.	Why does the professor suggest that the students refer to their lab workbook?
Answer	**C**	To find a list of important plant nutrients

Audio	34.	According to the professor, why are roots important to plants?
Answer	**A**	To absorb water and nutrients
	C	To suspend the plants in the solution

LISTENING 7 "LIBRARY"

Audio Conversation

Narrator:	Listen to part of a conversation between a librarian and a student.
Student:	Excuse me.
Librarian:	Yes?
Student:	Are you the reference librarian?
Librarian:	Yes. How can I help you?
Student:	Well, I'm looking for a book that compares Great Britain, Australia, Canada, and the United States. `Q35`
Librarian:	Okay. What exactly are you trying to compare?

	Student:	I'm not quite sure. How about the cost of living?
	Librarian:	Oh. Well cost of living is, uh, not very specific. I mean, what aspects of the cost of living do you need to find? Cost of living is a fairly broad topic.
	Student:	It is?
	Librarian:	Well, yes. Do you want this for personal information or is it for a class?
	Student:	It's for my economics class.
	Librarian:	Unhuh.
	Student:	With Professor Brooks.
	Librarian:	Oh, okay. Well, do you just need numbers . . . or is it a report . . . a narrative?
Q39	Student:	Just the numbers. I'm supposed to make a chart. It can be either a pie chart or a bar graph. And I have to have some demographic information, you know, in order to do the chart.
	Librarian:	So you want a general comparison. I'm trying to imagine what you'll put on the graph.
	Student:	Well, I'm not too clear about that. I was thinking I might make several graphs, you know, one for each country, with the cost of basic things on it, and then I could compare the graphs.
	Librarian:	Was that the assignment? Maybe if you could explain the assignment to me . . .
Q36	Student:	Okay. I, uh, I have it right here . . . somewhere. Just a minute. . . . Okay, here it is. Uh, it says, "make a pie chart or a bar graph with at least four parts. It should be large enough to share with the class."
	Librarian:	That's it?
	Student:	Unhuh. But it's for an economics class, and we have to be able to explain it to everyone. So that's why I was going for the cost of living and my major's international business so I was interested in comparing several countries.
	Librarian:	But the professor really only asked you for one chart.
	Student:	I guess so . . . but I'm trying to figure out how to compare those countries on one chart and it's not that easy.
	Librarian:	Okay. Well . . .
	Student:	You think I should just do the one chart then?
	Librarian:	It's usually better to follow the instructions for an assignment unless . . .
	Student:	Oh. Even if it's more than, uh, more than the professor asked for?
Q37	Librarian:	It's usually better to check with the professor first if you want to change the assignment.
	Student:	Okay then. I guess I need to choose one country and compare several factors for the one country.
	Librarian:	Or, if you want to compare several countries, you probably need to zero in on one factor.
	Student:	Yeah.
Q38	Librarian:	Like the average income for a family of four or . . .
	Student:	Oh I see. . . . Maybe I could compare the cost of a home.
	Librarian:	Right.
	Student:	So I could find that in an encyclopedia then.
	Librarian:	Well, maybe, but you want current data and I'm not sure that you'd find demographics on income and home prices in an encyclopedia. Anyway . . . look, why don't I show you where you can find some reference materials in economics? Then, you can browse for a while. Maybe you'll find something that sparks an idea. But if you don't, then just come back to my desk and I'll look with you.
	Student:	Thanks. That's great.

Audio   35. Why does the man approach the librarian?
Answer   **C**   He needs help finding some data. He wants to compare information about several countries.

Audio	36.	Listen again to part of the conversation and then answer the following question.
Replay		"Uh, it says, 'make a pie chart or a bar graph with at least four parts. It should be large enough to share with the class.'"
		"That's it?"
		"Unhuh."
Audio		What does the woman mean when she says this:
Replay		"That's it?"
Answer	B	She is expressing surprise by the stress and tone of her voice.

| **Audio** | 37. | What does the librarian imply? |
| **Answer** | D | The man should not change the assignment. |

| **Audio** | 38. | What example does the librarian give for the assignment? |
| **Answer** | B | Average family income in several countries |

| **Audio** | 39. | What will the man do with the information? |
| **Answer** | C | Draw a chart or a graph |

LISTENING 8 "ART HISTORY CLASS"

Audio Discussion

Narrator: Listen to part of a discussion in an art history class. The professor is talking about action art.

Professor:

In the 1950s, Abstract Expressionism emerged among a group of painters that, uh, came to be known as the New York School, although the members included artists from many regions of the United States and several European countries as well. In any case, we know that the brushstrokes were a significant feature of the work of Impressionist and Post Impressionist painters, and like them, the Abstract Expressionists were interested in the expressive qualities of paint, and particularly in the case of action painters or gesture painters . . . they were sometimes called gesture painters . . . and they developed new methods for applying the paint. They dripped, threw, sprayed, and, uh, splattered . . . paint on the canvas . . . with a view to expressing artistic . . . actions or gestures . . . as part of the creative process. Q40

   Now, according to your textbook, probably the best-known of the action painters was . . . who?

Student 1:   Pollock.

Student 2:   Jackson Pollock.

Professor:

No doubt about it. Pollock was a highly individual artist. He's famous for huge mural-sized works. And . . . to create them, he'd spread his unstretched canvas on the floor, and he'd approach the work from all four sides, walking around it and attacking it with commercial house paint in cans that he carried with him.

   He dripped the paint from sticks or brushes that he dipped in the cans or . . . or he threw the paint and splashed it in patterns . . . that, uh, . . . that reflected the motion of his arm and, uh, . . . and his body, as he engaged in his so-called action painting. I think you can see how the name applies to this method. So Pollock claimed that this process allowed him to be *in* the painting, not apart from it.

   Let me show you a picture of Pollock with a work in progress.

Photo of Jackson Pollock painting
Photograph by Hans Namuth
Courtesy Center for Creative Photography, University of Arizona
© 1991 Hans Namuth Estate

As you can see . . . and this is Pollock . . . he's stepping right onto the canvas, splattering and dripping the paint. He's focusing on the act of painting and he's using grand, rhythmic gestures . . . sort of similar to a dance. In fact, some critics referred to the work as a performance or a choreographed activity. He also used to pour the paint directly out of the can, and occasionally threw sand, broken glass, uh . . . pebbles, and string, and other objects . . . he would throw them onto the canvas.

So, how much of the action art was a result of decisions and how much was pure chance? What do you think?

Student 3:   Well, there was probably a little bit of both going on there.

Professor:
Probably so. But Pollock contended that he could control the flow of the paint with the motion of his arm and body . . . and that his work was *not* accidental. And it certainly *was* spontaneous in the sense that it happened very quickly and the decisions that he made were, uh, . . . were . . . of necessity, split second choices. So, I would say you're right, that action art, and Pollock's work in particular, is a combination of, uh, . . . of chance, of artistic intuition, and, uh, . . . and control. And I should point out that he was known to retouch a drip with the brush on occasion.

Now let me show you an example of the paintings themselves.

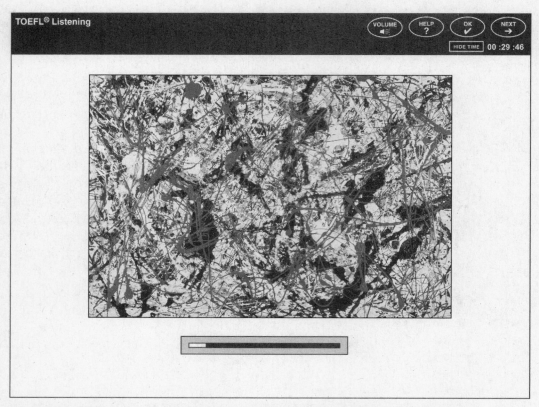

© 2006 The Pollock-Krasner Foundation/Artists Rights Society (ARS), New York

Professor: What do you see?

Student 2:   There's no visual center of attention.

Professor: Which means . . . ?

Student 2:   Which means . . . the image has no foreground, no background, no focus of attention.

Professor:
I see. However, I think you'll agree that it *does* have a, uh . . . a complex unity, a balance of form and color. Look at the patterns. Wouldn't you agree that they're caused by the separation and weaving of one pigment in another? And it was this . . . this . . . weaving that produced a number of tones from a minimal palette of paints. . . . Have any of you ever seen an original Pollock?

Student 3:   I have. I went to the Guggenheim Museum when I was in New York last year.

Professor: Could you tell the class a little about it?

Student 3:
Sure. I thought that the work looked like skeins of yarn. Because the dripping and the small objects produced . . . uh . . . uh . . .   Q43

Professor: Texture?

Student 3:
Yeah. Texture as well as form, like yarn. And I also remember the light that seemed to be *in* the canvas.

Professor:
And precisely because of the texture and light, it's really a disservice to see this as a flat slide.

Student 3:   Oh another thing. A lot of the paintings were identified by numbers instead of names.

Professor:

Oh, thanks for bringing that up. Some people think he did that because he didn't want to limit the imagination. He wanted others to view a painting, without prejudice, so to speak. But one piece has come to be called "Lavender Mist." I'm not really sure whether Pollock actually named it or not, but it's particularly interesting because the artist marked the image with his handprints. I think it's in your textbook, but again, seeing it with the texture of the paint is a different experience.

Okay, so, after the process of creation, we see beauty, order, unity, perhaps even rhythm in an incredible light emanating from the canvas. Pollock wanted to express his feelings rather then to merely illustrate them, and I think he *did* achieve that. And, whether you like them or not, and many critics argued and continue to argue their merits, but it's undeniable that works by Pollock are unique and recognizable . . . and virtually impossible to copy. It's also clear that he had a remarkable influence on later artists. Uh, later artists . . . color-field painters who adapted the paint-pouring methods . . . and modern artists who chose to work with allover patterns . . . and the performance artists who continue to push the envelope on activity and process.

Audio   40.   What is this discussion mainly about?
Answer   C   Abstract Expressionism

Audio   41.   To what did some critics compare Pollock's work?
Answer   B   Dancing, because the work appeared to be choreographed

Audio   42.   According to the professor, what defines action art?
Answer   A   Control
            C   Coincidence

Audio   43.   Listen again to part of the discussion and then answer the following question.
Replay   "Could you tell the class a little about it?"
            "Sure. I thought that the work looked like skeins of yarn. Because the dripping and the small objects produced . . . uh . . . uh . . . "
            "Texture?"
            "Yeah. Texture as well as form, like yarn."
Audio   Why does the professor say this:
Replay   "Texture?"
Answer   A   He is helping the student to find the exact word.

Audio   44.   What is interesting about the painting, "Lavender Mist?"
Answer   C   The artist's handprints

Audio   45.   What is the professor's opinion of Pollock?
Answer   B   He argues that Pollock's work was influential.

LISTENING 9 "ENGINEERING CLASS"

Audio Lecture
Narrator: Listen to part of a lecture in an engineering class.

Professor:
Because every earthquake presents us with unique conditions, it's difficult to anticipate the stresses that will ultimately affect the structures we design and build. So our challenge is to try to design a building that will be as . . . safe as possible . . . for all types of earthquakes. Besides that, during the past decade,

the expectations for earthquake-resistant structures have changed. Whereas in the past, it was considered adequate for a building not to collapse during an earthquake, now insurance companies and . . . and even clients . . . they're demanding buildings that will be able to maintain their structural integrity through an earthquake and, uh . . . remain sound . . . after the earthquake subsides.

So, in recent years we've developed several techniques for building more earthquake-resistant structures. For relatively small buildings, all we have to do, really, is bolt the buildings to their foundations and, uh . . . provide some support walls. Remember these walls are referred to as *shear walls* in your textbook. They're made of reinforced concrete, and by that I mean concrete with steel rods embedded in it. This not only strengthens the structure but . . . but it also diminishes the forces that tend to shake a building during a quake. And in addition to the shear walls that surround a building, shear walls can be situated in the center of a building around an elevator shaft or a stairwell. This is really an excellent reinforcement. It's commonly known as a *shear core*, and it contains reinforced concrete, too. [Q46]

Okay. Let's talk about walls. Walls can also be reinforced, using a technique called *cross-bracing*. Imagine steel beams that cross diagonally from the ceiling to the floor . . . and this happens on each story in a building. So before the walls are finished, you can see a vertical row of steel x's on the structure. And this cross-bracing tends to make a building very rigid, and consequently, very strong. [Q47]

But besides steel reinforcements, engineers have also devised *base isolators*, which are positioned below the building, and their purpose is to absorb the shock of the sideways shaking that can undermine a building and cause it to collapse. Most of the base isolators that are currently being used are made of alternating layers of steel and synthetic rubber. The steel is for strength, but, uh . . . the rubber absorbs shock waves. In higher buildings, a . . . a moat . . . of flexible materials allows the building to sway during seismic activity. Or . . . or large rubber cylinders support all of the corners of the building, and in between each floor, and they allow the building to sway during an earthquake. So, you can see that these alternatives are quite different from cross-bracing or shear walls. [Q48]

So the combination of reinforced structures and flexible materials has been proven to reduce earthquake damage. But even these engineering techniques are insufficient if the building has been constructed on filled ground. Soil used in fill dirt can lose its bearing strength when subjected to the shock waves of an earthquake, and the buildings constructed on it can literally disappear into the Earth. So, in areas where earthquakes are known to occur, it's important to understand the terrain, and you have to be sure that the ground is either solid or it's been adequately prepared. [Q49]

Okay, let's assume that we do everything right . . . we choose and prepare the construction site and we design a building with plenty of reinforcements and flexible materials. With cross-bracing, we probably have a building with the strength to hold up under earthquakes, even those of relatively high magnitudes. And while this is great for the building, what about the occupants? Well, the structure may be strong, but the furniture will probably be overturned or shifted during the earthquake and that could result in major injuries for the people inside. So, now that we've made progress in solving the problem of how to preserve the buildings, uh . . . one of the more recent areas of research is how to better protect the occupants during an earthquake. [Q50]

One interesting possibility is to design buildings that house a series of pistons, and these pistons are filled with fluid and controlled by sensors in a computer. So . . . by analyzing signals from the sensors, the computer should be able to determine the magnitude of an earthquake in progress . . . and when it does that, it can trigger electromagnets in the pistons to increase or decrease the . . . the rigidity of the shock absorbers . . . built into the structure. If the earthquake is minor, then the building can be programmed to sway gently, and the people and everything else inside get a safe ride. But during high-magnitude earthquakes, the shock absorbers can freeze the building to prevent it from shaking at all. So the beauty of the concept is that the computer sensors work very quickly, reacting within one one-thousandth of a second, and they can run on battery power since the electrical system usually fails during an earthquake. Will the concept work? Well, the National Science Foundation is supporting more research into the potential of pistons, and the results so far are promising. [Q51] [Q51]

Audio   46.   What is this lecture mainly about?
Answer   **C**   Earthquake-resistant structures

Audio	47.	Which technique is used to reinforce walls?
Answer	A	Cross-bracing

Audio	48.	Which two materials are used in base isolators?
Answer	A	Rubber
	B	Steel

Audio	49.	What happens to fill dirt during an earthquake?
Answer	C	It becomes unstable and collapses.

Audio **Replay**	50.	Listen again to part of the lecture and then answer the following question.
		"With cross-bracing, we probably have a building with the strength to hold up under earthquakes, even those of relatively high magnitudes. And while this is great for the building, what about the occupants? Well, the structure may be strong, but the furniture will probably be overturned or shifted during the earthquake and that could result in major injuries for the people inside."
Audio **Replay**		Why does the professor say this: "And while this is great for the building, what about the occupants?"
Answer	A	He is introducing a new major point—how to protect the occupants.

Audio	51.	What does the professor think about computer sensors for buildings?
Answer	B	He finds the research on sensors for pistons very encouraging.

➤ Speaking

Model Test 5, Speaking Section, CD 8, Track 2

INDEPENDENT SPEAKING QUESTION 1 "A TOURIST ATTRACTION"

Narrator 2: Number 1. Listen for a question about a familiar topic. After you hear the question, you have 15 seconds to prepare and 45 seconds to record your answer.

Narrator 1: If you were asked to choose one place in your country where you would take a tourist, which one would you choose? Why? What is especially impressive about the place? Use specific reasons and details to explain your choice.

Narrator 2: Please prepare your answer after the beep.

Beep

[Preparation time: 15 seconds]

Narrator 2: Please begin speaking after the beep.

Beep

[Recording time: 45 seconds]

Beep

INDEPENDENT SPEAKING QUESTION 2 "SUCCESS"

Narrator 2: Number 2. Listen for a question that asks your opinion about a familiar topic. After you hear the question, you have 15 seconds to prepare and 45 seconds to record your answer.

Narrator 1: Some people believe that the best way to succeed is to set goals and work hard to achieve them. Other people think that hard work is not as important as good luck. Which point of view do you think is true and why? Use specific reasons and examples to support your opinion.

Narrator 2: Please prepare your answer after the beep.

Beep

[Preparation time: 15 seconds]

Narrator 2: Please begin speaking after the beep.

Beep

[Recording time: 45 seconds]

Beep

INTEGRATED SPEAKING QUESTION 3 "AUTO REGISTRATION"

Narrator 2: Number 3. Read a short passage and listen to a talk on the same topic. Then listen for a question about them. After you hear the question, you have 30 seconds to prepare and 60 seconds to record your answer.

Narrator 1: A student meeting is planned to discuss the policy for vehicle registration. Read the policy in the college catalogue printed on page 400. You have 45 seconds to complete it. Please begin reading now.

[Reading time: 45 seconds]

Narrator 1: Now listen to a student who is speaking at the meeting. She is expressing her opinion about the policy.

Student:
Well, I don't mind paying a parking fee, and I even think that $20 is reasonable, but my concern is that some of us are using more than one car, and since the registration is for the car, not the student, well, then you have to pay $40 so you can drive both of your cars on campus, but you're only one student. See what I mean? Like me, sometimes I have to take my husband's car and one time last semester . . . I didn't have it registered and I got a ticket. I think that every student should pay a parking fee, and then just put a parking permit on the windshield of whatever car the student is driving that day, don't you?

Narrator 1: The student expresses her opinion of the policy for vehicle registration. Report her opinion and explain the reasons that she gives for having that opinion.

Narrator 2: Please prepare your answer after the beep.

Beep

[Preparation time: 30 seconds]

Narrator 2: Please begin speaking after the beep.

Beep

[Recording time: 60 seconds]

Beep

INTEGRATED SPEAKING QUESTION 4 "STRESS"

Narrator 2: Number 4. Read a short passage and then listen to part of a lecture on the same topic. Then listen for a question about them. After you hear the question, you have 30 seconds to prepare and 60 seconds to record your answer.

Narrator 1: Now read the passage about stress printed on page 401. You have 45 seconds to complete it. Please begin reading now.

[Reading time: 45 seconds]

Narrator 1: Now listen to part of a lecture in a psychology class. The professor is talking about an experiment.

Professor:
Let me tell you about a classic experiment on rats. I think it was first done in the early seventies by Weiss and reported in the *Scientific American*. Anyway, the rats were divided randomly into three groups. Rats in the first group were given shocks, but just before the shock was induced, they received a warning in the form of a tone. The second group of rats was also given shocks, but this group didn't receive the warning tone. And the final control group received no shocks, but they were exposed to the same warning tone as the first group. After a few weeks the rats were examined, and the animals that had received shocks with no warning were already showing severe signs of stomach ulcers. The other two groups of rats showed little or no instance of ulcers. According to Weiss, the experiment confirmed that unexpected events are more stressful than those that can be predicted. In related experiments, there was also evidence that even a small amount of control over the circumstances surrounding the stress can lower the negative effects. When rats were allowed to select their own rest and feeding times, they experienced less physical damage than did rats that received the same amount of rest and feeding at times that were selected for them.

Narrator 1: Explain the causes of stress and relate them to the experiment with rats.

Narrator 2: Please prepare your answer after the beep.

Beep

[Preparation time: 30 seconds]

Narrator 2: Please begin speaking after the beep.

Beep

[Recording time: 60 seconds]

Beep

INTEGRATED SPEAKING QUESTION 5 "ART PROJECT"

Narrator 2: Number 5. Listen to a short conversation. Then listen for a question about it. After you hear the question, you have 20 seconds to prepare and 60 seconds to record your answer.

Narrator 1: Now listen to a conversation between a student and her friend.

Friend:	What are you going to do for the project?
Student:	I don't know. I was hoping you could help me think of something.
Friend:	Well, you're such a good artist, you could talk about watercolor while you're doing one in front of the class. That would be totally awesome. If I were you, that's what I'd do.
Student:	Maybe, but what if I make a mistake in front of everyone?
Friend:	Come on. You're really talented. Besides, you wouldn't have to do much preparation beforehand.
Student:	True. And it fits in with what we've been talking about in class.
Friend:	Yeah. Or, how about this? You could bring in a photograph, a pencil drawing, and a watercolor of the same subject. Something simple so it wouldn't take so much time to do, like a flower. Then you could show the advantages and disadvantages of working with different materials.
Student:	I could do that one ahead of time.
Friend:	You could, but remember, it would take a lot more time.
Student:	Gee, thanks. I'll have to think about it, but these are both really good options.

Narrator 1: Describe the woman's problem and the two suggestions that her friend makes about how to handle it. What do you think the woman should do, and why?

Narrator 2: Please prepare your answer after the beep.

Beep

[Preparation time: 20 seconds]

Narrator 2: Please begin speaking after the beep.

Beep

[Recording time: 60 seconds]

Beep

INTEGRATED SPEAKING QUESTION 6 *"CAVERNS"*

Narrator 2: Number 6. Listen to part of a lecture. Then listen for a question about it. After you hear the question, you have 20 seconds to prepare, and 60 seconds to record your answer.

Narrator 1: Now listen to part of a lecture in a geology class. The professor is discussing caverns.

Professor:
Okay, as you'll recall, caves form in limestone when acidic groundwater follows some kind of weakness in the rocks. Now the rock formations in a cavern . . . that's the technical name that we use for a cave . . . the rock formations there are of two kinds . . . stalactites and stalagmites. Both of these formations are water that contains dissolved minerals that . . . that accumulate and build deposits. But stalactites hang down from the ceiling of the cavern, and stalagmites protrude up from the floor of the cavern. Well, these words sound a lot alike, and this can be confusing, so I always tell my students to remember that there is a *t* in stalactites, and the *t* has a tail that hangs down just like the stalactites that hang down from the ceiling of the cave, but there is an *m* in stalagmites and the points on an *m* stick up like the stalagmites that protrude up from the ground in a cave. And if that doesn't work for you, another way to remember the difference is that stalactite has a *c* in it, and so does the word *ceiling*, whereas stalagmite has a *g* in it, and so does the word *ground*. So stalactites drip down from the ceiling and stalagmites build up from the ground. So with these little tricks for remembering the difference, I expect you all to get this right on the next quiz.

Narrator 1: Using the main points and examples from the lecture, describe the two kinds of rock formations in a cavern, and explain how the professor helps his students remember the difference between the two.

Narrator 2: Please prepare your answer after the beep.

Beep

[Preparation time: 20 seconds]

Narrator 2: Please begin speaking after the beep.

Beep

[Recording time: 60 seconds]

Beep

➤ Writing

INTEGRATED ESSAY "EFFECTIVE DISCIPLINE"

First, read the passage on pages 404–405 and take notes.

 Model Test 5, Writing Section, CD 8, Track 3

Narrator: Now listen to a lecture on the same topic as the passage that you have just read.

Professor:
So now let's talk about how discipline relates to self-esteem. In studies of children, Coopersmith found that power and withholding of affection were associated with children who demonstrated low self-esteem, but management techniques were associated with children who exhibited high self-esteem. So, it seems that parents should use physical punishment and withholding of affection with caution, right? Well, most psychologists oppose physical punishment for children under the age of 2, and some psychologists believe that discipline should be achieved without any physical punishment for children of all ages, referencing the fact that discipline means "to teach" whereas punishment means "to harm." Anyway, it's generally agreed that reinforcement of good behavior is more effective than waiting for bad behavior that requires punishment. But when discipline *is* necessary, setting limits with negative consequences that are consistently enforced seems to promote healthy development of self-esteem in children, especially when these management techniques are supplemented with approval, attention, and affection. I mean, when parents try to catch their children in the act of doing something right and use that as a basis for positive reinforcement of their behavior.

➤ Example Answers and Checklists for Speaking and Writing

 Model Test 5, Example Answers, CD 8, Track 4

EXAMPLE ANSWER FOR INDEPENDENT SPEAKING QUESTION 1 "A TOURIST ATTRACTION"

Although a case could be made for showing a tourist the beautiful mountain region or the historic capital city in my country, I would probably take a tourist to my home because living with a family would give this visitor a perspective about my country that few tourists have. Shopping, eating meals together, um . . . interacting and participating in the usual everyday activities, attending religious services, and . . . and visiting friends in their homes, um, this would let the visitor live in my culture for awhile. I think this is more impressive than taking photos of places because you can see all of the usual tourist attractions in videos or magazines, but you can't understand how people live unless you live with them.

Checklist 1

✔ The talk answers the topic question.
✔ The point of view or position is clear.
✔ The talk is direct and well-organized.
✔ The sentences are logically connected.

✔ Details and examples support the main idea.
✔ The speaker expresses complete thoughts.
✔ The meaning is easy to comprehend.
✔ A wide range of vocabulary is used.
✔ There are only minor errors in grammar.
✔ The talk is within a range of 125–150 words.

EXAMPLE ANSWER FOR INDEPENDENT SPEAKING QUESTION 2 "SUCCESS"

I think it's important to set goals and work hard to achieve them. For one thing, goals help you think clearly about what you're doing. By identifying goals, you get organized. Another thing is the advantage of sharing goals with people who can help you. If others know what you're trying to do, sometimes they give you advice or assistance. As for good luck, I agree that a lucky opportunity or a chance meeting with a person who can help you is sometimes a key to success . . . but unless you know where you're going and what you want to achieve, you might not even recognize a lucky opportunity. So, in my opinion, the best way to succeed is to know what you want and work to create your own good fortune. Then, if luck shines on you, you'll just reach your goal sooner.

Checklist 2

✔ The talk answers the topic question.
✔ The point of view or position is clear.
✔ The talk is direct and well-organized.
✔ The sentences are logically connected.
✔ Details and examples support the main idea.
✔ The speaker expresses complete thoughts.
✔ The meaning is easy to comprehend.
✔ A wide range of vocabulary is used.
✔ There are only minor errors in grammar.
✔ The talk is within a range of 125–150 words.

EXAMPLE ANSWER FOR INTEGRATED SPEAKING QUESTION 3 "AUTO REGISTRATION"

To park on campus, students have to buy permits for each vehicle. They cost $20. The woman doesn't oppose the fee, but she believes that it . . . I mean the fee . . . it should cover all the vehicles that a student might need to use. She uses a personal example from last term when she had to drive her husband's car and she got a ticket even though she had a paid permit for her own car. So, um, so her solution is to pay for parking on campus and then display the permit on the vehicle that the student happens to be driving that day. That way, if there are several cars in the family, the student can drive any of them, using the same parking permit. In other words, she thinks that the $20 registration should be for the student who needs the parking space, not for the vehicle that the student's driving.

Checklist 3

✔ The talk summarizes the situation and opinion.
✔ The point of view or position is clear.
✔ The talk is direct and well-organized.
✔ The sentences are logically connected.
✔ Details and examples support the opinion.
✔ The speaker expresses complete thoughts.

✔ The meaning is easy to comprehend.
✔ A wide range of vocabulary is used.
✔ Errors in grammar are minor.
✔ The talk is within a range of 125–150 words.

EXAMPLE ANSWER FOR INTEGRATED SPEAKING QUESTION 4 "STRESS"

Stress is caused by changes in the environment that require people to adjust to new circumstances. It's interesting that these new conditions don't have to be negative. For example, you'd expect to have stress after a divorce or a health problem, but even moving to a new house or going on a trip can be stressful. Okay, in the experiment by Weiss, one group of rats was shocked after they heard a tone, so they knew that the shock was going to happen. Another group of rats heard the tone but didn't get the shock, and the other group received shocks at random without warning. So . . . the rats that received shocks without warning . . . they were the ones who developed ulcers but the other two groups had fewer ulcers or none at all. And this research proved that unexpected experiences are more stressful than those we can predict. Additional investigations also showed that even a little bit of control like choosing times to rest or eat could reduce stress.

Checklist 4

✔ The talk relates an example to a concept.
✔ Inaccuracies in the content are minor.
✔ The talk is direct and well-organized.
✔ The sentences are logically connected.
✔ Details and examples support the opinion.
✔ The speaker expresses complete thoughts.
✔ The meaning is easy to comprehend.
✔ A wide range of vocabulary is used.
✔ The speaker paraphrases in his/her own words.
✔ The speaker credits the lecturer with wording.
✔ Errors in grammar are minor.
✔ The talk is within a range of 125–150 words.

EXAMPLE ANSWER FOR INTEGRATED SPEAKING QUESTION 5 "ART PROJECT"

The woman's trying to decide what to do for her project and her friend makes a couple of suggestions. He encourages her to paint a watercolor in front of the class while she's giving a talk about watercolor. The advantage of that project is she wouldn't have to prepare very much before the presentation. The other idea is to show three different versions of one subject, like a flower . . . in watercolor, a pencil sketch, and maybe a photograph. She could talk about the pluses and minuses of working in each of the three media. Um, the advantage of the second project is that she could prepare it before class, but the problem is it would be more time-consuming. I think she should go with the second idea because she seemed nervous about doing a spontaneous watercolor, and even though it would take more time, showing the three pieces of art would be less stressful and the advanced preparation might influence the professor to give her a better grade.

Checklist 5

✔ The talk summarizes the problem and recommendations.
✔ The speaker's point of view or position is clear.
✔ The talk is direct and well-organized.

✔ The sentences are logically connected.
✔ Details and examples support the opinion.
✔ The speaker expresses complete thoughts.
✔ The meaning is easy to comprehend.
✔ A wide range of vocabulary is used.
✔ Errors in grammar are minor.
✔ The talk is within a range of 125–150 words.

EXAMPLE ANSWER FOR INTEGRATED SPEAKING QUESTION 6 "CAVERNS"

The rock formations in caverns are made up of water that's saturated with dissolved minerals. As they drip and deposit themselves in the cave, you'll notice some of them hang from the ceiling and some of them grow up from the floor. The terms for each of these deposits are so similar that the professor suggests some tricks to help keep them straight. *Stalactite* has the letter *t* in it, which reminds students of a tail that hangs down . . . but *stalagmite* has the letter *m* in it, which brings to mind two points that stick up. He also points out that *stalactite* has a *c* in it, like the word *ceiling*, and stalactites drip down from the ceiling, but *stalagmite* has a *g* in it, like the word *ground*, and stalagmites grow up from the ground. So . . . so these, uh, memory aids . . . they help us recall that stalactites are the rock formations that grow down from the cavern and stalagmites are the ones that grow up from the floor.

Checklist 6

✔ The talk summarizes a short lecture.
✔ Inaccuracies in the content are minor.
✔ The talk is direct and well-organized.
✔ The sentences are logically connected.
✔ Details and examples support the opinion.
✔ The speaker expresses complete thoughts.
✔ The meaning is easy to comprehend.
✔ A wide range of vocabulary is used.
✔ The speaker paraphrases in his/her own words.
✔ The speaker credits the lecturer with wording.
✔ Errors in grammar are minor.
✔ The talk is within a range of 125–150 words.

EXAMPLE RESPONSE FOR INTEGRATED ESSAY "EFFECTIVE DISCIPLINE"

Outline

Professor's view—effective discipline

• Reinforce correct behavior
• Coopersmith study
    Withholding of affection → low self-est.
    Management strategies → high self-est.
• Most psychologists no physical consequences
    children—2
• Consistent consequences/ limits

Common strategies

- Power = physical punishment
- Withdrawal affection
- Management strategies

Results in children

- Harsh power = aggressive + rebellious
- Withholding or threats/abandon = insecurity + dependence/approval

Behavior → disciplinary action clear
Consequences consistent
discipline "to teach"
punishment "to harm"

Map

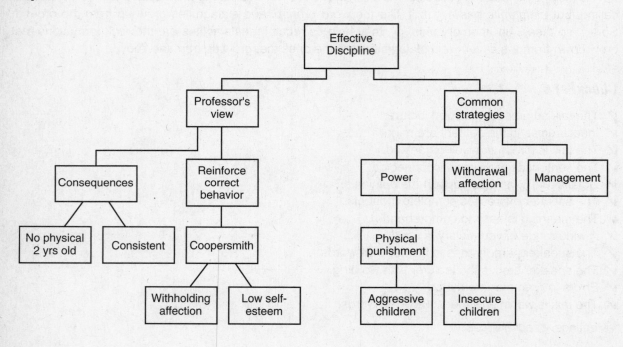

Example Essay

The professor advocates the reinforcement of correct behavior rather than the punishment of incorrect behavior. He refers to a study by Coopersmith in which children who experienced "withholding of affection" also showed signs of low self-esteem, whereas children who were disciplined using management strategies displayed high self-esteem. According to the lecture, most psychologists do not recommend physical consequences for children younger than two years old, and some oppose physical punishment for older children as well. When punishment is required, a consistent set of consequences for children who disregard the limits appears to engender positive self-esteem along with maturity.

Unfortunately, the three most common strategies that parents and caretakers use are, in order of frequency, power strategies, which include physical punishment; the withdrawal of affection; and management strategies. Children who are disciplined with harsh power strategies tend to become aggressive and rebellious. In contrast, children who experience the withholding of affection, including lack of communication or even threats of abandonment, can develop feelings of insecurity and dependence on others for approval in spite of model behavior while they are growing up.

In all forms of discipline, the relationship between the behavior and the disciplinary action should be clear and the consequences consistent, but, when making a choice for children, it may be worthwhile to reflect on the definition of *discipline*, which means "to teach" versus *punishment*, which means "to harm."

Checklist for Integrated Essay

✔ The essay answers the topic question.
✔ Inaccuracies in the content are minor.
✔ The essay is direct and well-organized.
✔ The sentences are logically connected.
✔ Details and examples support the main idea.
✔ The writer expresses complete thoughts.
✔ The meaning is easy to comprehend.
✔ A wide range of vocabulary is used.
✔ The writer paraphrases in his/her own words.
✔ The writer credits the author with wording.
✔ Errors in grammar and idioms are minor.
✔ The essay is within a range of 150–225 words.

EXAMPLE RESPONSE FOR INDEPENDENT ESSAY "TECHNOLOGICAL INNOVATIONS"

Outline

Computer

• Mail
• Meetings + conferences
• Language

Cheaper, easier to exchange information

Map

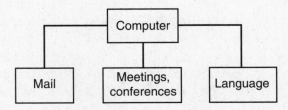

Cheaper, easier to exchange information

Example Essay

Without doubt, computers have changed the way that nations interact with each other in a global society. One type of communication that has been greatly affected by the computer is international mail. For example, prior to the widespread use of computers, a letter from the United States to my country would take weeks for delivery. I recall that the cost was almost $10 U.S. at a time when the same amount of money would buy groceries for a family for one week. Now mail can be delivered instantly at virtually no cost by electronic mail.

Another way that computers have affected international communication is in the way that people assemble in meetings and conferences. Before the introduction of computer technology, it was necessary to fly into a central location to conduct business or training. The time involved in travel was often ten times that of the actual meeting time. Now, through the miracle of teleconferencing, participants from many nations can meet in local sites and connect by means of satellite to a central conference facility. They can see each other on large screens and interact with each other from multiple sites around the world. After the initial investment in the equipment, a company can expect to save money because the travel budget can be adjusted down.

Finally, computers have influenced the language of communication around the world. Although English was a popular foreign language prior to the advent of the Internet, it is even more useful now. The computer keyboards in Roman letters are more efficient and, at least initially, the flood of information onto the "information highway" was often in the English language. To be connected in a global society increasingly means knowing English as a second language.

Computers have changed the way that nations interact with each other to send international mail, to attend world meetings and conferences, and to connect to the Internet. They have made it cheaper and easier to exchange information.

Checklist for Independent Essay

✔ The essay answers the topic question.
✔ The point of view or position is clear.
✔ The essay is direct and well-organized.
✔ The sentences are logically connected.
✔ Details and examples support the main idea.
✔ The writer expresses complete thoughts.
✔ The meaning is easy to comprehend.
✔ A wide range of vocabulary is used.
✔ Various types of sentences are included.
✔ Errors in grammar and idioms are minor.
✔ The essay is within a range of 300–350 words.

MODEL TEST 6: PROGRESS TEST

➤ Reading

READING 1 "EXOTIC AND ENDANGERED SPECIES"

1. **C** ". . . exotic species . . . a resident of an established community that was deliberately or accidentally moved from its home range and became established elsewhere." Choice A is not correct because it refers to an endangered species, not an exotic species. Choice B is not correct because exotic species are moved from their communities. Choice D is not correct because an exotic species becomes established, unlike most imports, which fail to thrive outside of their home range.

2. **D** "Unlike most imports, which can't take hold outside their home range, an exotic species permanently insinuates itself [the exotic species] into a new community." The pronoun "itself" does not refer to Choices A, B, or C.

3. **B** In this passage, *connect* is a synonym for "bond." Context comes from the result at the end of the same sentence. ". . . they started to import familiar animals."

4. **C** ". . . no natural predators . . . was the reality." Choice A is not correct because it refers to a solution for the problem, not why the plan failed. Choice B is not correct because Australians imported rabbits because they liked the familiar species. Choice D is not correct because it refers to the reason that the rabbits were introduced, not to why the plan failed.

5. **C** The rabbits create deserts by eating the vegetation, but they were not moved to deserts. Choice A is mentioned in paragraph 4, sentence 6. Choice B is mentioned in paragraph 4, sentence 7. Choice D is mentioned in paragraph 4, sentence 9.

6. **B** "Biting insects, mainly mosquitoes and fleas, quickly transmit the virus from host to host." Choice A is not correct because South American rabbits are the normal hosts for the myxoma virus. Choice C is not correct because it is the *O. cuniculus* rabbit that dies when infected. Choice D is not correct because resistant populations of *O. cuniculus* rabbits, not fleas, have an immunity to the virus.

7. **C** ". . . researchers are now questioning whether . . . it can . . . infect animals other than rabbits (such as humans)." Choice A is not correct because insects were not mentioned in the Spencer Gulf experiment. Choice B is not correct because the purpose of the experiment was to kill the rabbits. Choice D is not correct because 80 to 95 percent of the rabbits are being killed, but the small number with immunity is not identified as dangerous.

8. **C** In this passage, *results* is a synonym for "consequences." Context comes from the logical connection between researchers "questioning" and the phrase "long-term," which describes the "consequences."

9. **D** The farm and processing plant will manufacture products from kudzu, which will offer partial solutions. Choice A is not correct because kudzu was imported to control erosion, not for manufacture. Choice B is not correct because no argument is presented in defense of the decision. Choice C is not correct because it grows in Asia already.

10. **A** In this passage, *surpasses* is a synonym for "exceeds." Context comes from the logical relationship between "demand" and "supply."

11. **D** "When you hear someone bubbling enthusiastically about an **exotic species**, you can safely bet the speaker isn't an ecologist . . . they [exotic species] make native species **endangered species**." This introduction establishes the author's opinion that exotic species are often disruptive to the ecology.

12. **C** Vocabulary reference is a transitional device that connects the insert sentence with the previous sentence. The connection is the reference to "starch" in both the insert sentence and the previous sentence.

13. **E, B, C** summarize the passage. Choice A is a minor point that refers to major point C. Choice D is a detail that is not developed as a major point. Choice F is an important fact, but it is not a major point because is it not developed.

READING 2 "PALEOLITHIC ART"

14. **C** ". . . the remoteness and difficulty of access . . . suggest[s] . . . magical properties . . . rituals or dances." Choice A is not correct because they were probably used for rituals. Choices B and D are not mentioned or implied in the passage.

15. **D** Choice A is mentioned in paragraph 1, sentence 7. Choice B is mentioned in paragraph 1, sentence 8. Choice C is implied in paragraph 1, sentences 5 and 7.

16. **A** In this passage, *admission* is a synonym for "access." Context comes from the contrast with "remoteness" and "difficulty" in the same sentence.

17. **C** In this passage, *assist* is a synonym for "facilitate." Context comes from the contrast of "destruction" and "survival" in the same and following sentences.

18. **C** "A central problem for both the . . . theories is that the animals that seem to have been diet staples of Old Stone Age peoples are not those [animals] most frequently portrayed." The pronoun "those" does not refer to Choices A, B, or D.

19. **B** In this passage, the phrase *not believed* describes "discredited." Choice A describes *distracted*. Choice C describes *discouraged*. Choice D describes *disorderly*. Context comes from the parts of the word. The prefix *dis* means "not." The root *credit* means "believe."

20. **A** *It is true* paraphrases "cannot . . . be doubted" and *the paintings were meaningful* paraphrases "the paintings did have meaning."

21. **B** "Several observers have seen a primitive writing form in these representations of nonliving things." Choice A is not correct because they accompany the pictures of animals. Choice C is not correct because they may have had some other significance. Choice D is not mentioned or implied.

22. **C** "Some scholars have argued that the 'spots' which appear both within and without the horses' outlines, are painted rocks thrown at the animals." Choice A is true, but it is not the reason that the spots may represent a hunting scene. Choice B is not correct because the spots are drawn on the wall, not attached to it. Choice D is not correct because an interpretation of the geometric lines and figures in words is not mentioned.

23. **B** "Some scholars have considered them [positive imprints] 'signatures' of cult or community members, or . . . individual artists." Choices A and C are not correct because they are not mentioned or implied. Choice D is not correct because the author states that the "handprints . . . must have had a purpose."

24. **C** Because the author presents several different theories and does not offer a strong argument for any of them, the author's opinion is probably that the exact purpose of cave paintings is not known. Choice A is not correct because the author also presents the food-creation theory and the mythology theory as alternatives to the hunting ritual theory. Choice B is not correct because the mythology theory is not the only possibility discussed. Choice D is not correct because the author suggests several reasons why this theory cannot explain the narrow range of subjects or the inaccessibility of many of the paintings.

25. **B** *Example* is a transitional device that connects the insert sentence with the general statement in the previous sentence. The connection is between the general statement "animals that seem to have been diet staples . . . are not . . . portrayed" and the example that "red deer, not bison were eaten."

26. **B, D, A** summarize the passage. Choice C is true, but it is a minor point that is mentioned as evidence for Choice B. Choice E is not mentioned in the passage. Choice F is true, but it is a point that is used to develop the ideas in Choice A.

READING 3 "GROUP DECISION MAKING"

27. **A** "Groups accumulate more information, knowledge and facts . . . and often consider more alternatives." Choice B is not correct because a group tends to view a problem in more than one way. Choice C is not correct because making recommendations instead of decisions is not mentioned or implied in the passage. Choice D is not correct because each person has experience, but the experience of a group is not mentioned as a reason why a group is chosen to participate.

28. **B** ". . . people will . . . be more committed to a decision in which they have had a say than to a decision made for them." Choice A is true, but more ideas do not explain why the decisions are successful. Choice C is not correct because the help provided by a large number of people is not mentioned in the passage as an advantage during implementation. Choice D is not correct because implementation is successful in group decisions, but the decisions themselves may or may not be successful.

29. **B** In this passage, *significant* is a synonym for "considerable." Context comes from the reference to the "time required to make a decision" as a "disadvantage."

30. **D** In this passage, *As a result* describes "Consequently." Context comes from the conclusion that follows the word "Consequently."

31. **B** "One obvious disadvantage of group decision making is the time required to make a decision." Choice A is not correct because the implication is that sometimes a decision could have been made as effectively by an individual. Choice C is not correct because the "cost" refers to the time, not to the pay for group members. Choice D is not correct because groups tend to avoid disagreements.

32. **B** "All group members need to be encouraged and permitted to contribute." Choice A is not correct because the group should have goals, and personal goals by one member [the leader] should not dominate the discussion. Choice C is not correct because it is considered a disadvantage when an individual such as the group leader dominates the group. Choice D is not correct because expectations are not mentioned as a responsibility of the group leader.

33. **B** In this passage, *debatable* is a synonym for "controversial." Context comes from the contrast with "social pressure . . . to conform."

34. **A** "It occurs when groups are highly cohesive, have highly directive leaders, are insulated so they have no clear ways to get objective information, and—because they lack outside information—have little hope that a better solution might be found than the one [solution] proposed by the leader or other influential group members." The phrase "the one" does not refer to Choices B, C, or D.

35. **C** ". . . a group may try too hard to compromise . . . to maintain friendships and avoid disagreements." Choice A is not correct because the group may not make optimal decisions when the members try too hard to compromise. Choice B is not correct because groupthink requires agreement rather than compromise. Choice D is not correct because helping one member to reach a personal goal or win an argument would be the opposite of compromise.

36. **B** ". . . self-appointed 'mind guards' . . . bring pressure on dissenters." Choice A is not correct because people who conform will not necessarily pressure others. Choice C is not correct because "mind guards" use force to exert influence and may not be the most ethical members. Choice D is not correct because "mind guards" do not disagree with the group.

37. **C** ". . . decisions . . . are made without consideration of . . . alternative options." Choice A is not correct because the group exerts pressure on dissenters, but dissenters do not exert pressure on the group. Choice B is not correct because it is neither mentioned nor implied in the passage. Choice D is not correct because when groupthink takes place, poor decision making and wrong decisions occur.

38. **A** Generalization and example is a transitional device that connects the insert sentence with following sentences. "In fact, the traditional group is prone to a variety of difficulties" provides a general statement that introduces the disadvantages developed in the following sentences. Choices B, C, and D would interrupt the examples by inserting the generalization.

39. Advantages: **C, D, H**   Disadvantages: **A, B, E, F**   Not used: **G, I**

READING 4 "FOUR STAGES OF PLANETARY DEVELOPMENT"

40. **B**   "The moon, for example, is much like Earth, but its evolution has been dramatically altered by its smaller size." Choice A is not correct because the four stages are explained in the following paragraphs. Choice C is not correct because the Moon and all the terrestrial planets have passed through the same stages. Choice D is not correct because exploration is not mentioned in the passage.

41. **A**   "A meteorite hitting Earth at high velocity converts most of its [the meteorite's] energy of motion into heat." The pronoun "its" does not refer to Choices B, C, or D.

42. **A**   *The Earth was probably liquid* paraphrases "Earth may have been molten," and *the heat collected faster than it dissipated* paraphrases "this heat would have accumulated much more rapidly than it could leak away." In addition, *if the formation took place quickly* paraphrases "If Earth formed rapidly."

43. **B**   In this passage, *broken into small parts* describes the word "pulverized." Context comes from the reference to "battered."

44. **B**   Because radioactive elements continued to "warm and soften the rock layers," it must be concluded that radioactive matter generates intense heat. Choice A is not correct because all traces of early lava flooding caused by radioactive heating have been destroyed. Choice C is probably true, but the relative importance of the stages is not mentioned in the passage. Choice D is not correct because the heating, not the fracturing, is caused by radioactive decay.

45. **D**   In this passage, the phrase *most important* describes the word "dominant." Context comes from the contrast with the phrase "still occasionally" earlier in the sentence.

46. **B**   ". . . water fell as rain, filling the deepest basins to produce the first oceans." Choices A, C, and D are true, but they do not describe how the oceans formed.

47. **B**   ". . . this process [the presence of living matter] seems to be totally missing from other worlds in our solar system." Choice A is not correct because the author does not express doubt in her opinion. Choice C is not correct because she gives her opinion in the final sentence. Choice D is not correct because she states that living matter is "totally missing."

48. **A**   According to the passage, *cratering* is the second stage and *flooding* is the third stage. Choice B is not correct because slow surface evolution is the fourth stage, after *flooding*. Choice C is not correct because *differentiation* is the first stage, which comes before, not after *cratering*. Choice D is not correct because it is not a stage, although it is an important process.

49. **B**   "We do not know how the presence of living matter [which is peculiar to Earth] has affected the evolution of Earth." Choice A is mentioned in paragraph 1, sentence 1. Choice C is mentioned in paragraph 1, sentences 1 and 2. Choice D is mentioned in paragraph 4, sentence 8.

50. **D**   Addition is a transitional device that connects the insert sentence with the previous sentence. The reference to the way that the "mountains" and "continents" are "changing" in the previous sentence introduces the way that "air and water erode the surface and wear away geological features [like mountains and continents]" in the insert sentence. Choices A and B are not correct because they refer to flooding, not to the processes in slow surface evolution such as erosion. Choice C is not correct because the sentence does not include a reference to erosion and cannot introduce an additional sentence about erosion.

51. **A**   In this passage *different* is a synonym for "peculiar." Context comes from the phrase "On the other hand," which signals a contrast with the previous sentences that show similarities between Earth and the other planets.

52. **E, F, B**   summarizes the passage. Choice A is not correct because the stages are the same. Choice C is true, but it is a minor point that refers to major point E. Choice D is true, but it is a minor point that refers to major point F.

READING 5 "SPEECH AND WRITING"

53. **B**   In this passage, the phrase *come close to* is a synonym for "approximate." Context comes from the words "imperfectly" and "ideals" in the same sentence.

54. **D**   "When linguists study language, they take the spoken language as their best source of data and their object of description." Because they use the spoken language, researchers must prefer speech samples. Choice A is not correct because when researchers study Latin, they must make an exception [use written samples]. Choices B and C are not mentioned in the passage.

55. **A**   ". . . the majority of the Earth's inhabitants are illiterate." Choice B is not correct because illiterate populations are quite capable of spoken communication. Choice C is not correct because the majority of the Earth's inhabitants in the modern world are illiterate. Choice D is not correct because it is not mentioned in the passage.

56. **D**   *Both simple and complex writing systems* paraphrases "Writing systems [that] vary in complexity," and *require direct instruction* paraphrases "must all be taught."

57. **B**   In this passage, *thought* is a synonym for "deliberation." Context comes from the contrast with "spontaneous and simultaneous formulation of ideas" later in the sentence.

58. **C**   ". . . the association of writing with the standard variety is not a necessary one, as evidenced by the attempts of writers to transcribe faithfully the speech of their characters." Choice A is not correct because the speech of their characters is transcribed [written down]. Choice B is not correct because the examples are transcriptions of speech, not writing styles. Choice D is not correct because examples of the two varieties are not provided and could not be contrasted.

59. **B**   In this passage, *temporary* is a synonym for "transient." Context comes from the contrast with writing, which tends to "last."

60. **D**   "Writing could also change if it were made to follow the changes of speech. The fact that people at various times try to carry out spelling reforms amply illustrates this possibility [writing could change to follow the changes in speech]." Choice A is not correct because examples of British and American spelling are different. Choice B is not correct because pronunciation in British and American English is not compared. Choice C is not correct because spelling changes because of pronunciation, but pronunciation does not change because of spelling.

61. **A**   "The fact that people at various times try to carry out spelling reforms amply illustrates this possibility [writing could also change]." The phrase "this possibility" does not refer to Choices B, C, or D.

62. **C**   "It is a widely held misconception that writing is more perfect than speech." This opening statement expresses the author's opinion, which is developed in an essay with argument and persuasion. Choice A is not correct because the history of writing begins 1,200 years later than that of speech. Choice B is not correct because the author says that "the association of writing with the standard variety is not a necessary one." Choice D is not correct because the author points out that "Writing could also change if it were made to follow the changes of speech."

63. **C**   The author organizes the passage as a persuasive argument by explaining the reasons why speech is primary and then demonstrating why people have the "misconception" that writing is more perfect than speech. Choices A, B, and D are included as part of the argument.

64. **C**   Reference is a transitional device that connects the insert sentence with the previous sentence. *The Sumerians* in the insert sentence refers to "Sumer" in the previous sentence.

65.   Speech: **B, C, E, I**   Writing: **D, F, G**   Not used: **A, H**

➤ Listening

 Model Test 6, Listening Section, CD 8, Track 5, continued on CD 9, Track 1

LISTENING 1 "PROFESSOR'S OFFICE"

Audio Conversation

Narrator:	Listen to a conversation between a student and a professor.
Student:	Hi Dr. Davis. I'm a little early. Should I wait outside?
Professor:	No. Come on in. I'm free. What did you want to talk about?
Student:	Well, I've read the first couple of books you had on my list . . . the reading list for my independent study . . . and I was just wondering how you want me to report them to you. We didn't really talk about that.

Q1

Professor:	Well, I'm glad you stopped by. Let me think . . . didn't you have a project to do in addition to the reading list?
Student:	Yes. You said it could be a research paper or I could come up with a proposal for a different kind of project.
Professor:	That's right. So, the reading list is . . . background information then. Why don't you just come in when you finish the first part of the list. I think it was divided in two distinct parts . . . so just come in, and we'll talk about the readings.
Student:	You mean I should prepare a synopsis of each book and . . . and kind of report to you on each one?
Professor:	No, no. Nothing as formal as that. I was thinking more along the lines of a conversation. As I recall, the list has a focus, doesn't it?

Q4

Student:	Definitely. All of the books are novels and plays from the second half of the twentieth century.
Professor:	The Post Modern Period then. And all North American novelists and playwrights.
Student:	Right.
Professor:	So we should be able to find some common threads then. Remember, though, Post Modernism is very difficult to define precisely. Maybe we could start with a discussion of the themes that emerge in the collection of literature from that period.
Student:	That sounds interesting.
Professor:	I think so, too. And by the time you get through with the second half of the reading list and we get together again, maybe we can figure out whether we're looking at a logical extension of Post Modernism or whether there's actually a new movement there . . . in the readings on the second part. If you'll notice, there are quite a few minority writers represented, so you might want to think about what that means.
Student:	I noticed that in the list. The first part of the list has the usual North American writers and, of course, a good representation of women writers as you would expect, but the second part of the list includes a number of African-American authors, several Hispanic-American writers, and a few Oriental-Americans.

Q2

Professor:	It's a multiethnic mix.
Student:	Yeah.
Professor:	Good. So have you decided whether you want to do a paper or . . . something else perhaps?
Student:	To tell the truth, I'd really like to do something a little more creative. Maybe bring in some visuals on the computer as part of the . . . I don't know . . . I suppose you would call it a mixed media report. But I've never done anything like that before.

	Professor:	But that's what an independent study is designed to do. It's an opportunity to experiment and to have some one-on-one time with a professor.
	Student:	But a research paper is easier in some ways. At least I know that I can do a decent job. The computer project is unknown territory.
Q3	Professor:	True. But remember, it's unknown territory for all of us. I think I've heard some references to *Cybermodernism*, if you want to investigate some of the work that's being created in, as you call it, mixed media literature.
	Student:	Cybermodernism? Wow!
	Professor:	I think you'd find it interesting. Anyway, it's up to you. It's your project.
	Student:	Thanks. I'm really excited about doing this independent study. Actually, I'm spending more time on it than on any of my other classes.
Q5	Professor:	I've found that students usually invest more time and energy in a class that they can design. That's why I like to direct them. Oh, and Terry, if you run into any problems, don't wait until you're halfway through your reading list. Just stop by during my office hours. Maybe I can give you some references or at least a sounding board.
	Student:	Thanks. This is better than I even expected.

Audio 1. Why does the man go to see his professor?
Answer C To ask about the professor's requirements

Audio 2. How is the second part of the reading list different from the first part?
Answer A More minority authors are represented.

Audio Replay 3. Listen again to part of the conversation and then answer the following question.
"I think I've heard some references to *Cybermodernism*, if you want to investigate some of the work that is being created in, as you call it, mixed media literature."
"Cybermodernism? Wow!"
Audio Replay What does the man mean when he says this:
"Cybermodernism? Wow!"
Answer B His tone expresses interest and excitement.

Audio 4. What will the man probably do before the next meeting?
Answer D Prepare to talk with the professor

Audio 5. What can be inferred about the professor?
Answer B She is willing to help her students.

LISTENING 2 "ENVIRONMENTAL SCIENCE CLASS"

Audio Lecture
Narrator: Listen to part of a lecture in an environmental science class. The professor is talking about wind power.

Professor:
Q6 Today I want to talk with you about another renewable source of energy . . . wind power. This isn't a new concept. In fact, wind has been used for centuries to pump water and launch sailing vessels. But more recently, wind power has been used to generate electricity.

By the year 2000, California was using, maybe 15,000 wind turbines to produce about 400 megawatts of electricity. And that was happening at a cost that would be considered competitive with coal or nuclear power. And, although California currently leads the United States in harnessing wind power, there are several other areas that also hold considerable potential for increased production.

Texas and the Dakotas alone have enough wind potential to power the nation, but, since the winds there are so variable, well, wind power alone would be unreliable as a primary source of continuous energy. Nevertheless, it could be used as a secondary resource, along with fossil fuels. The strong and steady winds of the Pacific Northwest, especially in the Columbia River Basin . . . these winds would be ideal as a supplement to hydroelectric power when the river is experiencing periods of low water levels. Studies by the U.S. Department of Energy indicate that wind power generated from the Great Plains in the middle of the country could supply the continental United States with almost . . . 75 percent of the electricity required for the region.

[Q7]

In another section of the same report, it was noted that wind power is the world's fastest growing energy source. Since 1998, the capacity for wind energy has increased by more than 35 percent worldwide. And improvements in wind turbine technology in the past couple of decades has improved efficiency, cutting the cost dramatically, from roughly 40 cents to about 4 cents per kilowatt hour, and a new turbine design is being tested with a lower torque, so that may actually move the price closer to 3 cents.

Europe currently accounts for over 17 . . . Oh, sorry that's 70 . . . seven-zero percent of the world's wind power. India, China, Germany, Denmark, Italy, and Spain have published plans for major increases in wind-generated electricity projects in the next few years, and recent interest and exploration have been initiated in the United Kingdom and Brazil. Remote areas, especially islands, and other regions at a distance from electrical grids are vigorously exploring wind options. Clearly, the global implications not only for cheap energy but also for clean energy could be enormous. And, in some areas, the consumers are even willing to pay a subsidy for the pollution-free energy that wind provides their communities. In Colorado, for instance, through a program called Windsource, about 10,000 customers pay an additional $2.50 per month for every 100-killowatt hours of wind power. Legislation in several states in the United States now requires utility companies to guarantee that a percentage of their electricity will be generated from renewable sources like wind power.

[Q8]

Of course, there are some problems associated with wind power that do need to be considered. The blades on the turbines present a hazard to migrating birds. In some cases, the vibrations interfere with television reception in the area. And, there have been objections to wind farms because they produce noise and because they're not visually appealing to residents nearby. So, in addition to the studies to improve turbine design and energy efficiency, some of the attendant problems also require research and development. Regarding the noise, let me mention that design modifications, basically modifying the thickness of the turbine blades and making adjustments to the orientation of the turbines . . . these modifications have diminished the noise substantially in a number of sites. As for visual appeal, some creative ways to share the land to create a more attractive wind farm are being piloted.

[Q9]

So that brings us to the issue of storing wind power. And, although wind energy can be stored temporarily as battery power, the real challenge for wind power exploration will be how to level out the energy source. Alternatives for storage will be critical because, even in an area with steady winds, wind is still not totally reliable. But, the Tellus Institute has released promising results from studies to investigate the problem of intermittent wind. This is what they did. By dividing the wind turbines from one farm into two smaller farms with geographical separation, the capacity of the pair of farms increased by 33⅓ percent over the efficiency of the larger farm with the same number of turbines. So, by taking advantage of the slightly different wind patterns, a more continuous supply of wind power can be generated.

[Q10]

So where are we with all of this? Well, the research that will make wind power a viable option is underway but we need to continue to study . . . in order to solve some of the problems . . . before we can use wind power as a primary source of energy, globally.

[Q11]

Audio   6.   What aspect of wind power is the lecture mainly about?
Answer   **D**   Wind as a renewable energy option

Audio   7.   Which two regions of the United States have the greatest potential for supplying wind power?
Answer   **B**   The Midwestern Plains
            D   The Pacific Northwest

Audio Replay   8.   Listen again to part of the lecture and then answer the following question.

"Europe currently accounts for over 17 . . . Oh, sorry that's 70 . . . seven-zero percent of the world's wind power. India, China, Germany, Denmark, Italy, and Spain have published plans for major increases in wind-generated electricity projects in the next few years, and recent interest and exploration have been initiated in the United Kingdom and Brazil."

Audio Replay   Why does the professor say this:

"Europe currently accounts for over 17 . . . Oh, sorry that's 70 . . . seven-zero percent of the world's wind power."

Answer   C   He is correcting a previous statement.

Audio   9.   In the lecture, the professor identifies several problems associated with wind power. Indicate whether each of the following is one of the problems mentioned. Click in the correct box for each phrase.

Answer

	Yes	No
A Poor television reception	✔	
B Noisy turbines	✔	
C Expensive operating costs		✔
D Remote areas		✔
E Dangerous blades for birds	✔	

Audio   10.   How did the Tellus Institute solve the problem of intermittent wind?
Answer   D   By separating one wind farm into two locations

Audio   11.   What is the professor's opinion about the future of wind power?
Answer   A   He thinks that wind power will require more research before it becomes practical.

Listening 3 "Philosophy Class"

Audio Discussion
Narrator: Listen to part of a discussion in a philosophy class.

Professor:

Q12 The earliest Greek philosophers, also known as the pre-Socratic philosophers, they were very interested in determining the nature of the universe. Initially, Thales proposed that water was the original material from which all other material was derived, and by that he was referring not only to things on Earth but also in the heavens. He observed that life sprouts from a moist ground, unlike death that dries and shrivels into dust. The fact that water could transform itself into a solid as it does when it freezes into ice or it could change into air as it does when heated into steam, well, this convinced him that everything had originated as water and would eventually return to water. He believed that all things are living things, including rocks and metals, and so literally everything would transform itself into the original material, water, in a logical pattern of change.

A little later, Anaximander, and he was a student of Thales, so Anaximander was set on a path that involved questioning which of the elements was the most basic or fundamental. But he suggested that the universe was not originally made up of water as Thales had reasoned, but was a living mass, which he called the *infinite*. The word in Greek actually means "unlimited" but most translators have used the term *infinite* since it probably captures the meaning a little better in English. So Anaximander put forward what some believe is the first theoretical postulate . . . that the infinite was constantly in motion . . . up and down, back and forth. So, although the infinite had begun as a whole, the motion had caused pieces to be broken off to form all of the elements of the universe . . . the Earth, the Sun, stars. Then he specu-   Q13
lated that as the oceans had begun to evaporate, the first sea plants and animals had formed, and from them their descendants, the birds and land animals evolved, until finally, mankind was created.

Student 1:   That sounds a lot like evolutionary theory.

Professor:
Yes, it does. Probably the first instance of evolutionary theory among Europeans, although the Chinese philosophers had discussed this possibility earlier. Okay, so what do you think he postulated about the continued motion of the universe? Anyone?

Student 2:
I remember that part. He thought that all of these separate elements would eventually be put back together into the original infinite mass.

Professor:
Precisely right. But good students think for themselves, and some years later, Anaximander's student Anaximenes, criticized his teacher's view. He deduced that the original element of the universe was air, which was timeless and boundless, and in fact, alive. Because mankind and all the animals must breathe air in order to survive, he believed, therefore, that air had been transformed into blood, bone, and flesh. He also concluded that air was the origin of water, stone, and earth, and I think you can see the analogy with the parts of the body there. Furthermore, he contended that the solid condensations of air constituted the body of the world, but the ethereal quality of air constituted the spirit of the world, and it was the spirit that remained alive forever.

Now these three philosophers . . . Thales, Anaximander, and Anaximenes . . . they were all resi-dents of Miletus, and were very active beginning about 600 years before the Christian Era. So they were called the Milesian philosophers. And they all had different views, but they also had something in common.

Student 1:
Do you mean that they were all materialists? Because they were trying to explain the universe in terms   Q14
of perceivable elements like water and air?

Professor:
Good observation. Let's take that a step further. They all attempted to explain the unknown in terms of   Q15
the familiar instead of looking to the current mythologies or to a divine presence. And that's what is truly extraordinary about these pre-Socratic philosophers. A naturalistic account of the cosmos was pro-foundly different from the myths and legends of gods and goddesses that had been the basis for explaining the origin of the universe.

Student 2:   So what do you mean by naturalistic?

Professor:

I mean that they tried to use scientific arguments, and this marked a very new way of thinking. Unlike the exciting narratives of superhuman beings with the powers to create and change the universe, they proposed that the universe was made up of something very basic, and that it was constantly undergoing *natural* changes. The Milesians made a major contribution . . . and they did this by moving beyond the old mythologies and folktales, and some scholars even suggest that they were responsible for the beginnings of Western philosophy as we know it. Now when we talk about philosophy, it's important to point out that for many centuries philosophy was *not* a separate discipline from other areas of thought and knowledge. In fact, early philosophers were mathematicians, physicists, chemists, and biologists before

Q16 any of these sciences were identified as separate, uh, . . . subjects, or . . . fields of study. So the pre-Socratic philosophers were trying to discover a scientific basis for the universe long before the scientific method and the technologies were available to support their investigations. But, really, many scholars argue that these philosophers *did* initiate the process at least, and the process eventually resulted . . . years later . . . as the beginning of the physical sciences.

Q17   Okay, all of this appears on the surface to be very positive, right? But at the time, many philosophers as well as ordinary citizens were feeling much less comfortable with the very sparse tenants of emerging science than they had been with the rich and complicated stories that had explained the universe for them. Remember that this is all before Socrates, Aristotle, and Plato who were . . . by then . . . well, more able to expand on protoscientific thought and produce a massive and elaborate scientific alternative to the ancient beliefs.

Audio	12.	What is the discussion mainly about?
Answer	**C**	The nature of the universe

Audio	13.	Why does the student mention evolutionary theory?
Answer	**D**	He is comparing evolution to Anaximander's theory.

Audio	14.	Listen again to part of the discussion and then answer the following question.
Replay		"Do you mean that they were all materialists? Because they were trying to explain the universe in terms of perceivable elements like water and air?"
		"Good observation. Let's take that a step further."
Audio		Why does the professor say this:
Replay		"Good observation. Let's take that a step further."
Answer	**C**	She is going to expand on the comment. To "take a step further" means to "elaborate" or "provide details."

Audio	15.	What view did the three Milesian philosophers share?
Answer	**B**	They introduced a scientific approach to explaining nature.

Audio	16.	What can be inferred about the early Greek philosophers?
Answer	**A**	They were exploring the physical sciences.

Audio	17.	Listen again to part of the discussion and then answer the following question.
Replay		"Okay, all of this appears on the surface to be very positive, right? But at the time, many philosophers as well as ordinary citizens were feeling much less comfortable with the very sparse tenants of emerging science than they had been with the rich and complicated stories that had explained the universe for them."
Audio		What does the professor mean when she says this:
Replay		"Okay, all of this appears on the surface to be very positive, right?"
Answer	**B**	She is introducing doubt.

LISTENING 4 "PROFESSOR'S OFFICE"

Audio Conversation

Narrator: Now listen to a conversation between a student and a professor.

Student: Excuse me, Professor Jones. I was wondering whether I could talk with you for a minute? If you're busy now, though . . .

Professor: Sure, Anne. What's up?

Student: Well, I've been working on my research project. I'm doing it on decaffeinated beverages.

Professor: Oh, I remember. That's going to be interesting. How's it going?

Student: Good. I've got all the data, but the report is turning out to be fairly short. It took such a long time to do the research, I thought I'd have a lot more to write about. | Q18

Professor: Well, how long will it be, do you think?

Student: Probably five or six pages, and that includes a couple of pages with charts in them.

Professor: That sounds about right.

Student: It does?

Professor: Yes. Of course, it depends on what you included in the five pages. The issue here is whether the research design was well thought out, and whether you have all of the information in your report that you need to explain what you did . . . the approach . . . and the results that you found.

Student: Okay. I have a short introduction . . . just a few paragraphs really . . . so that's about caffeine, and then I talk about the benefits of decaffeination, and several ways to do that.

Professor: Unhuh. What else?

Student: Well, I explain my research design . . . and that's sort of a problem too because I'm not sure whether to make this sound like a book, you know, the way the studies are explained in our textbook, or whether I should just write it up as clearly as I can so that anyone would understand what I did.

Professor: I'd go for that option. In fact, why don't you ask a few friends to read it before you turn it in? If your friends get it, that's a good indication that you've explained it well, but if they have a lot of questions, then maybe you need to do some rewriting. And Anne, it's even better if your friends aren't chemistry majors like you are. | Q19

Student: Well, I would never have thought of that.

Professor: Then I'm glad I suggested it. By the way, did you include references at the end of your study?

Student: Just two. That's all I used.

Professor: Okay. Good. Just as long as you cite the references you used.

Student: Well, thanks. This is the first time I've ever done my own research. It was hard because I didn't have any experience, but it was fun, too. I was thinking about trying to get a part-time job as a lab assistant next year.

Professor: I think you'd be a good candidate. In fact, why don't you write up a draft of that report, and I'll look it over for you before you hand in the final copy. | Q20

Student: That would be perfect. I could bring it in on Monday since that's when you have your usual office hours. Would that be okay? | Q21

Professor: Yes, but that would only give you one day before the report is due.

Student: Oh right.

Professor: Okay then. Why don't you bring it to class on Friday?

Student: That would be great.

Professor:		And Anne, if you're really serious about that lab assistant position, I can give you some information about that when I see you.
Student:		I can't thank you enough.
Professor:		Not at all, Anne. You've got a lot going for you. I'm glad to help.

(Q22 marked in left margin beside "Professor:")

Audio   18.   Why does the woman want to talk with her professor?
Answer   C   She has some questions about the report she is writing.

Audio   19.   What advice does the professor give the woman?
Answer   A   Have some friends read the research

Audio   20.   What does the professor offer to do?
Answer   A   Read a draft of the report before the woman submits it

Audio   21.   Listen again to part of the conversation and then answer the following question.
Replay   "I could bring it in on Monday since that's when you have your usual office hours. Would that be okay?"
"Yes, but that would only give you one day before the report is due."
"Oh right."
Audio   Why does the professor say this:
Replay   "Yes, but that would only give you one day before the report is due."
Answer   A   His tone expresses reluctance because he realizes that she won't have time to revise the report.

Audio   22.   What is the professor's opinion of the woman?
Answer   B   He is very impressed with her attitude.

LISTENING 5 "BIOLOGY CLASS"

Audio Lecture
Narrator: Listen to part of a lecture in a biology class. The professor is talking about bacteria.

Professor:
Bacteria is the common name for a very large group of one-celled microscopic organisms that, we believe, may be the smallest, simplest, and perhaps even the very first forms of cellular life that evolved on Earth. Because they're so small, bacteria must be measured in microns, with one micron measuring about 0.00004 inches long. Most bacteria range from about 0.1 microns to about 4 microns wide and about 0.2 microns to almost 50 microns long. So how can we observe them? I'll give you one guess. Under the microscope, of course. As I said, bacteria are very primitive and simple. In fact, they're unicellular, which means that they're made up of a single cell. We think they probably evolved about three and a half billion years ago. Some of the oldest fossils are bacterial organisms. They've been found almost everywhere on Earth, including all the continents, seas, and fresh water habitats, and in the tissues of both plants and animals.

(Q25 marked in left margin)

Well, since they're so prevalent, you might ask, how do they reproduce? Okay, they grow in colonies and can reproduce, quite rapidly, in fact, by a process called *fission*. In fission, the cell, and remember, there's only one in bacteria, one cell. So the cell increases in size and then splits in two parts. Fission is also referred to in your text as *asexual budding*. Now you'll also read about *conjugation*, and that's when two separate bacteria exchange pieces of DNA, so there are two ways that reproduction can occur, but we think that fission is more common.

(Q25 marked in left margin)

Okay. Bacteria were virtually unknown until about 1600 when microscopes were introduced, and at that time, bacteria were observed and classified into three main types according to their shapes, and that classification hasn't really changed that much over the years. So that's what I want to talk about today—the main types of bacteria. The slides that I'm going to show you are enlargements of bacteria that I observed under the microscope in the lab earlier today. Now, this first slide is an example of *bacilli*.

Q23

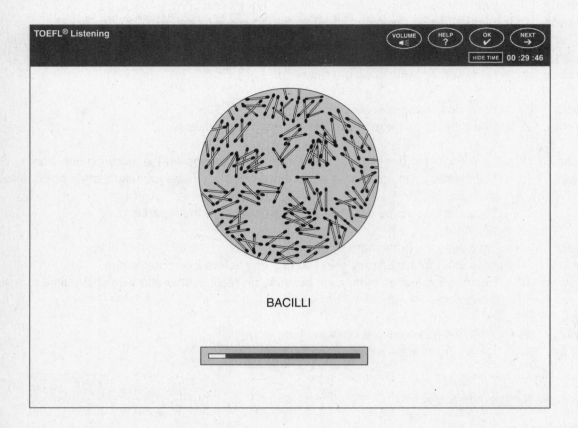

The bacilli are a group of bacteria that occur in the soil and air. As you can see, they're shaped like rods, and if you were to see them in motion, they'd be rolling or tumbling under the microscope. Of course, you can't see that because this is a still visual, but later, when you go into the lab, you'll see that rolling motion in examples of bacilli. These are kind of a greenish blue, but some are yellow. So don't try to identify them by their color. Look at the shape. These bacilli are largely responsible for food spoilage.

Okay, the next slide is a very different shape of bacteria. It's referred to as the *cocci* group, and it tends to grow in clusters or chains, like this example. This specimen is one of the common streptococci bacteria that cause strep throat.

Q24

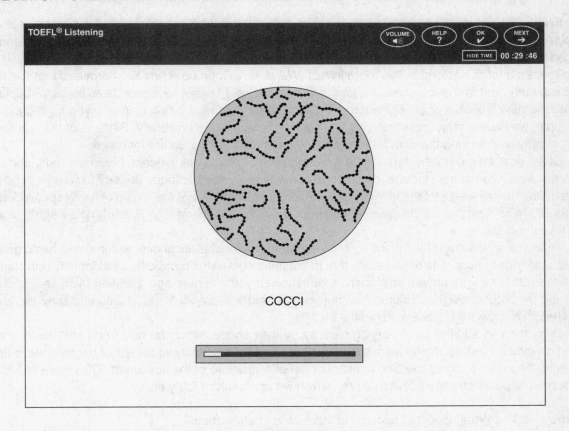

COCCI

Finally, let's look at the spiral-shaped bacteria called the *spirilla*.

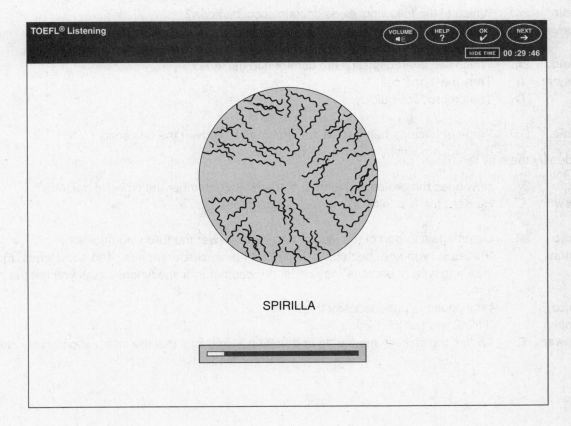

SPIRILLA

This is the spirilla. They look a little like corkscrews, and they're responsible for a number of diseases in humans. But I don't want you to get the wrong idea. It's true that some species of bacteria *do* cause diseases, but for the most part, bacteria are benign.

There's a lot of bacteria in this room in fact. We all have it on us. They live harmlessly on the skin, in the mouth, and in the intestines. In fact, bacteria are very helpful to researchers because bacterial cells resemble the cells of other life forms in many ways, and may be studied to give us insights. For example, we have a major research project in genetics here at the university. Since bacteria reproduce very rapidly, we're using them to determine how certain characteristics are inherited. `Q26`

Okay, now, let me review these three types with you . . . cocci are spheres, bacilli are rods, and spirilli are spirals. One of my students came up with a way to remember them. Just try to visualize the first letter in the name of each of the different types: Cocci starts with *C* like the shape of half a sphere. Bacilli starts with a straight line on the *B*, and a rod is straight. Spirilla starts with *S*, and that's a spiral shape. If it helps you, use it. `Q27`

In any case, although I want you to know the three major classifications, within these basic groups there are virtually hundreds of variations that make them somewhat more difficult to identify and classify than the rather straightforward specimens that I showed you a minute ago. Because, you see, bacteria can join in chains, clusters, pairs. And sometimes, more than one type of bacteria may be found together in a specimen. I think you get the picture. `Q28`

Okay then, in addition to identifying bacteria by their shape, which we now know isn't really a very good method for distinguishing them easily, if we really want to identify what type of bacteria we're dealing with, it's better to study the biochemistry or genetic structure of the specimen. They have one chromosome of double-stranded DNA in a ring, which we can analyze fairly easily.

Audio	23.	What aspect of bacteria is this lecture mainly about?
Answer	**D**	The three major types of bacteria

Audio	24.	Which of the following slides contain cocci bacteria?
Answer	**B**	The cocci bacteria are shown in this slide.

Audio	25.	Which two characteristics are common in bacteria?
Answer	**A**	They have one cell.
	C	They reproduce quickly.

Audio	26.	Why are bacteria being used in the research study at the university?
Answer	**C**	Bacteria are similar to other life forms.

Audio	27.	How does the professor help the students to remember the types of bacteria?
Answer	**C**	He uses the first letter to represent the shape.

Audio **Replay**	28.	Listen again to part of the lecture and then answer the following question. "Because, you see, bacteria can join in chains, clusters, pairs. And sometimes, more than one type of bacteria may be found together in a specimen. I think you get the picture."
Audio **Replay**		Why does the professor say this: "I think you get the picture."
Answer	**D**	To "get the picture" means "to understand." He thinks that the information is very clear.

LISTENING 6 "HISTORY CLASS"

Audio Lecture
Narrator: Listen to part of a lecture in a history class.

Professor:

Q29 Frontier home design in the United States was greatly influenced by the provisions of the Homestead Act of 1862. The legislation gave settlers the right to open land but mandated that homesteaders build a structure that was at least ten by twelve feet and included at least one glass window, and they had to live on their homestead and improve the land for five years before their claim was recognized. Of course, when they first arrived, most homesteaders lived in their wagons or pitched tents until they filed claims and planted crops. And even then, knowing that fully half of the homesteaders wouldn't make it through the five years required to complete their claims, homesteaders tended to view the construction of their homes as semi-permanent dwellings . . . more likely they'd build something better later or try to improve on what they'd built initially if they made it through the first five years. So, in addition to the requirements in the Homestead Act, the settlers needed a home that was easy to build, cheap, and maybe even disposable.

Q30   Well, the log cabin is the construction that comes to mind when we think of Western settlements, but the plains and the prairies had so few trees that log construction was almost impossible. So the sod
Q31 house was a practical solution for homesteaders on flat, treeless land. So how do you build a sod house? Well, first you wait for a rain that makes the earth soft, then you use a sod cutter to form sod bricks about
Q34 two or three feet square and a few inches thick. Then, you stack the bricks to form walls, and weave branches or twigs and grass into a roof that's finally covered with sod as well. Now, there were tremendous advantages to this type of construction. In the first place, it was very cheap . . . there are journals
Q32 from the 1800s that document construction prices at about $2.50, and most of that was for the glass window. And, it took very little time to build, probably a day or two. And the thick walls actually kept the house quite cool in the summer and fairly warm in the winter. If a better home could be built later, the sod house would simply dissolve into the soil. But there were serious disadvantages as well. Even well-built roofs leaked onto the dirt floors, forming mud puddles, and sometimes the roof even collapsed from the water weight. Or, in dry spells, the dirt crumbled from the roof into the home. Not to mention the infestations of insects and even snakes that inhabited the dirt walls.

Q31   So, those settlers who arrived in wooded areas opted to build log cabins instead of sod homes. Like the sod construction, the log cabin could be built in a few days, using simple tools, often only an axe. But it was much more comfortable. There's evidence that the first log cabins were introduced by Swedish
Q34 settlers as early as the 1700s but other immigrant settlers quickly adopted the construction. First, you build a foundation of rocks to keep the logs away from dampness that might cause them to rot. Then, you cut down the trees and square off the logs, cutting notches in the top and bottom of each end so they could fit together when they were stacked at the corners and it also had the advantage of assuring structural integrity. And there were several types of notching techniques that were used, depending on the skill of the builder. In any case, with notching, no nails were required and that was good since nails
Q34 had to be shipped into towns and then transported out to the new settlements. But there were gaps in the walls so these had to be filled by a technique called *chinking*. In *chinking*, grass, hay, moss and mud were worked into rolls about a foot long and maybe four inches wide and then they were inserted into the cracks between the logs. These rolls were commonly referred to as *mud cats* and were very effective in keeping out the cold and keeping in the heat. Of course, the tighter the logs, the fewer chinks were required, and that's important because the chinks were the weakest part of the cabin, and with the expansion and contraction that resulted from freezing and thawing, well, chinking tended to deteriorate and needed constant maintenance and repair.

    Okay, there was usually a stone or brick fireplace along one wall. And the roof was usually made of wood shingles. So you can imagine, this was quite an improvement over the sod house. The advantages were that the home could be kept clean. Even though the floor was usually dirt or gravel because flat boards were difficult to obtain, it was still an effective shelter to keep out the rain and dust.

Later, at the end of the 1800s, when the railroads brought materials such as asphalt shingles, tar paper, and finished boards to the frontier, the sod house was abandoned for one-room board shanties, covered with tar paper. Whether this was an improvement is subject to debate. For one thing, since they were often built without foundations, the harsh winds of the prairies literally blew the shanties away. Still, many settlers considered the shacks preferable to the old soddies even though they weren't as easy to heat and cool. To go back to the log cabin for a minute, the effect of new construction materials on the log cabin was . . . aesthetic . . . as well as practical. The logs were often covered on the outside by finished boards and on the inside with plaster, which gave the cabins a more finished look and improved insulation. And by this time the old one-room ten-by-twelve was also being replaced with larger homes with several rooms. The frontier settlers had weathered the hardships of their first five years, they'd received their claims, and they and their homes were a permanent part of the great western expansion. `Q33`

Audio	29.	What is the lecture mainly about?
Answer	C	Frontier homes in the West

Audio	30.	How does the professor organize his lecture?
Answer	D	He contrasts several types of homes in the West—log cabins, sod houses, and board shacks.

Audio	31.	What does the professor imply about construction materials for early homes?
Answer	A	Settlers used the materials from the natural environment.

Audio	32.	What is the evidence for the inexpensive price of a sod home?
Answer	D	Personal records and accounts—journals

Audio Replay	33.	Listen again to part of the lecture and then answer the following question. "Later, at the end of the 1800s, when the railroads brought materials such as asphalt shingles, tar paper, and finished boards to the frontier, the sod house was abandoned for one-room board shanties, covered with tar paper. Whether this was an improvement is subject to debate."
Audio Replay		Why does the professor say this: "Whether this was an improvement is subject to debate."
Answer	B	To demonstrate uncertainty

Audio	34.	In the lecture, the professor identifies attributes for different frontier homes. Indicate whether each attribute refers to a sod house or a log cabin. Click in the correct box for each phrase.
Answer		

	Sod House	Log Cabin
A A mud roof	✔	
B A rock foundation		✔
C Chinked walls		✔
D Notching techniques		✔
E Thick brick insulation	✔	

➤ Speaking

 Model Test 6, Speaking Section, CD 9, Track 2

INDEPENDENT SPEAKING QUESTION 1 "A GOOD SON OR DAUGHTER"

Narrator 2: Number 1. Listen for a question about a familiar topic. After you hear the question, you have 15 seconds to prepare and 45 seconds to record your answer.

Narrator 1: In your opinion, what are the characteristics of a good son or daughter in a family? Use specific examples and details to explain your answer.

Narrator 2: Please prepare your answer after the beep.

Beep

[Preparation time: 15 seconds]

Narrator 2: Please begin speaking after the beep.

Beep

[Recording time: 45 seconds]

Beep

INDEPENDENT SPEAKING QUESTION 2 "JOB OPPORTUNITIES"

Narrator 2: Number 2. Listen for a question that asks your opinion about a familiar topic. After you hear the question, you have 15 seconds to prepare and 45 seconds to record your answer.

Narrator 1: Some people are attracted to jobs that include a great deal of travel. Other people prefer jobs that allow them to return to their homes every evening. Which type of job opportunity would you prefer and why? Use specific reasons and examples to support your opinion.

Narrator 2: Please prepare your answer after the beep.

Beep

[Preparation time: 15 seconds]

Narrator 2: Please begin speaking after the beep.

Beep

[Recording time: 45 seconds]

Beep

INTEGRATED SPEAKING QUESTION 3 "EXCUSED ABSENCE"

Narrator 2: Number 3. Read a short passage and listen to a talk on the same topic. Then listen for a question about them. After you hear the question, you have 30 seconds to prepare and 60 seconds to record your answer.

Narrator 1: The professor's attendance policy is published in the course syllabus. Read the policy in the course syllabus printed on page 450. You have 45 seconds to complete it. Please begin reading now.

[Reading time: 45 seconds]

Narrator 1: Now listen to a student who is talking with friends about the policy.

Student:
On the one hand, it's good that you can be absent once without explaining why, but on the other hand, you can't be absent more than one time without getting a lower grade, so, I'd rather have the option of explaining my problem to the professor if I need to be absent, and then try to figure out a way to make up the work. Look, if I'm sick for two weeks, I don't think it's fair for the professor to lower my grade as long as I keep up with the class. Or, if you have a legitimate reason not to be there—like a family emergency or something. I don't think you should have to choose between your health or your family and your grade in the class.

Narrator 1: The student expresses his opinion of the professor's policy for excused absences. Report his opinion and explain the reasons that he gives for having that opinion.

Narrator 2: Please prepare your answer after the beep.

Beep

[Preparation time: 30 seconds]

Narrator 2: Please begin speaking after the beep.

Beep

[Recording time: 60 seconds]

Beep

INTEGRATED SPEAKING QUESTION 4 "INSECTS"

Narrator 2: Number 4. Read a short passage and then listen to part of a lecture on the same topic. Then listen for a question about them. After you hear the question, you have 30 seconds to prepare and 60 seconds to record your answer.

Narrator 1: Now read the passage about insects printed on page 451. You have 45 seconds to complete it. Please begin reading now.

[Reading time: 45 seconds]

Narrator 1: Now listen to part of a lecture in a biology class. The professor is talking about insects.

Professor:
Strictly speaking, a spider is not an insect. True, it is an invertebrate and an arthropod, but it belongs to a class identified as *arachnids*. Arachnids are not included in the insect world because their body structure is very different. The bodies of spiders are divided into two parts—the . . . a head with a fused thorax, which is all one structure, and the second part is a separate abdomen joined to the large head-thorax part by a narrow stalk. The head contains what many researchers now believe is a highly developed brain. There are no antennae, but four pairs of eyes and eight legs covered with fine, sensitive hairs more than compensate for the absence of the antennae. These hairy legs and feet explore the environment sending sensory messages back to the brain. Okay . . . the abdomen—remember that's the second part of the spider—it includes not only the digestive and reproductive systems but also the silk glands that allow spiders to spin their webs. So, as you see, even though spiders and insects are commonly grouped together as bugs, they are really not the same. An oversimplification is that spiders have too many legs and not enough wings. In reality, the entire body structure is quite different.

Narrator 1: Describe the structure of an insect and explain why a spider is not strictly considered an insect.

Narrator 2: Please prepare your answer after the beep.

Beep

[Preparation time: 30 seconds]

Narrator 2: Please begin speaking after the beep.

Beep

[Recording time: 60 seconds]

Beep

INTEGRATED SPEAKING QUESTION 5 "MEETING PEOPLE"

Narrator 2: Number 5. Listen to a short conversation. Then listen for a question about it. After you hear the question, you have 20 seconds to prepare and 60 seconds to record your answer.

Narrator 1: Now listen to a conversation between a student and his friend.

Student:	Can you believe that I've been here almost a whole semester, and you're the only friend I've made.
Friend:	No. How can that be?
Student:	I don't know. You know me better than anyone here at school. I thought maybe you could give me some advice.
Friend:	Sure. Um, well, do you belong to any clubs or any organizations on campus? That's always a good way to meet people.

Student:	No. I don't have a lot of time to, you know, go to meetings.
Friend:	Neither do I, but I do play inter-mural sports.
Student:	What's that?
Friend:	It's just a group that meets regularly to play basketball. Of course, there are lots of other teams, besides basketball, I mean. You could join a football team, or soccer . . . uh baseball, volleyball. Just go over to the Recreation Center and sign up. They'll put you on a team. You could use some time away from the books.
Student:	I'd like to do that, but . . .
Friend:	Well, since you don't want to take time away from your studies, why don't you join a study group, or get one going in one of your classes? That way, you wouldn't feel like you are wasting time, and besides, the people you meet will be serious students, so maybe they would be better friends for you anyway.

Narrator 1: Describe the man's problem, and the two suggestions that his friend makes about how to handle it. What do you think the man should do, and why?

Narrator 2: Please prepare your answer after the beep.

Beep

[Preparation time: 20 seconds]

Narrator 2: Please begin speaking after the beep.

Beep

[Recording time: 60 seconds]

Beep

INTEGRATED SPEAKING QUESTION 6 "SKINNER BOX"

Narrator 2: Number 6. Listen to part of a lecture. Then listen for a question about it. After you hear the question, you have 20 seconds to prepare, and 60 seconds to record your answer.

Narrator 1: Now listen to part of a lecture in a psychology class. The professor is discussing the Skinner Box.

Professor:
There have been several references to the Skinner Box in your textbook because a lot of behavioral modification experiments still use similar devices, even today, so let's just take a few minutes and make sure that everyone understands exactly what a Skinner Box is and how it works. The box which was named for B. F. Skinner, the American psychologist who developed it . . . it was used in Skinner's original experiment in 1932, and its construction hasn't changed much from that time. It's just a small, empty box, really, except for a bar with a cup underneath it. So picture this: In Skinner's experiment, a rat that had been deprived of food for twenty-four hours was placed in the box. As the animal began to explore its new environment, it accidentally hit the bar, and a food pellet dropped into the cup. The rat ate the pellet and continued exploring for more food. After hitting the bar three or four times with similar results, the animal started hitting the bar with intention instead of by accident. It had learned it could get food by pressing the bar. In other words, the food stimulus reinforced the bar pressing response. So . . . many

psychology experiments were modeled after Skinner's original research. Um, various animals have been placed in modified Skinner Boxes and presented with conditions that will result in a reward—food or some other desirable object or experience. In most of the behavior modification experiments in your book, you'll see a citation for Skinner's classic study.

Narrator 1: Using the main points and examples from the lecture, describe the Skinner Box, and then explain how the device is used in psychology experiments.

Narrator 2: Please prepare your answer after the beep.

Beep

[Preparation time: 20 seconds]

Narrator 2: Please begin speaking after the beep.

Beep

[Recording time: 60 seconds]

Beep

➤ Writing

INTEGRATED ESSAY "PRIMORDIAL SOUP"

First, read the passage on pages 454–455 and take notes.

   Model Test 6, Writing Section, CD 9, Track 3

Narrator: Now listen to a lecture on the same topic as the passage that you have just read.

Professor:
Most textbooks that have been published within the past fifty years include the Miller-Urey experiment because it was such a groundbreaking discovery at the time, and researchers honestly believed that they were on the verge of discovering the origin of life. But the current view of the Miller-Urey experiment is, let's say, skeptical. And there are several serious objections that we really need to deal with before we move on. First, the laboratory atmosphere that Miller and Urey created was charged with continuous electrical energy, but even though the atmosphere of early Earth was subjected to frequent electrical storms, they were probably not continuous. So, some scientists argue that, although amino acids and other organic compounds may have been formed in the early history of Earth, they probably would not have been produced in the amounts seen in the experimental environment. Some scientists are also concerned about the fact that oxygen was reduced from the atmosphere in the Miller-Urey experiment. What if the premise that the mixture of gases simulated that of early Earth were false? Then, of course, everything else in the experiment is flawed.

And here's another problem. Because several meteorites have fallen to Earth since the publication of the Miller-Urey experiment, there has been interest in analyzing them for amino acid content, and amino acids have been found in them. Well, that proves that amino acids are able to survive in severe conditions in space. So what does that mean? Some scientists think that the early Earth was similar to asteroids and comets that contain amino acids so they may have been present from the moment that the Earth was formed. Others point to the possibility that organic compounds escaped from within meteorites in impact sites where they hit the surface of the newly forming planet Earth.

The truth is that we just don't know how the first cell was formed, and we really aren't sure how that cell reorganized into larger living structures. So, although the Miller-Urey experiment is interesting, it probably does not hold the promise of unlocking the mystery of life on our planet.

➤ Example Answers and Checklists for Speaking and Writing

Model Test 6, Example Answers, CD 9, Track 4

EXAMPLE ANSWER FOR INDEPENDENT SPEAKING QUESTION 1 "A GOOD SON OR DAUGHTER"

The role of a good son or daughter changes over the years. Initially, being an obedient child is probably all that a parent requires. But when a child grows up and begins to become independent, then a good son or daughter is a person who has good character—who does well in school or succeeds in a career and demonstrates the personal qualities that the parents have tried to teach. Um . . . a good son or daughter is also a good parent when they have children of their own. When parents see their grandchildren being brought up well, uh, they know that they have provided a good example. And . . . and when the parents become old and need care, a good son or daughter won't be too busy to spend time with them and provide them with help.

Checklist 1

✔ The talk answers the topic question.
✔ The point of view or position is clear.
✔ The talk is direct and well-organized.
✔ The sentences are logically connected.
✔ Details and examples support the main idea.
✔ The speaker expresses complete thoughts.
✔ The meaning is easy to comprehend.
✔ A wide range of vocabulary is used.
✔ There are only minor errors in grammar.
✔ The talk is within a range of 125–150 words.

EXAMPLE ANSWER FOR INDEPENDENT SPEAKING QUESTION 2 "JOB OPPORTUNITIES"

Although a job that involves travel seems glamorous to people who spend day after day in an office, it really isn't for me. For one thing, traveling for business usually means going to the same places repeatedly and staying in the same, tired hotel rooms. Besides that, the pace of a business trip doesn't allow much time to see anything besides the inside of an office building and the road to the airport. And eating in restaurants isn't that healthy, and traveling all the time is exhausting. No, I'd rather have a job opportunity that . . . that would let me sleep in my own bed and, uh, eat my own cooking. Um . . . but ideally, the job would also include a three-week paid vacation so . . . I could travel to a destination of my choice and relax.

Checklist 2

✔ The talk answers the topic question.
✔ The point of view or position is clear.
✔ The talk is direct and well-organized.
✔ The sentences are logically connected.
✔ Details and examples support the main idea.
✔ The speaker expresses complete thoughts.
✔ The meaning is easy to comprehend.
✔ A wide range of vocabulary is used.
✔ There are only minor errors in grammar.
✔ The talk is within a range of 125–150 words.

EXAMPLE ANSWER FOR INTEGRATED SPEAKING QUESTION 3 "EXCUSED ABSENCE"

According to the professor's policy, students can be absent from one class without explaining unless there's a test scheduled and then the professor expects students to go to her office to give her an explanation for being out of class and arrange for making up the test. Also, being absent more than once could mean that your grade could be lowered by one letter for each time you miss class. The student doesn't agree with the excused absence policy because he thinks that his grade shouldn't be affected by absence if he makes up the work. Um . . . from his point of view, a valid reason for absence, uh, like an emergency, a family problem, or illness, uh, that shouldn't jeopardize his grade unless he fails to keep up with the class or his work's unsatisfactory.

Checklist 3

✔ The talk summarizes the situation and opinion.
✔ The point of view or position is clear.
✔ The talk is direct and well-organized.
✔ The sentences are logically connected.
✔ Details and examples support the opinion.
✔ The speaker expresses complete thoughts.
✔ The meaning is easy to comprehend.
✔ A wide range of vocabulary is used.
✔ Errors in grammar are minor.
✔ The talk is within a range of 125–150 words.

EXAMPLE ANSWER FOR INTEGRATED SPEAKING QUESTION 4 "INSECTS"

Insects are arthropods with a three-part body structure—a head, a thorax, and an abdomen. The head has a pair of eyes and a pair of antennae, and three pairs of legs and two pairs of wings are usually attached to the thorax. Now, although a spider is also an arthropod, it isn't considered an insect, uh, because, um, because it only has a two-part body structure. The head and the thorax are joined together on a spider and attached to its abdomen by a thin stem. And a spider doesn't have antennae but it does have four pairs of eyes. Instead of six legs, it has eight, hairy legs that are used kind of like an insect uses its antennae to explore the environment. A spider doesn't have wings. It has a unique glandular system that allows it to spin its webs. So, because of this very different body structure, a spider is not really an insect.

Checklist 4

✔ The talk relates an example to a concept.
✔ Inaccuracies in the content are minor.
✔ The talk is direct and well-organized.
✔ The sentences are logically connected.
✔ Details and examples support the opinion.
✔ The speaker expresses complete thoughts.
✔ The meaning is easy to comprehend.
✔ A wide range of vocabulary is used.
✔ The speaker paraphrases in his/her own words.
✔ The speaker credits the lecturer with wording.
✔ Errors in grammar are minor.
✔ The talk is within a range of 125–150 words.

EXAMPLE ANSWER FOR INTEGRATED SPEAKING QUESTION 5 "MEETING PEOPLE"

The man's problem is that he hasn't been very successful meeting people and making friends. He's been on campus for an entire semester, and the woman's the only friend he has. She suggests that he participate in some clubs, but he's reluctant to spend the time required for meetings. The woman plays inter-mural basketball. She says that there are a lot of sports options at the Recreation Center. Another possibility that she recommends is for the man to join a study group. That way, he'd meet some serious students and he'd still be using the time to study for classes while he was getting to know people. I think that the man should join a group to play sports for an hour twice a week because he probably needs the exercise, and he should also try to get into a study group because he'll probably have more in common with the people who are using their time to study for their classes.

Checklist 5

✔ The talk summarizes the problem and recommendations.
✔ The speaker's point of view or position is clear.
✔ The talk is direct and well-organized.
✔ The sentences are logically connected.
✔ Details and examples support the opinion.
✔ The speaker expresses complete thoughts.
✔ The meaning is easy to comprehend.
✔ A wide range of vocabulary is used.
✔ Errors in grammar are minor.
✔ The talk is within a range of 125–150 words.

EXAMPLE ANSWER FOR INTEGRATED SPEAKING QUESTION 6 "SKINNER BOX"

A Skinner Box is a small box that's empty except for a cup and a bar. When the bar over the cup is depressed, a food pellet drops into the cup. An animal that's placed in a Skinner Box will explore the environment for food, and at some point, will accidentally hit the bar, releasing the pellet. So . . . after the animal hits the bar about three or four times and it's rewarded with food, then it learns how to find food, using the bar, and it begins to hit the bar on purpose. The Skinner Box, or something like it, it's commonly used in psychology experiments that involve behavior modification. By presenting a subject with the opportunity for a reward, the behavior that produces the reward is reinforced. In the case of the classic experiment, the subject's opportunity for a reward is a food pellet, and the behavior that's reinforced is pressing the bar, but many types of rewards and behaviors have been used.

Checklist 6

- ✔ The talk summarizes a short lecture.
- ✔ Inaccuracies in the content are minor.
- ✔ The talk is direct and well-organized.
- ✔ The sentences are logically connected.
- ✔ Details and examples support the opinion.
- ✔ The speaker expresses complete thoughts.
- ✔ The meaning is easy to comprehend.
- ✔ A wide range of vocabulary is used.
- ✔ The speaker paraphrases in his/her own words.
- ✔ The speaker credits the lecturer with wording.
- ✔ Errors in grammar are minor.
- ✔ The talk is within a range of 125–150 words.

EXAMPLE RESPONSE FOR INTEGRATED ESSAY "PRIMORDIAL SOUP"

Outline

Summary reading

- Miller-Urey
- Create conditions life in E's atmosphere
    Water, methane, hydrogen, ammonia
    Heat + electrical charges
- Weeks amino acids
- Posited
    Simple life forms in oceans
    Comets + meteorites amino acids
- Referred to as "primordial soup"
    Living structures on E ← natural evolution atmosphere

Lecture
Criticism → procedure + conclusions

- Procedure
    Constant electrical stimulation
    Acids more concentrated
    Amount oxygen reduced → incorrect proportions
- Conclusions
    E similar to meteorites = amino acids from beginning
    Acids deposited meteorite crash on landmasses

Map

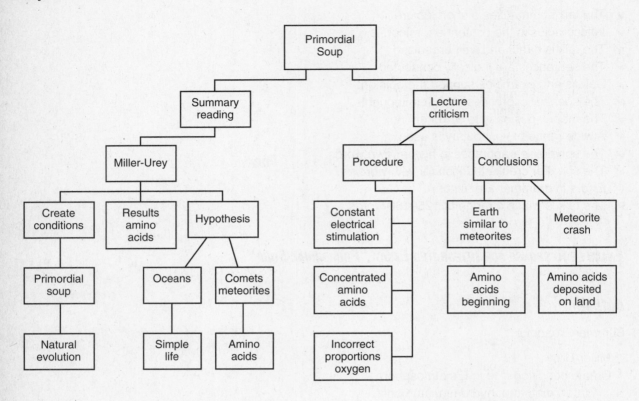

Example Essay

The Miller-Urey experiment was an attempt to recreate the conditions under which life may have evolved in the Earth's atmosphere. First, water, methane, hydrogen, and ammonia were heated and electrical charges were administered to simulate strong electrical storms that were probably part of early conditions. At the end of a few weeks, amino acids were identified in the liquid. Miller and Urey posited that simple life forms could have been nurtured in the early oceans, and furthermore, that comets and meteorites could have added more amino acids to the oceans. The mixture, referred to as "primordial soup," seemed to suggest that living structures on Earth could have developed from the natural evolution of the atmosphere.

Recent criticism of Miller and Urey calls into question both the procedure for the experiment and the conclusions. First, the mixture was subjected to constant electrical stimulation; however, storms in the early atmosphere were probably not continuous. Second, the amino acids that were created in the laboratory were probably more concentrated than those produced in the natural environment. Third, there is some question about the amount of oxygen that was reduced from the experimental mixture, a serious concern since the proportions would have to be the same for a simulation to be achieved. Finally, some researchers suggest the possibility that early Earth was similar to meteorites, and consequently, may have contained amino acids from the beginning or amino acids may have been deposited when meteorites crashed into the landmasses of a young planet Earth.

Checklist for Integrated Essay

✔ The essay answers the topic question.
✔ Inaccuracies in the content are minor.
✔ The essay is direct and well-organized.
✔ The sentences are logically connected.

✔ Details and examples support the main idea.
✔ The writer expresses complete thoughts.
✔ The meaning is easy to comprehend.
✔ A wide range of vocabulary is used.
✔ The writer paraphrases in his/her own words.
✔ The writer credits the author with wording.
✔ Errors in grammar and idioms are minor.
✔ The essay is within a range of 150–225 words.

EXAMPLE RESPONSE FOR INDEPENDENT ESSAY "LEARNING A FOREIGN LANGUAGE"

Outline

Advantages own country

- Teacher has similar experience—can use L1
- Cheaper than foreign travel
- Less stressful

Advantages foreign country

- Natural speech—accent + idioms
- Cultural context—behaviors
- Opportunities

My opinion—intermediate proficiency own country + advanced abroad

Map

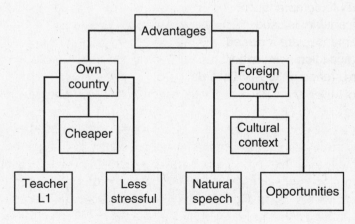

Intermediate own country
Advanced abroad

Example Essay

There are many advantages to learning a language in your own country. In the first place, it is quite a lot cheaper than it would be to travel to the country where the language is spoken. The cost of airfare, living accommodations, food, and tuition at a foreign school can be prohibitively high. In addition, there is less stress involved in learning in a familiar environment. Studying abroad requires that you speak the foreign language all the time to accomplish basic activities. Although it is an opportunity to use the language daily in a real setting, it can be very wearing. Finally, it is advantageous to have teachers who speak your native language because they have gone through the same stages of learning the foreign language that you are experiencing, and they know how to explain the new language by relating it to the native language.

Nevertheless, an argument can be made for learning a language in the country in which it is spoken. Only there can you truly hear the accent and idioms of natural speech. Being surrounded by the foreign language allows you to acquire nuances that elude the classroom. It is also beneficial to learn the language within the context of the culture so that you can learn the behaviors that accompany language. For example, learning how to order in a restaurant when you are right there with native speakers will also let you see how to behave in a restaurant in the foreign country. Finally, there are often opportunities that occur while you are in another country. Friendships can result in invitations to spend time with native speakers in their homes, and possibilities can present themselves for work or study in the foreign country.

In my opinion, the best way to learn a language is to achieve an intermediate level of proficiency in your own country and then to travel to the country where the language is spoken to make progress from the intermediate to the advanced level. By using this plan, you can benefit from the advantages of both options.

Checklist for Independent Essay

✔ The essay answers the topic question.
✔ The point of view or position is clear.
✔ The essay is direct and well-organized.
✔ The sentences are logically connected.
✔ Details and examples support the main idea.
✔ The writer expresses complete thoughts.
✔ The meaning is easy to comprehend.
✔ A wide range of vocabulary is used.
✔ Various types of sentences are included.
✔ Errors in grammar and idioms are minor.
✔ The essay is within a range of 300–350 words.

MODEL TEST 7: PROGRESS TEST

➤ Reading

READING 1 "THE HYDROLOGIC CYCLE"

1. **B**   *Solar energy is the source of power for the hydrologic cycle* paraphrases "The hydrologic cycle is driven by solar energy" and *begins by evaporating water from plants, soil, oceans, and freshwater sources* paraphrases "evaporates water from oceans, freshwater bodies, soils, and vegetation."

2. **D**   "The hydrologic cycle is the transfer of water from the oceans to the atmosphere to the land and back to the oceans." Choices A and B are not correct because they are not complete since they refer to only part of the cycle. Choice C is not correct because it refers to water sources, not the process.

3. **D**   "Of the total 1.3 billion km water on Earth, about 97 % is in oceans, and about 2% is in glaciers and ice caps. The rest [of the water] is in freshwater on land and in the atmosphere." The pronoun phrase "The rest" does not refer to Choices A, B, and C.

4. **B**   ". . . the building of large dams and reservoirs, can change the amount of water evaporated into the atmosphere and change the location and amount of precipitation on land." Choice A is not correct because pavement increases flooding. Choice C is not correct because it refers to the purpose of the man-made water sources, not to their effect on the water cycle. Choice D is not correct because aqueducts transport water from the mountains, but they do not improve the flow into the oceans.

5. **C**   ". . . water on land [freshwater] is important in moving chemicals, sculpturing landscape, weathering rocks, transporting sediments, and providing our water resources." Choice A is not correct because the rate of evaporation is not compared. Choice B is not correct because 97% of the water is in oceans, not freshwater sources. Choice D is true, but it is not the reason why freshwater is considered important.

6. **B**   In this passage, *part* is a synonym for "component." Context comes from the references to "percentages."

7. **C**   In this passage, *basic* is a synonym for "fundamental." Context comes from the usage with "unit," which is often described as "basic" or "fundamental."

8. **A**   "A drainage basin is usually named for its main stream or river, such as the Mississippi River drainage basin." The phrase "such as" signals an example. Choices B, C, and D are true, but they are not the reason that the author mentions the Mississippi River.

9. **D**   ". . . this relatively small amount of water in the global water cycle [0.001% of the total water on Earth] . . . produces all our freshwater resources." Choice A is not correct because the residence time of 9 days is more than one week. Choice B is not correct because both glaciers and oceans are unsuitable for human use. Choice C is not correct because only a relatively small amount of water is in the global water cycle at any one time.

10. **C**   ". . . the problem is water's availability in the right place at the right time in the right form." Choice A is not correct because total water abundance is not the problem. Choice B is not correct because people, plants, and animals compete for water, but there is no evidence in the paragraph that plants and animals are using the water that humans require. Choice D is not correct because the age of water is not mentioned as a safety hazard.

11. **C**   In this passage, *important* is a synonym for "significant." Context comes from the numbers in the fraction.

12. **C**   Cause and effect is a transitional device that connects the insert sentence with the previous sentence. The cause is "distribution of water on land is far from uniform" and the result is water

shortages in some areas. Choices A, B, and D are not correct because the cause and result are not in consecutive order.

13. **C, E, A** summarize the passage. Choice B is a minor point that refers to major point C. Choice D can be inferred from the passage, but it is not developed as a major point. Choice F is true but it is not mentioned in the passage.

READING 2 "PIAGET'S COGNITIVE DEVELOPMENT THEORY"

14. **C** We *engage in both organization of what we see and experience* paraphrases ". . . we organize our observations and experiences" and *adaptation of novel ideas* paraphrases "we also *adapt our thinking to include new ideas*."

15. **A** The concepts are explained by the girl's new experience with the hammer as she ". . . fits her behavior into the information she already has (assimilation)" and "adjustments . . . alter slightly her conception of the world (accommodation)." Choice B is not correct because the concepts, not the demonstration, are the lesson. Choice C is not correct because the girl solves the problem of how to use a new tool. Choice D is not correct because the example demonstrates the ways that people adapt, not the stages of development.

16. **A** In this passage, *change* is a synonym for "alter." Context comes from the reference to "adjustments" in the same sentence.

17. **B** "Some objects such as fingers and the mother's breast, can be sucked, but others [other objects], such as fuzzy blankets, should not be sucked." The noun "others" does not refer to Choices A, C, and D.

18. **C** In this passage, *different* is a synonym for "distinct." Context comes from the reference to "different" in the next sentence.

19. **B** In this passage, *complex* is a synonym for "sophisticated."

20. **B** ". . . *operations*, the Piagetian term for internalized mental actions." Choice A is not correct because symbolic thought occurs in a later stage, after operations. Choice C is not correct because it occurs in an earlier stage, before operations. Choice D is not correct because the reasoning that children can perform in operational stages does not explain the term operations.

21. **B** ". . . concrete operational thinkers cannot imagine the steps necessary to complete an algebraic equation, which is too abstract for thinking at this stage." Choice A is not correct because algebra requires formal, not concrete, operational thinking. Choice C is not correct because a child of 10 has reasoning abilities, if they are applied to concrete examples. Choice D is not correct because it is the abstract nature of the steps, not the number of steps, that makes algebra too difficult for a 10-year old.

22. **C** "They might think about what an ideal parent is like and compare their parents to this ideal standard." Choice A is true, but it is not the reason that the author mentions parents. Choices B and D are not mentioned in the passage.

23. **A** Because the formal operational stage is the last stage in Piaget's theory, and the age range is between 11 and 15, it must be concluded that people who are older than 15 have completed all of the stages. Choice B is not correct because the age range for the formal operational stage is between 11 and 15. Choice C is not correct because logical reasoning replaces intuitive thought in the concrete operational stage from 7 to 11 years of age. Choice D is not correct because there is no evidence to support this conclusion in the passage.

24. **C** Choice A is mentioned in paragraph 5, sentence 2. Choice B is mentioned in paragraph 1, sentence 8. Choice D is mentioned in paragraph 6, sentence 4.

25. **C** Chronological order is a transitional device that connects the insert sentence with the following sentence. "At the beginning" should appear in the sentence before "At the end" in reference to the sensorimotor stage.

26.   Concrete operational stage: **C, D, G**   Formal operational stage: **B, E, H, I**   Not used: **A, F**

READING 3 "CONQUEST BY PATENTS"

27. **D** ". . . patents are about the control of technology." Choices A and B are not correct because protests and lawsuits are caused by patents, but they are not the reason for patents to exist. Choice C is not correct because the "incentive and reward" to inventors is the reason touted [publicized] but not the real reason.

28. **D** "In the 1760s . . . Arkwright invented the water-powered spinning frame, a machine destined to bring cotton-spinning out of the home and into the factory. It [a machine] was an invention." The pronoun "It" does not refer to Choices A, B, or C.

29. **A** *Among the laws to protect Britain from competition* paraphrases "To protect its [Britain's] competitive advantage . . . Parliament enacted a series of restrictive measures," and *the textile industry* paraphrases "manufactured cloth." . . . *a ban on exporting Arkwright equipment* paraphrases "the prohibition of the export of Arkwright machinery" and the *[ban on] emigration of former employees* paraphrases "the emigration of any workers who had worked in factories using it [Arkwright machinery]."

30. **C** ". . . Samuel Slater, who had worked for years in the Arkwright mills, left England . . . disguised as a farmer . . . he was an intellectual property thief." Choice A is not correct because Slater established the textile mill in America, not in Great Britain. Choice B is not correct because Slater was the only worker from Britain. Choice D is not correct because Slater broke the law.

31. **A** In this passage, *discoveries* is a synonym for "innovations." Context comes from the introduction in the first paragraph that explains the "rights" for "inventors."

32. **B** "By the early 1970s . . . U.S. industry demanded greater protection for its idea-based products." Choice A is not correct because the free exchange was favored earlier in the history of the United States. Choice C is not correct because the United States pushed for standards in international trade agreements. Choice D is not correct because the United States blamed the Third World nations for piracy.

33. **A** ". . . a counterclaim that these were 'natural' or 'raw' materials and therefore did not qualify for patents." Choice B is not correct because a high percentage of the materials originated in plant and animal germplasm taken from the developing world. Choice C is not correct because barely a cent of royalties had been paid. Choice D is a claim against pirates in the Third World, but it is not a justification for using plants and animals from the developing world.

34. **B** "Such unacknowledged and uncompensated appropriation they named 'biopiracy.'" Choices A, C, and D are not part of the author's definition.

35. **B** In this passage, *assist* is a synonym for "facilitate." Context comes from logical reasoning in the sentence that suggests a positive effect. Choice D can be eliminated because it would have a negative effect.

36. **D** In this passage, *ideas* is a synonym for "notions." Context comes from the reference to the abstract concepts of "property and creativity."

37. **A** The word "Conquest" conveys the idea of domination, power, and unfair practices. Choices B and C are true, but they do not explain the use of the word "Conquest." Choice D is not correct because the trade agreements prevent developing nations from exerting the power that they might obtain through ownership of valuable resources.

38. **A** Chronological order as well as cause and effect are transitional devices that connect the insert sentence with the previous and following sentences. "Arriving in the U.S." in the insert sentence would have to follow the reference in the previous sentence to the time when Slater "left England for the New World." The recreation of the factory in the insert sentence was the cause that "enabled the production of commercial-grade cotton cloth in the New World" mentioned in the following sentence.

39. **A, D, F** summarize the passage. Choices B and C provide an example that develops major point A. Choice E is a detail that supports major point D.

➤ Listening

 Model Test 7, Listening Section, CD 9, Track 5, continued on CD 10, Track 1

LISTENING 1 "PROFESSOR'S OFFICE"

Audio Conversation

Narrator:	Listen to a conversation between a student and a professor.
Professor:	Okay Chris. Do you understand why I asked you to see me?
Student:	I guess so. I did something in class . . . I apologize.
Professor:	But do you understand what's bothering me?
Student:	No, not really. I like your class.
Professor:	I'm glad you do. But Chris you're disturbing the other students with your constant talking.
Student:	I am?
Professor:	Yes. I've had several people complain about it. They're missing key parts of the lecture because you're talking.
Student:	But I'm talking about the lecture. I'm not just making conversation.
Professor:	Look, Chris. It doesn't matter. When *I* am talking, *you* should be listening.
Student:	Well, I'm sorry. Sometimes I don't get a word or a phrase so I ask someone about it.
Professor:	Okay. I really don't think you're creating a disturbance on purpose. If I did, I'd simply ask you to drop the class. Period.
Student:	Oh please don't do that.
Professor:	That's not my plan, but it has to be an option. Look, maybe you need to record the lectures. I don't mind if you do that. Then, you can fill in the blanks when you listen the second time instead of asking your neighbor during the class.
Student:	That's a great idea. I really wanted to do that, but I was thinking you probably wouldn't want me to.
Professor:	And another thing. If you have questions, I need you to write them down and make an appointment to talk with me about them. That's why I have office hours twice a week. Just call the department, and we'll arrange a time.
Student:	Excuse me, Dr. Pierce. Can I tell you something? Uh, I'm embarrassed to ask you questions.
Professor:	Why in the world would that be? I ask for questions at the end of every lecture. I encourage students to use my office hours . . .
Student:	I know you do. It's just that where I went to school before I came here, if you asked a professor a question, it was an insult because . . . because it implied that he hadn't explained everything well. You see, if the professor does a good job on the lecture, everything will be clear and no one will need to ask a question.
Professor:	I see. Well, it's different here. I'm not saying that your other experience is wrong . . . I'm just saying that we do things differently at the university in this country. In my class I don't expect you to understand everything in the lectures. And I don't take it as a challenge when someone asks a question. I view the question as . . . kind of a compliment . . . because it means that person is very interested and is really trying to learn. That's the kind of student I want.
Student:	So, I can ask you questions in class?

Q1

Q2

Q3

Q4

Professor:		Or in my office. Just don't ask other students questions while I'm trying to give my lecture. That does upset me.
Student:		Oh, Professor Pierce. I'm so sorry. I was trying to be respectful. I'm interested in the class and I want to know everything.
Professor:		I see that. Now I'm asking you to show your interest and respect in a different way. I want you to ask me the questions at the times that I provide for question-and-answer—at the end of the lecture and during my office hours.
Q5	Student:	And I can record the lectures?
	Professor:	Yes. Just don't make a lot of noise in class, okay?
	Student:	Oh no, I won't. Thank you so much.

Audio	1.	Why does the man go to see his professor?
Answer	D	His professor asked him to come to the office.

Audio **Replay**	2.	Listen again to part of the conversation and then answer the following question. "I like your class." "I'm glad you do. But Chris you are disturbing the other students with your constant talking." "I am?"
Audio **Replay**		Why does the student say this: "I am?"
Answer	B	The student's tone expresses surprise.

Audio **Replay**	3.	Listen again to part of the conversation and then answer the following question. "I really don't think you're creating a disturbance on purpose. If I did, I'd simply ask you to drop the class. Period." "Oh please don't do that." "That's not my plan, but it has to be an option."
Audio **Replay**		What does the professor mean when she says this: "That's not my plan, but it has to be an option."
Answer	A	She is warning the student that she could take more serious action.

Audio	4.	How does the professor feel about questions in class?
Answer	B	She thinks that students who ask questions are showing interest.

Audio	5.	What will the man probably do during the next class?
Answer	B	He will tape record the lecture.

LISTENING 2 "ART CLASS"

Audio Lecture
Narrator: Listen to part of a lecture in an art class.

Professor:

Q6 Symmetry is a concept that, yes, is expressed in the graphic arts, but to understand its fundamental nature, we must go beyond art. We find symmetry in nature, it reverberates in music, translates into
Q7 choreography for dance, and . . . underlies basic mathematical formulas. But I'm getting ahead of myself. Let's begin with a dictionary definition of symmetry. And I'm reading here from the *American Heritage Dictionary of the English Language*: Symmetry is "exact correspondence of form and con-

stituent configuration on opposite sides of a dividing line or plane or about a center or an axis." And it's also identified in the same source as "beauty as a result of balance or harmonious arrangement." So we experience beauty and harmony when symmetry of form is expressed, and the form may be interpreted by any of the senses as, uh, harmonious. But in this class we're going to focus on symmetry in the visual arts, and that's symmetry in a visual plane.

Let's just look at some examples. In general, there are four types of symmetry in a plane, and a pattern is symmetrical if there's at least one type of symmetry. So, let me show you the four types since it's much easier to understand when you see them.

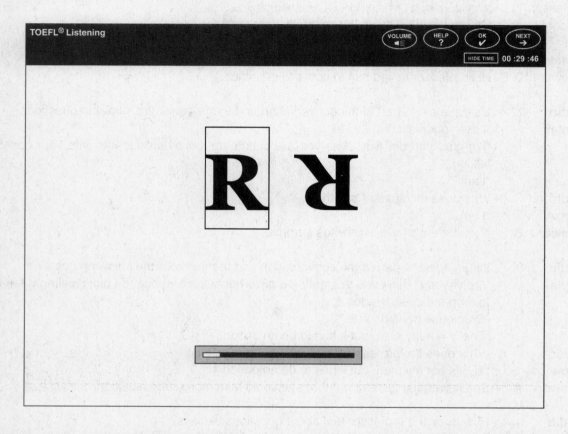

This is *rotation* symmetry. For this example, I used the letter *R*, but any object could have been used. And in the rotation, the object, in this example, the letter *R*, is turned around a center. In this case, there's a right angle, but any angle could have been selected.

Reflection is . . . wait a minute. Okay, here's the slide.

Q8

Reflection is what we see in a mirror, so every reflection has a mirror line. A reflection of the letter *R* is a mirror image or a backwards letter *R*. So, unlike the rotation around a circle, this type of symmetry flips the object over.

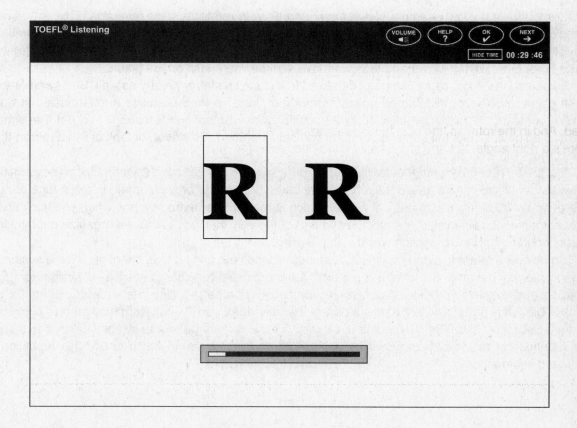

Here's a *translation*. To translate an object means that we move it, but we do it without rotation or reflection. It's simply placed somewhere else on the plane. And for our purposes, we're talking about a flat plane. So, in this example, uh, we just moved it over a little bit.

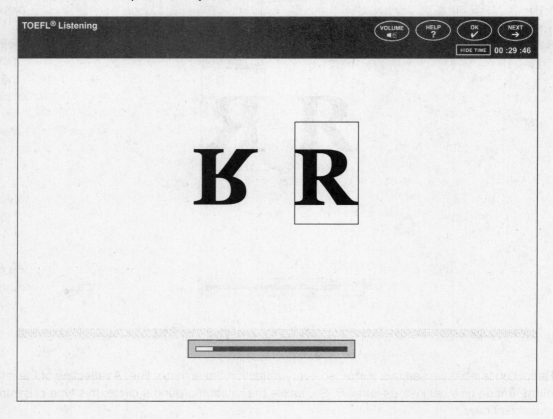

Okay, this is my last example of symmetry and it's referred to as *glide* reflection. This is the most complex type of symmetry because it involves two steps instead of one. A glide reflection is a combination of a reflection and a translation along the direction of the mirror line. So, uh, you can see the two steps here. First, we flip it over and then we move it somewhere else on the plane.

Of course these concepts can be generalized to include spatial symmetry as well. But, symmetry on a flat plane involves positioning all points around the plane so their positions in relationship to each remain constant . . . although their absolute positions may be subject to change. To put it in simple terms, if an object looks the same to you after you spin it around, flip it over, or look at it in a mirror, then that object probably has symmetry.

Symmetry is such a fundamental organizing principle that an object with symmetry can be identified . . . without our being able to see the, uh, . . . the entire object. Our brains somehow piece together the missing pieces to form a symmetrical whole. Which is really rather extraordinary, when you think about it. At some very basic level, symmetry may be part of the way that we . . . that we organize our thinking. And of course, that would explain why it's so pleasing. 　Q9

So now let's return to symmetry in art. Symmetry stands out and attracts attention. It's the system of organization for patterns. But what is a pattern? A *pattern* has three characteristics—a system for organization, and like we said before, this is often symmetry, but a pattern also has a basic unit, that is, uh, it's an object that's the smallest discrete part of the image. As you'll recall from the types of symmetry that we discussed, the letter *R* was the basic unit. Okay, finally, a pattern has repetition, which can be the repetition of a unit or a group of units. And, uh, this repetition, in much of art, this repetition is arranged symmetrically. 　Q10

Just look around the classroom. Look at the tiles on the floor. Here you see a symmetrical design with four repeating tiles. The tiles were not placed at random. There's a pattern here with all three characteristics of a pattern—first, there's a unit, a basic unit, of four tiles; second, there's repetition of the tiles with solid tiles surrounding them; and, uh, third, there's symmetry . . . within the four tiles, which to be specific, looks like rotation symmetry to me.

Q11   Now, for your studio assignment, I want you to draw a pattern that has as its organizing principle, a symmetrical design. It can be either in color or in black and white, but it must fit on a piece of standard 8½ by 11-inch paper. On a second sheet of paper, I want you to identify the type of symmetry that you used. Perhaps some of you will want to experiment with several types of symmetry, but if you do, please be sure to identify each of them clearly in your narrative. For this first effort, I recommend that you stick to something relatively simple, like the tile floor. So, when you come to class next week, be ready to share your design with three other people in a group. Then I'll collect them at the end of the hour.

Audio	6.	What is this lecture mainly about?
Answer	A	All of the other choices are mentioned in relationship to the main topic: Symmetry in the visual arts.
Audio Replay	7.	Listen again to part of the lecture and then answer the following question.
		"We find symmetry in nature, it reverberates in music, translates into choreography for dance, and . . . underlies basic mathematical formulas. But I'm getting ahead of myself. Let's begin with a dictionary definition of symmetry."
Audio Replay		What does the professor mean when he says this: "But I'm getting ahead of myself."
Answer	D	He wants to talk about that subject later.
Audio	8.	Which of the following slides represents reflection symmetry? Click on the correct diagram.
Answer	C	Reflection symmetry is shown in diagram C.
Audio	9.	How is it possible to recognize an object when only part of it is visible?
Answer	A	The brain recognizes symmetry and visualizes the whole.
Audio	10.	In addition to a system for organization, what characteristics define a pattern?
Answer	A	A basic unit
	C	Repetition
Audio	11.	What assignment does the professor give his students?
Answer	D	They have to design a pattern that includes symmetry.

LISTENING 3 "BIOLOGY CLASS"

Audio Lecture
Narrator: Listen to part of a lecture in a biology class.

Professor:
By studying the fossil record we can read the history of life on Earth. Interestingly enough, it appears that there are long periods in which not very much change occurs; then sporadic brief periods in which there are mass extinctions of species followed by diversification of the groups that survived. How does this happen? Well, sometimes a habitat is destroyed or the environment changes. Did you know that if the temperature of the ocean falls by even a few degrees, many species will die? Incredible, isn't it? Or, even when the environment is relatively stable, biological conditions can change when other species

evolve in different directions. For example, let's see, when a similar species evolves by developing a shell, then the related species without shells may be more vulnerable to predators and could become extinct as a result of changes in the other species. So you can see that extinction is a natural conse- | Q12
quence of history. It's, well, inevitable. But sometimes mass extinctions occur and most of the known species are lost. And this is very different.

Let me mention two such mass extinctions. First, the Permian mass extinction, which occurred | Q13
about 250 million years ago. According to fossil records, more than 90 percent of the marine species and about 30 percent of the orders of insects . . . perished. Then about 65 million years ago, the Cretaceous mass extinction claimed more than half of the marine species and many terrestrial species of plants and animals, including the dinosaurs.

So what causes mass extinction? This isn't an easy question to answer. You see, it's obvious from | Q14
the fossil records that species exist during a certain geological time period, and then, they disappear, and we have solid evidence for that. But *why* they disappear is, well, more speculative. In the Permian, several extreme conditions may have converged, including the merging of the continents into one large land mass. As you can imagine, such a radical change in the distribution of land and water would have disturbed habitats and caused the climate to change. There's also evidence that volcanic activity during this period may have produced enough carbon dioxide to cause global warming, which in turn would have affected the temperature and depth of the oceans, and it, and I'm referring here to global warming, so it probably also caused the oxygen levels in the oceans to decrease. All of these conditions could have converged to extinguish an enormous number of species at the same time. That's mass extinction.

And, a similar set of conditions may also have contributed to the mass extinction in the Cretaceous period as well. We can gather data that convinces us about continental drift . . . that it occurred along with receding seas along the continental coastlines. In addition, we know that cooler climate was prob- ably the result, at least in part, of . . . increased volcanic eruptions, and these eruptions probably released enough material into the atmosphere to block the sunlight. Having said all of that, many scien- | Q15
tists now favor a very different hypothesis. They theorize that maybe a large asteroid collided with the Earth. Advocates of the so-called *impact hypothesis* speculate that there were two events that caused the mass extinction. First, the impact probably caused a fire storm of such proportion that most of the life in North America would have been decimated within minutes. Second, they postulate that an enormous cloud of fallout could have blocked out the sunlight and . . . that the impact was, in fact, large enough to . . . darken the Earth . . . and we're talking about months or even years. So the result . . . of the darkness, I mean . . . that would have caused a reduction in photosynthesis, which, in turn, would have created a disruption in the food chain. Now, such a disruption would have affected many species.

So the advocates of the impact hypothesis . . . they put forward evidence that a thin layer of clay, | Q16
rich in iridium deposits, uh, can be found in the geologic material that separates the Mesozoic and the Cenozoic eras—precisely the time period for the Cretaceous mass extinction. So what's special about this clay? Well, iridium is a very rare element on Earth, but it's quite common in meteorites and other extraterrestrial debris that's been analyzed. So, it's possible that this sediment is the remains of the impact. The fact that there was more serious damage to the species in the Western Hemisphere could also be explained by the *point* of impact, and the fact that the dust cloud could have caused more acidic precipitation nearer the area of impact. Or, there may have been a number of calamities that converged simultaneously, disrupting planetary balances.

But whatever the cause or causes, the fact remains that the mass extinctions occurred, and they | Q17
influenced the biological diversity of our planet in profound ways. The species that survived, whether because they had genetic advantages or because they were fortunate enough to be farther from the catastrophes . . . these species became the ancestors of the species that have played important roles in biological evolutionary history.

Audio   12.   What aspect of the fossil record is this lecture mainly about?
Answer   **B**   The other points relate to the main topic of the lecture: Mass extinctions.

Audio	13.	Identify the main periods of mass extinction.
Answer	**A**	Permian
	C	Cretaceous

Audio	14.	Listen again to part of the lecture and then answer the following question.
Replay		"You see, it's obvious from the fossil records that species exist during a certain geological time period, and then, they disappear, and we have solid evidence for that. But *why* they disappear is, well, more speculative."
Audio		Why does the professor say this:
Replay		"But *why* they disappear is, well, more speculative."
Answer	**A**	The word "speculative" expresses uncertainty.

Audio	15.	What is the impact hypothesis?
Answer	**D**	The premise that an asteroid crashed, blocking the sunlight on Earth

Audio	16.	What is the evidence for the impact hypothesis?
Answer	**A**	The clay from the Cretaceous Period contains an element that is rare on Earth.

Audio	17.	What can be inferred about the professor's opinion?
Answer	**C**	He thinks that mass extinctions were important to evolution.

LISTENING 4 "STUDENTS ON CAMPUS"

Audio Conversation

Narrator: Listen to part of a conversation between two students.

Q18 Man: Hi. How did your presentation go?

Woman: Really well.

Man: See. I told you.

Woman: I know, but I was really nervous.

Man: So what happened?

Woman: Well, the T.A. asked for volunteers to go first, and I raised my hand right away because I wanted to get it over with before I got any more nervous than I already was.

Man: So you went first.

Q19 Woman: Yeah. And I used a lot of visuals. I had about twenty slides on PowerPoint, and that really helped me to stay on track. I mean, I didn't read the slides to the class or anything, but, you know, some of the titles kind of jogged my memory . . . so I knew what I wanted to say while each slide was shown.

Man: That's the beauty of PowerPoint.

Q20 Woman: Of course, I'm always afraid the computer program won't work . . . and then there I am without anything. But, I made overheads, you know, copies of all the slides, just in case.

Man: So you could have used the overhead projector as a back up. Good idea.

Woman: And I had most of the stuff on handouts so they could follow along without spending a lot of time taking notes. That way I could move along faster and get more in in ten minutes.

Man: Yeah. Ten minutes isn't very long when you're trying to present something as complex as population density.

Woman: That's for sure. The maps really helped.

Man: A picture's worth a thousand words.

Woman: So true.

Man: Listen, I can't remember whether you had a group or you had to present all by yourself.

Woman:	You had a choice, but I decided to do my own presentation. I don't know. Group projects are really popular but . . . you know.	Q21
Man:	I hear you. I'd rather take responsibility for the whole presentation, if I were you.	
Woman:	No surprises that way.	
Man:	Is that one of your handouts? . . . Wow. That looks fantastic.	
Woman:	It's easy. PowerPoint has an option for putting the slides on a handout.	
Man:	Still, it looks so . . . professional.	
Woman:	Thanks.	
Man:	So did you have any questions after the presentation?	
Woman:	Not really. I think people were mostly just wanting to get on with their own presentations.	Q22
Man:	But they seemed interested.	
Woman:	Oh, yeah. And the T.A. said something about "getting off to such a good start," so I felt good about that.	

Audio   18.   What are the students discussing?
Answer   B   The other choices relate to the main topic of discussion: The woman's presentation.

Audio   19.   Which strategy does the woman use for her presentation?
Answer   C   Show visuals to explain the points

Audio   20.   Why did the woman make overhead copies of the slides?
Answer   B   She was afraid that the computer program would fail.

Audio   21.   Listen again to part of the conversation and then answer the following question.
Replay   "You had a choice, but I decided to do my own presentation. I don't know. Group projects are really popular but . . . you know."
   "I hear you."

Audio   What does the man mean when he says this:
Replay   "I hear you."
Answer   D   He understands the woman's point of view and may even imply agreement. "I hear you" is an idiomatic way to say, "I understand."

Audio   22.   Why didn't the class ask questions after the presentation?
Answer   D   They were anxious to make their presentations.

LISTENING 5 "SOCIOLOGY CLASS"

Audio Discussion

Narrator: Listen to part of a discussion in a sociology class. The professor is talking about gangs.

Dr. Jackson:	Last class, I asked you to read some articles about gang activity. We're trying to come up with a definition, so let's just go around the table and share what we found. Tracy, will you begin please?	Q23
Tracy:	Okay. Um, actually, I read a review of the research for sociological studies on gang activity, and I found that gangs have been prevalent for much longer than I'd assumed. I was so surprised. For some reason, I thought that gang activity was a fairly recent phenomenon, but actually, one of the largest studies was carried out by Thrasher in 1936.	Q24
Dr. Jackson:	Good. Good. I'm pleased that you found that. Thrasher's study is a classic research investigation. Can you summarize the findings? Of the Thrasher study?	
Tracy:	Sure. First, I should say that the study included more than 1300 gangs with more than 25,000 members. So . . . according to Thrasher, a gang is a group that may form spontaneously, but after that, it will . . . integrate . . . and that happens through conflict and	

violence. Over time, a spirit of solidarity and an attachment to a local territory kind of forms. What's most interesting, besides the long history of gangs in the United States, the interesting part . . . it's the fact that not much has changed over the years. And, oh yes, gang behavior seems pretty similar even across cultures.

Dr. Jackson:	That *is* interesting.
Bill:	Dr. Jackson, may I go next? I have just a brief comment that seems to fit in here.
Dr. Jackson:	Please.
Bill:	Well, another classic study, much later, about 1987 or 8, I think, by Joan Moore . . . that study indicated that gang behavior is probably caused by normal adolescent insecurities . . . the desire for peer approval, respect, support, acceptance, and, in some cases, protection, if the neighborhood is perceived as dangerous. It seems that gangs take the place of the more childish cliques . . . those in-groups that develop in high schools.
Dr. Jackson:	Good point. And if we can refer back to the Thrasher study, he also suggested that gangs actually form in play groups where children of a very young age begin with the usual games like hide-and-seek or kickball, and progress as they get older to playing craps or engaging in petty theft on the street. Now, back to Moore. Bill?
Bill:	Right. Well . . .
Dr. Jackson:	What about Moore's definition of a gang? That relates to the Thrasher study.
Bill:	Oh, I see what you mean. I have that right here. Moore defined a gang as an "unsupervised peer group who is socialized by the streets rather than by conventional institutions," and I was thinking that the institutions might be schools, churches, organized clubs like boys' clubs. And one other thing, Moore emphasized that the gang had to define itself as a gang, you know, with some kind of criteria for membership that would be recognized by all of the gang members.
Dr. Jackson:	Such as?
Bill:	Such as participating in a crime, either stealing something and bringing it back to the gang, or . . . or even killing someone in an initiation.
Sandy:	Dr. Jackson, I looked up the definitions of gang members by police departments and law enforcement agencies.
Dr. Jackson:	Oh, great. Let's hear it.
Sandy:	Okay. Well, according to the California Youth Gang Task Force, for example, a gang member will be recognizable because of gang-related tattoos, clothing, and paraphernalia like scarves and hats that identify a particular gang and, sometimes these are called the colors, so that allows other people to confirm that the people with the colors on . . . that they have a right to be on the gang's turf. And, to follow up on Tracy's comments about the history of gangs, it looks like these criteria have been in place for a long, long time.
Dr. Jackson:	Good job. So far, what I'm hearing though, what I'm hearing refers to gang membership in general. So now let's talk about the ages of gang members. Typically, who belongs to a gang?
Tracy:	Well, this was an eye-opener. There seem to be stages, or maybe not stages, but at least categories of gang membership. It starts about age 10 or 12, which fits in with what you were saying earlier about play groups. So these kids are playing together and they start writing graffiti on their school lockers or their notebooks, and they look up to the gang members who are about 14–20. So the little kids are "Peewees" and the teenagers are called "Gang Bangers." But the members who are 20–25 years old. They're the "Hardcores," and most of the gangs that I read about didn't have very many members over 25 years old. So I would say that, in general, gang membership is for young men.
Dr. Jackson:	Thanks for your assessment of membership by age. And I would certainly agree with you. But what about females? Did anyone find any research on their role in gang activity?

Bill:	I did. And there are a few girl gangs—that's what they called them in the references . . . but I found that females are generally not considered members of the male-dominated gang. They're viewed as more of a support system, and an extended social group—friends and girlfriends to party with.
Sandy:	That's what I found, too. And another interesting thing. Maybe this is naïve, but I sort of imagined that gang activity was always . . . always criminal activity. But, uh, according to a study by . . . it was James Lasley . . . he looked at gangs in Los Angeles about ten years ago . . . and anyway, he found that they spent a lot of time hanging out, listening to music, drinking beer, and just partying with their girlfriends. And he made another good point. Since they don't have spending money, to go places like the movies or ball games, the neighborhood is their . . . entertainment.
Bill:	Yeah. I read that study. Didn't he say that some of the criminal activity was for fun . . . not really for financial gain?
Sandy:	Exactly. And there seems to be very little planning. Just kind of going with whatever turns up. Of course, there are instances of crimes for revenge or honor to maintain the reputation of the gang, but a lot of the time, crimes simply occur while gang members are looking for something to do.

Q27

Q28

Audio	23.	How does the professor organize the discussion?
Answer	**A**	By defining gang activity, using information from articles

Audio	24.	What was surprising about Thrasher's study?
Answer	**D**	The fact that gang activity has been prevalent for so long

Audio	25.	According to the study by Moore, what causes gang activity?
Answer	**B**	Normal feelings of insecurity in teens

Audio	26.	Listen again to part of the discussion and then answer the following question.
Replay		"And one other thing, Moore emphasized that the gang had to define itself as a gang, you know, with some kind of criteria for membership that would be recognized by all of the gang members."
		"Such as?"
Audio		Why does the professor say this:
Replay		"Such as?"
Answer	**B**	To encourage the student to give an example

Audio	27.	What is the role of women in gangs?
Answer	**C**	They are a support system for the gangs.

Audio	28.	In the discussion, the students identify aspects of gang activity. Indicate whether each of the following is one of the aspects. Click in the correct box for each phrase.
Answer		

	Yes	No
A A replacement for high school cliques	✔	
B A group socialized on the streets	✔	
C A peer group that is 14–20 years old		✔
D Young people who have dropped out of school		✔
E A group that makes careful plans		✔

LISTENING 6 "ANTHROPOLOGY CLASS"

Audio Discussion

Narrator: Listen to part of a discussion in an anthropology class. The professor is talking about totem poles.

Professor:

Some of the largest and most elaborate totem poles are those carved by the Haida people who live on Queen Charlotte Island about 150 kilometers west of the coast of British Columbia, as well as on the smaller islands along the West Coast of Canada. These islands are densely covered with huge red cedar trees that have served for many years as the material for the poles. Some of the totem poles are as tall as the trees themselves.

Q29   Historically, the Haida have carved and raised the totem poles for several important reasons . . . to honor an elder who's died, to record family ancestry and the accomplishments of the clan, to serve as a reminder for ancient stories that are part of an oral tradition, and . . . to recognize a person who's sponsored a Potlach ceremony. As an aside, the Potlach is a celebration that includes feasting and the
Q30   exchange of gifts. There might also be singing, story telling, and dancing, and I'll go into that more a bit later in the semester.

But back to the significance of the totem poles. When you see a totem pole, it's obvious that the carvings depict figures of animals and humans, stacked one on top of the other. It's probably less clear
Q31   that the selection and placement of the carved figures is deeply symbolic. So to really understand how important the totem poles are in Haida culture and to have an insight into the symbolism, I want you to think about all of the symbols in a European coat of arms. For example, the Coat of Arms of Canada includes a unicorn and a lion, a fleur de lis, and maple leaves. What's the point? Anyone? Come on. I'll give you one guess.

Student 1:

Do you mean that this coat of arms is a symbol . . . uh, I mean it identifies the *people* of Canada?

Professor:

Precisely. And that's what a totem pole does as well. It identifies the people of the family or clan or village in a symbolic way. The raven and the eagle are usually incorporated in the pole because the Haida people traditionally belong to one or the other of these two important clans. Other animals may recall a time before people lived on the earth, when birds and animals talked with each other and supernatural events explained history and provided examples for religious teachings.

But some symbols and the stories associated with them . . . these are known only to the owner of the pole, and of course, to the carver. Although some symbolic meanings are repeated, such as the association of healing power with the wolf or dignity with the bear, still, it's just not possible to recreate a story merely by looking at the pole. So, unless the stories are passed down to relatives or recorded by an anthropologist, then the meaning attached to an individual totem pole can be . . . lost.

Student 2:

Excuse me, I keep thinking about that old expression, *low man on the totem pole.* How does that fit in . . . to the symbolism, I mean.

Professor:

Q32   I knew someone would bring that up. Okay. *Low man on the totem pole* means "a person with very little status" but actually, we know that this expression isn't at all in keeping with the tradition of carving totem poles. In fact, the lower figures on the totem pole are usually the *most* important.

Student 3:   Why?

Professor:

For a very practical reason. Not symbolic at all. Remember the size of a totem pole? Well, it's often carved by more than one artist, usually a master carver and a number of apprentices, and the master carver is the one who carves the bottom ten feet of the pole, leaving the upper figures to the less experienced apprentices. The most elaborate carving and therefore, the most important figures are at the bottom of the pole where people are able to see them more clearly than they can see the figures at the top. In fact, many totem poles have a thunderbird at the top, which serves as a cap. As the lord of the sky, this choice is logical, but most of the time, it has very little significance in the story of the pole and it might be the . . . the crudest carving.

Q33

Student 3:   So did the Haida people worship the totem poles?

Professor:

That's another old myth. Totem poles were *not* worshiped and were *not* used to frighten away evil spirits as some early records supposed.

Now, no one knows exactly how long the Haida have been carving totem poles, and the reason for this is that a cedar pole that's been exposed to the elements . . ., uh, it will decay in fewer than one hundred years, so archeologists don't have a physical record of totem poles over the centuries. Probably the best description that we have of the tradition dates back to the late 1700s when European sailing vessels began trading with the Haida, and we know from ships' journals that totem poles were a well-established tradition at that time. Some of them were painted and others weren't, so that option seems to have been left to the discretion of the owner and the carver.

Okay, it's almost time for the bell to ring, but I want to mention that although our discussion has focused on the Haida, interestingly enough, many other aboriginal people have a history of carving totem poles as well. Just off the top of my head, I'd have to include the Tlingit and Tsimshian people of Alaska and the Salish people of Western Washington and British Columbia. And . . . the Maori people of New Zealand . . . and the . . . the Ainu people from Northern Japan. But that isn't an inclusive list by any means.

Q34

Audio   29.   Which of the following is an important reason the Haida people carve totem poles?
Answer   **C**   To recall traditional stories

Audio   30.   Listen again to part of the discussion and then answer the following question.
Replay   "As an aside, the Potlach is a celebration that includes feasting and the exchange of gifts. There might also be singing, story telling, and dancing, and I'll go into that more a bit later in the semester."
Audio   What does the professor mean when he says this:
Replay   "As an aside, the Potlach is a celebration that includes feasting and the exchange of gifts."
Answer   **A**   An "aside" is information that does not directly relate to the topic.

Audio   31.   Why does the professor mention the coat of arms of Canada?
Answer   **A**   To compare the symbolism to that of a totem pole

Audio   32.   What does the saying *low man on the totem pole* mean?
Answer   **C**   A person who has the least status among the members

Audio   33.   Why do the master carvers work on the bottom figures?
Answer   **B**   The figures near the bottom are more visible to the public.

Audio	34.	Listen again to part of the discussion and then answer the following question.
Replay		"Just off the top of my head, I'd have to include the Tlingit and Tsimshian people of Alaska and the Salish people of Western Washington and British Columbia. And . . . the Maori people of New Zealand . . . and the . . . the Ainu people from Northern Japan. But that isn't an inclusive list by any means."
Audio		What does the professor mean when he says this:
Replay		"Just off the top of my head, I'd have to include the Tlingit and Tsimshian people of Alaska and the Salish people of Western Washington and British Columbia."
Answer D		He is informing the students that there may be more information that he is not able to recall right now. "Off the top of my head" is an expression that speakers use when they are providing information spontaneously.

LISTENING 7 "PROFESSOR'S OFFICE"

Audio Conversation

Narrator:	Listen to a conversation in a professor's office.
Student:	Thanks for seeing me.
Professor:	No problem. What . . .
Student:	I'm here. Oh excuse me.
Professor:	Go ahead.
Q35 Student:	I'm here because, well, I just don't seem to be able to keep up, with the assignments, I mean.
Professor:	I see. Is that just in my class or is this a general problem?
Student:	Oh, no. I'm getting behind in my assignments in *all* my classes. There's just so much. It's overwhelming.
Professor:	Hmnn.
Q35 Student:	But I came to you because I thought you . . . you could give me some advice.
Professor:	Well, I'll try. So how many classes are you taking?
Q36 Student:	Four, which is about average, I think.
Professor:	And what are they?
Student:	Sorry?
Professor:	Which classes are you taking?
Student:	Oh. Well, I have Western Civilization, World Literature, um, your class in Psychology of course, and Philosophy.
Q37 Professor:	Unhuh. Well, that's the problem. All of your courses are reading-intensive classes.
Student:	If you mean that I have a lot of reading to do, that's the truth.
Professor:	Look, when you registered, did you talk with your advisor?
Student:	Not really.
Professor:	But you had to have your advisor's signature in order to complete the registration process . . .
Student:	Yeah, but I just had him sign it. I . . . I didn't really make an appointment or anything. See, I thought the best thing to do was to get all of my required courses out of the way so I could spend the last two years concentrating on my major.
Q37 Professor:	And that's a good plan, but the problem is that you selected four courses that have heavy reading assignments and probably papers to write in addition to tests, right?
Student:	Right. But most courses have a lot of reading, don't they?

Professor:	Some have more than others, and that's what I mean by a reading-intensive class. Listen, if you had taken a lab course, like . . . like Botany or Chemistry, well, then you would have had one course with a textbook and another course with a small lab manual. Now you'd have had to spend time in the lab to finish your experiments but you would have received credit for two courses and you wouldn't have had any papers to write—just tests.
Student:	Oh, I see, and with the literature, I have eight books to read, plus the textbook, and there are . . . how many? . . . four or five books in your class.
Professor:	So when you register, you really need to think about the course requirements so you aren't putting all of your reading-intensive courses together in the same semester.
Student:	Like I did this time. So, maybe it's not that I'm such a slow reader. Maybe I just have too much to read.
Professor:	Could be. In any case, the schedule has to be at least a part of the problem.
Student:	So what should I do now?
Professor:	Okay, well, how are you doing in your classes?
Student:	I'm getting Bs and Cs but I know I could get As if I had more time in the day. And I'm really worried about those Cs.
Professor:	Well, here's a possibility. Why don't you drop one of your courses? The one that takes the most time.
Student:	That would be my literature class.
Professor:	You could take it next semester. It's offered every term, and you would have some of the reading done already.
Student:	But wouldn't that mess up my graduation date?
Professor:	I don't know. You'd have to check that with your advisor to be sure.
Student:	But maybe the professor would be upset, about my dropping the class. Then next semester, when I show up again . . .
Professor:	You could talk with the professor and explain your plan. But if you decide to do this, you'll need to do it right away because there's a cut-off date for dropping a course and I think it's the end of this month.
Student:	I wish I hadn't gotten myself into this.
Professor:	Well, the main thing is to learn from it.
Student:	So next semester I could take some reading-intensive courses and some that are . . . less reading-intensive.
Professor:	And you should really see your academic advisor when you're selecting courses next time—to talk, I mean. Not just for a signature.

Q38

Q39

Audio	35.	Why does the man go to see his professor?
Answer	**C**	He would like some advice about his classes.

Audio	36.	Listen again to part of the conversation and then answer the following question.
Replay		"So how many classes are you taking?"
		"Four, which is about average, I think."
		"And what are they?"
		"Sorry?"
Audio		Why does the man say this:
Replay		"Sorry?"
Answer	**B**	"Sorry" indicates that he does not understand. He is asking the woman to explain.

Audio	37.	What is the man's problem?
Answer	**D**	He took classes with heavy reading assignments.

Audio   38.   What does the professor suggest?
Answer   **C**   Immediate withdrawal from one of the courses

Audio   39.   What can we infer about the situation?
Answer   **A**   The student will probably talk with his advisor before registration next term.

LISTENING 8 "PSYCHOLOGY CLASS"

Audio Lecture
Narrator: Listen to part of a lecture in a psychology class.

Professor:

Q41 The National Institute of Mental Health has been doing some interesting research on chemicals in the brain, the neurotransmitters, uh, by looking at brain images, and . . . at least some of the research has shown that the brain circuits responsible for sleep, appetite, concentration, and, uh, . . . and mood . . . they are altered during depressed states. So, basically, we've concluded that depression is caused by chemical imbalances in the brain. But we're still unclear about what triggers those imbalances in the first place.

Some types of depression appear to be genetically inherited, but often there's no family history of depression, or, conversely, a person with a family history may never develop a depressive disorder. So . . . It's a thorny problem.

Q40 Here at the university, we've been studying a disorder called *seasonal affective disorder*. Norman Rosenthal first identified this disorder in the mid 80s. **Q41** The theory is that a decrease in light during the long winter months may be responsible for triggering a chemical imbalance that in turn may cause depression among those people with a predisposition to depression. Supposedly, there's an area of the brain called the *suprachiasmatic nucleus*, which is very close to the retina of the eye, so this area of the brain responds to light by sending a signal to the pineal gland, and the signal causes the gland to sup-**Q42** press the secretion of a hormone called *melatonin*. To make a long story short, the more light, the less melatonin in the blood.

Q43 Okay, the acronym for seasonal affective disorder that's being used in the field is S.A.D. We didn't come up with that, and in fact, I personally think that it's an inappropriate way to refer to such a serious type of depression since it sounds rather mild, and seasonal affective disorder can be a very severe and debilitating disorder for some people. In fact, in extreme cases, it's life-threatening when patients become suicidal.

So anyway, as you can appreciate, the winter here is very dark, cold, and gray. By spring, almost everyone is tired of the gloom, but for some people, those suffering with seasonal affective disorder, it can be a serious problem. People with seasonal affective disorder experience deep and prolonged depression throughout the winter months, with what looks like a spontaneous alleviation of the condition . . . when spring arrives. Before the disorder was identified, it was rather a mystery for friends and family since the depression appeared to vanish only to return several months later.

Q44 Now, although previous research isn't conclusive, we do know that younger people, especially younger women, these women are at a higher risk for developing the disorder, and for being affected by it in a more severe form. If I recall, about 75 percent of those affected are women, with a typical age of onset about thirty years old. Other factors that contribute to the problem, apart from the long, dark days of course, these factors include heredity and stress.

What are the symptoms? Well, the usual spectrum of problems associated with depression—anxiety, lack of concentration, a tendency to sleep more and eat more, cravings for food with a high sugar content. This may be accompanied by weight gain. On the other hand, some people actually lose their appetites and tend to lose a significant amount of weight. We also see lower energy levels and for some people, a dull headache may accompany the problem.

So building on the research studies that identified the symptoms of seasonal affective disorder and the high-risk profile, we decided to undertake a longitudinal study of 120 subjects, and our research is really focusing on therapies that might help those people affected by S.A.D. Traditionally, psychotherapy has been used to identify and modify behaviors that contribute to depression, and it's been somewhat successful with patients identified with seasonal affective disorder, especially when used in combination with relaxation and stress reduction therapies. Antidepressant drug therapy has also been proven to reduce depression in studies of people who had seasonal disorders. But we've been using phototherapy almost exclusively with the subjects in our studies. It's very simple really. We've supplied each subject with a light box that provides the same type of natural lighting that would normally be shining through the window during the spring and summer. The subjects have been instructed to turn on the light box for two hours and then simply go about their activities in the room where the box is placed. They're not supposed to use the box like a sun lamp—no staring into the light, either with the eyes closed or open. They just ignore it once it's turned on.

So . . . although we're still evaluating our data from the first group of subjects, we have a few preliminary findings that I'll share with you today. First, we think that it's probably better to be exposed to the light box during the morning hours. Second, we're noticing a relationship between sleep patterns and seasonal depression, so maintaining a regular schedule for sleep seems to be a helpful therapy in conjunction with the light treatment. We're also fairly sure that the duration of light therapy can be modified for individuals. . . . Some subjects who were exposed to the light for less than two hours did very well while others showed no evidence of relief until they reestablished the two-hour treatments. One interesting possibility that we're working on is whether fluorescent lights might work as well as full spectrum light with the ultraviolet rays filtered out. In our first trials, we used UV light exclusively, but now we have some trials underway with fluorescent light, and the results so far are encouraging. I'm also happy to report that there are few subjects who are experiencing side effects. There's no evidence of eye damage. We've been careful to filter out any potentially damaging UV rays. And, in fact, the only negative side effect was minor headache that seemed to disappear after a few treatments.

Q45

So . . . next semester, we plan to begin the second stage of our studies, and we'll be comparing the degree of depression on the part of subjects undergoing light treatments with control groups who will receive either drug treatments or psychotherapy. What we really want to know is whether light treatments alone are as effective as the other options for therapy.

Audio	40.	What is this lecture mainly about?
Answer	B	Seasonal affective disorder

Audio	41.	What are neurotransmitters?
Answer	B	Chemicals in the brain

Audio	42.	What happens when there is a reduction of light during the winter months?
Answer	A	A decrease in melatonin may cause a chemical imbalance.

Audio	43.	Why does the professor think that the acronym S.A.D. is unsuitable?
Answer	B	It does not reflect the seriousness of the problem.

Audio	44.	Listen again to part of the lecture and then answer the following question.
Replay		" . . . although previous research isn't conclusive, we do know that younger people, especially younger women, these women are at a higher risk for developing the disorder, and for being affected by it in a more severe form. If I recall, about 75 percent of those affected are women, with a typical age of onset about thirty years old."
Audio		What does the professor mean when she says this:
Replay		"If I recall, about 75 percent of those affected are women, with a typical age of onset about thirty years old."
Answer	D	She is expressing uncertainty about the information.

Audio   45.   In the lecture, the professor reports the preliminary results of her research. Indicate whether each of the following is one of the findings.
Click in the correct box for each sentence.

Answer

	Yes	No
A Morning exposure for the treatment is superior.	✔	
B A regular sleep schedule supports therapy.	✔	
C Eye damage occurs in only a few subjects.		✔
D Sessions of less than two hours are preferable.		✔
E Fluorescent lighting cannot be used for therapy.		✔

LISTENING 9 "PHYSICS CLASS"

Audio Discussion
Narrator: Listen to part of a discussion in a physics class.

Professor Blake:
Okay, you'll remember that when Einstein was doing his research, uh, the strong and weak forces—they hadn't been identified yet, but still, he had some questions about the two forces that were generally accepted at the time—electromagnetism and gravity. You see, Einstein thought that nature, or rather a theory of nature, a good theory of nature had to be much simpler and, to use his term, more "elegant." So he spent the next thirty years in an effort to arrive at a . . . a unified field theory that he assumed . . . that . . . that would demonstrate how these two forces were really defined by one underlying principle.

Q46   So, today, and that would be about sixty years later, a group of physicists believe that they are close to finding that principle in something called *the theory of everything.*

[Laughter]

That's okay. A lot of other equally distinguished physicists are also laughing at this idea. But, anyway, for the first time in the history of our field, we have, uh, at least, uh, a structure, a framework, with the potential to explain every fundamental characteristic of the universe. You see, until fairly recently, we've been conceptualizing the particles, that is, the protons, neutrons, electrons, quarks, and everything else . . . we've been viewing them as points—very tiny points. But string theory assumes that if we could really take a look at the particles, and uh, that would have to be with technology that we haven't yet discovered, but if we could, then we'd see that the particles aren't points at all but . . . but strings and

Q47   these strings are looped back into themselves. Look, think of the strings like a very thin rubber band. Oh, and . . . and these strings vibrate.

Jim:
So everything in the universe is made up of the same thing then? It's all a combination of . . . of strings?

Professor Blake:
According to the theory, yes. But of course . . . we *see* differences, and those differences, uh, they're accounted for because the vibrations of the strings are different.

Jim: So in physics, you buy into the theory of everything or . . . or what?

Professor Blake:
Well, Jim, the choice isn't that clear. Um, not at all. There are a lot of scientists in between, and by that I mean that they see the theory of everything in a more limited way. They think that string theory, and understand that string theory is incorporated into the theory of everything . . . um, that string theory can explain all of the properties of the forces that cause the particles to interact and influence each other. Yes, Ellen. Did you have a comment?

Ellen:
Well, a question, really. Wouldn't it be true that if you understand everything about the . . . I think you called it the fundamental characteristics of the universe . . . so if you understand that, don't you understand everything?

Jim:
Wait a minute. So that would mean that we know it all now and there isn't anything else to discover, right? Because, uh, everything is physics . . . everything is just a reaction between vibrating strings.

Ellen:
I see your point, but you could . . . you might look at it as a . . . as a . . . starting place to, uh, to build our knowledge. Dr. Blake, you said that it'd be a structure, didn't you? So we'd have to fill in a lot of information but . . . we'd have a structure to start with. In my math class we were talking about string theory because some of the recent advances in mathematics have been possible because of string theory.

Professor Blake:
True enough. And, string theory isn't finished by any means. It's evolved from the beginning when we first started to think about it and, uh, the early models that included both open strings and the closed strings that I just described to you—the ones that look like a thin rubber band. And there's a lot of discussion about vibration or rather various types of vibration. Then there's the possibility of branes— b-r-a-n-e-s—which are kind of like closed strings with a membrane over them.

Jim:
But all of this is theoretical, right? Because we don't have the technology to observe strings—closed or open—and we certainly can't verify that there are branes out there.

Ellen:
Sure. But there are some very complex and . . . and . . . persuasive, uh, mathematical formulas, and they're presented in support of the theories. It isn't like someone's just dreaming this up without calculations.

Jim:
But I don't see why we should accept calculations when some of those calculations require us to think beyond what we can observe.

Professor Blake:
And many physicists would agree with you, Jim. String theory's unverified. Richard Feynman wrote a very interesting book, *The Character of Physical Law*, and to Feynman, to him, the test of any scientific theory has to be whether the consequences agree with the measurements we take in experiments. Of course, that assumes that the experiment was performed correctly and, uh, that the calculations were done without error, but anyway, I think you see the point.

Q48 Ellen: So you're saying that string theory requires further developments?

Professor Blake: What do *you* think?

Jim:
Q49 Well, I tend to be an empirical scientist. I'm a biology major, and I just want to take something into the lab and dissect it.

Professor Blake: Fair enough.

Ellen:
Q50 But I'm a physics major and . . . the idea of a theory of everything appeals to me. I know that we can't observe strings . . . yet . . . but maybe that's just a problem with the technology and . . . and eventually, we may be able to observe strings in the laboratory or . . . or we could find a way to observe strings in a natural setting and . . .

Jim: Come on. It's just conjecture.

Professor Blake:
Well, in fairness, any new theory has to begin as conjecture, but the real question is, can string theory pass through the developmental stages to a point where it can be verified or rejected. And, uh, these developments could be in the area of technology like Ellen suggests or perhaps they could be new methods of performing calculations and, uh, deriving the mathematical predictions. What I'm going to suggest is that we take a look at the web site that supplements your textbook. There are videos as well as animations and it includes a really good history of string theory, uh, but that's not why I want you to see it. I think the site demonstrates where we need to go from here if we're going to pursue an ultimate
Q51 theory, a . . . a theory of everything, if you will. And it's fairly objective so it should provide us with some interesting data for both sides of the debate.

Audio   46.   What is the discussion mainly about?
Answer A   The theory of everything

Audio   47.   How does the professor explain the closed string?
Answer C   He compares it with a thin rubber band.

Audio   48.   Listen again to part of the discussion and then answer the following question.
Replay   "So you're saying that string theory requires further developments?"
                  "What do *you* think?"
Audio   Why does the professor say this:
Replay   "What do *you* think?"
Answer D   He does not want to influence the woman's thinking.

Audio   49.   According to the discussion, what reason does the man give for rejecting string theory?
Answer B   Strings have not been observed in a laboratory.

Audio   50.   What can be inferred about the students?
Answer C   They have reached different conclusions about the theory.

Audio   51.   Why does the professor suggest that the students visit a web site?
Answer B   The web site should provide objective data, which they can use for the next discussion.

➤ Speaking

Model Test 7, Speaking Section, CD 10, Track 2

INDEPENDENT SPEAKING QUESTION 1 "A BOOK"

Narrator 2: Number 1. Listen for a question about a familiar topic. After you hear the question, you have 15 seconds to prepare and 45 seconds to record your answer.

Narrator 1: Think about a book that you have enjoyed reading. Why did you like it? What was especially interesting about the book? Use specific details and examples to support your response.

Narrator 2: Please prepare your answer after the beep.

Beep

[Preparation time: 15 seconds]

Narrator 2: Please begin speaking after the beep.

Beep

[Recording time: 45 seconds]

Beep

INDEPENDENT SPEAKING QUESTION 2 "FOREIGN TRAVEL"

Narrator 2: Number 2. Listen for a question that asks your opinion about a familiar topic. After you hear the question, you have 15 seconds to prepare and 45 seconds to record your answer.

Narrator 1: Some people think that it is better to travel as part of a tour group when they are visiting a foreign country. Other people prefer to make their own travel plans so that they can travel independently. Which approach do you think is better and why? Use specific reasons and examples to support your opinion.

Narrator 2: Please prepare your answer after the beep.

Beep

[Preparation time: 15 seconds]

Narrator 2:   Please begin speaking after the beep.

Beep

[Recording time: 45 seconds]

Beep

INTEGRATED SPEAKING QUESTION 3 "OLD MAIN"

Narrator 2: Number 3. Read a short passage and listen to a talk on the same topic. Then listen for a question about them. After you hear the question, you have 30 seconds to prepare and 60 seconds to record your answer.

Narrator 1: A public meeting is planned to discuss alternatives for renovating the original building on campus. Read the notice from the college newspaper printed on page 495. You have 45 seconds to complete it. Please begin reading now.

[Reading time: 45 seconds]

Narrator 1: Now listen to a professor who is speaking at the meeting. She is expressing her opinion about the proposals.

Professor:
Although there may be some practical reasons for tearing down the structure surrounding the clock tower, I urge the committee to consider the historical importance of Old Main and opt for renovation of the original structure. I think we all agree that the brick structure is quite beautiful and basically sound. Only a few minor repairs would be necessary to preserve it. The cost of new electrical and plumbing systems for the old structure would be less than the cost of a new building with the same systems. And if a new building were to be erected, the clock tower would seem out of place somehow.

Narrator 1: The professor expresses her opinion of the plan for the renovation of Old Main. Report her opinion and explain the reasons that she gives for having that opinion.

Narrator 2: Please prepare your answer after the beep.

Beep

[Preparation time: 30 seconds]

Narrator 2: Please begin speaking after the beep.

Beep

[Recording time: 60 seconds]

Beep

INTEGRATED SPEAKING QUESTION 4 "PANGEA"

Narrator 2: Number 4. Read a short passage and then listen to part of a lecture on the same topic. Then listen for a question about them. After you hear the question, you have 30 seconds to prepare and 60 seconds to record your answer.

Narrator 1: Now read the passage about Pangea printed on page 496. You have 45 seconds to complete it. Please begin reading now.

[Reading time: 45 seconds]

Narrator 1: Now listen to part of a lecture in a geography class. The professor is talking about Pangea.

Professor:
The theory of *continental drift* posits that 250 million years ago the continents were all connected in one gigantic continent, which we refer to as Pangea, and that was surrounded by one huge ocean called Panthalassa. At that time, the northernmost region of the continent corresponded to a landmass that included most of the modern continent of Asia, and Europe was south of the Asian region instead of north as it is now. So Asia and Europe were connected to the west with what is now North America. Africa and the Arabian Peninsula were positioned south of Europe with South America to the west, India to the east, and Antarctica and Australia south and southeast. Then, about 200 million years ago, this super continent began to separate into a northern continent and a southern continent. The northern continent was made of what is currently North America, Greenland, Europe, and Asia, and the southern continent included Antarctica, Australia, India, and South America. By 135 million years ago, the two continents had moved into positions that began to resemble the map that we see today, with seven continents.

Narrator 1: Explain how plate tectonics relates to the theory of *continental drift*.

Narrator 2: Please prepare your answer after the beep.

Beep

[Preparation time: 30 seconds]

Narrator 2: Please begin speaking after the beep.

Beep

[Recording time: 60 seconds]

Beep

INTEGRATED SPEAKING QUESTION 5 "HEADACHES"

Narrator 2: Number 5. Listen to a short conversation. Then listen for a question about it. After you hear the question, you have 20 seconds to prepare and 60 seconds to record your answer.

Narrator 1:   Now listen to a short conversation between a student and her friend.

Friend: Are you still having headaches?
Student: Yeah. I'm taking Tylenol every day.
Friend: That doesn't sound good. Why don't you go over to the health center?
Student: I keep thinking it'll go away. Probably just a tension headache. I feel really stressed out this semester.
Friend: Well, you're probably right, but it still wouldn't hurt to get a checkup. Maybe the doctor will refer you for an eye exam. I used to get headaches from eyestrain, especially when I was using my computer a lot. And guess what? I needed to get my glasses changed.
Student: No kidding? I hadn't thought about that, but I do notice that it gets worse after I've been using my computer.

Friend:	Well, then. That's important to mention when you see the doctor at the health center.
Student:	You think I should still go to the health center? I mean, if it's my eyes, I . . . I could just make an appointment with the eye doctor.
Friend:	You could, but you really aren't sure what it is. I'd go to the doctor at the health center, and I'd ask for a referral to the eye doctor. Besides, if you get referred, I think your student health insurance will pay most of the cost of new glasses.

Narrator 1: Describe the woman's problem, and the two suggestions that her friend makes about how to handle it. What do you think the woman should do, and why?

Narrator 2: Please prepare your answer after the beep.

Beep

[Preparation time: 20 seconds]

Narrator 2: Please begin speaking after the beep.

Beep

[Recording time: 60 seconds]

Beep

INTEGRATED SPEAKING QUESTION 6 "FAX MACHINES"

Narrator 2: Number 6. Listen to part of a lecture. Then listen for a question about it. After you hear the question, you have 20 seconds to prepare, and 60 seconds to record your answer.

Narrator 1: Now listen to part of a lecture in a business class. The professor is discussing the way that a fax machine transmits and receives data.

Professor:
Okay, to illustrate my point that many new machines are simply combinations of machines that are already available, let's talk about the fax machine. To understand how a fax machine works, I'd like you to think of it as three machines . . . a copier, a modem, and a printer. First, the data is copied. How does that happen? Well, when you load paper into the fax machine, a light shines on it and optical sensors read whether a specific point on the paper is black or white. These sensors communicate the digital information into a microprocessor, where a copy of the page is made of black or white dots. Thus, you see that in the first step, the fax machine functions like a copier. Next, the fax machine works like a modem. Remember, a modem takes a black-and-white image and converts this digital data into an analog signal, that is, electronic impulses that can be sent over a phone line. The fax machine calls another fax machine to transmit, using two different types of tones to represent the black and white dots in the document. For example, it might send an 800-Hertz tone for white and a 1,300-Hertz tone for black. The last part of a fax machine is the printer. After the receiving fax machine answers the sending fax machine, it begins to accept the electronic impulses, and then it converts them back to the black-and-white dots in a digital image. Finally, it prints the image out on paper just like any other printer.

Narrator 1: Using the main points and examples from the lecture, describe the three parts of a fax machine and then explain how the fax process works.

Narrator 2: Please prepare your answer after the beep.

Beep

[Preparation time: 20 seconds]

Narrator 2: Please begin speaking after the beep.

Beep

[Recording time: 60 seconds]

Beep

➤ Writing

INTEGRATED ESSAY "PROBLEM SOLVING"

First, read the passage on pages ⌐99–500 and take notes.

Model Test 7, Writing Section, CD 10, Track 3

Narrator: Now listen to a lecture on the same topic as the passage that you have just read.

Professor:
Now that you've read the article on problem solving, let's talk about the role of breaks. We all know that taking a break is a good strategy for solving a problem, but how does a break really influence the solution? Well, some researchers feel that rest allows the brain to analyze the problem more clearly. We're advised to "sleep on it" when a problem is difficult to solve. Okay, but what if there's some type of *incubation effect* during sleep that allows the brain to continue working on a solution? Here's what I mean. F. A. Kekule was puzzled by the structure of benzene. One night, he dreamed about a snake biting its tail while whirling around in a circle. And when he awoke, it occurred to him that the carbon atoms of benzene might be arranged in a ring. He attributed the solution of the problem directly to the dream. But Kekule's experience and others like it present researchers with a dilemma because there's disagreement about whether unconscious mental activity exists. Were the dreamers really asleep or were they relaxed but awake when they solved the problem?

Two explanations have been proposed to explain why a break supports problem solving while we're awake. One possibility is that during the break, information may appear that provides a solution. For example, Buckminster Fuller was looking at a triangle when he saw the structure of multiple triangles as the solution for constructing a geodesic dome. Of course, another possibility is much more simplistic. It could be that the value of taking a break is as basic as interfering with an ineffective pattern of thinking. By focusing on something else, we may return to the problem in a different frame of mind and think about it in a different, and more productive, way.

➤ Example Answers and Checklists for Speaking and Writing

 Model Test 7, Example Answers, CD 10, Track 4

EXAMPLE ANSWER FOR INDEPENDENT SPEAKING QUESTION 1 "A BOOK"

The Power of Positive Thinking by Dr. Norman Vincent Peale is one of my favorite books. Um . . . according to Dr. Peale, a positive outlook is essential to a happy, successful life. But what is especially interesting about the book are the practical strategies that help maintain an optimistic approach to living, even when, uh, things don't happen to be going well. He recommends reflection on all the aspects of life that are positive, and cultivating an "attitude of gratitude." He also recommends positive statements and mental pictures to encourage and motivate and . . . and to replace negative thoughts that come to mind.

Checklist 1

✔ The talk answers the topic question.
✔ The point of view or position is clear.
✔ The talk is direct and well-organized.
✔ The sentences are logically connected.
✔ Details and examples support the main idea.
✔ The speaker expresses complete thoughts.
✔ The meaning is easy to comprehend.
✔ A wide range of vocabulary is used.
✔ There are only minor errors in grammar.
✔ The talk is within a range of 125–150 words.

EXAMPLE ANSWER FOR INDEPENDENT SPEAKING QUESTION 2 "FOREIGN TRAVEL"

I've taken several tours, but I prefer to make my own travel plans because . . . I don't want to spend a lot of time at tourist hotels. In my experience, large hotels insulate travelers from the foreign culture. Instead of eating typical food, they prepare special meals for the tourists. And when I'm with groups of tourists, it's less likely that local people will approach me to talk. On my own, I've had some wonderful conversations with locals. Another reason that I like to travel independently is because I'm kind of . . . a spontaneous person, so I like to take advantage of opportunities that present themselves on the trip.

Checklist 2

✔ The talk answers the topic question.
✔ The point of view or position is clear.
✔ The talk is direct and well-organized.
✔ The sentences are logically connected.
✔ Details and examples support the main idea.
✔ The speaker expresses complete thoughts.
✔ The meaning is easy to comprehend.
✔ A wide range of vocabulary is used.
✔ There are only minor errors in grammar.
✔ The talk is within a range of 125–150 words.

EXAMPLE ANSWER FOR INTEGRATED SPEAKING QUESTION 3 "OLD MAIN"

The professor doesn't support the plan to demolish the main structure of Old Main and build a new structure around the original clock tower. She presents three arguments. Um . . . first, she says that the brick structure now standing is strong and it would require only minor repairs. And second, she points out that the electrical and plumbing problems in the old building could be repaired for less than the . . . the expenditure for a new building. Finally, she opposes the construction of a new building around the original clock tower because she thinks that the tower would be . . . would look odd in the new setting. She would probably support the alternative plan, which is, um . . . to repair the original building.

Checklist 3

✔ The talk summarizes the situation and opinion.
✔ The point of view or position is clear.
✔ The talk is direct and well-organized.
✔ The sentences are logically connected.
✔ Details and examples support the opinion.
✔ The speaker expresses complete thoughts.
✔ The meaning is easy to comprehend.
✔ A wide range of vocabulary is used.
✔ Errors in grammar are minor.
✔ The talk is within a range of 125–150 words.

EXAMPLE ANSWER FOR INTEGRATED SPEAKING QUESTION 4 "PANGEA"

According to the theory of plate tectonics, the outer layer of the Earth is made up of plates that are continually moving, and consequently, changing the relative position of the land and oceans. Building on this theory, scientists have proposed that about 250 million years ago, there was only one landmass, a huge continent that they have named Pangea, and it included all of the continents that we observe today. But about 200 million years ago, the plates caused Pangea to drift and break into a Northern continent that included North America, Greenland, Asia, and Europe, and a Southern continent that contained South America, India, Antarctica, and Australia. By about 135 million years ago, the plates had separated the landmasses into more or less the seven continents that we recognize today and positioned them fairly close to their current locations.

Checklist 4

✔ The talk relates an example to a concept.
✔ Inaccuracies in the content are minor.
✔ The talk is direct and well-organized.
✔ The sentences are logically connected.
✔ Details and examples support the opinion.
✔ The speaker expresses complete thoughts.
✔ The meaning is easy to comprehend.
✔ A wide range of vocabulary is used.
✔ The speaker paraphrases in his/her own words.
✔ The speaker credits the lecturer with wording.
✔ Errors in grammar are minor.
✔ The talk is within a range of 125–150 words.

EXAMPLE ANSWER FOR INTEGRATED SPEAKING QUESTION 5 "HEADACHES"

The woman's suffering from daily headaches, and she's controlling the pain by taking Tylenol. The man suggests that she make an appointment with a doctor at the health center because the problem should be diagnosed by a professional, but he also mentions the possibility that the doctor might refer her for an eye exam. Apparently, the problem's worse when she's been staring at the computer for long periods of time. Um . . . he reminds her that if the doctor at the health center refers her for the eye exam, the student health insurance may pay a large percentage of the cost for glasses. So . . . I think the woman should take the man's advice because eyestrain's a common problem for college students, and she probably *does* need an eye appointment, but by going to the doctor at the health center first, she can be certain that there isn't something more serious going on, and if she needs glasses, the referral will probably allow her to use her insurance benefit.

Checklist 5

✔ The talk summarizes the problem and recommendations.
✔ The speaker's point of view or position is clear.
✔ The talk is direct and well-organized.
✔ The sentences are logically connected.
✔ Details and examples support the opinion.
✔ The speaker expresses complete thoughts.
✔ The meaning is easy to comprehend.
✔ A wide range of vocabulary is used.
✔ Errors in grammar are minor.
✔ The talk is within a range of 125–150 words.

EXAMPLE ANSWER FOR INTEGRATED SPEAKING QUESTION 6 "FAX MACHINES"

A fax machine has three parts. The fax that's sending text and images has sensors to read black-and-white points on paper and communicate the patterns digitally to a microprocessor, and the microprocessor . . . it recreates the images in black-and-white dots. So this part of the process is like a copy machine. So then the digital information . . . I mean the image in black-and-white dots . . . it's converted into an analog signal that's made up of electronic impulses. The impulses are sent over a phone line, like a modem. Then the fax machine that's sending the information connects with another fax machine that's receiving the information. They communicate with two tones, one that signals a black dot and another that signals a white dot. And the fax machine that receives the tones begins to print the dots on paper in the same way that any printer produces an image. So a fax is really a combination copier, modem, and printer.

Checklist 6

✔ The talk summarizes a short lecture.
✔ Inaccuracies in the content are minor.
✔ The talk is direct and well-organized.
✔ The sentences are logically connected.
✔ Details and examples support the opinion.
✔ The speaker expresses complete thoughts.
✔ The meaning is easy to comprehend.
✔ A wide range of vocabulary is used.
✔ The speaker paraphrases in his/her own words.
✔ The speaker credits the lecturer with wording.
✔ Errors in grammar are minor.
✔ The talk is within a range of 125–150 words.

EXAMPLE RESPONSE FOR INTEGRATED ESSAY "PROBLEM SOLVING"

Outline

Sleeping

- Rest to function at higher capacity
- "Incubation effect"—Kekule structure benzene
- "Functional fixedness" released

Waking

- Input during break—Fuller geodesic dome
- Interruption unsuccessful process
- Different "mental set"

Map

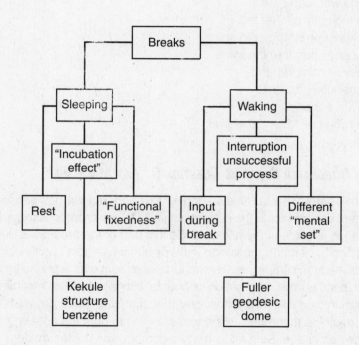

Example Essay

Although researchers do not agree about the way that a break contributes to problem solving, it is clear that breaks during sleeping hours and those that we take during waking hours are both helpful. The value of sleep may be related to the brain's requirement for rest in order to function at a higher capacity. On the other hand, it is possible that there is an "incubation effect," that is, that the brain continues to problem solve at a different level of consciousness during a sleep break. For example, Kekule had insight into the structure of benzene during a dream. Although researchers are not in agreement as to the level of unconscious activity of dreamers, and some argue that dreamers who solve problems are not really asleep, it remains that the sleep break was helpful. It may even be that "functional fixedness" described in the text is somehow released in sleep so that preconceived notions are less limiting.

In contrast, breaks during waking hours appear to be more straightforward. Sometimes input during the break period will contribute to the solution. For example, Fuller's inspiration for the geodesic dome occurred while he was looking at a triangle during a break. However, merely interrupting an unsuccessful problem-solving process could be helpful. By taking a break, we may be more willing to abandon a strategy that is not working, or, as the text states, we return to the problem with a different "mental set."

Checklist for Integrated Essay

✔ The essay answers the topic question.
✔ Inaccuracies in the content are minor.
✔ The essay is direct and well-organized.
✔ The sentences are logically connected.
✔ Details and examples support the main idea.
✔ The writer expresses complete thoughts.
✔ The meaning is easy to comprehend.
✔ A wide range of vocabulary is used.
✔ The writer paraphrases in his/her own words.
✔ The writer credits the author with wording.
✔ Errors in grammar and idioms are minor.
✔ The essay is within a range of 150–225 words.

EXAMPLE RESPONSE FOR INDEPENDENT ESSAY "STUDY ABROAD"

Outline

Like

- Improve language proficiency
- Participate in culture
- College courses

Dislike

- Miss family
- Rely on fast food
- Compete with students

Map

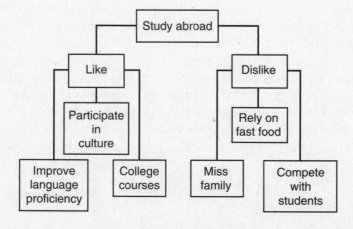

Example Essay

Living abroad provides many opportunities and challenges. When I study abroad, I look forward to making friends. By getting to know people, I will be able to improve my English language proficiency. There are idioms and words that are best learned within the context of real conversations with native speakers. I also look forward to being a participant in a new culture. At the end of my stay, I hope that I will understand the culture in a different and deeper way than is possible when information is derived from only movies and books. In addition, I am excited about studying on a foreign campus. I expect the college courses to be challenging, and I am eager to learn about the latest technological advances in my field of study.

I am realistic about the disadvantages of foreign study, however. I know that I will miss my family very much. It will be too expensive to return to my country to spend holidays with them, and I will be very lonely during the times when I know that they are gathered for special celebrations. Another aspect of the experience that I do not look forward to is the reliance on fast food that is so typical of college students. Pizza, hamburgers, and other junk foods are easier to find and prepare than the meals that I enjoy in my country, but they aren't as good, and they probably aren't as healthy. Finally, I imagine that my life will be very stressful because I will be competing with students who know the language of the classroom and are accustomed to the expectations that the professors have for their students. I am a competitive person by nature, and I am apprehensive about my ability to compete with my classmates.

Once I am living abroad, I will no doubt find many other opportunities to take advantage of and many challenges that I must confront. Nevertheless, I expect my experience to be overwhelmingly positive, and I intend to see the lessons in both adventures and adversity.

Checklist for Independent Essay

✔ The essay answers the topic question.
✔ The point of view or position is clear.
✔ The essay is direct and well-organized.
✔ The sentences are logically connected.
✔ Details and examples support the main idea.
✔ The writer expresses complete thoughts.
✔ The meaning is easy to comprehend.
✔ A wide range of vocabulary is used.
✔ Various types of sentences are included.
✔ Errors in grammar and idioms are minor.
✔ The essay is within a range of 300–350 words.

8

SCORE ESTIMATES

IMPORTANT BACKGROUND INFORMATION

It is not possible for you to determine the exact score that you will receive on the TOEFL. There are three reasons why this is true. First, the testing conditions on the day of your official TOEFL will affect your score. If you are in an uncomfortable room, if there are noisy distractions, if you are upset because you arrived in a rush, or if you are very nervous, then these factors can affect your score. The administration of a model test is more controlled. You will probably not be as stressed when you take one of the tests in this book. Second, the model tests in the book are designed to help you practice the most frequently tested item types on the official TOEFL. Because they are constructed to teach as well as to test, there is more repetition in TOEFL model tests than there is on official TOEFL tests. Tests that are not constructed for exactly the same purposes are not exactly comparable. Third, the TOEFL scores received by the same student will vary from one official TOEFL examination to another official TOEFL examination by as many as twenty points, even when the examinations are taken on the same day. In testing and assessment, this is called a standard error of measurement. Therefore, a TOEFL score cannot be predicted precisely, even when two official tests are used. But, of course, you would like to know how close you are to your goal. To do that, you can use the following procedure to estimate your TOEFL score. An estimate is an approximation.

PROCEDURE FOR SCORING

The official TOEFL® iBT tests have either a longer Reading section or a longer Listening section. The extra part on each test contains experimental questions that will not be graded as part of your score. You will need to do your best on all of the questions because you will not know which questions are experimental. The model tests in this book have either a longer Reading section or a longer Listening section. Use the procedure below with the charts on the following pages to determine your score estimate for each TOEFL® iBT model test.

1. Count the total number of correct answers for the Reading section Parts I and II.
2. Count the total number of correct answers for the Reading section Parts I and III for the model tests with a long Reading section.
3. Add the two totals for the Reading section and divide by 2 to calculate the Reading section average for the model tests with a long Reading section.

4. Count the total number of correct answers for the Listening section Parts I and II.
5. Count the total number of correct answers for the Listening section Parts I and III for the model tests with a long Listening section.
6. Add the two totals for the Listening section and divide by 2 to calculate the Listening section average for the model tests with a long Listening section.
7. Rate each question for the Speaking section on a holistic scale 0–4.
8. Add the six scores and divide by 6 to calculate the Speaking section average.
9. Rate each essay for the Writing section on a holistic scale 0–5.
10. Add the two scores and divide by 2 to calculate the Writing section average.
11. Refer to the reference charts on the following pages to find the scaled scores for each section *average*.
12. Finally, add the scaled scores for all four sections.

REFERENCE CHARTS

Reading

Correct Answers	Scaled Score
39	30
38	29
37	29
36	28
35	27
34	27
33	26
32	25
31	24
30	23
29	23
28	22
27	22
26	21
25	20
24	20
23	19
22	19
21	18
20	18
19	17
18	17
17	16
16	16
15	15
14	15
13	14
12	13
11	12
10	11
9	10
8	9
7	8
6	6
5	5
4	4
3	3
2	2
1	1
0	0

Listening

Correct Answers	Scaled Score
34	30
33	29
32	28
31	28
30	27
29	26
28	25
27	25
26	24
25	23
24	22
23	22
22	21
21	21
20	20
19	19
18	19
17	18
16	17
15	17
14	16
13	15
12	15
11	14
10	13
9	13
8	12
7	11
6	9
5	8
4	6
3	5
2	4
1	2
0	0

Speaking

Holistic Rating	Scaled Score
4.0	30
3.5	27
3.0	23
2.5	19
2.0	15
1.5	11
1.0	8
0	0

Writing

Holistic Rating	Scaled Score
5.0	30
4.5	28
4.0	25
3.5	22
3.0	20
2.5	17
2.0	14
1.5	11
1.0	8
0	0

EXAMPLES FOR SCORING MODEL TESTS

Example of iBT Model Test with Long Reading Section

Reading Section	Correct Answers	Scaled Score
Reading Parts I and II	37	
Reading Parts I and III	35	
Average number of correct answers	36	28

Listening Section		
Listening Parts I and II	30	
Listening Parts I and III	N/A	
Average number of correct answers	30	27

Speaking Section	Holistic Rating	
Speaking Question 1	4	
Speaking Question 2	4	
Speaking Question 3	3	
Speaking Question 4	3	
Speaking Question 5	4	
Speaking Question 6	3	
Average number of ratings	3.5	27

Writing Section		
Integrated essay	4	
Independent essay	5	
Average number of ratings	4.5	28

TOTAL
Add scaled scores for all sections   110

Example of iBT Model Test with Long Listening Section

Reading Section	Correct Answers	Scaled Score
Reading Parts I and II	36	
Reading Parts I and III	N/A	
Average number of correct answers	36	28

Listening Section	Correct Answers	Scaled Score
Listening Parts I and II	29	
Listening Parts I and III	31	
Average number of correct answers	30	27

Speaking Section	Holistic Rating	
Speaking Question 1	4	
Speaking Question 2	4	
Speaking Question 3	3	
Speaking Question 4	3	
Speaking Question 5	4	
Speaking Question 6	3	
Average number of ratings	3.5	27

Writing Section	Holistic Rating	
Integrated essay	4	
Independent essay	5	
Average number of ratings	4.5	28

TOTAL
Add scaled scores for all sections   110

FEEDBACK

A new feature of the TOEFL score report is feedback. A general analysis of your strengths and weaknesses will be included with the numerical score. The computer program on the CD-ROM that supplements this book provides feedback along with an automatic score report at the end of each model test.

OPTIONS FOR PERSONAL EVALUATION

SPEAKING

➤ Speak Up!

Speak Up! is a teacher-based evaluation, using the same criteria that raters use to score the official TOEFL Speaking section.

For more information on *Speak Up!*, visit *www.teflprep.com*.

WRITING

➤ Score It Now!

Score It Now! is an Internet-based essay evaluation using E-rater, a computerized scoring program that provides immediate scores for essays on a scale of 5–1 and general suggestions for improving essay writing skills. For a fee of $10, you can select from several authentic TOEFL essay topics, submit two essays, and receive two scores. Although the essays are not timed, you should complete them within thirty minutes in order to simulate a TOEFL writing experience. You should also take the time to read the sample essays that received scores of 5.

For more information on *Score It Now!*, visit *www.ets.org/scoreitnow*.

➤ Write Now!

Write Now! is a teacher-based evaluation, using the same criteria that raters use to score the official TOEFL essays.

For more information on *Write Now!*, visit *www.teflprep.com*.

RESOURCES

GLOSSARY OF CAMPUS VOCABULARY

academic advisor   n.   a person who helps students make decisions about their academic programs
   Example: Dr. Jones is the *academic advisor* for the engineering students.
   Suggestion: You should see your *academic advisor* before you decide.
   Assumption: Dr. Jones is your *academic advisor*?
   Problem: I can't see my *academic advisor* until Friday.

ace   v.   to receive a grade of A
   Example: I *aced* that exam.
   Suggestion: Find someone who *aced* the course to help you.
   Assumption: Kathy *aced* her computer science class?
   Problem: If I don't *ace* the final, I'll get a B in the class.

admissions office   n.   the administrative office where students apply for admission to a college or university
   Example: I have an appointment at the *admissions office* to review my application.
   Suggestion: Why don't you go over to the *admissions office*?
   Assumption: You mean you couldn't find the *admissions office*?
   Problem: I need to get to the *admissions office* before five o'clock.

all-nighter   n.   a study session that lasts all night
   Example: We had to pull an *all-nighter* to get ready for the final exam.
   Suggestion: If I were you, I wouldn't pull another *all-nighter*.
   Assumption: So you did pull another *all-nighter*.
   Problem: I have to pull an *all-nighter* in order to be ready for the final exam.

article   n.   a publication about an academic subject
   Example: We read six *articles* in addition to the reading in the textbook.
   Suggestion: You had better read the *articles* that were assigned.
   Assumption: You read the *articles* already?
   Problem: I need to read the *articles* again.

assignment   n.   work that must be done as part of the requirements for a class
    Example: The *assignment* was to read two chapters in the textbook.
    Suggestion: You had better read the *assignment* before class.
    Assumption: So you did read the *assignment* after all.
    Problem: I can't finish the *assignment* before class.

assistant professor   n.   a college or university teacher who ranks above a lecturer and below an associate professor
    Example: Dr. Green is an *assistant professor*.
    Suggestion: Why don't you find out whether he is a lecturer or an *assistant professor*?
    Assumption: You mean Dr. Green isn't an *assistant professor*?
    Problem: I need to find out whether Dr. Green is an *assistant professor*.

assistantship   n.   an opportunity for a graduate student to teach or do research in exchange for a stipend
    Example: Terry got an *assistantship* from State University.
    Suggestion: If I were you, I would apply for an *assistantship*.
    Assumption: So you did get an *assistantship* from State University.
    Problem: The *assistantship* doesn't pay as much as I thought it would.

associate professor   n.   a college or university teacher who ranks above an assistant professor and below a professor
    Example: Dr. Peterson is an *associate professor* now, but she will be promoted to a full professor at the end of the year.
    Suggestion: You could ask the secretary if Dr. Peterson is an *associate professor*.
    Assumption: Dr. Peterson isn't an *associate professor*, is she?
    Problem: If Dr. Peterson is an *associate professor*, I used the wrong title in my letter to her.

audit   v.   to attend a course without credit
    Example: It usually costs as much to *audit* a course as to take it for credit.
    Suggestion: You could *audit* the course if you don't need the credit.
    Assumption: You mean you are *auditing* the course?
    Problem: If I *audit* the course, I won't get credit for it.

bear   n.   a difficult class
    Example: That computer science course was a *bear*.
    Suggestion: I heard that Dr. Young's class is a real *bear*, so I would advise against it this semester.
    Assumption: Your roommate thought this class was a *bear*?
    Problem: Two of the classes I am in are real *bears*.

be behind   v.   to be late; to have a lot of work to do
    Example: I *am behind* in my physics class.
    Suggestion: You *are behind* in your psychology class so you should study.
    Assumption: Bill *is behind*?
    Problem: I can't go to the party because I *am behind* in my classes.

bike   n.   an abbreviation of the word *bicycle*
  Example: Many students ride their *bikes* on campus.
  Suggestion: You could park your *bike* outside the student union building.
  Assumption: Your *bike* was locked?
  Problem: I can't ride my *bike* to the pizza parlor because there isn't any parking for
                    it.

bike rack   n.   the metal supports where bicycles are parked
  Example: That *bike rack* is full, but there is another one by the library.
  Suggestion: If I were you, I would use the *bike rack* closest to the door.
  Assumption: The *bike rack* was moved from in front of the library?
  Problem: The *bike racks* at my dormitory will not hold all of the students' bikes.

blackboard   n.   the writing surface in the front of the classroom
  Example: Dr. Mitchell always writes the important words on the *blackboard*.
  Suggestion: You had better copy everything the instructor writes on the *blackboard*.
  Assumption: You mean you copied all of the material that was on the *blackboard*?
  Problem: I can't see what is written on the *blackboard*.

book   n.   a written work
  Example: The *books* for this class cost eighty dollars.
  Suggestion: You shouldn't wait too long to buy your *books*.
  Assumption: You didn't buy all of your *books*?
  Problem: I can't buy all of my *books* with only fifty dollars.

book bag   n.   a bag in which to carry books and school supplies
  Example: This *book bag* is very heavy.
  Suggestion: Why don't you buy a sturdy *book bag* so it will last longer?
  Assumption: Your brand new *book bag* fell apart?
  Problem: I can't carry all of my books at one time because my *book bag* is too small.

bookstore   n.   the store on campus where students buy their textbooks
  Example: The *bookstore* opens at seven in the morning.
  Suggestion: You should be at the *bookstore* before it opens so that you can get a used
                    book.
  Assumption: You mean that you were at the *bookstore* early and there were still no
                    used books?
  Problem: The *bookstore* is too far from my apartment for me to walk.

break   n.   a pause in work or study
  Example: Let's take a *break* after we finish our homework.
  Suggestion: If I were you, I would take a *break* before I began a new project.
  Assumption: You mean you're taking a *break* right now?
  Problem: I can't take a *break* until I complete this section of the problem.

bring up v. to improve
Example: If Jack doesn't *bring up* his grades, he won't get into graduate school.
Suggestion: If you want to *bring up* your grades, you will have to study more.
Assumption: You *brought up* your grades without studying?
Problem: If I don't study more, I won't be able to *bring up* my grades.

cafeteria n. a restaurant where students can select food from several choices and carry their meals on trays to their tables
Example: Let's order a pizza instead of going to the *cafeteria*.
Suggestion: Why don't we meet in the *cafeteria* before going to see our advisor?
Assumption: You mean you like the food in the *cafeteria*?
Problem: I can't meet you in the *cafeteria* because I have to speak with my professor after class.

call on v. to acknowledge in class; to invite to speak
Example: The professor *calls on* students who sit in the front more often than those who sit in back.
Suggestion: If you want the professor to *call on* you frequently, then sit in the front of the room.
Assumption: You sat in the front of the room and weren't *called on*?
Problem: I didn't know the answer when the professor *called on* me.

call the roll v. to read the names on a class roster in order to take attendance
Example: Some professors don't *call the roll*, but Dr. Peterson always does.
Suggestion: You should always find out whether or not the professor *calls the roll*.
Assumption: You mean you weren't there when Dr. Peterson *called the roll*?
Problem: I need to get to class earlier so that I will be there when Dr. Peterson *calls the roll*.

campus n. the buildings and grounds of a college or university
Example: State University has a beautiful *campus*.
Suggestion: You should see the *campus* before you decide to apply to school here.
Assumption: You mean you walked the entire *campus* by yourself?
Problem: I can't go with you to see the *campus* if you go this afternoon.

campus security n. the police on campus
Example: In an emergency, call *campus security*.
Suggestion: You had better call *campus security* to report that your bicycle is missing.
Assumption: The *campus security* is understaffed, isn't it?
Problem: Carol had to call *campus security* to help her get her car started.

carrel n. a private study space in the stacks of the library
Example: There are never enough *carrels* for all of the graduate students.
Suggestion: You should go to the library early in the evening if you want a *carrel*.
Assumption: You mean the *carrels* are free?
Problem: There aren't enough *carrels* in the library.

chapter   n.   a division in a book
> Example: The professor assigned three *chapters* in the textbook.
> Suggestion: If I were you, I would set aside several hours to read all of the *chapters* assigned today.
> Assumption: So you did allow enough time to finish the *chapters.*
> Problem: I have to go to the lab, and I am in the middle of a *chapter.*

cheat   v.   to act dishonestly
> Example: Students who *cheat* may be expelled from the university.
> Suggestion: You should not *cheat* because the penalty is serious.
> Assumption: Gary was expelled because he *cheated*?
> Problem: I know that some of my friends *cheated*, but I don't know what to do about it.

cheating   n.   a dishonest act
> Example: Sharing answers on an exam is *cheating.*
> Suggestion: You could sit alone during the exam so that the professor knows you are not *cheating.*
> Assumption: You consider copying a few sentences from a book *cheating*?
> Problem: Should I report it to the professor if I see someone *cheating*?

check out   v.   to borrow
> Example: You must have a library card to *check out* books.
> Suggestion: If you want to *check out* books for your research paper, you had better go to the library soon.
> Assumption: So you didn't go to the library to *check out* the books you needed?
> Problem: I need a new library card to be able to *check out* books.

class   n.   the meeting place and the content of a course
> Example: We have three *classes* together this term.
> Suggestion: You could arrange your schedule so that you have three *classes* on the same day.
> Assumption: So you wanted your *classes* to be on Friday.
> Problem: I have to work on Tuesdays and Thursdays, so I can't have *classes* on those days.

class discussion   n.   an exchange of ideas during a class
> Example: Dr. Green often has *class discussions* instead of lectures.
> Suggestion: If I were you, I would prepare for a *class discussion* in tomorrow's class.
> Assumption: You prepared for the *class discussion*, didn't you?
> Problem: I am not ready for the *class discussion* today.

closed out   adj.   to be denied access to a class
> Example: Register early so that you aren't *closed out* of the classes you want.
> Suggestion: Why don't you plan to register tomorrow before you are *closed out* of the classes you need to graduate?
> Assumption: Sue registered early to avoid being *closed out* of her classes?
> Problem: I was *closed out* of the English class I needed.

coed adj. an abbreviation for *coeducational,* which is a system of education in which both men and women attend the same school or classes
  Example: Most of the schools in the United States are *coed.*
  Suggestion: If I were you, I would live in a *coed* dormitory.
  Assumption: You mean you don't attend a *coed* school?
  Problem: My parents don't want me to live in a *coed* dormitory.

college n. a school that grants a bachelor's degree; an undergraduate division or a school within a university
  Example: Steve applied to the *college* of business at State University.
  Suggestion: You need to apply to the *college* of nursing early.
  Assumption: So you did apply to several *colleges* after all.
  Problem: The *college* of education requires three letters of recommendation.

commencement n. a graduation ceremony
  Example: Larger colleges and universities usually have *commencement* more than once each year.
  Suggestion: You had better be early for *commencement* because it starts on time.
  Assumption: So you did attend last year's *commencement* exercises.
  Problem: I don't have a cap and gown for *commencement.*

committee n. a group of professors who guide a graduate student's program and approve the thesis or dissertation
  Example: Bill's *committee* signed his dissertation today.
  Suggestion: You should be prepared before you meet with your *committee.*
  Assumption: Your *committee* didn't approve your dissertation topic?
  Problem: I need to do more research before I meet with my *committee.*

computer n. a programmable electronic machine that calculates, processes, and stores information
  Example: At some universities, students must bring their own *computers* with them to school.
  Suggestion: If I were you, I would purchase a *computer* before going to college.
  Assumption: You mean you don't know how to use a *computer?*
  Problem: I need to have my *computer* repaired.

computer disk n. a magnetic disk on which computer data is stored
  Example: It's a good idea to save a copy of your papers and projects on a *computer disk.*
  Suggestion: You should always have extra *computer disks.*
  Assumption: You mean you didn't save your work on a *computer disk?*
  Problem: I can't print my paper until I find my *computer disk.*

counselor n. a person who gives advice, often of a personal nature
  Example: See your advisor for academic advice and a *counselor* for personal advice.
  Suggestion: Why don't you speak with your *counselor* about the problems with your roommate?
  Assumption: You mean you have to make an appointment before seeing your *counselor?*
  Problem: I can't see my *counselor* until tomorrow.

course n.   a class
  Example: How many *courses* are you taking this semester?
  Suggestion: If I were you, I would take fewer *courses* this semester.
  Assumption: You registered for your *courses* already?
  Problem: I need to take *courses* that apply to my major.

course request (form) n.   a form used to register for a class
  Example: A student's academic advisor usually signs a *course request* form.
  Suggestion: You should pick up a *course request* form from the registrar's office today.
  Assumption: So you did pick up your *course request* form.
  Problem: I need to speak with my advisor about my *course request* form.

cram v.   to study at the last minute
  Example: Nancy always *crams* for the quizzes in her math class.
  Suggestion: Why don't you study each night instead of *cramming* the night before the test?
  Assumption: You mean you *crammed* for the biology final?
  Problem: I need to be more organized so I won't have to *cram* for my tests.

credit n.   a unit of study
  Example: I have thirty *credits* toward my master's degree.
  Suggestion: Why don't you check your *credits* with your advisor?
  Assumption: You mean you have enough *credits* to graduate?
  Problem: I have to take thirty more *credits* in my major area.

credit hour n.   the number that represents one hour of class per week for one term
  Example: This course is three *credit hours*.
  Suggestion: You could take eighteen *credit hours* this semester.
  Assumption: So you did complete fifteen *credit hours* last summer.
  Problem: I can't take enough *credit hours* to graduate this semester.

curve n.   a grading system that relies on the normal curve of distribution, resulting in a few A grades, the majority C grades, and a few failing grades
  Example: Grading on the *curve* encourages competition.
  Suggestion: Forget about the *curve*, and just do your best.
  Assumption: Dr. Graham grades his tests on the *curve*?
  Problem: Since the exams were graded on the *curve*, a 95 was a B.

cut class v.   to be absent from class, usually without a good excuse
  Example: My roommate *cut class* on Monday because he didn't come back to campus until late Sunday night.
  Suggestion: You had better not *cut class* on Thursday.
  Assumption: You *cut class* to sleep in?
  Problem: I can't *cut class* because I have too many absences.

dean n. an administrator who ranks above a department chair and below a vice president
    Example: The *dean* called a meeting with the department chair.
    Suggestion: You should meet with the *dean* about your problem.
    Assumption: So you did speak with the *dean*.
    Problem: Vicki has to prepare a presentation for the *dean*.

dean's list n. the honor roll at a college or university
    Example: You must maintain a 3.5 grade point average to be on the *dean's list*.
    Suggestion: You had better improve your grades if your want to make the *dean's list*.
    Assumption: Jack made the *dean's list* last semester?
    Problem: I can't make the *dean's list* this semester.

declare v. to make an official decision about a major field of study
    Example: Most students *declare* their major in their third year at the university.
    Suggestion: If I were you, I would *declare* my major before I take any more classes.
    Assumption: You mean you *declared* your major last year?
    Problem: Joe needs to *declare* his major soon.

degree n. an academic title awarded to a student who completes a course of study
    Example: The three most common *degrees* are a bachelor's, a master's, and a doctorate.
    Suggestion: You should get your *degree* before you get married.
    Assumption: So you did graduate with a *degree* in music theory.
    Problem: I can't get a good job without a *degree*.

department n. a division of a college or university organized by subject
    Example: The English *department* offers classes for international students.
    Suggestion: Why don't you check the *department's* phone number again?
    Assumption: So you worked in the English *department* office.
    Problem: I can't find the list of the *department* offices.

department chair n. a university administrator for a division of a college or university
    Example: The professors in a department report to the *department chair*.
    Suggestion: You could speak to the *department chair* about auditing the class.
    Assumption: You mean Dr. Carlson is the new *department chair*?
    Problem: I can't meet with the *department chair* until after registration.

diploma n. the certificate of completion for a degree
    Example: Students receive their *diplomas* at the graduation ceremony.
    Suggestion: You should get your *diploma* framed.
    Assumption: So you did show your family your *diploma*.
    Problem: I need to mail this form and pay my fees before I can get my *diploma*.

dissertation n. a thesis that is written in partial fulfillment of the requirements for a doctorate.
    Example: Dr. Green wrote his *dissertation* on global warming.
    Suggestion: If I were you, I would consider several ideas before selecting a *dissertation* topic.
    Assumption: You mean you already started your *dissertation*?
    Problem: I can't find enough research on my *dissertation* topic.

distance learning   n.   courses organized so that students can complete the requirements by computer, or other media, often without going to campus

Example: There are several *distance learning* opportunities for working adults.
Suggestion: Why don't you sign up for that course through *distance learning*?
Assumption: So you did take that *distance learning* class.
Problem: I can only take three *distance learning* classes.

division   n.   a group of departments in a college or university

Example: The *division* of modern languages includes both the Spanish department and the French department as well as the German department.
Suggestion: Why don't you go to the *division* of math and sciences to find more information about biology instructors?
Assumption: You mean you've already spoken to Dr. Conrad about the entrance exam for the *division* of social sciences?
Problem: I need to find out what opportunities the *division* of modern languages offers for foreign study.

doctorate   n.   the degree after a master's degree awarded to an academic doctor

Example: Karen will receive her *doctorate* in the spring.
Suggestion: You should meet with your academic advisor to discuss a *doctorate.*
Assumption: So you did receive your *doctorate* from State University.
Problem: I must complete my dissertation before I get my *doctorate*.

dorm   n.   an abbreviation for *dormitory*

Example: Living on campus in a *dorm* is often cheaper than living off campus.
Suggestion: You should live in a *dorm* for at least one year.
Assumption: You lived in a *dorm* for four years?
Problem: Sue needs to apply now for a room in the *dorm*.

draft   n.   a preliminary copy of a paper or other written document

Example: A good student does not turn in a first *draft* of a paper.
Suggestion: You should edit each *draft* on the computer.
Assumption: You wrote the first *draft* in one night?
Problem: I can't turn in my essay because I have only the first *draft* written.

drop   v.   to withdraw from a course

Example: If you *drop* a course early in the term, you may get a partial refund.
Suggestion: If I were you, I would *drop* the class immediately.
Assumption: You mean you *dropped* the class because it was too hard?
Problem: Bill needs to *drop* one of his classes because he is taking too many credit hours.

drop out   v.   to withdraw from a college or university

Example: Mark *dropped out* because he needed to work full-time.
Suggestion: You could *drop out* and then reenter next semester.
Assumption: Diane *dropped out* after her junior year?
Problem: I have to *drop out* because I don't have enough money for tuition.

due   adj.   expected on a certain date
    Example: The assignment is *due* on Friday.
    Suggestion: Why don't you turn in the paper before it's *due*?
    Assumption: You mean the project is *due* this week?
    Problem: I can't complete the assignment by the *due* date.

elective (course)   n., adj.   an optional academic course
    Example: In the junior year, most students are taking *elective* courses as well as
                   requirements.
    Suggestion: Take some *elective* classes in your areas of outside interest.
    Assumption: So you did take an *elective* in art appreciation.
    Problem: I can't take any *elective* classes this semester.

enroll   v.   to register for a course or a university program
    Example: Only a few students *enroll* in seminars.
    Suggestion: Why don't you *enroll* early before the class fills up?
    Assumption: You mean you didn't *enroll* in the computer class?
    Problem: I can't *enroll* in that class without taking the introductory class first.

essay   n.   a short composition on a single subject, usually presenting the personal opinion of
             the author
    Example: An *essay* is often five paragraphs long.
    Suggestion: If I were you, I would make an outline before writing the *essay*.
    Assumption: So you did get an A on the *essay*.
    Problem: I have to write an *essay* for my class on Friday.

exam   n.   an abbreviation for *examination*
    Example: The professor scheduled several quizzes and one *exam*.
    Suggestion: You had better prepare for the *exam* in chemistry.
    Assumption: You studied for the physics *exam*?
    Problem: I have to meet with my study group before the *exam*.

excused absence   n.   absence with the permission of the professor
    Example: Dr. Mitchell allows every student one *excused absence* each semester.
    Suggestion: You could take an *excused absence* in your Friday class so we could leave
                   early.
    Assumption: You mean you have two *excused absences* in biology?
    Problem: I already have one *excused absence* in Dr. Mitchell's class.

expel   v.   to dismiss from school
    Example: Gary was *expelled* because he cheated on an exam.
    Suggestion: You should avoid getting *expelled* at all costs.
    Assumption: Gary was *expelled* from the university?
    Problem: I would be *expelled* if I helped you.

extension n. additional time
> Example: We asked Dr. Peterson for an *extension* in order to complete the group project.
> Suggestion: You should organize your time so that you will not have to ask for an *extension*.
> Assumption: You mean your request for an *extension* was denied?
> Problem: I need to meet with my professor to discuss an *extension*.

faculty member n. a teacher in a college or university
> Example: Dr. Baker is a *faculty member* at State University.
> Suggestion: Why don't you ask a *faculty member* for directions?
> Assumption: You didn't meet any of the new *faculty members* when you visited the campus?
> Problem: I don't know the other *faculty members* in my department very well.

fail v. to receive an unacceptable grade
> Example: If Mary gets another low grade, she will *fail* the course.
> Suggestion: You had better complete the project or you will *fail* the class.
> Assumption: You mean you *failed* the exam?
> Problem: I have to study tonight, or I will *fail* the test tomorrow.

fee n. a charge for services
> Example: You must pay a *fee* to park your car on campus.
> Suggestion: If I were you, I would pay my *fees* before the late penalty applies.
> Assumption: You mean there are *fees* for using the recreational facilities?
> Problem: I need to go to the business office to pay my *fees*.

field trip n. a trip for observation and education
> Example: The geology class usually takes several *field trips* to the museum.
> Suggestion: You should wear sturdy shoes on the *field trip*.
> Assumption: You didn't sign up for the *field trip* to the art gallery?
> Problem: I have to go on a *field trip* Saturday morning, but my boss won't let me off work.

fill-in-the-blank (test) n., adj. an objective test in which the student completes sentences by writing in the missing words
> Example: Dr. Stephens always gives *fill-in-the-blank* tests during the semester, but he gives short-essay finals.
> Suggestion: You had better study the definitions for the *fill-in-the-blank* portion of the test.
> Assumption: You mean the test was all *fill-in-the-blank*?
> Problem: Kathy needs to do better on the *fill-in-the-blank* questions.

final (exam) n. the last examination of an academic course
> Example: The *final* will include questions from the notes as well as from the textbook.
> Suggestion: You should use both your notes and the text to review for the *final exam*.
> Assumption: You finished your *final* in an hour?
> Problem: I have to prepare for two *final exams* on the same day.

fine   n.   a sum of money paid for violation of a rule
Example: The *fine* for keeping a library book after the due date is one dollar per day.
Suggestion: You should move your car to avoid a *fine*.
Assumption: You mean you were charged a *fine* for parking there?
Problem: I need to pay my *fines* before the end of the semester.

fraternity   n.   a social organization for male college students
Example: Bill is going to join a *fraternity*.
Suggestion: You could join a professional *fraternity*.
Assumption: You were invited to join three *fraternities*?
Problem: I can't afford to join a *fraternity*.

fraternity row   n.   a street where many fraternity houses are located
Example: I live on Fifth Street, near *fraternity row*.
Suggestion: Why don't you walk down *fraternity row* to look at the homecoming decorations?
Assumption: Isn't Ken going to live on *fraternity row* next year?
Problem: I can't find a place to park on *fraternity row*.

freshman   n.   a first-year college student
Example: Most of the students in Manchester Hall are *freshmen*.
Suggestion: You should establish good study habits while you are a *freshman.*
Assumption: Didn't you live in a dorm when you were a *freshman*?
Problem: The *freshmen* have to take requirements.

full-time   adj.   the number of hours for standard tuition at a college or university, usually 9 hours for a graduate student and 12–15 hours for an undergraduate student
Example: Tom is a *full-time* student this semester.
Suggestion: If I were you, I would register as a *full-time* student this semester.
Assumption: You mean the scholarship is only available to *full-time* students?
Problem: I need to register as a *full-time* student to be eligible for a loan.

get behind   v.   to be late or off schedule
Example: I am *getting behind* in my math class.
Suggestion: You had better study this weekend or you will *get behind* in English.
Assumption: Ken *got behind* in his classes?
Problem: I *got behind* in French, and now my class is really confusing.

get caught up   v.   to bring up to date
Example: We are going to *get caught up* in our classes this weekend.
Suggestion: Why don't you *get caught up* in English before you start your next project?
Assumption: Sue *got caught up* over vacation?
Problem: I need to *get caught up* before final exams.

G.P.A.   n.   abbreviation for grade point average
Example: Kathy's *G.P.A.* as an undergraduate was 4.0, but she isn't doing as well in graduate school.
Suggestion: You should be concerned about your *G.P.A.*
Assumption: Laura's *G.P.A.* dropped last semester?
Problem: I can't raise my *G.P.A.* if I take calculus.

grade point average   n.   a scale, usually 0–4, on which grades are calculated
   Example: If students' *grade point averages* fall below 2.0, they will be placed on probation.
   Suggestion: If I were you, I would speak to my academic advisor about your *grade point average.*
   Assumption: You mean your *grade point average* is more important than work experience?
   Problem: I need to improve my *grade point average.*

grades   n.   a standard number or letter indicating a student's level of performance
   Example: We will get our *grades* in the mail a week after the semester is over.
   Suggestion: You should check the *grades* that the professor posted.
   Assumption   Our *grades* are already in the mail?
   Problem: I have to have better *grades* to get into the college of business.

graduate school   n.   a division of a college or university to serve students who are pursuing masters or doctoral degrees
   Example: I would like to apply to *graduate school* after I complete my bachelor's degree.
   Suggestion: Why don't you work a year before applying to *graduate school*?
   Assumption: So Tracy did get accepted to *graduate school.*
   Problem: I have to get letters of recommendation to apply to *graduate school.*

graduate student   n.   a student who is pursuing a master's or doctorate
   Example: *Graduate students* must maintain higher grades than undergraduate students.
   Suggestion: You had better work with the other *graduate students* on this project.
   Assumption: You mean only *graduate students* are allowed to take this class?
   Problem: All of the students in the class are *graduate students* except me.

grant   n.   funds for research or study
   Example: Carol received a *grant* for her research in psychology.
   Suggestion: You should apply for a summer *grant.*
   Assumption: You mean there are *grants* available for undergraduate students?
   Problem: Bill needs to write a proposal before Tuesday if he wants to be considered for a *grant.*

group project   n.   an assignment to be completed by three or more students
   Example: I prefer to work on *group projects* instead of on assignments by myself.
   Suggestion: You should select your *group project* before midterm.
   Assumption: You've chosen your *group project* already?
   Problem: The *group project* will take more time than I thought.

hand back   v.   return an assignment
   Example: Dr. Graham always *hands back* our assignments the next day.
   Suggestion: You had better be there when Dr. Mitchell *hands back* your exam.
   Assumption: Dr. Mitchell hasn't *handed back* your exam yet?
   Problem: I can't find the exam that he *handed back.*

handout n. prepared notes that a teacher provides to the class
    Example: Dr. Stephen's *handouts* are always very helpful.
    Suggestion: You had better save all of your *handouts*.
    Assumption: You lost the *handouts*?
    Problem: I need to organize all of my *handouts* before I start to study for the final.

head resident n. the advisor for a dormitory
    Example: The *head resident* can help you resolve problems with your roommate.
    Suggestion: If I were you, I would introduce myself to the *head resident*.
    Assumption: So you did speak with the *head resident*.
    Problem: I can't find the *head resident*.

health center n. the clinic on campus to provide basic health care for students
    Example: We are going to the *health center* for a free eye examination.
    Suggestion: You had better go to the *health center* for that cough.
    Assumption: You mean the *health center* is closed?
    Problem: I am too sick to go to the *health center*.

health insurance n. protection for students who may need medical attention
    Example: *Health insurance* is required on most campuses.
    Suggestion: You need to purchase *health insurance* through the university.
    Assumption: You don't have *health insurance*?
    Problem: I have to earn some more money to pay for my *health insurance*.

hit the books v. to study very hard
    Example: I have to *hit the books* tonight and tomorrow to get ready for the midterm.
    Suggestion: You had better *hit the books* for Dr. Sheridan's exam.
    Assumption: You mean you didn't *hit the books* for the psychology exam?
    Problem: My friends have to *hit the books* this weekend so they can't go to the party with me.

homework n. schoolwork done at home
    Example: If I do my *homework* every day, I understand the lectures better.
    Suggestion: Why don't you do your *homework* before dinner?
    Assumption: There wasn't any *homework* last night, was there?
    Problem: I have to do my *homework* in order to be prepared for the class discussion.

honors adj. special recognition for exceptional students
    Example: Jane is an *honors* graduate.
    Suggestion: You could live in an *honors* dorm.
    Assumption: So you did enroll in the *honors* program.
    Problem: The courses in the *honors* program are much harder than the regular courses.

housing office n. an administrative office for residence halls and off-campus rentals
    Example: Let's go over to the *housing office* to ask about apartments near the campus.
    Suggestion: If I were you, I would check at the *housing office* for a dorm application.
    Assumption: You mean the *housing office* closed early?
    Problem: I need to speak with someone in the *housing office* about my application.

incomplete   n.   a grade in a course that allows students to complete requirements the following term
Example: I asked Dr. Young for an *incomplete* in his class.
Suggestion: You should request an *incomplete* at least two weeks before the end of the term.
Assumption: Bill took an *incomplete* in sociology last semester?
Problem: I can't ask Dr. Young for another *incomplete*.

instructor   n.   a college or university teacher who ranks below an assistant professor
Example: My *instructor* for math is from Hawaii.
Suggestion: You should check with the *instructor* to see if there is room in the class.
Assumption: The *instructor* was absent?
Problem: I can't seem to get along with my *instructor*.

interactive television (course)   n.   a distance learning course that is taught on two-way television connections
Example: The instructor for our *interactive television course* is on a campus about fifty miles away.
Suggestion: You could take that *course* on the *interactive television*.
Assumption: Dr. Stephen's *course* is offered on *interactive television?*
Problem: *Interactive television courses* make me uncomfortable.

interlibrary loan   n.   a system that allows students on one campus to borrow books from other libraries on other campuses
Example: It takes at least a week to receive a book by *interlibrary loan*.
Suggestion: You could see if the book is available through *interlibrary loan*.
Assumption: Your *interlibrary loan* books arrived in time?
Problem: I can't seem to find the desk for *interlibrary loans*.

internship   n.   a training opportunity for an advanced student or a recent graduate
Example: Bill got an *internship* at the University Hospital.
Suggestion: You should apply for an *internship* very early.
Assumption: You are getting paid for your *internship?*
Problem: I need to serve a two-year *internship*.

junior   n., adj.   a third-year college student
Example: When I am a *junior*, I plan to study abroad for a semester.
Suggestion: You could concentrate on your major your *junior* year.
Assumption: A *junior* can study abroad?
Problem: I need to carry eighteen credit hours both semesters of my *junior* year.

keep grades up   v.   to maintain a good grade point average
Example: If Joanne doesn't *keep her grades up*, she will lose her scholarship.
Suggestion: You need to study harder if you want to *keep your grades up*.
Assumption: Kathy didn't *keep her grades up* this semester?
Problem: I can't *keep my grades up* and work full-time.

lab   n., adj.   abbreviation for laboratory
    Example: The course includes a five-hour *lab*.
    Suggestion: You had better allow sufficient time for your biology *lab*.
    Assumption: You missed the last *lab* session?
    Problem: I need to find a partner for my psychology *lab*.

lab assistant   n.   a graduate student who helps in the lab
    Example: Bill is Dr. Peterson's *lab assistant*.
    Suggestion: You could ask the *lab assistant* for help.
    Assumption: You are the *lab assistant*, aren't you?
    Problem: I need to speak with the *lab assistant* before class.

laboratory   n.   a classroom equipped for experiments and research
    Example: The physics *laboratory* at State University is very old.
    Suggestion: You could meet your biology study group in the *laboratory*.
    Assumption: The *laboratory* isn't closed Saturday, is it?
    Problem: I have to get directions to the *laboratory*.

lab report   n.   a written description of the laboratory activities
    Example: Our *lab reports* are due every Friday.
    Suggestion: If I were you, I wouldn't wait to start my *lab report*.
    Assumption: You mean the *lab reports* have to be typed?
    Problem: I have to turn in my *lab report* tomorrow.

learning assistance center   n.   an area used for tutoring and special programs to help
                                            students with their classes
    Example: I have to meet my tutor at the *learning assistance center* at four o'clock.
    Suggestion: You should go to the *learning assistance center* for help in the morning.
    Assumption: So Nancy did go to the *learning assistance center* for tutoring.
    Problem: The tutors at the *learning assistance center* are all juniors and seniors, so I
                    don't qualify.

lecture   n.   a presentation for a class, delivered by the professor
    Example: The *lectures* are really interesting, but I don't enjoy the labs as much.
    Suggestion: You should take more notes during Dr. Mitchell's *lectures*.
    Assumption: The *lecture* is canceled for today?
    Problem: I can't keep up with the *lectures*.

lecturer   n.   a college or university teacher, usually without rank
    Example: Mr. Lewis is only a *lecturer*, but his classes are very good.
    Suggestion: If I were you, I would speak with the *lecturer* about your questions.
    Assumption: The *lecturer* isn't here?
    Problem: I can't take notes because the *lecturer* speaks too fast.

library   n.   the building on campus where books and other research materials are kept
    Example: Vicki has a job in the *library*.
    Suggestion: Your study group could reserve a study room in the *library*.
    Assumption: You mean the *library* is within walking distance?
    Problem: I need to return my books to the *library*.

library card   n.   an identification card that permits the holder to borrow books and materials from the library

Example: Without a *library card*, you can't borrow books here.
Suggestion: You should get a *library card* right away.
Assumption: So you did bring your *library card* with you.
Problem: I can't use my *library card* because I owe a fine.

library fine   n.   a payment for returning books and materials after the due date

Example: You can't get your grade report unless you pay your *library fines*.
Suggestion: You should pay your *library fines* immediately.
Assumption: You owe ten dollars in *library fines*?
Problem: Nancy needs to pay her *library fines* before she checks out any more books.

lost and found   n.   an area on campus where items are kept for their owners to reclaim

Example: Maybe someone picked up your book and took it to the *lost and found*.
Suggestion: Why don't you check at the *lost and found* for your backpack?
Assumption: You mean Sue's wallet wasn't at the *lost and found*?
Problem: Sue needs to fill out a report at the *lost and found*.

lower-division (course)   adj.   introductory-level courses for first- and second-year students

Example: Seniors don't usually take *lower-division* courses.
Suggestion: You should take *lower-division* classes your first year.
Assumption: You mean all of the *lower-division* classes are full?
Problem: I have to take a *lower-division* class before I can take the advanced course.

major   n.   a field of study chosen as an academic specialty

Example: My *major* is environmental studies.
Suggestion: You should declare your *major* by your junior year.
Assumption: You mean you have to declare a *major* to graduate?
Problem: I have to tell my advisor my *major* tomorrow.

makeup test   n.   a test taken after the date of the original administration

Example: Dr. Stephens usually allows her students to take a *makeup test* if there is a good reason for being absent.
Suggestion: You could speak with Dr. Stephens about taking a *makeup test*.
Assumption: Dr. Peterson let you take a *makeup test*?
Problem: Dana needs to take a *makeup test* before spring break.

married student housing   n.   apartments on or near campus for married students

Example: There is usually a waiting list to be assigned to *married student housing*.
Suggestion: If I were you, I would get an application for *married student housing* today.
Assumption: You mean there are no vacancies in *married student housing*?
Problem: We need to pick up an application for *married student housing*.

Mickey Mouse course n.   a very easy course
Example: This is a *Mickey Mouse course,* but it is on my program of study.
Suggestion: Why don't you take one *Mickey Mouse course* this semester just for fun?
Assumption: You thought physics was a *Mickey Mouse course*?
Problem: I have to take this *Mickey Mouse course* to fulfill my physical education requirement.

midterm n.   an exam that is given in the middle of the term
Example: I got an A on my *midterm* in accounting.
Suggestion: Why don't you study with your study group for the music theory *midterm*?
Assumption: You mean Sue failed her economics *midterm*?
Problem: I have three *midterms* in one day.

minor n.   a secondary area of study
Example: With a major in international business, I decided to do my *minor* in English.
Suggestion: You should *minor* in economics since you're studying prelaw.
Assumption: You mean you've completed all of your *minor* classes?
Problem: I need one more class to complete my *minor*.

miss (class) v.   to be absent
Example: My roommate is *missing* a lot of classes lately.
Suggestion: If I were you I wouldn't *miss* Dr. Mitchell's class today.
Assumption: So you did *miss* class last Friday.
Problem: I can't *miss* any more of Dr. Mitchell's classes, or my grade will be lowered by one letter.

multiple-choice test n.   an objective test with questions that provide several possible answer choices
Example: We usually have *multiple-choice tests* in Dr. Graham's classes.
Suggestion: You had better study very carefully for Dr. Graham's *multiple-choice test*.
Assumption: It was a *multiple-choice test*?
Problem: I don't usually do well on *multiple-choice tests*.

notebook n.   a bound book with blank pages in it for notes
Example: I lost the *notebook* with my biology notes in it.
Suggestion: You should make sure that your *notebook* is well organized.
Assumption: You lost your *notebook*?
Problem: I need to organize my *notebook* this weekend.

notebook computer n.   a computer the size of a notebook
Example: Joe has a *notebook computer* that he uses in class.
Suggestion: Why don't you use my *notebook computer* to see whether you like it?
Assumption: So you did purchase a *notebook computer*.
Problem: I can't possibly afford a *notebook computer* right now.

notes   n.   a brief record of a lecture to help students recall the important points
    Example: We didn't take *notes* in class today because most of the lecture was from the book.
    Suggestion: You should copy Tracy's *notes* before the next test.
    Assumption: You mean you lent your *notes* to someone?
    Problem: I need to recopy my *notes* this evening.

objective test   n.   a test with questions that have one possible answer, usually presented in a multiple-choice, matching, or true-false format
    Example: The final exam will be an *objective test*, not an essay test.
    Suggestion: You should probably prepare for an *objective test* in math.
    Assumption: The final exam was an *objective test*?
    Problem: I have to study harder for *objective tests*.

off campus   adj.   not on university property
    Example: There are some very nice apartments just *off campus* on State Street.
    Suggestion: You should come to campus early unless you want to park *off campus*.
    Assumption: You mean Carol doesn't want to live *off campus*?
    Problem: I need to live *off campus* to save money.

office   n.   a place for university faculty and staff to meet with students and do their work
    Example: Mr. Lewis has an *office* in Madison Hall.
    Suggestion: Most of the advisors' *offices* are in Sycamore Hall.
    Assumption: So you did find Mr. Lewis's *office* before he left for the day.
    Problem: I have to go to the business *office* tomorrow to ask about my bill.

office hours   n.   a schedule when faculty are in their offices to meet with students
    Example: *Office hours* are usually posted on the door of the professor's office.
    Suggestion: You should write down the instructor's *office hours* in your notebook.
    Assumption: You don't know Dr. Miller's *office hours*?
    Problem: I can't find my copy of Dr. Miller's *office hours*.

online course   n.   a course taught on the Internet
    Example: There is a separate list of *online courses* this semester.
    Suggestion: Why don't you consider an *online course* in economics?
    Assumption: Joe took an *online course* last year?
    Problem: I need a computer to take an *online course*.

on probation   prep. phrase   experiencing a trial period to improve grades before disciplinary action
    Example: Kathy is *on probation,* so she will probably be studying this weekend.
    Suggestion: You had better keep up your grades or you will end up *on probation*.
    Assumption: Sue couldn't be *on probation* again.
    Problem: I can't let my parents find out that I am *on probation*.

on reserve   prep. phrase   retained in a special place in the library, usually for use only in the library

Example:	Dr. Young always puts a lot of books *on reserve* for his classes.
Suggestion:	You could check to see if the book is *on reserve*.
Assumption:	You mean the articles are *on reserve*?
Problem:	I have to find out which books are *on reserve*.

open-book test   n.   a test during which students may consult their books and notes

Example:	*Open-book tests* are often longer than other tests.
Suggestion:	You should still prepare even though it is an *open-book test*.
Assumption:	You mean you didn't know it was an *open-book test*?
Problem:	I can't find my notes for the *open-book test*.

orientation   n.   a program for new students at a college or university during which they receive information about the school

Example:	I missed the first day of *orientation*, so I didn't get a map.
Suggestion:	You should sit near the front during *orientation*.
Assumption:	So you did go to freshman *orientation*.
Problem:	I have to go to *orientation* tomorrow evening.

override   n.   permission to enter a class for which the student does not qualify

Example:	Dr. Stephens will usually give you an *override* if you need the class.
Suggestion:	You should speak to the professor about getting an *override* for that class.
Assumption:	You mean your request for an *override* was denied?
Problem:	I need to get an *override* so that I can take that class.

paper   n.   a research report

Example:	The *papers* for this class should be at least ten pages long.
Suggestion:	You had better follow Dr. Carlyle's guidelines for this *paper*.
Assumption:	Laura turned in her *paper* late?
Problem:	I can't print my *paper* because I need an ink cartridge for my printer.

parking garage   n.   a structure for parking, usually requiring payment

Example:	The *parking garages* are too far away from the classrooms.
Suggestion:	You had better get a parking permit for the *parking garage*.
Assumption:	You mean you don't know which *parking garage* you used?
Problem:	I have to find a *parking garage* with a vacancy.

parking lot   n.   an area for parking

Example:	This *parking lot* is for students only.
Suggestion:	You should avoid leaving your car in the *parking lot* overnight.
Assumption:	You mean your car was towed from the *parking lot*?
Problem:	I have to leave early to get a spot in the *parking lot* beside the dorm.

parking permit   n.   permission to park in certain parking lots or garages

Example:	Your *parking permit* expires at the end of the month.
Suggestion:	If I were you, I would get a *parking permit* when you register.
Assumption:	My *parking permit* has expired?
Problem:	I need to pay my fines before they will issue me another *parking permit*.

parking space   n.   a designated area for one car
    Example: There is a car in my *parking space*.
    Suggestion: You should not use a reserved *parking space*.
    Assumption: So you did park in someone else's *parking space*.
    Problem: I can't find a *parking space*.

parking ticket   n.   notice of a fine due for parking in a restricted area
    Example: If you don't take care of your *parking tickets*, you won't be able to register for classes next semester.
    Suggestion: You could avoid getting *parking tickets* by using the student parking lots.
    Assumption: You mean Carol got a *parking ticket* because she didn't have a permit?
    Problem: I have to save money to pay my *parking ticket*s.

part-time   adj.   less than the full work day or school day
    Example: Laura has a *part-time* job after school.
    Suggestion: Why don't you get a *part-time* job to pay for your books?
    Assumption: You applied for a *part-time* job on campus?
    Problem: I need to find a *part-time* job this summer.

pass back   v.   to return tests and assignments to the owner
    Example: Dr. Young is going to *pass back* our quizzes today.
    Suggestion: You should ask Dr. Young for an appointment after he *passes back* the tests.
    Assumption: Dr. Young didn't *pass back* the papers?
    Problem: I have to get my paper from Dr. Young because I wasn't there when he *passed them back*.

placement office   n.   the office where students receive assistance in locating employment
    Example: Several companies are interviewing students at the *placement office* this week.
    Suggestion: Why don't you check the interview listing in the *placement office* on Monday?
    Assumption: Joe got his job through the *placement office*?
    Problem: I need to schedule an interview in the *placement office*.

plagiarize   v.   to use someone else's written work without giving that person credit
plagiarizing   n.   the use of someone else's work without giving that person credit
    Example: To avoid *plagiarizing*, always cite the source.
    Suggestion: If you change this sentence, it will keep you from *plagiarizing*.
    Assumption: You mean you know someone who *plagiarized*?
    Problem: The professor thought that I had *plagiarized* a report.

pop quiz   n.   a quiz that is given without notice
    Example: We had a *pop quiz* in our sociology class today.
    Suggestion: You should always be prepared for a *pop quiz*.
    Assumption: You passed all of the *pop quizzes*?
    Problem: I have to be on time to class in case there is a *pop quiz* at the beginning of class.

post (grade)   v.   to publish a list and display it in a public place
    Example: The grades for the exams are *posted* on Dr. Graham's door.
    Suggestion: You should see if the grades have been *posted* yet.
    Assumption: The assignments aren't *posted* yet, are they?
    Problem: I can't get to campus to see if the grades are *posted*.

prerequisite   n.   a course required before a student is eligible to take a higher-level
                            course
    Example: This English class has two *prerequisites*.
    Suggestion: You should check the *prerequisites* before seeing your advisor.
    Assumption: You took the *prerequisites* last year?
    Problem: I have to pass the *prerequisites* before I can register for the next class.

presentation   n.   a lecture, speech, or demonstration in front of the class
    Example: Your *presentation* in our anthropology class was very interesting.
    Suggestion: You could use more pictures in your *presentation*.
    Assumption: You mean your *presentation* is fifty minutes long?
    Problem: I need to get over my fear of public speaking before I give my
                        presentation.

professor   n.   a college or university teacher who ranks above an associate professor
    Example: Dr. Baker is a *professor* of English.
    Suggestion: Why don't you speak with your *professor* about the project?
    Assumption: The *professor's* office hours are posted, aren't they?
    Problem: I need to speak to my *professor* before class on Friday.

program of study   n.   a list of the courses that a student must take to fulfill the require-
                            ments for graduation
    Example: If you want to change your *program of study,* you must see your advisor.
    Suggestion: Why don't you review your *program of study* in your catalog?
    Assumption: The *program of study* is a four-year plan, isn't it?
    Problem: I need to become familiar with my *program of study*.

project   n.   an assignment that often involves the application of knowledge
    Example: We can do the *project* by ourselves or in a group.
    Suggestion: Why don't you and your study group do the *project* together?
    Assumption: You did the *project* that everyone is talking about?
    Problem: I have to present my *project* to the class.

quarter   n.   a school term that is usually ten to twelve weeks in length
    Example: This *quarter* has gone by very quickly.
    Suggestion: You could take fewer classes next *quarter*.
    Assumption: You mean you have to finish your thesis this *quarter*?
    Problem: I need to study harder next *quarter*.

quiz   n.   an evaluation that is usually shorter and worth fewer points than a test
Example: We have a *quiz* in our algebra class every week.
Suggestion: You should always be prepared for a *quiz*.
Assumption: The *quiz* doesn't include last night's reading, does it?
Problem: We have a *quiz* in chemistry this week.

registrar   n.   a university official in charge of keeping records
Example: You need to see the *registrar* about your grade change.
Suggestion: If I were you, I would check with the *registrar* about your transcript.
Assumption: So you did file a change of address with the *registrar*.
Problem: The *registrar* is unavailable until next week.

registration   n.   the process for enrolling in courses at a college or university
Example: *Registration* always takes longer than I think it will.
Suggestion: You should meet with your advisor before *registration*.
Assumption: You mean that early *registration* is available for graduate students?
Problem: I can't get to *registration* before noon.

report   n.   a written or oral presentation of results, either of research or experimentation
Example: Ken gave an excellent *report* in our management class today.
Suggestion: If I were you, I would allow more time for my next *report*.
Assumption: So you did listen to Ken's *report*.
Problem: I have to do five oral *reports* for speech class.

research   n.   investigation or study
Example: Dr. Peterson is going to give a lecture about her *research* on cross-cultural interaction.
Suggestion: You could use my class for your *research*.
Assumption: Your *research* is complete, isn't it?
Problem: I need more sources for my *research*.

research assistant   n.   a research position under the supervision of a faculty member
Example: The *research assistants* get to know the faculty better than the other graduate students do.
Suggestion: You could apply to be a *research assistant* next year.
Assumption: You mean Ken's a *research assistant*?
Problem: I need to speak to the *research assistant* who works in the psychology lab.

research paper   n.   a written report based on research
Example: Use at least ten references for your *research papers*.
Suggestion: You had better go to the library soon if you want that book for your *research paper*.
Assumption: You mean we have to present our *research paper* to the class?
Problem: I can't get started on my *research paper*.

resident advisor   n.   an advisor who lives in a dormitory in order to provide supervision and counseling for the students

Example: We call our *resident advisor* the "head resident."
Suggestion: Why don't you speak to the *resident advisor* about your problem?
Assumption: You live next door to the *resident advisor*?
Problem: I need to speak with the *resident advisor* regarding the desk in my room.

review session   n.   a study meeting to review material before a test, often led by the professor

Example: I'm on my way to a *review session* for my art appreciation class.
Suggestion: You could schedule a *review session* with your study group.
Assumption: The *review session* was productive?
Problem: I can't meet Thursday afternoon for the *review session*.

room and board   n.   fees for room rent and meals

Example: *Room and board* goes up every year.
Suggestion: You should plan to include the price of *room and board* in your budget.
Assumption: You mean your scholarship covers *room and board*?
Problem: I need to find a part-time job to pay for *room and board*.

roommate   n.   a person who shares a room or rooms

Example: I think Diane is looking for a *roommate*.
Suggestion: Why don't you and Diane get another *roommate*?
Assumption: You mean you're looking for another *roommate*?
Problem: I need a *roommate* to share my rent.

schedule   n.   a list of courses with days, times, and locations

Example: My *schedule* this semester allows me to work in the afternoons.
Suggestion: With your *schedule*, you could get a job at school.
Assumption: Your *schedule* doesn't include evening classes?
Problem: I can't fit that class into my *schedule*.

scholarship   n.   a grant awarded to a student

Example: Tracy got a *scholarship* to attend a special summer course abroad.
Suggestion: Why don't you apply for a *scholarship*?
Assumption: There aren't any *scholarships* available for international students, are there?
Problem: I have to turn the application in tomorrow to be eligible for the *scholarship*.

section   n.   one of several options for the same course

Example: Everyone wants to take the *section* that Mrs. McNiel teaches.
Suggestion: You could ask Mrs. McNiel to let you into her *section*.
Assumption: You mean there are no *sections* open in the morning?
Problem: I can't get into that *section* because it is closed.

semester   n.   a school term that is usually fifteen to eighteen weeks in length

Example: When the *semester* is over, I am going to visit my family.
Suggestion: You could sign up for more classes this *semester*.
Assumption: This *semester* ends before winter break, doesn't it?
Problem: I need to take eighteen credit hours next *semester*.

senior   n.   a fourth-year student
    Example: Laura will be a *senior* next semester.
    Suggestion: If I were you, I would take that class as a *senior.*
    Assumption: You mean Dana is a *senior*?
    Problem: I have to take five classes when I'm a *senior.*

short-essay test   n.   a test with questions that require a written response of one sentence
                                 to one paragraph in length
    Example: I would rather take a *short-essay test* than an objective test.
    Suggestion: You had better study your notes for Dr. Mitchell's *short-essay test.*
    Assumption: You think a *short-essay test* is easier than an objective test?
    Problem: I have three *short-essay tests* in that class.

shuttle   n.   a bus that has a short route around the campus area
    Example: Carol has a car, but she still uses the campus *shuttle* most of the time.
    Suggestion: If I were you, I would take the *shuttle* at night.
    Assumption: You mean there's no *shuttle* on Sundays?
    Problem: I need to leave early to catch the *shuttle.*

sign up (for a class)   v.   to enroll (in a class)
    Example: Let's *sign up* for the same geology class.
    Suggestion: You should *sign up* for Dr. Brown's music theory class.
    Assumption: So you did *sign up* for the field trip.
    Problem: I can't *sign up* for that class because it conflicts with my schedule.

skip class   v.   to be absent
    Example: Nancy has been *skipping class* again.
    Suggestion: If I were you, I wouldn't *skip class* this week.
    Assumption: Ken *skipped class* yesterday?
    Problem: Bill *skipped class* on the day of the test.

snack bar   n.   a small restaurant area where a limited menu is available
    Example: We usually meet at the *snack bar* for a quick lunch.
    Suggestion: You could meet me at the *snack bar.*
    Assumption: So you did go to the *snack bar* after class.
    Problem: I need to go to the *snack bar* between classes because I don't have a
                         break for lunch.

social security number   n.   a nine-digit number that is often used for student identification
                                 as well as for employment purposes
    Example: What is your *social security number*?
    Suggestion: You should memorize your *social security number.*
    Assumption: Your *social security number* is on your license, isn't it?
    Problem: Anna doesn't have a *social security number.*

sophomore   n.   a second-year college student
    Example: A full-time student is usually a *sophomore* by the third semester.
    Suggestion: You had better complete your general education classes by the end of
                  your *sophomore* year.
    Assumption: You mean Bill is only a *sophomore*?
    Problem: I can't take advanced psychology because I am only a *sophomore*.

sorority   n.   a social organization for female college students
    Example: About a dozen *sororities* are on campus.
    Suggestion: You should consider joining a *sorority*.
    Assumption: So you did join a *sorority*.
    Problem: *Sororities* require a lot of time.

spring break   n.   a short vacation in the middle of the spring semester
    Example: Some of my friends are going to Florida for *spring break*.
    Suggestion: Why don't you visit your family over *spring break*?
    Assumption: You got your research paper done over *spring break*?
    Problem: I have to work during *spring break*.

stacks   n.   the area of the library where most of the books are shelved
    Example: At a small college, the *stacks* are usually open to all of the students.
    Suggestion: You should look in the *stacks* for that book.
    Assumption: The librarian let you go up in the *stacks* to look for your own book?
    Problem: I need to find a carrel in the *stacks*.

student   n.   one who attends a school
    Example: State University has more than fifty-thousand *students* enrolled on the main
                  campus.
    Suggestion: If you tell them that you are a *student*, maybe you will get a discount.
    Assumption: You mean you aren't a *student*?
    Problem: I need to find five *students* to complete my study.

student I.D. number   n.   a number used for identification at a college or university, often a
                          social security number
    Example: Your social security number is your *student I.D. number*.
    Suggestion: You should write your *student I.D. number* on all of your papers.
    Assumption: Pat has a *student I.D. number*?
    Problem: I can't seem to remember my *student I.D. number*.

student services   n.   an administrative branch of a college or university that provides non-
                          instructional support services for students
    Example: I have to go over to *student services* to meet with a financial aid advisor.
    Suggestion: You had better go to *student services* to check on your dorm application.
    Assumption: The *student services* office is open during registration, isn't it?
    Problem: I have to go to the *student services* office before the end of the day.

student union n.   a building on campus where students can relax
    Example: There is a movie at the *student union* tonight.
    Suggestion: You could meet Ken in the *student union* before the concert.
    Assumption: You mean the *student union* is closed over the holidays?
    Problem: The *student union* closes at 10:00 P.M.

studies n.   research investigations
    Example: Many *studies* have been conducted here at State University.
    Suggestion: Why don't you speak with Dr. Mason about her *studies*?
    Assumption: So you did begin your *studies*.
    Problem: I have to complete my *studies* by the end of the semester.

study v.   to acquire knowledge or understanding of a subject
    Example: I have to *study* if I want to get a good grade in this class.
    Suggestion: Why don't you plan to *study* at my house this weekend?
    Assumption: You mean you *studied* for that test?
    Problem: I need to allow more time to *study*.

study date n.   a date in which the activity is studying
    Example: Joe and Diane have *study dates* most of the time.
    Suggestion: You could arrange a *study date* with Jack before the test.
    Assumption: You mean you don't have a *study date* tonight?
    Problem: I have to meet Jack at the library for our *study date.*

study lounge n.   a quiet area of a dormitory where students can go to study
    Example: Even the *study lounge* is noisy in this dorm.
    Suggestion: Why don't you meet me in the *study lounge* this evening?
    Assumption: Did you say that the *study lounge* is quiet?
    Problem: I can't concentrate in the *study lounge*.

subject n.   an area of study
    Example: Math is my favorite *subject*.
    Suggestion: Why don't you ask Tracy for help with the *subjects* she tutors?
    Assumption: You can get tutoring in all of the *subjects* taught at the university?
    Problem: I have to take a lot of classes in *subjects* that I don't really like.

summer school n.   the summer sessions, which are usually June through August
    Example: *Summer school* starts the second week of June this year.
    Suggestion: Why don't you take the art appreciation course in *summer school*?
    Assumption: You mean you've gone to *summer school* every summer?
    Problem: I can't go to *summer school* this year.

T.A. n.   an abbreviation for teaching assistant
    Example: Laura has applied to be Dr. Graham's *T.A.*
    Suggestion: You should see the *T.A.* if you have questions about the lecture.
    Assumption: So Bill did apply to be a *T.A.*
    Problem: I have to find Dr. Graham's *T.A.* before class tomorrow.

teaching assistant   n.   a graduate student whose teaching duties are supervised by a faculty member
Example:	We have a *teaching assistant* for the discussion session of this class.
Suggestion:	You had better speak with the *teaching assistant* before the next lab session.
Assumption:	You mean you haven't spoken with the *teaching assistant*?
Problem:	The *teaching assistant* is really difficult to understand.

tenure   n.   an academic rank that guarantees permanent status
Example:	Professor Peterson has *tenure*, but Mr. Lewis doesn't.
Suggestion:	Why don't you request the requirements for *tenure*?
Assumption:	You mean Dr. Peterson has *tenure*?
Problem:	Mr. Lewis will have to get his Ph.D. to qualify for *tenure*.

term   n.   a time period when school is in session, usually a quarter or a semester
Example:	Dana needs two more *terms* to graduate.
Suggestion:	Dana had better take statistics next *term*.
Assumption:	Nancy passed all of her classes last *term*?
Problem:	I have to complete my dissertation in three *terms*.

test   n.   an evaluation that is usually longer and worth more points than a quiz but shorter and worth fewer points than an exam
Example:	You will have a *test* every week in this class.
Suggestion:	If I were you, I would work with my study group before the *test*.
Assumption:	You mean you forgot about the *test*?
Problem:	I have to study for two *tests* next week.

textbook   n.   a book that is used for a course
Example:	The *textbooks* can be purchased at the bookstore or ordered over the Internet.
Suggestion:	You could purchase used *textbooks* for some of your classes.
Assumption:	You mean you had to buy new *textbooks*?
Problem:	I can't find good used *textbooks* anywhere.

thesis   n.   a written research report in partial fulfillment of a graduate degree
Example:	Tracy isn't taking any courses this semester because she is writing her *thesis*.
Suggestion:	You should get the handbook at the graduate school before starting your *thesis*.
Assumption:	Tracy isn't writing her *thesis* this semester, is she?
Problem:	I need to allow at least one semester to write my *thesis*.

transcript   n.   a printed copy of a student's grades
Example:	The admissions office requires two *transcripts* with every application.
Suggestion:	Why don't you request an extra copy of your *transcript*?
Assumption:	You mean you still haven't received your *transcripts*?
Problem:	I have to have those *transcripts* by next Monday.

transfer   v.   to change schools
     Example: It is better to *transfer* at the beginning of the third year.
     Suggestion: If I were you, I would *transfer* as soon as possible.
     Assumption: Dana *transferred* to State University?
     Problem: I can't *transfer* colleges because I would lose credits.

tuition   n.   fees for instruction at a school
     Example: The *tuition* is different from school to school.
     Suggestion: You should check the *tuition* before deciding on a college.
     Assumption: *Tuition* at private colleges is more?
     Problem: I need a scholarship to pay my *tuition*.

tuition hike   n.   an increase in the fees for instruction
     Example: There is a *tuition hike* every year at State University.
     Suggestion: You should sign the petition protesting the *tuition hike*.
     Assumption: You mean you graduated before the *tuition hike*?
     Problem: I can't afford another *tuition hike*.

turn in   v.   to submit an assignment
     Example: Please *turn in* your homework before you leave.
     Suggestion: You had better *turn in* your paper before the end of the day.
     Assumption: You mean I could have *turned in* my paper tomorrow?
     Problem: I have to *turn in* the paper by Friday or I will get an F.

tutor   n.   a private instructor, often another student
     Example: I have to meet my *tutor* at the library.
     Suggestion: Why don't you get a *tutor* for your accounting class?
     Assumption: You mean Jack is your *tutor*?
     Problem: I can't afford to hire a *tutor*.

tutoring   n.   private instruction
     Example: Nancy needs some *tutoring* in this class.
     Suggestion: You could earn extra money *tutoring* for math.
     Assumption: So you did get the *tutoring* job.
     Problem: *Tutoring* takes a lot of time.

undergrad   n., adj.   abbreviation for undergraduate
     Example: I think that Dana is an *undergrad*.
     Suggestion: You could still enroll for *undergrad* classes while you are waiting to hear
                      from the graduate school admissions office.
     Assumption: You mean you're an *undergrad*?
     Problem: I need to apply for an *undergrad* scholarship.

undergraduate (student)   n., adj.   a student pursuing a bachelor's degree
     Example: Some *undergraduates* require five years to complete a four-year program.
     Suggestion: You should look at more than one *undergraduate* program.
     Assumption: You mean you completed your *undergraduate* courses in three years?
     Problem: I can't complete my *undergraduate* degree before we move.

upper-division (course) adj. advanced courses for third- and fourth-year students
- Example: Most of the *upper-division* courses are numbered 400 or above.
- Suggestion: Why don't you take an *upper-division* music class?
- Assumption: You mean grammar is an *upper-division* course?
- Problem: Dana needs to take an *upper-division* math class.

withdraw v. to leave school
- Example: My roommate *withdrew* from school.
- Suggestion: You should *withdraw* so that you won't have failing grades on your transcript.
- Assumption: You mean your parents want you to *withdraw* from school?
- Problem: I have to *withdraw* from school at the end of the semester.

work-study adj. a special program that allows study time when there is nothing to do on the job
- Example: There are several *work-study* positions open in the finance office.
- Suggestion: Dana should apply for the *work-study* program next semester.
- Assumption: You mean Vicki's library job is a *work-study* position?
- Problem: The *work-study* students couldn't answer my questions.

Xerox (machine) n. a copy machine
- Example: There is a long line at the *Xerox* machine.
- Suggestion: You could use the *Xerox* machine in the library.
- Assumption: You mean there are only three *Xerox* machines on campus?
- Problem: I need to find a *Xerox* machine.

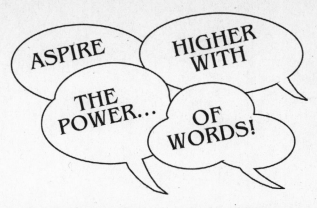

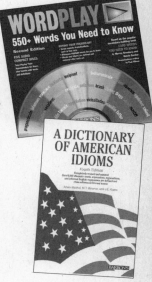